KIERKEGAARD'S INFLUENCE ON THE SOCIAL SCIENCES

Kierkegaard Research: Sources, Reception and Resources
Volume 13

Kierkegaard Research: Sources, Reception and Resources
is a publication of the Søren Kierkegaard Research Centre

Kierkegaard's Influence on the Social Sciences

Edited by
JON STEWART

ASHGATE

Published by
Ashgate Publishing Limited
Wey Court East
Union Road
Farnham
Surrey, GU9 7PT
England

Ashgate Publishing Company
Suite 420
101 Cherry Street
Burlington
VT 05401-4405
USA

www.ashgate.com

British Library Cataloguing in Publication Data
Kierkegaard's influence on the social sciences.
    Volume 13. – (Kierkegaard research)
    1. Kierkegaard, Søren, 1813–1855--Influence.
    2. Kierkegaard, Søren, 1813–1855--Knowledge--Social
    sciences. 3. Social sciences – History.
    I. Series II. Stewart, Jon (Jon Bartley)
    198.9-dc22

Library of Congress Cataloging-in-Publication Data
Kierkegaard's influence on the social sciences / [edited by] Jon Stewart.
        p. cm. — (Kierkegaard research ; v. 13)
    Includes indexes.
    ISBN 978-1-4094-3490-0 (hardcover : alk. paper) 1. Social
sciences—Research. 2. Social sciences—Philosophy, 3. Kierkegaard, Søren,
1813-1855. I. Stewart, Jon (Jon Bartley)
    H62.K474 2011
    300.92—dc23

                                                                        2011026577

ISBN 9781409434900

Cover design by Katalin Nun

Mixed Sources
Product group from well-managed
forests and other controlled sources
www.fsc.org Cert no. SA-COC-1565
© 1996 Forest Stewardship Council

Printed and bound in Great Britain by
MPG Books Ltd, Bodmin, Cornwall.

Contents

List of Contributors

Elisabetta Basso, Centre d'Archives de Philosophie, d'Histoire et d'Édition des Sciences, URS 3308, Centre International de Recherches en Philosophie, Lettres, Savoirs (Centre national de la recherche scientifique—École normale supérieure), Paris, France.

Dustin Feddon, M05 Dodd Hall, Department of Religion, Florida State University, Tallahassee, FL 32306-1520, USA.

Almut Furchert, Hong Kierkegaard Library, St. Olaf College, 1510 St. Olaf Avenue Northfield, MN 55057, USA.

Rick Anthony Furtak, Department of Philosophy, Colorado College, 14 E. Cache La Poudre, Colorado Springs, CO 80903, USA.

Diego Giordano, c/o Søren Kierkegaard Research Centre at the University of Copenhagen, Farvergade 27D, 1463 Copenhagen K, Denmark.

Poul Houe, Department of German, Scandinavian and Dutch, University of Minnesota, 205 Folwell Hall, 9 Pleasant Street S.E., Minneapolis, MN 55455-0124, USA.

Stuart Kendall, Visual and Critical Studies, California College of the Arts, 5212 Broadway, Oakland, CA 94618-1426, USA.

Søren Landkildehus, Hong Kierkegaard Library, St. Olaf College, 1510 St. Olaf Avenue Northfield, MN 55057, USA.

John Lippitt, School of Humanities, University of Hertfordshire de Havilland Campus, Hatfield, Herts AL10 9AB, UK.

J.D. Mininger, Faculty of Political Science and Diplomacy, Vytautas Magnus University, K. Donelaicio g. 58, 44248 Kaunas, Lithuania.

Edward F. Mooney, Department of Religion, Syracuse University, Syracuse, NY 13244, USA.

Simon D. Podmore, Trinity College, Broadstreet, Oxford, OX1 3BH, UK.

Anthony Rudd, Department of Philosophy, St. Olaf College, 1520 St. Olaf Avenue, Northfield, MN 55057, USA.

Leo Stan, Centre for the Study of Theory and Criticism, University of Western Ontario, Somerville House, Rm. 2345A, London, Ontario N6A 3K7, Canada.

Preface

Kierkegaard has long been known as a philosopher and theologian, but his contributions to psychology, anthropology, and sociology have also made an important impact on these fields. In many of the works of his complex authorship, Kierkegaard presents his intriguing and unique vision of the nature and mental life of human beings individually and collectively. Despite this, it must be said that in Kierkegaard studies, his influence on the social sciences generally remains a somewhat neglected field, especially in comparison to the vast wealth of philosophical or theological research. There are to date only a few full-length monographs dedicated to this dimension of his thought, and these have tended to focus primarily on the field of philosophical psychology.[1]

Some scholars are surprised to hear that there has actually been so little written about this subject since one frequently runs across titles that would seem to indicate a study of Kierkegaard's psychology. The explanation of this is a deceptive linguistic ambiguity. By the expression "Kierkegaard's psychology," one can mean, as we do here in this volume, Kierkegaard's contributions to the field of psychology via his psychological analyses as they appear in his works. But this same expression can also be taken to mean Kierkegaard's own psychological disposition. Indeed, many scholars, perhaps inspired by George Brandes' (1842–1927) famous book on Kierkegaard,[2] have treated him not as psychologist or a source of inspiration for psychological insight but rather, as it were, as a case study.[3] His life and complex

---

[1]   Kresten Nordentoft, *Kierkegaards psykologi*, Copenhagen: Gad 1972 (in English as *Kierkegaard's Psychology*, trans. by Bruce H. Kirmmse, Pittsburgh: Duquesne University Press 1978). Vincent A. McCarthy, *The Phenomenology of Moods in Kierkegaard*, The Hague: Martinus Nijhoff 1978. Wim Scholtens, *Alle gekheid op een stokje. Kierkegaard als psycholoog*, Baarn: Ten Have 1979. Harvie Ferguson, *Melancholy and the Critique of Modernity: Søren Kierkegaard's Religious Psychology*, London and New York: Routledge 1995. Karl Verstrynge, *De Hysterie Van De Geest: Melancholie en zwaarmoedigheid in het pseudonieme oeuvre van Kierkegaard*, Leuven: Peeters 2003. Michael Theunissen, *Der Begriff Verzweiflung. Korrekturen an Kierkegaard*, Frankfurt am Main: Suhrkamp 1993 (in English as *Kierkegaard's Concept of Despair*, trans. by Barbara Harshav and Helmut Illbruck, Princeton University Press 2005).

[2]   Georg Brandes, *Søren Kierkegaard. En kritisk Fremstilling i Grundrids*, Copenhagen: Gyldendal 1877.

[3]   See, for example, August Vetter, *Frömmigkeit als Leidenschaft. Eine Deutung Kierkegaards*, Leipzig: Insel 1928. Friedrich C. Fischer, *Die Nullpunkt-Existenz. Dargestellt an der Lebensform Sören Kierkegaards*, Munich: Beck 1933. Hjalmar Helweg, *Søren Kierkegaard—en psykiatrisk-psykologisk studie*, Copenhagen: H. Hagerups Forlag 1933. John Björkheim, *Søren Kierkegaard i psykologisk betydning*, Uppsala: Nyblooms Forlag

relationships provide ample material for investigations of this kind. Kierkegaard's constant self-reflection in his journals opens the door for many possible psychological analyses. Scholars never tire of speculating about the character of Kierkegaard's deeply religious father or his little-known mother, whom he never mentions, and their influence on his development and thinking. Likewise his strained relation with his elder brother Peter Christian Kierkegaard (1805–88) offers rich interpretative possibilities. Perhaps the favorite hobbyhorse in this regard is the issue of Kierkegaard's inability to marry Regine Olsen (1822–1904). Not least one should mention the question of his disputed mental condition towards the end of his life during his polemic with the Danish State Church, an issue that was taken up very early in the literature.[4] Many biographies seem to find it difficult to resist the temptation to do some psychologizing in order to explain the landmark events of his life, and this dimension constitutes a large part of the vast biographical literature on Kierkegaard.

Many later writers and thinkers, such as Kafka (1883–1924) and Lukács (1885–1971), have seen their own personal struggles reflected in the life of Kierkegaard, and thus it was natural for them to look to him for insight. A certain biographical or dispositional affinity led the Romanian author Mircea Eliade (1907–86) to approach Kierkegaard in this fashion. Strengthened by his own personal insight, Eliade follows the tradition of interpreting Kierkegaard's biography in terms of his psychology.

It has also been suggested that Kierkegaard's obsessive writing was the result of some physical or psychological condition.[5] Even during Kierkegaard's own lifetime, it was claimed that writing was for him a form of personal therapy to fulfill certain psychological needs or deficiencies in his personal relations. In an article in the context of the controversy surrounding *The Corsair*, the Danish critic Peder Ludvig Møller (1814–65), suggests: "Writing and producing seem to have become a physical need for him, or he uses it as medicine, just as in certain illnesses one uses bloodletting, cupping, steam baths, emetics, and the like. Just as a healthy person rests by sleeping, he seems to rest by letting his pen run, instead of eating and drinking, he satiates himself by writing...."[6] Thus the tradition of analyzing Kierkegaard psychologically is a very long one that was present almost from the very beginning.

1942. Ib Ostenfeld, *Angst-Begrebet i Søren Kierkegaard: Begrebet Angest*, Copenhagen: G.E.C. Gad 1933. Fanny Lowtzky, *Sören Kierkegaard. Das subjektive Erlebnis und die religiöse Offenbarung. Eine psychoanalytische Studie einer Fast-Selbstanalyse*, Vienna: Internationaler psychoanalytischer Verlag 1935. Ib Ostenfeld, *Søren Kierkegaards Psykologi. Undersøgelse og Indlevelse*, Copenhagen: Rhodos 1972 (in English as *Søren Kierkegaard's Psychology*, trans. and ed. by Alastair McKinnon, Waterloo: Wilfried Laurier University Press 1978. Marguerite Grimault, *La mélancholie de Kierkegaard*, Paris: Aubier 1965.

[4]   See Rasmus Nielsen, "Om S. Kierkegaards 'mentale Tilstand,' " *Nordisk Universitet-Tidskrift*, vol. 4, no. 1, 1858, pp. 1–29.

[5]   It has been speculated, for example, that Kierkegaard was an epileptic. See, for example, Leif Bork Hansen, *Søren Kierkegaards Hemmelighed og Eksistensdialektik*, Copenhagen: C.A. Reitzel 1994.

[6]   See P.L. Møller, "Et Besøg i Sorø," *Gæa. Æsthetisk Aarbog*, 1846, pp. 175–6. In *COR*, Supplement, p. 100.

Instead of these kinds of discussions about Kierkegaard's own psychology, most of the articles featured in the present volume explore the reception, more strictly speaking, of Kierkegaard's thought in the social sciences, where his works have served as inspiration for subsequent psychologists, anthropologists, and sociologists. With regard to the field of psychology or philosophical anthropology, *The Concept of Anxiety* and *The Sickness unto Death* have doubtless been the two most influential texts. With regard to the field of sociology, social criticism, or social theory, Kierkegaard's *A Literary Review of Two Ages* has also been regarded as offering valuable insights about some important dynamics of modern society.

Kierkegaard was influential for important schools of thought such as psychoanalysis or "depth psychology" developed in the work of figures such as Sigmund Freud (1856–1939) and Pierre Janet (1859–1947). While the use of Kierkegaard in these authors has been little explored, the present volume features pioneering articles about the role of Kierkegaard in the writings of later authors influenced by this school such as Jacques Lacan (1901–81) and Julia Kristeva (b. 1941). For example, Kierkegaard's concepts of repetition and anxiety were formative for Lacan's thought, while his theory of the ever-changing, dynamic development of the self has much in common with Kristeva's thinking. He has also played a role in developmental psychology in the work of Erik Erikson (1902–94), who was trained in psychoanalysis by Anna Freud (1895–1982). Erikson's theory of the stages of development of the individual may owe an important debt to Kierkegaard's psychological insights and famous theory of stages. Moreover, some elements of Kierkegaard's thought seem to lurk in the background of Erich Fromm's (1900–80) classic *Escape from Freedom*.[7]

Kierkegaard can also be seen as a source of inspiration for the school of analytical psychology, founded by Carl Jung (1875–1961). Kierkegaard's extensive use of narrative descriptions of individuals and their experiences in what would otherwise be regarded as philosophical or theological analyses can be seen as a forerunner of Jung's interest in the patient's biography and early childhood experiences. Kierkegaard can be seen as leading away from abstract theories and schemes in order to seek the solution in the private, individual experience of each human being. The inner workings of the human mind cannot be reduced to the physical organism but must be understood from the perspective of the life and experience of the individual.

Kierkegaard has also been regarded as a pioneer of existential psychology. His famous analyses of boredom, anxiety, and despair have played a major role in the development of this school. Thinkers such as Heidegger (1889–1976), Sartre (1905–80), Merleau-Ponty (1908–61), and Camus (1913–60) have been keen to take his analyses as the point of departure for their own considerations of human emotions and existence. Some of their insights were applied clinically by figures such as Ludwig Binswanger (1881–1966) and Viktor Frankl (1905–97).

Kierkegaard has also been hailed as an important forerunner of the closely related movement of humanistic psychology, made famous by Carl Rogers (1902–87) and Rollo May (1909–94). Rogers shared with Kierkegaard the conception of the irreducible nature of each single individual. He focused on individual freedom and

---

[7]   Erich Fromm, *Escape from Freedom*, New York: Rinehart & Co. 1941.

responsibility and refused to treat patients as objects. *The Concept of Anxiety* played an explicit and absolutely central role in the development of May's own theory of modern anxiety. Kierkegaard's influence is also clearly seen in the existential psychotherapy that has been popularized by Irvin Yalom (b. 1931) in the United States.

Kierkegaard has been associated with Christian psychology and different forms of pastoral care.[8] Scholars, pastors and counsellors have sought in Kierkegaard's writings concrete practices to help people in specific trying life situations. They have attempted to work out forms of therapy based on his thought.

But Kierkegaard's influence has in no way been limited to psychology. He has also served as a source of inspiration in sociology and the broad field of cultural criticism, for example, in the work of Jean Baudrillard (1929–2007). "The Seducer's Diary" from Part One of *Either/Or* was an important work for the development of Baudrillard's famous theory of seduction. Along similar lines, the interdisciplinary anthropologist Ernest Becker (1924–74) has made use of Kierkegaard in his influential work *The Denial of Death*.[9] Traces of Kierkegaard can also be found in the work of the British sociologist Anthony Giddens (b. 1938). In particular, inspirations for Giddens' account of anxiety, the self and the crisis can be found in Kierkegaard's writings. The French philosopher and social scientist René Girard (b. 1923) takes up the Kierkegaardian notions of defiance and despair from *The Sickness unto Death* and develops them in the context of his famous mimetic theory. Kierkegaard also plays a minor role in Max Weber's (1864–1920) classic of sociology, *The Protestant Ethic and the Spirit of Capitalism*. Finally, the sociologist and cultural critic Slavoj Žižek (b. 1949) makes use of a wide spectrum of concepts and ideas from Kierkegaard.

There are still some important areas in the social sciences where Kierkegaard's thinking could potentially bear fruit. Kierkegaard's theory of indirect communication is well known, but his ideas about communication have never been systematically applied to the field of linguistics. Similarly, he has much to say about ethics and the way in which people judge their best interests in relations to others, but no one has ever undertaken a detailed or systematic study of Kierkegaard's ideas in the context of economics. Drawing on Kierkegaard's analysis of modern society and his polemic with the press, some tentative attempts have been made to use of his ideas for the field of media studies,[10] but this remains also a potentially highly fruitful field that has yet to be fully explored.

Kierkegaard's importance for the social sciences has until now only been treated by scattered works. The present collection attempts to give as broad and systematic coverage of this reception as possible. It is hoped that these articles collectively will prove to be an important contribution to the field. But it seems clear that there is still much work to be done in this branch of Kierkegaard studies.

---

[8]   See C. Stephen Evans, *Søren Kierkegaard's Christian Psychology: Insight for Counseling and Pastoral Care*, Grand Rapids, Michigan: Regent College Publishing 1995. Helle Møller Jensen, *Sjælesorg mellem teori og praksis. En studie i sjælesorg under hensyntagen til Søren Kierkegaards brug af krops- og bevægelsesmetaforer i fire opbyggelige taler*. Ph.D. thesis, University of Aarhus, Denmark, 2006.
[9]   Ernest Becker, *The Denial of Death*, New York: The Free Press 1973.
[10]   See Hubert Dreyfus, "Kierkegaard and the Internet: Anonymity vs. Commitment in the Present Age," *Kierkegaard Studies Yearbook*, 1999, pp. 96–109.

Acknowledgements

The present volume represents the fruit of the collective labor of many people, and I would like here to gratefully acknowledge their work. I am most thankful for the selfless efforts of the following individuals: Lee C. Barrett, Ingrid Basso, Maria Binetti, Patrizia Conforti, Markus Kleinert, Anne Rachut, Peter Šajda, Jeanette Schindler-Wirth, Gerhard Schreiber, Heiko Schulz, Françoise Surdez, Margherita Tonon, and Karl Verstrynge. They helped to locate references and photocopy texts that were needed for the individual articles. Peter Šajda did an exhaustive literature search and provided the authors with outstanding preliminary bibliographies for their articles; this work made the articles of the present volume much stronger and more thorough than they would otherwise have been. I am thankful to Poul Houe and Curtis Thompson for their useful comments on and constructive suggestions for the Preface. Katalin Nun single-handedly did the tedious electronic editing for this volume. Her efforts are much appreciated. I am also deeply grateful to the other members of the production team, our proofreaders, Finn Gredal Jensen and Philip Hillyer and our typesetter Nicholas Wain. In the name of everyone involved in the editorial and advisory board, I would like to sincerely thank the authors of this volume for sharing their enormous expertise in this context. Through their efforts, an important contribution has been made to our understanding of Kierkegaard's influence on the social sciences.

List of Abbreviations

ASKB   *The Auctioneer's Sales Record of the Library of Søren Kierkegaard*, ed. by
        H.P. Rohde, Copenhagen: The Royal Library 1967.

BA   *The Book on Adler*, trans. by Howard V. Hong and Edna H. Hong, Princeton:
        Princeton University Press 1998.

C   *The Crisis and a Crisis in the Life of an Actress*, trans. by Howard V. Hong
        and Edna H. Hong, Princeton: Princeton University Press 1997.

CA   *The Concept of Anxiety*, trans. by Reidar Thomte in collaboration with
        Albert B. Anderson, Princeton: Princeton University Press 1980.

CD   *Christian Discourses*, trans. by Howard V. Hong and Edna H. Hong,
        Princeton: Princeton University Press 1997.

CI   *The Concept of Irony*, trans. by Howard V. Hong and Edna H. Hong,
        Princeton: Princeton University Press 1989.

CIC   *The Concept of Irony*, trans. with an Introduction and Notes by Lee M.
        Capel, London: Collins 1966.

COR   *The Corsair Affair; Articles Related to the Writings*, trans. by Howard V.
        Hong and Edna H. Hong, Princeton: Princeton University Press 1982.

CUP1   *Concluding Unscientific Postscript*, vol. 1, trans. by Howard V. Hong and
        Edna H. Hong, Princeton: Princeton University Press 1982.

CUP2   *Concluding Unscientific Postscript*, vol. 2, trans. by Howard V. Hong and
        Edna H. Hong, Princeton: Princeton University Press 1982.

CUPH   *Concluding Unscientific Postscript*, trans. by Alastair Hannay, Cambridge
        and New York: Cambridge University Press 2009.

EO1   *Either/Or*, Part I, trans. by Howard V. Hong and Edna H. Hong, Princeton:
        Princeton University Press 1987.

EO2   *Either/Or*, Part II, trans. by Howard V. Hong and Edna H. Hong, Princeton:
        Princeton University Press 1987.

EOP   *Either/Or*, trans. by Alastair Hannay, Harmondsworth: Penguin Books
        1992.

EPW   *Early Polemical Writings*, among others: *From the Papers of One Still
        Living; Articles from Student Days; The Battle Between the Old and the
        New Soap-Cellars*, trans. by Julia Watkin, Princeton: Princeton University
        Press 1990.

EUD   *Eighteen Upbuilding Discourses*, trans. by Howard V. Hong and Edna H. Hong, Princeton: Princeton University Press 1990.

FSE   *For Self-Examination*, trans. by Howard V. Hong and Edna H. Hong, Princeton: Princeton University Press 1990.

FT   *Fear and Trembling*, trans. by Howard V. Hong and Edna H. Hong, Princeton: Princeton University Press 1983.

FTP   *Fear and Trembling*, trans. by Alastair Hannay, Harmondsworth: Penguin Books 1985.

JC   *Johannes Climacus, or De omnibus dubitandum est*, trans. by Howard V. Hong and Edna H. Hong, Princeton: Princeton University Press 1985.

JFY   *Judge for Yourself!*, trans. by Howard V. Hong and Edna H. Hong, Princeton: Princeton University Press 1990.

JP   *Søren Kierkegaard's Journals and Papers*, vols. 1–6, ed. and trans. by Howard V. Hong and Edna H. Hong, assisted by Gregor Malantschuk (vol. 7, Index and Composite Collation), Bloomington and London: Indiana University Press 1967–78.

KAC   *Kierkegaard's Attack upon "Christendom," 1854–1855*, trans. by Walter Lowrie, Princeton: Princeton University Press 1944.

KJN   *Kierkegaard's Journals and Notebooks*, vols. 1–11, ed. by Niels Jørgen Cappelørn, Alastair Hannay, David Kangas, Bruce H. Kirmmse, George Pattison, Vanessa Rumble, and K. Brian Söderquist, Princeton and Oxford: Princeton University Press 2007ff.

LD   *Letters and Documents*, trans. by Henrik Rosenmeier, Princeton: Princeton University Press 1978.

LR   *A Literary Review*, trans. by Alastair Hannay, Harmondsworth: Penguin Books 2001.

M   *The Moment and Late Writings*, trans. by Howard V. Hong and Edna H. Hong, Princeton: Princeton University Press 1998.

P   *Prefaces / Writing Sampler*, trans. by Todd W. Nichol, Princeton: Princeton University Press 1997.

PC   *Practice in Christianity*, trans. by Howard V. Hong and Edna H. Hong, Princeton: Princeton University Press 1991.

PF   *Philosophical Fragments*, trans. by Howard V. Hong and Edna H. Hong, Princeton: Princeton University Press 1985.

PJ   *Papers and Journals: A Selection*, trans. by Alastair Hannay, Harmondsworth: Penguin Books 1996.

PLR   *Prefaces: Light Reading for Certain Classes as the Occasion May Require*, trans. by William McDonald, Tallahassee: Florida State University Press 1989.

PLS   *Concluding Unscientific Postscript*, trans. by David F. Swenson and Walter Lowrie, Princeton: Princeton University Press 1941.

PV   *The Point of View* including *On My Work as an Author*, *The Point of View for My Work as an Author*, and *Armed Neutrality*, trans. by Howard V. Hong and Edna H. Hong, Princeton: Princeton University Press 1998.

PVL   *The Point of View for My Work as an Author* including *On My Work as an Author*, trans. by Walter Lowrie, New York and London: Oxford University Press 1939.

R   *Repetition*, trans. by Howard V. Hong and Edna H. Hong, Princeton: Princeton University Press 1983.

SBL   *Notes of Schelling's Berlin Lectures*, trans. by Howard V. Hong and Edna H. Hong, Princeton: Princeton University Press 1989.

SLW   *Stages on Life's Way*, trans. by Howard V. Hong and Edna H. Hong, Princeton: Princeton University Press 1988.

SUD   *The Sickness unto Death*, trans. by Howard V. Hong and Edna H. Hong, Princeton: Princeton University Press 1980.

SUDP   *The Sickness unto Death*, trans. by Alastair Hannay, London and New York: Penguin Books 1989.

TA   *Two Ages: The Age of Revolution and the Present Age. A Literary Review*, trans. by Howard V. Hong and Edna H. Hong, Princeton: Princeton University Press 1978.

TD   *Three Discourses on Imagined Occasions*, trans. by Howard V. Hong and Edna H. Hong, Princeton: Princeton University Press 1993.

UD   *Upbuilding Discourses in Various Spirits*, trans. by Howard V. Hong and Edna H. Hong, Princeton: Princeton University Press 1993.

WA   *Without Authority* including *The Lily in the Field and the Bird of the Air, Two Ethical-Religious Essays, Three Discourses at the Communion on Fridays, An Upbuilding Discourse, Two Discourses at the Communion on Fridays*, trans. by Howard V. Hong and Edna H. Hong, Princeton: Princeton University Press 1997.

WL   *Works of Love*, trans. by Howard V. Hong and Edna H. Hong, Princeton: Princeton University Press 1995.

WS   *Writing Sampler*, trans. by Todd W. Nichol, Princeton: Princeton University Press 1997.

Jean Baudrillard:

The Seduction of Jean Baudrillard

Stuart Kendall

French cultural critic Jean Baudrillard (1929–2007) developed an original method of cultural criticism in significant part from his reading of Søren Kierkegaard's fictional presentation of the act of seduction in "The Seducer's Diary." For Baudrillard, seduction came to serve as an analogue to critical thought in general and a precursor to an entire range of what he later called "fatal strategies" of individual freedom. Though crucial to his own development, Baudrillard's reading of Kierkegaard in general and of "The Seducer's Diary" in particular was not itself a critical or thorough reading. Rather, he subjected the text to a species of speculative interpretation and used it as the basis for protracted extrapolation into a wide range of other cultural spheres and critical concerns. This in mind, it is unsurprising that tracing Baudrillard's engagement with Kierkegaard should tell us more about Baudrillard and his readers than it does about Kierkegaard.

I.

Across more than fifty books and pamphlets published between 1968 and his death in 2007, Jean Baudrillard established an international reputation as a critic of contemporary culture. Principally though often inaccurately identified with postmodernism, Baudrillard's writings amalgamate and transcend several distinct critical and creative discourses—Marxism, psychoanalysis, semiology, anthropology, media studies, pataphysics—to forge an original and unclassifiable, interdisciplinary form of post-Marxist cultural criticism. Trained as a sociologist, Baudrillard taught for more than twenty years at the University of Paris, most notably at the Nanterre campus, as his international reputation spread. In the decades prior to his death, Baudrillard traveled widely, as a lecturer and visiting professor, in the United States, Japan, Brazil, Spain, Chile, Venezuela, Columbia, and Australia, among other locales, while continuing to produce trenchant and often controversial cultural commentary on such events as the 1991 war in the Persian Gulf and the attack on the World Trade Center in 2001.

Born in July 1929 and raised in Northeastern France, mainly in Reims, which had been home to Georges Bataille (1897–1962) and Roger Caillois (1913–78) before him, Baudrillard taught German in French lycées and became known as a translator of German writers and philosophers—Peter Weiss (1916–82), Bertolt

Brecht (1898–1956), and Karl Marx (1818–83) most frequently—before pursuing studies in sociology at the Sorbonne. Baudrillard defended his dissertation on the ideological formation of consumer goods in 1966 before a committee composed of Roland Barthes (1915–80), Pierre Bourdieu (1930–2002), and Henri Lefebvre (1901–91), all of whom were at or near the height of their ascendancy and influence at that time.

Baudrillard was also active as a leftist militant during these years. He founded the Maoist *Association populaire franco-chinoise* with Félix Gauttari (1930–92) and others in 1962 and helped edit its bulletin. He participated in the events of May 1968, but, as the workers' movement turned toward reform, he lost his faith in the revolutionary project and the theoretical models that inspired it. Over the next decade, in a series of increasingly radical books and essays running from *The System of Objects* (1968) to *In the Shadow of the Silent Majorities or the End of the Social* (1978), Baudrillard subjected the major critical discourses of the modern era to coruscating criticism, clearing the path for a still more radical turn that was to come.

Baudrillard's career can be broken into periods roughly corresponding to the periodicals to which he contributed during each period. During the 1960s, his years of political militancy, he wrote literary reviews for Jean-Paul Sartre's *Les Temps modernes*. During the 1970s, as he moved further and further from the Marxist milieu, his journal was the Situationist inspired *Utopie*. During the 1980s, as Baudrillard formulated his notions of seduction, simulation, and fatal strategies, he published in *Traverses*. By the 1990s, increasingly renowned, at once an *éminence gris* and an *enfant terrible*, Baudrillard published a column in left-center French daily, *Libération*. Through the years his books were often, though by no means exclusively, composed of articles originally published in these and other venues. Hubert Tonka in France and Sylvère Lotringer in the United States played a significant role in cultivating Baudrillard's reputation by editing and promoting collections of his essays. Partly as a result of this, Baudrillard's international reputation and influence initially surged in areas—like art and aesthetic theory—that were of comparatively minor significance to him.

Baudrillard's own interests and influences have often been difficult for international critics and commentators unfamiliar with French intellectual history to parse. Baudrillard has very often been extremely reticent, when not in fact secretive about them. To anticipate our trajectory, we may observe that the term "secretive" here derives, for Baudrillard, from his reading of Kierkegaard. Baudrillard's influences have also been obscure because they are both myriad and diffuse. He borrows insights and strategies from an extraordinarily wide range of fields, combines them with literary flair in often startling ways, and attains insights that appear to stand on their own, if in need of careful analysis and explication. Baudrillard developed his secretive or reticent style as an increasingly self-conscious method of post-avant-gardist cultural activism.

Without access to the cultural sources and hence the context of his thought, Anglophone commentators in particular have often taken his work at face value without perceiving its highly stylized contours and effects. The diversity and expanse of Baudrillard's work has also, I believe, frustrated his critics and supporters, who typically content themselves with an understanding of Baudrillard derived from one period or another of his work, or even simply from one book or, sadly, remark.[1]

Baudrillard's critics, pro and contra, have also been frustrated by his fundamental critical strategy, which effectively eviscerates the discourses and cultural practices at the center of his analysis. Piece by piece, essay by essay, book by book, Baudrillard pushed his thought through new and shifting horizons of concern, tearing at both the tools and terrain of critical cultural studies from within. His work is Marxist, semiological, psychoanalytic, sociological, philosophical, and literary by turns, without ever settling into a single mode of analysis or expression or letting any of these modes of analysis stand. Unsurprisingly, readers committed to these discourses might find something of interest somewhere in his vast *corpus*, much to lament, and even more that seems either banal or mystifying, without necessarily taking an interest in the whole *corpus*.

Baudrillard's first book, *The System of Objects*, based on his dissertation, extends Roland Barthes' semiological method of the ideological formation of consumer culture, first explored in Barthes' *Mythologies* (1957), across the entire range of consumer goods. In subsequent work, Baudrillard subjected his own methods to auto-critique, most famously revealing Marxism itself as a "mirror" complicit with the mode of production it sought to attack.

Baudrillard's strategies in his early books derive from Roland Barthes' semiology but also from Theodor Adorno's (1903–69) negative dialectics and from the cultural program of the Frankfurt School in general, most notably Herbert Marcuse's (1898–1979) interpretation of "one-dimensional" consumer society. But his methods and orientation already also included reference to classical figures in French sociology, like Emile Durkheim (1858–1917) and, more significantly, Marcel Mauss (1872–1950), as well as more obscure figures from the fringes of the Surrealist movement, like Roger Caillois and Georges Bataille. Baudrillard's thought had also been marked by an early interest—and thesis on—Friedrich Nietzsche (1844–1900) as well as a fascination with the theatrical and poetic writings of Alfred Jarry (1873–1907) and Antonin Artaud (1896–1948), known respectively for their inventions of Pataphysics and the Theater of Cruelty. In later works, as we will see, Baudrillard would add Jorge Luis Borges (1899–1986) and Søren Kierkegaard to this list of critical influences.

From these sources, Baudrillard derived a view of culture based on the opposition of two distinct modes of exchange, respectively identified with various aspects of primitive and modern cultures. (Primitive, for Baudrillard, following Claude Lévi-Strauss (1908–2009), is not a derogatory term.) Modern cultures, in Baudrillard's view, are predicated on utilitarian forms of exchange, based on false equivalencies, which are themselves traceable to structures of replication and representation. The commodity form is only one example of this kind of structure. Modern cultures are cultures of production, wherein production is always the production of a false equivalence: labor produces goods, the unconscious produces consciousness; signs

---

[1]   Here I am thinking of Douglas Kellner in particular. See, for example, Mike Gane's discussion of Kellner's writings about Baudrillard in Mike Gane, *Baudrillard: Critical and Fatal Theory*, London: Routledge 1991, pp. 47–54.

circulate in endless exchange. Criticism itself collaborates in this system to the extent that it replicates the forms of the systems under scrutiny. At best, critical discourses can only function as tools for the reform of structures that circumscribe the entire scope of the debate.

Primitive cultures, on the other hand, are not based on representations but rather on myths and symbols. Primitive cultures do not produce representations but rather present myths. Myths are presented in rituals, which, as enactment and reenactment, are always simultaneously more and less than they seem to be. Primitive cultures are cultures based on mythic or what Baudrillard calls symbolic exchange rather than on utilitarian exchange. Modern culture is itself predicated on the eradication of symbolic exchange. In modern cultures, myths and symbols are recast as representations, which nevertheless cannot quite achieve the stability of pure equivalencies. Thus modern cultures retain and attempt to control or contain elements—objects and structures—of symbolic exchange in uneasy equilibrium. Modern cultures turn symbols into commodities through production. Primitive cultures, on the other hand, submit to a more ambiguous and equivocal logic that Baudrillard designated, at least initially, with a term he borrowed from Kierkegaard: "seduction."

II.

The place and role of Kierkegaard's thought in Baudrillard's *corpus* is limited but, in its way, decisive. Kierkegaard and specifically Kierkegaard's "The Seducer's Diary" serves a key function in Baudrillard's formulation of his notion of seduction in *Seduction*. This text is itself pivotal in Baudrillard's work. Thereafter Baudrillard makes passing remarks about Kierkegaard or based on this thought, in both texts and interviews, in the early 1980s and intermittently over the following twenty years. Thus while Kierkegaard no longer occupies center stage in Baudrillard's evolving thought after *Seduction*, he never exits entirely. More importantly, however, the themes and even techniques that Baudrillard derives from his reading of Kierkegaard's work remain fundamental to the perspective he developed and deepened after his encounter with it. I am suggesting that a great deal of Baudrillard's later work—work produced after 1979—can be read in light of Kierkegaard, though not necessarily directly. As we will see, this suggestion is entirely in keeping with the specific themes and notions that Baudrillard derives from Kierkegaard, most importantly, that of the secret. Kierkegaard may be an unstated and thus "secret" reference for much of Baudrillard's later work.

Before examining Baudrillard's reading of Kierkegaard, we might remark that Kierkegaard's influence on his work has received almost no sustained attention from his critics and commentators. Indeed, when Baudrillard's critics do mention Kierkegaard, they generally do so only in passing, before moving on to the themes and topics that truly interest them in Baudrillard's work. This oversight is consistent with the critical approach to Baudrillard's work in general. His critics have, by and large, been far more interested in Baudrillard's topics and remarks than in the sources and contexts of those remarks. Critics, commentators, and interviewers as well have often followed their own interests through Baudrillard's *corpus* rather than attempting to situate Baudrillard's work in a larger intellectual frame. This has been particularly problematic in regard to Kierkegaard's influence on Baudrillard, since readers of the latter share few if any of the concerns of the former. As noted above, even Baudrillard himself evidences far less than a thorough, let alone critical, understanding of Kierkegaard's work.

Douglas Kellner provides a good example of a critic whose approach to Baudrillard does not extend to the Danish theologian. In his book, *Jean Baudrillard: From Marxism to Postmodernism and Beyond*, Kellner remarks:

> Baudrillard utilizes Søren Kierkegaard's highly masculinist and misogynist text "The Seducer's Diary" as the basis for his model of seduction. He takes Kierkegaard's aesthete (a barely disguised alter ego) who devises incredibly complicated strategies and ruses to fascinate an "innocent" young virgin in a long series of preludes to the eventual sexual conquest as the model for the highly ritualistic game that he is valorizing as the alternative to the order of production.[2]

Kellner's sarcastic and dismissive remarks here are hardly sympathetic to either of the authors in question. Indeed, they barely evidence any familiarity with or insight into Kierkegaard's text whatsoever. Needless to say, this is Kellner's sole remark about Kierkegaard in his two-hundred-page appraisal of Baudrillard's work, and it constitutes more attention than most commentators apply.

But as noted, Baudrillard's interest in Kierkegaard, though perhaps decisive and certainly pivotal, has been far from consistent. His first reference to Kierkegaard, in *Consumer Society*, is no more than a passing remark, observing the irony that Kierkegaard's works might sell well.[3] Van Gogh's paintings figure in the same quip as an analogue from the visual arts. Baudrillard's next reference to Kierkegaard comes almost a decade later, in *Seduction*, where "The Seducer's Diary" serves as the central reference within the book as a whole.[4] Even in *Seduction*, however, Baudrillard works from Kierkegaard's text rather than toward it; he develops his own thought based on Kierkegaard's text by drawing it out, adding examples or otherwise expanding its notions, rather than attempting to understand, interpret, or explain Kierkegaard's own purposes.

Baudrillard next references Kierkegaard in a text entitled *Please Follow Me*, which he published as part of photographer Sophie Calle's *Suite Venitienne*. This text also figures in Baudrillard's major book *Fatal Strategies*. The reference to

---

[2]   See Douglas Kellner, *Jean Baudrillard: From Marxism to Postmodernism and Beyond*, Cambridge and Palo Alto: Polity Press and Stanford University Press 1989, pp. 146–7.

[3]   Jean Baudrillard, *La société de consummation*, Paris: Editions Denoël 1970, p. 152. (English translation: *Consumer Society: Myths and Structures*, trans. by Chris Turner, London: Sage 1998, p. 102.)

[4]   Jean Baudrillard, *De la séduction*, Paris: Galilée 1979. (English translation: *Seduction*, trans. by Brian Singer, New York: St. Martin's Press 1990, p. 18; pp. 80ff.; p. 98; p. 101; p. 105; p. 115; p. 117.)

Kierkegaard here is again to "The Seducer's Diary," to a passage that Baudrillard had previously referenced in *Seduction*.[5]

Over the next twenty years, Baudrillard continued to make passing references to Kierkegaard and his work in texts and interviews. Twice—in *Cool Memories III* and *Cool Memories IV*—he references the problem of repetition.[6] And twice again he references the notion of secrecy; in *Fragments* and *Cool Memories V*.[7] *Cool Memories V* also includes a passing reference to "The Seducer's Diary."[8] Baudrillard's book *Impossible Exchange* attributes a comment to Kierkegaard about individuals who cannot face the Last Judgment.[9] Another passing remark, in an interview originally published in 1983, identifies Kierkegaard with a previous era in the history of thought, when "philosophy could express itself."[10]

In *The Ecstasy of Communication*, the summary document Baudrillard submitted as his *Habilitation* (required for supervising doctoral research in the French university system), Baudrillard recalls Kierkegaard only in reference to "The Seducer's Diary" and his treatment of it in *Seduction*.[11] This seems entirely appropriate. Aside from the passing remarks described above, Baudrillard's interest in Kierkegaard was focused on "The Seducer's Diary" and confined to *Seduction*. It seems likely that

---

[5]   See Jean Baudrillard, *Les strategies fatales*, Paris: Grasset 1983. (English translation: *Fatal Strategies*, trans. by Philip Beitchman and W.G.J. Niesluchowski, New York: Semiotext(e) and Pluto 1990, p. 129; p. 132; p. 135; Jean Baudrillard and Sophie Calle, *Suite Venitienne: Please Follow Me*, Paris: Editions de l'Etoile 1983, p. 76, English translation by Dany Barash and Danny Hatfield, Seattle: Bay Press 1988 (reprinted in Jean Baudrillard, *Fatal Strategies*, trans. by Philip Beitchman and W.G.J. Niesluchowski, New York: Semiotext(e) 1990, pp. 128–37).

[6]   See Jean Baudrillard, *Cool Memories*, vols. 1–5, Paris: Galilée 1987–2005, vol. 3, *Fragments: 1990–1995* (1995), p. 45. (English translation: *Cool Memories*, vols. 1–5, trans. by Emily Agar and Chris Turner, vols. 1–4 were published in London and New York: Verso 1990–2003, vol. 5 was published in Cambridge: Polity Press 2006, vol. 3: *Fragments: 1990–1995* (1997), trans. by Emily Agar, pp. 34–5.) Jean Baudrillard, *Cool Memories*, vol. 4: *1995–2000* (2000), p. 113. (*Cool Memories*, vol. 4: *1995–2000*, trans. by Chris Turner (2003), pp. 87–8.)

[7]   Jean Baudrillard, *D'un fragment l'autre: Entretiens avec François L'Yvonnet*, Paris: Albin Michel 2001, p. 158. (English translation: *Fragments: Conversations with François L'Yvonnet*, trans. by Chris Turner, London: Routledge 2004, p. 104.) Baudrillard, *Cool Memories*, vol. 5: *2000–2004* (2005), p. 26. (*Cool Memories*, vol. 5: *2000–2004*, trans. by Chris Turner (2006), p. 14.)

[8]   Baudrillard, *Cool Memories*, vol. 5: *2000–2004*, pp. 29–30. (*Cool Memories*, vol. 5: *2000–2004*, p. 17.)

[9]   Jean Baudrillard, *Échange impossible*, Paris: Galilée 1999, p. 66. (English translation: *Impossible Exchange*, trans. by Chris Turner, London: Verso 2001, p. 47.)

[10]   See "Revenge of the Crystal," interview with Guy Bellavance, *Parachute*, June–August 1983. (Reprinted in *Baudrillard Live: Selected Interviews*, ed. by Mike Gane, London: Routledge 1993, p. 50.)

[11]   Jean Baudrillard, *L'Autre par lui-même: Habilitation*, Paris: Galilée 1987, pp. 57–8. (English translation: *The Ecstasy of Communication*, trans. by Bernard and Caroline Schutze, New York: Semiotext(e) 1988, p. 65.)

Baudrillard did not devote any sustained attention to Kierkegaard's work other than while writing *Seduction* in the late 1970s.

Baudrillard himself does not in fact specify the works or editions of works by Kierkegaard that he has read or when he read them, through citations or otherwise. Nor does he reference any secondary literature or scholarship devoted to Kierkegaard that has influenced his own thought. "The Seducer's Diary" was first translated into French by Jean-Jacques Gateau (1887–1967), as *Le Journal du Séducteur*.[12] Fourteen years later, the entirety of *Either/Or* appeared in French translation.[13] More recently, during the years when Baudrillard himself was writing about Kierkegaard, Paul-Henri Tisseau and Else-Marie Jacquet-Tisseau translated Kierkegaard's complete works in twenty volumes for Éditions de L'Orante (1966–87). Baudrillard might have read any one or even several of these translations, but he offers no direct citations or specific remarks. His practice here is in keeping with the common French habit of imprecise citation in writings like these.

At least two writers who influenced Baudrillard a great deal were also interested, at key moments, in Kierkegaard: namely, Georges Bataille and Theodor Adorno. Bataille, however, and somewhat surprisingly given his interests, does not write about Kierkegaard's "Seducer's Diary," and Baudrillard's use of that text is distinct enough from Adorno's to refute the notion of Adorno having influenced Baudrillard's use of Kierkegaard in any meaningful way.[14] For Adorno, Kierkegaard's significance is in his ability to demonstrate the relationship between abstract spirit and the radical particularity of experience in this world. Baudrillard, however, makes no reference to Adorno's writings about Kierkegaard, though he freely admits Adorno's general influence on the orientation of his work.

III.

All of this in mind, looking back, it seems highly surprising that a dissident Marxist sociologist like Jean Baudrillard should have turned to a writer like Søren Kierkegaard precisely when and in the specific way that he did. As I have remarked, *Seduction* is a strange and pivotal text in Baudrillard's *corpus*. It marks a distinct break from his previous strategies and style of cultural criticism and should be understood as marking the passage to a new phase in his thought. The passage in question can be characterized as a one from the position of the critical subject to that of a cultural object. For the first decade of Baudrillard's writing career, he endeavored to speak in the tradition of critical consciousness, exemplified by Theodor Adorno. From that position, in each of his major works, he reprised and rejected the major assumptions of the reigning critical discourses of his day—Marxism, semiology,

---

[12]   Søren Kierkegaard, *Le Journal du Séducteur*, trans. by Jean-Jacques Gateau, Paris: Stock 1929.

[13]   Søren Kierkegaard, *Ou bien...ou bien*, trans. by F. Prior and M.H. Guignot, Paris: Gallimard 1943.

[14]   Theodor W. Adorno, *Kierkegaard. Konstruktion des Aesthetischen*, Frankfurt am Main: Suhrkamp Verlag 1962. (English translation: *Kierkegaard: Construction of the Aesthetic*, trans. by Robert Hullot-Kentor, Minneapolis: University of Minnesota Press 1989.)

sociology, and psychoanalysis—each of which was revealed, in distinct ways, to be a mode of representation based on the production of limited or false consciousness. After this period, Baudrillard would speak differently; he would endeavor to speak not as a subject but as an object, less as a producer than as a product, using the act of writing as what he called a "fatal strategy." The French title of Baudrillard's *Habilitation*—*L'Autre par lui-même* (the other by himself)—neatly summarizes his new perspective, in particular as it recalls French poet Arthur Rimbaud's (1854–91) famous claim, "*je est un autre*" (I is an other).[15] Baudrillard's passage to the position of an object is a passage away from critical consciousness toward a provocative new style of theory-literature.

Just prior to *Seduction*, Baudrillard published a collection of poetry, *L'Ange du Stuc*, and then in 1980, the year after *Seduction*, he began his *Cool Memories* series of loosely dated aphoristic fragments. Baudrillard ultimately published five volumes in the series between 1987 and 2005, and it is difficult to read them without thinking of "The Seducer's Diary." Kierkegaard's fictional editor, "A," had introduced that diary by saying: "Therefore, his diary is not historically accurate or simply narrative; it is not indicative but subjunctive."[16] Aside from the final word, the description applies as neatly to Baudrillard's *Cool Memories* series as it does to "The Seducer's Diary." Both works are reflective without being systematic or exhaustive; psychological, philosophical and at times theological; historical—in the sense of self-consciously framing episodes in the moral history of their times—and literary, without placing the entire burden of interest on their literary merits alone. Kierkegaard's work is "subjective" in the sense that it records the inner life of its author, the seducer. Baudrillard endeavors to be objective, not in the traditional scientific sense of that term, but in a new sense connoting radical alienation.

The *Cool Memories* series begins with the observation: "This is where the rest of life begins."[17] This is the rest of life, for the author, because, as he observes, it is likely that he has written the best book he will write, visited the most beautiful place he will ever visit, and been wounded in love more deeply than he ever will be again. What remains is the rest, "something extra" which is not without its charm. *Cool Memories* is a record of what remains and as such the writings contained therein never sparkle, hurry, or enthuse. The writing is "aesthetic," in Kierkegaard's sense, in its careful and intricate observation of the multiple surfaces—physical and psychological—of life, but it does not find deliverance in that aestheticism. In *Cool Memories*, people and things are enigmatic, including the author himself. Indeed, the author does not try to make his observations cohere into a full, personal or subjective world-view. The writings are instead presented as fragments. Though Baudrillard never discusses the connection, the *Cool Memories* series can, and I think should, be read as its author's continuation and update of Kierkegaard's "The Seducer's Diary."

Baudrillard has to *update* Kierkegaard's *Diary* in part because he affiliates Kierkegaard and the *Diary* with an earlier and now vanished era in culture. In the

---

[15]   See Arthur Rimbaud's famous letter to his friend Paul Demeny from May 15, 1871, reprinted in Arthur Rimbaud, *Oeuvres*, Paris: Garnier 1960, pp. 344ff.
[16]   *SKS* 2, 294 / *EO1*, 304.
[17]   Baudrillard, *Cool Memories*, vol. 1, p. 11. (*Cool Memories*, vol. 1, p. 3.)

"Revenge of the Crystal" interview cited above, Baudrillard identified Kierkegaard with a previous, "Romantic" era in the history of thought—"the beautiful period of subjective irony, of radical subjectivity"—which, he claims, is now over. In *Seduction*, he consistently associates "The Seducer's Diary" with an earlier era in thought. In previous eras, seduction was "*hot*, while that of our modern idols is *cold*, being at the intersection of two cold mediums, that of the image and that of the masses."[18] The terms "hot" and "cold" derive from Marshall McLuhan's (1911–80) language in media studies, but they correspond clearly enough to the previous dichotomy: the Romantic era of radical subjectivity was an era of *hot* or "high impact" experience, thought and representation; the modern era of objective irony is a cold era of images and of the masses. The masses, it should be remembered, are not a class; for Baudrillard, they are incapable of developing critical self-consciousness, which derives from an understanding of class-based identity.

Baudrillard's continued insistence that Kierkegaard belongs to a previous era in the history of thought evidences more than a little nostalgia for that era, and something more than nostalgia. Baudrillard's critical enterprise entails a search for symbolic or ritual forms of *contemporary* cultural expression that may be associated with that previous era and, more distantly, with primitive cultures. It is, in other words, important that Kierkegaard not be modern. Baudrillard's appeal to Kierkegaard is in part an attempt to reach beyond modern thought to find another kind of critical thinking. In *Fatal Strategies*, Baudrillard links his use of the term "symbolic" with Kierkegaard's notion of the aesthetic.[19] The aesthetic and the symbolic are both descriptors of "fatal strategies"; they do not promise any transcendence, but they nevertheless "hold the secret."[20]

With all of this in mind, it is unsurprising that Baudrillard remained uninterested in developing a more thorough or critical approach to Kierkegaard's work. As an atheist, Baudrillard took no interest in Kierkegaard's theological work or in his attacks on the religious institutions of Denmark. And as a critic of modern thought and culture, he took no interest in Kierkegaard's more commonly celebrated contributions to that thought. Rather, Baudrillard remained focused on the critical resource that he discovered in "The Seducer's Diary."

That resource was, of course, the notion of seduction. Baudrillard needed that particular resource at that particular moment in his own work as a lever against three contemporary cultural institutions: psychoanalysis, feminism, and the philosophical project of Michel Foucault (1926–84). In *Symbolic Exchange and Death* (1976), his major work immediately preceding *Seduction*, Baudrillard discussed the psychoanalytic theme of the death drive as an aspect of symbolic exchange. *Seduction* continues this reflection by pursuing the theme of seduction as the "lost object" of psychoanalysis.[21] Sigmund Freud (1856–1939) himself had abandoned the theory of seduction in 1907, and it had remained outside of psychoanalytic theory until Jacques Lacan (1901–81) brought it back in both theory and practice. Baudrillard's

---

[18]   Baudrillard, *De la séduction*, p. 132. (*Seduction*, p. 95.)
[19]   Baudrillard, *Les Stratégies fatales*, p. 191. (*Fatal Strategies*, p. 132.)
[20]   Ibid.
[21]   Baudrillard, *De la séduction*, p. 80. (*Seduction*, p. 55.)

turn to the theory of seduction is another appeal to and critique of the institution of psychoanalysis, particularly as embodied in the late 1970s, in the texts and practices of Lacan.

The theory of seduction was also a useful lever in Baudrillard's critique of third-wave feminism. Third-wave feminism was in need of critique, in Baudrillard's view, because it sought a specious equality for its constituency. Rather than celebrating the freedoms and pleasures historically enjoyed by women, third-wave feminism sought to transform women into the equivalent of men in the workforce, and to transform female practices of seduction, among other pleasures, into modes of phallic sexuality. The liberation and valorization of the female orgasm is in fact a reduction of modes of pleasure. In this argument, the coincidence of women's liberation and the spread of pornography is entirely unsurprising. In pornography, the body is reduced to a pure object devoid of transcendence, meaning, or value. In liberation, women have been freed to become members of an alienated workforce. In both cases, what has been lost is the symbolic or aesthetic value of unique personal experience. Though this critique was in fact a defense of the heterogeneity of female experience in the modern world, feminists greeted it with outrage.

Baudrillard also developed his theory of seduction as a response to the philosophical project of Michel Foucault, particularly his *History of Sexuality*, the first volume of which appeared in 1976. Baudrillard's first remarks on seduction appeared in a corrosive review article devoted to that work, published as *Forget Foucault* in 1977.[22] Foucault's mistake, in Baudrillard's estimation, was to reduce sexuality to a species of power struggle and to attempt to liberate sexuality as a means of resistance to social power structures. Baudrillard turned to the theory of seduction as an alternative. Seduction, he said, has nothing to do with power. But Baudrillard does not mention Kierkegaard in his article on Foucault, which might suggest that he did not begin to consider Kierkegaard's text until after December 1976, when he wrote that piece.

With all of this in mind, we can say that Baudrillard's appeal to Kierkegaard's "Seducer's Diary" is thus more than a little over-determined, and this, among other things, makes *Seduction* a very strange book. It offers pointed critiques of psychoanalysis, pornography, and feminism, as well as modern mass media and social and political practices, and stands in line with his earlier critiques of psychoanalysis, Marxism, and contemporary French philosophy (as practiced by Foucault). Against all of these discourses, Baudrillard developed his theory of seduction based on Kierkegaard's text, without bothering to advance a critical interpretation of Kierkegaard's work in general.

For Baudrillard, the theory of seduction proposes a gesture—seduction—that is irreducible to the modern logic of production and representation, and hence also power in all of its guises. Seduction may produce results but the seducer does not produce those results himself or herself. Seduction in fact governs provocation, rather than production. It provokes actions on the part of the individual who has been seduced. Seduction is also distinct from sexuality. Where sex begins, seduction has

---

[22]   Jean Baudrillard, *Oublier Foucault*, Paris: Galilée 1977. (English translation: *Forget Foucault*, trans. by Nicole Dufresne, New York: Semiotext(e) 1987.)

ended. Seduction certainly involves the body, but it does not reduce the body to an object, certainly not to a mere sex object, as does pornography. Seduction inevitably enlists the whole body—and all other manner of allurements besides—rather than just the genitalia. It creates an entire range of specific and individual meanings that adhere to the objects of the world, as when at the end of "The Seducer's Diary," Johannes has his servant replicate the room in which his seduction of Cordelia largely took place by surrounding her with objects that will speak to her of specific moments in their relationship.

Seduction is in this way a game of signs in which the seducer surrounds himself or herself with potential signs that must be activated by the one who is being seduced. If the signs are too overt, the seduction enters the realm of pornography, a simple offering of sex. If the signs fail to communicate their intended meanings, they fail to seduce. The signs must scintillate or suggest, promise or provoke, without ever delivering precisely what they promise.

The provocation involved in seduction entails an actual relationship, filled with specific points of encounter. This, too, distinguishes seduction from the easy sexuality available through pornography. In pornography, sex is equal and anonymous, a matter of quantity rather than unique quality. What matters is the nudity of the desired object and that is all. If any additional qualities are present, they threaten to tip the exchange into the realm of the symbolic, to lend one or another of the partners in the act a modicum of power over the other.

Seduction, on the other hand, thrives on this imbalance without succumbing to the exploitation of power. Over and over again in "The Seducer's Diary," one wonders whether Johannes should be credited with the seduction at the heart of the text or if Cordelia might herself not have been the responsible party. Her physical beauty and charm can be said to have seduced him and thus initiated the whole affair well before she herself even became aware of her effect on him. Johannes, of course, behaves in a calculated manner so as to seduce Cordelia, to lead her along a path, but even this path evolves slowly and in specific response to Cordelia's actions and responses to Johannes. Neither one of the pair can be said to have been solely responsible for the precise way the events unfolded that summer.

In "Either/Or: Peripeteia of an Alternative in Jean Baudrillard's *De La Séduction*," Louise Burchill argues that Baudrillard has misunderstood the dialectical nature of Kierkegaard's argument and procedure in "The Seducer's Diary" and *Either/Or* as a whole, and she is perhaps correct in this assertion.[23] But her criticism is not really to the point. Baudrillard's interest is in the process by which the seduction unfolds rather than in the conclusions that Kierkegaard might anticipate us drawing from it. Seduction, in Baudrillard's rather precisely limited reading, is, once again, a fatal strategy. It is a kind of an action that does not benefit from or lead to a transcendence of any kind. It never escapes the aesthetic realm, the realm of things in this world.

---

[23]   See Louise Burchill, "Either/Or: Peripeteia of an Alternative in Jean Baudrillard's *De La Séduction*," in *Seduced and Abandoned: The Baudrillard Scene*, ed. by Andre Frankovits, Glebe, Australia: Stonemoss Publishers 1984, pp. 87–100. (Reprinted in *Jean Baudrillard*, ed. by Mike Gane, London: Sage Publications 2000 (*Sage Masters of Modern Social Thought*, vol. 3), pp. 183–98.)

Against the Hegelian notion of dialectics, Baudrillard proposes what he calls a "double spiral."[24] In the double spiral, each pole in an action—like an act of seduction—is ultimately and indeed inevitably reversible. Johannes is simultaneously led by and leading Cordelia throughout the tale. He can never achieve anything that she does not permit him to achieve, yet his thoughts and deeds are never any more fully circumscribed by her than hers are by him. The limited freedoms of this kind of "spiral" relationship describe Baudrillard's critical procedure for the rest of his career. A provocateur, he endeavors to lead us astray, to seduce us and provoke our interest, to undermine our expectations and our assumptions by activating those expectations and assumptions themselves.[25]

Baudrillard is arguably best known in the Anglophone world for his book *Simulacra and Simulation*.[26] The terms of this title advance Baudrillard's theory of seduction into new realms, without substantially altering it. The gesture of simulation—as a literary trope—is itself a method of seduction. In *Seduction*, he speculates:

> Can one imagine a theory that would treat signs in terms of their seductive attraction, rather than their contrasts and oppositions? Which would break with the spectacular nature of the sign and the encumbrance of the referent? And in which the terms would play amongst themselves within the framework of an enigmatic duel and an inexorable reversibility?[27]

Contrasts and oppositions describe the mechanics of the Hegelian dialectic. Baudrillard's appeal to attraction and reversibility is an appeal to the spiral logic of seduction.

The perspective is partly expressed in a passage from Kierkegaard that Baudrillard quotes twice, in *Seduction* and in the *Please Follow Me* portion of *Fatal Strategies*: "There is a mirror on the opposite wall; she [Cordelia] is not contemplating it, but the mirror is contemplating her."[28] As a critic, Baudrillard becomes the mirror of his world but also its provocative seducer, anticipating its changes of mood and orientation, all while remaining invisible to that world, in some way outside the frame of its vision. The seducer is not part of the power structure, not truly implicated in or circumscribed by the dialectics of action and response.

Another passage from Kierkegaard that Baudrillard quotes twice, in *Fragments* and in *Cool Memories V*, offers a justification for this perspective: "He who speaks of himself should never say the whole truth; he should keep it secret and divulge

24   Baudrillard, *L'Autre par lui-même*, pp. 68–9. (*The Ecstasy of Communication*, p. 79.)
25   These themes are explored in Jørgen Dehs, "Cordelia, c'est moi, Kierkegaard og Baudrillard," in *Denne slyngelagtige eftertid. tekster om Søren Kierkegaard*, vols. 1–3, ed. by Finn Frandsen and Ole Morsing, Århus: Slagmark 1995, vol. 3, pp. 541–54.
26   Jean Baudrillard, *Simulacres et simulation*, Paris: Galilée 1981. (English translation: *Simulacra and Simulation*, trans. by Sheila Faria Glaser, Ann Arbor, Michigan: University of Michigan Press 1994.)
27   Baudrillard, *De la séduction*, p. 141. (*Seduction*, p. 103.)
28   *SKS* 2, 305 / *EO1*, 315. See Baudrillard, *De la Séduction*, p. 144 (*Seduction*, p. 105) and Baudrillard, *Les stratégies fatales*, p. 196 (*Fatal Strategies*, p. 135).

only fragments."[29] For Baudrillard, this notion describes a practice of "scrupulous delicacy" in which the author, like the seducer, knows what to say and what not to say in order to provoke the necessary response from his target. This delicacy is of the essence of seduction, and it is of the essence of the double spiral of Baudrillard's critical enterprise. The strategy of the double spiral is one of simultaneous advance and retreat. Every provocative assertion—each attack—inevitably entails a reversal—the reversal or overturning of the object or ideology in question—but also a withdrawal, as Baudrillard withdraws from the field of critical engagement rather than seeking to recapitulate the terms of the whole. The curious nostalgic tone of his work also derives in part from this strategy. It is as if Baudrillard were always writing *after* the object in question, even, as in *L'Autre par lui-même*, after his own work, or, as in *Cool Memories*, after his life.

The secret—the truth—is never really revealed, and in fact, for Baudrillard, as for Nietzsche, the truth is that there is not any. That is the real secret. Transcendence is itself a myth and a provocation designed to lure us into the symbolic order. Only the movement of the spiral is real.

With all of this in mind, it would be disinguous of me to suggest that Kierkegaard's place in Baudrillard's work is in fact that of a secret, a secret key that might unlock Baudrillard's *corpus*, or even a few corners of it. And yet, as I have attempted to show, this is in fact the case, at least to some extent. Kierkegaard is surely there behind Baudrillard's theory of seduction, his notion of a non-dialectical "spiral" of reversible provocation and response, his seductive practice of cultural criticism, and his fragmentary diaries, placid mirrors of our world. For all of that, Kierkegaard's influence certainly cannot be said to circumscribe Baudrillard's vast *corpus*.

---

[29]　　See Baudrillard, *D'un fragment l'autre: Entretiens avec François L'Yvonnet*, p. 158. (*Fragments: Conversations with François L'Yvonnet*, p. 104; and Baudrillard, *Cool Memories*, vol. 5, *2000–2004*, p. 26. (*Cool Memories*, vol. 5, *2000–2004*, p. 17.)

Bibliography

I. References to or Uses of Kierkegaard in Baudrillard's Corpus

La société de consommation, Paris: Editions Denoël 1970, p. 152. (English translation: *Consumer Society: Myths and Structures*, trans. by Chris Turner, London: Sage 1998. p. 102.)

De la séduction, Paris: Galilée 1979, p. 33; pp. 110ff.; pp. 135ff.; p. 157; pp. 159ff. (English translation: *Seduction*, trans. by Brian Singer, New York: St. Martin's Press 1990, p. 18; pp. 80ff.; pp. 98ff.; p. 115; pp. 117ff.)

Les strategies fatales, Paris: Grasset 1983, p. 187; p. 191; p. 196. (English translation: *Fatal Strategies*, trans. by Philip Beitchman and W.G.J. Niesluchowski, New York: Semiotext(e) and Pluto 1990, p. 129; p. 132; pp. 135–6.)

L'Autre par lui-même: Habilitation, Paris: Galilée 1987, p. 57. (English translation: *The Ecstasy of Communication*, trans. by Bernard and Caroline Schutze, New York: Semiotext(e) 1988, p. 65.)

Cool Memories, vols. 1–5, Paris: Galilée 1987–2005, vol. 3 (*Fragments: 1990–1995*), p. 45; vol. 4 (*1995–2000*), p. 113; vol. 5 (*2000–2004*), p. 26; pp. 29–30. (English translation: *Cool Memories*, vols. 1–5, trans. by Emily Agar and Chris Turner, vols. 1–4 were published in London and New York: Verso 1990–2003, vol. 5 was published in Cambridge: Polity Press 2006, vol. 3 (*Fragments: 1990–1995*), pp. 34–5; vol. 4 (*1955–2000*), pp. 87–8; vol. 5 (*2000–2004*), p. 14; p. 17.)

Baudrillard Live: Selected Interviews, ed. by Mike Gane, London: Routledge 1993, see p. 50. (English translation: "The Revenge of the Crystal" interview with Guy Bellavance, *Parachute*, June–August, 1983; Reprinted in *Revenge of the Crystal: A Baudrillard Reader*, London: Pluto 1989, p. 17.)

Échange impossible, Paris: Galilée 1999, p. 66. (English translation: *Impossible Exchange*, trans. by Chris Turner, London: Verso 2001, p. 47.)

D'un fragment l'autre: Entretiens avec François L'Yvonnet, Paris: Albin Michel 2001, p. 158. (English translation: *Fragments: Conversations with François L'Yvonnet*, trans. by Chris Turner, London: Routledge 2004, p. 104.)

Jean Baudrillard and Sophie Calle, *Suite Venitienne. Please Follow Me*, Paris: Editions de l'Etoile and Cahiers du Cinema 1983, p. 76. (English translation by Dany Barash and Danny Hatfield, Seattle: Bay Press 1988; reprinted in *Fatal Strategies*, trans. by Philil Beitchman and W.G.J. Niesluchowski, New York: Semiotext(e) 1990, pp. 128–37.)

II. Sources of Baudrillard's Knowledge of Kierkegaard

Adorno, Theodor W., *Kierkegaard. Konstruktion des Ästhetischen*, Tübingen: J.C.B. Mohr 1933.

— *Dialektik der Aufklärung. Philosophische Fragmente* (co-authored with Max Horkheimer), Amsterdam: Querido Verlag N.V. 1947, p. 23; pp. 210–11.

— *Minima moralia. Reflexionen aus dem beschädigten Leben*, Berlin and Frankfurt am Main: Suhrkamp 1951, p. 131; p. 157; p. 249; pp. 288–92; pp. 430–1.

Barthes, Roland, *Sur Racine*, Paris: Éditions du Seuil 1963, p. 40.

— *Fragments d'un discours amoureux*, Paris: Éditions du Seuil 1977, p. 248.

— *Leçon*, Paris: Éditions du Seuil 1978, pp. 15–16; pp. 27–8.

— *Sollers écrivain*, Paris: Éditions du Seuil 1979, p. 31.

Bataille, Georges, *L'Expérience intérieure*, Paris: Gallimard 1943, p. 29; p. 72; p. 170, note (in *Œuvres Complètes*, vols. 1–12, Paris: Gallimard 1970–88, vol. 5, p. 24; p. 56; p. 128, note).

Benjamin, Walter, *Das Passagen-Werk*, in *Gesammelte Schriften*, vols. 1–7, ed. by Rolf Tiedemann and Hermann Schweppenhäuser with Theodor W. Adorno and Gershom Scholem, Frankfurt am Main: Suhrkamp 1982, vol. 5, pp. 429–31.

— *Ursprung des deutschen Trauerspiels*, Berlin: Ernst Rowohlt Verlag 1928, pp. 233–4.

Deleuze, Gilles, *Nietzsche et la philosophie*, Paris: Presses Universitaires de France 1962, pp. 41–3; 107, note 2.

— *Le bergsonisme*, Paris: Presses Universitaires de France 1966, p. 38, note 2; p. 53.

— *Différence et répétition*, Paris: Presses Universitaires de France 1968, pp. 12–20; p. 38; p. 39, note 1; pp. 126–7; p. 289, note 1; pp. 347–8; p. 377; p. 397.

— *Logique du sens*, Paris: Minuit 1969, p. 349.

— *Cinéma 1. L'image-mouvement*, Paris: Minuit 1983, pp. 158–64; pp. 184–5.

— *Cinéma 2. L'image-temps*, Paris: Minuit 1985, p. 224, note 30; pp. 227–8; pp. 230–1.

— *Pourparlers 1972–1990*, Paris: Minuit 1990, p. 84.

— *Deux régimes de fous. Textes et entretiens 1975–1995*, Paris: Minuit 2003, p. 192; p. 264; p. 307.

Derrida, Jacques, *L'écriture et la différence*, Paris: Seuil 1967, p. 51; p. 143; pp. 161–5.

— *Glas*, Paris: Galilée 1974, pp. 224–5; pp. 258–9.

— *Passions*, Paris: Éditions Galilée 1993, pp. 57–8; p. 84.

— *Force de loi*, Paris: Galilée 1994, p. 58.

— *Adieu à Emmanuel Lévinas*, Paris: Galilée 1997, p. 24; pp. 166–7; p. 209.

— *Donner la mort*, Paris: Galilée 1999.

Heidegger, Martin, *Sein und Zeit*, Halle: Niemeyer 1927, pp. 175–96, see also p. 190, note 1; p. 235, note 1; and p. 338, note 1.

Kierkegaard, Søren, *Le journal d'un séducteur*, trans. by Jean-Jacques Gateau, Paris: Club français du livre 1962.

Lacan, Jacques, *Le Séminaire. Livre II. Le Moi dans la théorie de Freud et dans la technique psychanalytique. 1954–1955*, Paris: Le Seuil 1978, p. 110; pp. 124–5.

— *Le Séminaire. Livre X. L'Angoisse. 1962–1963*, Paris: Éditions de Seuil 2004, p. 385.

— *Le Séminaire. Livre XI. Les Quatre Concepts fondamentaux de la psychanalyse*, Paris: Le Seuil 1974, p. 59.

— *Le Séminaire. Livre XVII. L'envers de la psychanalyse*, Paris: Le Seuil 1991, pp. 51–2; pp. 168–9.

Marcuse, Herbert, *Reason and Revolution: Hegel and the Rise of Social Theory*, New York: Oxford University Press 1941, pp. 262–7.

Sartre, Jean-Paul, *L'être et le néant. Essai d'ontologie phénoménologique*, Paris: Gallimard 1943 (*Bibliothèque des Idées*), pp. 58–84; pp. 94–111; pp. 115–49; pp. 150–74; pp. 291–300; pp. 508–16; pp. 529–60; pp. 639–42; pp. 643–63; pp. 669–70; pp. 720ff.

— *L'existentialisme est un humanisme*, Paris: Nagel 1946, pp. 27–33.

— *Situations I*, Paris: Gallimard 1947, pp. 154–5; pp. 162–3; pp. 168ff.

III. Secondary Literature on Baudrillard's Relation to Kierkegaard

Burchill, Louise, "Either/Or: Peripeteia of an Alternative in Jean Baudrillard's *De La Séduction*," in *Seduced and Abandoned: The Baudrillard Scene*, ed. by Andre Frankovits, Glebe, Australia: Stonemoss Publishers 1984. (Reprinted in Mike Gane, *Jean Baudrillard*, London: Sage Publications 2000 (*Sage Masters of Modern Social Thought*, vol. 3), pp. 183–98.)

Dehs, Jørgen, "Cordelia, c'est moi, Kierkegaard og Baudrillard," *Denne slyngelagtige eftertid. tekster om Søren Kierkegaard*, vols. 1–3, ed. by Finn Frandsen and Ole Morsing, Århus: Slagmark 1995, vol. 3, pp. 541–54.

Gane, Mike, *Baudrillard: Critical and Fatal Theory*, London: Routledge 1991, pp. 159–66.

Kellner, Douglas, *Jean Baudrillard: From Marxism to Postmodernism and Beyond*, Cambridge and Palo Alto: Polity Press and Stanford University Press 1989, pp. 146–7.

Morris, Meaghan, "Banality in Cultural Studies," *Block*, vol. 14, pp. 15–26.

Ernest Becker:

A Kierkegaardian Theorist of Death and Human Nature

Rick Anthony Furtak

The writings of Ernest Becker (1924–74) are distinguished by an intense and fervent sincerity that ought to be appreciated by anyone who values these same qualities in Kierkegaard's thought. And if Kierkegaard's works are difficult to classify within the boundaries of any single intellectual discipline, then Becker is a worthy heir to the Kierkegaardian legacy in that respect as well. His admirers, who tend to regard Becker as an underappreciated genius, span an eclectic variety of fields. Although he was formally educated as a cultural anthropologist, Becker—who viewed his own project as an attempt to develop a scientific understanding of the human being—has left a legacy in many areas within the social sciences and humanities. While Becker is not exactly recognized as a canonical figure in any one category of academic scholarship, recent works have sought to appropriate his ideas for philosophy,[1] literary studies,[2] religious thought,[3] healthcare,[4] and educational theory,[5] as well as numerous branches

---

[1]   See, for example, Frederick Sontag, *The Return of the Gods: A Philosophical/ Theological Reappraisal of the Writings of Ernest Becker*, New York: Peter Lang 1989. See also E. Doyle McCarthy, "The Sources of Human Destructiveness: Ernest Becker's Theory of Human Nature," *Thought*, vol. 56, 1981, pp. 44–57; and Maxine Sheets-Johnstone, "Death and Immortality Ideologies in Western Philosophy," *Continental Philosophy Review*, vol. 36, 2003, pp. 235–62.

[2]   See Kirby Farrell, *Play, Death, and Heroism in Shakespeare*, Chapel Hill, North Carolina: University of North Carolina Press 1989; and Ron Evans, *The Creative Myth and the Cosmic Hero: Text and Context in Ernest Becker's The Denial of Death*, New York: Peter Lang 1992.

[3]   See, for example, Stephen W. Martin, *Decomposing Modernity: Ernest Becker's Images of Humanity at the End of an Age*, Toronto: Institute for Christian Studies 1997; Sally A. Kenel, *Mortal Gods: Ernest Becker and Fundamental Theology*, Lanham, Maryland: University Press of America 1988; and Jarvis Streeter, *Human Nature, Human Evil, and Religion: Ernest Becker and Christian Theology*, Lanham, Maryland: University Press of America 2008.

[4]   See Neil Elgee, "Mortality Anxiety: An Existential Understanding for Medical Education and Practice," in *Death and Denial*, ed. by Daniel Liechty, Westport, Connecticut: Praeger Publishers 2002; Harry J. Berman, "Generativity and Transference Heroics," *Journal of Aging Studies*, vol. 9, 1995, pp. 5–11; and Steen Halling, "Meaning Beyond Heroic Illusions?: Transcendence in Everyday Life," *Journal of Religion and Health*, vol. 39, 2000, pp. 143–58.

[5]   Michael Alan Kagan, *Educating Heroes: The Implications of Ernest Becker's Depth Psychology of Heroism for Philosophy of Education*, Durango, Colorado: Hollowbrook

of social and clinical psychology.[6] It is in the last of these categories that Becker's influence has been the most visible within the human sciences, and this influence is principally based upon Becker's 1973 book, *The Denial of Death*,[7] which is also the text in which Becker engages significantly with Kierkegaard. Accordingly, my main focus in this article will be on Kierkegaard's importance for the formation of Becker's psychological ideas, as evidenced in the relevant portions of *The Denial of Death*.

Writings from the early 1960s show Becker developing in incipient form some of the insights that would come to their fruition a decade later in *The Denial of Death*, which was awarded the Pulitzer Prize for General Nonfiction in 1974. A journal entry written in Rome during a formative period in Becker's life refers to Kierkegaard as one example of the "truly Olympian and free souls" who have recognized that atheism is untenable, since every professed atheist must effectively believe in something larger than himself "in order to be sustained in his own meaning," even if it is nothing more than technological progress or public opinion.[8] He continued to reflect on this theme after returning to the USA,[9] and in his 1969 book *Angel in Armor* he remarked that "no person is strong enough to support the

---

Publishing 1994. See also Jonathan Kermiet, *The Image of Man in Ernest Becker's Work and Its Implications for Health Education*, M.A. Thesis, University of Maryland, College Park, Maryland 1977.

[6]   "Terror Management Theory" is the name for an entire research program in academic psychology that has been spawned from Becker's ideas: for a synopsis and bibliography, see Sheldon Solomon et al., "The Cultural Animal: Twenty Years of Terror Management Theory and Research," in *Handbook of Experimental Existential Psychology*, ed. by Jeff Greenberg et al., New York: Guilford Press 2004, pp. 13–34. Cf. Sheldon Solomon, Jeff Greenberg, and Tom Pyszczynski, "Tales from the Crypt: On the Role of Death in Life," *Zygon*, vol. 33, 1998, pp. 9–44. Other examples of Becker's influence in psychology include, for example, Steven J. Bartlett, "The Humanistic Psychology of Human Evil: Ernest Becker and Arthur Koestler," *Journal of Humanistic Psychology*, vol. 48, 2008, pp. 340–63; Patrick H. Munley and Phillip D. Johnson, "Ernest Becker: A Vital Resource for Counseling Psychology," *Counseling Psychology Quarterly*, vol. 16, 2003, pp. 363–72; Neil J. Elgee, "Laughing at Death," *Psychoanalytic Review*, vol. 90, 2003, pp. 475–97; LeRoy Aden, "The Challenge of Becker: A New Approach to Pastoral Care," *Journal of Psychology and Christianity*, vol. 3, 1984, pp. 74–9; G.W. Hartz, "The Denial of Death: Foundations for an Integration of Psychological and Theological Views of Personality," *Journal of Psychology and Theology*, vol. 8, 1980, pp. 53–63; Daniel Liechty, *Transference and Transcendence: Ernest Becker's Contribution to Psychotherapy*, Lanham, Maryland: Rowman and Littlefield 1995; and Jerry S. Piven, *The Psychology of Death in Fantasy and History*, Westport, Connecticut: Praeger Publishers 2004.

[7]   Ernest Becker, *The Denial of Death*, New York: Free Press 1973. By 1997, when this book was reissued by the same publisher, with a new Foreword by Sam Keen, it had sold over half a million copies.

[8]   Journal entry dated 25 April 1964, in Robert Kramer (ed.), "The Journals of Ernest Becker, 1964–1969," *Journal of Humanistic Psychology*, vol. 47, 2007, pp. 430–73, at pp. 436–7.

[9]   Becker was an American who taught briefly at Syracuse University after earning his Ph.D. there, and then subsequently at the University of California at Berkeley, San Francisco State University, and eventually Simon Fraser University in Vancouver, Canada.

meaning of his life unaided by something outside him," but that to "drop the pretense of self-sufficiency" would require a person to build himself anew "on entirely new foundations of meaning." Just after saying this, Becker adds that Kierkegaard is "a greater psychologist than Freud" because he grasped this in a way that Freud did not.[10] In *The Birth and Death of Meaning*, he calls Kierkegaard "one of the greatest modern theorists of anxiety," which according to Becker was seen by Kierkegaard as a "response to man's condition," especially to human "finitude."[11] Although each of these themes is mentioned only briefly prior to *The Denial of Death*, they would become some of the dominant motifs of Becker's major work.

The one place in Becker's writings where he engages in a sustained dialogue with Kierkegaard is during a remarkable, though relatively short, chapter of *The Denial of Death*.[12] Before we turn exclusively to that chapter, let me sketch some of the overall argument of Becker's book. He begins with the claim that knowledge of our mortality is a distinctive feature of human beings: "man [*sic*] is not just a blind glob of idling protoplasm, but a creature with a name who lives in a world of symbols... and not merely matter. His sense of self-worth is constituted symbolically, [feeding] on an abstract idea of his own worth"; although we are biological organisms, then, we also long for "cosmic significance."[13] This need to feel that our lives are meaningful is only amplified insofar as we grasp our "abject finitude,"[14] which coexists uneasily with our most noble capacities and highest aspirations:

> We might call this existential paradox the condition of *individuality within finitude*. Man has a symbolic identity that brings him sharply out of nature. He is a symbolic self, a creature with a name, a life history. He is a creator with a mind that soars out to speculate about atoms and infinity, who can place himself imaginatively at a point in space and contemplate bemusedly his own planet....Yet, at the same time...man is a worm and food for worms.[15]

Our "self-consciousness," combined with our bodily nature and the mortality that it represents, confronts us with a truly "excruciating dilemma":

> This is the paradox: [the human being] is out of nature and hopelessly in it; he is dual, up in the stars and yet housed in a heart-pumping, breath-gasping body that once belonged to a fish and still carries the gill-marks to prove it. His body is a material fleshy casing that is alien to him in many ways—the strangest and most repugnant way being that it aches and bleeds and will decay and die. Man is literally split in two: he has an awareness of his own splendid uniqueness in that he sticks out of nature with a towering majesty,

---

10   Ernest Becker, *Angel in Armor: A Post-Freudian Perspective on the Nature of Man*, New York: George Braziller 1969, p. 130.

11   Ernest Becker, *The Birth and Death of Meaning: An Interdisciplinary Perspective on the Problem of Man*, 2nd ed., New York: Free Press 1971, p. 42. (This reference to Kierkegaard does not appear in the first edition of this work: *The Birth and Death of Meaning: A Perspective in Psychiatry and Anthrolopogy*, New York: Free Press 1962.)

12   Becker, "The Psychoanalyst Kierkegaard," in *The Denial of Death*, pp. 67–92.

13   Ibid., p. 3.

14   Ibid., p. 33.

15   Ibid., p. 26.

and yet he goes back into the ground a few feet in order blindly and dumbly to rot and disappear forever. It is a terrifying dilemma to be in and to have to live with.[16]

This anxious sense of our creaturely vulnerability and eventual death is the consequence of our status as a type of living being that has attained self-awareness and knows that it is mortal. Continuing to expand on this "existential paradox," Becker sets "the freedom of thought" alongside "the body, [which] represents determinism and boundness."[17] As a result of this divide between "symbols (freedom) and body (fate)," the human being is plagued by a "confusion over the meaning of his life."[18] The realm of bodily limitation and fragility threatens us with a sense of nothingness and insignificance. In order not to be overcome by this dreadful feeling of the transience and futility of human life, we are in need of some reassurance that our lives are not merely fleeting and meaningless, and Becker does not hesitate to describe what we seek as a kind of "redemption."[19] Every human ideology, or framework of belief, is therefore essentially religious, whether or not it acknowledges this, because of the need that it attempts to address: namely, the need to feel that one's life, albeit finite, is significant in the scheme of things.[20] Each cultural or personal interpretive scheme, if we rely upon it in order to make sense of existence, is thus "a living myth of the significance of human life."[21] Devotion to the goal of providing for one's family in a capitalist society, or to the goal of serving dutifully as a police officer in an atheist state, could qualify as "religious" if it provides one with an "ultimate concern" and is therefore effectively functioning as a god.[22] In this sense, Becker says, our best "scientific picture of the human condition…coincides exactly with the religious understanding of human nature."[23] That is, a psychological description of the human being explains our theological impulse, that is, our tendency to ground our self-understanding in something beyond ourselves.

Obviously, the "science of man" for which Becker was searching throughout his career could not be value-neutral, because it would have to come to terms with this problem of meaning: that is, our need to find meaningful and convincing

---

[16]   Ibid., pp. 26–7.

[17]   Ibid., pp. 41–2.

[18]   Ibid., p. 44.

[19]   Ibid., p. 167. See also Daniel Liechty, "Introduction" to *The Ernest Becker Reader*, ed. by Daniel Liechty, Seattle: University of Washington Press 2005, pp. 11–23, see especially pp. 15–19.

[20]   See Becker, *The Denial of Death*, pp. 5–6. Cf. Liechty, "Introduction," p. 21.

[21]   Becker, *The Denial of Death*, p. 7.

[22]   The phrase is from Paul Tillich, *The Dynamics of Faith*, New York: Harper 1958. Becker appeals to Tillich's notion of faith repeatedly throughout *The Denial of Death*; see, for example, p. 68; p. 130; p. 175; pp. 277–80.

[23]   Quoted by Sam Keen in "A Conversation with Ernest Becker," *Psychology Today*, vol. 7, no. 2, 1974, pp. 71–80 (reprinted in *The Ernest Becker Reader*, ed. by Liechty, pp. 219–29, at p. 219). See also Becker, *The Denial of Death*, p. 196: "psychology has to give way to 'theology.' " He quotes Otto Rank, *Beyond Psychology*, New York: Dover 1958, p. 194, to the effect that man is a "theological being" and that the "need for a truly religious ideology" is "inherent in human nature."

interpretations of our lives, in spite of our mortality and creatureliness. In the human sciences, Becker maintains, we must reject the presumption that "science has no business talking about values."[24] Keeping in mind this qualified, or expanded, definition of the scientific, we can see what Becker means in claiming that Kierkegaard's work furnishes us with acute "empirical analyses of the human condition."[25] This claim appears on the first page of the chapter in which Becker delves into Kierkegaard's writings to show their relevance for psychology or (one might say) philosophical anthropology. It is followed by the remark that Kierkegaard was "post-Freudian" in an uncanny sense, because he not only anticipated some central insights of psychoanalytic theory but actually saw further than Freud himself in certain respects.[26] Just as Becker's engagement with Kierkegaard is almost entirely confined to this one chapter, the range of Kierkegaardian texts on which Becker relies is almost exclusively limited to *The Concept of Dread*, that is, *The Concept of Anxiety*, and *The Sickness unto Death*, both of which he read in Walter Lowrie's translations.[27] Nonetheless, it is clear from this chapter of *The Denial of Death* that Kierkegaard's work had a decisive impact on Becker's thinking. Furthermore, although Becker disregarded the issue of pseudonymity, he was sufficiently well-attuned to the content of Kierkegaard's writings that, at one point, he correctly guesses what English word was intended when Lowrie's edition contains a similar, plausible word due to a typographical error.[28]

Becker begins his reading of Kierkegaard by associating our "fallen" condition with the awareness of our mortality: "if Adam eats of the fruit of the tree of knowledge God tells him, 'Thou shalt surely die.' "[29] Repeating what by now is a familiar theme, Becker comments that the human being "was given a consciousness of his individuality [and] at the same time he was given the consciousness…of his own death and decay." This "existential paradox" of the human condition, as Becker named it earlier, has "one great penalty for man: it [gives] him *dread*, or anxiety."[30]

---

24   Ernest Becker, *The Structure of Evil: An Essay on the Unification of the Science of Man*, New York: George Braziller 1968, p. 385.

25   Becker, *The Denial of Death*, p. 67.

26   Ibid., p. 68.

27   See Søren Kierkegaard, *The Concept of Dread*, trans. by Walter Lowrie, Princeton: Princeton University Press 1957 [1946]; Søren Kierkegaard, *The Sickness unto Death*, in *Fear and Trembling and The Sickness unto Death*, trans. by Walter Lowrie, Princeton: Princeton University Press 1954. For the original Danish text of *The Concept of Anxiety* and *The Sickness unto Death*, see *SKS* 4, 307–461 and *SKS* 11, 113–242.

28   The passage is from *The Sickness unto Death*, p. 169 in the 1954 Lowrie edition: Becker quotes as it appears, "[the self] tries itself out with floundering in the possible," and adds after "tries" the comment, "[*sic*: 'tires'?]"—which is more accurate. Lowrie had it right in an earlier edition of *The Sickness unto Death*, which appeared in one volume by itself: see Kierkegaard, *The Sickness unto Death*, trans. by Walter Lowrie, Princeton: Princeton University Press 1946, p. 54: "[t]he self…tires itself out with floundering in the possible." See *SKS* 11, 151 / *SUD*, 36. The Hongs have "it flounders around in possibility until it is exhausted"; "*det spræller sig træt i Mulighed*" is how the phrase reads in the Danish.

29   Becker, *The Denial of Death*, p. 69. Cf. Gen 2:17.

30   Ibid., p. 69.

Referring to *The Concept of Anxiety*, he notes that the human being, according to Kierkegaard, is a "synthesis of the soulish and the bodily," and therefore experiences anxiety; "if man were a beast or an angel," that is, if he were either without self-awareness or entirely non-animal, then "he would not be able to be in dread."[31] Since we cannot be "straightforwardly an animal or an angel," Becker adds, our self-consciousness is terrifying: "death is man's peculiar and greatest anxiety."[32] Hence, we are inclined to block out any awareness of our mortality, and in *The Concept of Anxiety* this is described as "shut-upness"; so Becker proposes that "by 'shut-upness' Kierkegaard means what we today refer to [as] repression," and he points to Kierkegaard's portrayal of "a partisan of the most rigid orthodoxy," for whom "truth is an ensemble of ceremonies," as an example of the repressed person who has a "closed personality."[33] Key to Becker's analysis of Kierkegaard's text is its linking of "shut-upness" with "untruth," which is "precisely unfreedom."[34] He continues: "Kierkegaard gives us some portrait sketches of the styles of denying possibility," and "is intent on describing what we today call 'inauthentic' men, [who] follow out the styles of automatic and uncritical living in which they were conditioned as children."[35] For further illustration, Becker now turns to *The Sickness unto Death* and its portrayal of the all-too-human forms of despair.

Quoting from the discussion of how necessity's despair is to lack possibility, and finitude's despair is to lack infinitude, Becker points out the "dull security" of the figure who follows "the others" and lives after their fashion but fails to become a self. He observes that "for Kierkegaard 'philistinism' was triviality, man lulled by the daily routines of his society, content with the satisfactions that it offers him: in today's world the car, the shopping center, the two-week summer vacation."[36] Volunteering additional examples of his own, Becker writes that such a figure is the "culturally normal" man, who "imagines that he has an identity if he pays his insurance premium, that he has control of his life if he guns his sports car or works his electric toothbrush."[37] Such a person "dares not stand up for his own meanings" because it is more comforting to live "embedded in a safe framework of social and cultural obligations and duties."[38] He is weighed down by necessity, and yet everything seems trivial: so to avoid the dizzying threat of too much symbolic possibility, "[h]e holds onto the people who have enslaved him in a network of crushing obligations, belittling interaction, precisely because these people *are his*

---

[31]   Kierkegaard, *The Concept of Dread*, p. 39; p. 139 (see *SKS* 4, 349 / *CA*, 43 and *SKS* 4, 454 / *CA*, 155).
[32]   Becker, *The Denial of Death*, pp. 69–70.
[33]   Ibid., pp. 70–1. Becker quotes from *The Concept of Dread*, pp. 110–14; and p. 124 (see *SKS* 4, 424–9 / *CA*, 123–8 and *SKS* 4, 440 / *CA*, 139–40).
[34]   Kierkegaard, *The Concept of Dread*, p. 114 (see *SKS* 4, 429 / *CA*, 128). "Shut-upness" is Lowrie's rendering of *Indesluttethed*.
[35]   Becker, *The Denial of Death*, p. 73.
[36]   Ibid., p. 74.
[37]   Ibid., 79. Becker cites Kierkegaard, *The Sickness unto Death*, pp. 166–7; and pp. 170–4 (see *SKS* 11, 149–51 / *SUD*, 33–5 and *SKS* 11, 153–7 / *SUD*, 37–42).
[38]   Becker, *The Denial of Death*, p. 79.

shelter, his strength, his protection against the world."[39] Referring back to his own chief explanatory paradigm, Becker summarizes as follows:

> Kierkegaard is painting for us a broad and incredibly rich portrait of types of human failure, ways in which man succumbs to and is beaten by life and the world; beaten because he fails to face up to the existential truth of his situation—the truth that he is an inner symbolic self, which signifies a certain freedom, and that he is bound by a finite body, which limits that freedom. The attempt to ignore either aspect of man's situation, to repress possibility or to deny necessity, means that man will live a lie, fail to realize his true nature, be "the most pitiful of all things."[40]

If philistinism overcompensates to avoid the despair of too much possibility, the other extreme is infinitude's despair, in which one becomes fantastic and attempts "to deny the limitations of the finite." This also "exaggerate[s] one half of the human dualism at the expense of the other," and what someone suffering from this form of despair needs is "an acknowledgment of reality, the reality of one's limits."[41] Taken to psychotic or pathological extremes, the despairs of possibility/infinitude and of necessity/finitude would, respectively, culminate in schizophrenia and depression. Becker's use of these diagnostic terms might seem contrary to the spirit of Kierkegaard's writings; however, his aim is not to medicalize the different modes of despair but to argue that underlying common mental disorders are spiritual afflictions based upon different ways of failing to come to terms with one's existential predicament.

Mental and spiritual health, on Becker's view, would depend on living with a full awareness of both our creaturely finitude and our need to work out some relation to a transcendent source of meaning. Kierkegaard has "no easy idea of what 'health' is,"[42] but he makes it clear that it cannot be the "fictitious" well-being of the "normal," well-adjusted person. Because we are entirely finite, and utterly self-aware and conscious, we cannot honestly deny one or another side of human nature for the sake of attaining equanimity: "anxiety is the result of the perception of the truth of one's condition," and self-awareness "means full fear and trembling, at least some of the waking day."[43] It would be obviously false for us not to acknowledge our corporeality, since this would require a willful self-deception; on the other hand, if we give up on finding ultimate significance and try to narrow down our meanings "to the body and to this world alone," Becker argues that we will either be dissatisfied with mundane reality or else idolatrously devoted to something finite, as exemplified in the "deification" of another person or in zealous patriotism, just to name two instances.[44] If we could achieve a credible redemption, it would have to combine a

---

[39]   Ibid., p. 80.
[40]   Ibid., p. 75.
[41]   Ibid., pp. 76–7. On "philistinism," see Kierkegaard, *The Sickness unto Death*, pp. 184–7 (see *SKS* 11, 165–8 / *SUD*, 50–3).
[42]   Becker, *The Denial of Death*, pp. 86–7.
[43]   Ibid., p. 59.
[44]   Ibid., p. 168; p. 148; see also p. 128; and p. 160. Cf. Liechty, "Introduction," p. 22: "The drama of human spirituality" is based in the fact that "we may choose the security of idols or the adventure of faith."

full awareness of both our most lofty possibilities and our most base limitations.[45] And these supremely demanding criteria, in Becker's view, can be fulfilled only by Kierkegaardian faith.

If anxiety "reveals the truth of [one's] situation," then—in the words of *The Concept of Anxiety*, as Lowrie renders it and Becker quotes—someone who has been "educated" by dread, or anxiety, "knows more thoroughly than a child knows the alphabet that he demands of life absolutely nothing, and that terror, perdition, annihilation, dwell next door to every man."[46] Henceforth, he will "interpret reality differently" than before.[47] When half-gods go, the gods arrive: that is, someone who has faced up to his or her own nothingness will no longer be contented with making an idol of social stature, deifying a movie star, or accumulating petty symbols of wealth. He or she will need deeper and more real sources of assurance, in order to feel that life is not in vain:

> This is Kierkegaard's message, the culmination of his whole argument about the dead-ends of character, the ideal of health, the school of anxiety, the nature of real possibility and freedom. One goes through it all to arrive at faith, the faith that one's very creatureliness has some meaning to a Creator; that despite one's true insignificance, weakness, death, one's existence has meaning in some ultimate sense because it exists within an eternal and infinite scheme of things brought about and maintained to some kind of design by some creative force.[48]

Even though this notion of religious faith might sound exceedingly vague, it captures the crucial idea that individual existence is of absolute significance, which is said by Kierkegaard to be *the* principle on which Christianity is based.[49] According to Becker, the human being "attains cosmic significance by affirming its connection with the invisible mystery at the heart of creation. This is the meaning of faith. At the same time it is the meaning of the merger of psychology and religion in Kierkegaard's thought."[50] Lest it appear as if he is offering too easy a solution to the human dilemma, or the "existential paradox," Becker points out and endorses the statement that faith does not annihilate anxiety, but constantly renews itself out of anxiety's dying gasp.[51]

Ernest Becker died of cancer six months shy of his fiftieth birthday, in the midst of writing a book that sought to develop the political implications of *The Denial of Death*,[52] and his ambitious intellectual project could not be articulated any further.

---

[45]   As Becker puts it, "psychological rebirth" would require being subjected "to the terrifying paradox of the human condition, since one must be born not as a god, but as a man, or as a god-worm, or a god who shits. Only this time without the neurotic shield that hides the full ambiguity of one's life." Becker, *The Denial of Death*, p. 58.

[46]   Ibid., p. 88.

[47]   Ibid. Quoting Kierkegaard, *The Concept of Dread*, p. 140 (see *SKS* 4, 455 / *CA*, 156).

[48]   Becker, *The Denial of Death*, p. 90.

[49]   Notebook entry from 1847; see *SKS* 20, 88, NB:123 / *JP* 2, 1997. Cf. *SKS* 23, 374, NB19:70 / *JP* 2, 2165. See also Luke 12:17.

[50]   Becker, *The Denial of Death*, p. 91.

[51]   Becker cites Kierkegaard, *The Concept of Dread*, p. 104 (see *SKS* 4, 419 / *CA*, 117).

[52]   This unfinished manuscript was edited and published posthumously, see Ernest Becker, *Escape from Evil*, New York: Free Press 1975.

There remained some unresolved questions that his theory had not answered, and not only minor ones. Giving a nod to Jacques Choron, Becker admits that it may never "be possible to decide whether the fear of death is or is not the basic anxiety," thus granting what is potentially a major concession.[53] We might speculate about what Kierkegaard would say about this, and whether he would wish that Becker had revised his view so as to depict anxiety as not necessarily being about death "as such," but this is debatable.[54] More important, among the divergences between Kierkegaard's work and Becker's own, is the tendency in Becker's writings to describe world-views as irrational or illusory byproducts of a repressed death anxiety, as if no belief system can offer us more than "the illusion of meaning."[55] In his deathbed interview with Becker, Sam Keen invokes Kierkegaard's name as he challenges Becker with respect to this bias:

> You say man lives on two levels. He is an animal and a symbol-maker, hence he lives in one world of fact and another of illusion….But it seems to me you fall into the old positivist distinction between fact and interpretation or data and meaning. I doubt that we have anything like a raw world of facts to which we then add a layer of symbolic interpretations….As Kierkegaard might have said, "Where do you, Ernest Becker, a historical individual, stand in order to give so certain a separation of fact and illusion?"[56]

Becker, who had already taken issue with Freud's claim that religion is an "illusion," saying that "it represents on the contrary the furthest reach of the self, the highest [ideal] man can achieve,"[57] pauses in response to this question. Finally, he replies: "Yes, I see. That is a very good point. I don't really know how to answer that. What you are saying is that the symbolic transcendence of death may be just as true as the fact of death." He adds that a religious faith without "false consolations" is something that he has striven to maintain throughout his adult life.[58] And he concedes that, as long as our beliefs are not predicated on a denial of certain truths about the human condition, most notably the truth about our mortality, then there is no good reason to dismiss our interpretations of that condition as untruthful simply because they are underdetermined by objective fact. Insofar as he assented to such a view, Becker might have arrived at an even more truly Kierkegaardian perspective than his written works would sometimes indicate. In any event, his work has been instrumental in conveying certain elements of Kierkegaard's thought to a broader audience in the social sciences—to a degree that the professedly "unscientific" Dane would probably never have imagined.

---

[53]   Becker, *The Denial of Death*, p. 15. He is citing Jacques Choron, *Death and Western Thought*, New York: Collier Books 1963, p. 17.

[54]   Cf. Robert C. Solomon, *True to Our Feelings: What Our Emotions are Really Telling Us*, New York: Oxford University Press 2007, p. 41.

[55]   See *The Denial of Death*, p. 80. This way of thinking has continued to inform Terror Management Theory (see n. 6 above), as is noted by Eugene Webb, "Ernest Becker and the Psychology of Worldviews," *Zygon*, vol. 33, 1998, pp. 71–86.

[56]   Keen, "A Conversation with Ernest Becker," in *The Ernest Becker Reader*, p. 224.

[57]   Becker, *The Denial of Death*, p. 174.

[58]   Keen, "A Conversation with Ernest Becker," in *The Ernest Becker Reader*, pp. 224–5.

Bibliography

I. References to or Uses of Kierkegaard in Becker's Corpus

The Structure of Evil: An Essay on the Unification of the Science of Man, New York: George Braziller 1968, p. 270.

Angel in Armor: A Post-Freudian Perspective on the Nature of Man, New York: George Braziller 1969, p. 130; p. 185.

The Birth and Death of Meaning: An Interdisciplinary Perspective on the Problem of Man, 2nd ed., New York: Free Press 1971, p. 42; p. 144. (These references to Kierkegaard do not appear in the first edition of this work: *The Birth and Death of Meaning: A Perspective in Psychiatry and Anthropology*, New York: Free Press 1962.)

The Denial of Death, New York: Free Press 1973, pp. 67–92; pp. 169–75; pp. 196–200; p. 205; p. 258.

II. Sources of Becker's Knowledge of Kierkegaard

May, Rollo, *The Meaning of Anxiety*, revised ed., New York: W.W. Norton 1977 [1950], pp. xiv–xv; p. xxi; p. 15; pp. 20–1; pp. 26–8; pp. 32–51; pp. 58–9; pp. 65–6; p. 99; p. 113; p. 123; p. 125; p. 133; p. 151; p. 158; p. 192; p. 207; pp. 218–20; p. 229; p. 244; p. 247; p. 265; p. 365; p. 370; p. 376; p. 379; pp. 384–5; p. 390; pp. 392–3.

Miller, Libuse Lukas, *In Search of the Self: The Individual in the Thought of Kierkegaard*, Philadelphia: Muhlenberg Press 1962.

Rohde, Peter P. (ed.), *The Diary of Søren Kierkegaard*, trans. by Gerda M. Andersen, New York: Philosophical Library 1960.

Shestov, Lev, *Athens and Jerusalem*, trans. by Bernard Martin, Athens, Ohio: Ohio University Press 1966, see especially pp. 229ff.

III. Secondary Literature on Becker's Relation to Kierkegaard

Bellinger, Charles, *The Unrepentant Crowd: Søren Kierkegaard and Ernest Becker on the Roots of Political Violence*, M.A. Thesis, Pacific School of Religion, Berkeley, California 2007.

Furtak, Rick Anthony, *Wisdom in Love: Kierkegaard and the Ancient Quest for Emotional Integrity*, Notre Dame, Indiana: University of Notre Dame Press 2005, p. 82; p. 118; p. 188.

Harvey, Van A., *Feuerbach and the Interpretation of Religion*, New York: Cambridge University Press 1995, pp. 295–7; pp. 304–6.

Hughes, Glenn, *Transcendence and History: The Search for Ultimacy from Ancient Societies to Postmodernity*, Columbia, Missouri: University of Missouri Press 2003, pp. 205–7.

Loy, David R., *Lack and Transcendence: The Problem of Death and Life in Psychotherapy, Existentialism, and Buddhism*, Amherst, New York: Prometheus Books 2003, p. 19.

Martin, Stephen W., *Decomposing Modernity: Ernest Becker's Images of Humanity at the End of an Age*, Toronto: Institute for Christian Studies 1997, p. 47; pp. 78–80.

Mooney, Edward F., *Knights of Faith and Resignation: Reading Kierkegaard's Fear and Trembling*, Albany, New York: State University of New York Press 1991, p. 59; p. 157.

Mullen, John Douglas, *Kierkegaard's Philosophy: Self-Deception and Cowardice in the Present Age*, Lanham, Maryland: University Press of America 1995, p. 6; p. 62; p. 165.

Schneider, Kirk J., *The Paradoxical Self: Toward an Understanding of Our Contradictory Nature*, Amherst, New York: Humanity Books 1999, p. 7; p. 177.

Sontag, Frederick, "The Metaphysics of Psychology," *International Philosophical Quarterly*, vol. 22, 1982, pp. 35–40.

— "Life and Death," *American Journal of Theology and Philosophy*, vol. 4, 1983, pp. 55–63.

— *The Return of the Gods: A Philosophical/Theological Reappraisal of the Writings of Ernest Becker*, New York: Peter Lang 1989, p. 105; p. 128.

Westphal, Merold, *God, Guilt, and Death: An Existential Phenomenology of Religion*, Bloomington, Indiana: Indiana University Press 1984, pp. 95–106.

Yalom, Irvin D., *Existential Psychotherapy*, New York: Basic Books 1980, p. 493.

Ludwig Binswanger:

Kierkegaard's Influence on Binswanger's Work

Elisabetta Basso

> People are always shouting that a melancholiac
> should fall in love, and then his melancholy would all
> vanish. If he actually is melancholy, how would it be
> possible for his soul not to become melancholically
> absorbed in what has come to be the most important
> of all to him?
>
> Søren Kierkegaard, *Repetition*[1]

In "Dream and Existence"[2]—the work of Ludwig Binswanger (1881–1966) which represents the programmatic manifesto of the Swiss psychiatrist's anthropological program, well known as *Daseinsanalyse*—there is a Kierkegaard quotation in exergue,[3] from then on he would remain one of the most constant references in all Binswanger's work. Now, in spite of such an imposing presence, the role and the weight of the Danish philosopher on Binswanger's thought is still today almost completely neglected by both Kierkegaardian and Binswangerian secondary

I wish to express my gratitude to the Howard V. and Edna H. Hong Kierkegaard Library, St. Olaf College, Northfield, Minnesota and especially to Cynthia Wales Lund, without whose kind and valuable bibliographical aid I could not have written this article. A special thanks also to Peter Moench, who revised it.

[1]   *SKS* 4, 13–14 / *R*, 136.

[2]   Ludwig Binswanger, "Traum und Existenz," *Neue Schweizer Rundschau*, vol. 23, 1930, pp. 673–85; pp. 766–79 (in his *Ausgewählte Werke in vier Bänden*, vols. 1–4, ed. by Hans-Jürg Braun, Heidelberg: Asanger 1992–94, vol. 3, pp. 95–119; English translation: "Dream and Existence," in *Being-in-the-World. Selected Papers of Ludwig Binswanger*, trans. by Jacob Needleman, New York: Harper & Row 1963, pp. 222–48; This translation was revised by Keith Hoeller in *Review of Existential Psychology and Psychiatry*, vol. 19, no. 1, 1984–85, pp. 81–105, special issue on "Dream and Existence." Here, I will refer to this latest edition).

[3]   "Above all, we must keep firmly in mind what it means to be a human being." As Keith Hoeller remarks in his "Foreword" to Binswanger's "Dream and Existence" (pp. 13–14)—referring to Herbert Spiegelberg's *Phenomenology in Psychology and Psychiatry: A Historical Introduction* (Evanston, Illinois: Northwestern University Press 1972, p. 194)—this quotation is from chapter 2 of the *Concluding Unscientific Postscript*: "The Subjective Truth, Inwardness; Truth is Subjectivity" (*SKS* 7, 182 / *CUP1*, 198).

literature. Usually the literature confines itself to tracing it back generally to the "origins of the existential movement in psychology,"[4] or to the introduction of phenomenology in psychology and psychiatry.[5]

The reasons for this neglect are probably different in the cases of Binswanger and Kierkegaard. With regard to the "philosophical" influences on Binswanger's thought, the name of the Swiss psychiatrist has been—and still is—more obviously connected to the phenomenological projects of Edmund Husserl (1859–1938) and Martin Heidegger (1889–1976), to whom he expressly and programmatically referred throughout the course of his many-sided research on the epistemological status of psychology and psychiatry. With regard to Kierkegaard, by contrast, the most obvious approach—in considering a "psychiatric" reception of his thought— has been to deal with him as a clinical case, either according to a biographical point of view, or according to the model of psychiatrists' studies on philosophers and artists: one could consider, for instance, Karl Jaspers' (1883–1969) essay on Strindberg and Van Gogh,[6] or the innumerable examples that psychoanalysis in particular, since its origins, has elaborated in this respect. Especially in the past, there have been indeed such approaches to Kierkegaard's work, some with the explicit purpose of considering Søren Kierkegaard from a psychiatric or a psychoanalytical perspective.[7] As all Kierkegaard scholars know, such an attempt to reduce his thought to the expression of a mental illness was already made in 1845 by the literary critic Peter Ludvig Møller (1814–65), who published a critical review of *Stages On*

---

[4]   Cf. Rollo May, "The Origins and Significance of the Existential Movement in Psychology," in *Existence—A New Dimension in Psychiatry and Psychology*, ed. by Rollo May, Ernest Angel, and Henri F. Ellenberger, New York: Basic Books 1958, pp. 3–36. Gordon Marino also points out Kierkegaard's work—in particular *The Concept of Anxiety*—as "the source book of existential psychology and psychoanalysis"; see Gordon Marino, "Anxiety in *The Concept of Anxiety*," in *The Cambridge Companion to Kierkegaard*, ed. by Alastair Hannay and Gordon D. Marino, Cambridge: Cambridge University Press 1998, pp. 308–28, see p. 308.

[5]   Cf. Spiegelberg, *Phenomenology in Psychology and Psychiatry*.

[6]   Karl Jaspers, *Strindberg und Van Gogh. Versuch einer pathographischen Analyse unter vergleichender Heranziehung von Swedenborg und Hölderlin*, Bern et al.: Bricher 1922 (*Arbeiten zur angewandten Psychiatrie*, vol. 5). (English translation: *Strindberg and Van Gogh: An Attempt of a Pathographic Analysis with Reference to Parallel Cases of Swedenborg and Hölderlin*, trans. by Oskar Grunow and David Woloshin, Tucson, Arizona: University of Arizona Press 1977.)

[7]   Marguerite Grimault drew up an almost complete historical bibliography (up to 1965) of the principal attempts which have been made by psychiatrists and psychoanalysts to analyze the "case" Kierkegaard: see her *La mélancolie de Kierkegaard*, Paris: Aubier 1965, pp. 63–186 (Chapter 1: "Le point de vue des psychanalystes" and Chapter 2: "Le point de vue des psychiatres et de quelques autres," of Part II: "Bibliographie historique et critique des principales études de psychopathologie sur le cas Kierkegaard"). See also Ib Ostenfeld, *Søren Kierkegaards psykologi*, Copenhagen: Rhodos 1972. (English translation: *Søren Kierkegaard's Psychology*, trans. and ed. by Alastair McKinnon, Waterloo: Wilfrid Laurier University Press 1978.) Ostenfeld's aim is to show that Kierkegaard's life and work can be adequately explained in terms of normal psychology and that he was an essentially healthy and stable individual.

Life's Way in his *Gæa, Aesthetic Yearbook 1846*, where he considered Kierkegaard's philosophical work as a personal therapeutic activity.[8]

Now, it is clear even just from a first glance at Binswanger's reading of Kierkegaard that it does not correspond to any of the above-mentioned approaches. This reading would seem to be, instead, much more similar in some respects to the point of view of psychologists who recognize a special interest in Kierkegaard's own psychological thinking.[9] One can consider, in this respect, Binswanger's statement in "The Case of Ellen West," according to which schizophrenia is "that sickness of the mind which Kierkegaard, with the keen insight of a genius, described and illuminated from all possible aspects under the name of 'Sickness Unto Death,' " and "no document could more greatly advance the existential-analytic interpretation of schizophrenia."[10] In any event, even if it is true that the most quoted of Kierkegaard's

---

[8]   See Peter Ludvig Møller, "A Visit to Sorø: Miscellany," *Gæa: Æsthetisk Aarbog*, 1846, pp. 144–87 / *COR*, Supplement, pp. 96–104 (partial translation). Kierkegaard reacted to Møller's attack by publishing an anonymous article in *Fædrelandet*, no. 2078, December 27, 1845 (reprinted in *SKS* 14, 79–84) / *COR*, 38–46), which in its turn attacked Møller in his private life, and this article sparked off the well-known "Corsair Affair."

[9]   Cf. above all Rollo May, *The Meaning of Anxiety*, New York: W.W. Norton 1996 [1950], pp. 31–45. See also Roland David Laing, *The Divided Self: A Study of Sanity and Madness*, London: Tavistock 1960. Especially focused on Kierkegaard's psychological thought is the work of Kresten Nordentoft, *Kierkegaards psykologi*, Copenhagen: G.E.C. Gad 1972. (English translation: *Kierkegaard's Psychology*, trans. by Bruce H. Kirmmse, Pittsburgh: Duquesne University Press 1972). Nordentoft is the only one who explicitly refers to Kierkegaard's presence in Binswanger's work (Nordentoft, *Kierkegaard's Psychology*, pp. 233–9). Here he expresses his "reservations about Ludwig Binswanger when he says that he knows of no other book which is more capable than *The Sickness unto Death* of making a contribution to the Dasein-analytic interpretation of schizophrenia," because actually "Kierkegaard has nowhere put forth anything which claims to be a coherent theory of madness in the strict sense" (ibid., p. 233). In any event, he argues that even if "it is too narrow to view *The Sickness unto Death* purely and simply as a book about schizophrenia…, nevertheless, the idea is obvious and fascinating, and some of his statements can contribute to the description to the schizophrenic process" (ibid., p. 234). Bruno Avrain, in his *Kierkegaard et Freud*, Paris: Alba nova 1988, uses Kierkegaard's unconscious religious need in order to oppose to Freud's view of religion as collective neurosis the idea that it is the repression of such a religious need that is the cause of neurosis, and not vice versa. Also, C. Stephen Evans situates Kierkegaard's view of the "unconscious" with respect to some other major psychological perspectives, and especially to psychoanalysis: cf. "Kierkegaard's View of the Unconscious," in *Kierkegaard in Post/Modernity*, ed. by Martin J. Matuštik and Merold Westphal, Bloomington, Indiana: Indiana University Press 1995, pp. 76–97; now in *Søren Kierkegaard: Critical Assessments*, vols. 1–4, ed. by Daniel W. Conway and K.E. Gover, London and New York: Routledge 2002, vol. 2 (*Epistemology and Psychology: Kierkegaard and the Recoil from Freedom*), pp. 72–92.

[10]   See Ludwig Binswanger, "Der Fall Ellen West. Eine anthropologisch-klinische Studie," *Schweizer Archiv für Neurologie und Psychiatrie*, vol. 53, 1944, pp. 255–77; vol. 54, 1944, pp. 69–117 and pp. 330–60; vol. 55, 1945, pp. 16–40, see vol. 54, 1944, p. 100 (in Binswanger, *Ausgewählte Werke in vier Bänden*, vol. 4, pp. 73–209, see p. 136; English translation: "The Case of Ellen West," in *Existence—A New Dimension in Psychiatry and Psychology*, p. 297.) The complete Binswanger quotation is the following: "One may say that in this document Kierkegaard has recognized with intuitive genius the approach of

works by Ludwig Binswanger are the "psychological" ones, it would be wrong to reduce Binswanger's reading of the Danish philosopher to the extrapolation of a series of ready-made theories, concepts, and categories, in order to apply them to the field of psychopathology. In turning to Kierkegaard's speculation, Binswanger never intended to test or acknowledge the "validity" of Kierkegaardian psychological insights and theses. More subtly and deeply, the connection between the two thinkers can be recognized at an epistemological level; here one sees the main problem which concerned Binswanger from the first decades of the twentieth century, namely, the problem of how to elaborate a *scientific* method for psychology while considering it as a "science of the spirit/mind" (*Geisteswissenschaft*), according to Wilhelm Dilthey's (1833–1911) paradigm. In this regard, we agree with those Kierkegaard scholars who point out that Kierkegaard's "psychology" does not correspond to modern psychology, and if we are to apply an established use of the word "psychology" to Kierkegaard's "psychological works," "it must be that of Hegel, for whom psychology is part of an all-embracing science of man as emerging self-conscious spirit."[11]

Binswanger received his first training in psychiatry at the beginning of the twentieth century in one of the most distinguished European psychiatric institutes, the Burghölzli in Zürich, which was directed by the famous Swiss psychiatrist Eugen Bleuler (1857–1939) and his young assistant, Carl Gustav Jung (1875–1961), who supervised Binswanger's degree in Medicine in 1907. Before his degree in Medicine in Zürich, Binswanger had studied at the Universities of Lausanne and Heidelberg. After he left the Burghölzli, he worked some months in Jena, at the University Psychiatric Hospital directed by his uncle, Otto Binswanger. Then he reached the psychiatric institute directed by his father in Switzerland, the Bellevue in Kreuzlingen (founded by his grandfather in 1857), where he would remain until his death in 1966. Thanks to Bleuler, the Burghölzli was the first university clinic to apply Freud's psychoanalytical theories to psychiatric diseases. This would have great importance for Binswanger's own research, since in Freud's method he could find at the same time a systematic approach to the psyche, and the concern for the singularity of the lived experiences he was looking for in order to reform an academic psychiatry which was positivistically orientated according to the model of the medical sciences. So, at the origins of Binswanger's psychiatric concern, there was the problem of how to reconcile the living *singularity* of the "case," namely, the singular psyche, with the *universality* of science. This was the question that Binswanger put to psychiatry and tried to answer throughout his theoretical activity: how could it be possible to *explain* the singular?

It was also the question that, at the same time, the German psychiatrist Karl Jaspers tried to answer, by elaborating an "*understanding* psychology" (*verstehende Psychologie*), which concluded, however, with the powerlessness of psychiatry

---

schizophrenia; for at the root of so many 'cases' of schizophrenia can be found the 'desperate' wish—indeed, the unshakable command to one's *Eigenwelt*, *Mitwelt*, and 'fate'—*not* to be oneself, as also can be found its counterpart, the desperate wish to *be* oneself."

[11]   Cf. Alastair Hannay, "Pathology of the Self," in his *Kierkegaard*, London and New York: Routledge & Kegan Paul 1982, pp. 157–8 (reprinted in *Søren Kierkegaard: Critical Assessments of Leading Philosophers*, vol. 2, ed. by Conway, pp. 157–8).

to cope with illness exactly because of the chasm of the boundless mutability and incommunicability of the singular.[12] While Jaspers argued that it was impossible to formulate any *laws* in the field of psychology, Binswanger objected that, on the contrary, such a formulation of scientific laws was possible for psychology: the question was to find some laws which would be adequate to the particular "object" of psychological inquiry, namely, the *psychic*.[13] Freud's "psychoanalysis," in this regard, for the young Binswanger, was the perfect example of the possibility of collecting *scientifically* and *systematically* the material of experience—namely, the "real lived experience of real and individual persons"[14]—"under rational themes and sense connections" (*Sinnzusammenhänge*).[15] It is exactly such a quest for the "*structural* connections and principles,"[16] or for the "rational and *a priori laws*"[17] which govern the organization and functioning of the psyche, that would lead Binswanger towards *Gestalt* psychology and towards Husserl's phenomenology.[18] In Binswanger's perspective, the great common intuition of Freud's methodology, *Gestalt* psychology and Husserlian phenomenology was the idea that

> the experience [*Erleben*] of something and the knowledge about such an experience cannot be understood on the basis of a "cause" which would be not this same lived experience….[They] are an *originary phenomenon* which is not further derivable; the science of "life" can be conceived on the basis of such a phenomenon, but inversely, this phenomenon cannot be explained by such a science.[19]

[12]   See Karl Jaspers, "Kausale und 'verständliche' Zusammenhänge zwischen Schicksal und Psychose bei der Dementia praecox (Schizophrenie)," *Zeitschrift für die gesamte Neurologie und Psychiatrie*, vol. 14, pp. 158–263 (published also in his *Gesammelte Schriften über Psychopathologie*, Berlin: Springer 1963, pp. 329–413).

[13]   Cf. Ludwig Binswanger's reply to Jaspers: "Bemerkungen zu der Arbeit Jaspers' 'Kausale und verständliche Zusammenhänge zwischen Schicksal und Psychose bei der Dementia praecox (Schizophrenie),' " *Internationale Zeitschrift für ärztliche Psychoanalyse*, vol. 1, 1913, pp. 383–90.

[14]   Ludwig Binswanger, "Erfahren, Verstehen, Deuten in der Psychoanalyse," *Imago*, vol. 12, nos. 2–3, 1926, pp. 223–37, see p. 229 (in his *Ausgewählte Werke in vier Bänden*, vol. 3, pp. 3–16, p. 9; published also in Ludwig Binswanger, *Ausgewählte Vorträge und Aufsätze*, vols. 1–2, Bern: Francke 1947–55, vol. 2, pp. 67–80).

[15]   Binswanger, "Erfahren, Verstehen, Deuten in der Psychoanalyse," p. 233 (in his *Ausgewählte Werke in vier Bänden*, vol. 3, p. 12).

[16]   Ludwig Binswanger, "Welche Aufgaben ergeben sich für die Psychiatrie aus den Fortschritten der neueren Psychologie?," *Zeitschrift für gesamte Neurologie und Psychiatrie*, vol. 91, nos. 3–5, 1924, pp. 402–36 (in his *Ausgewählte Vorträge und Aufsätze*, vol. 2, pp. 111–46).

[17]   See Binswanger, "Erfahren, Verstehen, Deuten in der Psychoanalyse," p. 235 (in his *Ausgewählte Werke in vier Bänden*, vol. 3, p. 13).

[18]   To understand the way in which Binswanger establishes a link between *Gestalt* psychology and Husserlian phenomenology, see his review of Eugène Minkoswki's work, *La schizophrénie. Psychopatologie des schizoïdes et des schizophrènes* (Paris: Payot 1927) that appeared in *Schweizer Archiv für Neurologie und Psychiatrie*, vol. 22, 1928, pp. 158–63, see p. 161.

[19]   Ludwig Binswanger, "Lebensfunktion und innere Lebensgeschichte," *Monatsschrift für Psychiatrie und Neurologie*, vol. 68, 1928, pp. 52–79, see p. 64 (in his *Ausgewählte Werke*

Such a conception, however, together with a closer adherence to Husserl's principle according to which the *phenomenon* must be grasped "in a more original and full way" apart from "any indirect hypostatization,"[20] would lead Binswanger—during the 1920s—to distance himself from the Freudian theory of instincts, in which one could recognize again the mark of a positivistic and reductionist view of the psyche. In this regard, the impact of Heidegger's *Being and Time* (1927) marks a further turning point in Binswanger's speculation, since the Heideggerian "analytic of *Dasein*" would have enabled phenomenology to make use of its theoretical instruments for an analysis of the existential and biographical actuality. According to Binswanger's reading of Heidegger, both psychoanalytical and phenomenological notions should be directed towards an anthropological research project oriented to the study of the "*Being-in*" (*Dasein*), namely, the being of man "in the world." The Binswanger essay which opens such a new speculative phase is "Dream and Existence" (1930), and the theme of the dream plays an important role in this regard, since his interest in it led Binswanger to conduct research in the field of literary history and history of the "spirit,"[21] which took him towards that *praktisches Menschenkenntnis* which defines anthropologically his reception of Heidegger's philosophical plan.

In order to understand the importance that Kierkegaard has in Binswanger's work, one has to point out the methodological and epistemological approach in which the Swiss psychiatrist assimilates different philosophical perspectives and makes use of them in an original way. The most evident and well-known example of that, is exactly his reception of Husserl's concept of *essence* (*Wesen*, εἶδος) and Heidegger's *Dasein* as a kind of methodological instrument or "systematic clue" to be used in order to understand the different forms or "styles" in which people organize and structure their existence as *being-in-the-world*.[22] Hence *Dasein*, conceived as the *structure* of existence, could guide the psychiatrist through the various expressions of mental diseases, furnishing him with the structural kernel or *a priori* element, which would be the key to penetrate and understand them, but also to classify them from a scientific point of view.

In this sense, we could suggest that Binswanger's reception of Kierkegaard, methodologically, is quite similar to Husserl's and Heidegger's, although the Swiss psychiatrist never wrote anything specially focused on Kierkegaard or on his direct connection to him. In this regard, I think we could borrow from Michel Foucault

---

in vier Bänden, vol. 3, pp. 71–94; published also in Binswanger, *Ausgewählte Vorträge und Aufsätze*, vol. 1, pp. 50–73). All translations from Binswanger's works are mine, unless otherwise noted.

20   Ludwig Binswanger, "Über Phänomenologie," *Zeitschrift für die gesamte Neurologie und Psychiatrie*, vol. 82, 1923, pp. 10–45, see p. 34 (in his *Ausgewählte Werke in vier Bänden*, vol. 3, p. 57).

21   See in particular Ludwig Binswanger, *Wandlungen in der Auffassung und Deutung des Traumes von den Griechen bis zum Gegenwart*, Berlin: Springer 1928.

22   Ludwig Binswanger, "Über die daseinsanalytische Forschungsrichtung in der Psychiatrie," *Schweizer Archiv für Psychiatrie und Neurologie*, vol. 57, 1946, pp. 209–35, see p. 220 (in his *Ausgewählte Werke in vier Bänden*, vol. 3, pp. 231–57, see p. 242; English translation: "The Existential Analysis School of Thought," in *Existence—A New Dimension in Psychiatry and Psychology*, pp. 191–212, see p. 201).

(1926–84) the remark that he made in 1984 about the relation of his own thought to Heidegger's: "I think it is important to have a small number of authors with whom one thinks, with whom one works, but about whom one does not write. Perhaps I'll write about them one day, but at such a time they will no longer be instruments of thought for me."[23]

What is undeniable, in any event, is the fact that Kierkegaard is almost everywhere present in Binswanger's work, in a way which evolves with the development of this work. In this regard, and in order to facilitate our task of detecting such a Kierkegaardian presence, we can subdivide Binswanger's work at least into three large phases, in each of which Kierkegaard's concepts play a particular role.

The first phase, which we could locate during the first two decades of the twentieth century, would correspond to the time when Binswanger was looking for a method for a psychology as "human science," which would be adequate to *understand* the authentically *human* nature of the *psyche*. As we have already seen, at this stage of his research, the Swiss psychiatrist adhered to the Freudian approach, in which he could find at the same time a sustained attention to the human being as a *person*, and a systematic method of analysis. And indeed the very first occurrence of the name of Kierkegaard in Binswanger's work is in his *Introduction to the Problems of General Psychology* (1922),[24] where he points out the importance which the literary and poetic sources—especially the Romantic *Realpsychologie*—had for the Diltheyan perspective of a *geisteswissenschaftlich* psychology.[25] Jaspers too, in his *General Psychopathology* (1913), mentioned the Danish philosopher several times—always together with Friedrich Nietzsche (1844–1900)—as one of the great "psychologists" as "self-revealers,"[26] and it is exactly in this same context and sense that Binswanger mentions both Kierkegaard and Jaspers.[27] What Binswanger especially appreciates in Kierkegaard, at this stage of his development, is his ethic of the *individual*, since it

---

[23]   Michel Foucault, "Le retour de la morale," in his *Dits et écrits, 1954–1988*, vols. 1–4, ed. by Daniel Defert and François Ewald, Paris: Gallimard 1994, vol. 4, p. 703. (English translation: "Final Interview," trans. by Thomas Levin and Isabelle Lorenz, in *Michel Foucault—Politics, Philosophy, Culture: Interviews and Other Writings, 1977–1984*, ed. by Lawrence D. Kritzman, New York: Routledge 1988, p. 250.)

[24]   Ludwig Binswanger, *Einführung in die Probleme der allgemeinen Psychologie*, Berlin: Springer 1922. Perhaps it is not superfluous to remark that such a volume was dedicated by Binswanger to both Eugen Bleuler and Sigmund Freud. Binswanger mentions Kierkegaard in Chapter IV: "Das fremde Ich und die wissenschaftliche Darstellung der Person. Einleitung" (p. 225); § II. 6: "Das Verstehen des seelischen Zusammenhangs" (p. 296); and § III: "Der Begriff der Person" c) "Person und Ästhetik. Der ästhetische Begriff der Persönlichkeit. Person und Kultur" (p. 322; p. 324).

[25]   See ibid., chapter II, § 1: "Die 'inhaltliche Wirklichkeit' des Seelenlebens (Dilthey) und das generalisierende Verfahren," pp. 31ff.

[26]   Karl Jaspers, *General Psychopathology*, trans. by J. Hoenig and Marian W. Hamilton, Baltimore and London: Johns Hopkins University Press 1997, p. 773. (German original: *Allgemeine Psychopathologie*, 9th ed., Berlin: Springer 1913.)

[27]   See Binswanger, *Einführung in die Probleme der allgemeinen Psychologie*, p. 296. Binswanger mentions the three authors together also in his later "Karl Jaspers und Psychiatrie," *Schweizer Archiv für Neurologie und Psychiatrie*, vol. 51, 1943, pp. 1–13; published also in *Karl Jaspers in der Diskussion*, ed. by Hans Saner, Munich: Piper 1973, pp. 21–32, see p. 26).

does not correspond to an *individualistic* world-view "in the sense of Max Stirner's" (1806–56), nor to "a hedonistic morality,"[28] but to the idea that "the individual can become aware of himself only by himself."[29]

What is interesting in this context is the fact that Binswanger considers Kierkegaard's psychological insights to be the very core of such an ethics: "The ingenious psychologist that Kierkegaard was [Binswanger remarks] is revealed not least of all in the closeness to real life that characterizes his ethics!"[30] This attitude towards Kierkegaard's ethics and religious thought remains unchanged throughout Binswanger's work. It is true that during the 1940s again—in considering schizophrenia in Kierkegaardian terms, as "the 'desperate' wish *not* to be oneself"[31]— the Swiss psychiatrist remarked:

> Even the physician of the soul who does not concur in the purely religious conception and interpretation of this "illness," who does not regard "the self" as eternal in the religious sense, does not believe in the religious sense in the power which posited it, who does not see in the human being a synthesis of the temporal and the eternal in the religious sense, but rather conceives existentially of despair in the sense of the sickness unto death—even such a physician, too, is deeply indebted to this work of Kierkegaard.[32]

In any event, during this first phase of Binswanger's thought, Kierkegaard is mentioned just in order to mark the *anthropological* direction on which the new psychology would set out: "The problems—as Kierkegaard says—could never more 'outrun one another, as if it were a matter of arriving first at the masquerade'; on the contrary, now we know somehow 'where we properly belong,' where we come from and what we want to achieve through our research."[33] So, Kierkegaard is compared

---

[28]   See Binswanger, *Einführung in die Probleme der allgemeinen Psychologie*, p. 322.

[29]   Ibid., p. 324. Here Binswanger quotes several passages from "The Balance between the Esthetic and the Ethical in the Development of the Personality," in *Either/Or*, Part 2.

[30]   Binswanger, *Einführung in die Probleme der allgemeinen Psychologie*, p. 324.

[31]   *SKS* 11, 46 / *SUD*, 49.

[32]   See Ludwig Binswanger, "Der Fall Ellen West. Eine anthropologisch-klinische Studie," *Schweizer Archiv für Neurologie und Psychiatrie*, vol. 53, 1944, pp. 255–77; vol. 54, 1944, pp. 69–117 and pp. 330–60; vol. 55, 1945, pp. 16–40, see vol. 54, 1944, pp. 100–1 ("The Case of Ellen West," pp. 297–8.) See also Ludwig Binswanger, "Der Fall Ellen West. Eine anthropologisch-klinische Studie," *Schweizer Archiv für Neurologie und Psychiatrie*, vol. 54, 1944, p. 95 ("The Case of Ellen West," pp. 292–3): "We must neither tolerate nor disapprove of the suicide of Ellen West, nor trivialize it with medical or psychoanalytic explanations, nor dramatize it with ethical or religious judgments. Indeed, the statement by Jeremias Gotthelf applies well to an existential totality such as Ellen West: 'Think how dark life becomes when a poor human wants to be his own sun'; or the dictum of Kierkegaard: 'However low a man has sunk, he can sink ever lower, and this *can* is the object of his dread.' But this growing dark and this sinking must not be understood by existential analysis by way of religion or ethics, but must be viewed and described anthropologically."

[33]   Ludwig Binswanger, "Welche Aufgaben ergeben sich für die Psychiatrie aus den Fortschritten der neueren Psychologie?" *Zeitschrift für gesamte Neurologie und Psychiatrie*, vol. 91, nos. 3–5, 1924, pp. 402–36, see p. 402 (in his *Ausgewählte Vorträge und Aufsätze*, vol. 2, p. 112). Cf. *SKS* 4, 317 / *CA*, 9.

to the "passionate religious *pathos* of Augustine, the brilliant 'poetic imagination' of Shakespeare, the philosophical prophecies of Nietzsche, but also to the sceptical, unbiased, attentive and narrative 'soul mood' [*Seelenstimmung*] of Montaigne."[34]

However—according to Binswanger—despite the importance of such spiritual attitudes for the new "*understanding*" psychology, all of them are lacking in "what only a science could afford: the elaboration, transmission, and diffusion of scientific *method*, the articulation and organization of the so obtained notions in a *theoretical and meaningful context*, and then the reflection on the *knowledge process*."[35] Therefore, such a humanistic tradition in which Binswanger places Kierkegaard did not systematize and organize its anthropological insights in the way Freud did. The Swiss psychiatrist will reassert this position in his book from 1928, *Changes in Concept and Interpretation of Dream from the Greeks to the Present*, where he remarks that if Freud had confined his analysis to the "study in depth of the man's life-history" without elaborating a scientific method, "he would not have gone really beyond other authors, like Nietzsche, Dostoevsky, Kierkegaard and other great moralists and poets."[36]

Such an attitude towards the Danish philosopher would change during the second and most extensive phase of Binswanger's work, which corresponds—as we have already anticipated above—to the Heideggerian "turn" of "Dream and Existence." According to Heidegger's *analytic of Dasein*, which aims to "radiograph" the *structure* of the human *being-in-the-world*, now Binswanger reread his own adherence to the scientific program of both Husserl's deduction of the *essence* of phenomena, and Freud's determination of *typical* psychic mechanisms, by the analysis of the *forms* or *styles* of existence which characterize every individuality as "modes of the human being." This way of considering *existence* in regard both to the individuality and the universality of the human being can be associated, according to Binswanger, "with the names—to cite only a few—of Heraclitus, Plato, Hegel, Kierkegaard, and Heidegger."[37] The meaning of Kierkegaard in this context is twofold, since Binswanger mentions the Danish philosopher at the same time together with, and against Hegel. The first sense concerns the aim of approaching the problem of dreams starting from the concept of "spirit." What Kierkegaard and Hegel—but also Kierkegaard and the other authors just mentioned—would have in common is the idea that the dream corresponds to "the possibility of a nonspiritual manner of being human."[38] Even if Binswanger does not mention it explicitly, it

---

[34]   Ludwig Binswanger, "Erfahren, Verstehen, Deuten in der Psychoanalyse," *Imago*, vol. 12, nos. 2–3, 1926, pp. 223–37, see p. 224 (in his *Ausgewählte Werke in vier Bänden*, vol. 3, p. 3).

[35]   Binswanger, "Erfahren, Verstehen, Deuten in der Psychoanalyse," *Imago*, vol. 12, p. 224 (in his *Ausgewählte Werke in vier Bänden*, vol. 3, p. 4).

[36]   Binswanger, *Wandlungen in der Auffassung und Deutung des Traumes*, p. 68.

[37]   Binswanger, "Traum und Existenz," *Neue Schweizer Rundschau*, vol. 23, 1930, pp. 673–85; pp. 766–79, see p. 772 (in his *Ausgewählte Werke in vier Bänden*, vol. 3, p. 112; "Dream and Existence," p. 97).

[38]   Binswanger, "Traum und Existenz," *Neue Schweizer Rundschau*, vol. 23, 1930, p. 772 (in his *Ausgewählte Werke in vier Bänden*, vol. 3, p. 112; "Dream and Existence," p. 97).

is quite clear—when he writes that "dreaming 'is' 'life-function' "[39]—that he refers to *The Concept of Anxiety*'s analysis of "innocence," namely, to the idea that spirit is dreaming when man is "physically qualified in immediate unity with his natural condition."[40] According to Binswanger, "an individual turns from mere self-identity to becoming a self or 'the' individual, and the dreamer awakens in that unfathomable moment when *he decides* not only to seek to know 'what hit him,' but seeks also to strike into and take hold of the dynamics of the events."[41] The core of the argumentation here is very close to Kierkegaard's, since Binswanger thinks that such a waking up is *spiritual*, and that subjectivity must develop by virtue of the Kierkegaardian "passion of inwardness."[42] According to Binswanger, the difference between Kierkegaard and Hegel appears clearly here in this kind of a Kierkegaardian progress of a subjectivity which works "through objectivity *and out of it again*."[43] So, if Binswanger chooses Kierkegaard, it is exactly because "as psychotherapists, we must go beyond Hegel, for we are not dealing with *objective* truth, with the congruence between thinking and Being, but with 'subjective truth,' as Kierkegaard would say."[44]

---

[39]   Binswanger, "Traum und Existenz," *Neue Schweizer Rundschau*, vol. 23, 1930, p. 778 (in his *Ausgewählte Werke in vier Bänden*, vol. 3, p. 118; "Dream and Existence," p. 102).

[40]   *SKS* 4, 347 / *CA*, 41: "Innocence is ignorance. In innocence, man is not qualified as spirit but is physically qualified in immediate unity with his natural condition. The spirit in man is dreaming."

[41]   Binswanger, "Traum und Existenz," *Neue Schweizer Rundschau*, vol. 23, 1930, p. 778 (in his *Ausgewählte Werke in vier Bänden*, vol. 3, p. 118; "Dream and Existence," p. 102). Such a conception will be reasserted by Binswanger in his essay on Freud's conception of man in the light of anthropology, see Ludwig Binswanger, "Freuds Auffassung des Menschen im Lichte der Anthropologie," *Nederlands Tijdschrift voor de Psychologie*, vol. 4, nos. 5–6, 1936, pp. 266–301, see p. 297 (published also in Binswanger, *Ausgewählte Vorträge und Aufsätze*, vol. 1, pp. 159–89; English translation: *Being-in-the-World*, p. 176): "We see then that what Freud, following Fechner's model, elevated to the pleasure principle is *one* and *only* one particular mode of human existence or being-in-the-world. It was this mode that Heraclitus singled out and defined anthropologically as man's existence in the '*idios*'-cosmos, as the reversion to the private world. Sleeping, dreaming, the surrender to passion and sensory pleasure are what Heraclitus cites as instances of this form of being. What is involved here is a form of selfhood in which the self in its historicity is not yet presentationally apparent (cf. Kierkegaard's concept of repetition), but is merely 'momentarily' arrested and caught up. What is involved, in other words, is a form of being that can be characterized as being-overcome or being-overpowered. It is thus a form of passivity, the passive givenness of human beings to their momentary being."

[42]   Binswanger, "Traum und Existenz," *Neue Schweizer Rundschau*, vol. 23, 1930, p. 776 (in his *Ausgewählte Werke in vier Bänden*, vol. 3, p. 116; "Dream and Existence," p. 101). p. 101. See *SKS* 7, 186 / *CUP1*, 203.

[43]   Binswanger, "Traum und Existenz," *Neue Schweizer Rundschau*, vol. 23, 1930, p. 776 (in his *Ausgewählte Werke in vier Bänden*, vol. 3, p. 116; "Dream and Existence," p. 101).

[44]   Binswanger, "Traum und Existenz," *Neue Schweizer Rundschau*, vol. 23, 1930, p. 776 (in his *Ausgewählte Werke in vier Bänden*, vol. 3, p. 116; "Dream and Existence," pp. 100–1). *SKS* 7 / *CUP1*, chapter 2: "Subjective Truth, Inwardness, Truth is Subjectivity"). Binswanger goes on as follows: "Only on the basis of such an insight can the psychotherapist himself turn

Nevertheless, it is very important to remark how such a Kierkegaardian "subjective truth," in Binswanger's perspective, deals with a kind of "objectivity" again, which is not Hegel's, but which still corresponds to Kierkegaard's idea according to which, in order to deal with human affairs, psychology must be enabled "at once to construct his example which even though it lacks factual authority nevertheless has an authority of a different kind."[45] This different kind of "spiritual" authority consists in the psychologist's ability "to create at once both the totality and the invariable from what in the individual is always partially and variably present,"[46] and it corresponds very well with Binswanger's *Daseinsanalyse*, according to which the psychologist has to go beyond the singular and contingent psychopathologic expressions in order to "look for the principle which rules the formation of the series."[47] And it is Kierkegaard again that the Swiss psychiatrist mentions in his essay on the "Flight of Ideas" (1932–33), where he points out that the psychologist can penetrate into the experience of "confusion" of ideas only if he is able to "penetrate into the existential-anthropological structure" of it, namely, "the *form* of being-a-man which we call confusion."[48]

This structure is determined by some *spatial* and *temporal* coordinates in which Binswanger recognizes—on the basis of the Heideggerian *Daseinsanalytik*—the general "*world-project*" of a particular *form* of existence, like mania, depression, obsessiveness, and so on. So existence is never just an objective "simple-presence"— as Heidegger would say—but a "temporalization of time." That is why—Binswanger affirms—the psychiatrist must "leave a *too* fixed link between the temporal qualities of permanence, reflexivity, duration and continuity (Kierkegaard), and the concept of form (purely personal and human, and artistic as well)."[49]

---

from a dreaming to a waking spirit, so that what Kierkegaard says of Lessing might be said of him: 'In neither accepting an unfree devotion nor recognizing an unfree imitation, he— himself free—enables everyone who approaches him to enter into free relation with him.' "

[45]   *SKS* 4, 359 / *CA*, 54.

[46]   *SKS* 4, 359 / *CA*, 55. Cf. also *SKS* 4, 378 / *CA*, 74: "Life is rich enough if only one understands *how to see*. One need not travel to Paris and London; besides, this would be of no help if one is unable to see."

[47]   Ludwig Binswanger, "Über Ideenflucht," *Schweizer Archiv für Neurologie und Psychiatrie*, vol. 27, no. 2, 1932, pp. 203–17; vol. 28, nos. 1–2, 1932, pp. 183–202; vol. 29, no. 1, 1932, pp. 1–37; 193–252; vol. 30, no. 1, 1933, pp. 68–85; see vol. 29, no. 2, 1932, p. 25 (in his *Ausgewählte Werke in vier Bänden*, vol. 1, see p. 132).

[48]   Binswanger, "Über Ideenflucht," *Schweizer Archiv für Neurologie und Psychiatrie*, vol. 28, no. 1, 1932, p. 25 (in his *Ausgewählte Werke in vier Bänden*, p. 132).

[49]   Binswanger, "Über Ideenflucht," in *Schweizer Archiv für Neurologie und Psychiatrie*, vol. 29, no. 2, 1932, p. 222 (in his *Ausgewählte Werke in vier Bänden*, p. 180). We find such a conception again in Binswanger's essay, "Das Raumproblem in der Psychopathologie," *Zeitschrift für die gesamte Neurologie und Psychiatrie*, vol. 145, 1933, pp. 598–647 (in his *Ausgewählte Werke in vier Bänden*, vol. 3, pp. 123–77; Published also in *Ausgewählte Vorträge und Aufsätze*, vol. 2, pp. 618–43), where he remarks that "in psychopathology we have to do with a kind of space which our special science and the science of nature in general have despised as not scientific," but which is actually, originally, behind such a "scientific" science. (Binswanger, "Das Raumproblem in der Psychopathologie," p. 620 (in his *Ausgewählte Werke in vier Bänden*, vol. 3, pp. 123–77, see p. 146).) That's the "*lived* space,"

In this context, Kierkegaard is mentioned also—together with Heidegger again—in order to oppose to such an experience of "existential loss of the self" a "principle of the *self*" as "existential realization," which consists in the awakening of the self from irresponsible and non-autonomous everyday life—that is, the "self as *'they are [Man]'* "—to the "*authentic* self."[50] Binswanger reasserts that in his works throughout the 1930s, where he remarks—for instance in his article on "Heraclitus' Conception of the Man" (1935)—that "the self cannot be discovered through everyday ways but must be searched laboriously, through great efforts, like something which is mostly distant from our everyday view."[51] In this respect, Binswanger considers

---

and Binswanger ascribed such an insight to authors like Plotinus, Saint Augustine, Herder, Franz von Baader, Dilthey, Scheler, but he also refers to "Pascal, Kierkegaard, and Newmann, as the greatest co-founders of the science we are talking about." (Ibid.) Concerning again the concept of "temporalization of time," Binswanger also refers to Kierkegaard in his essay "Über die daseinsanalytische Forschungsrichtung in der Psychiatrie," *Schweizer Archiv für Psychiatrie und Neurologie*, vol. 57, 1946, pp. 209–35, see p. 225 (in his *Ausgewählte Werke in vier Bänden*, vol. 3, pp. 231–57, see p. 247).

[50]   See Binswanger, "Über Ideenflucht," *Schweizer Archiv für Neurologie und Psychiatrie*, vol. 28, no. 2, 1932, p. 25 (in his *Ausgewählte Werke in vier Bänden*, vol. 1, p. 132): "We can and we must be brief for now, since 'everybody' nowadays speaks of such a principle. It is the principle of the *self* (we know that from Kierkegaard, Heidegger, Jaspers, and many others)." There is also another reference to Kierkegaard in Binswanger's "Über Ideenflucht" (*Schweizer Archiv für Neurologie und Psychiatrie*, vol. 28, no. 2, 1932, p. 201; in his *Ausgewählte Werke in vier Bänden*, vol. 1, p. 104): "The depressive's world becomes night. Kierkegaard too equates the deep melancholy with darkness and night (cf. the night of the absolute and the sunny brightness of happiness in his *Diaries*)."

[51]   Ludwig Binswanger, "Heraklits Auffassung des Menschen," *Die Antike*, vol. 9, no. 1, 1935, pp. 1–38, see p. 12 (in his *Ausgewählte Vorträge und Aufsätze*, vols. 1–2, 2nd ed., Bern: Francke 1961, vol. 1, p. 108). Binswanger quotes Kierkegaard exactly in such a context: "When Kierkegaard says about Heraclitus the obscure that he had deposited his thoughts in his books, and his books in Diana's temple, 'for his thoughts had been his armor in life, and therefore he hung them in the temple of the goddess' [*SKS* 4, 210 / *FT*, 123], the word 'armor'…is right on the mark: the linguistic clothes and Heraclitus' clothes of thought are not two different clothes put on separately one above the other, but they are one and the same armor, which was born—or better still, grown—from a solitary and bitter life, produced by the heroic act to bear it and by the decision to light it up through the philosophical awareness of self." See Binswanger, "Heraklits Auffassung des Menschen," *Die Antike*, vol. 9, no. 1, 1935, pp. 1–38, see p. 6 (in his *Ausgewählte Vorträge und Aufsätze*, 2nd ed., 1961, vol. 1, p. 103). Cf. also in Binswanger, "Heraklits Auffassung des Menschen," *Die Antike*, vol. 9, no. 1, 1935, pp. 1–38, see p. 13 (in his *Ausgewählte Vorträge und Aufsätze*, 2nd ed., 1961, vol. 1, p. 109): "Man is in the 'situation' of *phronesis*, namely, in the way of being of *phronein*, when he can concentrate apart from the stormy dispersion of existence in the way of being of the quiet awareness of truth…; only in such a 'quiet' is it possible to be oneself, is it possible that life composes itself in a 'constant' self. Yet such a way of being, whose possibility 'is' in every existence, is chosen only by few people; the larger part of them avoids it, and remains in the way of being of dispersion, into which it has blindly fallen. There is no doubt in which kind of being…Heraclitus sees the authentic, proper, full humanity…, the veritable determination of man. It is the way of being of the ἄριστοι (frag. 29), namely, the best, against which there is the multitude, the crowd, that is the πολλοί (frag. 2, 17, 29)….The Greek word οἱ πολλοί

Kierkegaard as a kind of heir of Heraclitus, as "the philosopher who first opened up to us the forms of the human being's historicity," who showed us that man "is founded in himself, in his 'self-consciousness,' " and that such a self-consciousness is a kind of prophet who "appears amid a noisy, thoughtless and pleasure-loving crowd incapable of judging responsibly, a crowd which does not listen to what he says, and which does not understand what he is going to teach, because (world) temporality is not and will never be the essence of the spirit, but always and only his trouble (Kierkegaard)."[52]

But one would be wrong to conclude that what Binswanger most appreciates in Kierkegaard is just a kind of "aristocratic" and wisdom ethics. What is most interesting in Binswanger's reading of Kierkegaard is the fact that he assimilates the opposition between the *authenticity of self-consciousness* and the *multitude's dispersion* from an epistemological point of view rather than an ethical one. So, when the Swiss psychiatrist quotes Kierkegaard's effort to "find the key to understand the contraposition between the Eleatics and Heraclitus,"[53] it is in order to show the possibility of attaining a *subjective truth* without thereby falling into the dispersion of the boundless mutability of a contingent individual. Read through Heidegger's *structural* analytic of existence, Kierkegaard's anthropological approach to "psychology" offered to Binswanger the answer to his own epistemological need to reconcile the individual singularity of the clinical cases with the universality of science.[54] Therefore, the Kierkegaardian "structural" approach according to which one cannot "view the particular" without keeping "*in mente*, at the same time, the totality,"[55] corresponds perfectly to Binswanger's approach to psychopathology, namely, to the need of understanding the "psychological" (particular) phenomena against the background of the "existential" (universal) ones. Throughout the 1930s and 1940s Binswanger always reasserts that the "existential analysis cannot

---

is equivalent to Kierkegaard's multitude, Jaspers' crowd, and somehow to Heidegger's ontological determination of the anonymous being of 'the they' [*Man-Sein*]."

[52]   Binswanger, "Heraklits Auffassung des Menschen," *Die Antike*, vol. 9, no. 1, 1935, pp. 1–38, see p. 37 (in his *Ausgewählte Vorträge und Aufsätze*, 2nd ed., 1961, vol. 1, p. 130).

[53]   Binswanger, "Heraklits Auffassung des Menschen," *Die Antike*, vol. 9, no. 1, 1935, p. 36 (in his *Ausgewählte Vorträge und Aufsätze*, 2nd ed., 1961, vol. 1, p. 130).

[54]   In this regard, one can agree with the approach of Vincent A. McCarthy to Kierkegaard's psychological concepts (*The Phenomenology of Moods in Kierkegaard*, The Hague, Boston: Martinus Nijhoff 1978), since he understands them as *structures* of experience; cf. in particular § 2, C: "The Idea of Anxiety. The Experience and Structure of Anxiety." Dealing with *moods* as "underlying structures" (p. 120), instead of looking for definitions of them, McCarthy enables us to grasp the very phenomenological meaning of them, that is, the meaning which Binswanger grasped too. It is also interesting to see the way in which he argues that "in opening any volume of Kierkegaard's works, one is plunged *in medias res* on every occasion" (p. 2), for that is also the *Daseinsanalyse's* methodological principle of *immanence*.

[55]   *SKS* 4, 379 / *CA*, 76. See also *SKS* 11, 196 / *SUD*, 82: "To begin to describe particular sins would be out of place," since "the main point is simply that the definition, like a net, embraces all forms."

be content with the psychological judgment."[56] That is why, in this phase of his research, he rereads also the Freudian psychopathological notions from such an existential perspective, and again with reference to Kierkegaard, as we can see in this passage from his essay on "Heidegger's Analytic of Existence and Its Meaning for Psychiatry" (1949):

> That human beings *can* become "neurotic" at all is also a sign of the thrownness of Dasein and a sign of its potentiality of fallenness—a sign, in short, of its finitude, its transcendental limitedness or unfreedom. Only he who scorns these limits—in Kierkegaard's terms—who is at odds with the fundamental conditions of existence, can become "neurotic," whereas only he who "knows" of the unfreedom of finite human existence and who obtains "power" over his existence within this very powerlessness is unneurotic or "free."[57]

And it is interesting to notice the importance that Binswanger accords to Kierkegaard for such a distinction between the "existential" and "psychological" point of view, as the Swiss psychiatrist observes in "The Case of Lola Voss": "Since what Kierkegaard called 'the mystery of existence'—that unfreedom makes a prisoner of itself—is valid for all human existence, schizophrenia merely represents a particularly intensive and peculiarly constituted variation of that change of freedom into unfreedom, or, as we express it, of existence into world."[58]

It is exactly such a *structural* principle which guides all of Binswanger's analyses of clinical cases, in which Kierkegaard is almost always present. We have already seen partly such an imposing presence in "The Case of Ellen West,"[59] but we can also think of "The Case of Ilse," where Binswanger remarks explicitly:

---

[56] Cf. Binswanger, "Der Fall Ellen West. Eine anthropologisch-klinische Studie," *Schweizer Archiv für Neurologie und Psychiatrie*, vol. 54, 1944, p. 97. ("The Case of Ellen West," p. 294).

[57] Ludwig Binswanger, "Die Bedeutung der Daseinsanalytik Martin Heideggers für das Selbstverständnis der Psychiatrie," in Carlos Astrada et al., *Martin Heideggers Einfluß auf die Wissenschaften*, Bern: Francke 1949, pp. 58–72, see p. 70 (published also in his *Ausgewählte Vorträge und Aufsätze*, vol. 2, pp. 264–78; English translation: "Heidegger's Analytic of Existence and Its Meaning for Psychiatry," trans. by Jacob Needleman, in his *Being-in-the-World*, pp. 206–21, see p. 218).

[58] Ludwig Binswanger, "Studien zum Schizophrenienproblem. Der Fall Lola Voss," *Schweizer Archiv für Neurologie und Psychiatrie*, vol. 63, 1949, pp. 29–97, see p. 69 (published also in Ludwig Binswanger, *Schizophrenie*, Pfullingen: Neske 1957, study no. 4, pp. 289–358; English translation: "The Case of Lola Voss," trans. by Ernest Angel, in his *Being-in-the-World*, p. 314).

[59] There are further references to Kierkegaard in Binswanger, "Der Fall Ellen West. Eine anthropologisch-klinische Studie," *Schweizer Archiv für Neurologie und Psychiatrie*, vol. 54, 1944, p. 96 ("The Case of Ellen West," p. 294). See furthermore the quotation in "Der Fall Ellen West," *Schweizer Archiv für Neurologie und Psychiatrie*, p. 360 ("The Case of Ellen West," p. 341), which Binswanger attributes to *Philosophical Fragments*, but which actually is in the *Concluding Unscientific Postscript*: "Kierkegaard could rightly say that in insanity 'the small finiteness has been fixated—which can never happen with [the inwardness of] infinity." See *SKS*, 7, 178 / *CUP1*, 194. Concerning the conception of "fixation," see also Binswanger, "The Case of Ellen West," p. 299; p. 303; p. 326, where he

A great mind developed both a new philosophical concept of illness and an understanding of insanity as mental disease. We are thinking of Kierkegaard and of his concept of sickness unto death, of the "desperate" wish to-be-oneself and to-be-not-oneself. This "illness" and its ingenious description and philosophical-theological interpretation appear to us as one of the most important contributions to the purely "anthropological" understanding of certain clinical forms of insanity, and particularly of schizophrenia.[60]

The Swiss psychiatrist reasserts the same conception in his analysis of "The Case of Jürg Zünd," where he remarks—in considering the concept of anxiety from the Kierkegaardian point of view—that "anxiety and suddenness are just two different expressions for the same existential phenomenon: the first would be formulated from a psychological point of view, the latter from an existential-analytical one."[61] That means that one can consider two forms of "psychology," according to whether one considers the "real moment" of a psychopathological expression, or its "possibility." As Binswanger says, referring explicitly to the Danish philosopher again: "Every real moment of despair is to be traced back to its possibility."[62] That is why Binswanger's

---

refers to Kierkegaard's *Philosophical Fragments*. His actual reference is again to the *Postscript*, see *SKS* 7, 178 / *CUP1*, 194. See also Binswanger, "Der Fall Ellen West," *Schweizer Archiv für Neurologie und Psychiatrie*, p. 31 ("The Case of Ellen West," p. 356).

[60]   Ludwig Binswanger, "Wahnsinn als lebensgeschichtliches Phänomen und als Geisteskrankheit," *Monatsschrift für Psychiatrie und Neurologie*, vol. 110, 1945, pp. 129–60, see p 160. (English translation: "Insanity as Life-Historical Phenomenon and as Mental Disease: The Case of Ilse," in *Existence—A New Dimension in Psychiatry and Psychology*, pp. 214–36, see pp. 235–6.) Here Binswanger writes also: "As to insanity in the clinical sense, we refer to Kierkegaard's notes on the lack of 'inwardness of infinity' in insanity and on the contradiction that something is here focused upon objectively which, at the same time, is grasped with passion; or, in other words, that 'the small infinity has been fixated,' " and he refers in particular to Kierkegaard's *Philosophical Fragments* again, I, 2. Actually, he means the *Postscript*, that is, *SKS*, 7, 178 / *CUP1*, 194.

[61]   Ludwig Binswanger, "Der Fall Jürg Zünd," *Schweizer Archiv für Neurologie und Psychiatrie*, vol. 56, 1946, pp. 191–220; vol. 58, 1947, pp. 1–43; vol. 59, 1947, pp. 21–36, see vol. 58, 1947, p. 37 (in *Schizophrenie*, pp. 189–288, see pp. 262–3). In this essay, there are two other references to Kierkegaard: the first concerns the Kierkegaardian concept of "anxiety about the good" (Binswanger, "Der Fall Jürg Zünd," *Schweizer Archiv für Neurologie und Psychiatrie*, vol. 58, 1947, p. 2 (in *Schizophrenie*, p. 231)). The latter is about the idea that "we can know what is typical for a schizophrenic existence through the 'normal psychic life'" (Binswanger, "Der Fall Jürg Zünd," *Schweizer Archiv für Neurologie und Psychiatrie*, vol. 58, 1947, p. 29 (in *Schizophrenie*, p. 480)), and in this regard, Binswanger quotes *Stages on Life's Way*: "When someone is stuck in something and does not know which end is up, when everything has become so devastatingly relative that it seems as if one is being suffocated, then it may be expedient to act suddenly at one point just to get something moving and some life in all that dead flesh." Cf. *SKS* 6, 438 / *SLW*, 475. "If one does not know whether one is sick or well, if this condition tends to make no sense, it is good to risk doing something desperate suddenly. But even if one acts without deliberation, there is still a kind of deliberation." Cf. *SKS* 6, 438 / *SLW*, 475–6.

[62]   Binswanger, "The Case of Ellen West," p. 305. Binswanger here is clearly referring to *The Sickness unto Death*, see *SKS* 11, 132 / *SUD*, 17.

clinical cases always give the impression of lacking the "concreteness" which should characterize sick people. What Binswanger actually aims to do is take the singular biography of his patients as the occasion of presenting such *possibilities of existence* or, that is, the "transcendental organization" of every singular lived experience. One can just consider the way in which he defines his analysis of Suzanne Urban's case, as the "historical transformation of an individual mode of being as the 'paradigmatic ground' of the human destiny's *existential possibility*. In such a way [he says] we set out the *phenomenological nature* of our analysis."[63]

Such an approach is particularly clear in Binswanger's work on *Henrik Ibsen and the Problem of Self-Realization in Art* (1949), where the Norwegian dramatist is taken as a paradigmatic example in order to focus on the "human being's essential and *a priori* features" which determine the different modes of existing, and in particular the mode of "self-realization."[64] But what is also interesting in this book is the way in which Binswanger compares Ibsen to Kierkegaard, according to "a sequence which starts from Socrates and leads to Kierkegaard, Nietzsche, Jaspers and Heidegger."[65] According to Binswanger, what the Danish philosopher and Ibsen hold in common is the following:

> Like Kierkegaard behind his pseudonyms, [Ibsen] should have never been discovered, and he did not want to be discovered personally either. What should occur to Kierkegaard as to Ibsen, in order to be able to "be productive," was their existence's

---

[63]   See Ludwig Binswanger, "Der Fall Suzanne Urban," *Schweizer Archiv für Neurologie und Psychiatrie*, vol. 69, 1952, pp. 36–77; vol. 70, 1952, pp. 1–32; vol. 71, 1952, pp. 57–96, see vol. 71, 1952, p. 57 (in *Ausgewählte Werke in vier Bänden*, vol. 4, p. 287). Binswanger mentions *The Concept of Anxiety* both in "Der Fall Suzanne Urban" (Binswanger, "Der Fall Suzanne Urban," *Schweizer Archiv für Neurologie und Psychiatrie*, vol. 69, 1952, p. 58 (in *Ausgewählte Werke in vier Bänden*, vol. 4, p. 236)) and in his "The Case of Lola Voss," where it also concerns the Kierkegaardian dialectic of closure or "demonic"; see Binswanger, "Studien zum Schizophrenienproblem. Der Fall Lola Voss," *Schweizer Archiv für Neurologie und Psychiatrie*, see p. 65 ("The Case of Lola Voss," in his *Being-in-the-World*, p. 310). On *The Concept of Anxiety*, concerning the concept of "the sudden," see also Binswanger's "Studien zum Schizophrenienproblem. Der Fall Lola Voss," *Schweizer Archiv für Neurologie und Psychiatrie*, see pp. 50–51 ("The Case of Lola Voss," p. 295); on fate as Kierkegaard's "nought of anxiety" (Binswanger, "Studien zum Schizophrenienproblem. Der Fall Lola Voss," *Schweizer Archiv für Neurologie und Psychiatrie*, see p. 52 ("The Case of Lola Voss," p. 297). About Kierkegaard's concept of "repetition," see Binswanger, "Studien zum Schizophrenienproblem. Der Fall Lola Voss," *Schweizer Archiv für Neurologie und Psychiatrie*, see p. 59 ("The Case of Lola Voss," p. 304). About the notion of "superstition," see Binswanger, "Studien zum Schizophrenienproblem. Der Fall Lola Voss," *Schweizer Archiv für Neurologie und Psychiatrie*, see p. 70 ("The Case of Lola Voss," p. 314). Finally, on the "fundamental conditions" of existence, see Binswanger, "Studien zum Schizophrenienproblem. Der Fall Lola Voss," *Schweizer Archiv für Neurologie und Psychiatrie*, see p. 70 ("The Case of Lola Voss," p. 315).

[64]   See Ludwig Binswanger, *Henrik Ibsen und das Problem der Selbstrealisation in der Kunst*, Heidelberg: Lambert Schneider 1949, p. 44.

[65]   Ibid., p. 11. Just above he compared Kierkegaard also to Lessing, according to Ibsen's idea that what is most important in freedom is the struggle to obtain it, and that "self-realization is a ceaseless and interminable *widening* of oneself." (See ibid., p. 10.)

"unendurable" oppression in the form of not being understood, their suffering because of their contemporaries' "incomprehension," together with the indomitable wish, on the contrary, to be quite "completely" understood by them....Both of them...belong to the *artistic* form of confession, and thereby to the self-realization in it. Nevertheless, the artist does not feel understood in his deepest intimacy, when it occurs in his behaving and acting's "innermost" reasons and intentions—that is the most subjective character of his subjectivity—but, on the contrary, only when he is understood in the objectivity by which and in which his subjectivity consolidates, realizes or "forms" itself by art.[66]

It is exactly such an "objectivity"—under the form of the study of the *structural forms* of existence—that Binswangerian *Daseinsanalyse* was looking for, and we can find such a perspective again in Binswanger's work, *Three Forms of Frustrated Existence: Extravagance, Idiosyncrasy and Affectation* (1956). What the Swiss psychiatrist is interested in is not considering those psychopathological expressions from a "medical-psychiatric point of view"—according to which they would be just "pathological 'defectiveness,' morbid 'deviations' or 'symptoms' "—but transposing them "in the wider frame of the structure of the human existence or 'being-in-the-world,' which Heidegger so rigorously, systematically and ingeniously 'revealed' in his existential analytic."[67] And in order to define the meaning of such a perspective, Binswanger claims that one might have to trace it back "to Plato and Aristotle (or better still, Heraclitus); but such notions are also the basis of the Kierkegaardian doctrine of 'possibility' as the 'hardest category,' and especially of Heidegger's existential analytic."[68]

---

[66]   Ibid., p. 35. Other references to Kierkegaard are on p. 36 (about Ibsen's own relationship to Kierkegaard's work); on p. 39 (a quotation from the *Concluding Unscientific Postscript*, see *SKS* 7, 180 / *CUP1*, 197: "Only momentarily can a particular individual, existing, be in a unity of the infinite and the finite that transcends existing. This instant is the moment of passion"); on p. 54 (dealing with the "structural features" of the human being, Binswanger mentions dizziness as an expression of anxiety, and he cites *The Concept of Anxiety*, see *SKS* 4, 365 / *CA*, 61); and on p. 79 (about the concept of "repetition").

[67]   Ludwig Binswanger, *Drei Formen missglückten Daseins: Verstiegenheit, Verschrobenheit, Manieriertheit*, Tübingen: Niemeyer 1956, p. X (in his *Ausgewählte Werke in vier Bänden*, vol. 1, p. 238).

[68]   Binswanger, *Drei Formen missglückten Daseins*, p. X (in his *Ausgewählte Werke in vier Bänden*, vol. 1, p. 238). There are some other references to Kierkegaard in this work; Binswanger writes about the concept of *anxiety* as the desperate wish to *be* oneself in *The Sickness unto Death* (Binswanger, *Drei Formen missglückten Daseins*, p. 115 (in his *Ausgewählte Werke in vier Bänden*, vol. 1, p. 345); He mentions the Kierkegaardian notion of *aesthetic* (Binswanger, *Drei Formen missglückten Daseins*, p. 149 (in his *Ausgewählte Werke in vier Bänden*, vol. 1, p. 375); on the experience of the "mere desire" see Binswanger, *Drei Formen missglückten Daseins*, p. 155 (in his *Ausgewählte Werke in vier Bänden*, vol. 1, p. 381). There is also a passage from *The Concept of Anxiety* concerning the "spiritlessness" (Binswanger, *Drei Formen missglückten Daseins*, p. 187 (in his *Ausgewählte Werke in vier Bänden*, vol. 1, pp. 408–9): "The lostness of spiritlessness is the most terrible of all, because the misfortune is precisely that spiritlessness has a relation to spirit, which is nothing. To a certain degree, spiritlessness may therefore possess the whole content of spirit, but note well, not as spirit but as the haunting of ghosts, as gibberish, as a slogan, etc. It may possess the truth, but note well, not as truth but as rumor and old wives'

Within this "existential-analytical" phase of Binswanger's work, one could recognize a kind of "subphase," which would correspond to the great work of 1942 on the *Basic Forms and Cognition of Human Existence*.[69] Here the "principle of the self"—that is, the "supreme principle" of *Dasein*—is problematized and deepened by the concept of *"being-with"* [*Mitsein*] in a way that leads Binswanger to object that Heidegger's concept of *Dasein* fails to account for the very "foundation" of the human being, that is intersubjectivity. Such a critical remark includes Kierkegaard's concept of the *self* too,[70] since Binswanger here looks at it as the origin of Heidegger's *Dasein*:

> Therefore, for us the principle which led Heidegger to conceive the *Mineness* as the ontological interpretation of *Dasein* falls. Besides, such a way of understanding *Dasein* is connected to Kierkegaard's model, which—as is well known—sees man's "fundamental consciousness" in his consciousness to be an individual, to disclose oneself or to become transparent to oneself as individual.[71]

That is why Binswanger proposes—after he remarked in Kierkegaard the priority of the relation between *self* and *world* to that between *me* and *you*—to turn Kierkegaard's statement according to which "the person who can scarcely open himself cannot love,"[72] into *"the person who can scarcely love cannot open himself,"* because "love and self-revelation are the same."[73] It is not the intention of this article to discuss or study in depth this position. What is interesting in this context is to notice how the Swiss psychiatrist compares Kierkegaard to Heidegger in a way that could finally contribute to clarify his attitude towards the German philosopher, an attitude which is still nowadays one of the most discussed questions among both Binswanger and Heidegger scholars. So, it would be interesting to explore how Binswanger's reading of Kierkegaard is indebted to his reading of Heidegger, that is, if he read Kierkegaard through Heidegger, or vice versa.[74] One cannot avoid remarking, for instance, the similarity between Binswanger's statement about Kierkegaard's understanding of

---

tales" (cf. *SKS* 4, 397–8 / *CA*, 94). Finally, in a footnote, Binswanger also writes about the stages of despair in *The Sickness unto Death* (p. 411).

[69]   Ludwig Binswanger, *Grundformen und Erkenntnis menschlichen Daseins*, Zürich: Niehans 1942 (in his *Ausgewählte Werke in vier Bänden*, vol. 2).

[70]   It is a problem which is still discussed today among Kierkegaard scholars; see, for instance, Pia Søltoft, "Anthropology and Ethics: The Connection between Subjectivity and Intersubjectivity as the Basis of a Kierkegaardian Anthropology," in *Anthropology and Authority: Essays on Søren Kierkegaard*, ed. by Poul Houe, Gordon D. Marino, and Sven Hakon Rossel, Amsterdam, Atlanta: Rodopi 2000, pp. 41–8.

[71]   Binswanger, *Grundformen und Erkenntnis menschlichen Daseins*, p. 58 (in his *Ausgewählte Werke in vier Bänden*, vol. 2, p. 49).

[72]   See *SKS* 3, 158 / *EO2*, 160.

[73]   Binswanger, *Grundformen und Erkenntnis menschlichen Daseins*, pp. 128–9 (in his *Ausgewählte Werke in vier Bänden*, vol. 2, pp. 114–15).

[74]   On Heidegger's reception of Kierkegaard concerning in particular *The Concept of Anxiety*, see Dan Magurshak, *"The Concept of Anxiety*: The Keystone of the Kierkegaard-Heidegger Relationship," in *The Concept of Anxiety*, ed. by Robert L. Perkins, Macon, Georgia: Mercer University Press 1985 (*International Kierkegaard Commentary*, vol. 8), pp.

schizophrenia as we have found it in "The Case of Ellen West," and Heidegger's statement in *Being and Time* according to which "the man who has gone farthest in analyzing the phenomenon of anxiety—and again in the theological context of a 'psychological' exposition of the problem of original sin—is Søren Kierkegaard."[75] What is clear is that Binswanger's reading of Kierkegaard is in many ways indebted to that of Heidegger. However, in such a context, we must confine ourselves to noting that Binswanger here claims that Heidegger secularized Kierkegaard's religious idea of existence.[76]

167–95, which can also be useful in order to problematize Binswanger's reception of both Heidegger and Kierkegaard.

[75]   See Martin Heidegger, *Sein und Zeit*, ed. by Friedrich-Wilhelm von Herrmann, Abteilung 1, vol. 2, in Martin Heidegger, *Gesamtausgabe*, Frankfurt am Main: Klostermann 1975ff., see p. 191, note 4. (English translation: *Being and Time*, trans. by John Macquarrie and Edward Robinson, Oxford: Basil Blackwell 1962, p. 191.)

[76]   There exist some critical interpretations, however, which emphasize the fundamental role that Lutheranism might have had also in Heidegger's conception of existence as "care." See Roberta De Monticelli, "Binswanger et le pari de la phénoménologie psychiatrique," in *Les Études Philosophiques*, vols. 1–2, 1994, p. 230. But one can also think of Jean Wahl's essay, "Heidegger et Kierkegaard. Recherche des éléments originaux de la philosophie de Heidegger," *Recherches Philosophiques*, vol. 2, 1932–33, pp. 349–70. (Published also in Jean Wahl, *Études kierkegaardiennes*, 2nd ed., Paris: Vrin 1949 [1938], pp. 455–476; and in his *Kierkegaard. L'un devant l'autre*, Paris: Hachette 1998, pp. 69–95.) There are again a lot of other references to Kierkegaard in Binswanger's *Grundformen und Erkenntnis menschlichen Daseins*. Thus, he writes about the concept of "the closedness" (*Grundformen und Erkenntnis menschlichen Daseins*, p. 123 (in his *Ausgewählte Werke in vier Bänden*, vol. 2, p. 109)); about Mozart's Don Juan (*Grundformen und Erkenntnis menschlichen Daseins*, p. 189 (in his *Ausgewählte Werke in vier Bänden*, vol. 2, p. 170, note 41)); about Kierkegaard's concept of the "nothingness of anxiety" (*Grundformen und Erkenntnis menschlichen Daseins*, p. 236 (in his *Ausgewählte Werke in vier Bänden*, vol. 2, p. 212)); and about the conflict between the "theological self" and the multitude (*Grundformen und Erkenntnis menschlichen Daseins*, p. 243 (in his *Ausgewählte Werke in vier Bänden*, vol. 2, pp. 218–19)), where he compares Kierkegaard to Saint Augustine. On Kierkegaard's religious concepts of "sin" and "guilt," see Binswanger, *Grundformen und Erkenntnis menschlichen Daseins*, p. 246 (in his *Ausgewählte Werke in vier Bänden*, vol. 2, p. 221)). Binswanger compares Pascal's concept of *moi haïssable* to Kierkegaard's "desperate self" (*Grundformen und Erkenntnis menschlichen Daseins*, p. 400, note 16 (in his *Ausgewählte Werke in vier Bänden*, vol. 2, p. 362, note 16)). He also compares Kierkegaard's concept of "self-knowledge" to that of Saint Paul, Augustine, Pascal, Malebranche and Hamann (*Grundformen und Erkenntnis menschlichen Daseins*, p. 420 (in his *Ausgewählte Werke in vier Bänden*, vol. 2, p. 379)). Binswanger also remarks that Kierkegaard's concept of the "self-knowledge" does not correspond to Hamann's concept of "self-loving" (*Grundformen und Erkenntnis menschlichen Daseins*, p. 422 (in his *Ausgewählte Werke in vier Bänden*, vol. 2, p. 381)). He writes also about Kierkegaard's "being-to-oneself" as pseudonym (*Grundformen und Erkenntnis menschlichen Daseins*, p. 473, note 3 (in his *Ausgewählte Werke in vier Bänden*, vol. 2, p. 411, note 3)); about Kierkegaard's concept of "repetition," which Binswanger compares to Heidegger's (*Grundformen und Erkenntnis menschlichen Daseins*, p. 473 (in his *Ausgewählte Werke in vier Bänden*, vol. 2, p. 427)); about Kierkegaard's concept of subjectivity as inwardness or as passion (p. 480; *Ausgewählte Werke in vier Bänden*, vol. 2, p. 433); and about Feuerbach's and Kierkegaard's struggle

We can find some other information about the way in which Binswanger conceives his reading of both Kierkegaard and Heidegger in his work of 1956: "The Man in Psychiatry."[77] This essay is a kind of retrospective explanation of the importance of the two authors for existential-analytical psychiatry, in which Binswanger takes Kierkegaard as one of the examples of "the way which can lead us to set out correctly the question of man together with the question of the insane man."[78] The Swiss psychiatrist takes up *The Concept of Anxiety* again, and he quotes in particular Kierkegaard's statement, "the physician at an insane asylum who is foolish enough to believe that he is eternally right and that his bit of reason is ensured against all injury in this life is in a sense wiser than the demented, but he is also more foolish, and surely he will not heal many."[79] The only physician who really can understand madness is the one who has "sympathy," but "this sympathy [Binswanger says quoting Kierkegaard] is true only when one admits rightly and profoundly to oneself that what happened to one human being can happen to all."[80]

We can remark here the same position which we have already found in Binswanger's works during the 1940s, and which consists in the idea that "one can understand madness only on the basis of our common human lot,"[81] that is, existence in both its different and common *figures* and *structures*. But what changes now in Binswanger's attitude towards Kierkegaard is his consideration in relation to Heidegger, a consideration which seems to be more similar to the one which we find in Binswanger's works during the 1920s. Now the example of Kierkegaard, according

---

against Hegel's system (*Grundformen und Erkenntnis menschlichen Daseins*, p. 498 (in his *Ausgewählte Werke in vier Bänden*, vol. 2, p. 449)). There are also several references to Kierkegaard in order to explain the concept of "existential cognition and existence" (pp. 545ff.; *Ausgewählte Werke in vier Bänden*, vol. 2, pp. 493ff.). One can also mention a reference to Kierkegaard's concept of "repetition" (*Grundformen und Erkenntnis menschlichen Daseins*, p. 552, note 2 (in his *Ausgewählte Werke in vier Bänden*, vol. 2, p. 499, note 2) and another one to Kierkegaard's "passion of subjectivity," p. 508)). For a long quotation from *Repetition* see *Grundformen und Erkenntnis menschlichen Daseins*, p. 562 (in his *Ausgewählte Werke in vier Bänden*, vol. 2, p. 549) and *Grundformen und Erkenntnis menschlichen Daseins*, p. 639 (in his *Ausgewählte Werke in vier Bänden*, vol. 2, p. 619). Cf. *SKS* 4, 23 / *R*, 146. Kierkegaard is mentioned together with Heidegger again in order to oppose his conception of existence with another one focused on the concept of "love" (*Grundformen und Erkenntnis menschlichen Daseins*, p. 605 (in his *Ausgewählte Werke in vier Bänden*, vol. 2, p. 580)). Finally, he writes about the concept of "repetition" again in *Grundformen und Erkenntnis menschlichen Daseins*, p. 682 (in his *Ausgewählte Werke in vier Bänden*, vol. 2, p. 629).

[77]   See Ludwig Binswanger, "Der Mensch in der Psychiatrie," *Schweizer Archiv für Neurologie und Psychiatrie*, vol. 77, pp. 123–38 (in his *Ausgewählte Werke in vier Bänden*, vol. 4, pp. 57–72).

[78]   Binswanger, "Der Mensch in der Psychiatrie," *Schweizer Archiv für Neurologie und Psychiatrie*, vol. 77, p. 123 (in his *Ausgewählte Werke in vier Bänden*, vol. 4, p. 57).

[79]   *SKS* 4, 359 / *CA*, 54.

[80]   Ibid. Quoted by Binswanger in "Der Mensch in der Psychiatrie," *Schweizer Archiv für Neurologie und Psychiatrie*, vol. 77, p. 123 (in his *Ausgewählte Werke in vier Bänden*, vol. 4, p. 57).

[81]   Binswanger, "Der Mensch in der Psychiatrie," *Schweizer Archiv für Neurologie und Psychiatrie*, vol. 77, p. 124 (in his *Ausgewählte Werke in vier Bänden*, vol. 4, p. 58).

to Binswanger—as important as it is in order to give a direction to the new humanistic psychiatry—"is just the prelude to the understanding of the authentic and essential fundament and ground of psychiatry, namely, the *Da-sein*."[82] Heidegger's analysis of existence, not Kierkegaard's, radically discloses to us what *being a man* means: only with Heidegger does the human concern change from being "philosophical, religious and humanistic," to being "a rigorously scientific concern."[83]

This sort of statement about Kierkegaard is the last in Binswanger's work, since during the last phase of his speculation—which corresponds to his works from the 1960s: *Melancholy and Mania* (1960)[84] and *Delusion* (1965)[85]—Binswanger gives up existential-anthropological analysis in order to begin a study of the cognitive and structural principles of consciousness according to Husserl's later genetic phenomenology. The criticisms that Binswanger now uses against the "utility" of Heidegger's *existential* point of view for the psychiatrist's concerns are relevant for Kierkegaard as well, and the only reference to the Danish philosopher during this last phase of Binswanger's thought is made in *Melancholy and Mania* in order to remark that melancholic anxiety is "something more than and different from an original or essential anxiety."[86] It is more properly a "natural phenomenon," a "deviation from the *conditions of the natural experience*,"[87] which does not correspond to Heidegger or Kierkegaard's structure of development of the authentic *self*.[88]

So, one could conclude such an excursus on Binswanger's psychological-existential questioning of the self with the same statement with which Kierkegaard concluded his "simple psychological deliberation" of 1844: "Here this deliberation ends, where it began. As soon as psychology has finished with anxiety, it is to be delivered to dogmatics."[89] But instead of dogmatics, one has now to choose—according to Binswanger's concern—a new kind of "scientific" psychology.

---

[82]   Binswanger, "Der Mensch in der Psychiatrie," *Schweizer Archiv für Neurologie und Psychiatrie*, vol. 77, p. 125 (in his *Ausgewählte Werke in vier Bänden*, vol. 4, p. 58).

[83]   Binswanger, "Der Mensch in der Psychiatrie," *Schweizer Archiv für Neurologie und Psychiatrie*, vol. 77, p. 125 (in his *Ausgewählte Werke in vier Bänden*, vol. 4, p. 59).

[84]   Ludwig Binswanger, *Melancholie und Manie. Phänomenologische Studien*, Pfullingen: Neske 1957 (in his *Ausgewählte Werke in vier Bänden*, vol. 4, pp. 351–428).

[85]   See Ludwig Binswanger, *Wahn. Beiträge zu seiner phänomenologischen und daseinsanalytischen Erforschung*, Pfullingen: Neske 1965 (in his *Ausgewählte Werke in vier Bänden*, vol. 4, pp. 429–539).

[86]   Binswanger, *Melancholie und Manie*, p. 57 (in his *Ausgewählte Werke in vier Bänden*, vol. 4, p. 381).

[87]   Binswanger, *Melancholie und Manie*, p. 57 (in his *Ausgewählte Werke in vier Bänden*, vol. 4, p. 381).

[88]   Binswanger, *Melancholie und Manie*, p. 60 (in his *Ausgewählte Werke in vier Bänden*, vol. 4, p. 383).

[89]   *SKS* 4, 461 / *CA*, 162.

Bibliography

I. References or Uses of Kierkegaard in Binswanger's Corpus

Einführung in die Probleme der allgemeinen Psychologie, Berlin: Springer 1922, p. 225; p. 296; p. 322; p. 324.

"Welche Aufgaben ergeben sich für die Psychiatrie aus den Fortschritten der neueren Psychologie?," *Zeitschrift für gesamte Neurologie und Psychiatrie*, vol. 91, nos. 3–5, 1924, pp. 402–36, see p. 402 (in his *Ausgewählte Vorträge und Aufsätze*, vols. 1–2, Bern: Francke 1947–55, vol. 2, pp. 111–46, see p. 112).

"Erfahren, Verstehen, Deuten in der Psychoanalyse," *Imago*, vol. 12, nos. 2–3, 1926, pp. 223–37, see p. 224 (in his *Ausgewählte Werke in vier Bänden*, vols. 1–4, ed. by Hans-Jürg Braun, Heidelberg: Asanger 1992–94, vol. 3, pp. 3–16, see p. 3; published also in his *Ausgewählte Vorträge und Aufsätze*, vols. 1–2, Bern: Francke 1947–55, vol. 2, pp. 67–80).

Wandlungen in der Auffassung und Deutung des Traumes von den Griechen bis zum Gegenwart, Berlin: Springer 1928, p. 68.

"Traum und Existenz," *Neue Schweizer Rundschau*, vol. 23, 1930, pp. 673–85; pp. 766–79, see p. 673; p. 772; p. 776 (in his *Ausgewählte Werke in vier Bänden*, vol. 3, pp. 95–119, see p. 95; p. 112; p. 116; English translation: "Dream and Existence," in *Being-in-the-World. Selected Papers of Ludwig Binswanger*, trans. by Jacob Needleman, New York: Harper & Row 1975 [1963], pp. 222–48; this translation was revised by Keith Hoeller in *Review of Existential Psychology and Psychiatry*, vol. 19, no. 1, 1984–85, special issue on "Dream and Existence").

"Über Ideenflucht," *Schweizer Archiv für Neurologie und Psychiatrie*, vol. 27, no. 2, 1932, pp. 203–17; vol. 28, nos. 1–2, 1932, pp. 183–202; vol. 29, no. 1, 1932, pp. 1–37; pp. 193–252; vol. 30, no. 1, 1933, pp. 68–85; see vol. 28, no. 2, 1932, p. 201; vol. 29, no. 1, 1932, p. 25; vol. 29, no. 2, 1932, p. 222 (in his *Ausgewählte Werke in vier Bänden*, vols. 1–4, ed. by Hans-Jürg Braun, Heidelberg: Asanger 1992–94, vol. 1, pp. 2–231, see p. 104; p. 132; p. 180; published also as *Über Ideenflucht*, Zürich: Orel Füssli 1933 (reprinted, New York: Garland 1980)).

"Das Raumproblem in der Psychopathologie," *Zeitschrift für die gesamte Neurologie und Psychiatrie*, vol. 145, 1933, pp. 598–647, see p. 620 (in his *Ausgewählte Werke in vier Bänden*, vols. 1–4, ed. by Hans-Jürg Braun, Heidelberg: Asanger 1992–94, vol. 3, pp. 123–77, see p. 146; published also in his *Ausgewählte Vorträge und Aufsätze*, vols. 1–2, Bern: Francke 1947–55, vol. 2, pp. 618–43).

"Heraklits Auffassung des Menschen," *Die Antike*, vol. 9, no. 1, 1935, pp. 1–38, see p. 6; p. 12; p. 13; pp. 36–7 (in his *Ausgewählte Vorträge und Aufsätze*, vols. 1–2, 2nd ed., Bern: Francke 1961, pp. 98–131, see p. 108; p. 109; p. 130).

"Freuds Auffassung des Menschen im Lichte der Anthropologie," *Nederlands Tijdschrift voor de Psychologie*, vol. 4, nos. 5–6, 1936, pp. 266–301, see p. 297 (in his *Ausgewählte Vorträge und Aufsätze*, vols. 1–2, Bern: Francke 1947–55, vol. 1, pp. 159–89, see p. 186; English translation: "Freud's Conception of Man in the Light of Anthropology," in *Being-in-the-World. Selected Papers of Ludwig Binswanger*, trans. by Jacob Needleman, New York: Harper & Row 1975 [1963], pp. 149–81).

Grundformen und Erkenntnis menschlichen Daseins, Zürich: Niehans 1942, p. 58; p. 123; pp. 128–9; p. 189; p. 236; p. 243; p. 246; p. 400; p. 420; p. 422; p. 473; pp. 480–1; p. 498; pp. 545–8; p. 552; p. 562; p. 605; p. 639; p. 682 (in his *Ausgewählte Werke in vier Bänden*, vols. 1–4, ed. by Hans-Jürg Braun, Heidelberg: Asanger 1992–94, vol. 2, p. 49; p. 109; pp. 114–15; p. 170; p. 212; pp. 218–19; p. 221; p. 362; p. 379; p. 381; p. 411; p. 427; p. 433; p. 449; pp. 493–6; p. 499; p. 508; p. 549; p. 580; p. 619; p. 629).

"Der Fall Ellen West. Eine anthropologisch-klinische Studie," *Schweizer Archiv für Neurologie und Psychiatrie*, vol. 53, 1944, pp. 255–77; vol. 54, 1944, pp. 69–117; pp. 330–60; and vol. 55, 1945, pp. 16–40, see vol. 54, 1944, p. 95; p. 96; pp. 100–2; p. 106; p. 108; p. 343; p. 360; vol. 55, 1945, p. 31 (in his *Ausgewählte Werke in vier Bänden*, vols. 1–4, ed. by Hans-Jürg Braun, Heidelberg: Asanger 1992–94, vol. 4, pp. 73–209, see pp. 131–2; pp. 136–8; p. 142; p. 143; p. 166; p. 184; p. 201; published also in his *Schizophrenie*, Pfullingen: Neske 1957; English translation: "The Case of Ellen West," in *Existence—A New Dimension in Psychiatry and Psychology*, ed. by Rollo May, Ernest Angel and Henri F. Ellenberger, New York: Basic Books 1958, pp. 237–364).

"Wahnsinn als lebensgeschichtliches Phänomen und als Geisteskrankheit," *Monatsschrift für Psychiatrie und Neurologie*, vol. 110, 1945, pp. 129–60, see p. 160.

"Der Fall Jürg Zünd," *Schweizer Archiv für Neurologie und Psychiatrie*, vol. 56, 1946, pp. 191–220; vol. 58, 1947, pp. 1–43; and vol. 59, 1947, pp. 21–36, see vol. 58, 1947, p. 2; p. 29; pp. 36–8 (in his *Schizophrenie*, Pfullingen: Neske 1957, study no. 3, pp. 189–288, see p. 231; pp. 262–3; p. 480).

"Über die daseinsanalytische Forschungsrichtung in der Psychiatrie," *Schweizer Archiv für Psychiatrie und Neurologie*, vol. 57, 1946, pp. 209–35, see p. 225 (in his *Ausgewählte Werke in vier Bänden*, vols. 1–4, ed. by Hans-Jürg Braun, Heidelberg: Asanger 1992–94, vol. 3, pp. 231–57, see p. 247).

"Über den Satz von Hofmannsthal: 'Was Geist ist, erfaßt nur der Bedrängte,' " *Studia Philosophica*, vol. 8, 1948, pp. 1–11, see p. 3 (in his *Ausgewählte Werke in vier Bänden*, vols. 1–4, ed. by Hans-Jürg Braun, Heidelberg: Asanger 1992–94, vol. 3, pp. 265–73, see p. 267; published also in his *Ausgewählte Vorträge und Aufsätze*, vols. 1–2, Bern: Francke 1947–55, vol. 2, pp. 243–51).

"Die Bedeutung der Daseinsanalytik Martin Heideggers für das Selbstverständnis der Psychiatrie," in Carlos Astrada et al., *Martin Heideggers Einfluß auf die Wissenschaften*, Bern: Francke 1949, pp. 58–72, see p. 70 (in his *Ausgewählte Vorträge und Aufsätze*, vols. 1–2, Bern: Francke 1947–55, vol. 2, pp. 264–78, see p. 275; English translation: "Heidegger's Analytic of Existence and Its Meaning for Psychiatry," in his *Being-in-the-World. Selected Papers of Ludwig*

Binswanger, trans. by Jacob Needleman, New York: Harper & Row 1975 [1963],
  pp. 206–21).
Henrik Ibsen und das Problem der Selbstrealisation in der Kunst, Heidelberg:
  Lambert Schneider 1949, pp. 10–11; pp. 35–6; p. 39; p. 54; p. 79.
"Studien zum Schizophrenienproblem. Der Fall Lola Voss," *Schweizer Archiv für
  Neurologie und Psychiatrie*, vol. 63, 1949, pp. 29–97, see pp. 50–1; p. 52; p. 59;
  p. 65; p. 69; p. 70; p. 76 (in his *Schizophrenie*, Pfullingen: Neske 1957, pp. 289–
  358, see p. 300; p. 310; p. 317; p. 319; p. 324; p. 331; pp. 333–4; p. 339; p. 479;
  pp. 484–5; English translation: "The Case of Lola Voss," trans. by Ernest Angel,
  in his *Being-in-the-World*, see p. 295; p. 297; p. 304; p. 310; pp. 314–15; p. 321).
"Daseinsanalytik und Psychiatrie," *Der Nervenarzt*, vol. 22, 1951, pp. 1–10, see
  p. 2 (in his *Ausgewählte Vorträge und Aufsätze*, vols. 1–2, Bern: Francke 1947–
  55, vol. 2, pp. 279–302, see p. 282).
"Der Fall Suzanne Urban," *Schweizer Archiv für Neurologie und Psychiatrie*, vol.
  69, 1952, pp. 36–77; vol. 70, 1952, pp. 1–32; and vol. 71, 1952, pp. 57–96, see
  vol. 69, 1952, p. 58 (in his *Ausgewählte Werke in vier Bänden*, vols. 1–4, ed.
  by Hans-Jürg Braun, Heidelberg: Asanger 1992–94, vol. 4, pp. 210–332, see
  p. 236; published also in his *Schizophrenie*, Pfullingen: Neske 1957, study no.
  5, pp. 359–470).
Drei Formen missglückten Daseins, Tübingen: Niemeyer 1956, see p. X; p. 115;
  p. 149; p. 155; p. 187; p. 189 (republished as *Formen mißglückten Daseins*,
  in his *Ausgewählte Werke in vier Bänden*, vols. 1–4, ed. by Hans-Jürg Braun,
  Heidelberg: Asanger 1992–94, vol. 1, p. 238; p. 345; p. 375; p. 381; pp. 408–9;
  p. 411).
"Der Mensch in der Psychiatrie," *Schweizer Archiv für Neurologie und Psychiatrie*,
  vol. 77, 1956, pp. 123–38, see pp. 123–5; pp. 134–6 (in his *Ausgewählte Werke in
  vier Bänden*, vols. 1–4, ed. by Hans-Jürg Braun, Heidelberg: Asanger 1992–94,
  vol. 4, pp. 57–72, see pp. 57–9; pp. 68–70; published also as *Der Mensch in der
  Psychiatrie*, Pfullingen: Neske 1957).
Melancholie und Manie. Phänomenologische Studien, Pfullingen: Neske 1957, see
  p. 60 (republished as "Melancholie und Manie," in his *Ausgewählte Werke in vier
  Bänden*, vols. 1–4, ed. by Hans-Jürg Braun, Heidelberg: Asanger 1992–94, vol.
  4, pp. 351–428, see p. 383).

II. Sources of Binswanger's Knowledge of Kierkegaard

Heidegger, Martin, *Sein und Zeit*, Halle: Niemeyer 1927, pp. 175–96, see also
  p. 190, note 1; p. 235, note 1; p.338, note 1.
Jaspers, Karl, *Allgemeine Psychopathologie*, 9th ed., Berlin: Springer 1973 [1913],
  p. 262;
p. 274; pp. 291–2; p. 300; pp. 354ff.; p. 589; p. 613; pp. 630–1; pp. 646–7; p. 649;
  p. 680; p. 686.
Kierkegaard, Søren, *Gesammelte Werke*, vols. 1–12, trans. and ed. by Hermann
  Gottsched and Christoph Schrempf, Jena: Diederichs 1909–22.

— *Auswahl aus seinen Bekenntnissen und Gedanken*, ed. by Fritz Droop, Munich: Müller 1914 (*Bibliothek der Philosophen*, vol. 11).

III. Secondary Literature on Binswanger's Relation to Kierkegaard

Basso, Elisabetta, "Il sogno e il dramma immanente del destino. 'Un saggio di ricerca frammentaria,' " in Ludwig Binswanger, *Il sogno. Mutamenti nella concezione e interpretazione dai Greci al presente*, trans. and ed. by Elisabetta Basso, Macerata: Quodlibet 2009, pp. 117–48.

Basso, Elisabetta, "Le rêve comme argument: les enjeux épistémologiques à l'origine du projet existentiel de Ludwig Binswanger," *Archives de Philosophie*, vol. 73–4, 2010, pp. 655–86, see pp. 677–9.

Besoli, Stefano, "Sull'ambiguità del comprendere. In margine ad alcune considerazioni binswangeriane," *Comprendre*, vols. 16–18, 2006–08, pp. 34–53, see p. 39.

D'Ippolito, Bianca Maria, *La cattedrale sommersa. Fenomenologia e psicopatologia in Ludwig Binswanger*, Milan: Franco Angeli 2004, p. 58; p. 61; pp. 83–5; p. 89; p. 107; p. 136; p. 147; pp. 186–7; p. 220.

Herzog, Max, *Weltenwürfe. Ludwig Binswangers phänomenologische Psychologie*, Berlin and New York: De Gruyter 1992, p. 110; p. 139; p. 146; p. 149; p. 184; p. 207.

Hoeller, Keith, "Foreword" to Keith Hoeller, Jacob Needleman, Michel Foucault, and Ludwig Binswanger, *Dream and Existence*, Seattle, Washington: Review of Existential Psychology & Psychiatry 1986, pp. 13–14.

Holzhey-Kunz, Alice, "Einleitung," in Ludwig Binswanger, *Ausgewählte Werke in vier Bänden*, vols. 1–4, ed. by Hans-Jürg Barun, Heidelberg: Asanger 1992–94, vol. 4, pp. 13–55.

May, Rollo, *The Origins and Significance of the Existential Movement in Psychology*, in *Existence—A New Dimension in Psychiatry and Psychology*, ed. by Rollo May, Ernest Angel and Henri F. Ellenberger, New York: Basic Books 1958, pp. 3–36.

Nordentoft, Kresten, *Kierkegaard's Psychology*, trans. by Bruce H. Kirmmse, Pittsburgh: Duquesne University Press 1972, see pp. 233ff. (Original Danish: *Kierkegaards psykologi*, Copenhagen: G.E.C. Gad 1972.)

Sonnemann, Ulrich, *Existence and Therapy: An Introduction to Phenomenological Psychology and Existential Analysis*, New York: Grune & Stratton 1954, p. 145.

— *Negative Anthropologie. Vorstudien zur Sabotage des Schicksals*, Reinbek bei Hamburg: Rowohlt 1969, p. 124; p. 128.

Spiegelberg, Herbert, *Phenomenology in Psychology and Psychiatry: A Historical Introduction*, Evanston, Illinois: Northwestern University Press 1972, p. XXVIII; p. XXIX; p. XXX; p. XXXVIII; p. 121; p. 150; p. 159; pp. 162–3; p. 303; p. 311.

Mircea Eliade:

On Religion, Cosmos, and Agony

Leo Stan

Born in 1907 in Bucharest, Mircea Eliade exhibited the first signs of his astonishing intellectual gifts at an incredibly young age. He published his first newspaper article when he was 14. Before turning 16, his works included newspaper articles on entomology, literary criticism, alchemy, and the history of religions. While still in secondary school, he began to try his hand at literature and wrote his first novel, to be published just a few years afterwards. Starting with 1925, he enrolled in the Literature and Philosophy Department of Bucharest University, from which he graduated in 1928 with a thesis on *Italian Philosophy, from Marsilio Ficino to Giordano Bruno*. Prior to the university period Eliade entertained a passionate interest in Oriental culture and religions, reading everything he could find on the subject. In the year of his graduation this passion was rewarded with a scholarship that allowed him to go to India as a student of Surendranath Dasgupta. Here he elaborated a comparative analysis of Yoga techniques.[1] The topic enthralled him to such an extent that he spent six months in an *ashram* at Rishikesh where what he learned *in abstracto* became a lived experience. However, almost unfathomably, in 1932 he decided to return home where a year later, he obtained a doctoral degree from the University of Bucharest. An outstanding career followed during the period between the wars. Books on religious topics, novels, academic articles, university lectures, public conferences, a tireless journalistic activity—they all created for him the allure of a myth, revered to this very day in some Romanian circles. World War II found him abroad as a cultural attaché in the Romanian Legations in London and Lisbon. In 1945 he left Portugal for Paris where he spent eleven years, lecturing at the Sorbonne and publishing assiduously on various topics in the phenomenology and history of religion. From 1957 on, he held a permanent professorship at the University of Chicago, Divinity School. He died in 1986. It is also important to remember that Eliade was a prolific diarist. The publication of his autobiographical authorship is still under way, although an impressive part is already available. Besides his monumental correspondence,

I wish to express my gratitude to The Social Sciences and Humanities Research Council of Canada for financial support in writing this material.

[1]   The results of this research were published after Eliade's return to Romania. Mircea Eliade, *Yoga. Essai sur les origins de la mystique indienne*, Paris: Librairie Orientaliste Paul Geuthner and Bucharest: Fundaţia pentru literatură şi artă 1936. This book became the basis for Eliade's classical work, *Le Yoga. Immortalité et liberté*, Paris: Payot 1954.

Eliade's journalistic authorship still awaits its complete critical publication.[2] Given the gargantuan proportions of Eliade's appetite for knowledge, the encounter with Søren Kierkegaard was bound to happen sooner or later.

And it happened sooner rather than later. The reasons are legion and cover a broad psychologico-philosophical spectrum. First of all, the commonalities started from the biographical level. In their ineffable intimacy, Mircea Eliade and Kierkegaard believed that spiritual achievements cannot be actualized without a heroic sacrifice of eroticism and of one's bourgeois existence, although the Romanian author quickly realized the excessiveness of such conviction. Both were innately wistful and perceived their melancholy as a confirmation of but also an obstacle to, their brilliance. From very early on, they realized that the true meaning of philosophy and religion cannot be other than existential and subjectivity-oriented.[3] Similarly to Kierkegaard, Eliade pursued a stormy, iconoclastic, and even bellicose journalistic activity,[4] being the target of a great deal of malicious or ridiculing attacks in the press.[5] We should add that neither Eliade nor Kierkegaard was ever content with modernity and its alleged gains. What they additionally shared was a fervent belief in the primacy of the spiritual and the religious over secular science and politics.[6] Also their *oeuvre* testifies to a genuine reverence for the truths hidden in classical mythology and fairy-tales. Finally, their appreciation for literature was so absorbing that they entwined their philosophical authorship with authentic literary accomplishments.

As already stated, Eliade's success was due to his immense knowledge and encyclopedic aspirations.[7] In his analysis of Eliade's early authorship, Florin Ţurcanu convincingly shows how erudition becomes the chief ideal that the young Eliade ceaselessly and fervently upholds among the peers of his generation. Thus, to Eliade's mind, aside from the traditional humanistic education, the true intellectual should handle with the same masterfulness the newly discovered Oriental philosophy and the mythical thought nestled in folklore.[8] Moreover, he or she was expected to be up to date with the emerging Italian and Spanish thinkers. The achievements and general history of science should not be ignored either. One could easily argue that Eliade accomplished this desideratum. If we browse only through his newspaper

---

2   Sorin Alexandrescu, *Mircea Eliade dinspre Portugalia*, Bucharest: Humanitas 2006, pp. 113–17.

3   For Eliade's early creed about the indissoluble link between spirituality and the concrete individual selfhood, see, for example, Mircea Eliade, *Itinerariu spiritual. Scrieri de tinereţe 1927*, Bucharest: Humanitas 2003, p. 390.

4   See in this sense, Mac Linscott Ricketts, *Mircea Eliade: The Romanian Roots, 1907–1945*, Boulder: Columbia University Press 1988 (*Eastern European Monographs*), pp. 276–82; pp. 302–5; p. 1120.

5   Ricketts, *Mircea Eliade*, pp. 1087–8.

6   Eliade, Itinerariu spiritual, p. 266.

7   See Florin Ţurcanu, "Erudiţie şi jurnalism. Publicistica lui Mircea Eliade în anii 1926–1928," *Sud-Estul şi contextul european*, vol. 3, 1995, pp. 87–94; see p. 91.

8   Mircea Popescu, "Eliade and Folklore," in *Myths and Symbols: Studies in Honor of Mircea Eliade*, ed. by Joseph M. Kitagawa and Charles H. Long, Chicago and London: University of Chicago Press 1969, pp. 81–90.

articles between 1926 and 1928, we find analyses of authors as dissimilar as Julius Evola, Anatole France, Georg Brandes, Amiel, Remy de Gourmont, Chuang Tzu, Lao Tzu, Milarepa, Asvagosha, Raffaele Pettazzoni, Ernesto Buonaiuti, Giovanni Gentile, Rudolf Steiner, alongside the autochthonous literary scene and a host of historians of philosophy, of science, or of religion. Kierkegaard's authorship itself, which was vastly unknown in Romania at the time, figured in Eliade's must-read list as a crucial formative stage in becoming a cultural virtuoso.[9]

I. A Successful Attempt at Indirect Communication

The spring Sunday of March 4, 1928 represents a landmark for Kierkegaard's entry into the Romanian cultural milieu.[10] On this date, the newspaper *Cuvântul* hosted an article with the glamorous title, "Sören Kierkegaard. Fiancé, Pamphleteer, and Hermit."[11] Much later its author would boast of being the first to have introduced the Danish genius to the Romanian audience, a fact that is not entirely accurate.[12] Before dealing with the content, we should remember that at the time, Eliade was desperately trying to put an end to an erotic affair—which seemed to him intellectually emasculating—with a young girl by the name of Rica Botez.[13] Thus, like Kierkegaard long before him, Eliade was trying to communicate with the beloved indirectly.[14] However, it is important to point out that, whereas the dialectical *telos* of Kierkegaard's writings was to initiate Regine Olsen into the ultimacy of the God-relationship, Mircea Eliade, while drawing on the example of Pygmalion, sought to mold Rica in accord with his virile intellectualist ideals. And yet, this aspect does not compromise the historico-cultural importance of Eliade's text.

---

[9]   Eliade also used Kierkegaard as a weapon against the monopoly of the French culture. See Eliade, *Itinerariu spiritual*, p. 381.

[10]   A comprehensive survey of Eliade's biography and intellectual activity during this period can be found in Ricketts, *Mircea Eliade*, pp. 197–325.

[11]   Mircea Eliade, "Sören Kierkegaard—Logodnic, pamfletar şi eremit," *Cuvântul*, vol. 4, no. 1035, 1928, p. 1 (reprinted in Mircea Eliade, *Virilitate şi ascezā. Scrieri de tinereţe 1928*, Bucharest: Humanitas Publishers 2008, pp. 68–72; all further references are to this edition). The reader should also be aware that Eliade's encounter with the Christian rebel of Copenhagen was anticipated by a few thematic commonalities which unfortunately, cannot be dealt with here.

[12]   Ţurcanu ("Erudiţie şi jurnalism," p. 93, note 16) observes that the first public mention of Kierkegaard in Romania appears in an article by Mihail Ralea, published in *Viaţa românească*, vol. 19, nos. 6–7, 1927. See also Mircea Eliade, *Ordeal by Labyrinth: Conversations with Claude-Henri Rocquet*, trans. by Derek Coltman, Chicago and London: University of Chicago Press 1982, p. 17, where Eliade mistakenly states that the article was published in 1925 or 1926.

[13]   Their relation is described under a novelistic veil in Eliade's unpublished novel, *Gaudeamus*, written that very year. See Mircea Eliade, *Romanul adolescentului miop*, Bucharest: Minerva 1989, pp. 215–465. For further details, see Ricketts, *Mircea Eliade*, pp. 198–215.

[14]   Ricketts, *Mircea Eliade*, pp. 214–15.

In general, the article gives the reader a rough idea of the pivotal events in Kierkegaard's life: the somber relation to his gloomy father, the traumatizing experience with Regine, the *Corsair* affair, the anti-ecclesiastical revolt, and a supposedly failed encounter with Christian religiosity. From a thematic perspective, Eliade gives an overview of the threefold structure of existence, the gloomy picture of Kierkegaard's Christianity, and the intricacies of seduction, on which, for reasons that should be obvious, the author dwells quite a bit.

The article commences with Michael Kierkegaard's calamitous saga which triggered, according to Eliade, Søren's own "spiritual tragedy."[15] The youngest son of the family makes his way into existence in a "gloomy, quiet household which was terrified by the anger of the insulted [God],"[16] while his entire childhood could not have been more "somber and bleak."[17] Next, Eliade—whose deference towards academia never knew any doubts—holds that upon the dreadful discovery of the paternal enigma, the son decides to atone for family sins by...completing his theology degree. Eliade's quick sketch of Kierkegaard's entry into maturity is, indeed, memorable:

> With a soul unsettled by doubts and the restlessness of potentialities, while being overwhelmed by the terror of boredom—which was acquired in childhood and adolescence, but also dilated by phantasms—and torn apart by loneliness, Sören timidly entered the scene of life, yet eager for enjoyments, caresses, and the warmth of love. He was tempted by *everything* but did not dare to taste any fruit, for he dreaded the shadow of destiny. He withdrew into himself and realized he was rebellious, terrified, impenetrable, irrevocably wistful, probably destined to a hardened solitude, to suffering, and perhaps, to genius.[18]

One cannot fail to recognize here a few salient features that admittedly confirm Kierkegaard's lasting place in the history of European pessimism. And yet, Eliade might pass too quickly over a certain trait of Kierkegaard's personality, which prodigiously found its way into the written works, namely, his polemical sarcasm and vigorous irony. Eliade seems unaware that Kierkegaard looked for viable alternatives to Romantic self-dissolving apathy.[19] Also, Eliade ignores—and maybe he could not have known—that Kierkegaard disengaged from the world on soteriological grounds, that is, as penance for his early rambunctious and *bon vivant* lifestyle, not to mention the nocturnal escapades that preceded his father's death. At any rate, it is highly plausible that this aesthetic episode had a portentous share in Kierkegaard's proverbial "thorn in the flesh." Last but not least, when read in light of contemporary scholarship, Eliade's view of Kierkegaard's solitude as insurmountable is equally open to debate.[20]

---

[15] Eliade, *Virilitate şi asceză*, p. 69. Throughout this article, unless otherwise stated, all translations from the Romanian are mine.

[16] Ibid.

[17] Ibid.

[18] Ibid.

[19] See *SKS* 1, 308ff. / *CI*, 272ff.

[20] See, for instance, Jørgen Bukdahl, *Søren Kierkegaard and the Common Man*, trans. by Bruce H. Kirmmse, Grand Rapids, Michigan: Eerdmans 2001; *Encounters with Kierkegaard: A Life Seen by His Contemporaries*, trans. and ed. by Bruce H. Kirmmse, Princeton, New

Moving to the delicate topic of eros, Eliade claims that Regine Olsen mediated Kierkegaard's encounter with "the vagarious, warm, and dazzling voluptuousness of life."[21] His affection for her, Eliade adds, was expected to bring a ray of light into the dark world of the genius. If Søren's "soul was bleak and tormented, the fiancée's love spread out and pacified."[22] But as an incurable melancholic, who is unworthy of Regine's pure feelings, the fiancé decides to break the engagement. Eliade's conspicuously romantic narrative has it that, while "frightened by that year of happiness,"[23] but also nourished by an "arduous inner life,"[24] Kierkegaard commits to paper "The Seducer's Diary" and "In vino veritas." His unacknowledged purpose is to dupe both the beloved and the public into thinking that he is a mere aesthete, simply "a man who reaps without delay every enjoyment available, who believes as much in love as in the *necessary* mobility of love."[25] However, Eliade is perceptive enough to specify that, upon discovering that the innocent girl has given herself to "an obscure philistine,"[26] the deceitful seducer is left only with his writing. Moreover, according to Eliade, the engagement's denouement had a dramatic effect on Kierkegaard, so much so that it gave birth to definitive insights into the bottomless depths of subjectivity.[27]

Another debatable conjecture concerns Kierkegaard's loss of faith. Eliade writes that "Sören Kierkegaard knew the sweetness and serenity of Jesus for a very short time (1847–48), namely when he wrote the book series crowned by *Christian Discourses*. From that moment on and until his death," we read further, "he became terribly distraught, petrified by the immensity of the meaning of Christianity."[28] As the unhappy love represents a genuine "catalyst for his latent genius,"[29] Eliade's Kierkegaard opts for a reclusive existence but makes sure he avoids the anchoritic path. After the traumatic collision with the *Corsair*, his predicament became even higher. "He could not find any relief in Christianity, his loneliness was more and more oppressive, whilst his wretched soul ardently felt the absence of love."[30] The clash with the established church is described in similar apocalyptic tones. Eliade notes that on the occasion of Mynster's burial and Martensen's funerary speech, "Sören could not contain his fury against a Church that granted the title of sainthood

---

Jersey: Princeton University Press 1996. Of some relevance here is also Habib C. Malik, *Receiving Søren Kierkegaard: The Early Impact and Transmission of His Thought*, Washington, D.C.: Catholic University of America Press 1997.

[21]   Eliade, *Virilitate şi asceză*, p. 69.

[22]   Ibid.

[23]   Ibid.

[24]   Ibid.

[25]   Ibid., p. 69.

[26]   Ibid., p. 70.

[27]   Ibid.: "What we might call Sören Kierkegaard's 'philosophy,' [namely] his view of the aesthetic, the ethical, and the religious…was definitively established during these crisis years." See also Ricketts, *Mircea Eliade*, p. 284.

[28]   Eliade, *Virilitate şi asceză*, p. 71.

[29]   Ibid.

[30]   Ibid., p. 72.

to a commoner."[31] Once *The Moment* became public, every Dane should have been able to ascertain that "Christianity has ceased to exist: the Church [service] implies a remunerated job and Christians are irretrievably mediocre."[32] When the perpetrator of this spiritual upheaval tragically dies, continues Eliade, the battle "plunges into the very soul of Denmark."[33] Thus, a whole nation comes to perpetuate Kierkegaard's troubled existence.

As to Kierkegaard's philosophy proper, Eliade briefly peruses the tripartite division of human existence. He starts by applauding Kierkegaard's aestheticism because of its "plural and refreshing dynamism."[34] I have already stated that, being committed to a relationship, about which he was not very enthusiastic, Eliade will expatiate more than anything else on the ambiguous attractiveness of seduction. Referring exclusively to the intellectual seducer from *Either/Or*, Part 1 and "In vino veritas," Eliade portrays him as "a subtle, refined, and enigmatic erudite."[35] Since capable of flawlessly manipulating the soul of his victims, Johannes appears to Eliade as the obdurate advocate of voluptuousness and unlimited erotic freedom. However, Eliade is not so naïve to forget that Kierkegaard's lofty seducer "wants Cordelia's perfect body only,"[36] and that "for just a night."[37] Despite his refinement, Johannes is no different from any other libertine: he lost all interest in Cordelia after he carnally possessed her, and immediately set out to pursue the next target. Eliade has a curious and even unintelligible solution for the tension between the flesh and the spirit within the personality of the seducer. He explains that "virgins," who probably stand for carnality, "must be seduced solely by masculine *souls*."[38] Here the commentator might allude to his own understanding of eroticism and cultural *paideia*,[39] rather than decrypt the intricacies of Kierkegaard's reflective seduction.

Upon elaborating Kierkegaard's ethics, Eliade is visibly disappointed. He remarks that the second stage is particularized by a "severe immobility (*staticism*)"[40] and an "extreme, incommunicable individualism,"[41] both issuing from a "protracted painful experience."[42] Besides, Eliade warns us that the passage from one stage to another should not be understood along the lines of evolutionary causality. "The ethical," he writes, "is not obtained from the aesthetic by means of an evolution of

---

31   Ibid.
32   Ibid., p. 72.
33   Ibid.
34   Ibid., p. 71.
35   Ibid., p. 70.
36   Ibid.
37   Ibid.
38   Ibid., pp. 70–1.
39   See in this sense Mircea Eliade, "Apology for Virility," *Gîndirea*, nos. 8–9, August–September 1928 (reprinted in Eliade, *Virilitate şi asceză*, pp. 230–52). See also Mircea Eliade, *Memorii*, 3rd ed., Bucharest: Humanitas 2004, pp. 138–9. (English translation in his *Autobiography*, vols. 1–2, trans. by Mac L. Ricketts, San Francisco: Harper & Row 1981, vol. 1, p. 134.)
40   Eliade, *Virilitate şi asceză*, p. 71.
41   Ibid.
42   Ibid.

sorts, while the religious is not an ordinary overcoming of the ethical."[43] Rather, inasmuch as existential transitions emerge thanks to a leap or an "unintelligible transfiguration,"[44] each individual "experientially subscribes only to the values of that stage."[45] In consequence, according to Eliade, we should conceive the three stages as "fully separated"[46] from one another.

When he probes the religious territory, Eliade observes that Kierkegaard's God is able to interfere in the leap from one existence sphere to another. Pertinently enough, he writes that this deity "breaks into the world, into history, and the individual's life as the paradox."[47] However, from here Eliade infers that the Kierkegaardian religion is "unconceivable, irrational, absurd."[48] As rooted in the person's living experience and not in a rigorous dogma, Kierkegaard's Christianity strikes one as "stupendous, oppressive, and annihilating."[49] That is how Eliade comes to the realization that Kierkegaard completely disregards the ecclesiastical dimension of Christian life.[50]

Now, before turning to the next segment of our subject, a few comments are necessary. That Eliade intuited the perennial value of Kierkegaard's philosophy so early in his career is in itself a remarkable exploit. Although for us today most of his judgments seem stereotypical and significantly outdated, they must have sounded like breaking news to Romania in the late 1920s. Many of Eliade's contemporaries (like Emil Cioran (1911–95), for instance) chanced upon Kierkegaard's ideas for the first time through this short piece.[51] My second remark regards Eliade's sources. These are, I hypothesize, twofold. First, in the article Eliade admits that he consulted the extant Italian and German translations, but without providing any bibliographical details.[52] On the other side, from a historical standpoint, we may surmise that Eliade's soon to be university professor and mentor, Nae Ionescu (1890–1940), might have had a momentous say in this enterprise.[53]

---

[43] Ibid.

[44] Ibid.

[45] Ibid.

[46] Ibid.

[47] Ibid.

[48] Ibid.

[49] Ibid. Eliade also states that Kierkegaard fell victim to a similar "spiritual agony." (Ibid., p. 72.) Kierkegaard thus appears "an ascetic tormented by Cordelia's face, [and] a loner hardened by sufferings." (Ibid., p. 72.) However, Eliade insists as much on the fact that Kierkegaard was never an anchorite. Moreover, he wrongs Cordelia with Regine.

[50] Ricketts (*Mircea Eliade*, pp. 291–3) offers a useful summary of Eliade's view of religiousness at the time. Eliade tends to conceive the Christian religion either as a mystical experience (that is, as wisdom doubled by sainthood), which is accessible to a few, or as a path that goes through the ecclesia, which is meant for the many and is based on liturgical rites.

[51] Ţurcanu, "Erudiţie şi journalism," p. 90; Emil M. Cioran, "Beginnings of a Friendship," in *Myths and Symbols: Studies in Honor of Mircea Eliade*, pp. 407–14; p. 409. The same may be true of Eugène Ionesco, the future father of the theater of the absurd.

[52] Eliade, *Virilitate şi asceză*, p. 70. Later, Eliade will clarify that he consulted the Italian translations of "The Musical Erotic" and "The Diary of the Seducer," from *Either/Or*, Part 1 and of "In vino veritas" from the *Stages*. See note 73 below.

[53] Kierkegaard's plausible influence on Nae Ionescu deserves a separate study. Let it suffice to remember that in *The Portuguese Diary* Eliade explicitly links Kierkegaard to

As regards the article's content, three elements are of particular interest. First, it is unclear why Eliade affirms that Kierkegaard understands the ethical in terms of stagnation, extreme individualism, and ineffability. It is well-known that, in *Fear and Trembling*, the ethical is explicitly equated with sociality and discursive intelligibility, whereas only religiousness (exemplified through Abraham's absurd faith) is thought in terms of inward incommunicability. Further, in *Either/Or*, Part 2, Judge William's ethics is precisely the opposite of Eliade's interpretation; namely, the ethicist is an individual who deliberately assumes his interactive, social, historical environs, possessing therefore a highly dynamic interiority. Worthy of mention is also William's volubility in detailing his *Weltanschauung*. The second limitation concerns the mythical figure of Don Juan. Even if he had access to "The Musical Erotic" chapter from *Either/Or*, Part 1, Eliade is completely silent about Kierkegaard's reflections on Mozart's *Don Giovanni*, which are indispensable to the Kierkegaardian treatment of seduction.[54] The third observation is connected with the first. When indicting Kierkegaard for a subjectivist static ethics, Eliade shows that he had no knowledge of Kierkegaard's considerations on this matter from the *Postscript*. For, had he read this book, Eliade would have discovered a depiction of ethics as intimately linked to the subject's becoming and existential possibilities. Consequently, he could not claim that the ethical is marked by immobility. Moreover, in the same book Eliade might have come across the fundamental distinction between religiousness A and B, with fundamental consequences for his own theories on religious phenomena, in general, and archaic spirituality or magical thought, in particular.[55]

---

the memory of his former professor, whom he praises for having defended the autarchy of religious phenomena vis-à-vis traditional metaphysics and ethics. According to Eliade, what might bring Ionescu and Kierkegaard together is their quintessential reflections on religiousness, and thereby their "validation of extra-rational experiences." Mircea Eliade, *Jurnalul portughez şi alte scrieri*, vols. 1–2, ed. by Sorin Alexandrescu, Bucharest: Humanitas 2006, vol. 1, p. 292. (Throughout this article all references to *Jurnalul portughez* pertain to volume 1 only.) At the same time, Eliade mentions Ionescu's merit of having introduced and popularized "theological doctrines and terminology amongst laymen," which cannot be said of Kierkegaard. Ibid. Also, Eliade's suspicion that Kierkegaard ceased to believe in God might be patterned on Nae Ionescu's biography. See ibid, p. 285; pp. 291–2. Indispensible details on Nae Ionescu and his possible mediation of Kierkegaard in Eliade's intellectual trajectory can be found in Florin Ţurcanu, *Mircea Eliade. Le prisonnier de l'histoire*, Paris: Éditions la Découverte 2003, pp. 46–70.

[54]   *SKS* 2, 55–81 / *EO1*, 47–75. Eliade will later admit of his familiarity with Kierkegaard's "The Musical Erotic," although we cannot know for sure whether he read this piece prior to the 1928 article.

[55]   In fact, fruitful parallels can be drawn between Eliade's depiction of magical thought and Kierkegaard's religiousness A. See Eliade, *Virilitate şi asceză*, pp. 230–43; pp. 275–8. Ricketts, *Mircea Eliade*, p. 229; p. 253; pp. 283–4. *SKS* 7, 505–10 / *CUP1*, 555–61. For Eliade's theories on magic, see Mircea Eliade, *Occultism, Witchcraft, and Cultural Fashions: Essays in Comparative Religions*, Chicago and London: University of Chicago Press 1976; Mircea Eliade, *Zalmoxis, the Vanishing God: Comparative Studies in the Religions and Folklore of Dacia and Eastern Europe*, trans. by Willard R. Trask, Chicago and London: University of Chicago Press 1972.

The next major chapter of Eliade's reception is radically different. Its frame is apocalyptic, while Kierkegaard's impact on Eliade will be more intimate than ever before. We shall see that in a time when Eliade traverses a true limit-situation in Jaspers' sense, the Kierkegaardian *corpus* acquires an almost cathartic value for his distressed soul.

II. The Lusitanian Gethsemane

The Portuguese Diary, wherein the interaction between Eliade and Kierkegaard reaches its apex, has recently become available to Romanian readers in a complete critical edition.[56] The journal spans the years 1941 to 1945, when, we remember, Eliade worked as a cultural attaché for the Romanian consulate in Lisbon. The inestimable value of the book resides in the revelation of an absolutely unknown Eliade. What concerns us here is that Eliade's position vis-à-vis Kierkegaard takes a dramatic turn. The encounter with the Danish thinker, apart from its intellectual fertility, will facilitate a temporary psychological equipoise in the midst of a total disaster. More exactly, with Kierkegaard's help Eliade will try to rationalize the irrational *par excellence*, that is, the contingency of death, the absurdity of war, and the terror of history.[57]

But first a few provisos. In his minute and insightful commentary, Sorin Alexandrescu affirms that *The Portuguese Diary* recounts "a *secular* scenario of [Christ-like] Passion, death, and resurrection."[58] Alexandrescu uses the term "Apocalypse" or the expression "an unfathomable abyss of suffering"[59] to characterize Eliade's ordeal during this time. Such dramatic and definitive pronouncements are no exaggeration. For, halfway through his stay in Portugal, Eliade witnesses the slow agony and eventual death of his first wife in parallel with the slow but sure defeat of Romania in World War II. Romania's geopolitical downfall will also precipitate the process by which Eliade's firmly built reputation simply goes to waste. Thus *The Portuguese Diary* is the story of a threefold death: erotic, political, and professional.

Eliade met Nina Mareş at a Christmas soirée in the winter of 1932–33. She was a fresh divorcée and had a daughter—Adalgiza, a name with intriguing resonances in Romanian—from her previous marriage. Nina earned her living as a clerk-typist and secretary for a telephone company. Approximately six years before the abovementioned date, her heart and psychic balance had been shattered by a love affair with a younger lieutenant. In the aftermath of their separation, she was hospitalized for several months due to a nervous breakdown. When they were introduced, Eliade

---

[56] Eliade arrived in Lisbon on February 10, 1941. He came from London where he had held the same position from April 1940. On Eliade's stay in London and Lisbon, see also Ţurcanu, *Mircea Eliade. Le prisonnier de l'histoire*, pp. 302–42; and Ricketts, *Mircea Eliade*, pp. 1093–9.

[57] For Eliade's views of sacred and profane history, in general, see Douglas Allen, *Myth and Religion in Mircea Eliade*, New York: Routledge 2002, pp. 211–65. See also Alexandrescu, *Mircea Eliade*, p. 208.

[58] Alexandrescu, *Mircea Eliade*, p. 227.

[59] Ibid., p. 211.

was in the middle of another affair with the theater actress, Sorana Țopa.[60] He wavered a great deal when having to choose between the latter—a dreamy sophisticated woman—and the more down-to-earth Nina. Eventually, he found Nina more suitable to his personality and married her in October 1934. Eliade's marital instinct turned out to be impeccable. Nina was more than what a prominent intellectual might expect from his life partner in those times.[61] She distinguished herself through a complete dedication to her studious husband. What she had to offer was not only an elysian bourgeois existence, but also—which is not a mere trifle—her unconditional faith in Mircea's great intellect and academic success. Her devotion was so self-effacing that sacrifices must have seemed a matter of course.[62] For instance, upon getting pregnant, it seems that Eliade hinted at a possible abortion, which Nina immediately carried out. Much later, while in Lisbon, she developed uterine cancer, of which she died in November 1944 after a prolonged agony.[63] Eliade heard about the disease only very shortly before her death because she had managed to hide the brutal truth so as not to encumber his study and career. Nonetheless, when realizing the nature of her illness and its inevitable outcome, Eliade became obsessed with his contribution to her death.[64] In the diary, he mentions an incommunicable secret that tears him apart, most probably referring to this disturbing possibility.[65]

Between 1941 and 1942 Nina appears only now and then in *The Portuguese Diary*. Beginning with 1943, as her physical state worsens, her presence becomes more conspicuous and moves to the center of attention during 1944. Even if long before her death Eliade was already battling depression, insomnia, and a ruinous sentiment of intellectual failure, his dark moods aggressively got the upper hand as Nina grew more ill and had to be hospitalized. His affection became more compelling than ever, while the beloved's bodily degradation and his utter powerlessness invaded his conscious life. Sorin Alexandrescu mentions in this respect Eliade's cyclothymic attacks, "sleeplessness, lack of focus, melancholy, vagotonia, irascibility, neurasthenia."[66] Even the capacity to empathize with his fellow countrymen, who were defeated and massacred in the war, had completely vanished.[67]

---

[60]   An expressionist portrait of Sorana Țopa is drawn by Cioran, "Beginnings," pp. 411–12.

[61]   For a confirmation in this regard, see Eliade, *Memorii*, p. 278 (*Autobiography*, vol. 1, p. 275).

[62]   Eliade, *Memorii*, pp. 275–80. (*Autobiography*, vol. 1, pp. 271–7.) Other interesting details are offered by Ricketts, *Mircea Eliade*, pp. 541–51; p. 1121; and Alexandrescu, *Mircea Eliade*, p. 214.

[63]   Eliade, *Memorii*, pp. 389–90. (*Autobiography*, vol. 2, pp. 105–6.)

[64]   Alexandrescu, *Mircea Eliade*, p. 210. Elements of Eliade's tragic relation to Nina appear in his novel, *Nuntă în cer* [A Celestial Wedding] (1946); Mircea Eliade, *Maitreyi. Nuntă în cer*, Bucharest: Minerva 1986, pp. 173–336.

[65]   Eliade, *Jurnalul Portughez*, p. 288. It also seems that as early as 1927–28 Eliade wondered "if [he] was cursed to repay with misfortune those [he] loved and who loved [him]." Eliade, *Memorii*, p. 131. (*Autobiography*, vol. 1, p. 126.)

[66]   Alexandrescu, *Mircea Eliade*, p. 219. See also ibid, pp. 220–3.

[67]   Eliade, *Jurnalul Portughez*, pp. 297–8; p. 304; p. 306.

In this period, Eliade turns to the Bible, preponderantly to Paul's letters. The wisdom of Job, Isaiah, and Ecclesiastes also makes perfect sense to him.[68] However, the manifold attempts at rationalizing the calamity[69] alternate with feelings of utter dejection, abandonment, and hopelessness. It would, therefore, be no exaggeration to call the timespan between 1944 and 1945 Eliade's Gethsemane.[70] It is in this highly traumatic context that Kierkegaard's books were voraciously read by Eliade for the sake of psychological comfort and existential intelligibility.[71] However, in what follows I hope to show how and why this encounter is rather ambiguous. Regardless of the personal meaningfulness he drew from Kierkegaard, Eliade was critical towards the Danish thinker, particularly due to the latter's emphasis on the Christic suffering mimesis to the detriment of all cosmological, symbolic, and liturgical considerations.[72] In the closing pages, I analyze the pertinence of Eliade's critiques and the different perspective on religiousness they might spring from.

Without a doubt, *The Portuguese Diary* represents a trustworthy testimony to Eliade's psycho-intellectual affinity with Kierkegaard. Eliade's tenacious fascination with him most probably began in 1925 and lingered for a considerable time.[73] Thus, no sooner than September 1942, Eliade admits of "his incessant engrossment with [André] Gide and Kierkegaard."[74] Three months later he goes as far as confessing that he never ever had enough of Kierkegaard.[75] At the summit of his inward turmoil, "aside from the Bible, [he] can read only authors like Kierkegaard and Shestov."[76] The captivation becomes so consuming that he ploughs through Kierkegaard's books "every night in bed."[77] This unfeigned interest can also be deduced from the quotations Eliade transcribes in the diary using the French translations. There is a total of eleven such instances, two from *Repetition*,[78] one from *Practice in*

---

[68]   Relevant in this sense is Eliade, *Jurnalul Portughez*, pp. 270–1; p. 304; p. 313; Alexandrescu, *Mircea Eliade*, p. 215.

[69]   See Eliade, *Jurnalul Portughez*, pp. 270–1; Eliade, *Memorii*, p. 391 (*Autobiography*, vol. 2, pp. 106–7).

[70]   See also Alexandrescu, *Mircea Eliade*, p. 217.

[71]   Eliade, *Memorii*, p. 390. (*Autobiography*, vol. 2, p. 106.)

[72]   Here Eliade exhibits essential affinities with Martin Buber's indictment that Kierkegaard defends a purportedly acosmic religiousness. See Martin Buber, *Between Man and Man*, trans. by Ronald Gregor Smith, London: Routledge and Kegan Paul 1947, pp. 40–82.

[73]   In *Jurnalul Portughez*, pp. 289–90, Eliade acknowledges that he came across Kierkegaard for the first time in 1925, when he read the Italian translation of *The Diary of the Seducer*. See Søren Kierkegaard, *Il diario del seduttore*, trans. by Luigi Redaelli, Turin: Fratelli Bocca 1910 (2nd ed., 1921). Soon afterwards Eliade acquired two other Italian translations, namely, *In vino veritas*, trans. by Knud Ferlov, Lanciano: R. Carabba 1910 (2nd ed., 1919, 3rd ed., 1922); and *L'erotico nella musica*, trans. by Gualtiero Petrucci, Genoa: A.F. Formiggini 1913.

[74]   Eliade, *Jurnalul Portughez*, p. 135. See also ibid., p. 297.

[75]   Ibid., p. 163; p. 301.

[76]   Ibid., p. 306.

[77]   Ibid., p. 328. The entry is dated February 13, 1945. See also Alexandrescu, *Mircea Eliade*, p. 218.

[78]   Eliade, *Jurnalul Portughez*, p. 281.

Christianity,[79] four from the journals,[80] and one from *The Point of View*.[81] The remaining three are not explicitly referenced by Eliade, but are probably taken from the journals.[82] From what these quotations put forward, we can guess that Eliade appreciated Kierkegaard's link between God and the infinite possibility, the qualitative discrepancy between cowardice and madness, the definition of faith as "an absurd struggle for the possible,"[83] the incommensurability between erudition in Christian matters and following Christ, the equation of Christianity with a "radical cure"[84] from which everyone flees, the fact that Kierkegaard is "condemned"[85] to be himself (which is God's will), the communicative virtues of friendship, the existential tasks and gratuitous generosity of every genuine writer, and finally, the nonconformist nature of an authentic genius. *Nota bene*, no quotation is reproduced with a critical aim in mind. Instead, each reflects Eliade's state of mind or is used as a prop for his intuitions, whether intellectual or sapient.

In a different perspective, Eliade values Kierkegaard's stress on subjectivity, which arguably "goes hand in hand with a tendency in Indian philosophy to find the absolute within the subjective."[86] Somewhat related is Eliade's realization, vis-à-vis "the singularity of the God- or fate-chosen person, of the genius, of the saint, of 'the individual' (in Kierkegaard's sense), his absolute incorruptible solitude, his cursed incapacity to communicate with his fellows etc."[87] Kierkegaard is also eulogized by Eliade for having "offered the most insightful analyses of religious pathos (*sentimentului*), and contributing like nobody else in the nineteenth century…to the substantiation of the autonomy of religious experience, to its definitive dissociation from ethics and metaphysics."[88] Eliade's encomium includes the intimate connection between religiosity and danger, realized by Kierkegaard in his heroic pursuit of the "idea for which to live and die."[89] According to Eliade, it is this connection that probably fuelled Kierkegaard's "resistance against the daily press and [social] environment."[90]

---

[79]   Ibid., p. 305.
[80]   Ibid., p. 297; p. 307; p. 309; p. 310. The edition Eliade most probably refers to is Søren Kierkegaard, *Journal. Extraits 1. 1834–1846*, trans. by Jean Jacques Gateau and Knud Ferlov, Paris: Gallimard 1941.
[81]   Eliade, *Jurnalul Portughez*, pp. 315–16.
[82]   Ibid., p. 280; p. 289; p. 291. I am grateful to Jon Stewart for the bibliographical information regarding the available French, Italian, and German translations of Kierkegaard's works during the period covered by this article.
[83]   Ibid., p. 289.
[84]   Ibid., p. 307. See *Pap.* I A 89 / *JP* 1, 415.
[85]   Eliade, *Jurnalul Portughez*, p. 309.
[86]   Ibid., p. 138.
[87]   Ibid., p. 302.
[88]   Ibid., p. 291.
[89]   Ibid., p. 306. In December 1944, Eliade wonders why he did not have Kierkegaard's (and Nietzsche's) audacity "to philosophize starting from personal experiences, and to adopt an aphoristic, fragmentary style." Eliade, *Jurnalul Portughez*, p. 272.
[90]   Eliade, *Jurnalul Portughez*, p. 316. This is an obvious allusion to the *Corsair* affair and probably to *The Moment* period. In this regard, Eliade reminds us that Kierkegaard was

In the midst of the crisis briefly outlined above, Eliade finds the energy to sketch a study, wherein Kierkegaard's three-leveled stages should be compared with "the four necessary steps of self-fulfillment in the Judaic tradition."[91] These steps are: discipleship, marriage (including parenthood), the retreat from civic life, and the ascetic period that follows the death of one's spouse. Interesting as this parallel may seem, Eliade conjectures that the Mosaic tradition, although it lacks the aesthetic stage in Kierkegaard's sense, "brings to perfection the religious modality insofar as one dies alone, in reclusion, face to face with God."[92] As such, the Hebrew believer "is not asocial, since he fulfilled all of his civil duties."[93] The immediate implication is that next to Judaism, Kierkegaard's Christianity *is* asocial and disregards civic obligations.[94] Eliade thus coheres with the massive cohort of commentators who chastise Kierkegaard for his extremist individualism.

It is now time to address the tremendous relevance Kierkegaard acquired in Eliade's personal life. An important parallelism in this regard envisions the erotic-marital domain. Eliade feels that his loss of Nina is not far from Kierkegaard's loss of Regine:

> I will always be grateful to Kierkegaard for having the courage to confess in 1848 that he knows of no greater danger than that of religiousness, and for having said that his break with Regine Olsen is a world event infinitely more important than the birth of Alexander the Great. Following Kierkegaard's example, I could confess that the loss of Nina surpasses [in significance] even my country's catastrophes which occurred one after the other ever since 1940.[95]

A few days afterwards, Eliade adds the following lines:

> Kierkegaard's tragedy is not that he lost Regine Olsen by giving her up, but rather that he met her, that he loved her and was loved back. His ensuing sufferings and drama derive from the irrevocable fact that, upon being introduced, he fell in love with her. This aspect could never be eradicated. [Therefore,] my tragedy did not come to fruition on 20 November 1944[96] but rather on 25 December 1932 when my friendship with

---

the first to make explicit the rift between modernity and true Christianity. Eliade, *Jurnalul Portughez*, p. 234.

[91]   Ibid., p. 296.

[92]   Ibid.

[93]   Ibid.

[94]   However, Eliade's opposition to Kierkegaard's Christianity is not absolute. A proof in this regard is Eliade's unequivocal appreciation for Peter's denial of Christ as depicted in *Practice in Christianity* (*SKS* 12, 112 / *PC*, 103–4). The edition Eliade most probably used is Søren Kierkegaard, *L'Ecole du christianisme, par Anti-Climacus*, trans. by Paul-Henri Tisseau, Bazoges-en-Pareds: privately published 1936. What Eliade finds particularly "interesting" is "Kierkegaard's observation…that Peter would not have doubted Christ, had he considered him a mere human being, regardless of how perfect." Kierkegaard's Peter, Eliade correctly points out, "is troubled exclusively by the Son of God." Eliade, *Jurnalul Portughez*, p. 303.

[95]   Eliade, *Jurnalul Portughez*, p. 306.

[96]   The date of Nina's death.

Nina became love, and that was conducive both to our marriage with its joys, and to my [present] melancholy.[97]

Like Kierkegaard more than a century before, Eliade considers the secret of his life—most probably tied, I believe, to the horrific possibility of having "killed" Nina by forcing her to go through with an abortion[98]—atrocious and inadmissible.[99] The difference, however, is quite important here. Eliade equates the "thorn in the flesh" with an "actual," though indirect and unpremeditated, murder of the beloved. Kierkegaard, however, rationalizes his life-long ordeal as the divine punishment that has befallen his family due to a supposedly unforgivable sin perpetrated by his father.[100] Further, by breaking the engagement (indeed, a symbolic crime), Kierkegaard wished to awaken his fiancée to the possibility of religion. Still, if Kierkegaard the writer was expected to arise from the ashes of Kierkegaard the fiancé, as Joakim Garff astutely observed,[101] not very different were Eliade's own hopes immediately after his wife's death.

The personal comparisons go beyond this topic. For example, in January 1945, after realizing that the substance of Kierkegaard's and of his own authorship is emphatically biographical,[102] Eliade asks himself: "Why aren't I able to use my despair, melancholy, and even my breakdowns (*căderi*) to create and write as Kierkegaard did?"[103] Yet, soon afterwards, he comes to think the opposite, namely, that his "duty is to work,"[104] because melancholy and every other suffering are "given to me so that I bring a true *oeuvre* to fulfillment."[105] Simultaneously, Eliade wishes, and quite adamantly so, "not to be confounded with Kierkegaard."[106] Irrespective of "a shared passion and even obsession for…the real around us, for the concreteness and evanescence of the fragmentary and the finite,"[107] Eliade openly assumes "the possibility that the fragment coincide with the Whole,"[108] while Kierkegaard rejects

---

[97]   Eliade, *Jurnalul Portughez*, p. 319.

[98]   Sorin Alexandrescu observes that Eliade's subsequent sense of guilt is generalized to every single love relationship he was involved in. Soon enough, this generalization turns into an obsession that he is cursed "to kill everything he lays his hands on." Alexandrescu, *Mircea Eliade*, p. 217.

[99]   Eliade, *Jurnalul Portughez*, p. 288.

[100]   I hereby leave aside, though without contesting, the possibility that Kierkegaard could have also referred to an alleged adventure in a brothel. The same holds for the "syphilis hypothesis." See in this respect, Joakim Garff, *Søren Kierkegaard: A Biography*, trans. by Bruce H. Kirmmse, Princeton and Oxford: Princeton University Press 2005, pp. 102–11 and pp. 340–53; and Henning Fenger, *Kierkegaard, the Myths and Their Origins: Studies in the Kierkegaardian Papers and Letters*, trans. by George C. Schoolfield, New Haven and London: Yale University Press 1980, see especially chapter 3.

[101]   Garff, *Søren Kierkegaard: A Biography*, p. 240; p. 347; pp. 432–3.

[102]   Eliade, *Jurnalul Portughez*, p. 297.

[103]   Ibid., pp. 288–9.

[104]   Ibid., p. 317.

[105]   Ibid.

[106]   Ibid., p. 284.

[107]   Ibid.

[108]   Ibid.

it. Moreover, Eliade, this time as a historian of religion, feels compelled to observe that Kierkegaard

> comments on Abraham's and Job's example to the point of exasperation while delving (but only reflectively) into an Absurdity which ostensibly allows him to regain Regina [*sic*] Olsen. However, my observation would be that Abraham and Job have both a vast prehistory behind them; the fact that humans fulfilled "repetition"[109] through a series of rites…, and consequently, that this "repetition," together with its annihilation of "history," with its suspension and regeneration of time, has been available not solely to a handful of divinely chosen people, but also to the entire archaic humankind.[110]

On the other side, Eliade is envious not only of Kierkegaard's prolificacy but also of his work discipline. On January 10, 1945 (at the peak of his purgatorial experience), he reminds himself that "Kierkegaard has written *Enten-Eller* in approximately eleven months."[111] Eliade does not hesitate to go into the mathematical details of this performance, calculating how many pages a day the Danish author must have written in order to achieve his goal. As a result, Eliade bemoans that he could never equal this record as he is deprived of "what Kierkegaard had to a prodigious degree: the continuity of work."[112] In this sense, Eliade remarks that beginning with *Either/Or* and until the completion of the *Postscript*, Kierkegaard wrote incessantly and rigorously for four and a half years.[113] Even so, Eliade's rather candid discontent comes to a halt on February 4, 1945, when he enters the following remark in his diary:

> From Kierkegaard's confessions, I understand that for almost five years he wrote a number of hours every single day, that he set himself this goal in order to withstand his inner prodigality; as a matter of fact, had he surrendered to his inspiration, he would have written night and day, to the point of complete exhaustion and madness. This writing schedule explains much of Kierkegaard's prolixity. Perhaps, if he fully surrendered [to his inspiration], he would have written more concisely, more abruptly.[114] But as it was, his long daily hours allowed him every digression, every fantasy and marginal detour. There are in *Enten-Eller* unreadable pages, and even in books which are very dense, such as *Practice in Christianity*, the inspiration is sometimes wilting, the style is gloomy, while repetitions abound.[115]

---

[109]   In April 1947 Eliade discovers the notion of "repetition" in Heidegger's *Sein und Zeit* but makes no mention of Kierkegaard's homonymous book or category. Mircea Eliade, *Jurnal 1941–1969*, Bucharest: Humanitas 2004, p. 111. (English translation: *Journal I. 1945–1955*, trans. by Mac L. Ricketts, Chicago and London: University of Chicago Press 1990, pp. 52–3.) See also Mircea Eliade, *Cosmos and History: The Myth of the Eternal Return*, 2nd ed., trans. by Willard R. Trask, New York: Harper & Row 1959, pp. 1–48.)

[110]   Eliade, *Jurnalul Portughez*, p. 284.

[111]   Ibid., p. 294.

[112]   Ibid.

[113]   Ibid., pp. 294–5.

[114]   Obviously, Eliade contradicts himself here. What he must have meant is: "Perhaps, if he did not surrender to his inspiration."

[115]   Eliade, *Jurnalul Portughez*, p. 316. This entry is prefigured by a cursory remark on January 25 (p. 307), according to which reading Kierkegaard's diary is highly burdensome.

The worst experience in this respect occurs when Eliade peruses the chapter, "Guilty?/Not Guilty?" from the *Stages*, which makes a terrible impression on him. After admitting that this text "is simply unbearable,"[116] Eliade confesses:

> I can barely read a few pages [from "Guilty?/Not Guilty?"]. Afterwards I happily get back to the Bible. Sometimes, Kierkegaard's prolixity exceeds even the extreme limit of decency. I wish a "complete edition" were put together comprising all of his readable writings. It would be a wonderful two-volume piece.[117]

Verbosity and an impenetrable eloquence constitute a mere prelude to Eliade's even deeper revisionist evaluation. What seems to bother him as well, are Kierkegaard's egocentrism[118] and distaste for Goethe,[119] who was a true icon for Eliade. A comparable point of contention is Kierkegaard's imperviousness to anything related to rites and foundational myths,[120] an issue to which we will come back. Furthermore, in *The Portuguese Diary* Eliade reiterates (twice) his early tenet on Kierkegaard's loss of faith;[121] this entitles us to assume that even when his familiarity with Kierkegaard's *oeuvre* acquired a greater depth, Eliade never questioned the views he expressed in 1928.

A series of questions should be raised at this point. First, do not these dissatisfactions throw an ambiguous light on the fact that Eliade claimed to have found Kierkegaard's works *meaningful* precisely when his search for God and for religious assuagement held sway? Second, how are we to judge Eliade's reception of the *Postscript*,[122] where Kierkegaard (indeed, pseudonymously) develops the inaccessibility of the other's inwardness? Did not Eliade learn from this book that no one can ever state something irrefutable about the subjective actuality of others and therefore, of their faith? Thirdly, why is Eliade unreceptive to the Kierkegaardian paradigm of a *struggling faith*, of a relation to God, which is, to be sure, undermined by anxiety, despair, and doubt, but is also full of joy, hope, and salvific expectations by virtue of the divine infinite agape?[123] On this model, is not Kierkegaard's faith

---

[116]   Eliade, *Jurnalul Portughez*, p. 328.

[117]   Ibid. See also ibid., pp. 289–90: "Kierkegaard elates me but he also exasperates me. He is laconic and prolix, full of pathos, ironic, and dull. Sometimes, he is absolutely unreadable. The commentaries he makes about some books published in his own time are of no interest to me….My relation to Kierkegaard lasted for twenty years now, but to this very day I have not read him exhaustively. There is something that escapes me, that prevents me from devouring his books; it may be his irony…or perhaps his prolixity, stagnation, or artificial euphoria."

[118]   Ibid., p. 140.

[119]   Eliade reminds himself that "to exist à la Goethe" was the worst qualification Kierkegaard could use about someone; it so appears that none other than bishop Mynster was knighted with that title. Eliade, *Jurnalul Portughez*, p. 301.

[120]   Ibid., p. 284.

[121]   Ibid., p. 285; p. 291.

[122]   The *Postscript* had been available in French since 1941 and is explicitly quoted in *Jurnalul Portughez*. See note 143 below.

[123]   This is rather confusing since Eliade is as aware of the agapeic gist of the Christian religion. See Mircea Eliade, *Oceanografie*, Bucharest: Humanitas 2003 [Bucharest: Cultura Poporului 1934], p. 77.

rather exemplary, given its impetus to permanent critical introspection, its acute awareness of sin, but also its obdurate certainty that to a God who is love everything remains possible, including our (unmerited) redemption?

The plausible answer to these queries must take into account Eliade's suspicions of Kierkegaard's purported acosmism. Generally speaking, one of Eliade's most enduring beliefs and theoretical positions is that the mysteries put forward by various religious traditions are necessarily and inextricably tied to "the cosmos."[124] In a journal entry, the principal theme of which is Kierkegaard's resistance to ritual acts and mythological narratives, Eliade reaffirms his "unwillingness to abandon the finite, [its] splendid thrilling fragmentariness."[125] For Eliade, worldliness is imbued with a religious significance that awaits its skillful decipherer. Perhaps, owing to his perennial preoccupation with the Renaissance ideal, which treats artworks, literary creations, scientific inquiries, religious life, and philosophical ratiocination as organically interconnected and as different ways of actualizing the spiritual potential of humankind, Eliade tends to advocate a crypto-pantheistic phenomenology. There is a sense in which his monumental analysis of religion—in tandem with his tentative theories on human creativity—hinges on the underlying creed that this world counts at least as much, if not more, than the ones beyond. Most interesting, however, is that, although he acknowledges that "his main concern is salvation from history,"[126] the soteriology Eliade envisages does not orbit around the Christological postulates, with which Kierkegaard struggled throughout his whole life, but rather around "the [religious] symbol, the myth, the ritual—the archetypes."[127]

That said, on January 9, 1945, after a lengthy *lamentatio* about his melancholy, carnal temptations, and dread of dilettantism, Eliade suddenly asks himself: "Why does Christianity—and particularly, *true* Christianity—connect *suffering* with God's *love*?"[128] Then, he wonders whether "the Judaic perspective, in which the human love for God becomes manifest through alleviation, happiness, and prosperity, was not, religiously speaking, closer to the truth."[129] In this way, Eliade surmises that "the religious experience that salvages the concrete and material goods"[130] is much more relevant and true to the spirit of religion than the total renunciation of worldliness for the sake of redemption. Consequently, if asked to choose between Christianity and

---

[124] Eliade, *Jurnalul Portughez*, p. 312. See also ibid., p. 232. A major reason for advocating this view must have been the particular Christianity Eliade ascertained in the religious identity of Romanians. He speaks of the latter's immemorial chthonic ties and especially of the "naturalness" of their Christian faith which "transfigures the Cosmos without, however, destroying or repudiating it." Alexandrescu, *Mircea Eliade*, p. 38. Thus, Romanians venerated a perfectly harmonious universe, while resistant against any interference of existential despair in religious matters.

[125] Eliade, *Jurnalul Portughez*, p. 283. Hence Eliade's intention to expand upon "the religious and metaphysical nature of our most obscure experiences (*trăiri*), that is, of eating, sex, and anger." Ibid., p. 234.

[126] Ibid., p. 232.

[127] Ibid.

[128] Ibid., p. 293; first emphasis added.

[129] Ibid.

[130] Ibid.

Judaism, Eliade confesses he would definitely opt for the latter, without realizing that he hereby throws a dubious light on the *Christian* consolations he searched for when witnessing Nina's agony.[131]

This is the context in which Eliade rebuts Kierkegaard for completely blinding himself to the mundane implications of religious existence, and for manically stressing the crucifying martyrdom of faith. On January 4, 1945, after quoting Kierkegaard's statement that "to believe in spite of reason is martyrdom,"[132] Eliade initiates an imaginary dialogue with his Danish interlocutor. The exchange consists of a succession of questions, while its tone is equally passionate and recriminatory:

> Don't you [Kierkegaard] feel sometimes the irresistible attraction of the irrational, which invites one to omit reason, to contradict it or to ignore it completely?[133] Doesn't this attraction give you any joy, any emotion? Moreover, doesn't faith—which is a creative act because through it you assert your freedom, you acquire a new mode of living—let you experience any beatitude? Just because reason is always on your side will every act of faith always be mortifying? What about the liberation through the paradoxicality of faith, the enthusiasm with which every believer affirms the absurd…, the plenary, almost orgiastic, feeling of creatureliness, the feeling that your faith is creative at its core, that the world *is made in accord with* your belief, that your free act of faith is not only soteriological, but also cosmological—do not all of these cause you any joy? You believe and confess your faith, but these bring you no alleviation; rather, they make you feel a genuine martyrdom because you simply have faith "in spite of reason."[134]

---

[131]   Eliade, in fact, acknowledges that religious faith is incomparably better than any other means to cope with suffering. *Jurnalul Portughez*, p 289; p. 292; p. 304; p. 308. In *Itinerariu spiritual*, p. 409, Eliade also admits that Christianity has a distinct and salutary capacity to assume the burden of mortality.

[132]   Eliade, *Jurnalul Portughez*, p. 284.

[133]   Here we should not forget that Eliade has been significantly influenced by Miguel de Unamuno's and Lev Shestov's reception of Kierkegaard. See in this sense, Ricketts, *Mircea Eliade*, p. 1106. See also Mircea Eliade, *Jurnal 1970–1985*, Bucharest: Humanitas 1993, pp. 33–4 (English translation: *Journal III. 1970–1978*, trans. by Teresa Lavender Fagan, Chicago and London: University of Chicago Press 1989, pp. 28–9); and Eliade, *Jurnalul Portughez*, p. 286; p. 298.

[134]   Eliade, *Jurnalul Portughez*, p. 284–5. A similar dissatisfaction is expressed ten days later, when Eliade chides Kierkegaard for his "sickly dread of any concrete joy" and for "the complete withdrawal from [this] life." Ibid, p. 301. In February 1945, Eliade contests with the same vehemence Kierkegaard's view that the imitation of Christ necessitates suffering and martyrdom. (This critique is all the more surprising given that *Practice in Christianity* is deemed by Eliade "an excellent book from all points of view." Eliade, *Jurnalul Portughez*, p. 303.) Instead, Eliade holds that "regardless of the sufferings one is to endure, the heart of the militant Christian *must* be continually joyful before God." Eliade, *Jurnalul Portughez*, p. 311. Ironically, this is exactly what Kierkegaard affirms in *Christian Discourses*. *SKS* 10, 107–66 / *CD*, 95–159. Another irony is that, while a student in Bucharest, Eliade considered suffering and anxiety indispensible to the spiritualization of personhood. Ricketts, *Mircea Eliade*, pp. 249–50; p. 261; Eliade, *Oceanografie*, pp. 53–6; pp. 194–6. Moreover, as late as January 1946 Eliade compares Kierkegaard's category of despair with "the despair of the African who, after having knocked on all the doors of the sacred, turns to the Supreme Being…as a last resort." Eliade, *Jurnal 1941–1969*, p. 69. (*Journal I*, p. 13.)

Historically speaking, critiques of this nature came from two contemporaries of Eliade. The first is Martin Buber, who accused Kierkegaard of embracing a quietist outlook on religiosity, and of estranging the Christian religion from its creationistic roots.[135] Eliade might have been familiar with these indictments, though Buber's name never surfaces in *The Portuguese Diary*. Secondly, by pure coincidence, in 1940 Theodor Adorno attacked Kierkegaard on comparable grounds, although his criticisms were formulated from the vantage of social justice and economical inequality.[136] As I have addressed Buber's and Adorno's dissatisfaction with Kierkegaard elsewhere,[137] I shall concentrate solely on Eliade's suspicions.

Basically, what Eliade reacts against is Kierkegaard's unworldly metaphysics and morbid representation of Christianity. In so doing, he invokes the religious paradigm embodied by Abraham and Job. Additionally, he reads the teaching of Christ exclusively within a Hebraic perspective which, we said, revolves around worldly bliss.[138]

If we take into consideration the troubled psychological state in which Eliade makes these statements, then his omissions, misunderstandings, and even distortions of Kierkegaard may seem natural. Nonetheless, it remains important to see what Eliade leaves aside in his pantheistic offensive. First, he completely bypasses the centrality of worldliness in Kierkegaard's *Fear and Trembling*. A thoughtful reading of this book—to which he had access at the time—should have made him realize that Kierkegaard actually cherishes his intuitions. Specifically, Kierkegaard is fully aware that within the limits of the Abrahamic faith: "[temporality], finitude—that is what it is all about."[139] Kierkegaard also knows that a full-fledged renunciation does not always elicit a morose interaction with the world. The most pertinent example here is the Kierkegaardian knight of faith, whose familiarity with and reveling in, the mundane surpass in depth and joy those of anyone else precisely because he appropriates the finite as *divine gift*. Secondly, Eliade does not clarify how it is possible to deem a religious experience paradoxical if one is to completely dismiss reason and abandon oneself to a beatific enjoyment of finitude. Thirdly, Eliade turns a blind eye to Kierkegaard's theory, put forth in *Philosophical Fragments*, that reason is by its very nature self-sacrificial. Through the *Fragments* Eliade could have discovered that by letting the paradox present itself to consciousness, reason opens the self to the utter otherness of the divine.[140] The same book may have also

---

[135]   Buber, *Between Man and Man*, pp. 40–82.

[136]   Theodor W. Adorno, "On Kierkegaard's Doctrine of Love," *Studies in Philosophy and Social Science*, vol. 8, 1940, pp. 413–29. My assumption is that Eliade did not know Adorno's text since it is hard to believe that he had access to German academic journals while in Lisbon during a global war. An even more convincing proof is that Kierkegaard's *Works of Love*, the sole focus of Adorno's criticisms, never surfaces in Eliade's comments.

[137]   Leo Stan, *Either Nothingness or Love: On Alterity in Søren Kierkegaard's Writings*, Saarbrücken: VDM Verlag Dr. Müller 2009, chapter 7.

[138]   See Eliade, *Jurnalul Portughez*, p. 294; p. 296.

[139]   *SKS* 4, 143 / *FT*, 49.

[140]   *SKS* 4, 242–3 / *PF*, 37. *SKS* 4, 249 / *PF*, 44. *SKS* 7, 320–1 / *CUP1*, 349–51.

substantiated Eliade's supposition that religious faith is fundamentally regenerative, bringing forth an authentic rebirth of one's whole being.[141]

Now, it is easier to understand why Eliade is rather reluctant about conceiving human ordeals within a Christian horizon. Even though he links Christianity with "the paradox of being human,"[142] he does not suspect, especially after having read the Kierkegaardian works cited throughout *The Portuguese Diary*,[143] that the paradoxical nature of humankind may owe as much, if not more, to Christian soteriology than to Hebraic creationism. Another oversight concerns the Christian category of *skandalon*, whose mistranslation into Romanian Eliade explicitly deplores. Symptomatic here is that he pays absolutely no attention to the cardinal importance of the scandal or offense of Christianity in Kierkegaard's *corpus*, although *Practice in Christianity* crosses his gaze just a few days later.[144] Equally noticeable, albeit much less imputable, is the absence from *The Portuguese Diary* of any reference to Kierkegaard's *Works of Love*. Though the first French translation of this book came out in 1945, Eliade could have familiarized himself with its main problematic, if not through the German translation, which had been available since 1890 and was republished in 1924, then via Jean Wahl's exegesis, of which he sounds very enthused.[145] A deeper knowledge of *Works of Love* would have made Eliade reconsider some of his judgments regarding the implicit absence of sociality from Kierkegaard's religious thought.[146] Another telling omission concerns Kierkegaard's use of pseudonymity, of which Eliade does not utter a word. Moreover, *The Point of View of My Work as an Author*, which mainly deals with the problem of existential (or indirect) communication should have been of tremendous interest to Eliade, granted his intense preoccupation with the philosophical challenges of existentiality.[147]

Finally, it defies the understanding why Eliade was completely impervious to the ironic subtleties and, especially, to the comical overtones of Kierkegaard's rhetoric.[148] After all, he admits of having purchased *Prefaces* and the *Postscript*,

---

[141]   Eliade, *Jurnalul Portughez*, p. 313. *SKS* 4, 227–30 / *PF*, 19–22.

[142]   Eliade, *Jurnalul Portughez*, p. 299. Kierkegaard would have fully agreed with Eliade on this point.

[143]   In January 1945 Eliade admits that in the previous year he purchased "approximately twelve volumes" by Kierkegaard in the French translation. Of these he mentions the *Postscript*, *Either/Or*, *Practice in Christianity*, and the *Journals*. Eliade, *Jurnalul Portughez*, p. 289. For the specific titles and editions Eliade refers to, see the bibliography of Jon Stewart's "France: Kierkegaard as a Forerunner of Existentialism to Poststructuralism," in *Kierkegaard's International Reception*, Tome I, *Northern and Western Europe*, ed. by Jon Stewart, Aldershot: Ashgate 2009 (*Kierkegaard Research: Sources, Reception and Resources*, vol. 8), pp. 460–5. See also note 73 above for other books Eliade read during his student years.

[144]   Eliade, *Jurnalul Portughez*, p. 304; p. 305. Notably enough, Eliade seems unaware of the intimate connection between the Christian *skandalon* and paradoxicalness.

[145]   Eliade, *Jurnalul Portughez*, p. 289. Jean Wahl, *Études kierkegaardiennes*, Paris: Aubier 1938, pp. 711–14.

[146]   See Eliade, *Jurnalul Portughez*, p. 296.

[147]   Ibid., p. 135; p. 282.

[148]   That is all the more surprising since Eliade does mention Kierkegaard's "biting, quasi-paradoxical" aphorisms and irony, both traced back to the "caustic spirit of romantics."

where he could have found a side of Kierkegaard's authorship that is infinitely incongruent with his tenebrous picture of the Dane's world.[149] At this point, one might suspect that Eliade has not read all the books he mentions in the journal. However, one would thus forget that the erudite historian of religions was an avid reader (a quality he admires in Kierkegaard, as well).[150] Besides, if we embrace this objection, then Eliade's praise of Jean Wahl's *Études Kierkegaardiennes*,[151]—a book which offers a panoramic glace at Kierkegaard's *corpus* and engages with its main themes, categories, and problems—becomes somewhat untrustworthy.

III. Conclusions

To be sure, Eliade had every right to take pride in having introduced Kierkegaard's biography and authorship to the Romanian interwar audience, not to mention the personal benefits he drew from this timely encounter. Above I addressed the way in which Eliade's appropriation of Kierkegaard developed along two main lines. We encountered first, Eliade's use of Kierkegaard as a potential subversion of the French monopoly within Romanian culture, but also as a necessary step in one's intellectual formation. Second, the Kierkegaardian *corpus* exhibited its balsamic virtues when the inevitability and grotesqueness of death rendered Eliade's life simply hellish. It is important to know that the biographical relevance disappears when Eliade leaves Lisbon for Paris, where he would launch his imposing scholarly career.

It is now time to risk a few hypotheses on the reasons for Eliade's misreadings, an issue which deserves a separate and comprehensive treatment. First, we should never lose sight of the fact that throughout his entire activity Eliade pursued a comparative approach to religious phenomena. His ultimate end was thus to develop a unitary and universalist theory of the sacred. When he returned from India, Eliade's comprehension of religion became more ecumenical.[152] The realization that

---

Eliade, *Virilitate și asceză*, p. 69. The reason for this opacity might be rather personal. "I feel no attraction to irony," Eliade openly confesses. Eliade, *Jurnalul Portughez*, p. 290.

[149]   In a 1927 article ("Amiel. Note II") Eliade alleges that Kierkegaard's authorship is traversed by a tragic crimson thread, giving the *Postscript* as an example. Eliade, *Itinerar spiritual*, p. 296. This reference can certainly bewilder us since Johannes Climacus has made a longstanding career as a humorist who knows everything about his profession, including its ties to the religious. See for instance, *SKS* 7, 457–61 / *CUP1*, 504–8. See also Hugh Pyper, "Beyond a Joke: Kierkegaard's *Concluding Unscientific Postscript* as a Comic Book," in *Concluding Unscientific Postscript*, ed. by Robert L. Perkins, Macon, Georgia: Mercer University Press 1997 (*International Kierkegaard Commentary*, vol. 12), pp. 149–68.

[150]   Eliade, *Jurnalul Portughez*, p. 289: "We should not forget that Søren Kierkegaard was stimulated not only by coffee, but also by extensive readings. This existentialist had a library of over 20,000 volumes. He was ceaselessly reading or skimming through in order to stimulate himself, to [be able to] offer a rejoinder, to spice up the conversation." The reader should also be aware that Eliade's estimation of the enormous size of Kierkegaard's personal library is a vast exaggeration.

[151]   In a diary entry dated January 8, 1945, Eliade reverently admits that he had owned Wahl's book "for a long time." Eliade, *Jurnalul Portughez*, p. 289.

[152]   Ricketts, *Mircea Eliade*, pp. 71–2.

sacredness has a myriad of manifestations and historical forms acquired indelible contours in his mind.[153] After the war, when Kierkegaard starts to vanish from Eliade's attention, phenomenology and the history of religions appear to him as the most suitable tools in coming to terms with religious phenomena.[154] Besides, Eliade proposes a radical reconsideration of archaic religions. His scrupulous and sympathetic analyses of tribal religiosity side by side with the major Eastern traditions and the three monotheisms alive today, can be regarded as integral to his passionate quest for a new humanism underpinned by shared universal values.[155]

By contrast, Kierkegaard's thought remains exceptionally Christian, despite Climacus' theorizing of religiousness A. Moreover, worthy of note is Eliade's indebtedness to the Eastern Orthodox tradition,[156] on the basis of which he identified Christianity with a Christ-centered mysticism that prioritized the possibility of human deification and one's living relationality to the Cosmos.[157] Eliade's appreciation of the fundamental importance of the Church was not less sincere;[158] hence the frustration with Kierkegaard's anti-ecclesiastical streak.[159] And perhaps, his resistance against Kierkegaard's personalist-militant, pathos-filled, and sacrificial interpretation of *imitatio Christi* at the expense of Christian cosmology should be read against the same background.

However, Eliade's reception of Kierkegaard is complex enough to include momentous affinities. My conjecture is that the latter's recondite ground chiefly issues from the fundamental intuition of *the irreducibility of religion*. Throughout their authorship, both Kierkegaard and Eliade have insisted that the religious experience gestures towards an utterly heterogeneous reality that cannot be understood solely in terms of science, interpersonal or virtue ethics, sociology, and psychology.[160] As Kierkegaard a century before, Eliade was cognizant of Christianity's dualistic understanding of spirit.[161] The salvific meaning of Christ's historicity was not entirely foreign to him either,[162] although he never thought it through to its ultimate consequences. The fact, openly acknowledged by Eliade, that Christianity appears as sheer folly when put into practice, has a Kierkegaardian flavor.[163] That said,

---

[153]   Ibid., p. 255.

[154]   See Eliade, *Memorii*, p. 391. (*Autobiography*, vol. 2, p. 107.)

[155]   Ricketts, *Mircea Eliade*, p. 311; p. 317; p. 1122; Eliade, *Memorii*, p. 392 (*Autobiography*, vol. 2, p. 108); Eliade, *Itinerariu spiritual*, p. 256.

[156]   See, for instance, Mircea Eliade, *Profetism românesc*, vols. 1–2, Bucharest: Roza Vînturilor 1990; vol. 1, p. 58; and Eliade, *Itinerariu spiritual*, p. 328.

[157]   Ricketts, *Mircea Eliade*, pp. 261–2; p. 265; p. 269; p. 275; p. 278.

[158]   Alexandrescu, *Mircea Eliade*, p. 62; p. 66; Ricketts, *Mircea Eliade*, p. 293. "The return to the Church is redemptive and necessary," Eliade stated as early as November 1927. Eliade, *Profetism românesc*, vol. 1, p. 55.

[159]   Mircea Eliade, *Drumul spre centru*, ed. by Gabriel Liiceanu and Andrei Pleșu, Bucharest: Univers 1991, p. 284.

[160]   Ricketts, *Mircea Eliade*, p. 258; p. 267; p. 291.

[161]   Ibid., p. 263. By "dualism" I mean strictly the postlapsarian antagonism between flesh and spirit. See 1 Cor 15:50. Phil 3:3. Heb 2:14.

[162]   Ricketts, *Mircea Eliade*, p. 268.

[163]   Ibid., p. 272.

one can parallel what Eliade called the paradoxical structure of hierophany[164] with Kierkegaard's expatiations on the God-man's offensive paradoxicality. That Eliade disregarded Kierkegaard's edifying meditations on "the lilies in the field and the birds of the air" should not deter us from seeing them as a *confirmation* of Eliade's conjectures regarding the concealment of sacredness within the profane.[165] For us today, all these elements undoubtedly imply that the philosophical dialogue between Kierkegaard and Eliade goes beyond the territory of their captivating biographies.

---

[164]   Ibid., p. 1096.
[165]   Leo Stan, "The Lily in the Field and the Bird of the Air: An Endless Liturgy in Kierkegaard's Authorship," in *Kierkegaard and the Bible*, Tome II, *The New Testament*, ed. by Lee C. Barrett and Jon Stewart, Aldershot: Ashgate 2010 (*Kierkegaard Research: Sources, Reception and Resources*, vol. 1), pp. 55–78.

Bibliography

I. References to or Uses of Kierkegaard in Eliade's Corpus

"Sören Kierkegaard—Logodnic, pamfletar şi eremit," *Cuvântul*, vol. 4, no. 1035, 1928, p. 1. (Reprinted in Mircea Eliade, *Virilitate şi asceză. Scrieri de tinereţe 1928*, Bucharest: Humanitas Publishers 2008, pp. 68–72.)

Oceanografie, Bucharest: Humanitas 2003 [Bucharest: Cultura Poporului 1934], pp. 21–2; pp. 198–9; p. 201.

Drumul spre centru, ed. by Gabriel Liiceanu and Andrei Pleşu, Bucharest: Univers 1991, p. 145. (Originally published as *Fragmentarium*, Bucharest: Vremea 1939.)

Drumul spre centru, ed. by Gabriel Liiceanu and Andrei Pleşu, Bucharest: Univers 1991, p. 480. (Originally published as *Comentarii la legenda Meşterului Manole*, Bucharest: Publicom 1943.)

Drumul spre centru, ed. by Gabriel Liiceanu and Andrei Pleşu, Bucharest: Univers 1991, p. 284; p. 308. (Originally published as *Insula lui Euthanasius*, Bucharest: Fundaţia Regală pentru Literatură şi Artă 1943.)

Le Mythe de l'éternel retour, Paris: Gallimard 1949, pp. 162–4. (English translation: *Cosmos and History: The Myth of the Eternal Return*, 2nd ed., trans. by W.R. Trask, New York: Harper & Row 1959, pp. 109–10.)

Mythes, rêves et mystères, Paris: Gallimard 1957, pp. 26–7. (English translation: *Myths, Dreams and Mysteries*, trans. by Philip Mairet, New York and Evanston, Illinois: Harper & Row 1960, pp. 30–1.)

Traité d'histoire des religions, Paris: Payot 1964, p. 330. (English translation: *Patterns in Comparative Religion*, trans. by Rosemary Sheed, Cleveland: World Publishing Co. 1958, pp. 393–4.)

Jurnal 1970–1985, ed. by Mircea Handoca, Bucharest: Humanitas 1993, pp. 33–4; p. 481. (English translation: *Journal III. 1970–1978*, trans. by Teresa Lavender Fagan, Chicago and London: University of Chicago Press 1989, pp. 28–9; and *Journal IV. 1979–1985*, trans. by Mac L. Ricketts, Chicago and London: University of Chicago Press 1990, p. 108.)

Europa, Asia, America...Corespondenţă, vols. 1–3, Bucharest: Humanitas 1999–2004, vol. 3, p. 396.

Jurnal 1941–1969, ed. by Mircea Handoca, Bucharest: Humanitas 2004, pp. 111–12; p. 441; p. 468. (English translation: *Journal I. 1945–1955*, trans. by Mac L. Ricketts, Chicago and London: University of Chicago Press 1990, p. 53; and *Journal II. 1957–1969*, trans. by Fred H. Johnson Jr., Chicago and London: University of Chicago Press 1989, pp. 164–5; pp. 191–2.)

Memorii, 3rd ed., Bucharest: Humanitas 2004, pp. 132–4; p. 141; p. 277; p. 390. (English translation: *Autobiography*, vols. 1–2, trans. by Mac L. Ricketts, San

Francisco: Harper & Row 1981, vol. 1, p. 127; p. 129; p. 136; p. 274; vol. 2, p. 106.)

Jurnalul portughez și alte scrieri, ed. by Sorin Alexandrescu, Bucharest: Humanitas 2006, p. 135; p. 138; p. 140; p. 163; p. 234; p. 272; pp. 280–1; pp. 283–6; pp. 288–92; pp. 294–8; pp. 301–3; pp. 305–7; pp. 309–11; p. 316; p. 319; p. 328.

II. Sources of Eliade's Knowledge of Kierkegaard

Kierkegaard, Søren, *Il diario del seduttore*, trans. by Luigi Redaelli, Turin: Fratelli Bocca 1910.

— *In vino veritas*, trans. by Knud Ferlov, Lanciano: R. Carabba 1910.

— *L'erotico nella musica*, trans. by Gualtiero Petrucci, Genoa: Formiggini 1913.

— *La Répétition. Essai d'expérience psychologique par Constantin Constantius*, trans. by Paul-Henri Tisseau, Paris: Alcan 1933.

— *Crainte et Tremblement. Lyrique-dialectique, par Johannes de Silentio*, trans. by Paul-Henri Tisseau, Paris: Fernand Aubier; Éditions Montaigne 1935.

— *L'Ecole du christianisme par Anti-Climacus*, trans. by Paul-Henri Tisseau, Bazoges-en-Pareds: le Traducteur 1936.

— *Point de vue explicatif de mon oeuvre: communication directe, rapport historique*, trans. by Paul-Henri Tisseau, Bazoges-en-Pareds: le Traducteur 1940.

— *Journal. Extraits 1. 1834–1846*, trans. by Jean Jacques Gateau and Knud Ferlov, Paris: Gallimard 1941.

— *Post-scriptum aux Miettes philosophiques*, trans. by Paul Petit, Paris: Mesmil 1941.

— *Coupable? Non coupable? Une histoire de la souffrance: expérience psychologique par Frater Taciturnus*, trans. by Paul-Henri Tisseau, Bazoges-en-Pareds: P.-H. Tisseau 1942.

— *L'alternative. Un fragment de vie. Publié par Victor Eremita. Deuxième partie: Contenant les papiers de B: lettres à A*, trans. by Paul-Henri Tisseau, Bazoges-en-Pareds: le Traducteur 1940.

— *Ou bien...ou bien*, trans. by F. Prior, O. Prior and M.H. Guignot, Paris: Gallimard 1943.

Wahl, Jean, *Études kierkegaardiennes*, Paris: Aubier 1938.

III. Secondary Literature on Eliade's Relation to Kierkegaard

Altizer, Thomas J.J., *Mircea Eliade and the Dialectic of the Sacred*, Westport: Greenwood Press Publishers 1975, pp. 54–6; pp. 60–1; pp. 65–6; pp. 73–80.

Davenport, John J., "The Essence of Eschatology: A Modal Interpretation," *Ultimate Reality and Meaning: Interdisciplinary Studies in the Philosophy of Understanding*, vol. 19, no. 3, 1996, pp. 206–39.

Diaconu, Madalina, "Kierkegaard-Rezeption in Rumänien," *Revue Roumaine de Philosophie*, vol. 45, nos. 1–2, 2001, pp. 149–64.

Dobre, Catalina Elena, "Kierkegaard and the Romanian Culture," *Acta Kierkegaardiana*, vol. 2, 2007, pp. 257–69.

Irina, Nicolae, "Romania: A Survey of Kierkegaard's Reception, Translation and Research," in *Kierkegaard's International Reception*, Tome II, *Southern, Central and Eastern Europe*, ed. by Jon Stewart, Aldershot: Ashgate 2009 (*Kierkegaard Research: Sources, Reception and Resources*, vol. 8) pp. 301–4.

Erik Erikson:

Artist of Moral Development

Edward F. Mooney

I. Introduction

Erik Erikson was born in Germany in 1902. He died in Massachusetts in 1994, having produced a rich body of work that included the widely read *Childhood and Society*, *Young Man Luther*, and *Gandhi's Truth*.[1] He is best known for a theory of identity-formation achieved through stages of development from infancy through old age, and is credited with coining the notion of "identity crisis," and its off-spring, "mid-life crisis." Although the themes of self-knowledge and self-realization are as old as any literature we possess, casting them in terms of a now ubiquitous discourse of "identity," even of "identity politics," owes a great deal to the popular and academic discussions of Erikson's work in the 1950s and 1960s when he achieved something of celebrity status.[2] Erikson conceives of the several stages of development as a tenuous equilibrium between opposed forces that remain in dynamic conflict.

The sketch that Erikson provides of any single stage in development is "dialectical" rather than "essentialist" and static. Likewise, relations *among* unfolding stages are dynamic and dialectical. Later stages take up or subsume earlier ones (and their tensions) rather than supplanting, superseding, or erasing them. An infant's battle between trust and mistrust, for example, continues in various reconfigurations throughout life. Kierkegaard readers might think here of a particular section title in Kierkegaard's *Either/Or*, Part Two, "The Balance between the Esthetic and the Ethical in the Development of the Personality." We can imagine Erikson having a section title introducing "the balance between intimacy and isolation in the development of love as central to personality in early adulthood."

There is a basis in Erikson's experience for rough parallels between his interest in moral-psychological development and Kierkegaard's interests. His mother, a Danish Jew, read Kierkegaard aloud to Erikson in his early years.[3] Late in life,

---

[1]   See Erik Erikson, *Childhood and Society*, New York: Norton 1950; Erik Erikson, *Young Man Luther: A Study in Psychoanalysis and History*, New York: Norton 1958; and Erik Erikson, *Gandhi's Truth: On the Origin of Militant Nonviolence*, New York: Norton 1969.

[2]   The best account of Erikson's life, writing, cultural sources and impact is Lawrence J. Friedman, *Identity's Architect: A Biography of Erik Erikson*, New York: Scribners 1999.

[3]   See Friedman, *Identity's Architect*, pp. 29–31; p. 41. Indicative of the creative literary and moral-religious temperament that rubbed off on her son, she read Brandes and Emerson, as well.

Erikson began taking notes for an extended study of Kierkegaard, but his powers were failing.[4] He published nothing from these notes. In the mid 1970s he was asked by his Episcopalian parish in Tiburon, a small town just north of San Francisco, where he had settled for retirement, to give an informal seminar on Kierkegaard's theology. He asked his neighbor, the Kierkegaard scholar Arnold Come, to join in the effort. He confided to Come that what he most admired in Kierkegaard was his critical acumen and exploratory, open-ended imagination. As a psychoanalyst, Erikson recognized and admired Kierkegaard's great skill in taking up the deepest moral-religious issues while steadfastly avoiding creedal or simplistic conclusions that would shut off dialogue. As Erikson read him, Kierkegaard's "answers" were always tantalizingly incomplete and never one-sided—that is, never undialectical. In Erikson's view, that was a great virtue.[5]

For Erikson, this focus on negotiating tensions in the achievement of identity reflects a Kierkegaardian temperament fostered informally in childhood. More explicitly, it reflects his initiation into Viennese psychoanalysis, a movement dedicated to exploring the self (or soul) especially in its torments or sickness, with an aim toward health and healing. Erikson's sense that achieving personal equilibrium was a life-long task and a passage through stages has roots in his early life, which set for him an unusually dramatic context for working toward identity.

II. Life and Works

For most of his early school years and into young adulthood, Erikson was Erik Homberger. He became "Erikson" only after becoming a United States citizen in 1939 (he emigrated in 1933). He was born out of wedlock to Karla Abrahamsen, daughter of prominent Danish Jewish parents, the family known for philanthropy toward Jewish refugees from Russia. At the time of his birth, she was married to a German-Jewish stockbroker. His biological father was a Dane known mysteriously only as "Erik." For the duration of her long life, and to Erikson's chagrin, his mother adamantly refused to reveal anything about his biological father. Her Danish family remained silent, as well.

At birth, Erikson was officially registered as "Erik Salomonsen," reflecting his mother's married name, and became "Erik Homburger" at the age of seven when his mother remarried, and he was formally adopted by his stepfather. At that point he forfeited any chance to claim Danish citizenship through his mother. Hitler was making Germany and Austria uninhabitable by the 1930s. Denmark provided a few months' haven before his emigration to the United States. Raised an orthodox German Jew, he was teased by Christian classmates for being Jewish, and at temple-school for being tall, blond, and blue-eyed—a "goy." Like William James, another prominent psychologist, early on he pursued a wandering artistic career as

---

4   Ibid., pp. 448–9.

5   See Arnold Come, letter to the editor, *New York Review of Books*, vol. 46, no. 18, 1999. See also the discussion of Kierkegaard's importance to Erikson in Carol Hren Hoare, *Erikson on Development in Adulthood: New Insights from the Unpublished Papers*, Oxford: Oxford University Press 2002, p. 83; pp. 176–9; p. 183; p. 212.

a painter. In his twenties he became attracted to the budding practice and theory of psychoanalysis, a movement that focused, of course, on ameliorating inner conflict; he began the regimen of daily analysis.

His burden, quite clearly, was to sort out the several conflicting strands of his complex inheritance. He had three fathers, we might say, one utterly unknown, one known only in his earliest years, and a step-father who for all his kindness could not fill the gap created by a man who had abandoned him and whose identity had been absolutely erased. He had a Danish mother, now German, twice married, and carrying the blemish of bearing a child out of wedlock. That would color his own sense of legitimacy. He was protected from the facts until he left home, but his blond hair and blue eyes must have raised his suspicions much earlier. He was accepted neither as fully Jewish nor fully German.

In mid-life Erikson converted to Christianity; his wife, Joan Serson, was Episcopalian, daughter of a minister. A Canadian-American, she was studying modern dance in Germany and Austria in pursuit of a Ph.D. from Columbia. Upon discovering that she was pregnant, they were married in 1930 in Germany in civil, Christian and Jewish ceremonies. To compound the question of religious, familial, and national identity, he then faced the question of what it was to become American. He took up the task with characteristic energy and resolve.

It was a formidable, and as he would come to see it, a creative task to sort through these inherited and adopted social and cultural traditions, and to mull over the imprints, longings, and aspirations related to them. The job was ongoing—to weave a viable sense of self. He would see his never-finishable project not in terms of overcoming sickness, neurosis, or pathology, but as an artistic endeavor. We might think that he was saddled with an unusually complicated inheritance at an unusually tumultuous time in history—a kind of chaos from which to compose an identity. One can sense from the writing that flowed from his practice as an attentive child analyst, however, that he came to see that it is broadly human to inherit a convoluted past that then accompanies a child or youth into their future. The child is father and mother to the man or woman who will be.[6]

Erikson undertook training analysis with Anna Freud. He graduated from the Vienna Psychoanalytic Institute in early 1933, the year that Freud's books (along with others) were burned. Anti-Semitism was increasing by the day. As a Jew associated with a "decadent Jewish school of thought," he was at risk and left with his wife and young son first for Denmark and then for the United States. In December 1933 he became the first child analyst at Massachusetts General Hospital in Boston. There was a growing interest in psychoanalysis in the United States and few analysts from Vienna. He was a talented practitioner and teacher—and always restless. The next year Erikson accepted an appointment in the Medical School at Yale. Subsequently, his interest in child development and education took a cross-

---

[6]   Wordsworth says famously, "The child is father to the man." Kierkegaard says "the one who will work gives birth to his own father." See *FTP*, 57 (*SKS* 4, 123 / *FT*, 27). Erikson inhabits the German Romantic tradition from Schiller to Nietzsche that sees becoming oneself, or giving birth to oneself, as a poetic task. For discussion, see *Philosophical Romanticism*, ed. by Nikolas Kompridis, London and New York: Routledge 2006.

cultural and anthropological bent. He traveled West to participate in a study of Native American ways of childrearing, living on-site among the Sioux in South Dakota. Some years later, with the help of the anthropologist Alfred Kroeber (1876–1960), he learned from the Yurok in Northern California.

In 1939, Erikson accepted a position at the University of California, Berkeley. His widely read *Childhood and Society* came out in 1950. It became a widely used college text in departments of sociology, anthropology, and education, as well as in psychology—increasingly when it came out as a paperback in the mid 1960s. Refusing to comply with the McCarthy-era demand for anti-communist loyalty oaths from all faculty, he resigned from the University in 1950. Erikson subsequently taught for a number of years at Harvard and worked with troubled children at the Austin Riggs Center in western Massachusetts. He returned to the San Francisco Bay area in the early 1970s, living in Tiburon with his wife, daughter, and sons. A dozen years later he returned to Cambridge, Massachusetts, by then an old man in physical and mental decline. He died and was buried on Cape Cod in the tiny village of Harwich.

Although he was always connected with research institutions, Erikson considered himself less a "scholar's scholar" known for rigorously conducted studies, than as an innovative teacher, observer, and healer, and what today we would call a public intellectual.[7] He could claim among his older enthusiastic supporters in the 1930s and 1940s the broadly interdisciplinary and widely-discussed anthropologists, Margaret Mead (1901–78) and Ruth Benedict (1887–1948).[8] Both encouraged his fledging efforts to write in a way that would be broadly accessible and that would mesh psychological with social-psychological and anthropological developmental configurations. Later, he would return the favor, playing a formative role in the careers of Robert Coles (born 1929), Robert Jay Lifton (b. 1926), and Carol Gilligan (b. 1936).[9] Like Erikson, each of these psychologists were concerned with an interdisciplinary approach to the development not just of children or youth but of adults, a moral trajectory that would open possibilities for moral growth and for that sort of conviction on which a viable identity can be built.

---

[7]   In addition to Erikson's *Childhood and Society*, *Young Man Luther*, and *Gandhi's Truth*, other of his works were widely read and discussed, among them, *Identity and the Life Cycle*, New York: Norton 1959; and *Insight and Responsibility*, New York: Norton 1964. See also *Ideas and Identities: The Life and Work of Erik Erikson*, ed. by Robert S. Wallerstein and Leo Goldberger, Bloomington, Indiana: Indiana University Press 1998; *The Erik Erikson Reader*, ed. by Robert Coles, Oxford: Blackwell 2000; and Erik Erikson, *Vital Involvement in Old Age* (with Joan M. Erikson and Helen Q. Kivnick), New York: Norton 1986.

[8]   See Friedman, *Identity's Architect*, pp. 131–9.

[9]   See Robert Coles, *Erik Erikson, the Growth of his Work*, Boston: Atlantic-Little Brown 1970; Carol Gilligan, *In a Different Voice*, Cambridge, Massachusetts: Harvard University Press 1982; Robert Jay Lifton, *The Life of the Self: Toward a New Psychology*, New York: Simon and Schuster 1976.

III. Psychological Development as Moral Itinerary

Taking an extended historical perspective, Erikson's sketch of psychological growth is an elaborate schema of virtues. One need not picture "virtues" as moralistically demanding or punishing ideals imposed and sanctioned by a culture or religious institution. One can think of them as Erikson does, as the strengths or capacities that a sensitive observer will find in the make-up of persons who achieve some degree of fulfillment in their lives. Their authority does not lie in institutional edicts or in the privileged insight of specialists, but in the grain of commonplace experience (though the lessons of such experience may remain underappreciated and underdescribed). Sometimes their authority lies in the transcendent luminosity of transcultural exemplars like Jesus, Socrates, or Gandhi. At the level of ordinary experience, we could safely venture that any relatively fulfilled life will achieve some degree of love or intimacy, some capacity for sustained work and play, some knack for hopefulness and trust, even as these are haunted by doubt or despair. Erikson offers a schema of such virtues as desiderata that are more or less universal. The theme of a minimally fulfilled life would be based in observation and one's reading, and be offered as something factual that simultaneously has normative force. It is better to have families that instill trust in infants than families that instill doubt and mistrust. Of course there will be cultural variation in the balance of these virtues and in the modes of their expression. The full list of virtues, the sort of schema Erikson sketches in his eight-stage overview of the life-cycle, will surely vary, especially as he moves past childhood to early adulthood and maturity. But it is highly plausible, perhaps as certain as any generalization about things human can be, that the ideal that infants attain basic trust is a cross-cultural universal. In any case, the bare possibility of variation in moral schemata does not lessen the plausibility of there being core virtues. Erikson's schema can be taken as a provisional universal, the burden placed on the critic to show that societies can flourish without infants developing trust (say), or hope, and a sense of initiative and purpose (for instance). He offers a heuristic, an alluring invitational proposal for understanding moral maturation. It remains open to elaboration, exploration, and experimental (or experiential) critique, confirmation, and refutation.[10]

Plato proposes wisdom, moderation, and courage as basic virtues. The Gospels add faith, hope, and love (or charity). Aristotle would add friendship. Erikson's schema will seem more psychological than Plato's or Aristotle's, and less religious than those of the Gospels, but there is considerable overlap. For instance, Erikson has a place for neighbor love, *eros*, and *philia*—though these are not his terms of art.[11] And he expands "the virtues" in relatively new directions. For instance his

---

[10]   If not exactly a scientific confirmation, the wide appeal of his schema is registered in the appearance of a television film based on his work. See John Hubley, "Everybody Rides the Carousel" (documentary film 1976, DVD 1999). That broad appeal is also registered in the appearance of Kit Welchman, *Erik Erikson Worked for his Life, Work, and Significance*, Philadelphia: Open University Press 2000.

[11]   The recent raft of publications on Kierkegaard's *Works of Love* can be seen as framing Kierkegaard broadly in a virtue tradition. For just one study, see M. Jamie Ferreira, *Love's Grateful Striving: A Commentary on Kierkegaard's Works of Love*, Oxford: Oxford University

elaboration of love would include a prominent place for maternal, paternal, and intergenerational generative bonds of affection. If his schema can reach back to Classical Greek and Gospel traditions, it also has more recent nineteenth-century predecessors. It bears comparison, as we have seen, with Kierkegaard's quasi-developmental theory of stages on life's way, and when Erikson underlines the importance of play in development, we should hear echoes of Schiller's "play impulse" and of Nietzsche's proposal that a childlike free play is essential to adult creativity.[12]

In the last third of his career, Erikson moved beyond studies based on observation of children and youth to take up the formation of history-shaping moral-religious leaders. The eight-stage schema of moral maturation still animates his thinking, but writing *Young Man Luther* and *Gandhi's Truth* required the skills of a biographer and historian as well as of a developmental psychologist. These books were received by some as contributions to psycho-history, a term that had some cachet at the time. His choice of figures to study is not accidental. Erikson hoped his depictions of moral-religious greatness could illuminate and energize an American culture that especially in the 1960s and 1970s was in tumultuous and often violent search of its own identity.[13] The country had recently suffered the assassinations of Martin Luther King and John and Robert Kennedy, cities were burning, and violent anti-war protests had begun, bringing many deaths in their wake. These events would resonate with Erikson's experience 30 years earlier. While in Vienna he had begun taking notes on Hitler's extraordinary ability to captivate wayward, otherwise directionless youth. These became a chapter in *Childhood and Society*. What would a counter-Hitler look like? His books on Gandhi and Luther, written during America's time of troubles, and his later lectures on Jefferson and notes on Jesus, were attempts, in effect, to display the charisma of luminously effective moral-religious leaders.[14] Their early experiences and inner "self-work" was meshed in his narratives with the historical context of the societies that challenged and shaped them. He was dedicated to the study of moral individuals of great stature. He was equally dedicated to bring useful beacons of hope to a country still struggling to find itself, to settle its moral itinerary.

Press 2001. For accounts of the virtues in Kierkegaard, see also *Kierkegaard after MacIntyre*, ed. by John J. Davenport and Anthony Rudd, Chicago: Open Court 2001.

[12]   Nietzsche's three-stage schema of moral development, camel–lion–child, is found in the first sections of *Thus Spoke Zarathustra*.

[13]   The 1970 biography of Erikson by Robert Coles is dedicated to California migrant worker organizer, Caesar Chavez. Chavez, Gandhi, and Martin Luther King epitomized for Erikson the hope of non-violent social change, an alternative to the disasters of Nazism, McCarthyism, Stalinism, and the more violent fringes of the new left and Black Power movements.

[14]   See Erik Erikson, "The Galilean Sayings and the Sense of 'I,'" *Yale Review*, vol. 70, no. 3, 1981, pp. 321–62, Erik Erikson, "Reflections on Dr. Borg's Life Cycle," *Deadalus*, vol. 105, no. 2, 1976, pp. 1–28. Erikson was invited to give the prestigious National Endowment for the Humanities Jefferson Lectures in 1973, following Lionel Trilling who gave the first set of annual lectures. Trilling's topic was "Sincerity and Authenticity." Aptly enough, Erikson chose to speak on Jefferson. They were published as *Dimensions of a New Identity: The Jefferson Lectures in the Humanities*, New York: Norton 1974.

Although Erikson never presumed to speak even as a minor prophet in his adopted country, many took his diagnosis of moral failure and more importantly, his positive vision of transforming change and healing, as deeply and religiously inspiring.

IV. The Nature of a Developmental Stage

Each stage (or phase) in moral growth is a rough equilibrium achieved through struggle, an equilibrium that contains or moderates the parties to that struggle and that serves as a platform for further growth. For example, in the first year of life an infant struggles with trust and mistrust. Adults come and go, give warmth and then leave, provide food and withhold it, prevent pain and cause it—or at least fail to dependably remove it. An infant's success in handling issues of trust and mistrust in the first months of life will be crucial to its flourishing as an infant, as a creature who learns more or less to handle the dark, aloneness, hunger, and pain. And it is clear that success or failure at this early stage of maturation can have massive consequences for the success of the adult in handling adult matters of trust/mistrust. There is struggle early on that reappears all the way through the extended life-cycle.

Now achieving a minimally happy resolution or negotiated equilibrium in the infant's struggles with mistrust and trust will depend greatly on general circumstance—material conditions, for instance, adequate food and protection from temperature extremes—and on the specific ability of caregivers to provide reliable patterns of nourishment, security, and comfort. A caregiver's predictable attention and responsiveness is crucial if the infant is to trust that someone leaving a room has not left for good, or that weaning is not utter abandonment. Degrees of mistrust may remain, but one works for a predominance of trust. Erikson calls the successful negotiation of this earliest conflict the emergence of hope—a necessary virtue if one is to take the world then and later on as at least partially reliable. Mothering or fathering that is erratic, inconsistent, or decidedly deficient can instill a lasting and inordinately intense sense of anxiety and worthlessness. We might think of teenage suicide as partly a matter of failure to find the world trustworthy: one cannot find heart to trust life, to trust common reasons to live, or to trust those whom one knows: there is no reason not to die.

Given the fluidity and amorphous nature of shifts through trust and mistrust, one might want to expand the vocabulary available to mark this struggle. Trust is plausibly allied with courage and patience; mistrust, with anxiety, doubt, and fear. Hope is plausibly allied with self-confidence and optimism. We could expand, more or less indefinitely, the array of descriptive terms available to anyone seeking to capture this early struggle. This suggests that "trust" and "mistrust" are labels giving focus to a loosely constructed, open-ended associative field. But there are limits to credible expansion of descriptors. An infant can be pleased by music, but its orienting associative field cannot include the concept of Beethoven's 139 being pleasing, or of a stroke victim's first steps being an occasion for delight. Erikson's immediate trio of trust, mistrust, and hope, are suggestive starting points for understanding an infant's work with an elusive and often disappointing world.

A Kierkegaardian might be excused for sensing a too-neat three-step dialectic, as if we were witnessing a sort of Hegelian itinerary of human spirit's struggle to find itself among others. In *Childhood and Society* one finds the progress of moral maturation depicted in a schematic checker-board chart of three-step progressions. This chart is predictably reproduced in summaries of Erikson's views. The eight-tiered, three-step chart functions like a set of telegraphic abbreviations, or PowerPpoint bullets. The heart of the matter lies in his thick descriptions, as he knew. Erikson knew that in actual cases, things are seldom so simple. The pair "trust/mistrust" is a shorthand for an array of associated terms and phenomena. Development is nuanced, subtle, and elusive in the particular case—not a lockstep across well-marked parade grounds. It is telling that late in his career, Erikson came to chart his own moral itinerary. He schematized his development in six stages (as we will see below) and particular stages were no longer titled in terms of the virtues laid out in *Childhood and Society* and so much discussed in the 1960s. The eight-stage schema was not set in stone.

Exploring the full complexity of trust or mistrust, shame, guilt, autonomy, or courage, can be the goal of a lengthy piece of literature, especially as these underlie post-childhood lives. An extraordinary imagination might make headway in giving a narrative of a single infant's or child's struggles—Erikson gives us a keen observer's account—but infants cannot tell us much about their rudimentary experience, even though pre-verbal cries, coos, and gestures (the brightness of a smile, the tightness of a fist) can give us clues. In the hands of a great novelist, the struggles between trust/mistrust, autonomy/shame, or initiative/guilt can come into vivid relief in narratives of the experience and behavior of more developed individuals. *The Brothers Karamazov*, for example, can be read as a masterpiece in the depiction of these early-established virtues (and their contraries) as they flower (or fade). Even such a massive work of genius, however, teaches us humility in our presumed knowledge of the human heart. It can raise as many questions as answers about moral-psychological development. And if this is true of Dostoevsky's work, it must also be true of developmental accounts generally. Subtle portraits of the self, soul, or personality in transit can seem strangely unfinished, open-ended— even as trust or love, shame or self-doubt have an open-ended structure. Erikson's scheme of conflicting self-factors and their ideal resolution or tempering must be taken as heuristic in pointing us toward ever-more refined sensitivities to patterns of perception, affect, and comportment that nevertheless remain elusive and complex.

V. An Eight-Stage Cycle

Infancy is the first stage of the life-cycle. As we have seen, in good enough circumstances the struggle is between trust and mistrust, and issues, optimally, in confidence and hope. A Kierkegaardian will trace the interplay of doubt and mistrust that will surface later in a sense of melancholy or despair. The virtue of basic trust, or a knack for hope, serves as an underlying platform, stable or unreliable, for the next phase of development.

A stage-two toddler (roughly, age 1½–2) struggles with autonomy and shame. She will advance from crawling to running here and there, testing the world and herself. If she is successful, she will have a sense of autonomy rather than a will-shattering shame (at failures) and doubt. Self-initiative or will is developed even in following out the simple impulse to dash across open space towards the safety of an immovable couch. Erikson designates will (or self-initiative) as the virtue providing the platform for the next phase of growth.

The third stage of growth, the pre-school years falling between age 3 and 5, is marked by the struggle between initiative and guilt, and its successful negotiation Erikson calls "purpose." A preschooler struggles with the tasks of dressing herself, building with blocks, or playing make-believe with others. Guilt attaches to an inevitable sense that there is much that is expected that one cannot accomplish, and that the initiatives one undertakes are so often ill-conceived and poorly executed. One feels "guilt" if one cuts oneself with a paring knife, or tumbles painfully while racing down the stairs. Success in these struggles issues in a sense that one can undertake tasks and see them to completion—eating an apple (if not paring it), racing on the lawn (if not down the stairs). One develops a fledgling sense of purpose.

The grade-school child inhabits stage four. Stacked on the continuing challenges of earlier stages, the task now is to sustain initiative and purpose in larger projects, where industry vies against a sense of inferiority. One measures one's performance against peers, in the classroom, say, or on the athletic field. A successful negotiation of the industry/inferiority struggle yields the virtue of competence. Erikson's choice of "industry" as his operative label for this stage brings to mind as its contrast the neglected medieval vice of *acedia*—a listlessness, apathy, or melancholy. Perhaps the familiar doldrums of adolescence have their roots in an earlier stage-four failure of industry. What Erikson calls "inferiority" may be related to a later, adolescent listlessness.

A stage-five teenager will face the issue of identity head on (though in a wider sense, identity has been at issue all along). One begins to come into one's own, paradoxically, by negotiating one's loyalty to others. Identity, for Erikson, is never a solo achievement, but always a dialogical or relational affair, where connection with others is an essential part of the process. A teenager faces options for identity, previously unavailable. One can consider and negotiate loyalty to one's parents versus loyalty to one's rebellious pals, loyalty to one's parent's patterns of religiosity, consumerism, or grooming—or dogged loyalty to their opposites. One can consider, more or less explicitly, how much one's family's class standing or ethnicity matters, and how much to pledge to develop one's academic, artistic, or athletic talents. Then there is the dramatic and intense matter of gender differentiation. If one is biologically male, will one chart a super-masculine course or a more nurturing "feminine" one? Are there inklings or strong feelings of same-sex attraction? Biological females will face parallel struggles in working out gender identification. Erikson sees the struggle as between identity and role-confusion, and the achieved equilibrium he calls "fidelity"—a relatively stable identity that establishes a sense of where one "fits in" or "belongs," that rests on what one shall care about, to what or to whom shall one be faithful.

At this stage, differences of culture, class, and ethnicity, even of living in this decade rather than that, become massive and inescapable. However complicated it may be to describe practices across cultures for instilling trust in infants, the matter of describing the attainment of gender identity presents challenges of an altogether different order. Here place-specific descriptions of practices and options will outrun attempts at broad generalization. And this increasing requirement to account for variation and particularity in a moral itinerary will carry on through the remaining stages of the life-cycle.

The young adult (stage six) has the challenge of balancing intimacy and isolation. On the one hand, there is a felt-need, at least in European-based cultures, for aloneness and isolation to consolidate identity on one's own; on the other hand, there is the pull of intimate relations in work, family, and romance. When successfully negotiated, one achieves the virtue of love. This is a broad virtue realized in a youth's budding romantic relations, and also in intergenerational familial love (of younger siblings or cousins, who reciprocate, and of aunts and grandparents, whom one trusts will also reciprocate). It is realized in love of work with others, a capacity for affinity (or *philia*) in one's relations with teammates, neighbors, and co-workers, and in one's knack for cultivating friendships. The struggle of intimacy and isolation arises as one negotiates whom one should date, if anyone, and what sort of life is appealing (the relative isolation of a scholar or the more gregarious life of a saleswoman). When, if ever, will one settle down? In modern democratic nations, the option of staying in school well past adolescence can be a tactic for ducking or delaying a conventional expectation that one settle into building a career or enjoying a sustaining intimate relationship, or raising a family of one's own. Love, as a resolution, accordingly, encompasses far more than romance. It is the glue of sociality across many fronts as one matures into full adulthood.

Erikson's stage seven, mid to late adulthood, is marked by what becomes known as the mid-life crisis. If love successfully emerges at the threshold of adult life, as a care for work and others that is vitally sustained, in mid-life the challenge is to maintain that care against the encroachments of tedium, boredom, and decline. Erikson tags this crisis as the struggle between generativity and stagnation. One assesses what one has accomplished in life, what remains to be done, and where one has failed. Erikson sees a sense of fulfillment arising as one transfers energy from one's own career to assisting a younger generation.

Old age, stage eight, offers the chance to enjoy a measure of wisdom as the foreknowledge and actual impingement of disease and death arrive. Erikson frames the struggle as between integrity and despair. The challenge is to sustain poise through the adversities of age rather than falter in bitterness, disgust, or despair. Some handle death and decline reasonably well. Others can be bitter, unhappy, dissatisfied, not only with their infirmities (loss of hearing or sight or continence, for instance) but also with the dark sense of what they have failed to accomplish within their life-time.

VI. Hope for the Soul

Long after the eight-stage life-cycle was first outlined in *Childhood and Society*, and its mid-phases elaborated in the books on Luther and Gandhi, Erikson found he had more to say about old age, as he entered that phase of life. His thoughts appear strikingly in an essay on Ingmar Bergman's film, "Wild Strawberries."[15] The

---

[15]   See Erikson, "Reflections on Dr. Borg's Life Cycle."

film depicts an old doctor facing death, reliving memories of youthful love, and wondering if an honorary degree he is about to receive can mean much in the face of personal uncertainty. The essay reads as his reflections on his own wanderings through mists of non-being, through the shadows of death. In notes for this essay, Erikson praises the film for exhibiting "the most perfect combination of artistic form and psychological comprehension + existential religiosity."[16] It is not hard to imagine that Erikson would want these words to convey the ambition of his own later writing.

The spiritual and existential, even religious hues of his reflections on the film are more explicit in notes he published on the theme of Jesus' Galilean proverbs and sayings. These notes relied on scholarship that attempted to sort what the historical figure said from later additions and revisions. Erikson proposes that Jesus inaugurates a new sense of "I," and "I" related to an other, and free of those boundaries the protection of which leads one person to oppose, combat, or stand at cross-purposes with another. A kind of universal acceptance and openness to something like the Quaker "inner light," and perhaps something like Quaker peacefulness and patience, and capacity to listen beyond rancor or judgmentalism, seemed to pervade this new sense of "I." Perhaps Erikson explores and offers this new "I" as a more luminous sense of identity than any he had yet elaborated, and a sense of "I" that he must have hoped he came some distance toward inhabiting.

In the psychoanalytic community, Erikson has been labeled a Neo-Freudian and "ego psychologist." His amendments to Freud would include his expanding the stages of psychic development beyond childhood into adulthood and old age, and his stress on healthy negotiations of psychic conflict. In addition, Erikson accords significant initiative to a well-developed ego that needs to concede oversight neither to the passions of the id (or libido) nor to the super-ego (the punishing moralist and conscience, as well as the guardian of ideals). The stress on the ego's capacity to muster a strength of its own against encroachments of either id or super-ego are part and parcel of Erikson's alertness to more or less successful negotiations of psychic struggle at each stage of the life-cycle.

Although a reader of Kierkegaard will have "stages on life's way" in mind as he takes up Erikson's map of personality development, Erikson sees himself not as a theologian and not primarily as a religious writer (though he veered in this direction later). Professionally, he takes himself for most of his career to be a psychologist or psychoanalyst expanding Freud's stage theory of infancy far beyond childhood, through to old age.[17] He seeks narratives, after *Childhood and Society*, of entire lives, and also expands Freud by stressing the social, political, and religious contexts of development. It is noteworthy that Erikson gave momentum to the fledgling field of psychobiography and psychohistory with his studies of Luther's conversion and what he called "Gandhi's Truth." He cast these lives not as laboring under religious illusion (as a rigid Freudian would insist), but as exemplary, broadly successful, spiritually and morally luminous.

---

[16]   Friedman, *Identity's Architect*, p. 444.

[17]   For a late, quasi-religious essay, see Erikson's "The Galilean Sayings and the Sense of 'I.'"

He describes Gandhi's success in terms that side-step a secular–religious divide. Hope, for example, is both a religious and a secular virtue. Anxiety and doubt can appear in a religious as well as in a secular register. Where Kierkegaard might see despair as a rebellion against God, or as a refusal to avow the self one is, Erikson would see it as closer to anxiety, a pervasive undercurrent one negotiates (or fails to negotiate) through the struggles that impinge at any stage in the life-cycle: struggles between trust and mistrust, initiative and guilt, and so forth. Erikson seemed to highlight the successful negotiation of inner struggle, rather than its failure in neurosis or pathology. Kierkegaard seems to have less confidence in a positive outcome of these negotiations. Success will be at best elusive. Ways to fail at becoming a self are easier to tally than ways to achieve a satisfying balance in self-development.

Erikson had spent a lifetime describing the life-cycle generally, and the lives of Luther, Jefferson, and Gandhi, in particular. He found himself late in life sketching out the stages of his own moral (and spiritual) development. As we have mentioned, he felt no need to make this sketch conform to the schema that he had made famous. In place of an eight-stage emergence of virtues, he characterized his development in stages that do not mention virtues. In non-technical terms that any conventional biographer might adopt, Erikson divides his life into six phases: (1) Childhood, Youth, Early Adulthood (1902–27), (2) Training in Freud's Vienna (1927–33), (3) Making of *Childhood and Society* (1933–50), (4) Clinician of Voice and Identity (1950–60),[18] (5) Professor-Ethical Philosopher (1960–75),[19] and (6) Old Age (1976–94).[20]

In 1987 an article on Erikson appeared in *The New York Review of Books*, aptly titled "The Artist as Analyst." The author was the prominent developmental psychologist Jerome Bruner (b. 1915). He wrote that "Erikson must surely be the most distinguished living psychoanalyst."[21] Erikson hoped that despite reasons for despair, he had matured as a teacher holding out the promise of health, a non-creedal answer to "the sickness unto death." In tone, he had none of Kierkegaard's pervasive irony, and was seldom as prophetically polemical or as darkly pessimistic, embattled and acerbic as Kierkegaard became toward the end of his life. Yet Erikson was neither uncritical of his times nor of theories of self and society. It was no accident that out of a lifetime admiration, Erikson, began work specifically on Kierkegaard in his years of retirement. That work remained no more than notes and a short typescript, unfortunately.[22] Overall, we might see at the core of Erikson's gentle sensibility a generous, kindly hope. That is the virtue that most conspicuously threads through his career as a psychologist, anthropologist, ethical philosopher, and even, for many of his admirers in the post-war decades, a (minor) prophet. At the least, he was a man of wisdom and a consummate teacher and healer.

---

[18]   During these years, Erikson worked at the Austen Riggs Center for troubled adolescents, in western Massachusetts.

[19]   This period was at Harvard and later in Tiburon, California.

[20]   The Eriksons moved from Tiburon, to Cambridge, Massachusetts, in 1987, where they shared a house with Dianne Eck, a young professor of religion, and her spouse, the Rev. Dorothy Austin.

[21]   Jerome Bruner, *The New York Review of Books*, December 3, 1987, p. 8.

[22]   See note 4, above.

Bibliography

I. References to or Uses of Kierkegaard in Erikson's Corpus

Young Man Luther: A Study in Psychoanalysis and History, New York: Norton 1958, pp. 13–15; p. 59; p. 71; p. 150; p. 214; pp. 240–3; p. 252.

Insight and Responsibility: Lectures on the Ethical Implications of Psychoanalytic Insight, New York: Norton 1964, p. 202; p. 204.

"The Ontogeny of Ritualization in Man," *Philosophical Transactions of the Royal Society of London*, 1966, pp. 337–49.

Gandhi's Truth: On the Origins of Militant Nonviolence, New York: Norton 1969, p. 108; p. 125; p. 128.

Life History and the Historical Moment, New York: Norton 1975, p. 31; p. 107; p. 122; p. 161.

"Reflections on Dr. Borg's Life Cycle," *Deadalus*, vol. 105, no. 2, 1976, pp. 1–28.

"The Galilean Sayings and the Sense of 'I,' " *Yale Review*, vol. 70, no. 3, 1981, pp. 321–62.

II. Sources of Erikson's Knowledge of Kierkegaard

Geismar, Eduard, "Wie urteilte Kierkegaard über Luther," *Jahrbuch der Luther-gesellschaft*, vol. 10, 1928, pp. 1–27.

Kierkegaard, Søren, *Søren Kierkegaards Papirer*, vols. 1–16, ed. by P.A. Heiberg, V. Kuhr, and E. Torsting, Copenhagen: Gyldendal 1909–48.

— *The Journals of Søren Kierkegaard: A Selection*, ed. and trans. by Alexander Dru, London: Oxford University Press 1938.

III. Secondary Literature on Erikson's Relation to Kierkegaard

Allen, Kenneth Ralph, *Identity and the Individual. Personhood in the Thought of Erik Erikson and of Søren Kierkegaard*, Ph.D. Thesis, Boston University Graduate School, Boston 1967.

Coles, Robert, *Erik Erikson, the Growth of his Work*, Boston: Atlantic-Little Brown 1970, pp. 3–11; p. 204; p. 320.

Friedman, Lawrence J., *Identity's Architect: A Biography of Erik Erikson*, New York: Scribners 1999, pp. 372–3; p. 389; p. 403; p. 439; pp. 448–9.

Hannay, Alastair, *Kierkegaard*, London: Routledge & Kegan Paul 1982, p. 287.

Hoare, Carol Hren, *Erikson on Development in Adulthood: New Insights from the Unpublished Papers Oxford*, New York: Oxford University Press 2002, p. 83; pp. 176–9; p. 183; p. 212.

Erich Fromm:

The Integrity of the Self and the Practice of Love

John Lippitt

I. Life and Works

Erich Fromm (1900–80) was a psychoanalyst and social psychologist associated with the Frankfurt School of social theory and often credited with forging key links between Marxist and Freudian thought. Born to Orthodox Jewish parents, Fromm briefly studied law and jurisprudence at the University of Frankfurt am Main and then, at Heidelberg, sociology under Max Weber's brother Alfred (1868–1958), psychology under Karl Jaspers (1883–1969) and philosophy under Heinrich Rickert (1863–1936). After earning his Ph.D. in sociology from Heidelberg in 1922, Fromm went on—under the influence of Frieda Reichmann, whom he later married—to train as a psychoanalyst and to begin his own clinical practice. At this time he was also appointed by Max Horkheimer (1895–1973), as chief psychological expert of the Frankfurt Institute for Social Research (the so-called "Frankfurt School").[1]

When the Nazis came to power in Germany, the Frankfurt School moved to Geneva and then the USA, becoming established at Columbia University in 1934. Following an invitation from the Chicago Psychoanalytic Institute to give a series of lectures in 1933, Fromm moved from Switzerland to the USA, holding throughout the 1940s a series of teaching positions at Columbia, Michigan, Yale, and New York Universities and Bennington College, Vermont. He became a US citizen in 1940, but in 1950 moved to Mexico, its climate better suiting his second wife's health needs. Fromm taught at the National Autonomous University in Mexico City (UNAM) until 1965 (afterwards becoming professor emeritus there), while also holding various posts in the USA and maintaining his psychoanalytic practice. Fromm's political engagements during this time included the international peace movement, and arguing against both Western capitalism and Soviet Communism in the American Socialist Party. After retirement from UNAM, Fromm wrote productively, including during the very last years of his life after his move, along with his third wife, back to Switzerland in 1974. He died in 1980, a few days short of his eightieth birthday.

---

[1]   See Rainer Funk, "Erich Fromm's Life and Work," in *Erich Fromm and Critical Criminology: Beyond the Punitive Society*, ed. by Mathieu Deflem, Kevin Anderson, and Richard Quinney, Urbana and Chicago: University of Illinois Press 2000, p. 7.

Amongst the most significant of Fromm's works for our purposes are his first important monograph, *Escape from Freedom* or *The Fear of Freedom*[2] and *The Art of Loving*,[3] both of which we shall discuss in some detail below. Other important texts include *Man for Himself*,[4] where Fromm developed a humanistic ethics and "characterology" that goes beyond Freud's libido theory; *Psychoanalysis and Religion*,[5] an extension of the ideas of *Man for Himself* beyond ethics into religion; *The Sane Society*,[6] which discusses alienation in capitalist and bureaucratic society and argues for a democratic and humanistic socialism; *You Shall Be as Gods*,[7] which argues for a variety of non-theistic religions; and *To Have or To Be?*,[8] in which the acquisitive, materialistic "having" mode is contrasted unfavorably with the "being" mode manifested in shared experience and rooted in love. As will be seen from the above, one of Fromm's abiding concerns was the relation between the individual and society. But perhaps to put it thus is slightly misleading. As Rainer Funk explains, for Fromm:

> It was no longer valid to say "here I am and there is society"; but rather, "I am primarily a reflection of society, in that my unconscious is socially determined and I therefore reflect and realize the secret expectations, requirements, wishes, fears, and strivings of society in my own passionate strivings." In reality, none of the following—not the apparent separation of society and individual, not the apparent separation of conscious and unconscious, not the apparent separation of society and unconscious—actually exist. All of these dimensions are in the social unconscious of every single human being.[9]

One commentator has described Fromm as "[t]he psychoanalyst who probably thought the most about the relationship of culture and the individual."[10]

Though initially influenced by Freud, like many other psychoanalysts, Fromm eventually broke with Freudian thought. The reasons are complex, but one key aspect is given towards the end of *The Fear of Freedom*:

> We believe that man is *primarily* a social being, and not, as Freud assumes, primarily self-sufficient and only secondarily in need of others in order to satisfy his instinctual needs.

---

[2]   Erich Fromm, *Escape from Freedom*, New York: Rinehart & Co. 1941 (published in the UK and other parts of the English-speaking world as *The Fear of Freedom*, London: Routledge and Kegan Paul 1942).

[3]   Erich Fromm, *The Art of Loving: An Inquiry into the Nature of Love*, New York: Harper and Row 1956.

[4]   Erich Fromm, *Man for Himself: An Inquiry into the Psychology of Ethics*, New York: Rinehart and Co. 1947.

[5]   Erich Fromm, *Psychoanalysis and Religion*, New Haven, Connecticut: Yale University Press 1950.

[6]   Erich Fromm, *The Sane Society*, New York: Holt, Rinehart and Winston 1955.

[7]   Erich Fromm, *You Shall Be as Gods: A Radical Interpretation of the Old Testament and Its Tradition*, New York: Holt, Rinehart and Winston 1966.

[8]   Erich Fromm, *To Have or to Be?*, New York: Harper and Row 1976.

[9]   Funk, "Erich Fromm's Life and Work," p. 9.

[10]   James W. Jones, *Terror and Transformation: The Ambiguity of Religion in Psychoanalytic Perspective*, Hove and New York: Taylor and Francis 2002, p. 46.

In this sense, we believe that individual psychology is fundamentally social psychology or…the psychology of interpersonal relationships; the key problem of psychology is that of the particular kind of relatedness of the individual toward the world, not that of satisfaction or frustration of single instinctual desires.[11]

This focus on selfhood as relational might already ring some Kierkegaardian bells: we shall return to this in more detail below.

II. En passant: Fromm on Kierkegaard[12]

In *The Denial of Death*, Ernest Becker (1924–74) cites Kierkegaard as an important precursor to psychoanalysis.[13] Kierkegaard is routinely cited as an early "depth psychologist" and of course addresses at length such topics as anxiety and despair. Yet in common with other psychoanalysts such as Jung and Kristeva, Fromm has little to say in any detail about Kierkegaard. Rarely does the latter receive more than one reference in any given Fromm text, and often, when he is mentioned, it is on a list of (allegedly) comparable thinkers, Nietzsche and Marx being probably the most common bedfellows. For instance, Kierkegaard is mentioned explicitly just once in *The Fear of Freedom*, being listed, along with Nietzsche and Kafka, as one of the "visionary thinkers"[14] who had already foreseen some of the themes of twentieth-century life that Fromm seeks to describe and diagnose in this book. Kierkegaard, we are told, "describes the helpless individual torn and tormented by doubts, overwhelmed by the feeling of aloneness and insignificance."[15] Another comparison with Nietzsche occurs in *Psychoanalysis and Religion* where, talking about the—in many ways regrettable—development of psychology as a science, Fromm complains, "Notwithstanding exceptional figures like Nietzsche and Kierkegaard, the tradition in which psychology was a study of the soul concerned with man's virtue and happiness was abandoned."[16] Kierkegaard starts to emerge as being, for Fromm, an insightful yet largely ignored figure, a man before his time.[17] A

---

[11]   Fromm, *Escape from Freedom*, p. 290. (*The Fear of Freedom*, p. 247.)

[12]   For enormous help in tracking down the references to Kierkegaard in Fromm's writings, I am extremely grateful to Fromm's literary executor, Rainer Funk.

[13]   Ernest Becker, *The Denial of Death*, New York: Simon and Schuster 1973, chapter 5, pp. 67–92.

[14]   Fromm, *Escape from Freedom*, p. 133. (*The Fear of Freedom*, p. 114.)

[15]   Ibid.

[16]   Fromm, *Psychoanalysis and Religion*, pp. 5–6.

[17]   Other places where Kierkegaard is mentioned in passing as one on a list of thinkers are as follows. He is listed amongst those, including Marx and Nietzsche again, but also Kant, Darwin, Bergson, Joyce and Picasso, who express "Western man's desire to relinquish false gods, to do away with illusions and to grasp himself and the world as part of a total reality." See Erich Fromm, *Sigmund Freud's Mission*, New York: Harper and Row 1959, p. 116. Later, he is one of those—along with humanist socialism, Schweitzer, Russell and Einstein—the underlying theme of whose thought is "the concept of the unity of the human race, and of humanity contained in each individual as a potential." See Erich Fromm, "Humanism and Psychoanalysis," *Contemporary Psychoanalysis*, vol. 1, no. 1, 1964, p. 71. He is also claimed

further such comparison is with both Marx and Nietzsche as a significant protestor against alienation.[18] In the nineteenth century, the prophetic voices of this trio were "muted by the apparent success of capitalist industrialism," but such protests against "the dehumanization of man" were heard more loudly during and after World War II.[19] Indeed, earlier in the same chapter, Fromm claims,

> the whole existentialist philosophy, from Kierkegaard on, is, as Paul Tillich puts it, "an over one-hundred-years-old movement of rebellion against the dehumanization of man in industrial society." Actually, the concept of alienation is, in nontheistic language, the equivalent of what in theistic language would be called "sin": man's relinquishment of himself, of God within himself.[20]

Marx is portrayed here as an alternative to Kierkegaard: both are concerned with "the salvation of the individual," Marx's primary concern with capitalist society being "its destruction of individuality and its enslavement of man...by things and circumstances of their own making."[21] (This, as we shall see from Section III, is a return to a central theme of *The Fear of Freedom*.) But earlier, in the preface, Kierkegaard has been unfavorably compared to Marx, as being insufficiently attuned to the importance of class and social issues: "in contrast to Kierkegaard and others, Marx sees man in his full concreteness as a member of a given society and of a given class, aided in his development by society, and at the same time its captive."[22] This theme, of Marx as going beyond Kierkegaard in an important respect, is repeated a year later:

> Precisely because alienation has reached a point where it borders on insanity in the whole industrialised world, undermining and destroying its religious, spiritual, and political traditions and threatening general destruction through nuclear war, many are better able to see that Marx had recognized the central issue of modern man's sickness; that he had not only seen, as Feuerbach and Kierkegaard had, this "sickness" but that he had shown that contemporary idolatry is rooted in the contemporary mode of production

---

to keep company with Spinoza, Kant, Feuerbach, Marx, Freud and Scheler in teaching, like St. John Chrysostom before them, that "sin was to consider man as a means or a tool." See *The Nature of Man*, ed. by Erich Fromm and Ramon Xirau, New York: Macmillan 1968, p. 12. Finally, in a posthumously published paper written in 1969, Fromm quotes R.D. Laing's view that Kierkegaard—like Marx, Nietzsche, Freud, Heidegger, Tillich and Sartre—had the realization that "Humanity is estranged from its authentic possibilities. This basic vision prevents us from taking any unequivocal view of the sanity of common sense, or of the madness of the so-called madmen." See Erich Fromm, "The Dialectic Revision of Psychoanalysis," in his *The Revision of Psychoanalysis*, ed. by Rainer Funk, Boulder: Westview Press 1992 [1969], p. 61. Kierkegaard was, of course, an influence on what is probably Laing's best-known book, *The Divided Self*.

[18] Erich Fromm, *Marx's Concept of Man*, New York: Frederick Ungar 1961, p. 72.

[19] Ibid.

[20] Ibid., p. 47.

[21] Ibid., p. 49.

[22] Ibid., pp. v–vi.

and can be changed only by the complete change of the economic-social constellation together with the spiritual liberation of man.[23]

Nevertheless, Kierkegaard continues to be credited for recognizing the importance of maximizing "individuality." Demonstrating that he views it as possible to be a "humanist" in a theistic as well as a non-theistic sense, Fromm claims, "Some Humanist thinkers—among them Leibniz, Goethe, Kierkegaard and Marx— particularly stressed the need to develop individuality to the greatest possible extent in order to achieve the highest harmony and universality."[24] However, rather dubiously with respect to Kierkegaard, he adds: "all Humanists have shared a belief in the possibility of man's perfectibility, which, whether they believed in the need for God's grace or not, they saw as dependent upon man's own efforts (which is why Luther was not a Humanist)."[25] Kierkegaard's proximity to Luther on such a point appears not to be recognized. Similarly, in *The Nature of Man*, Kierkegaard appears on another list of philosophers who perceive that "man *makes himself*; that man is the author of his own history."[26] This is perhaps because Fromm associates Kierkegaard with the existentialists, and we are told that they "have told us that we lack an essence, that we are in the first instance an existence, that is, that we are that which we make of ourselves during the course of our life."[27] It is hard to avoid the conclusion that Kierkegaard is here being turned into Sartre. On the other hand, Fromm goes on to gloss the idea that "man is historical and temporal" in a way that does bring us closer to a Kierkegaardian view: "Man no longer *is* rational; he *becomes* rational. He no longer *is* social; he *becomes* social. He no longer *is* religious; he *becomes* religious."[28]

Finally, there is what appears to be the only explicit reference to a specific Kierkegaard text in Fromm's work. *The Art of Being* contains a short chapter entitled "To Will One Thing," and *Purity of Heart* is referenced in a footnote.[29] Willing one thing is heralded as "[t]he first condition for more than mediocre achievement in any field, including that of the art of living."[30] There is a reference here to the problem of double-mindedness: "Where energies are split in different directions, an aim is not only striven for with diminished energy, but the split of energies has the effect of weakening them in both directions by the constant conflicts that are engendered."[31]

---

[23]   Erich Fromm, *Beyond the Chains of Illusion: My Encounter with Marx and Freud*, New York: Simon and Schuster 1962, p. 59.

[24]   See Fromm's "Introduction" to *Socialist Humanism: An International Symposium*, ed. by Erich Fromm, New York: Doubleday 1965, p. vii.

[25]   Ibid.

[26]   Fromm, *The Nature of Man*, p. 6.

[27]   Ibid.

[28]   Ibid., p. 7.

[29]   Erich Fromm, *The Art of Being*, New York: Continuum 1992, p. 31, note. As the editor's foreword (by Rainer Funk) explains, this text consists of selected chapters that Fromm wrote at the time (1974–76) that he was composing *To Have or to Be?* but which were not included in that earlier text. *The Art of Being* was published posthumously.

[30]   Ibid.

[31]   Ibid.

However, Fromm does not seem concerned with the full Kierkegaardian resonances of that term: his subsequent discussion is not committed to the idea that only the good can genuinely be willed without double-mindedness.

In sum, the generally passing nature of Fromm's references to Kierkegaard leads one to suspect that his knowledge of the latter was not especially detailed. As an educated German who came to intellectual maturity in the first half of the twentieth century, Fromm could not have avoided knowing something of Kierkegaard, and he seems in general to have liked what he saw. But his personal library seems to have contained relatively few Kierkegaard titles.[32] Fromm's reading of Kierkegaard may have been inspired by the personal contact he had with Paul Tillich and Reinhold Niebuhr.[33]

Despite the paucity of explicit references to Kierkegaard in *The Fear of Freedom*, that book develops a number of Kierkegaardian themes and there remain numerous significant points of contact between Fromm's thought and Kierkegaard's. Let us turn, then, to two such themes: the loss of the self through "automaton conformity" and the central importance of love, aspects of which I shall supplement with a more detailed discussion of what is arguably Fromm's best-known book, *The Art of Loving*.[34]

III. Selfhood: "automaton conformity" and the Loss of the Self

An absolutely central idea to the thought of both Kierkegaard and Fromm is the importance of becoming a (genuine) self. Selfhood, far from being a "given," is a goal, a task. This theme, which runs throughout Kierkegaard's work, receives one of its most famous articulations at the start of *The Sickness unto Death*. The self is a synthesis of ostensible opposites—finite and infinite; freedom and necessity; temporal and eternal—that must be held together in a (creative) tension. In thus relating to itself and willing to be itself, the self "rests transparently in the power that established it."[35] (This is later defined as faith.[36]) This last vital point—the

---

[32]   I advance this claim with considerable caution. The two-thirds of Fromm's final library archived in Germany contains a German-language anthology of Kierkegaard's writings, Søren Kierkegaard, *Religion der Tat. sein Werk in Auswahl*, ed. by Eduard Geismar, Stuttgart: Alfred Kröner Verlag 1948 [1930]; Søren Kierkegaard, *Fear and Trembling and The Sickness unto Death*, trans. by Walter Lowrie, New York: Doubleday Anchor 1954; Søren Kierkegaard, *Purity of Heart is to Will One Thing*, trans. by Douglas V. Steere, New York: Harper & Brothers 1956; and Søren Kierkegaard, *Either/Or*, vols. 1–2, trans. by David F. Swenson, Lillian Marvin Swenson, and Walter Lowrie, New York: Anchor Books 1959. *Religion der Tat* and *Purity of Heart* contain various underlinings, but *Either/Or* does not. However, this does not account for the books Fromm had to leave in Europe when moving to the USA in 1934; some not taken to Mexico in 1950; or the remaining one-third of his final library that remains in Mexico. I am grateful to Rainer Funk for this information.

[33]   This has been suggested to me by Rainer Funk in a personal correspondence.

[34]   This book is a long-standing bestseller and now being marketed in a series with the title "Classics of Personal Development."

[35]   *SKS* 11, 129 / *SUD*, 13.

[36]   *SKS* 11, 164 / *SUD*, 49.

unapologetic insistence on our utter dependence upon God—is what will ultimately divide Fromm from Kierkegaard. The self-knowledge that *Sickness* urges upon us is that our true position is dependency. The human self being "a derived, established relation,"[37] we must acknowledge our creatureliness and—as Augustine insists in the *Confessions*—find our rest and contentment therein. (Or as Kierkegaard puts it in the title of an upbuilding discourse, "To Need God is a Human Being's Highest Perfection."[38]) Both the resistance to this idea, and the delicate balance needed between these aspects of selfhood, mean that we are far more likely than not to fall into some version(s) or other of the forms of despair Anti-Climacus catalogues in *Sickness*. And notwithstanding the crucial difference mentioned above, there remain important parallels between Kierkegaard and Fromm on this last point. We might say that they agree on the diagnosis of the disease, if not on the cure. More specifically, what Fromm calls "automaton conformity" sounds like one of the varieties of Anti-Climacean despair. In noting this below, we shall see that Fromm's remark explicitly about Kierkegaard above is somewhat misleading, insofar as it downplays the importance of self-deception and the ability to "hide" from oneself the feelings there described.

We will best understand Fromm's concerns about "automaton conformity" by understanding the central ideas of *The Fear of Freedom*. The book, says Fromm, is about "the meaning of freedom for modern man,"[39] and its central thesis is as follows:

> modern man, freed from the bonds of pre-individualistic society, which simultaneously gave him security and limited him, has not gained freedom in the positive sense of the realization of his individual self; that is, the expression of his intellectual, emotional and sensuous potentialities. Freedom, though it has brought him independence and rationality, has made him isolated and, thereby, anxious and powerless. This situation is unbearable and the alternatives he is confronted with are either to escape from the burden of this freedom into new dependencies and submission, or to advance to the full realization of positive freedom which is based upon the uniqueness and individuality of man.[40]

"Automaton conformity," for Fromm, is one of main "mechanisms of escape"[41] to which modern man succumbs in order to escape the burden of freedom. Indeed, it is "the solution that the majority of normal individuals find in modern society."[42] Here, Fromm is returning to a theme which, he claims in *Beyond the Chains of Illusion*, had occupied him as a young man at the end of World War I: "the wish to understand the irrationality of human mass behaviour."[43] Yet what he says about it sounds strikingly Kierkegaardian:

---

[37]   *SKS* 11, 130 / *SUD*, 13.

[38]   *SKS* 5, 291–316 / *EUD*, 297–326.

[39]   Fromm, *Escape from Freedom*, p. vii. (*The Fear of Freedom*, p. ix.)

[40]   Fromm, *Escape from Freedom*, p. viii. (*The Fear of Freedom*, p. x.)

[41]   Fromm, *Escape from Freedom*, p. 185. (*The Fear of Freedom*, p. 159.)

[42]   Fromm, *Escape from Freedom*, p. 185. (*The Fear of Freedom*, p. 160.)

[43]   Fromm, *Beyond the Chains of Illusion*, p. 6.

the individual ceases to be himself; he adopts entirely the kind of personality offered to him by cultural patterns; and he therefore becomes exactly as all others are and as they expect him to be. The discrepancy between "I" and the world disappears and with it the conscious fear of aloneness and powerlessness.[44]

Comparing such people to animal camouflage, Fromm goes on to claim: "The person who gives up his individual self and becomes an automaton, identical with millions of other automatons (*sic*) around him, need not feel alone and anxious any more. But the price he pays…is high; it is the loss of his self."[45]

This idea will be very familiar to readers of Kierkegaard. As well as the famous attack on "the crowd," we might recall the confused and inauthentic relation to ethical demands ridiculed by Climacus in the *Postscript* when he compares those whose ethical behavior is purely a function of how they see others behave, like children at a party whose mother has told them to "mind your manners and watch the other polite children and behave as they do."[46] Such a person "would never do anything first and would never have any opinion unless he first knew that others had it."[47] Most importantly of all, perhaps, compare the idea, in *Sickness*, that "[e]very human being is primitively intended to be a self, destined to become himself."[48] Yet it is vital not to be "ground down smooth" rather than merely "ground into shape."[49] Anti-Climacus expresses a concern about the kind of despair—that of lacking "infinitude"—which

> seems to permit itself to be tricked out of its self by "the others." Surrounded by hordes of men, absorbed in all sorts of secular matters, more and more shrewd about the ways of the world—such a person forgets himself, forgets his name divinely understood, does not dare to believe in himself, finds it too hazardous to be himself and far easier and safer to be like the others, to become a copy, a number, a mass man.[50]

Just as Fromm notes that "automaton conformity" is the most common "mechanism of escape" from the burden of freedom, so Anti-Climacus claims, "this form of despair goes practically unnoticed in the world."[51]

Fromm's concern is essentially with a lack of originality and authenticity, essentially what Kierkegaard is highlighting in his criticisms of those who lack *Primitivitet*. Amongst the examples he gives of "automaton" thinking is a person judging, say, a Rembrandt as beautiful not because of any genuine inner response but because he knows he is supposed to find it so. Or, in photographing a well-known piece of scenery, reproducing the picture as he has seen it countless times before on postcards.[52] But there are deeper existential concerns with people not knowing who

---

[44]   Fromm, *Escape from Freedom*, pp. 185–6. (*The Fear of Freedom*, p. 160.)
[45]   Fromm, *Escape from Freedom*, p. 186. (*The Fear of Freedom*, p. 160.)
[46]   *SKS* 7, 222 / *CUP1*, 244.
[47]   Ibid.
[48]   *SKS* 11, 149 / *SUD*, 33.
[49]   Ibid.
[50]   *SKS* 11, 149 / *SUD*, 33–4.
[51]   *SKS* 11, 149 / *SUD*, 34.
[52]   Fromm, *Escape from Freedom*, p. 193. (*The Fear of Freedom*, p. 166.)

they really are, for instance, the man who believes that he "wants" to get married but who is "actually…caught up in a sequence of events which leads to marriage and seems to block every escape."[53] His true uncertainties only come to the fore with the "cold feet" he discovers on the morning of the wedding, but "if he is 'sensible' this feeling only lasts for a few minutes, and he will answer the question whether it is his intention to marry with the unshakable conviction that it is."[54] This is but one example, claims Fromm, of countless instances in everyday life in which people seem to make genuinely free decisions, but are in fact following internal or external pressures of "having" to want the thing they are going to do:

> As a matter of fact, in watching the phenomenon of human decisions, one is struck by the extent to which people are mistaken in taking as "their" decision what in effect is submission to convention, duty or simple pressure. It almost seems that "original" decision is a comparatively rare phenomenon in a society which supposedly makes individual decision the cornerstone of its existence.[55]

Later, Fromm makes an equivalent point with respect to genuine and pseudo-emotions.[56] In such ways, "the original self is completely suffocated by the pseudo -self."[57] And for Fromm, "the psychoanalytic procedure is essentially a process in which a person tries to uncover this original self."[58] Fromm claims that Freud focused excessively on the repression of the "bad," but not sufficiently on the extent to which the "good" are also subject to repression under social pressures and fear of ridicule or attack.[59]

Fromm returns to this theme in his discussion of "the illusion of individuality" in democratic society. "The right to express our thoughts," he points out, "means something only if we are able to have thoughts of our own."[60] "Originality" does not mean that an idea has never previously been thought, but "that it is the result of [a person's] own activity and in this sense is his thought."[61] There can be a lack of originality in willing as well as in thinking and feeling, as when people do not ask themselves whether the aims they pursue—more money, a bigger house, a better car—are what they really want. Fromm's key thought here is also one that seems to run through Kierkegaard's work, about the deep desire for meaning human beings have, and yet how they often hide from themselves these "frightening"[62] central questions about the "meaning of life." The key point is that conformity and the loss of the self are mutually reinforcing: "He thinks, feels, and wills what he believes he is supposed to think, feel, and will; in this very process he loses his self upon

---

[53] Fromm, *Escape from Freedom*, p. 201. (*The Fear of Freedom,* p. 173.)

[54] Ibid.

[55] Ibid.

[56] Fromm, *Escape from Freedom*, p. 244. (*The Fear of Freedom,* p. 210.)

[57] Fromm, *Escape from Freedom*, p. 205. (*The Fear of Freedom*, p. 177.)

[58] Fromm, *Escape from Freedom*, p. 206, note. (*The Fear of Freedom*, p. 177, note.)

[59] Ibid.

[60] Fromm, *Escape from Freedom*, p. 241. (*The Fear of Freedom*, p. 207.)

[61] Fromm, *Escape from Freedom*, p. 242. (*The Fear of Freedom*, p. 209.)

[62] Fromm, *Escape from Freedom*, p. 252. (*The Fear of Freedom*, p. 217.)

which all genuine security of a free individual must be built."[63] However, at the same time, "The loss of the self has increased the necessity to conform, for it results in a profound doubt of one's own identity."[64] It is in this context that Fromm could echo the following, famous words from *Sickness*: "The greatest hazard of all, losing the self, can occur very quietly in the world, as if it were nothing at all. No other loss can occur so quietly; any other loss—an arm, a leg, five dollars, a wife, etc.—is sure to be noticed."[65]

Fromm returns to this theme in *The Nature of Man*, where he associates talk of "one" (as opposed to "I") with "the world of gossip, of meaningless talk in which no one in particular is responsible for anything."[66] And he explicitly connects this with Kierkegaard:

> Kierkegaard had already seen that such an attitude can provide us with a sort of pleasure. Such is, in his words, the world of the "aesthetic man"; in other words, of the man who cannot find himself and wants to find his being in experiencing all things, thus losing his being and his identity. But this "experiencing" without beginning or end, which Kierkegaard symbolized in the attitude of the Don Juan, tends to create sadness, the "sadness of the hedonist," so similar to the "suffering" described in the teaching of Buddha. This sadness consists in the absence of self. And sadness is, according to Kierkegaard, and to Spinoza, the most negative of our passions, the passion most clearly against the course of life.[67]

We turn now to another topic crucial to both Fromm and Kierkegaard: love.

IV. Love

A comparative discussion of our two thinkers' views on love could justifiably take up an entire book. In the space available here, I shall limit myself to a discussion of the following overlapping themes: love as active (the "works" of love); preferential and non-preferential forms of love; and the importance, in the context of loving others, of distinguishing "good" and "bad" forms of self-love. The two most important Fromm texts for our purposes here shall be *The Fear of Freedom* and, especially, *The Art of Loving*.

---

63   Fromm, *Escape from Freedom*, p. 254. (*The Fear of Freedom*, p. 219.)
64   Ibid.
65   *SKS* 11, 148 / *SUD*, 33.
66   Fromm, *The Nature of Man*, p. 16.
67   Ibid.

A. Love and its Works: The Brother and the Neighbor

For both thinkers, love must be manifested in its "works," hence Kierkegaard's idea that love is "known only by its revealing fruits"[68] and Fromm's insistence that the "art of loving" must be realized in *practice*[69] and that basic to this is "activity."[70]

In *The Fear of Freedom* Fromm, following Freud, notes the centrality of both love and work to human life. Indeed, he presents "the spontaneity of love and productive work"[71] as the only alternative to the kind of dangerous, identity-threatening escape mechanism exemplified by "automaton conformity." Love and productive work are the "foremost expressions" of the "spontaneous relationship to man and nature" that Fromm commends, "a relationship that connects the individual with the world without eliminating his individuality."[72] Fromm stresses the "supreme role of love" in the Christian world-view, and castigates Calvin—one of the figures who comes in for the most flak in Fromm's work[73]—for failing to recognize this, "in blatant contradiction to the New Testament."[74] Given the importance of love to Kierkegaard's thought—not only in *Works of Love* but throughout the *corpus*—this is one place at which one might have hoped for a more detailed engagement with Kierkegaard on Fromm's part. However, let us note some important links.

What is love, for Fromm? He denies that love is something "caused" by an object. Rather, it is "a lingering quality in a person which is only actualized by a certain 'object.' "[75] (That is, the object actualizes what is already there in potentiality, rather than being its efficient cause.) Love is a "passionate affirmation" of such an object; "an active striving and inner relatedness, the aim of which is the happiness, growth, and freedom of its object."[76] Interestingly, Fromm is suspicious of the Kierkegaardian idea that erotic love [*Elskov*] and friendship are "natural" (rooted in "drives and inclination"),[77] whereas universal love ("brotherly" love is the term Fromm tends to use for neighbor-love) is beyond what is merely natural. Fromm further glosses this "lingering quality" as "a readiness which, in principle, can turn to any person and object including ourselves."[78] Indeed, he claims that "exclusive love is a contradiction in itself."[79] The romantic myth of only one other we can love

---

68   *SKS* 9, 16 / *WL*, 8.

69   Fromm, *The Art of Loving*, Chapter 4, pp. 107–33.

70   Fromm, *The Art of Loving*, p. 128.

71   Fromm, *Escape from Freedom*, p. 23. (*The Fear of Freedom*, p. 18.)

72   Fromm, *Escape from Freedom*, p. 30. (*The Fear of Freedom*, p. 24.)

73   Both Luther and Calvin are described as being amongst the ranks of "the greatest haters" in history (ibid., p. 82), but Fromm finds Calvin's doctrine of predestination to be particularly repulsive. See especially ibid., pp. 76–8, as well as the criticism of Calvin in *Psychoanalysis and Religion*, pp. 35–6.

74   Fromm, *Escape from Freedom*, p. 88. (*The Fear of Freedom*, p. 75.)

75   Fromm, *Escape from Freedom*, p. 114. (*The Fear of Freedom*, p. 98.)

76   Ibid.

77   *SKS* 9, 51 / *WL*, 44.

78   Fromm, *Escape from Freedom*, p. 114. (*The Fear of Freedom*, pp. 98–9.)

79   Fromm, *Escape from Freedom*, p. 114. (*The Fear of Freedom*, p. 99.)

encourages a kind of love which is "not love but a sado-masochistic attachment."[80] Fromm asserts: "Love for one person implies love for man as such. Love for man as such is not...an abstraction coming 'after' the love for a specific person, or an enlargement of the experience with a specific 'object'; it is its premise, although, genetically, it is acquired in the contact with concrete individuals."[81] In other words, Fromm claims that brotherly love is the "most fundamental" type of love. On one level, this echoes Kierkegaard's idea that many varieties of love can be traced to a common point of origin: "Just as the quiet lake originates deep down in hidden springs no eye has ever seen, so also does a person's love originate more deeply in God's love. If there were no gushing spring at the bottom, if God were not love, then there would be neither the little lake nor a human being's love."[82] Yet on another level—the matter of God being the ultimate source of this love—the two thinkers are in profound disagreement.

A further similarity, however, is that Fromm echoes the concerns about selfishness and neediness that run through Kierkegaard's discussion of erotic love and friendship as forms of—often disguised—self-love. Contrasting love at its purest with love of one's flesh and blood, an animal for its young, and the child for the parents on whom he is dependent, Fromm claims: "Only in the love of those who do not serve a purpose, love begins to unfold."[83] But the conclusion that brotherly or neighbor-love is without purpose seems unwarranted. There are several such purposes that such love could serve. Clearly, if as Kierkegaard claims such love is a duty, then the "purpose" question is answered. But even outside such a view, one's sense of well-being or satisfaction may be served by acts or "works" of love. (Hence the fascinating but extremely complex question of the relationship between ostensibly "selfless" love and eudaimonism.[84]) Further, as Ilham Dilman has pointed out, Fromm's claim that such fundamental love is pure because it is without purpose is inconsistent with his earlier claim, central to the book, that love is "the answer to the problem of human existence."[85]

B. Self-Love

Both Fromm and Kierkegaard have interesting takes on self-love that draw our attention to what is either wrong or simplistic about the common tendency to equate self-love with selfishness. One of the claims for which *The Art of Loving* is best known is that one cannot properly love others until one loves oneself. This basic thought has become a banal cliché, but we shall see that what Fromm means by the

---

[80]   Fromm, *Escape from Freedom*, p. 115. (*The Fear of Freedom*, p. 99.)

[81]   Ibid.

[82]   *SKS* 9, 18 / *WL*, 9–10.

[83]   Fromm, *The Art of Loving*, p. 48.

[84]   And hence the exact meaning and import of Jesus' saying that "whosoever will save his life shall lose it, and whosoever will lose his life for my sake shall find it" (Matt 16:25).

[85]   See Fromm, *The Art of Loving*, p. 7. See also Ilham Dilman, *Love: Its Forms, Dimensions and Paradoxes*, Basingstoke and New York: Macmillan 1998, p. 129.

idea, and the role it plays in his thought, is both more interesting and more subtle than a contemporary reader might expect.

In *The Fear of Freedom*, Fromm noted an apparent paradox arising from the historical account he gives there: that Protestantism, with its official focus on sacrifice and asceticism, actually gives rise to a system—modern capitalism—marked by "an extreme degree of egotism and by the pursuit of self-interest."[86] Modern capitalist man has become "a servant to ends which were not his,"[87] and yet subjectively believes himself to be motivated by his own self-interest. This paradox requires us to look closely at "the psychological intricacies of the problem of selfishness."[88] It is here that Fromm directs at Luther, Calvin, Kant, and Freud a charge that has also (wrongly) been directed at Kierkegaard: that they assume selfishness and self-love to be one and the same.

As noted above, for Fromm the self is as much a proper object of love as any other.[89] This has implications for "the affirmation of my own life, happiness, growth, freedom."[90] If one possesses this "readiness," one possesses it in relation to oneself: "if he can only 'love' others, he cannot love at all."[91] It is from this basis that Fromm argues that self-love is something quite distinct from selfishness: indeed, he claims, selfishness is the very opposite of true self-love. For Fromm, selfishness is a kind of greediness, and greed is a "bottomless pit"[92] that can never be filled. The selfish person is consumed with a restless, never satisfied anxiety ultimately resulting from dissatisfaction with himself. Ditto the narcissist: according to Fromm, narcissism too is "an overcompensation for the basic lack of self-love."[93] Thus Freud is wrong when he claims that the narcissist has withdrawn love from others and directed it on to himself: according to Fromm, he loves neither others nor himself.[94] It is for this reason that Fromm claims that *"Selfishness and self-love, far from being identical, are actually opposites."*[95]

Fromm claims that psychological observation simply does not support the thesis that love for oneself and love for others stand in contradiction to each other.[96] But he has a more basic logical point, which parallels Kierkegaard's emphasis on the "as yourself" of the second love commandment. Fromm rejects Tillich's suggestion that the term "self-love" would be better replaced by a phrase such as "natural self-affirmation" or "paradoxical self-acceptance" on two grounds. First, the term "self-love," understood as a virtue rather than a vice,[97] very clearly expresses the idea that

---

[86]   Fromm, *Escape from Freedom*, p. 113. (*The Fear of Freedom*, p. 98.)

[87]   Ibid.

[88]   Fromm, *Escape from Freedom*, p. 114. (*The Fear of Freedom*, p. 98.)

[89]   But can I have such an apparently generic relation to myself? On this question Kierkegaard, in such works as *The Sickness unto Death* is arguably more probing than Fromm.

[90]   Fromm, *Escape from Freedom*, p. 115. (*The Fear of Freedom*, p. 99.)

[91]   Ibid.

[92]   Fromm, *Escape from Freedom*, p. 115. (*The Fear of Freedom*, p. 100.)

[93]   Fromm, *Escape from Freedom*, p. 116. (*The Fear of Freedom*, p. 100.)

[94]   Ibid.

[95]   Fromm, *The Art of Loving*, p. 60, emphasis in original.

[96]   Fromm, *The Art of Loving*, p. 59.

[97]   Fromm, *The Art of Loving*, p. 58.

"love is an attitude which is the same toward all objects, including myself";[98] "I am a human being too."[99] Second, the term has a history rooted precisely in the second biblical love commandment and the subsequent tradition.[100] Fromm understands the commandment to imply that "respect for one's own integrity and uniqueness, love for and understanding of one's own self, cannot be separated from respect and love and understanding for another individual. The love for my own self is inseparably connected with the love for any other being."[101] Ultimately, "an attitude of love towards themselves will be found in all those who are capable of loving others."[102]

So what of the original paradox? How can it be that modern man engages in behavior ultimately damaging to himself, while all the time believing that this is in his self-interest? Fromm's answer is that modern man acts in the interests of the *social* self, "a self which is constituted by the role the individual is supposed to play and which in reality is merely the subjective disguise for the objective social function of man in society."[103] (Recall our discussion of "automaton conformity" and the links with *Sickness* above.) *Selfishness in the modern world constitutes feeding the social self at the expense of frustrating the real self.*[104] This latter has been reduced to fragments—intellect and will power—to the exclusion of other parts of "the total personality." The undeniable mastery of nature that modern man has achieved has been accompanied by his becoming "estranged from the product of his own hands."[105] The world he has built—a world of factories, houses, mass-produced cars, and clothes—has become his master;[106] he has become an instrument for the purposes of the "machine" he has built. "He keeps up the illusion of being the centre of the world, and yet he is pervaded by an intense sense of insignificance and powerlessness which his ancestors once consciously felt towards God."[107] Thus, for Fromm, the general tenor of manipulation and instrumentality that pervades a society in which the laws of the market reign supreme applies also to the individual's relation to himself. Man "sells himself and feels himself to be a commodity."[108] This has profound impacts: a person's self-confidence becomes dependent upon what others think of him—his perceived value in the marketplace—and his self-esteem is dependent upon his popularity.[109] All of this is a very long way from true self-love.

In returning to this theme in *The Art of Loving*, Fromm wants to show his reader "that all his attempts for love are bound to fail, unless he tries most actively to develop his total personality...that satisfaction in individual love cannot be attained

98   Fromm, *The Art of Loving*, p. 57, note.
99   Fromm, *The Art of Loving*, p. 58.
100   Fromm, *The Art of Loving*, pp. 58–9.
101   Ibid.
102   Fromm, *The Art of Loving*, p. 59.
103   Fromm, *Escape from Freedom*, p. 117. (*The Fear of Freedom*, p. 101.)
104   Ibid.
105   Ibid.
106   Fromm, *Escape from Freedom*, p. 117. (*The Fear of Freedom*, p. 101.)
107   Fromm, *Escape from Freedom*, p. 118. (*The Fear of Freedom*, pp. 101–2.)
108   Fromm, *Escape from Freedom*, p. 119. (*The Fear of Freedom*, p. 103.)
109   Fromm, *Escape from Freedom*, pp. 119–20. (*The Fear of Freedom*, pp. 103–4.)

without the capacity to love one's neighbour, without true humility, courage, faith and discipline."[110]

The centrality of "character" to Fromm's thought, together with the idea that "maturity" is necessary to live well, leads to the thought that "the ability to love as an act of giving depends on the character development of the person."[111] This alone suggests that there is a kind of self-love (in the form of self-care) necessary properly to love others. The key concepts in this "character development" as well as care ("the active concern for the life and growth of that which we love"[112]) are responsibility (a voluntary act that is a response "to the needs, expressed or unexpressed, of another human being"[113]); respect (the non-exploitative concern that the other person "should grow and unfold as he is...for his own sake, and in his own ways, and not for the purpose of serving me";)[114] and knowledge (which includes the ability to see below the surface of the loved one, for example that her anger masks a deeper anxiety).[115] There are similarities with Kierkegaard, especially in *Works of Love*, in all of this.

Particularly worthy of note is Fromm's claim that respect for others is only possible if "*I* have achieved independence; if I can stand and walk without needing crutches, without having to dominate and exploit anyone else."[116] Here, then, is one concrete sense in which I can only love others if I (properly) love myself: if I have found myself sufficiently worthy to be a project on which I have done substantial ethical work. In other words, Fromm enables us to see the possibility not only that there can be a kind of self-love that is *acceptable* (because it is non-selfish), but that there are aspects of proper self-love and self-care that may actually be *necessary* in order to love others. ("If an individual...can love *only* others, he cannot love at all."[117])

Self-love is, of course, a key topic in *Works of Love*. As noted, Kierkegaard's valorization of non-preferential neighbor-love has often seen him accused of devaluing preferential love such as erotic love and friendship as merely "natural" or "pagan." I side with those numerous recent commentators (perhaps most prominent amongst them Jamie Ferreira) who have argued, against critics such as Adorno and Løgstrup,[118] that Kierkegaard is not dismissing erotic love and friendship *per se*.[119] But our focus here will be upon the claim that such preferential loves are actually disguised forms of self-love: "Just as self-love selfishly embraces this one and only

---

[110]   Fromm, *The Art of Loving*, p. xix.

[111]   Fromm, *The Art of Loving*, p. 26.

[112]   Ibid.

[113]   Fromm, *The Art of Loving*, p. 28.

[114]   Fromm, *The Art of Loving*, p. 28.

[115]   Fromm, *The Art of Loving*, p. 29.

[116]   Fromm, *The Art of Loving*, p. 28.

[117]   Fromm, *The Art of Loving*, p. 60.

[118]   Theodor W. Adorno, "On Kierkegaard's Doctrine of Love," *Studies in Philosophy and Social Science*, vol. 8, 1939–40, pp. 413–29; Knud Ejler Løgstrup, *The Ethical Demand*, ed. by Hans Fink and Alasdair MacIntyre, trans. by Theodor I. Jensen and Gary Puckering, Notre Dame: University of Notre Dame Press 1997.

[119]   M. Jamie Ferreira, *Love's Grateful Striving: A Commentary on Kierkegaard's Works of Love*, Oxford: Oxford University Press 2001.

self that makes it self-love, so also erotic love's passionate preference selfishly encircles this one and only beloved, and friendship's passionate preference encircles this one and only friend."[120] (On this point, compare Fromm: "If a person loves only one other person and is indifferent to the rest of his fellow men, his love is not love but a symbiotic attachment, or an enlarged egotism."[121]) Combine Kierkegaard's association of erotic love and friendship with self-love, and a further tendency in the secondary literature to conflate self-love with selfishness,[122] and we get the worry that Kierkegaard is claiming erotic love and friendship to be necessarily selfish. If this were Kierkegaard's position, small wonder it meets with resistance.

Yet as Ferreira notes, Kierkegaard makes an important distinction between "proper [*rette*]"[123] and "selfish"[124] forms of self-love. Consequently, she argues, we should read his attacks on self-love as typically assuming that it is the latter he has in mind.[125] Critics are mistaken to suppose that Kierkegaard believes the self-love involved in preferential love is necessarily selfish. Ferreira puts the point thus: "It is entirely possible that I could enjoy a relationship based on preference without ever actually being selfish, as long as I would in principle be willing to let another be the source of my preferred one's good if it were indeed better for my preferred one that this should happen."[126] Selfishness in preferential love-relationships, on this view, seems to amount to either ignoring the good of the other, or devaluing it in relation to my own good.

Several important points arise in relation to this debate. A full discussion of them would take us beyond the scope of this article, but let me briefly touch upon three. First, we should acknowledge that in *Works of Love* Kierkegaard is not as clear as he might be about respecting his own distinction between self-love *per se* and selfish (or otherwise "bad") self-love: he often uses the general term "self-love" to refer to the latter, more limited kind. Second, we have noted the tendency in the secondary literature to categorize this "bad" kind of self-love as "selfish." But for much of what we want to object to, "selfishness" is the wrong term. It does not seem to capture many of the examples Kierkegaard himself uses of "bad" self-love. None of "the bustler" who "wastes his time and powers in the service of futile, inconsequential pursuits"; "the light-minded person" who "throws himself almost like a nonentity into the folly of the moment"; "the depressed person" who "desires to be rid of life, indeed, of himself"; or the person who "surrenders to despair"[127] seem well described by the term "selfish." As I have argued elsewhere, an important distinction needs to be

---

[120]   *SKS* 9, 60 / *WL*, 53.

[121]   Fromm, *The Art of Loving*, p. 46.

[122]   See, for instance, Ferreira, *Love's Grateful Striving*, see especially p. 31 and Sylvia Walsh, *Living Christianly: Kierkegaard's Dialectic of Christian Existence*, University Park: Pennsylvania State University Press 2005, p. 79.

[123]   *SKS* 9, 20 / *WL*, 18.

[124]   *SKS* 9, 31 / *WL*, 23. *SKS* 9, 60 / *WL*, 53. *SKS* 9, 152 / *WL*, 151.

[125]   M. Jamie Ferreira, "The Problematic Agapeistic Ideal—Again," in *Ethics, Love and Faith in Kierkegaard*, ed. by Edward F. Mooney, Bloomington, Indiana: Indiana University Press 2008, p. 97.

[126]   Ibid., p. 100.

[127]   *SKS* 9, 30–1 / *WL*, 23.

made between selfishness and other vices of self-focus, such as self-centeredness.[128] In short, selfishness is only one of a number of vices of self-focus that proper self-love would need to avoid. Third, Ferreira's position above (and this is quite common amongst commentators) seems to be that I am being selfish unless I put the good of the other above my own good. But are there not circumstances in which this involves an inappropriate degree of self-sacrifice? One aspect of *Works of Love* that makes Kierkegaard's position less extreme than, say, Anders Nygren[129] is the strength of his emphasis on the "as yourself" of the love commandment: each of us can say of ourselves that "I am a neighbor too." We should be troubled by any account of self-love that effectively overlooks this. What we need to avoid is feeling—as arguably in Lévinas—perpetually held hostage by the other. Recent feminist theology is a particularly enlightening source of the idea that there are forms of self-sacrifice so extreme that by valorizing and following them, we fall into a variety of sin just as dangerous as that emanating from pride and self-aggrandizement.[130] And in so doing, we fail to see, as Richard Kearney memorably puts it, that "not every other is innocent and not every self is an egoistic emperor."[131]

With regard to the second point above, Fromm illustrates in two particularly memorable ways the importance of distinguishing between selfishness and self-centerdness. In *The Art of Loving*, he discusses "neurotic 'unselfishness' ":

> a symptom of neurosis observed in not a few people who usually are troubled not by this symptom, but by others connected with it, such as depression, tiredness, inability to work, failure in love relationships, and so on. Not only is unselfishness not felt as a "symptom"; it is often the one redeeming character trait on which such people pride themselves. The "unselfish" person "does not want anything for himself"; he "lives only for others," is proud that he does not consider himself important. He is puzzled to find that in spite of his unselfishness he is unhappy, and that his relationships to those close to him are unsatisfactory. Analytic work shows that his unselfishness is not something apart from his other symptoms but one of them, in fact often the most important one; that he is paralyzed in his capacity to love or enjoy anything; that he is pervaded by his hostility towards life and that *behind the facade of unselfishness a subtle but not less intense self-centredness is hidden*. This person can be cured only if his unselfishness too is interpreted as a symptom along with the others, so that his lack of productiveness, which is at the root of both his unselfishness *and* his other troubles, can be corrected.[132]

---

[128]   John Lippitt, "True Self-Love and True Self-Sacrifice," *International Journal for Philosophy of Religion*, vol. 66, 2009, pp. 125–38.

[129]   Anders Nygren, *Agape and Eros*, trans. by Philip Watson, New York and Evanston: Harper and Row 1969 [1953].

[130]   See, for instance, Valerie Saving Goldstein, "The Human Situation: A Feminine View," *Journal of Religion*, vol. 40, no. 2, 1960, pp. 100–12; Barbara Hilkert Andolsen, "*Agape* in feminist ethics," in *Feminist Theological Ethics: A Reader*, ed. by Lois K. Daly, Louisville, Kentucky: Westminster John Knox Press 1994, pp. 146–59; Erin Lothes Biviano, *The Paradox of Christian Sacrifice: The Loss of Self, the Gift of Self*, New York: Crossroad 2007.

[131]   Richard Kearney, *Strangers, Gods and Monsters*, London and New York: Routledge 2003, p. 67.

[132]   Fromm, *The Art of Loving*, pp. 61–2, first emphasis mine.

The effect of such "unselfishness" on others is damaging, particularly in such a mother on her children. Fromm claims that the children are adversely affected by the mother's "hidden hostility towards life…and eventually they become imbued with it themselves":[133] precisely the opposite of the mother's intentions.

Conversely—and this is the second illustration—surely the most extreme form of self-centerdness is narcissism. Fromm describes overcoming one's narcissism as "the main condition for the achievement of love."[134] Further, "The narcissistic orientation is one in which one experiences as real only that which exists within oneself, while the phenomena in the outside world have no reality in themselves, but are experienced only from the viewpoint of being useful or dangerous to one."[135] Narcissism's opposite, the desirable pole, is what Fromm calls "objectivity," though what he means is not that variety of objectivity to which Climacus takes exception, but simply "the faculty to see people and things *as they are*,"[136] rather than as distorted by one's own desires and fears. This gloss nicely echoes what Kierkegaard means when he talks about our duty to love the actual people that we see,[137] rather than reducing the other to the same (as Lévinas would put it). In Kierkegaard's words, the concern is as follows: "*in loving the actual individual person it is important that one does not substitute an imaginary idea of how we think or could wish that this person should be. The one who does this does not love the person he sees but again something unseen, his own idea or something similar.*"[138] But it is also important to note that Fromm connects his discussion of overcoming narcissism with an emphasis, echoing Kierkegaard, on the need to get beyond only preferential love: "I cannot be truly objective about my family if I cannot be objective about the stranger, and vice versa."[139]

Such non-preferential love, argues Fromm, requires objectivity (in the above sense), reason (the faculty to think objectively), and humility (the emotional attitude behind it). But all these—indeed the practice of the art of loving as a whole—are dependent upon the practice of what Fromm calls "rational faith."[140] He defines this as "not primarily belief in something, but the quality of certainty and firmness which our convictions have…a character trait pervading the whole personality."[141] As a humanist, Fromm's conception of faith obviously lacks the transcendental dimension of Kierkegaardian faith (see section V below), but for our purposes here, note that one important dimension of faith for Fromm is faith in an enduring self, and this faith in ourselves is for him an important dimension of self-love. Moreover, in parallel to love, "Only the person who has faith in himself is able to be faithful to others."[142] Readers of Kierkegaard will be well aware of the parallels between faith and love

---

[133]   Ibid., p. 62.
[134]   Ibid., p. 118.
[135]   Ibid.
[136]   Ibid.
[137]   *SKS* 9, 156–74 / *WL*, 154–74.
[138]   *SKS* 9, 162 / *WL*, 164, emphasis in original.
[139]   Fromm, *The Art of Loving*, p. 120.
[140]   Fromm, *The Art of Loving*, p. 121.
[141]   Ibid.
[142]   Fromm, *The Art of Loving*, p. 123.

that run throughout his work, so it is interesting in this respect to note that one of the culminating ideas of *The Art of Loving* is that love is an act of faith, and that "whoever is of little faith is also of little love."[143] The Kierkegaardian idea of faith as trusting risk—think of Climacus' 70,000 fathoms—is also present in Fromm's idea, present as a theme that frames *The Art of Loving*, that whereas most people's conscious fear is of not being loved, "*the real, though usually unconscious fear is that of loving*. To love means to commit oneself without guarantee, to give oneself completely in the hope that our love will produce love in the loved person."[144] It is in this sense, for Fromm, that love is an act of faith.

C. A Coda on Erotic Love

Alongside this goes a skepticism about the dangers of "erotic love" ("the craving for complete fusion, for union with one other person"[145]) that is in some sense more extreme than Kierkegaard's. After all, Kierkegaard does describe erotic love as "undeniably life's most beautiful happiness."[146] Fromm describes it as "perhaps the most deceptive form of love there is,"[147] in large part because the experience of such love is often confused with a naively romantic notion of "falling in love." But as Fromm notes, "After the stranger has become an intimately known person there are no more barriers to be overcome."[148] It is hard not to be reminded of Johannes the Seducer here. And Fromm is more explicit than Kierkegaard about the potentially misleading nature of sexual desire. Noting the association of love with sexual desire in the minds of most people, Fromm claims that they "are easily misled to conclude that they love each other when they want each other physically."[149] The following related thought seems decidedly Kierkegaardian: "If the desire for physical union is not stimulated by love, if erotic love is not also brotherly love, it never leads to union in more than an orgiastic, transitory sense."[150] Here we might recall the Seducer's last diary entry, expressing as it does something close to contempt for the object of his seductive project:

> now it is finished, and I never want to see her again. Once a girl has given away everything, she is weak, she has lost everything....I do not want to be reminded of my relationship with her; she has lost her fragrance...nothing is more revolting than the feminine tears and pleas that alter everything and yet are essentially meaningless. I did love her, but from now on she can no longer occupy my soul.[151]

---

143   Fromm, *The Art of Loving*, p. 128.
144   Fromm, *The Art of Loving*, p. 127, emphasis in original.
145   Fromm, *The Art of Loving*, pp. 52–3.
146   *SKS* 9, 266 / *WL*, 267.
147   Fromm, *The Art of Loving*, p. 53.
148   Ibid.
149   Fromm, *The Art of Loving*, p. 54.
150   Ibid.
151   *SKS* 2, 432 / *EO1*, 445.

Similarly, Fromm claims that the supposed union is nothing but an illusion: "without love this 'union' leaves strangers as far apart as they were before—sometimes it makes them ashamed of each other, because when the illusion has gone they feel their estrangement even more markedly than before."[152] In contrast to Freud, for whom tenderness was a sublimation of the sexual instinct, Fromm claims, "it is the direct outcome of brotherly love, and exists in physical as well as in non-physical forms of love."[153]

Fromm's discussion of exclusiveness in erotic love also warrants mention since it provides a possible gloss on what the controversial claim in *Works of Love* that the lover is "first and foremost the neighbor" might amount to. Fromm claims that exclusiveness, while often "possessive attachment," the kind of combined egoism which so troubles Kierkegaard, in which a couple simply "solve the problem of separateness by enlarging the single individual into two"[154]—does not *have* to mean that. Here is his alternative: "Erotic love is exclusive, but it loves in the other person all of mankind, all that is alive. It is exclusive only in the sense that I can fuse myself fully and intensely with one person only. Erotic love excludes the love for others only in the sense of erotic fusion, full commitment in all aspects of life—but not in the sense of deep brotherly love."[155]

Fromm adds another concern to Kierkegaard's worries about erotic love as preferential: the problems arising from capitalism. Since our whole culture is based upon "the idea of a mutually favourable exchange,"[156] this economic model is imported into romantic relationships. People look for a "good deal" in the relationships market, seeking out such commodities in a partner—toughness, sexiness, ambition, tolerance—as may be valued by the fashions of their society. "Two persons thus fall in love when they feel that they have found the best object available on the market, considering the limitations of their own exchange values. Often, as in buying real estate, the hidden potentialities which can be developed play a considerable role in this bargain."[157] This element is not so loud in Kierkegaard, though we might recall *Fear and Trembling*'s "frogs in life's swamp"—and the contempt in which the young lad holds them.[158]

V. Fromm and Kierkegaard: Some Key Differences

For all the points of contact between them, there are perhaps two major themes that divide Fromm and Kierkegaard on the matters here discussed. First, Fromm is far more centrally concerned with historical factors and underlying social structures

---

152   Fromm, *The Art of Loving*, pp. 54–5.
153   Fromm, *The Art of Loving*, p. 55.
154   Ibid.
155   Fromm, *The Art of Loving*, p. 55.
156   Fromm, *The Art of Loving*, p. 3.
157   Fromm, *The Art of Loving*, pp. 3–4.
158   *SKS* 4, 136 / *FT*, 41.

than is Kierkegaard.[159] Second, and more obviously, their views of religion are very different. In closing, let us consider each in turn.

Fromm's account of modern freedom grows out of an account of the collapse of the assumptions of the medieval world and the growth of Lutheranism and Calvinism. In this sense, his world-view has a significant overlap with that of Max Weber.[160] And whereas *Works of Love* seems to be addressing the individual reader, Fromm sees major social changes as necessary before genuine love can be more commonplace. He roots the problem of "aloneness" in capitalist society, and key ideas—such as the view of the self as a commodity to be packaged for others' approval—stem from this perspective. At the end of *The Art of Loving*, he insists: "Those who are seriously concerned with love as the only rational answer to the problem of human existence must, then, arrive at the conclusion that important and radical changes in our social structure are necessary, if love is to become a social and not a highly individualistic, marginal phenomenon."[161]

As to religion, while descended from a long line of rabbis and fascinated with religious questions—his doctoral dissertation was on the social-psychological function of the law in the community life of diaspora Jews—Fromm's views on religion are often excessively sweeping and somewhat dismissive. In *The Fear of Freedom*, religion seems to be treated as of at best instrumental value when Fromm lists it amongst those things (nationalism being another) that are "refuges from what man dreads most: isolation."[162] One is reminded here of Freud's reductionist view of religion as psychological consolation.[163] The section on "love of God" in *The Art of Loving* involves a very broad-brush account of matriarchal and patriarchal, Eastern and Western, forms of religion in which the influence of Freud still seems too prevalent. In effectively ranking religions in a hierarchy, Fromm indulges, like his erstwhile mentor, in a high degree of psychological over-generalization. Moreover, consider this summary of his view of freedom: "Positive freedom...implies the principle that there is no higher power than this unique individual self, that man is the centre and purpose of his life; that the growth and realization of man's individuality is an end that can never be subordinated to purposes which are supposed to have greater dignity."[164] Hardly a view that Kierkegaard, with his resolute emphasis on our creatureliness and radical dependence upon God, could accept. While in

---

[159]   Recall his comparison of Marx and Kierkegaard in Section II.

[160]   Max Weber, *The Protestant Ethic and the Spirit of Capitalism*, London: Routledge 2001 [1930]. Though for Fromm's attempt to distinguish his position from Weber's; see Fromm, *Escape from Freedom*, pp. 296–7 (*The Fear of Freedom*, pp. 251–2).

[161]   Fromm, *The Art of Loving*, p. 132. Fromm develops this theme in more detail in his *The Sane Society*.

[162]   Fromm, *Escape from Freedom*, p. 20 (*The Fear of Freedom*, p. 15).

[163]   See Sigmund Freud, *The Standard Edition of the Complete Psychological Works of Sigmund Freud*, vols. 1–24, ed. and trans. by James Strachey, London: Hogarth Press 1953–74, see especially "Obsessive Actions and Religious Practices," vol. 9 (1907), pp. 115–28; *Totem and Taboo*, in vol. 13 (1913), pp. 1–162; *The Future of an Illusion*, in vol. 21 (1927), pp. 3–58; *Civilization and its Discontents*, in vol. 21 (1930), pp. 59–214; and *Moses and Monotheism*, in vol. 23 (1939), pp. 7–137.

[164]   Fromm, *Escape from Freedom*, p. 265 (*The Fear of Freedom*, p. 228).

Psychoanalysis and Religion Fromm recognizes the importance of religion—"there is no one without a religious need, a need to have a frame of orientation and an object of devotion"[165]—he relies upon a distinction between "authoritarian" and "humanistic" religion that has been much criticized as excessively simplistic.[166] Authoritarian religion involves "recognition on the part of man of some higher unseen power as having control of his destiny, and as being entitled to obedience, reverence, and worship."[167] The essence of such a view, for Fromm, is "despising everything in oneself."[168] By contrast, "humanistic" religion is "centred around man and his strength."[169] In theistic forms of such religion, God is "a symbol of *man's own powers*."[170] Fromm includes the teachings of Jesus here,[171] though his justification for doing so is rather thin.[172] In his discussion of dependence, Fromm says:

> [I]t is one thing to recognise one's dependence and limitations, and it is something entirely different to indulge in this dependence, to worship the forces on which one depends. To understand realistically and soberly how limited is our power is an essential part of wisdom and maturity; to worship it is masochistic and self-destructive. The one is humility, the other self-humiliation.[173]

But there is more assertion than argument in Fromm's claim that worship is necessarily masochistic. James W. Jones suggests that we need the distinction between "submission" and "surrender" argued for by Emmanuel Ghent.[174] What Fromm describes above counts as the former, but "surrender…involves the choice to give oneself over to a powerful aesthetic, romantic, or spiritual experience" and as such "is an essential aspect of any transforming experience."[175] The inability to do so "might itself be regarded as psychologically problematic."[176]

To be fair to Fromm, we should acknowledge that some of Kierkegaard's more extreme claims in valorizing self-denial do seem to fall foul of a problem Fromm might help us to diagnose.[177] Ultimately, though, Anti-Climacus' essentially

---

[165]   Fromm, *Psychoanalysis and Religion*, p. 25.

[166]   To be fair to Fromm, he does say that this is "only one distinction"—but nevertheless "one which in my opinion is the most important." See Fromm, *Psychoanalysis and Religion*, p. 34.

[167]   Ibid., p. 34.

[168]   Ibid., p. 36. Calvin in particular once again comes in for particular criticism here.

[169]   Ibid., p. 37.

[170]   Ibid.

[171]   Ibid.

[172]   Ibid., pp. 48–9.

[173]   Ibid., p. 53.

[174]   Emmanuel Ghent, "Masochism, submission and surrender," *Contemporary Psychoanalysis*, vol. 24, 1990, pp. 108–36; cited in Jones, *Terror and Transformation*, p. 67.

[175]   Ibid.

[176]   Ibid.

[177]   Consider for instance the claims that to be truly Christian, self-denial must involve rejection by "the world": "all denial that finds support in the world is not Christian self-denial." See *SKS* 9, 195 / *WL*, 196. In places, Kierkegaard seems to come dangerously close to valorising self-denial purely for its own sake, a view that might not unreasonably be charged

Augustinian focus on "resting transparently in the power that created" us betokens a very different view of our dependence to that of Fromm. And for all his praise for certain varieties of religion and the interesting points of contact between our two thinkers, it seems likely that Kierkegaard would suspect that ultimately there is a God-shaped hole in Fromm's thought.

---

with spiritual masochism. For more on this, see John Lippitt, " 'Love's Blank Checks': Frankfurt, Kierkegaard, Self-Love and Self-Denial," in *Living Reasonably, Loving Well: Conversing with Frankfurt and Kierkegaard*, ed. by Myron Penner and Søren Landkildehus, Bloomington, Indiana: Indiana University Press, forthcoming.

Bibliography

I. References to or Uses of Kierkegaard in Fromm's Corpus

Escape from Freedom, New York: Rinehart & Co. 1941, p. 133 (published in the UK and other parts of the English-speaking world as *The Fear of Freedom*, London: Routledge and Kegan Paul 1942, p. 114).

Psychoanalysis and Religion, New Haven, Connecticut: Yale University Press 1950, p. 5.

Sigmund Freud's Mission: An Analysis of His Personality and Influence, New York: Harper and Row 1959, p. 116.

Marx's Concept of Man, New York: Frederick Ungar 1961, p. v; pp. 46–7; p. 72.

Beyond the Chains of Illusion: My Encounter with Marx and Freud, New York: Simon and Schuster 1962, p. 56; p. 59.

"Humanism and Psychoanalysis," *Contemporary Psychoanalysis*, vol. 1, no. 1, 1964, pp. 69–79, see p. 71.

The Nature of Man, ed. by Erich Fromm and Ramon Xirau, New York: Macmillan 1968, pp. 225–30.

"The Dialectic Revision of Psychoanalysis," in his *The Revision of Psychoanalysis*, ed. by Rainer Funk, Boulder: Westview Press 1992, pp. 11–80; see p. 61.

The Art of Being, New York: Continuum 1992 (published posthumously), p. 31, note.

II. Sources of Fromm's Knowledge of Kierkegaard

Collins, James Charles, *The Mind of Kierkegaard*, Chicago: Regnery 1953.

Jaspers, Karl, *Reason and Existenz*, trans. by William Earle, New York: Noonday Press 1957, pp. 19–50; p. 51; p. 64; pp. 127–30; p. 133; p. 135; p. 137; p. 143.

Kierkegaard, Søren, *The Concept of Dread*, trans. by Walter Lowrie, London: Oxford University Press 1944.

— *A Kierkegaard Anthology*, ed. by Robert Bretall, Princeton, New Jersey: Princeton University Press 1946.

— *Religion der Tat. Sein Werk in Auswahl*, ed. by Eduard Geismar, Stuttgart: Alfred Kröner Verlag 1948 [1930].

— *Journals*, trans. by Alexander Dru, New York: Oxford University Press 1951.

— *Either/Or*, vols. 1–2, trans. by David F. Swenson, Lillian Marvin Swenson, and Walter Lowrie, Princeton, New Jersey: Princeton University Press 1959.

Lowrie, Walter, *Kierkegaard*, vols. 1–2, New York: Harper 1962.

Price, George Henry, *The Narrow Pass: A Study of Kierkegaard's Concept of Man*, New York: McGraw-Hill 1963.

Wahl, Jean, *Études kierkegaardiennes*, Paris: Aubier 1938.

III. Secondary Literature on Fromm's Relation to Kierkegaard

Koskinen, Lennart, *Søren Kierkegaard och existentialismen—om tiden, varat och evigheten*, Nora: Nya Doxa 1994, p. 93.

Anthony Giddens:
Kierkegaard and the Risk of Existence

Søren Landkildehus

As an unperfect actor on the stage,
Who with his fear is put beside his part,
Or some fierce thing replete with too much rage,
Whose strength's abundance weakens his own heart;
So I, for fear of trust forget to say
The perfect ceremony of love's rite…

Shakespeare, Sonnet 23.

I. Overture

Anthony Giddens (b. 1938) is a strong voice in British sociology. Connecting insights from a broad spectrum of other thinkers he has managed to give birth to a popularization of key modern sociological terms. In the following, I trace the influence of Kierkegaard's thought on Giddens' treatment of the self and society in *Modernity and Self-Identity*.[1] Giddens mentions Kierkegaard explicitly only a few times. The aim of the present work is to track parallels which might indicate a more thorough-going inheritance than acknowledged in Giddens' exploitation of Kierkegaard's thought. This is done, however, with caution since what might look like unacknowledged inheritance is a representation of a conglomerate of ideas, which for all its striking similarities does not allow the critic to draw any conclusion.

The core idea that guides the rehearsal of the thoughts and representations which respectively Kierkegaard and Giddens have published, is *mise-en-scène* as the interplay between the concepts of crisis, reflexivity, and self. There are different takes on the status of this interplay. For Kierkegaard the interplay is normatively tragic. The risks of existence are the pain of abandonment and the perdition of despair.[2] For Kierkegaard, the ethical task for a human being is to transcend the isolation of modernity.[3] This transcendence involves faith and a holism of the spiritual. Thus, Kierkegaard's normative claim will be construed as tragic *repentance* for the loss of existential composure. For Giddens the interplay is descriptively tragic. The risks

---

[1]   Anthony Giddens, *Modernity and Self-Identity*, Cambridge: Polity Press 1991.
[2]   See *SKS* 2, 147 / *EO1*, 147. *SKS* 11, 131 / *SUD*, 15.
[3]   *SKS* 4, 355 / *CA*, 50.

of existence are societal structures which, intertwined, are the results of modernity. The increased reflexive nature of social existence leads to dilemmas of trust, risk-assessment, and self-fashioning. For Giddens, part of what enables coping with the anxieties of modernity is therapy, that is, what counters dilemmas of reflexivity is self-reflexivity. Thus, rather than questioning or revising the need for reflexivity, the descriptive tragic maps the *pain* of our current existential posture.

In what follows, I shall elaborate on the parallels of these two tragic takes on social existence. Although Kierkegaard has been criticized for lacking a social dimension in his thinking, the present work does not need to rely on such a dimension to sketch the contours of individual social existence. In one sense, Kierkegaard's tragic pain is that sociality is represented at various stages and in various guises as the community of the dead.[4] Consequently, Kierkegaard is a victim of modernity as an author of existential experiments where individuals *fail to connect* (to recall E.M. Forster's fateful epigram to *Howards End* in its negative form) and as an ordinary human being whose journals vividly describe an almost unendurable isolation.

II. Curtains: "The Crisis and A Crisis in the Life of an Actress"

In this section, I am going to track the idea of crisis as it appears in Giddens' *Modernity and Self-Identity* in parallel to the idea of crisis in Kierkegaard's piece on theater criticism, "The Crisis and a Crisis in the Life of an Actress." The in-between, as it were, of the parallels is a consideration of what might be considered a synoptic view on the modern individual, when seen refracted from the two thinkers. In the terminology of the theater, crisis is the point at which some dramatic conflict has reached its pinnacle, after which there can be some resolution. The normatively tragic claim is that such resolution can come about only through radical change, whereas the descriptively tragic claim involves coping with the fact that after one crisis is overcome a new build-up awaits.

A. Crises of High Modernity

"A 'crisis' exists whenever activities concerned with important goals in the life of an individual or collectivity suddenly appear inadequate."[5] Giddens characterizes High Modernity, which is what he calls our present age, as "replete with risks and dangers," a characterization which is aptly captured by the term "crisis."[6] We live, according to Giddens, in a culture of risk where rapid transformations disable means of future risk assessment.[7] The highly modern man is subject to crisis as a "more

---

4   *SKS* 9, 339–52 / *WL*, 345–58. Cf. also Hugh S. Pyper, "Cities of the Dead: the Relation of Person and Polis in Kierkegaard's *Works of Love*," in *Kierkegaard: The Self in Society*, ed. by George Pattison and Steven Shakespeare, Basingstoke: Macmillan Press 1998, pp. 125–38.
5   Giddens, *Modernity and Self-Identity*, p. 184.
6   Ibid., p. 12.
7   Ibid., p. 28.

or less continuous state of affairs,"[8] which means that the activities modern man instigates to achieve some goal may turn out to be inadequate.

Although modernity introduces the means by which many risks may be countered, that is, through mass-produced structures, organizations, and strategies, new risks are introduced due to the global nature of modern societies. Whereas we are dealing with basic risks of survival through urbanization and sanitation, new risks are introduced which face us in the new millennium, and which stem from global consumerism. Thus, just as we thought we could navigate knowledgeably providing shelter and food, global climate changes may threaten this navigability, which is taken for granted.

In Giddens' vocabulary, abstract systems such as symbolic tokens (for example, money) and expert systems (for example, banks) are *disembedding mechanisms*, which each in their own way separates time and space for social experience. Money challenges our understanding of time by being a means of credit, which means that the time of actual payment may be stretched over a lifetime; thus the reality of reckoning and transaction may be disembedded from *inter-human* social settings. Money challenges our sense of space in virtue of being a means of standard payment, which means that we may pay without being in close proximity to the recipient; thus the reality of someone reckoning or transacting with someone else is spatially disembedded.[9] Expert systems disembed our sense time and space by the very fact of monopolizing technical knowledge to which ordinary beings must have recourse in order to complete, for example, a financial transaction. According to Giddens, expert systems have colonized many of our social needs, such that reckoning with the state of our health, our loved ones, and even ourselves must be routed through someone with expert knowledge.[10]

When *bouleversement* such as the global financial meltdown of late 2008 happens, "crisis" describes when a collectivity does not have adequate means to achieve a goal, which here is sustaining growth. However, in any situation of crisis the main coping strategy is re-establishing *ontological security*, which is a sense of continuity in events, through the means of trust. Trust operates as a means by which we may face up to loss, and it generates efforts.[11] I shall return to trust later on, for now the idea is that coping with a crisis such as global financial meltdown involves trusting and facing the loss of the knowledge which had hitherto sustained the assessments of risks on the financial markets.

The upshot is that modernity is a setting in which, although the individual has access to knowledge, the *use-by date* of that knowledge is indefinite. The degrees to which this is an apt description of our time more than a general description of any hyper-capitalist society (compare Dickens' *Little Dorrit*, or Trollope's *The Way We Live Now*), would depend on other analyses than the feature of modernity, which is as old as modernity, namely, what one might call the separation of the mind-body through the disembedding mechanisms of doubt and individuality. For Giddens, the

8   Ibid., p. 12.
9   Ibid., p. 18.
10   Ibid.
11   Ibid., p. 41.

difference between modernity and High Modernity is that enduring the latter will see the individual set in a constructed locale of existence constituted by the media through which non-proximate events will have a proximate impact on individual lives. As a consequence, someone living in Denmark may listen to a podcast from Canada about the wildfires in Australia, which might induce the individual to donate money to reconstruction efforts. Perhaps the individual will decide not to donate money, but the issues are brought close enough that making decisions or taking action is pertinent. Qua individual, each one of us is disembedded from any particular sociality, but we belong to a globality where other societies representing "home" can substitute the one in which we are physically present.

In Ernst Cassirer's (1874–1945) *An Essay on Man*, the perspective on what crisis amounts to concerns the "complete anarchy of thought" which rules the "modern theory of man."[12] The crisis of modern man's ability to know (hereafter *knowledgeability*) is that expert systems abound to such a degree that no single human being needs to know anything further than where to search for answers. Cassirer bemoans the loss of an intellectual center for human *knowledgeability*, but the kind of *deskilling* (a concept Giddens coins to describe this loss)[13] that is implied in the gradual transfer of power to expert systems, does not, according to Giddens, mean loss of power.[14] High modern man acquires new skills as required by the prevalent social structures. As an example, the general loss of classical knowledge in modern-day Europe does not entail a loss of people's *knowledgeability* regarding the classics, rather the means of acquisition has changed, and so the phenomenal expression of classical knowledge has changed. Whereas once the ability to know the classics consisted in being well-read, the same ability now consists in knowing which search-engine to use, for the high modern individual *reskilling* ("the reacquisition of knowledge and skills")[15] is always an option.[16] However, Cassirer would not have been satisfied with this. What for High Modernity is a change in how to navigate the expert systems, is for Cassirer a change in the nature of the ability to navigate. The very ability to make informed choices requires the kind of intellectual center, which would be the result of pre-high modern *Bildung*. Consequently, for both Giddens and Cassirer "crisis" denotes a specific situation of an individual.[17]

Understanding the individual in crisis does not, according to Giddens, require "us to resort to an arcane philosophical anthropology," but rather the socio-psychological structures of high modern man seem to reveal both the means by which crises are perpetuated and how to achieve successful coping strategies.[18] But where such strategies as trust are concerned it remains unclear to what extent Giddens is merely arbitrarily borrowing without acknowledging from Niklas Luhmann (1927–98),

---

[12]   Ernst Cassirer, *An Essay on Man: An Introduction to a Philosophy of Human Culture*, New Haven, Connecticut: Yale University Press 1944, p. 21.
[13]   See Giddens, *Modernity and Self-Identity*, p. 22.
[14]   Ibid., pp. 137–9.
[15]   Ibid., p. 7.
[16]   Ibid., p. 141.
[17]   Cf. the discussion of Cassirer's "crisis" in Steve G. Lofts, *Ernst Cassirer: A "Repetition of Modernity,"* Albany: State University of New York Press 2000, pp. 23–34.
[18]   Giddens, *Modernity and Self-Identity*, p. 41.

or to what extent generally available criteria can determine which analysis of trust we accept.[19] Cassirer, on the other hand, would point to the need for philosophical anthropology as crucial for navigating at all. It is in understanding man as playing an originating factor in the structures of modernity that we may learn how and why these structures are not harmonically calibrated. However, if we are wary of such anthropological slogans as ζῷον πολιτικόν or *animal rationale*, then Cassirer's *animal symbolicum* will be profoundly unsatisfying. The reduction of politics, rationality, and communication to "the animal" is in point of fact the sort of disembedding mechanism, which individuality perpetrates. In one sense, which I shall return to later on, sociality is not a structure of the individual, but rather the other way round, which would imply that communication, politics, and rationality are not instantiated by individuals. Individuals are instantiated by communication, politics, and rationality: in speaking, being with others, and thinking, I am individualized. However, being individualized enables influencing sociality partly by creatively reskilling, for example, to communicate, and partly through creating the expert systems that will handle communication, politics, and rationality or help reskilling individuals.

B. A Synoptic View of the Modern Individual and His Audience

The "I" of Giddens' High Modernity is an "actor [who] must maintain constant vigilance in order to be able to 'go on' in social life…maintaining habits and routines is a crucial bulwark against threatening anxieties, yet by that very token it is a tensionful phenomenon in and of itself."[20] Without drawing too strong of a parallel, the *actor* on the stage of social performance contains many of the *aesthetic-metaphysical* dialectic movements which are present in Kierkegaard's critique of actresses in "The Crisis and a Crisis in the Life of an Actress." The occasion for Kierkegaard's piece is Johanne Luise Heiberg's (1812–90) repeat performance of her debut role as Shakespeare's Juliet. There was a gap of 17 years between the two performances, and Kierkegaard's interest is in the clash between the outward demands of the role, viz. youthfulness, and the inward demands of the role, viz. character. Kierkegaard's argument is that Heiberg in the repeat performance displays the outward demands in virtue of her mastery of expressing the inward demands.

An actress, Kierkegaard says, possesses various indefinite qualities which dialectically determine the relationship between the individual actress and *the audience*, which is Kierkegaard's preferred notion for the social world.[21] First, to a certain degree an actress must possess luck.[22] With her various sleights of hand, tosses of the head, her walk, her voice, and her gestures (to name a few of what Kierkegaard lists), the actress must have luck on her side to come across as a competent representation of what she enacts. Naturally, there is skill at play when

---

[19]   See Nils Mortensen's introduction to Niklas Luhmann, *Tillid–en mekanisme til reduktion af social kompleksitet*, Copenhagen: Hans Reitzels Forlag 1999, p. 9.
[20]   Giddens, *Modernity and Self-Identity*, p. 39.
[21]   See *SKS* 8, 86–7 / *TA*, 90.
[22]   *SKS* 14, 96 / *C*, 308.

controlling the environment for acting out some character; the actress is schooled in the many intricate and indefinite ways to make the appropriate impression.[23] However, luck as a dialectical movement determines both the skill of the actress and the skill of the critic (others, sociality, etc.). For the high modern actor "going on" in social life is a hyper-real theatrical performance, the histrionics of which depend on bodily control.[24] Luck and the manipulation of fortuitous events are crucial determinants of how well one comes across to the audience of social life.

Secondly, an actress must have the quality of being able to "go on," which Kierkegaard discusses in terms of restlessness. The actress "goes on" without haste, accidents, or stress, because restlessness is that by which she reveals animation, motivation, and joy, that is, to say a youthful restlessness.[25] Such "light" restlessness is a means by which the actress may skirt the insecurities that would threaten to induce her to make haste, to make unmotivated errors, and to betray that she is unhappy, that is, the shadowy side of restlessness. The ability to pull off "going on" produces in the audience a "calmness" with an accompanying forbearance, because there is a flow to the activities. The restless youthfulness of animation, motivation, and joy is immediately appealing, whereas the shadowy restlessness is disturbing. Thus, when Giddens describes the phenomenon of the social performance, which implies a division between self-identity and performing in social contexts, he warns of those who come to realize that the flow of their activities is "put on or false."[26] The high modern actor on the global scene may lose sight of the flow of his activities and develop serious dissociative traits.

Thirdly, an actress needs to embody the thoughts and ideas of the play. According to Kierkegaard, the capacity of doing this is *expressiveness of soul*: the actress gives soul to the words of the play, in such a way as to not only take "the author's words correctly from his mouth, but she gives them back to him...in the co-knowledge of ingeniousness."[27] Thus, the actress "relates herself soulfully to the author's words, but she relates herself to herself in the something more that very properly may be called resonance in relation to the lines and consonance in relation to the whole character."[28] Whereas Kierkegaard is conscious of his errand as a theater critic, the characterization of what it means "to give soul" to scripted words can be transferred to the case of social norms and the subconscious dramas. As such Kierkegaard's actress is not an unsuitable parallel to Giddens' understanding of the self as narrator.[29] In manifold ways, the explicit communication of the self as a coherent narrative takes the words from the author's mouth and returns them to him. Understood in this way, self-narrative is a highly reflexive and continuous project.[30] (As an aside, the analysis of the Ratman case by Jonathan Lear would suggest that acting out

---

23   *SKS* 14, 99–100 / *C*, 313.
24   Giddens, *Modernity and Self-Identity*, pp. 56–7.
25   *SKS* 14, 97 / *C*, 309.
26   Giddens, *Modernity and Self-Identity*, p. 58.
27   *SKS* 14, 98–9 / *C*, 312.
28   *SKS* 14, 98 / *C*, 311–12.
29   Giddens, *Modernity and Self-Identity*, p. 76.
30   Ibid., pp. 75–6.

of character involves a kind of cognitive dissemblance, which may indicate that there is more to the story of what makes a harmonious actor in High Modernity than reliance on societal trust.[31]) The high modern actor is simultaneously the author and the performer of his own drama, with the caveat, naturally, that this authorship always already presupposes embeddedness in sociality.

Fourthly, the actress must possess "the proper rapport with onstage tension."[32] The burden of being staged, as it were, requires coping strategies which turn the tension to lightness. Thus, the actress might be anxious in the wings, "but onstage she is happy and light as a bird."[33] In the wings, or at rehearsal anxiety might show up, but Kierkegaard remarks that this is to be understood as elasticity: with the correct tension anxiety is an intensification.[34] Of course, this imagery invites thoughts of tensions so intense as to snap the elasticity of the individual, or thoughts of lack of tensions so profound as to render the elasticity of the individual too slack (essentially two common manifestations of stress). Viewing it through Giddens' terms, the "proper rapport with onstage tension" would be the routines of ontological security which manage bouts of anxiety. In cases where anxiety threatens self-identity, the rehearsed routines of social interaction may help to relieve the individual from the discomfort of anxiety. For the high modern actor, however, being in the wings is being onstage too. Consequently, it would be hard to distinguish when anxiety is a helpful elasticity for a pending performance, and when it is wrecking the *career* of a performing actor as a social being.

I have attempted to draw attention to the feature of modern life which increasingly determines the worth of the individual in relation to an audience. In this respect, I have found useful Kierkegaard's list of important attributes of an actress. The parallel transcends the works of both authors, since Kierkegaard's *aesthetic-metaphysical* considerations form part of theater criticism, whereas Giddens offers a study of the effects of modernity on self-identity in the age of High Modernity. The space *inbetween* allows us to view modern man as essentially captured by the *aesthetic-metaphysical* dialectic which renders individuals as actors (in all the multifariousness of sense that the word "actors" may carry) and the social order as audience to individual performances. The twist of High Modernity introduces a sort of rapid oscillation between being an actor and being part of the audience, where, given that the oscillation has high enough frequency, the two roles are indistinguishable. Nevertheless, part of Kierkegaard's errand when listing the attributes of an accomplished actress is to stage the possible kinds of development available: Kierkegaard's interest is in what he calls *metamorphosis*.

---

[31]   Jonathan Lear, *Open Minded: Working out the Logic of the Soul*, Cambridge, Massachusetts: Harvard University Press 1999, pp. 80–122.

[32]   *SKS* 14, 99 / *C*, 312.

[33]   Ibid.

[34]   *SKS* 14, 99 / *C*, 313.

C. The Metamorphoses of Performance

Throughout Kierkegaard's authorship the enigmatic word *metamorphosis* occurs at crucial junctures. In the discussion of Mozart, metamorphosis is declared a "better word" for "stages" in connection with the immediate erotic stage, since each of them represents a *transformative* revelation about what the immediate stage is.[35] For Judge William, metamorphosis is what happens in the movements of the spirit, and which reveals the heavy-mindedness that prevents individual transparency, and which, by its presence, indicates the possibility of becoming spiritually determined.[36] Johannes Climacus mentions briefly that in nature "there is no analogy to a human being's metamorphosis of development insofar as he undergoes the highest development: to subject himself to the absolute qualification of spirit."[37] Anti-Climacus remarks that the kind of despair which relates to something earthly might become stuck with the earthliness, and thus there is no "metamorphosis in which consciousness of eternity of the self breaks through, so that the fight could begin, which either intensifies despair to a higher form, or leads to faith."[38] As a result, metamorphosis indicates throughout the authorship an event of change, which however, may take different guises that we can paraphrase in the following manner: (1) Metamorphosis is transformation within a stage; thus the aesthetic as a stage can undergo various intensified changes in mood. (2) Metamorphosis is transformation between stages; thus change in awareness allows a critical stance on the aesthetic and/or the ethical. (3) Metamorphosis is transformation of the self; thus there is a possibility of transcendence. The crisis of an actress is a metamorphosis in two ways. Kierkegaard's usage of the term "crisis" refers to the original Greek meaning, that is, "turning point," which is used both in theater and in medicine when talking about breaking fevers. The turning point of an actress is, according to Kierkegaard, either the ingenious turn towards originality, which expresses the ideal, or the steady progress to roles which are congruent with the advancement in outward change.[39] Kierkegaard adds that the latter will interest an ethicist, because of the straightforward "perfectibility" of the development, whereas the former will interest the aesthetician, because the transformation expresses the ideal in its ideality.[40]

In Giddens' terms, a crisis is when a mismatch exists between actions and goals of some individual or collective, so that there is inadequacy of resources to obtain a desired end. This sense of crisis allows us to understand metamorphosis as a requirement in order to cope with various strains, risks, and anxieties.[41] Event by event the high modern actor is transformed to adapt to the rapid changes of the social

---

[35]   *SKS* 2, 80 / *EO1*, 73–4.

[36]   *SKS* 3, 184 / *EO2*, 189.

[37]   *SKS* 7, 503 / *CUP1*, 553.

[38]   *SKS* 11, 174 / *SUD*, 553.

[39]   *SKS* 14, 104–7 / *C*, 319–24.

[40]   Ibid.

[41]   The kind of metamorphosis Giddens would allow and the kinds Kierkegaard employs are essentially of different *sorts*. Metamorphosis is never instrumental in Kierkegaard's understanding, and thus not a form of coping strategy. I am grateful to Kirsten Klercke for alerting me to this.

world. In short, the high modern actor must continually undergo maturation, which requires creative skills on the part of the actor.[42]

The mirroring, I have provided here, sees Giddens' sociological study of the high modern actor dressed in theatrical terms and Kierkegaard's theatrical study of the actress Johanne Luise Heiberg expressing components of a sociological study. The question ought to be how well *such* a method of reading inheritances brings about worthwhile views of what might be considered the sources of some line of thought. The comparison of crises in Giddens and Kierkegaard should make us aware that, *given* that Giddens has read Kierkegaard, various trails of thought are likely to acquire a parallel reflection by which the reader may be led to speculate about a larger inheritance than acknowledged. The extent to which that would be a reasonable claim is not to be tested here.

III. The Present Stage: the Inbetween of Anxiety, Reflection, and Trust

The tragic interplay between crisis, reflexivity, and the self was said to have two forms which were either normative or descriptive, the positions of Kierkegaard and Giddens respectively. Normatively, the tragic sets a task for the individual for which he must take responsibility: the metamorphosis of the self. Descriptively, the tragic delineates the condition within which the individual finds himself thrown, to use Heidegger's term. Whereas the former includes the latter, the latter does not entail the former. In this section, I focus on the tragic nature of the interplay. Giddens relies on a description of anxiety as a fundamental phenomenon in the constitution of the self of High Modernity, and as such it is here we find direct acknowledgments of Kierkegaard.

A. Questioning Anxiety

Since Kierkegaard's groundbreaking work, analyses of anxiety have played a major part of explaining a fundamental feeling of being at odds with the reality within which we find ourselves. But whereas anxiety in Kierkegaard is a disease of freedom, in Freud a manifestation of repressed sexuality, in Heidegger a feature of the potential for authentic life, it is in Giddens a combination of these different conceptions.[43] Giddens' specific use of Kierkegaard is in framing what Giddens calls *existential questions* of which there are four categories: questions about *existence* as such, *human life, other persons*, and finally *self-identity*.

Giddens adds to Kierkegaard's analysis of anxiety in terms of freedom, according to which as a "phenomenon, anxiety derives from the capacity—and indeed, necessity—for the individual to think ahead, to anticipate future possibilities counterfactually in relation to present action."[44] However, more fundamentally, anxiety springs from the "very 'faith' in the independent existence of persons and

---

[42]   Giddens, *Modernity and Self-Identity*, p. 41.

[43]   Ibid., pp. 47–55.

[44]   Ibid.

objects that ontological security implies."[45] Thus, the first category of existential questions is about the awareness of beings, which according to Giddens is about activities: "in 'doing' everyday life" individuals answer the question about existence.[46] Anxiety is the fact of becoming aware of there being questions to answer, which are "lodged fundamentally on the level of behaviour."[47] In this sense, the discussion Kierkegaard carries out about Adam's leap of awareness is an instance of this kind of situation. The movement from innocence to the self-awareness of being *guilty* is facilitated by anxiety, which motivates by enticing the implicit "can" of possibility.[48] Consequently, the first category of existential questions covers individuals always already in action.

The second category is about human life. Giddens claims that all humans live in what he calls existential contradiction: though of a mere material origin, we are animated as self-conscious beings who are confronted with the temporal question of our mortality. As such, Giddens points out that it is not our biological demise which is problematic, but we are anxious about subjective death, which he claims is Kierkegaard's position.[49] It is not clear what exactly the exegetical foundation for this is, but Giddens mentions both the *Concluding Unscientific Postscript* and *The Sickness unto Death* as evidence that the sort of question which the second category poses is one of finitude. However, in key writings Kierkegaard is quite clear that death does not play the role that it does, for example, in Heidegger's analysis of Dasein. In *The Concept of Anxiety*, Kierkegaard says death is what terrorizes the spiritless bourgeois citizen, who is in an even worse situation than primitive Adam. The words of God's judgment of the certainty of death awaken anxiety by the fear of God's command, and so Adam would be anxious about what he does not understand. For the spiritless citizen, however, anxiety is not prompted by the representation of death as such, but disguised as that which enthuses all the careless joys and pleasures of that individual. In terms of what Giddens would call ontological security, that very structure is the disguised mortality of the spiritless citizen, and this is the terror for the bourgeoisie (one identified by the structure of affordability, the demise of which is also the demise of one's self). In *Three Discourses on Imagined Occasions*, the speech at a grave speaks at length about "Death's decision" (*Dødens Afgjørelse*). However, for Kierkegaard death is not just the deciding factor of our lives—we shall surely die—nor merely the factor of when—we do not know when we die—rather the decision of death is a doing [-*gørelse*] off [*af-*] of death.[50] We are called upon to make the decision of death to be able to have a true conception of how to live.[51] Seen with Kierkegaard's eyes, death as finitude is a mere Donne-esque comma, an

---

45   Ibid., p. 48.
46   Ibid.
47   Ibid.
48   *SKS* 4, 350 / *CA*, 44.
49   Giddens, *Modernity and Self-Identity*, pp. 49–50.
50   *SKS* 5, 442–69 / *TD*, 71.
51   *SKS* 5, 437 / *TD*, 62.

exhaling, before infinity as illustrated in John Donne's (1572–1631) tenth divine meditation's last line: "And death shall be no more, Death thou shalt die."[52]

Margaret Edson expresses the significance of this poignantly and beautifully in her play *WIT*, letting a professor teach the importance of scholarship and respect for sources in this manner:

> …it is ultimately about overcoming the seemingly insuperable barriers separating life, death, and eternal life. In the edition you chose, this profoundly simple meaning is sacrificed to hysterical punctuation:
>
> And Death—*capital D*—shall be no more—*semicolon!* Death—*capital D*—*comma*—thou shalt die—*exclamation point!*
>
> If you go in for this sort of thing, I suggest you take up Shakespeare. Gardner's edition of the Holy Sonnets returns to the Westmoreland manuscript source of 1610—not for sentimental reasons, I assure you, but because Helen Gardner is a *scholar*. It reads:
>
> And death shall be no more, *comma*, Death thou shalt die.
>
> *(As she recites this line, she makes a little gesture at the comma.)*
>
> Nothing but a breath—a comma—separates life from life everlasting. It is simple really. With the original punctuation restored, death is no longer something to act out on a stage, with exclamation points. It's a comma, a pause. This way, the *uncompromising* way, one learns something from this poem, wouldn't you say? Life, death. Soul, God. Past, present. Not insuperable barriers, not semicolons, just a comma.[53]

The *uncompromising* way of approaching the second category of existential questions is that a religious thinker such as Kierkegaard cannot be taken as party to a secular worry about finitude. Whereas it is a basic condition of the high modern individuals to be actors on the diffuse stage of sociality, and as a result they are required to act out death with exclamation points and insuperable barriers, Kierkegaard's point about death as a question is quite different, because it is a religious matter. The *uncompromising* approach would in this way become a challenge to the way we live now.

The third category of questions relates to other persons. Giddens claims that this category does not contain questions about whether there are others, or how intersubjectivity derives from subjectivity.[54] Rather the problem of the other "concerns the inherent connections which exist between learning the characteristics of other persons and the other major axis of ontological security" which is trust.[55] Trusting interpersonal relations is a necessary but unreliable element in the "sustaining of an 'observable/accountable' world" the occurrence of which is "miraculous," orderly, and brought on by the "achievement of everyday actors in an entirely routine way."[56] However constant, the orderly achievement is threatened by "the slightest glance of one person towards another, inflexion of the voice, changing facial expression or gestures of the body."[57] Thus, the third category of existential questions introduces

---

[52]   John Donne, *The Complete English Poems*, London: Penguin 1996, p. 313.
[53]   Margaret Edson, *WIT*, New York: Dramatists Play Service 1999, p. 14.
[54]   Giddens, *Modernity and Self-Identity*, pp. 50–1.
[55]   Ibid.
[56]   Ibid., p. 52.
[57]   Ibid.

anxiety in the guise of the fragility of interpersonal trust. Giddens does not enter into any comparison with Kierkegaard on this point, but if he did, Kierkegaard's portrayal of the Akedah, the offering of Isaac by Abraham, is the story of losing trust in the societal structure, which, according to Giddens, is part and parcel of ontological security. Consequently, Kierkegaard would be less impressed with the reliance on interpersonal relations for ontological security than is Giddens, because for Kierkegaard trust in the individual relationship with the divine supersedes that of interpersonal relationships.

Illustratively, Henrik Ibsen's (1828–1906) character Nora displays the kind of objection to Giddens which Kierkegaard might be taken to have. In *A Doll's House*, Nora undergoes a metamorphosis from devoted housewife to emancipated woman in a rebellion against being reduced to a doll in the puppet play of society:

> At home, Daddy used to tell me what he thought, then I thought the same. And if I thought differently, I kept quiet about it, because he wouldn't have liked it. He used to call me his baby doll, and he played with me as I used to play with my dolls. Then I came to live in your house..I lived by doing tricks for you, Torvald. But that's the way you wanted it. You and Daddy did me a great wrong.[58]

The patriarchal society represented by the Father-absent and the Father-present objectifies the woman who is a doll whether played with by the former or the latter. The only difference is that Nora was a doll child and now she is a doll wife, but it is a game-specifying difference of the kind which underlines what kind of use women have in patriarchal societies. Nora is a game-breaker, precisely because she loses social functionality and the trust of the patriarchal representative. This, however, affords Nora freedom: "If I'm ever to reach any understanding of myself and the things around me, I must stand alone."[59] Nora is here asking category one type existential questions, which is to say, Nora is not merely a functionality of others, but also in and of herself. Such questions override the urgency of category three type questions. Thus, when Torvald admonishes her by saying that she knows nothing of society, Nora can reply: "No, I don't. But I shall go into that too. I must try to discover who is right, society or me."[60] Getting answers to category one and two type questions seems to entail answering category three questions.

The case of category four questions is in many ways similar to that of category three, since for Giddens the issue of self-identity is one of having a reflexive project of autobiography; thus it is a question of whether one can begin such questioning without having answers to category one and two questions, which by their answer entail what kind of answer can be given to category three and four questions. Nevertheless, category four questions involve, Giddens claims, the "cognitive component of personhood," which means to have a "concept of a person" and not just being a person as a "reflexive actor."[61] Giddens claims that although the content

---

58   Henrik Ibsen, *Four Major Plays*, trans. by James MacFarlane and Jens Arup, Oxford: Oxford University Press 1998, p. 80.

59   Ibid., p. 81.

60   Ibid., p. 83.

61   Giddens, *Modernity and Self-Identity*, p. 53.

of that concept is subject to cultural variations, the crucial generality is the ability to use "I" in shifting contexts. Discontinuity, anxieties about being engulfed, and a general lack of biographical continuity are, according to Giddens, symptoms of a lack of the ability to use "I" in shifting contexts.[62] The existential question of category four is whether one is likely to sustain "a particular narrative," which requires undoubtedly "an unconscious aspect to this chronic 'work,' perhaps organised in a basic way through dreams."[63] Again, Kierkegaard is not mentioned in the discussion of category four questions, perhaps because Kierkegaard's conception of the self is religiously articulated or perhaps because the risk of existence Giddens sees in the fragmented self, which is discontinuous and Kafkaesque, without inner certainty of being alive, is not avoided by narratives in the way Giddens might think.[64] In this respect, Kierkegaard can offer a comment on the dream of personality which he claims is a byproduct of fantasy:

> In such a self-intuition of fantasy the individual is not a real figure, but a shadow, or more concisely: the real figure is invisibly present, and does not make do with casting shadows, but the individual has a plethora of shadows all of his likeness and in each their moment rightfully his self...this shadow existence demands satisfaction, and it is never beneficial for an individual if the shadow lacks the time to act itself out, yet it is rather tragic or comical if the individual made a mistake and acted itself out in the shadow.[65]

The multiple narratives an individual may engage in are shadows, each in their time as full an expression of that individual as possible, but they are not the self of that individual. The ability to use "I" across shifting contexts does not offer much of a constraint, when someone suffering from depression narrates only negative slants of past events, which otherwise are seen in richer light than the undermining self-doubting darkness of depression. Thus, the self is not reducible to a narrative, the character of which is subject to constant change: the only permanence of a narrative is its impermanence. Consider, for example, Samuel Beckett's (1906–89) *Krapp's Last Tape*. Krapp is a hyper-narrator of his many shadows, each of which is as tragic as the next. The repetition of sequences on the tape, on which he narrates past events, is a sort of mulling over Krapp's self-narrative that produces this comment from Krapp: "Just been listening to that stupid bastard I took myself for thirty years ago, hard to believe I was ever as bad as that."[66]

The high modern actor might be forced to act out the hyper-reflexivity which chronically answers the question of self-identity; however, rather than being a coping strategy with regard to the risks of existence it is just as likely a symptom of despair. Worrying about who one is might indicate that one has no answers to category three, two and one types of existential questions. Thus, rather than a means of coping with anxiety, self-narrative can be seen as a description of being in the grip of anxiety. As a result, the normative tragic would indicate that there is another

---

62   Ibid.
63   Ibid., p. 54.
64   Ibid., p. 53.
65   *SKS* 4, 30 / *R*, 154–5 (my translation).
66   Samuel Beckett, *Collected Shorter Plays*, New York: Grove Press 1994, p. 62.

option for answering the existential questions which points towards a transcendent understanding of human selves. Against this, the descriptive tragic merely describes the immanent possible moves for an actor on the stage of sociality.

B. Existential Espionage

The reason why Giddens would be unlikely to embrace Kierkegaard's normative tragic can be teased out of the following snippet, which one might detect as an unacknowledged reference to Kierkegaard:

> ...basic trust is fundamental to the connections between daily routines and normal appearances. Within the settings of daily life, basic trust is expressed as a bracketing-out of possible events or issues which could, in certain circumstances, be cause for alarm. What other people appear to do, and who they appear to be, is usually accepted as the same as what they are actually doing and who they actually are. Consider, however, the world of the spy who, in the interests of self-preservation, cannot accept the range of normal appearances in the way other people usually do. The spy suspends part of the generalised trust which is ordinarily vested in "things as they are," and suffers tortuous anxieties about what would otherwise be mundane events. To the ordinary person a wrong number may be a minor irritation, but to the undercover agent it may be a disturbing sign that causes alarm.[67]

Contrast this to the following description of the existential spy in Kierkegaard:

> The psychological observer ought to be more nimble than a tightrope dancer in order to incline and bend himself to other people and imitate their attitudes...he should sit entirely composed in his room, like a police agent who nevertheless knows everything that takes place. What he needs he can fashion at once; what he needs he has at hand at once by virtue of his general practice, just as in a well-equipped house one need not carry water from the street but has it on his level by high pressure. If he were to become doubtful, he is so well-oriented in human life and his eyes are so inquisitorially sharp that he knows where to look to discover easily a suitable individuality who can be useful for the imaginary construction [*Experimentet*].[68]

The isolated police spy, who sits at home, has by virtue of his psychological nimbleness the ability to make experiments of existential situations. The spy does not take things at face value; he does not accept that what people are and do is what they appear to be and do

Now, Giddens' diagnosis of the Kierkegaardian spy must be that his suspension of generalized trust is such that it will never be sufficient for the spy to accept mere descriptions of human existence, but that his vested interest is to unmask the fleeting world in which ordinary existence attempts to navigate as essentially in need of something else. That something else would be, paradoxically, trust. However, whereas for Giddens that trust is to be found in the interpersonal relations of sociality,

---

[67]   Giddens, *Modernity and Self-Identity*, p. 127.

[68]   *SKS* 4, 359–60 / *CA*, 54–5.

Kierkegaard thinks that faith in the divine is the sole means of trust sufficient and necessary for building a human life.

Taken in isolation, the problem Kierkegaard faces is that he presupposes the conclusion in his premises, and thus, when he exhorts the individual task of transcending the despair of immanence, he is begging the question. On the other hand, when Giddens is describing the risks of high modern existence he is relying on the premise that sociality constitutes an answer to the individual's existential problems, which is both uncritical and unambitiously narrow-minded.

IV. Exeunt—by Way of Conclusion

In the course of this article, I have done several things. The influence of Kierkegaard on Giddens' thinking is evidently limited to the analysis of anxiety. However, I tried out a parallel reading which might indicate more of a connection than is acknowledged. I chose the text of "The Crisis and a Crisis in the Life of an Actress," but I might have chosen the review of *Two Ages* to develop the idea of sociality as the audience, and the leveling tendency of the conglomerate of individuals which itself is impersonal. I am not convinced of how good a case may be mounted for arguing that Kierkegaard has influenced Giddens; rather the line I would take is to search out the territory inbetween the parallels.

Giddens' use of Kierkegaard is interesting, because Kierkegaard is usually very unhandy for Anglophone thinkers. It is unsurprising that Giddens rejects antiquated philosophical anthropologies, which I take to be a sleight-of-hand reference to the elaborate and Christian anthropology Kierkegaard expounds. Going into that particular aspect is, I guess, the direct way to complication. Nevertheless, it may be to the detriment of the use of Kierkegaard if one does not understand how the analysis of anxiety is reliant on the specific religious outlook Kierkegaard advocates.

I have chosen to couch my discussion in references to the theater—this might strike some as overkill. However, given Kierkegaard's many references to the theater and the implied "staging" of the high modern actor in Giddens, I found the temptation undeniable. Kierkegaard's theater is both the leveling audiences of the common man and the exalted attention of the divine. Whereas Giddens' actor must learn to perform with others, Kierkegaard's individual must learn to perform before God, perhaps after much rehearsal [*Indøvelse*] in Christianity.

Finally, there are but a few publications which mention the names Giddens and Kierkegaard on their pages but never in any comparative or systematic way, which is why a bibliography of secondary literature cannot be compiled.[69] In this sense, the present work is the occasion for asking whether there is more to be said about Giddens' work in relation to Kierkegaard scholarship.[70]

---

[69]   I owe Peter Šajda a debt of gratitude for the vast preparatory work he did in sifting through the secondary literature in order to find what has been written on Giddens and Kierkegaard.

[70]   I am grateful to the editors of this volume and to Kirsten Klercke for offering her insightful comments on an earlier draft.

Bibliography

I. References to or Uses of Kierkegaard in Giddens' Corpus

Modernity and Self-Identity—the Self and Society in the Late Modern Age, Cambridge: Polity Press 1991, p. 37; pp. 47–50; p. 59.

II. Sources of Giddens' Knowledge of Kierkegaard

May, Rollo, *The Meaning of Anxiety*, revised ed., New York: W.W. Norton 1977 [1950], pp. xiv–xv; p. xxi; p. 15; pp. 20–1; pp. 26–8; pp. 32–51; pp. 58–9; pp. 65–6; p. 99; p. 113; p. 123; p. 125; p. 133; p. 151; p. 158; p. 192; p. 207; pp. 218–20; p. 229; p. 244; p. 247; p. 265; p. 365; p. 370; p. 376; p. 379; pp. 384–5; p. 390; pp. 392–3.

MacIntyre, Alasdair, *After Virtue*, London: Ducksworth 1981.

Kierkegaard, Søren, *Concluding Unscientific Postscript*, trans. by David F. Swenson and Walter Lowrie, Princeton, New Jersey: Princeton University Press 1941.

— *The Concept of Dread*, trans. by Walter Lowrie, London: Macmillan 1944.

— *The Sickness unto Death*, trans. by Alastair Hannay, Harmondsworth: Penguin 1989.

III. Secondary Literature on Giddens' Relation to Kierkegaard

Craig, Anita, "The Possibilities for Personhood in a Context of (Hitherto Unknown) Possibilities," in *Kierkegaard: The Self in Society*, ed. by George Pattison and Steven Shakespeare, Basingstoke: Macmillan Press 1998, p. 55; p. 57; p. 67, note.

Ferguson, Harvie, *Melancholy and the Critique of Modernity*, London: Routledge 1995, p. 272.

Mehl, Peter John, *Thinking through Kierkegaard: Existential Identity in a Pluralistic World*, Chicago: University of Illinois Press 2005, p. 143.

René Girard:

From Mimetic Desire to Anonymous Masses

Diego Giordano

I. Girard's Life, Works, and Thought

René Noël Théophile Girard was born in the southern French city of Avignon, on Christmas day, 1923. His father, Joseph Frédéric Marie (1881–1962), was a historian and archivist-paleographer, director of the Calvet Library and Museum, and curator of the Palais des Papes in Avignon. His mother, Marie-Thérèse Fabre, was a fervent Catholic of Drôme and the first person to get a Bachelor's degree in this southeast French district.

In 1941 Girard received his Baccalaureate in Philosophy at Lycée Mistral of Avignon, and between 1943 and 1947 he studied medieval history at the École des chartes, Paris, obtaining the degree as archivist-paleographer with a thesis entitled *La vie privée à Avignon dans la seconde moitié du XVe siècle*.[1] In 1947, after having organized during the summer an exhibition of modern art and sculpture at Palais des Papes, he moved to the United States, to Indiana University, having been awarded a one-year fellowship.[2] Here, he carried out his historical research as a Ph.D. student, writing a thesis on the Americans' opinion of France during the first part of World War II (*American Opinion of France, 1940–1943*).[3] This topic, even though far from his later works, gives us the measure of the fascination exerted on Girard by the interaction among cultures and civilizations. At the time he was also assigned to teach French literature—the field that unveiled him as a literary critic—at Indiana University (1947–52) and Duke University (1952–53). In 1950, after having defended the thesis with which he obtained a doctorate in history, Girard began to publish articles both on historiography and literature and some articles

---

[1] With this thesis, which was defended at the École des chartes in March 1947, Girard obtained the qualification of *archiviste paléographe*, and was placed on the list (*ordre de mérite*) sixth out of seventeen; see *Chronique de l'Ecole des chartes et des archivistes-paléographes*, Paris: Bibliothèque de l'école des chartes 1948, vol. 107, no. 1, pp. 181–90.

[2] Later he was twice awarded a Guggenheim Fellowship (1960 and 1967).

[3] René Girard, *American Opinion of France, 1940–1943*, Bloomington: Indiana University 1950. (The dissertation is kept at Indiana University, Wells Library, Research Collection, Cat. No. D40 .G518.) An excerpt from this thesis was reprinted in the issue of *Les Cahiers de l'Herne* dedicated to Girard: *Cahier de L'Herne No. 89: René Girard*, ed. by Marc Anspach, Paris: Éditions de L'Herne (collection "Cahiers de L'Herne") 2008, pp. 41–3.

about reflections on art in André Malraux's novels.[4] But because of the delay in the publication of his research, he was not granted tenure at Indiana University. From 1953 to 1957 he occupied the position of assistant professor in French at Bryn Mawr College (Pennsylvania), and in the winter of 1959 he experienced a conversion to the Christian faith described in *Quand ces choses commenceront. Entretiens avec Michel Treguer* (1994)[5] and in *The Girard Reader* (1996).[6] From Bryn Mawr he moved to Johns Hopkins University where, after a few years he became a full professor (1961) and chair of the Department of Romance Languages (1965–68). Between 1961 and 1966 Girard published two important books: *Deceit, Desire and the Novel: Self and Other in Literary Structure* (1961),[7] in which starting from an analysis of the novel/romantic conception of love, he develops the theory of the triangular structure of desire based on a "mimetic" process of imitation; and *Resurrection from the Underground: Feodor Dostoevsky* (1963),[8] where, making use of the characters created by Fyodor Dostoevsky (1821–81) as human models, he tries to show how man is essentially a desiring being. The articles of this period as well are focused on great writers (Proust, Dante, Racine, Camus, Hugo), because Girard argues that literature, depicting its protagonists' entanglement in mimetic webs of desire and rivalry, easily allows one to unearth the mechanism through which the man acquires his desires.

In 1966 (October 18–21) at Johns Hopkins University Girard organized with Richard Macksey and Eugenio Donato a famous international and interdisciplinary conference on continental structuralism entitled "The Languages of Criticism and the Sciences of Man," in which, among the others, Roland Barthes (1915–80), Jacques Derrida (1930–2004), and Jacques Lacan (1901–81) took part.[9] During the Symposium, the main topics of which were structural linguistics and the relationship between authorship and language, Girard was profoundly fascinated by the paper

---

4   See, for example, René Girard, "L'histoire dans l'oeuvre de Saint-John Perse," *Romantic Review*, vol. 44, 1953, pp. 47–55; "Marriage in Avignon in the Second Half of the Fifteenth Century," *Speculum*, vol. 28, 1953, pp. 485–98; "Franz Kafka et ses critiques," *Symposium*, vol. 7, 1953, pp. 34–44; and "Valéry et Stendhal," *Publications of the Modern Language Association of America*, vol. 59, 1954, pp. 347–57.

5   René Girard, *Quand ces choses commenceront. Entretiens avec Michel Treguer*, Paris: Arléa 1994.

6   René Girard, *The Girard Reader*, ed. by James G. Williams, New York: Crossroad 1996.

7   René Girard, *Mensonge romantique et vérité Romanesque*, Paris: Grasset 1961. (English translation: *Deceit, Desire and the Novel: Self and Other in Literary Structure*, trans. by Yvonne Freccero, Baltimore: Johns Hopkins University Press 1965.)

8   René Girard, *Dostoievski: du double à l'unité*, Paris: Plon 1963. (English translation: *Resurrection from the Underground: Feodor Dostoevsky*, trans. and ed. by James G. Williams, New York: Crossroad 1997.)

9   See *The Structuralist Controversy: The Languages of Criticism and the Sciences of Man*, ed. by Richard Macksey and Eugenio Donato, Baltimore: Johns Hopkins University Press 1970. The contributions presented are by René Girard, Richard Macksey, Charles Morazé, Georges Poulet, Eugenio Donato, Lucien Goldmann, Tzvetan Todorov, Roland Barthes, Jean Hyppolite, Jacques Lacan, Guy Rosolato, Neville Dyson-Hudson, Jacques Derrida, Jean-Pierre Vernant, Nicolas Ruwet.

presented by Jacques Derrida.[10] In it Derrida offered a new philosophical approach, so-called "deconstructionism" (extensively handled the following year in *De la grammatologie*),[11] whose aim is to make a close comparison between texts and authors of Western philosophy, showing the implicit assumptions, the hidden prejudices, and the dormant contradictions of the culture and language in which, not too consciously, "we live." This contribution, with the other entitled "La pharmacie de Platon,"[12] in which Derrida discusses the Plato's authorship, considerably influenced Girard who turned his attention to the great Greek tragedians (Sophocles' *Oedipus* cycle and Euripides' *The Bacchae*). Starting from the ancient Greek religious practice of *Pharmakós*—with which a kind of human scapegoat (a slave, a cripple or a criminal) was chosen and expelled from the community at times of disaster—Girard was led to redefine his mimetic theory. It was revised to include the notions of collective violence against a single victim and of a *scapegoat mechanism*[13] as constant factors in human culture and relations.

These themes are studied in depth in one of Girard's more significant books, *Violence and the Sacred* (1972).[14] At this point Girard, who had definitively gone beyond the limits of literary criticism, can radically assume the Freudian and structuralist themes in order to rework them in a different and innovative synthesis. In *Violence and the Sacred* he criticizes Sigmund Freud (1856–1939), especially the theories put forward in *Totem and Taboo*,[15] and rereads the Freudian lesson through the lens of mimetic theory, underlining the fundamental unity of myths and rites.

According to Girard, Freud has correctly understood that the sacrifice is the memory of a founding collective killing, but this notion has to be understood by

---

[10]   Jacques Derrida, "La structure, le signe et le jeu dans le discours des sciences humaines," in Derrida, *L'écriture et la différence*, Paris: Éditions du Seuil 1967, pp. 409–28. (English translation: "Structure, Sign and Play in the Discourse of the Human Sciences," in *The Languages of Criticism and the Sciences of Man: The Structuralist Controversy*, ed. by Richard Macksey and Eugenio Donato, Baltimore: Johns Hopkins University Press 1970, pp. 247–65.)

[11]   Jacques Derrida, *De la grammatologie*, Paris: Les Éditions de Minuit 1967. (English translation: *Of Grammatology*, trans. by Gayatri Chakravorty Spivak, Baltimore: Johns Hopkins University Press 1976.)

[12]   Jacques Derrida, "La pharmacie de Platon," *Tel Quel*, no. 32, 1967, pp. 17–59, and no. 33, 1968, pp. 4–48; republished in Derrida, *La dissémination*, Paris: Éditions du Seuil 1972, pp. 69–197. (English translation: "Plato's Pharmacy," in *Dissemination*, trans. by Barbara Johnson, Chicago: University of Chicago Press 1981, pp. 61–171.)

[13]   The expression "scapegoat mechanism" was not coined by Girard himself but it belongs to Kenneth Burke (1897–1993), who used it in two books: *Permanence and Change* (1935) and *A Grammar of Motives* (1940). However, Girard takes this concept from Burke and develops it much more extensively as an interpretation of human culture.

[14]   René Girard, *La violence et le sacré*, Paris: Grasset 1972. (English translation: *Violence and the Sacred*, trans. by Patrick Gregory, Baltimore: Johns Hopkins University Press 1977.)

[15]   Sigmund Freud, *Totem und Tabu. Einige Übereinstimmungen im Seelenleben der Wilden und der Neurotiker*, Vienna: Hugo Heller & Cie 1913. (English translation: *Totem and Taboo: Resemblances between the Mental Lives of Savages and Neurotics*, trans. by Abraham A. Brill, New York: Moffat Yard & Co. 1918.)

means of psychoanalysis.[16] For the performance of a sacrifice a scapegoat is required. The ritual sacrifice, which corresponds to the original violence, is founded on a twofold substitution: the substitution of all members of a community with a single person who is the scapegoat, and the substitution of a sacrificial victim with the original victim. By means of his theory of an initial founding violence based on the scapegoat, Girard wants to explain the origin, nature and purpose of sacrifice and, at once, the genesis of myths and rituals. In other words Girard's hypothesis is that ritual scapegoating is a cultural solution to the contagious conflict engendered by mimetic desire. With the revelation of ritual killing as scapegoating, there is the opportunity for humans to confront both their violence and the violent solution to their violence. Sacrifice, that founds human culture, also has a sacred value because it permits the community to regain its lost peace. In this process the sacrificial victim plays a crucial role insomuch as it, catalyzing on itself all collective tensions, appears at the same time as source and solution of crisis.

In 1971 Girard left Johns Hopkins University to become a Distinguished Professor in the English Department at the State University of New York at Buffalo, where he remained until 1976. In 1976 he accepted a second appointment at Johns Hopkins University, with the title of John M. Beall Professor of the Humanities. A new phase of his life began. The English translation of *Violence and the Sacred* came out in 1977, and for the first time his thought became the subject of reviews, interviews, and scholarly forums in North America.

In 1978 he published *Things Hidden since the Foundation of the World*,[17] an atypical book in the form of a dialogue with two psychiatrists, Jean-Michel Oughourlian and Guy Lefort. In it Girard develops the implications of his mimetic theory, expanding them to fundamental anthropology, psychology and, for the first time, Christianity and the Judeo-Christian Scriptures. The *victimary*[18] mechanism is the missing link between the animal world and the human world. It permits one to venture an explanation of the hominization of primates, detecting in the process of collective reconciliation the birth of symbolic thought and language. The first hominids were different from primates for having genetically inherited a greater aptitude for imitation, which exposed them to frequent mimetic crises and triggered

---

[16]   According to Girard, the mimetic conception removes the desire from the object, and simultaneously it makes violence a consequence of rivalry, while the Oedipus complex postulated by Freud founds the desire on the objective value of the object (the mother); it has to presuppose the awareness of rivalry and its destructive results. The awareness, unlikely in a child, of wishing to possess his mother at the expense of killing the father, compels Freud to gradually introduce different psychical structures (instincts, drives, Id, super-ego). But, Girard argues, the theory of mimetic desire can be directly applied to the Oedipus complex in order to simplify it: if the child wants his mother it is because, in an imitative relationship with the father, he saw the father desire his mother.

[17]   René Girard, *Des choses cachées depuis la fondation du monde*, Paris: Grasset 1978. (English translation: *Things Hidden since the Foundation of the World: Research undertaken in collaboration with J.-M. Oughourlian and G. Lefort*, trans. by Stephen Bann and Michael Metteer, Stanford: Stanford University Press 1987.)

[18]   This term, Anglicized, derives from the Latin word *victimarius*, which in ancient Rome indicated the Minister of Sacrifice.

the victimary mechanism. This mechanism permits Girard to explain, for example: (1) the need of sacrificial victims by early human communities; (2) the passage from human victims to animal ones; (3) the birth of hunting to supply the victims; (4) the birth of cattle-breeding as casual result of acclimatization of a supply of victims; (5) the birth of agriculture. Girard shows that the origin of culture is neither economic nor sexual, but religious. The development of rites and prohibitions by proto-human and human groups assumes infinitely different forms, obeying in any case a very rigorous practical direction: the prevention of the return of mimetic crisis. In archaic religion it is therefore possible to trace the origin of all cultural foundations (philosophy, literature, politics, etc.).

As the theory of natural selection is the rational principle of explanation of the immense variety of life-forms, so the victimary mechanism is the rational principle of explanation of the immense variety of cultural forms. The analogy with Charles Darwin (1809–82) extends as well to the scientific statute of this theory, which is no more than a hypothesis not susceptible of being proven experimentally, but one that stands out for its prodigious explanatory power.[19] However, in *Things Hidden since the Foundation of the World*, for the first time Girard broaches the subjects of Christianity and Bible that will be further investigated some years later in *The Scapegoat*.[20]

In 1979 Girard became member of the American Academy of Arts and Sciences. In 1981 he organized at Stanford University an international Symposium on "Disorder and Order,"[21] and in the same year he accepted his last post as Andrew B. Hammond Professor of French Language, Literature, and Civilization at Stanford University, where he concluded his career in the summer of 1995.

During these years Girard organized many important international conferences (with Jean-Pierre Dupuy), held different academic positions,[22] and received awards and honorary doctorates. In the meantime he published *The Scapegoat* (1982), *Job,*

---

[19]   If Girard's theory appears as the natural prolongation of biology to social field, it is interesting to notice that recently biology has confirmed the hypotheses of Girard with the discovery of "mirror neurons."

[20]   René Girard, *Le bouc émissaire*, Paris: Grasset 1982. (English translation: *The Scapegoat*, trans. by Yvonne Freccero, Baltimore: Johns Hopkins University Press 1986.)

[21]   See *Disorder and Order: Proceedings of the Stanford International Symposium (September 14–16, 1981)*, ed. by Paisley Livingston, Saratoga, California: Anma Libri 1984 (*Stanford Literature Studies*, vol. 1). Girard's contribution, pp. 80–97, is entitled "Disorder and Order in Mythology."

[22]   1985: Director of Seminar, University of North Carolina. 1986: Co-director (with Jean-Pierre Dupuy) of the "Program of Interdisciplinary Research," Stanford University. In 1990 a group of scholars founded the "permanent" *Colloquium on Violence and Religion* (COV&R), of which Girard was made Honorary Chair. This international association is devoted to explore and develop Girard's mimetic theory and the relationship between violence and religion in the genesis and maintenance of culture. The association publishes *The Bulletin of the Colloquium on Violence and Religion* and *Contagion: Journal of Violence, Mimesis, and Culture.*

the Victim of His People (1985),[23] *A Theater of Envy: William Shakespeare* (1990),[24] and a very important set of interviews gathered in the book *Quand ces choses commenceront. Entretiens avec Michel Treguer* (1994).[25]

After retirement, and until the present day, Girard continues to be active both as writer[26] and as interlocutor in interviews and interdisciplinary dialogues.[27] For his studies and contributions to French culture and language he was elected, on March 17, 2005, an "immortal" member of the prestigious French Academy.[28]

II. Girard's Use of Kierkegaard: Paradigms of Social and Individual Conduct

Although René Girard's works contain only a few passing references to Søren Kierkegaard,[29] the relationship between them can be approached from various angles.[30] First of all, from a biographical point of view, we realize that both

---

[23]   René Girard, *La route antique des hommes pervers*, Paris: Grasset 1985. (English translation: *Job, the Victim of His People*, trans. by Yvonne Freccero, Stanford: Stanford University Press 1987.)

[24]   René Girard, *Shakespeare. Les feux de l'envie*, Paris: Grasset 1990. (English translation: *A Theater of Envy: William Shakespeare*, New York and Oxford: Oxford University Press 1991.)

[25]   René Girard, *Quand ces choses commenceront. Entretiens avec Michel Treguer*, Paris: Arléa 1994.

[26]   See, for example, René Girard, *Je vois Satan tomber comme l'éclair*, Paris: Grasset 1999. (English translation: *I See Satan Fall Like Lightning*, trans. by James G. Williams, Maryknoll: Orbis Books 2001.) *Le sacrifice*, Paris: Bibliothèque nationale de France 2003. *Dieu, une invention?* (with André Gounelle and Alain Houziaux), Ivry-sur-Seine: Editions de l'Atelier 2007.

[27]   See, for example, René Girard, *Um Longo Argumento do princípio ao Fim: Diálogos com João Cezar de Castro Rocha e Pierpaolo Antonello*, Rio de Janeiro: Topbooks 2000. (English translation: *Evolution and Conversion: Dialogues on the Origins of Culture*, London: Continuum 2008.) *Celui par qui le scandale arrive: entretiens avec Maria Stella Barberi*, Paris: Desclée de Brouwer 2001. *Verità o fede debole. Dialogo su cristianesimo e relativismo* (with Gianni Vattimo), ed. by Pierpaolo Antonello, Massa: Transeuropa Edizioni 2006. *Achever Clausewitz (entretien avec Benoît Chantre)*, Paris: Carnets Nord 2007.

[28]   See René Girard, *Le Tragique et la Pitié: Discours de réception de René Girard à l'Académie française et réponse de Michel Serres*, Paris: Editions le Pommier 2007.

[29]   See René Girard, "Camus's Stranger Retried," *Publications of the Modern Language Association of America*, vol. 79, no. 5, 1964, pp. 528–9; *Mensonge romantique et vérité Romanesque*, p. 64 (*Deceit, Desire and the Novel: Self and Other in Literary Structure*, p. 58); *To Double Business Bound: Essays on Literature, Mimesis, and Anthropology*, Baltimore: Johns Hopkins University Press 1978, pp. 26–7; *Le bouc émissaire*, p. 245 (*The Scapegoat*, p. 173). See also *The Girard Reader*, ed. by James G. Williams, New York: Crossroad 1996, p. 268; and Girard's "Foreword" to Robert Hamerton-Kelly, *The Gospel and the Sacred*, Minneapolis: Fortress Press 1994, p. xi.

[30]   Regarding the secondary literature on the relationship between Kierkegaard and Girard, we do not have a large quantity of material. Works in which a direct or passing comparison between the two authors is traceable are listed in the bibliography at the end of this article.

Kierkegaard and Girard nourished interests in various branches of the knowledge, such as literature, aesthetics, ethics, psychology, and theology. Secondly, on a methodological side, observing the way in which they discuss philosophical or theological subjects, we note the pre-eminence of literature as the key to approach problems. In his works the "writer" Kierkegaard constantly quotes classic literature, deriving from it principles, mottoes, or paradigmatic examples, useful for what he wants to demonstrate, while Girard, after having obtained fame just as a literary critic, develops his anthropological philosophy in close connection with literary contexts. Lastly, on a theoretical ground, the most relevant affinity between them can be detected in the special attention the two turn to an analysis of human behavior, starting from which it is possible to answer some questions concerning the individual and social existence.

In the article "Camus's Stranger Retried" (1964) Girard quotes a long passage[31] from *The Sickness unto Death*. It is the first time Girard refers to Kierkegaard. He takes the cue from the discussion of the notion of the "absurd" which is pervasive in all the works of Albert Camus (1913–60), and he carries out a comparative analysis of the psychological traits belonging to the main characters of the major literary works written by the Nobel laureate (such as *The Stranger* or *The Fall*). According to Girard, a young man who feels doomed to anonymity and mediocrity is compelled to repay with indifference the indifference of society, and, if he is also particularly talented, to antagonize society through a challenging attitude. In this connection, for the French philosopher what Kierkegaard writes apropos of *defiance* [*Trods*] is significant: "Even more relevant here than a purely psychiatric interpretation are the passages of *The Sickness unto Death* dedicated to what Kierkegaard calls 'defiance' or 'the despair of willing despairingly to be oneself.' "[32] In his analysis of the forms of despair,[33] Kierkegaard examines the type of despair known as defiance, identifying and describing the three major traits of the Absurd Man, later discussed by Camus: a rejection of escaping existence (suicide), a rejection of help from a higher power, and an acceptance of his absurd (and despairing) condition.[34]

In fact a form of despair, which is exactly opposed to mimetic behavior, is to want one's sorrow not to be recognized by society, or healed by another person, namely: "to be unwilling to hope in the possibility that an earthly need, a temporal cross, can come to an end. The despairing person who in despair wills to be himself is unwilling to do that,"[35] freezing oneself in the impossibility of doing anything:

---

[31]   Girard, "Camus's Stranger Retried," pp. 528–9.

[32]   Ibid., p. 528. Girard quotes from Kierkegaard's *Fear and Trembling, and The Sickness unto Death*, trans. by Walter Lowrie, Garden City, New York: Doubleday 1954, pp. 204–5, which corresponds to *SKS* 11, 181 / *SUD*, 67.

[33]   For Kierkegaard there are three manifestations of human despair over becoming a self: (1) "spiritlessness," the failure to realize one's possibility; (2) "weakness," the move to escape from one's self; and (3) "defiance," the attempt to affirm and master oneself by denying dependence upon God (and society).

[34]   See *SKS* 11, 184–5 / *SUD*, 71.

[35]   *SKS* 11, 184 / *SUD*, 70. See also *SKS* 11, 185 / *SUD*, 72: "…now it is too late, now he [the man in despair] would rather rage against everything and be the wronged victim of the whole world and of all life, and it is of particular significance to him to make sure that he has

Consequently, the self in despair is always building only castles in the air, is only shadowboxing. All these imaginatively constructed virtues make it look splendid; like oriental poetry, they fascinate for a moment; such self-command, such imperturbability, such ataraxia, etc. practically border on the fabulous.... In despair the self wants to enjoy the total satisfaction of making itself into itself, of developing itself, of being itself; it wants to have the honor of this poetic, masterly construction, the way it has understood itself. And yet, in the final analysis, what it understands by itself is a riddle.[36]

In *Deceit, Desire and the Novel*, Girard completely expounds his mimetic theory, which is the hinge for his later anthropological analysis of culture, society, and religion. According to Girard, our desires are copied from models or mediators whose objects of desire become our desired objects. Man in general is not able to desire by ignoring the others: the object and the aim of a desire is proposed or imposed by a third person, so the desiring structure is triangular, and it does not proceed along a straight line. The triangle, which is established among the desiring person, the desired object, and the mediator, constantly recurs in the structure of the novels of Cervantes, Flaubert, Stendhal, Proust, and Dostoevsky. Romantic criticism was not capable of underlining the desiring *mimesis*, but it concealed the mediator, setting up the romantic lie of the pure, direct and spontaneous desiring capacity. Believing in the autonomy of the desires of humans (and characters) is an error because jealousy and envy are inevitably aroused in the mimetic situation. Human desires are not innate; rather, we "borrow" our desires from those we imitate. In this process the mediator, that is, the person who is our model (but also other imitators of the same model), can become our rival or competes with us for getting what we want. The romantic concept of a spontaneous desire is illusory, while the fictional truth requires modeling itself upon a mirroring desire, because the essence of any desiring is mimetic.

In other words, for Girard, human culture is founded on an imitative behavior through which the human being determines his desires, basing them on the desires of the Other, who becomes the normative and paradigmatic point of reference for the development of personality. To this effect the mimetic theory seems to explain the psychological dynamics proposed by Kierkegaard with reference to despair as inability, by a human individual, to fix a model to imitate. Even more exactly, the only reference accessible to the despairing man, who consciously remains in despair, is ultimately only the self, in one's despair (self-despair). This conduct takes on a destructive tendency, since the model, whose behaviors and desires one wants to imitate, constitutes also the main "obstacle" to the complete fulfillment of the copied desire. This means that the despairing subject rejects looking outside himself or herself, to an external model, suppressing the will to act in the world, and consequently becoming the immediate "rival" of himself.[37] On this point Kierkegaard and Girard meet each other to the extent that they recognize that a

---

his torment on hand and that no one takes it away from him—for then he would not be able to demonstrate and prove to himself that he is right."

36   *SKS* 11, 183 / *SUD*, 69.

37   It follows that the Girardian figure of the "Double" cannot be used as regards the despairing man.

man must always have a prototype. The presupposition which both philosophers understand in a similar way is that humans historically attempt to find meaning in their lives. But for Kierkegaard the question is not whether or not one chooses a prototype but which prototype one chooses.[38]

The first chapter of *Deceit, Desire and the Novel*, devoted by Girard to expounding the "triangular desire" theory, opens with a quotation in which Don Quixote represents to his loyal squire Sancho the need to *imitate* the conduct of Amadis of Gaul, one of the most perfect "knight errants." And he goes on to say,

> the man who wishes to be known as careful and patient should and does imitate Ulysses, in whose person and works Homer paints for us a vivid portrait of carefulness and patience, just as Virgil shows us in the person of Aeneas the valor of a pious son and the wisdom of a valiant captain....In the same way Amadis was the pole, the star, the sun for brave and amorous knights, and we others who fight under the banner of love and chivalry should imitate him. Thus, my friend Sancho, I reckon that whoever imitates him best will come closest to perfect chivalry.[39]

This model is called by Girard the *mediator* of desire. Chivalric existence is the *imitation* of Amadis in the same sense that the Christian's existence is the imitation of Christ.

On a loose sheet of paper in which Kierkegaard talks just about the character of Don Quixote (and discusses the proposal to work out a comic novel entitled "A Literary *Don Quixote*"), it is possible to trace a considerable affinity with what Girard notices, referring to the human aptitude towards imitation: "Every time he would say something which *he thought* was something new but eventually turned out to be something old he had read (this aspect could be very interesting), someone else would already have said it."[40]

Also in *Deceit, Desire and the Novel*, talking about some Dostoevskian *stereotypical* characters who turn their attention towards a mediator whose desire is shaped by the relationship with the divine, Girard makes a brief mention of Kierkegaard:

> The hero turns passionately toward the Other, who seems to enjoy the divine inheritance. So great is the disciple's faith that he perpetually thinks he is about to steal the marvelous secret from the mediator. He begins to enjoy his inheritance in advance. He shuns the present and lives in the brilliant future. Nothing separates him from divinity, nothing but the mediator himself, whose rival desire is the obstacle to his own desire. Dostoyevsky's consciousness, like Kierkegaard's Self, cannot exist without an external prop.[41]

---

[38] Cf. Gregor Malantschuk, *Kierkegaard's Way to the Truth: An Introduction to the Authorship of Søren Kierkegaard*, trans. by Mary Michelsen, Montreal: Inter Editions 1987, p. 74. (Originally published as *Indførelse i Søren Kierkegaards Forfatterskab*, Copenhagen: Munksgaard 1953.)

[39] Girard, *Mensonge romantique et vérité Romanesque*, p. 11. (*Deceit, Desire and the Novel*, p. 1.)

[40] *Pap.* I A 146 / *JP* 1, 770.

[41] Girard, *Mensonge romantique et vérité Romanesque*, p. 64. (*Deceit, Desire and the Novel*, p. 58.) Cf. *SKS* 19, 417, NB5:113 / *JP* 4, 4148.

The passage ends with the main assertion, repeated at various times by Girard, according to which the choice always involves choosing a model, and true freedom lies in the basic choice between a human and a divine model.

But it is necessary to draw a distinction between the mimetic theory suggested by Girard and what Kierkegaard states apropos of imitation or the requirement of having a prototype of reference. Girard's mimetic theory is an operative paradigm he applies to different fields of knowledge in order to provide an exhaustive hermeneutic pattern capable of accounting for myth, religion, and literature. The foundation of this theory is in the conviction that human beings imitate more than they normally think, and that their conduct is not given by a purpose of differentiation as against the ethnic or social group they belong to, but just by the wish to conform to it. Contrariwise for Kierkegaard, imitation is limited to the following of Christ (*sequela Christi*), while the notion of prototype refers to martyrdom. Moreover, Kierkegaard identifies the martyr as a prototype not merely for the sake of imitation but first and foremost as an ideal, the value of which is in the great effort it demands from the single individual.

According to Girard, the mimetic process underlies even the genesis of religion and particularly of (1) ritual sacrifice, as reiteration of the original victimary event; (2) myth, as tale of that event from the point of view of the crowd; (3) prohibitions and laws, as ban of access to all those objects which caused rivalry and crisis. The religious course is slowly but gradually developed to every mimetic crisis, the solution of which restores a temporary peace. In this sense rituals and prohibitions are a sort of empirical knowledge about violence. Gospels are seemingly like any myth, with a victim lynched by a unanimous crowd, and this event is then celebrated as a ritual sacrifice (Eucharist) by the followers of the Christian religion.

Girard takes up this subject again in *The Scapegoat*, merging the mimetic theory with the victimary mechanism in his analysis of the Scriptures. According to him, the Gospels reveal all kinds of human relationships that at first seem incomprehensible and fundamentally irrational. These can and must ultimately be reduced to a single unifying factor: mimeticism.[42] The crowd plays a central role in the process triggered by mimeticism. Girard tries to show how the crowd is present in every "demonic" episode described in the Gospels. The same word "legion"[43] has negative connotations indicating the warlike mob or the hostile troop who crucified Christ.[44] Just talking about the anonymous (but unanimous) crowd, whose aim is to identify and kill the sacrificial victim, Girard makes a passing reference to Kierkegaard, writing that "the mob is the lie,"[45] in order to support his thesis. The expression used by Kierkegaard is "the crowd is untruth," and it is repeatedly asserted in "For the Dedication to 'That

---

[42]   Girard, *Le bouc émissaire*, p. 233. (*The Scapegoat*, p. 165.)

[43]   Mark 5:1–20; Matthew 8:28–34; Luke 8:26–39.

[44]   Girard, *Le bouc émissaire*, p. 244. (*The Scapegoat*, p. 173.)

[45]   Girard, *Le bouc émissaire*, p. 245. (*The Scapegoat*, pp. 173–4.) Girard gets this Kierkegaardian expression quoting Jean Starobinski, "La Démoniaque de Gérasa," *Analyse structurale et exégèse biblique: essais d'interprétation*, ed. by Roland Barthes et al., Neuchatel: Delachaux et Niestlé 1971, pp. 63–94. (English translation: "The Gerasene Demoniac," *Structural Analysis and Biblical Exegesis: Interpretational Essays*, ed. by Roland Barthes et al., trans. by Alfred M. Johnson, Pittsburgh: Pickwick 1974, pp. 57–84.) See also

Single Individual' " (1846),[46] which is the first "note" of *"The Single Individual":
Two "Notes" Concerning My Work as an Author*, a supplement to *The Point of View
for My Work as an Author*, a work published posthumously in 1859 by Kierkegaard's
brother, Peter Christian Kierkegaard. As a footnote indicates,[47] *The Single Individual*
was meant to accompany the dedication to "that individual" which is found in
Upbuilding Discourses in Various Spirits (1847).

The theme of the solitary individual was dealt with at length in the *Concluding
Unscientific Postscript*, but in *"The Single Individual"* Kierkegaard more
emphatically spells out the value of the individual versus the masses. In relation
to "the numeric masses," the individual person is of infinite importance. God
deals with, saves and judges individuals, while the masses have no real essence.
According to Kierkegaard, the crowd, since as existential category it is opposed to
that of the single individual, is synonymous with inauthenticity, irresponsibility, the
tyranny of people and the majority, the principle of evil and moral disintegration
of modern democracy. For Kierkegaard, as for Girard, the biblical episodes which
tell of Christ's suffering never hold a single man guilty, but rather the mob which
foments its violent conduct through its anonymity:[48]

> There is a view of life which conceives that where the crowd is, there is also the truth,
> and that in truth itself there is need of having the crowd on its side. There is another
> view of life which conceives that wherever there is a crowd there is untruth, so that (to
> consider for a moment the extreme case), even if every individual, each for himself in
> private, were to be in possession of the truth, yet in case they were all to get together in a
> crowd—a crowd to which any decisive significance is attributed, a voting, noisy, audible
> crowd—untruth would at once be in evidence.[49]

That means any idea, even a true one, that is asserted by a crowd, becomes untruth,
for the crowd cannot express the truth: "ethically and ethically-religiously the crowd
is untruth, the untruth of wishing to work by means of the crowd, the numerical, of
wishing to make the numerical the criterion which decides what truth is."[50]

We conclude our brief analysis, asserting that if the Gospels seem to gather up
all the characteristic elements of myths issuing from several cultures, in them the
prescriptive paradigm for social conduct has a revolutionary value, because the
victim is shown as innocent. The archaic myths were built on the lie of the victim's
guilt, for they told the event as seen from the crowd's perspective. This disavowal
lets the victimary mechanism (and the ritual sacrifice) be efficacious in producing
and preserving peace. On the contrary, the evangelical gospel (*evangelium*) asserts

---

Jean Starobinski, "The Struggle with Legion: A Literary Analysis of Mark 5:1–20," *New
Literary History*, vol. 4, 1973, pp. 330–56.

[46]   *SV1* XIII, 591–7 / *PV*, 105–12. Cf. also *Pap*. IX B 63,4–5, pp. 350–7.

[47]   *SV1* XIII, 591 / *PV*, 105.

[48]   Kierkegaard refers to Matthew 27:30. The "untrue" attitude of the crowd is already
described by Kierkegaard in *SKS* 20, 211–12, NB2:178 / *JP* 3, 2926 and *SKS* 20, 212,
NB2:178.a / *JP* 3, 2926. On the crowd's instability before Christ, cf. also *SKS* 12, 50–68 / *PC*,
36–55.

[49]   *SV1* XIII, 591 / *PV*, 105–6.

[50]   *SV1* XIII, 611–12 / *PV*, 125–6 (*Postscript to the "Two Notes,"* March 1855.)

categorically and unambiguously the victim's innocence, so undermining the sacrificial system (that is, the cultural order founded on sacrificial violence) on which the social order rests. Already the Old Testament shows the innocence of the victims (Abel, Joseph, Job, etc.), but it is only with the New Testament that the things hidden since the foundation of the world[51] are revealed: the foundation of the world order upon murder, described in all its harsh historicity in the Passion.

In other words, both for Girard and Kierkegaard in the Gospels the God of violence has disappeared and another God, totally extraneous to any logic of violence, is revealed. This shift is possible because the point of view of the crowd, which is the ground of collective violence as resolution for social crisis, is finally recognized as deceitful. The consequence is evident: only if Christians advocate a non-sacrificial reading of the Gospels, then the figure of Christ can become, in his subjectivity, the only efficacious model (or mediator) who allows for an escape from the untruth.

---

[51]   See Matthew 13:35: "…to fulfill what had been said through the prophet: 'I will open my mouth in parables, I will announce what has lain hidden from the foundation (of the world).'" For "the prophet" some textual witnesses read "Isaiah the prophet." The quotation is actually from Psalm 78:2. The psalm's title ascribes it to Asaph, the founder of one of the guilds of temple musicians. He is called "the prophet" (The *New American Bible* translates "the seer") in 2 Chronicles 29:30, but it is doubtful that Matthew averted to that; for him, any Old Testament text that could be seen as fulfilled in Jesus was prophetic.

Bibliography

References to or Uses of Kierkegaard in Girard's Corpus

"Camus's Stranger Retried," *Publications of the Modern Language Association of America*, vol. 79, no. 5, 1964, pp. 528–9.
Mensonge romantique et vérité Romanesque, Paris: Grasset 1961, p. 64. (English translation: *Deceit, Desire and the Novel: Self and Other in Literary Structure*, trans. by Y. Freccero, Baltimore: Johns Hopkins University Press 1965, p. 58.)
To Double Business Bound: Essays on Literature, Mimesis, and Anthropology, Baltimore: Johns Hopkins University Press 1978, pp. 26–7.
Le bouc émissaire, Paris: Grasset 1982, p. 245. (English translation: *The Scapegoat*, trans. by Yvonne Freccero, Baltimore: Johns Hopkins University Press 1986, p. 173.)
"Foreword" to Robert Hamerton-Kelly, *The Gospel and the Sacred: Poetics of Violence in Mark*, Minneapolis: Fortress Press 1994, p. xi.
"Epilogue" to *The Girard Reader*, ed. by James G. Williams, New York: Crossroad 1996, p. 268.

II. Sources of Girard's Knowledge of Kierkegaard

Camus, Albert, *Le Mythe de Sisyphe*, Paris: Gallimard 1942, p. 39; pp. 42–3; p. 51; pp. 56–61; p. 65; pp. 69–72.
Bataille, Georges, *L'Erotisme*, Paris: Union générale d'éditions 1965, p. 282.
Kierkegaard, Søren, *Fear and Trembling, and The Sickness unto Death*, trans. by Walter Lowrie, Garden City, New York: Doubleday 1954.
Lacan, Jacques, *Écrits*, Paris: Éditions du Seuil 1966, p. 46; p. 123; p. 293; p. 367; p. 519; p. 716.
Sartre, Jean-Paul, *L'être et le néant. Essai d'ontologie phénoménologique*, Paris: Gallimard 1943 (*Bibliothèque des Idées*), pp. 58–84; pp. 94–111; pp. 115–49; pp. 150–74; pp. 291–300; pp. 508–16; pp. 529–60; pp. 639–42; pp. 643–63; pp. 669–70; pp. 720ff.
Starobinski, Jean, "La Démoniaque de Gérasa," *Analyse structurale et exégèse biblique: essais d'interprétation*, ed. by Roland Barthes et al., Neuchatel: Delachaux et Niestlé 1971, pp. 63–94.

III. Secondary Literature on Girard's Relation to Kierkegaard

Baile, Gil, *Violence Unveiled: Humanity at the Crossroads*, New York: Crossroad 1995, p. 89; p. 91; p. 197; p. 280, note 14.

Bandera, Cesareo, "From Girard to Shakespeare, Kierkegaard, and Others," *South Central Review*, vol. 12, no. 2, 1995, pp. 56–68.

Bellinger, Charles K., "Toward a Kierkegaardian Understanding of Hitler, Stalin, and the Cold War," in *Foundations of Kierkegaard's Vision of Community*, ed. by George B. Connell and C. Stephen Evans, Atlantic Highlands, New Jersey: Humanities Press 1992, pp. 218–30.

— "The Crowd is Untruth: a Comparison of Kierkegaard and Girard," *Contagion: A Journal of Violence, Mimesis and Culture*, no. 3, 1996, pp. 103–19.

— *The Genealogy of Violence: Reflections on Creation, Freedom, and Evil*, Oxford: Oxford University Press 2001, pp. 72–86.

Gronhovd, Anne-Marie, "Isaac dans un imaginaire féminin: Les Images de Louise Bouchard," *The French Review*, vol. 71, no. 6, 1998, pp. 985–96.

Hamerton-Kelly, Robert, *Sacred Violence: Paul's Hermeneutic of the Cross*, Minneapolis: Fortress Press 1992, p. 166.

Keenan, Dennis King, *The Question of Sacrifice*, Bloomington: Indiana University Press 2005, pp. 25–56; pp. 149–54.

Luhrmann, Tanya Marie, "The Ugly Goddess: Reflections on the Role of Violent Images in Religious Experience," *History of Religions*, vol. 41, no. 2, 2001, pp. 114–41.

Mancinelli, Paola, "*Homo Absconditus Homo Revelatus*: Su Alcune Tracce Kierkegaardiane in René Girard," *NotaBene. Quaderni di Studi Kierkegaardiani*, vol. 2, 2002, pp. 127–37.

McCracken, David, *The Scandal of the Gospels: Jesus, Story, and Offense*, New York: Oxford University Press 1994, p. 9.

— "Scandal and Imitation in Matthew, Kierkegaard, and Girard," *Contagion: A Journal of Violence, Mimesis and Culture*, no. 4, 1997, pp. 146–62.

Milbank, John, "Stories of Sacrifice: From Wellhausen to Girard," *Theory, Culture & Society*, vol. 12, no. 4, 1995, pp. 15–46.

Mjaaland, Marius Timmann, "Ambivalence: On Sacrifice in Philosophy, Society, and Religion," *Neue Zeitschrift für Systematische Theologie und Religionsphilosophie*, vol. 50, nos. 3–4, 2008, pp. 189–95.

Pattison, George, *Kierkegaard, the Aesthetic and the Religious: From the Magic Theatre to the Crucifixion of the Image*, New York: St. Martin's Press 1992, pp. 125–56.

Pattison, George and Steven Shakespeare, "Introduction," in *Kierkegaard: The Self in Society*, ed. by George Pattison and Steven Shakespeare, New York: St. Martin's Press 1998, pp. 1–23.

Suchocki, Majorie Hewitt, *The Fall to Violence*, New York: Continuum 1994, p. 26; p. 29; p. 103n.

Webb, Eugene, *Philosophers of Consciousness: Polanyi, Lonergan, Voegelin, Ricoeur, Girard, Kierkegaard*, Seattle: University of Washington Press 1988, pp. 183–225.

Carl Gustav Jung:

A Missed Connection

Anthony Rudd

Carl Gustav Jung (1875–1961) was a Swiss psychologist and psychotherapist. He was born and brought up in the Swiss countryside where his father was a Reformed (that is, Calvinist) pastor. Although he had strong interests in the humanities, and in philosophy (especially Kant, Schopenhauer and Nietzsche),[1] Jung eventually focused on the study of medicine and went on to specialize in the then just emerging discipline of psychiatry. For a time (from 1907 to 1912) he was a close associate of Sigmund Freud (1856–1939), but he broke away from Freudian psychoanalysis and eventually became the founder of his own distinctive school, which he called "Analytical Psychology." Today, thousands of psychotherapists around the world have received an explicitly Jungian or "post-Jungian" training, and many thousands more use Jungian methods and techniques without being so formally or exclusively committed to Jung's principles. Some Jungian ideas have become part of the general stock-in-trade of psychotherapy, without even always being recognized as Jungian in origin.[2] Widely used methods of personality testing, such as the Myers-Brigg test, are directly derived from Jung's psychological typology. And some of Jung's ideas (such as the distinction between "introverts" and "extroverts")[3] have become part of the everyday "folk psychology" which people use to understand themselves and others quite apart from any therapeutic or academic context.[4]

---

[1]   See Sonu Shamdasani, *Jung and the Making of Modern Psychology: The Dream of a Science*, Cambridge: Cambridge University Press 2003, pp. 197–202; Marilyn Nagy, *Philosophical Issues in the Psychology of C.G. Jung*, Albany, New York: SUNY Press 1991, pp. 12–22.

[2]   For instance, he introduced the practice of "training analysis" whereby a trainee analyst must himself or herself undergo a process of analysis. See Shamdasani, *Jung and the Making of Modern Psychology*, p. 2.

[3]   This is elaborated in C.G. Jung, "Allgemeine Beschreibung der Typen," in his *Gesammelte Werke*, vols. 1–20, Olten: Walter Verlag 1971–94, vol. 6 (*Psychologische Typen*), pp. 357–443, §§ 621–740. (English translation: "General Description of the Types," in *The Collected Works of C.G. Jung*, vols. 1–20, ed. by Herberg Read, Michael Fordham, and Gerhard Adler, trans. by R.F.C. Hull, Princeton, New Jersey: Princeton University Press 1953–79, vol. 6 (*Psychological Types*), pp. 330–407, §§ 556–671.)

[4]   One sign of Jung's impact outside of therapeutic and academic contexts is that in 1967 he received the ultimate accolade of having his photo included in the montage of counter-cultural heroes that adorns the cover of the Beatles' *Sgt. Pepper* album.

As I will show in this article, there are many points of contact between Jung's thought and Kierkegaard's. Kierkegaard is correctly regarded as one of the pioneers of "depth psychology"; even apart from his two explicitly "psychological" works, *The Concept of Anxiety* and *The Sickness unto Death* (which deal with states— anxiety and despair—that are of direct interest to psychotherapists), he is throughout his work concerned with psychological issues. Indeed, the turn from metaphysics to psychology expressed in his focus on the subjectivity of the individual is at the heart of his thinking. As one commentator on Jung has put it:

> Philosophy has traditionally sought to transcend the particular individual in its quest for the universal forms of knowledge and being. Early in the nineteenth century, however, Kierkegaard alerted philosophy to the dangers inherent in this tradition and made a peculiar form of autobiography, his pseudonymous works, into material for thinking. Psychoanalysis is, in part, heir to this philosophical turn.[5]

I. Jung's Kierkegaardian Psychology

In what follows, I shall give a brief outline of some of Jung's main psychological ideas, emphasizing as I do so, the very striking parallels with aspects of Kierkegaard's thinking. (I will, in a sense, be using Kierkegaardian ideas to introduce Jungian ones.) I will organize this exposition under the following headings: A. Individualism; B. Emphasis on the Unconscious; C. Teleological and Non-Reductive View of the Psyche; D. Individuation and Becoming a Self; E. Subjectivity and Existential Engagement; and F. Religious Concerns.

A. Individualism

Both authors are concerned to address the individual, and they share a powerful distrust of "the crowd," of mass culture. Neither has much faith in collective political endeavors, and both have been criticized as a result for elitism or political indifference. There are, in particular, very striking parallels between Kierkegaard's analysis of his culture in the review of the novel *Two Ages* and Jung's account of his in *The Undiscovered Self.* Jung's dictum "the bigger the crowd, the more negligible the individual becomes"[6] is extremely Kierkegaardian. And the title of one of Jung's chapters, "Religion as the Counter-Balance to Mass-Mindedness,"[7] echoes Kierkegaard's insistence that to escape the implacable force of "leveling" one must "leap into the embrace of God."[8] Moreover, Jung shares Kierkegaard's concern that the drive to objective, scientific knowledge, as well as more purely

[5]   George B. Hogenson, *Jung's Struggle with Freud*, Notre Dame and London: University of Notre Dame Press 1983, pp. 3–4.
[6]   C.G. Jung, "Gegenwart und Zukunft," in his *Gesammelte Werke*, vol. 10 (*Zivilisation in Übergang*), p. 283, § 503. (English translation: "The Undiscovered Self (Present and Future)," in *The Collected Works of C.G. Jung*, vol. 10 (*Civilization in Transition*), p. 254, § 503 [*The Undiscovered Self*, trans. by R.F.C. Hull, London: Routledge 1958, p. 17].)
[7]   Ibid., Chapter 2.
[8]   *SKS* 8, 103 / *TA*, 108.

political and economic developments, are helping to undermine the status of the individual. "Judged scientifically, the individual is nothing but a unit which repeats itself *ad infinitum*....[But] for understanding, it is just the unique individual human being who, when stripped of all those conformities and regularities so dear to the heart of the scientists, is the supreme and only real object of investigation."⁹ Jung's claim that we cannot solve the problem by an "either/or" choice between science and individual understanding¹⁰ may be a dig at Kierkegaard (an ill-directed one, since Kierkegaard nowhere suggests we need to *reject* science or objectivity), but Jung's claim that "Under the influence of scientific assumptions...the individual...suffer[s] a leveling down" could not be more Kierkegaardian.¹¹

However, neither Kierkegaard nor Jung is an individualist in the sense of simply ignoring the deep rootedness of the individual in society. For neither of them is interested in encouraging a merely anti-social individualism, a willful egoism. (For Kierkegaard, of course, this would be a form of the aesthetic life.) Both thinkers insist that one needs to transcend the concerns of the ego. What exactly this involves we will consider shortly. But we should note here one of Jung's most distinctive ideas—that there is not only a personal but a collective unconscious. As I dig down deeper into my psyche, I find, not only contents that are personal to myself, but the "Archetypes" that are common to humanity as a whole. There is no close parallel to this idea in Kierkegaard's thinking,¹² but I do not think it stands in contradiction to anything in Kierkegaard. It is certainly compatible with his individualism, as it is with Jung's. The process of "individuation" for Jung is one in which I discover psychological contents that connect me, at a deep ontological level, with the rest of humanity. But in discovering them, I am faced with precisely the challenge of taking personal responsibility for not only the personal but also the collective aspects of my psyche.

B. Emphasis on the Unconscious

Jung's psychology, like Freud's, is in large measure, an investigation into the unconscious mind. Kierkegaard is undeniably a pioneer of such investigations. It is

---

9   Jung, "Gegenwart und Zukunft," in his *Gesammelte Werke*, vol. 10 (*Zivilisation in Übergang*), p. 280, § 497. ("The Undiscovered Self (Present and Future)," in *The Collected Works of C.G. Jung*, vol. 10 (*Civilization in Transition*), p. 251, § 497.) [*The Undiscovered Self*, p. 11].)

10   Jung, "Gegenwart und Zukunft," in his *Gesammelte Werke*, vol. 10 (*Zivilisation in Übergang*), p. 297, § 496. ("The Undiscovered Self (Present and Future)," in *The Collected Works of C.G. Jung*, vol. 10 (*Civilization in Transition*), p. 251, § 496 [*The Undiscovered Self*, p. 11].)

11   Jung, "Gegenwart und Zukunft," in his *Gesammelte Werke*, vol. 10 (*Zivilisation in Übergang*), p. 281, § 499. ("The Undiscovered Self (Present and Future)," in *The Collected Works of C.G. Jung*, vol. 10 (*Civilization in Transition*), p. 252, § 499 [*The Undiscovered Self*, p. 13].)

12   See *The Concept of Anxiety*, where Haufniensis insists that "the individual is both himself and the race....Perfection in oneself is therefore the perfect participation in the whole." (*SKS* 4, 33–5 / *CA*, 28–9.)

axiomatic to Kierkegaard that we have a nature and that there is a good for us, given that nature. However, we are mostly unaware of that nature and that good; and this is because we, in some sense, choose to be. Kierkegaard is fascinated, therefore, by our capacity for self-deception, and for what Freud would call repression. In *The Sickness unto Death* in particular he investigates the despair to which he claims we are all prone, mostly without being conscious of it.[13] Perhaps in this he is closer to Freud than to Jung, although a notable difference is that Freud thinks that we tend mostly to repress the id's demands for immediate sensual gratification, while Kierkegaard's concern is with our repression of the demands that moral and religious ideals make on us. Jung does recognize the mechanisms of repression and their role in building up the personal unconscious, but the collective unconscious he sees as a fundamental ontological fact about human nature, not something simply created by our desire not to recognize it. However, even here the contrast is not as sharp as it might at first seem. For the unconscious in Jung is probably best understood not simply as the unknown, but as that aspect of ourselves that we cannot or will not get into clear focus. As one commentator has put it: "unconsciousness, for Jung, describes the quality of a life that is lived but not yet reflectively known."[14] And there is a sense in Jung of an *imperative* to individuation—to the active taking of responsibility for all of what we are. This may not be so far removed from Kierkegaard's notion of despair being the failure to fully acknowledge the polarities which constitute our being, of which we cannot be simply or wholly unaware.

C. Teleological and Non-Reductive View of the Psyche

In contrast to most schools of twentieth-century psychology (including, for all their other differences, Psychoanalysis, Behaviorism and contemporary cognitive science), Jung rejects the notion that the psyche can be understood reductively— in terms of the supposedly more fundamental truths of the natural sciences: "The modern preference for physical grounds of explanation leads…to a 'psychology without a psyche'—I mean to the view that the psyche is nothing but a product of biochemical processes."[15] In contrast to what he acknowledges to be the characteristic "modern" view of psychology, Jung recommends that we "consider the possibility of a 'psychology with the psyche'—that is, of a field of study based on the assumption of an autonomous psyche."[16] Although neither Kierkegaard nor Jung attempts to solve the mind–body problem, Kierkegaard obviously, like Jung,

---

[13]   See *SKS* 11, 138–44 / *SUD*, 22–8. *SKS* 11, 157–62 / *SUD*, 42–7. I am assuming that both *The Sickness unto Death* and *The Concept of Anxiety* are only "weakly" pseudonymous and can be taken as expressions of Kierkegaard's own views.

[14]   See Roger Brooke, *Jung and Phenomenology*, London: Routledge 1991, p. 124.

[15]   C.G. Jung, "Das Grundproblem der gegenwärtigen Psychologie," in his *Gesammelte Werke*, vol. 8 (*Die Dynamik des Unbewußten*), p. 378, § 660. (English translation: "The Basic Postulates of Analytical Psychology," in *The Collected Works of C.G. Jung*, vol. 8 (*The Structure and Dynamics of the Psyche*), p. 344, § 660 (also in *Modern Man in Search of a Soul*, London: Routledge 1984, p. 207).)

[16]   Jung, "Das Grundproblem der gegenwärtigen Psychologie," in his *Gesammelte Werke*, vol. 8 (*Die Dynamik des Unbewußten*), p. 378, § 661. ("The Basic Postulates of Analytical

rejects any kind of natural-scientific reductionism and presupposes the autonomy of psychological explanation. One aspect of this anti-scientism is that both thinkers endorse a teleological view of the psyche. One of the central differences between Freud and Jung is that Jung insisted that the psyche must be understood as being oriented towards goals. Freud, with his scientistic orientation, rejected teleology in favor of (in principle) mechanistic explanations. In practice, this meant that he traced neuroses back to early childhood traumas. Jung agreed that sometimes one needed to be freed from the tyranny of the past, but he focused more on patients who, without any particular backward-looking cause, found themselves oppressed by their inability to move forward to a meaningful future.[17] Kierkegaard, of course, shares this teleological perspective; as noted above, his investigation of the unconscious presupposes a teleological understanding of the self.

D. Individuation and Becoming a Self

For both Kierkegaard and Jung, the ultimate *telos* for each of us is to become a self. Kierkegaard sets this out in the famous formulation at the start of *The Sickness unto Death*; a self is a synthesis of psychological factors ("the infinite and the finite...the temporal and the eternal...freedom and necessity"),[18] not just a passive synthesis, but an active process of consciously holding these factors together in creative tension— which is itself only possible through relating to God ("The power that established" the self).[19] But this is a goal to be achieved, not something that we just automatically are: "Considered in this way, a human being is still not a self."[20] Jung too sees selfhood as the *telos* of the human person—failure to achieve which can bring neurosis or depression even to those who have achieved the more conventionally recognized goals of success in career, family life, etc. The self, for Jung is the totality of the psyche (though he also sometimes talks of it as the organizing center of that totality):

> [T]he personality as a total phenomenon does not coincide with the ego, that is, with the conscious personality, but forms an entity that has to be distinguished from the ego... I have suggested calling the total personality, which, though present, cannot be fully known, the self. The ego is...subordinate to the self and is related to it like a part to the whole.[21]

Psychology," in *The Collected Works of C.G. Jung*, vol. 8 (*The Structure and Dynamics of the Psyche*), p. 344, § 661.)

[17]   Hence the tendency of Jungian analysts to specialize in the "mid-life crisis" of people who have achieved the standard social goals of establishing a career, family life, etc., but who then find themselves oppressed by a sense of emptiness. See, for example, James Hollis, *The Middle Passage: From Misery to Meaning in Midlife*, Toronto: Inner City Books 1993.

[18]   *SKS* 11, 129 / *SUD*, 13.

[19]   *SKS* 11, 130 / *SUD*, 14.

[20]   *SKS* 11, 129 / *SUD*, 13.

[21]   C.G. Jung, "Das Ich," in his *Gesammelte Werke*, vol. 9, Part 2 (*Aion. Beiträge zur Symbolik des Selbst*), p. 14, §§ 8–9. (English translation: "The Ego," in *The Collected Works of C.G. Jung*, vol. 9, Part 2 (*Aion: Researches into the Phenomenology of the Self*), p. 5, §§ 8–9.)

The self in that sense exists, even while we are unconscious of it; but to achieve self*hood* is to integrate the various aspects of the self, to consciously take them up as parts of who one is. One could perhaps say that for both Kierkegaard and Jung, one starts as a potential self, and has the task of fully *becoming* the self one can be. For Kierkegaard the failure to integrate and balance the various aspects of the personality leads to despair in its various forms.[22] So in *The Sickness unto Death* he sets out a schematic typology of persons, distinguished by which of their potentials they are overstressing and which they are neglecting. The aesthete is lost in imagination unconnected to reality; the "bourgeois philistine" lacks any imaginative sense for alternative possibilities, etc.[23] For Jung also, the process of individuation involves the recognition and integration of those aspects of one's personality that have been left relatively underdeveloped, but which are necessary to complement the more developed and acknowledged aspects of it:

> [T]he unconscious processes stand in a complementary relation to the conscious mind. I expressly use the word "complementary" and not "contrary" because conscious and unconscious are not necessarily in opposition to one another, but complement one another to form a totality, which is the *self*....The self is a quantity that is supraordinate to the conscious ego. It embraces not only the conscious, but also the unconscious psyche, and is therefore, so to speak, a personality which we *also* are.[24]

This connects Jung's explorations of the unconscious to his psychological typology. He distinguishes ideal types[25] along two main axes—introvert/extrovert and "rational"/"irrational,"[26] the rational being further broken down into "thinking" and "feeling" functions and the "irrational" into "sensation" and intuition." No one wholly conforms to these ideal types, and a healthy personality needs to include a balance of all these factors (though not necessarily in a precisely equal fashion). The less emphasized aspects of the personality will tend to get pushed into the unconscious and assume crude and undeveloped forms there, becoming what Jung calls "the shadow." But as complementary to the over-developed functions, they need to be integrated into the personality. A "rational" type needs to recognize his or her "irrational" side; a "rational" type who is predominantly oriented to thinking needs to recognize the complementary "feeling" aspect within the rational; an extrovert needs to recognize the introverted aspect of himself or herself. Thus Jung's description of psychological types is not simply a set of idealizations which real

---

22   "Possibility's Despair is to Lack Necessity....Necessity's Despair is to Lack Possibility," etc., see *SKS* 11, 151 / *SUD*, 35. *SKS* 11, 153 / *SUD*, 37.

23   See, for example, *SKS* 11, 152–3 / *SUD*, 156–7. *SKS* 11, / *SUD*, 41–2.

24   C.G. Jung, "Die Beziehungen zwischen dem Ich und dem Unbewußten," in his *Gesammelte Werke*, vol. 7 (*Zwei Schriften über analytische Psychologie*), p. 195, § 274. (English translation: "The Relations between the Ego and the Unconscious," in *The Collected Works of C.G. Jung* vol. 7 (*Two Essays on Analytical Psychology*), p. 177, § 274.)

25   "Ideal" in the sense in which a scientific model is an "idealization," abstracting from the more complex forms that actually exist. It is not, as we shall see, in any way an ideal goal, something one should strive to attain.

26   It should be noted that Jung is using these terms in a technical sense; there is nothing necessarily pejorative about "irrational" in this usage.

people may approximate to. For the closer real people come to approximating to these ideals the more pathologically one-sided they will be. Thus Jung's typology, like Kierkegaard's, is a gallery of pathological possibilities.

The similarities between Jung's and Kierkegaard's typologies are not merely structural but substantive as well (though of course they do not simply map onto one another in any neat and tidy way.) The best-known aspect of Jung's account is his description of introversion and extraversion. The ideal (and therefore one-sidedly) extraverted type is focused on externals and lacking self-awareness: "His whole consciousness looks outward, because the essential and decisive determination always comes from outside."[27] The danger here is that "a too extraverted attitude can also become so oblivious of the subject that the latter is sacrificed completely to so-called objective demands."[28] This means that the neglected introverted side of the personality is largely repressed, becoming unconscious, and is thus only able to develop in a crude way. But it makes itself felt, nonetheless, through a process of compensation for the one-sidedly extraverted nature of the conscious personality. But as a result, "the unconscious demands of the extravert have an exclusively primitive, infantile, egocentric character."[29] Jung's analysis of the pathologies of the one-sided extravert bear striking similarities to the critique that runs throughout Kierkegaard's whole work of those who, absorbed in externals (whether sensuality, work, duty or intellectual speculation) lack inwardness. Such people may "use their capacities, amass money, carry on secular enterprises, calculate shrewdly, etc., perhaps make a name in history, but themselves they are not; spiritually speaking, they have no self."[30] And Kierkegaard, like Jung, is well aware that the repressed aspects of the personality do not simply go away: "the anxiety that characterizes spiritlessness is recognized precisely by its spiritless sense of security. Nevertheless, anxiety lies underneath; likewise despair also lies underneath."[31] Jung insists that there are also corresponding dangers in a purely (one-sidedly) introverted attitude, which turns away from the outside world ("the object"):

> As a result of the ego's unadapted relation to the object…a compensatory attitude arises in the unconscious, which makes itself felt as an absolute and irrepressible tie to the object….It is now the unconscious that takes care of the relation to the object, and it does so in a way that is calculated to bring the [conscious ego's] illusion of power and [its] fantasy of superiority to utter ruin. In consequence, the ego's efforts to detach itself from the object and get it under control become all the more violent. In the end

---

[27] Jung, "Allgemeine Beschreibung der Typen," in his *Gesammelte Werke*, vol. 6 (*Psychologische Typen*), pp. 361–2, § 628. ("General Description of the Types," in *The Collected Works of C.G. Jung*, vol. 6 (*Psychological Types*), p. 334, § 563.)

[28] Jung, "Allgemeine Beschreibung der Typen," in his *Gesammelte Werke*, vol. 6 (*Psychologische Typen*), p. 364, § 632. ("General Description of the Types," in *The Collected Works of C.G. Jung*, vol. 6 (*Psychological Types*), p. 335, § 564.)

[29] Jung, "Allgemeine Beschreibung der Typen," in his *Gesammelte Werke*, vol. 6 (*Psychologische Typen*), p. 366, § 637. ("General Description of the Types," in *The Collected Works of C.G. Jung*, vol. 6 (*Psychological Types*), p. 338, § 571.)

[30] *SKS* 11, 150–1 / *SUD*, 35.

[31] *SKS* 11, 159 / *SUD*, 44.

it surrounds itself with a regular system of defenses….for the purpose of preserving at least the illusion of superiority.[32]

Kierkegaard certainly has more sympathy with the introverted than with the extraverted character. But he is also acutely aware of the dangers of excessive introversion. One example of this would be the aesthetic dreamer who loses reality by drifting too far into fantasy.[33] Another is what Kierkegaard describes as "inclosing reserve." This is the attitude of a self, shut up as behind a locked door, that is, in despair because it cannot (will not) express itself in the world or to others. In Kierkegaard's sketch, this character may be "a university graduate, husband, father, even an exceptionally competent public officeholder."[34] But this is a façade—what Jung calls a *persona*. It is hollow since the "inclosingly reserved" person does not fully inhabit or put himself into these relations to the outside world. But his self cannot flourish in this self-imposed isolation, for the need to express itself in relation to the world is a crucial part of the self. Moreover, Kierkegaard suggests that such a person may (as Jung would expect) become overpowered by a crude compensation. The despair "may break through," with the result that "a person in this kind of despair may hurl himself into life…a restless spirit who wants to forget…Or he will seek oblivion in sensuality."[35] A crude immersion in the external world attempts to compensate for the excessive introversion of a character whose isolation has become intolerable.

E. Subjectivity and Existential Engagement

Kierkegaard's emphasis on "subjectivity" is a call to serious self-examination. "Truth is subjectivity,"[36] in that the truth about oneself can only be grasped in a mood of serious self-concern, not in one of detached intellectual inquiry—an attitude that may be adopted precisely in order to evade the difficulty and pain of real self-knowledge. This is compatible with the recognition that "subjectivity is untruth" also;[37] that what one encounters in one's struggle to self-knowledge is precisely one's tendency to self-deception, to denial of (parts of) what one is. Jung also held these views together; indeed their conjunction is probably a necessary presupposition for any serious practice of psychotherapy. For a psychoanalytic or analytical psychological "cure" is not something that can be performed by the therapist on the patient (as a doctor might set a broken leg), but can only be achieved through the joint efforts of therapist and patient, with most of the effort coming from the latter. For both Freud and Jung, what is needed is not just that the patient acquires an intellectual

---

[32]   Jung, "Allgemeine Beschreibung der Typen," in his *Gesammelte Werke*, vol. 6 (*Psychologische Typen*), p. 412, § 697. ("General Description of the Types," in *The Collected Works of C.G. Jung*, vol. 6 (*Psychological Types*), pp. 378–9, § 626.)

[33]   *SKS* 11, 152–3 / *SUD*, 36–7.

[34]   *SKS* 11, 178 / *SUD*, 63–4.

[35]   *SKS* 11, 180 / *SUD*, 65–6.

[36]   *SKS* 7, 173–228 / *CUP1*, 189–251.

[37]   *SKS* 7, 189 / *CUP1*, 207.

recognition of the source of his or her problems, but that he or she "works through"[38] the issues in an intensely personal way. But Jungian analysis differs from classical Freudian analysis in that it typically takes place face to face, as an interchange between analyst and analysand, while in the classic Freudian mode, the analyst sits out of sight of the analysand, an (ideally) detached, objective observer. For Jung, the "counter-transference," the emotional involvement of the analyst with the patient, is as important as the "transference" itself, in which the patient projects his or her feelings onto the analyst.[39] As Kierkegaard reminds us, no one—analyst, scientist, metaphysician—escapes from being an existing human being, and, for Jung, the analyst cannot even be effective qua analyst if he or she retreats into a position of detached objectivity.

But the heart of the analytic work has to be done by the analysand, and this cannot be achieved if he or she adopts an attitude of detached observation to himself or herself. Jung gives a particularly good illustration of this—an example that is, moreover, deeply Kierkegaardian, since it involves an abstract intellectualizing by a patient, motivated precisely by a desire to repress an uncomfortable ethical insight:

> [A] highly intelligent young man...had worked out a detailed analysis of his own neurosis....He...asked me to tell him why he was not cured....I was forced to grant him that, if it were only a question of insight into the causal connections of a neurosis, he should in all truth be cured. Since he was not, I supposed that this must be due to the fact that his attitude to life was somehow fundamentally wrong....Jung then discovered that a poor school-teacher who loved him had cruelly deprived herself to indulge the young man in...visits to pleasure-resorts. His want of conscience was the cause of his neurosis, and it is not hard to see why scientific understanding failed to help him. His fundamental error lay in his moral attitude. He found my way of looking at the question shockingly unscientific....He supposed that by invoking scientific thought he could spirit away the immorality which he himself could not stomach.[40]

This must be regarded as a wonderfully Kierkegaardian case study!

F. Religious Concerns

The final, but centrally important connection to be noted between Kierkegaard and Jung is that both of them saw their psychological insights fitting into a religious context. Despite the efforts of some (over-) ingenious commentators to downplay his

---

[38] See Sigmund Freud, "Remembering, Repeating and Working Through," in the *Standard Edition of the Complete Psychological Works of Sigmund Freud*, vols. 1–24, ed. and trans. by James Strachey with Anna Freud, London: Hogarth Press 1953–74, vol. 12, pp. 145–56.

[39] See Christopher Perry, "Transference and Countertransference," in *The Cambridge Companion to Jung*, ed. by Polly Young-Eisendrath and Terence Dawson, 2nd ed., Cambridge: Cambridge University Press 2008, pp. 147–70.

[40] See C.G. Jung, "Das Grundproblem der gegenwärtigen Psychologie," in his *Gesammelte Werke*, vol. 8 (*Die Dynamik des Unbewußten*), p. 389, § 685. ("Basic Postulates of Analytical Psychology," in *The Collected Works of C.G. Jung*, vol. 8 (*The Structure and Dynamics of the Psyche*), pp. 355–6, § 685 (in *Modern Man in Search of a Soul*, pp. 223–4).

religious concerns, I take it to be obvious that Kierkegaard's thought is ultimately and indeed pervasively religious. Specifically, it is crucial for Kierkegaard that the self can only become whole—its potentially centrifugal elements can only hold together—if it is properly related to God. Jung's psychology also had a centrally religious aspect to it. His attitude differed sharply from that of Freud, who took for granted the falsity of all religious beliefs, saw them as delusions standing in the way of a proper understanding of our nature and situation, and was professionally interested only in why such obviously irrational beliefs came to be held.[41] Jung, on the contrary, saw religion as an expression of something fundamental to human nature: "[T]he human psyche, from time immemorial, has been shot through with religious feelings and ideas. Whoever cannot see this aspect of the human psyche is blind, and whoever chooses to explain it away, or to 'enlighten' it away, has no sense of reality."[42]

At the same time, just as Kierkegaard was intensely conscious of the way that Christian concepts (and indeed ethico-religious concepts in general) had been made banal and deprived of substantial meaning, so Jung was acutely aware of the contemporary sense of the "death of God." Medieval faith "no longer seems real to us, even in our dreams. Natural science has long ago torn this lovely veil to shreds.... Modern man has lost all the metaphysical certainties of his medieval brother."[43] But the religious need persists, however repressed or deprived of culturally established symbolic articulation, and that need is what Jung saw the discovery of oneself (one's self) and the individuation process as meeting:

> Among all my patients in the second half of life…there has not been one whose problem in the last resort was not that of finding a religious outlook on life. It is safe to say that every one of them fell ill because he had lost that to which the living religions of every age had given their followers, and none of them has been really healed who did not regain his religious outlook. This, of course, has nothing whatever to do with a particular creed or membership of a church.[44]

---

[41]   See Sigmund Freud, *The Future of an Illusion*, in *Standard Edition of the Complete Psychological Works of Sigmund Freud*, vol. 21.

[42]   C.G. Jung, "Der Gegensatz Freud und Jung," in his *Gesammelte Werke*, vol. 4 (*Freud und die Psychoanalyse*), p. 391, § 781. (English translation: "Freud and Jung: Contrasts," *The Collected Works of C.G. Jung*, vol. 4 (*Freud and Psychoanalysis*), p. 339, § 781 (in *Modern Man in Search of a Soul*, p. 140).

[43]   C.G. Jung, "Das Seelenproblem des modernen Menschen," in his *Gesammelte Werke*, vol. 10 (*Zivilisation im Übergang*), p. 98, §§ 162–3. (English translation: "The Spiritual Problem of Modern Man," in *The Collected Works of C.G. Jung*, vol. 10 (*Civilisation in Transition*) p. 81, §§ 162–3 (in *Modern Man in Search of a Soul*, p. 235).

[44]   C.G. Jung, "Über die Beziehung der Psychotherapie zur Seelsorge," in his *Gesammelte Werke*, vol. 11 (*Zur Psychologie westlicher und östlicher Religion*), p. 362, § 509. (English translation: "Psychotherapists or the Clergy?" in *The Collected Works of C.G. Jung*, vol. 11 (*Psychology and Religion: West and East*), p. 334, § 509 (in *Modern Man in Search of a Soul*, p. 264).

II. Jung's Response to Kierkegaard

Given all that they have in common, it is surprising that Jung has little to say explicitly about Kierkegaard, and that little is mostly hostile. But during Jung's student days in the 1890s, Kierkegaard was still little known outside of Scandinavia. He began to attract more attention in the German-speaking world after 1900, but it was not until after World War I that his became a household name amongst the intelligentsia. By then, Jung's main ideas were already formed, and, though he considerably elaborated on them, he showed little interest in considering new perspectives from philosophy or theology. This was despite the fact that some other eminent psychiatrists, such as Ludwig Binswanger (1881–1966) (who had studied with Jung) acknowledged Kierkegaard's influence,[45] and that the vogue for Kierkegaard in German philosophical circles really began with Karl Jaspers (1883–1969), who had been an influential psychiatrist before turning to philosophy.

There are precisely two references to Kierkegaard in Jung's 20-volume *Collected Works*. The first occurs in the important essay "Archetypes of the Collective Unconscious" (1934, revised 1954). There Jung considers how many Europeans, finding the symbolic language of Christianity worn bare and reduced to pious cliché by its familiarity, but needing some means by which to articulate their religious needs "become attracted by the symbols of the East...just as once before the heart and mind of antiquity were gripped by Christian ideas."[46] He goes on:

> There are many Europeans who began by surrendering completely to the influence of the Christian symbol until they landed themselves in a Kierkegaardian neurosis, or whose relation to God, owing to the progressive impoverishment of symbolism, developed into an unbearably sophisticated I-You relationship—only to fall victim in turn to the magic and novelty of Eastern symbols.[47]

Jung does not explain what he means by a "Kierkegaardian neurosis" (the sort of neurosis that Kierkegaard analyzed, or the sort of neurosis from which Jung supposed him to suffer); nor does he show any awareness that Kierkegaard was centrally concerned to respond to precisely the cultural situation Jung himself identifies in that passage—the banalization of Christian concepts through the fiction of a "Christian" society or culture.

The second reference to Kierkegaard comes in a rather similar context, in Jung's "Psychological Commentary on the Tibetan Book of the Great Liberation." Here again, Jung is contrasting "Western" and "Eastern" mentalities:

---

[45] See Reidar Thomte, "Historical Introduction" to *CA*, p. xviii.

[46] C.G. Jung, "Über die Archetypen des kollektiven Unbewußten," in his *Gesammelte Werke*, vol. 9, Part 1 (*Die Archetypen und das kollektive Unbewußte*), p. 18, § 11. (English translation: "The Archetypes and the Collective Unconscious," in *The Collected Works of C.G. Jung*, vol. 9, Part 1 (*The Archetypes and the Collective Unconscious*), p. 8, § 11.)

[47] C.G. Jung, "Über die Archetypen des kollektiven Unbewußten," in his *Gesammelte Werke*, vol. 9, Part 1 (*Die Archetypen und dar kollektive Unbewußte*), p. 18, § 11. (English translation: "The Archetypes and the Collective Unconscious," in *The Collected Works of C.G. Jung*, vol. 9, Part 1 (*The Archetypes and the Collective Unconscious*), p. 8, § 11.)

For [the Western mind] man is small inside; he is next to nothing; moreover, as Kierkegaard says, "before God, man is always wrong." By fear, reticence, promises, submission, self-abasement, good deeds and praise, he propitiates the great power which is not himself but *totaliter alter*, the wholly Other, altogether perfect.[48]

This reference is a bit more precise—it shows at least some awareness by Jung of a specific Kierkegaardian text, namely, the sermon "The Upbuilding that Lies in the Thought that, in Relation to God, We Are Always in the Wrong," from the second part of *Either/Or*.[49] And it gives us a clearer sense of what he might have meant by a "Kierkegaardian neurosis." It would seem to be something much like what Hegel calls "the unhappy consciousness"[50]—the attitude of someone who projects all that is of value outside himself and onto a purely external deity, before whom he then feels weak, sinful, and unworthy.[51]

At a number of places in his personal correspondence, Jung mentions Kierkegaard—usually in critical, even scathing, terms. He says at one point that he finds him "simply insupportable,"[52] and at another, describes him as a neurotic.[53] He does admit that "Kierkegaard was a stimulating and pioneering force precisely because of his neurosis," but then goes on to say that his "grizzling" or "moaning" enabled him to "settle everything in the study" so that he "need not do it in life."[54] This patronizing and insensitive comment can, sadly, be paralleled by comparably crude remarks on other philosophers—for example, "Heidegger's *modus philosophandi* is neurotic

---

[48]   C.G. Jung, "Psychologischer Kommentar zu: Das tibetische Buch der großen Befreiung," in his *Gesammelte Werke*, vol. 11 (*Zur Psychologie westlicher und östlicher Religion*), p. 519, § 772. (English translation: "Psychological Commentary on the Tibetan Book of the Great Liberation," in *The Collected Works of C.G. Jung*, vol. 11 (*Psychology and Religion: West and East*), p. 482, § 772.)

[49]   *SKS* 3, 320–32 / *EO2*, 339–54.

[50]   See G.W.F. Hegel, *Phenomenology of Spirit*, trans. by A.V. Miller, Oxford: Oxford University Press 1977, pp. 126–38.

[51]   This analysis was taken up by Feuerbach, who extended it, as Hegel did not, to Christianity as such, not just to a particular phase of Christianity. From Feuerbach, this theory of religion as alienation was of course taken up—more or less taken for granted—by Marx and Freud as the basis for their critiques of religion. Jung is closer to Hegel than to Feuerbach; he is far more positive about religion in general than Freud, and is willing indeed to find important psychological symbolism in Christianity in particular. However, he seems to find the Feuerbachian analysis convincing so far as some aspects at least of Christianity are concerned, and to see Kierkegaard simply as a preacher of this alienated and alienating religiosity.

[52]   C.G. Jung, *Briefe*, vols. 1–3, ed. by Aniela Jaffé and Gerhard Adler, Olten: Walter-Verlag 1972–73, vol. 1 (*1906–1945*), p. 294. (English translation: *Letters*, vols. 1–2, ed. by Gerhard Adler and Aniela Jaffé, trans. by R.F.C. Hull, Princeton, New Jersey: Princeton University Press 1973–75, vol. 1, p. 231 (letter to Rudolf Pannwitz, March 27, 1937).)

[53]   Jung, *Briefe*, vol. 1, p. 411. (*Letters*, vol. 1, p. 332 (letter to Arnold Künzli, March 16, 1943).)

[54]   Ibid.

through and through, and is ultimately rooted in his psychic crankiness."[55] In another letter Jung announces that "Kierkegaard's view that animals have no fear is totally disproved by the facts. There are whole species which consist of nothing but fear. A creature that loses its fear is condemned to death."[56] But although Kierkegaard (Haufniensis) does claim in *The Concept of Anxiety* that "anxiety is not found in the beast," this claim follows from his careful distinction between fear, which refers to "something definite," and anxiety, that is, the "freedom's actuality as the possibility of possibility."[57] Kierkegaard is clearly not denying the obvious facts about animal fear that Jung cites; and Jung's impression that he was shows that Jung can have had only the haziest idea of what Kierkegaard was saying in *The Concept of Anxiety*, to which the distinction between anxiety and fear is, of course, crucial.

It is not clear from these few references what, if anything, Jung had read of Kierkegaard; he had at least enough sense of him to find him seriously annoying, but his few off-hand comments tell us more about Jung himself than about Kierkegaard. Certainly they show little serious understanding of Kierkegaard on Jung's part; nor do they show Jung making any serious attempt to reach such an understanding. This is puzzling (not to say sad) just because there are, as noted above, so many important commonalities in the thought of Kierkegaard and Jung.

III. Religious Differences

Given all that Kierkegaard and Jung had in common, why was Jung so dismissive and/or hostile towards Kierkegaard? I think the most plausible answer to this question, although I am being (unavoidably) a little speculative here, can be found in their attitudes to religion. For it is here that I think we can find, for all their commonalities, the deepest points of contention between them. And these (as well as purely contingent factors such as simple ignorance and/or misunderstanding of Kierkegaard on Jung's part) may help to explain Jung's attitude. That Kierkegaard and Jung are both essentially religious psychologists is one of the most important things they have in common, but religion is, notoriously, at least as prone to divide as to unite, and there are substantial differences between Jung's and Kierkegaard's religious ideas. (Though, as I shall try to show, these are not perhaps as great as they might at first appear.)

One can start with a biographical speculation. Jung's father, as noted above, was a pastor in the Swiss Reformed (Calvinist) Church, in which the young Carl Jung was naturally raised. In his autobiography,[58] Jung records his disillusion with

---

[55]   Jung, *Briefe*, vol. 1, p. 410. (*Letters*, vol. 1, p. 331 (letter to Arnold Künzli, February 28, 1943).)

[56]   Jung, *Briefe*, vol. 1, p. 492. (*Letters*, vol. 1, p. 399 (letter to pastor Fritz Buri, December 10, 1945).)

[57]   *SKS* 4, 348 / *CA*, 42.

[58]   C.G Jung, *Erinnerungen, Träume, Gedanken*, ed. by Aniela Jaffé, Stuttgart and Zurich: Rascher Verlag 1962. (English translation: *Memories, Dreams, Reflections*, recorded and ed. by Aniela Jaffe, trans. by R. and C. Winston, London: Fontana Books, HarperCollins 1995. This book contains chapters written by Jung, and others written up by Jaffe from

the Church, which seemed to him to be spiritually empty, a place of mechanically observed routines.[59] He was baffled by what he saw as the contradictions in the official Christian doctrines he was taught.[60] Though he had a strongly religious sensibility, he could find nothing of the terror and mystery of his religious experience in either the teachings or the activities of the Church.[61] And he came to believe that his father had really lost his own faith and was desperately trying to deny that to himself while going through the motions of a pastor's professional existence.[62] In later life, Jung often expressed appreciation for the rich symbolism of Catholic liturgy, imagery, and ritual, which he saw as performing a psychologically valuable role which the more iconoclastic Protestant Churches had given up on.[63] He did sometimes continue to refer to himself as a "Protestant,"[64] for he felt that his religious sensibility had been inescapably marked by his upbringing and heritage; moreover, he saw himself as one who, in the spirit of Luther's original revolt, stood alone before God, without ecclesiastical intervention.[65] However, his attitude to the mainstream Protestant Churches remained generally unsympathetic, conditioned by his own childhood experience.

---

the transcripts of interviews she did with Jung; the whole being then edited by Jaffe. So it is not exactly a straightforward autobiography, and should be treated with some caution. (See Shamdasani, *Jung and the Making of Modern Psychology*, pp. 23–4.) But it would be extravagant to suggest that it can be dismissed or ignored.

[59]   Jung, *Erinnerungen, Träume, Gedanken*, pp. 51–2; pp. 58–61. (*Memories, Dreams, Reflections*, pp. 62–3; pp. 70–3.)

[60]   Jung, *Erinnerungen, Träume, Gedanken*, p. 52; p. 58 (*Memories, Dreams, Reflections*, p. 63; p. 70.)

[61]   Jung, *Erinnerungen, Träume, Gedanken*, pp. 47–8; pp. 51–2; p. 60. (*Memories, Dreams, Reflections*, pp. 58–9; pp. 62–3; p. 72.)

[62]   Jung, *Erinnerungen, Träume, Gedanken*, pp. 48–9; p. 61. (*Memories, Dreams, Reflections*, pp. 59–60; p. 73.)

[63]   For instance, C.G. Jung, "Das symbolische Leben," in his *Gesammelte Werke*, vol. 18 (*Das symbolische Leben*), tome 1, pp. 287–301, §§ 608–34. (English translation: "The Symbolic Life," in *The Collected Works of C.G. Jung*, vol. 18 (*The Symbolic Life: Miscellaneous Writings*), pp. 267–76, §§ 608–34.) See also Ann Lammers, *In God's Shadow: The Collaboration of C.G. Jung and Victor White*, New York: Paulist Press 1994, pp. 132–5. Focusing on Jung's relationship with the English Dominican theologian Victor White, this is one of the best studies of Jung's attitude to orthodox Christianity.

[64]   See, for example, Jung, "Über die Beziehung der Psychotherapie zur Seelsorge," in his *Gesammelte Werke*, vol. 11 (*Zur Psychologie westlicher und östlicher Religion*), pp. 368–9, § 522; p. 374–5 § 537. ("Psychotherapists or the Clergy?" in *The Collected Works of C.G. Jung*, vol. 11 (*Psychology and Religion: West and East*), p. 340, § 522; p. 347, § 537. (*Modern Man in Search of a Soul*, p. 273; p. 281.)

[65]   "A Protestant [is] a man who is defenceless against God and no longer shielded by walls or communities, he has a unique spiritual opportunity for immediate religious experience." See C.G. Jung, "Psychologie und Religion," in his *Gesammelte Werke*, vol. 11 (*Zur Psychologie westlicher und östlicher Religion*), p. 53, § 86. (English translation: "Psychology and Religion," in *The Collected Works of C.G. Jung*, vol. 11 (*Psychology and Religion: West and East*), p. 49, § 86.)

The wave of interest in Kierkegaard in post-World War I Europe had both philosophical and theological sources. Kierkegaard was an important influence not only on Jaspers and Heidegger, but on Karl Barth (1886–1968), and the radical "Crisis Theology" or "Neo-Orthodoxy" with which he was associated. Barth was Swiss and a prominent public figure; he and Jung were the only Swiss intellectuals of their day to enjoy real international fame and status. Jung refers to him occasionally, but generally with suspicion. In a letter he writes: "I wonder which devil Karl Barth (with his absolute God) worships in practice. It's very likely one of them has him by the collar."[66] Although Barth was concerned to shake the Protestant (and especially the Reformed) Church out of the stupor that had so depressed the adolescent Jung, it seems that the mature Jung associated Barth with a spiritually arid Calvinist orthodoxy. If, as seems possible, Jung's understanding of Kierkegaard was filtered, at least in good part, through broadly Barthian channels (that is to say, he understood Kierkegaard to a large extent as an intellectual ancestor of Barth), then that might explain his intensely negative reaction to Kierkegaard. Jung may have found that Kierkegaard carried with him too many deeply personal connotations— reminders of the dispiriting ecclesiastical background to his own childhood—for him to read Kierkegaard with any sympathy or open-mindedness. Instead, a sort of allergic reaction, a defensive gesture of repudiation, may have been triggered by the association of Kierkegaard, via Barth, with his own religious upbringing.

This is speculation, though I think it has some plausibility. We can get back to somewhat firmer ground by considering the actual differences between Jung's and Kierkegaard's religious ideas. These are certainly real, though not perhaps as great as they might at first appear. A first difference is that Kierkegaard is a committedly Christian thinker, and clearly differentiates (genuine) Christianity from all other religious outlooks. Jung, on the other hand, has an equally respectful interest in many different religions, and an exclusive commitment to none. (And he often shows a particular interest in and sympathy for marginal, esoteric or heretical movements, like alchemy and Gnosticism.) Secondly, Jung has often been charged with a sort of theological anti-realism; many have wondered about whether God, for Jung, is ultimately anything more than the self.[67] On this view, Jung, like Freud, is a reductionist, although a much subtler one. For him, there are genuinely religious needs and impulses in the human psyche, which are not just disguised expressions of more real forces such as infantile sexuality; but those religious impulses do not in the end refer to anything extra-psychical. The language of relation to God would thus express no more than a relationship to oneself. Martin Buber (1878–1965) criticizes Jung along these lines in his essay "Religion and Modern Thinking."[68] According

---

[66]   Jung, *Briefe*, vol. 1, p. 84. (*Letters*, vol. 1, p. 58 (letter to Albert Oeri, January 4, 1929).)

[67]   The self in the rich Jungian sense explicated above, of course; not just the ego.

[68]   Martin Buber, "Religion und Modernes Denken," *Merkur*, vol. 6, no. 2, 1952, pp. 101–20. (English translation: "Religion and Modern Thinking," in his *Eclipse of God: Studies in the Relation between Religion and Philosophy*, trans. by Eugene Kamenka and Maurice S. Friedman, Atlantic Highlands, New Jersey: Humanities Press International 1988, pp. 65–92). The first half of the essay deals with Sartre and Heidegger, the second half with Jung. I have focused on Buber's critique of Jung since it has acquired something of the status of a *locus*

to Buber, Jung "conceives of God not as a Being or Reality to which a psychical content corresponds, but rather as this content itself."[69] So, for him, "that which experiences the religious, the soul, experiences simply itself."[70]

A third point of difference is that Jung rejects the traditional idea of God as perfect. Rather, according to Jung, God, like us, has a dark "shadow" side, an element of evil within Himself.[71] Of course, what one makes of this claim depends on what one makes of the realism issue. Is Jung's account of God's shadow a sort of Gnostic theology in which the really existing, extra-psychic God has an evil side, or is it merely a description of the God-image as it exists in the human psyche? (Or, more specifically, is it a description of "God" (Jahveh), the literary character presented in the Bible, which is the primary form of the God-image in the West.) But in any case, according to Jung's critics, this idea leads to a fourth, this time ethical, difference between Jung and traditional orthodoxy. For on this view, Jung rejects the idea that we should strive to become good and eschew evil ("be ye perfect as your father in heaven is perfect"[72]), and proposes instead the goal of becoming integrated, which includes an acceptance of the evil as well as the good within one's nature. As Buber puts it, "The soul which is integrated in the Self as the unification in an all-encompassing wholeness of the opposites, especially the opposites good and evil, dispenses with the conscience as the court which distinguishes and decides between the right and the wrong."[73] Furthermore, all of this is for Jung an intra-psychic event. Buber complains that Jung is concerned only with the process of integration within the self, and fails to see it as essentially related to others: "[T]he self, even if it has integrated all of its unconscious elements, remains this single self confined within itself."[74] For Buber, by contrast, what is needed is "a genuine contact with the existing being who meets me…full and direct reciprocity with him. [A way that] leads from the soul which places reality in itself to the soul that enters reality."[75]

Although the differences between Kierkegaard and Jung are real, they can easily be exaggerated. On the first point, Kierkegaard does insist on the distinctiveness of the "paradoxical" religiousness of Christianity, but he remains respectful of non-Christian religiousness (the "Religiousness A" of the *Concluding Unscientific Postscript*, exemplified by his beloved Socrates). Non-Christian religions are not so much false as partial in their grasp of the truth; and Socrates had a genuine God-relationship, however limited. Though religiousness A may be inadequate from a

---

classicus; and because Buber, though (as we shall see) himself critical of Kierkegaard, was also deeply influenced by him. Buber's critique of Jung is distinctively Kierkegaardian in spirit, and so is particularly useful for our purposes here.

[69]   Buber, *Eclipse of God*, p. 80.

[70]   Ibid., p. 84.

[71]   An idea most fully addressed in Jung's *Answer to Job*. See C.G. Jung, *Antwort auf Hiob*, in his *Gesammelte Werke*, vol. 11 (*Zur Psychologie westlicher und östlicher Religion*), pp. 385–506, §§ 553–758. (English translation: *Answer to Job*, in *The Collected Works of C.G. Jung*, vol. 11 (*Psychology and Religion: West and East*), pp. 357–470, §§ 553–758.)

[72]   Matt 5:48.

[73]   Buber, *Eclipse of God*, p. 87.

[74]   Ibid., p. 89.

[75]   Ibid.

strictly Christian standpoint, its attainment is a significant spiritual accomplishment, a large step beyond the aesthetic or merely ethical standpoints on the way to becoming whole. And Jung, for his entire refusal to treat Christianity as having a special status, continued to call himself a Christian and even specifically a Protestant: "I am definitely inside Christianity....I am a Protestant in my soul and body."[76] For all his interest in certain aspects of Hinduism, Buddhism, and Taoism, he often claims that as a European, his religious outlook is necessarily shaped by Christianity, and that he can approach Eastern religious traditions only as an interested outsider.[77] Of course, this is a remark about himself, and his historical-cultural conditioning, not about the intrinsic value or disvalue of any particular tradition, and so a genuine difference between him and Kierkegaard remains.

As for the issue of realism, Jung's position is not, I think, as clearly anti-realist as has often been supposed. His statements on this matter are often vague and sometimes apparently conflicting,[78] but there is an underlying basic consistency in his thought. Although he often describes himself as a scientist, an "empiricist," his philosophical position is basically Kantian.[79] We cannot know what either the physical or the psychical is in itself, but we can study the ways in which they appear as phenomena to consciousness.[80] This is what both the physicist and the psychologist do. Metaphysical claims about the ultimate nature of that which appears phenomenally to us, or about realities that altogether transcend experience, can be neither affirmed nor denied: "Psychological truth by no means excludes metaphysical truth, though

---

[76]   Jung, *Briefe*, vol. 3, p. 63. (*Letters*, vol. 2, p. 334 (letter to Rev. H.L. Philp, October 26, 1956).)

[77]   See, for example, C.G. Jung, "Yoga und der Western," in his *Gesammelte Werke*, vol. 11 (*Zur Psychologie westlicher und östlicher Religion*), pp. 574–80, §§ 865–76 (English translation: "Yoga and the West," in *The Collected Works of C.G. Jung*, vol. 11 (*Psychology and Religion: West and East*), pp. 532–7, §§ 865–76); and C.G. Jung, "Geleitwort zu D.T. Suzuki: Die große Befreiung," in his *Gesammelte Werke*, vol. 11 (*Zur Psychologie westlicher und östlicher Religion*), pp. 598–602, §§ 902–7. (English translation: "Foreword to Suzuki's 'Introduction to Zen Buddhism,' " in *The Collected Works of C.G. Jung*, vol. 11 (*Psychology and Religion: West and East*), pp. 553–7, §§ 902–7.)

[78]   "As for his personal religious convictions, Jung made such apparently blatantly contradictory statements that even his closest students tend to retire in discouragement with the attempt to follow him." See Nagy, *Philosophical Issues in the Psychology of C.G. Jung*, p. 2.

[79]   See Shamdasani, *Jung and the Making of Modern Psychology*, pp. 163–202; Lammers, *In God's Shadow: The Collaboration of C.G. Jung and Victor White*, pp. 114–16; Nagy, *Philosophical Issues in the Psychology of C.G. Jung*, pp. 11–36.

[80]   Hence Jung sometimes describes himself as a "phenomenologist" (see, for example, Jung, "Psychologie und Religion," in his *Gesammelte Werke*, vol. 11 (*Zur Psychologie westlicher und östlicher Religion*), p. 1, § 2 ("Psychology and Religion," in *The Collected Works of C.G. Jung*, vol. 11 (*Psychology and Religion: West and East*), p. 2, § 2.), which is really less misleading than "empiricist." Cf. Brookes, *Jung and Phenomenology* for a detailed reading of Jung as (in practice, and despite various theoretical inconsistencies) a phenomenologist. This does not conflict with Jung's essential Kantianism, as phenomenology is itself a distinctively post-Kantian philosophy.

psychology, as a science, has to hold aloof from all metaphysical assertions."[81] It should be noted, though, that Jung does not claim that metaphysical statements are, as the logical positivists would say, meaningless; but he regards them as lying outside his competence as a scientist and doctor. Describing "metaphysicians" as those who "think they know about unknowable things in the Beyond," he continues: "I have never ventured to declare that such things do *not* exist; but neither have I ventured to suppose that any statement of mine could in any way touch them."[82] What he can assert is the reality of the God-image in the psyche, and the vital necessity for individuation of orienting oneself properly to it; but he can neither affirm nor deny the reality of an "objective" God corresponding to that image, or indeed, distorted or falsified by it.

A real difference between Jung and Kierkegaard remains. For Kierkegaard, it is only through relating to the genuinely extra-psychical reality of God that we can be made whole; the ontological question of the ultimate reality of God cannot be bracketed, since it is tied up with the existential issues of becoming a self. So, although Jung does not deny the extra-psychic reality of God, he does still differ from Kierkegaard, who thinks it necessary to positively affirm it. Again, though, the difference can be made to seem starker than it is. For Kierkegaard also dismisses any merely abstract or speculative approach to God and, like Kant and Jung, rejects the traditional metaphysical proofs of God.[83] A genuine relation to or knowledge of God is an existential or subjective one; which means that we relate to God only via the ways in which we are able to apprehend him (that is, through our God-images.) For Kierkegaard, though, it is crucial that what we relate to via our subjectivity is the real God, whereas Jung is content to set that question aside.

This connects to Buber's complaint that, more generally, Jung makes individuation a purely intra-psychical event, unconnected to any relationship with a real other. For Buber, God is such an other, but, crucially so are other finite selves, and he criticizes Kierkegaard for neglecting the importance of our relationships with finite others as well as with God. Taking Kierkegaard's own broken engagement as an example, Buber writes: "God wants us to come to him by means of the Reginas he has created and not by renunciation of them."[84] This criticism may be rather unfair, for whether or not Kierkegaard was right to break off with Regine Olsen, he was acutely aware that he was acting as "an exception," not proposing a policy of renunciation as generally valid. But it is interesting to find that Jung criticizes

---

[81]　　　C.G. Jung, "Symbole der Mutter und der Widergeburt," in his *Gesammelte Werke*, vol. 5 (*Symbole der Wandlung. Analyse des Vorspiels zu einer Schizophrenie*), p. 295, § 344. (English translation: "Symbols of the Mother and of Rebirth," in *The Collected Works of C.G. Jung*, vol. 5 (*Symbols of Transformation*), p. 231, § 344.)

[82]　　　C.G. Jung, "Religion und Psychologie: Eine Antwort an Martin Buber," in his *Gesammelte Werke*, vol. 18 (*Das symbolische Leben*), tome 2, p. 711, § 1503. (English translation: "Religion and Psychology: Reply to Martin Buber," in *The Collected Works of C.G. Jung*, vol. 18 (*The Symbolic Life*), p. 664, § 1503.)

[83]　　　See *SKS* 4, 244–9 / *PF*, 39–44. *SKS* 7, 186 / *CUP1*, 203–4. *SKS* 7, 304–6 / *CUP1*, 333–5.

[84]　　　Martin Buber, "The Question to the Single One," in his *Between Man and Man*, trans. by R.G. Smith, London: Fontana 1961, p. 73.

Kierkegaard in precisely the same terms in one of his letters: "when God appeared to him in the shape of 'Regina' he took to his heels. It was too terrible for him to have to subordinate his autocratism to the love of another person."[85] This itself suggests (again setting aside the question of whether Jung is fair to Kierkegaard here) that Jung does not deny that psychological wholeness may, or may in part, come about through the relationship to another person. And, as is shown by the case noted above of the intellectually acute but ethically clueless young man who was sponging off his impoverished lover, Jung was well aware that a bad relationship to another can cause, or preclude the healing of, a neurosis (a misrelation within oneself). Nevertheless, there is at least a difference of emphasis here. Buber stresses the ways in which the self can become whole through relations to others, while Jung is mainly concerned with the need to establish a healthy self-relation in order to then be able to relate well to others, instead of simply projecting one's inner conflicts onto them. But it does seem to me that these insights can be regarded as complementary, which makes the complete failure of mutual understanding which characterized the Jung–Buber debate particularly sad. (Similarly, Buber stresses the ways in which we can relate to God through relating properly to others, while Kierkegaard emphasizes how we need to relate rightly to God in order to relate rightly to other people. Again, it does not seem to me that we need be forced to an either/or here.)

That Jung sees God as having an evil side to him is, on the face of it, a serious divergence from Kierkegaard's view. For the latter, in the words of his favorite biblical quotation, God is "the father of lights, with whom there is no change or shadow of variation," and from whom "every good gift and every perfect gift," proceeds.[86] Following a long tradition of Christian Platonism, Kierkegaard sees God as "the Good" in the single-minded willing of which "Purity of heart" consists.[87] Jung, on the contrary, rejects the Platonic-Augustinian view that evil is a lack of goodness, rather than something real in itself. The traditional doctrine he took (falsely, I think) to involve a trivialization or glossing over of the reality of evil: "One could hardly call the things that have happened, and still happen, in the concentration camps of the dictator states an 'accidental lack of perfection'—it would sound like a mockery."[88] Jung at times seems to argue that the evil which so clearly characterizes the world must be traced back to some evil in the creator of that world: "In a monotheistic religion everything that goes against God must be traced back to God himself."[89] This kind of argument, though, would go against Jung's

---

[85]   Jung, *Briefe*, vol. 2, p. 366. (*Letters*, vol. 2, p. 145 (letter to pastor Willi Bremi, December 26, 1953).)

[86]   James 1:17. Kierkegaard uses this as the text for several of his upbuilding discourses. See *SKS* 5, 41–56 / *EUD*, 31–48. *SKS* 5, 129–42 / *EUD*, 125–39. *SKS* 5, 143–58 / *EUD*, 141–58.

[87]   *SKS* 8, 138ff. / *UD*, 24ff.

[88]   C.G. Jung, "Christus, ein Symbol des Selbst," in his *Gesammelte Werke*, vol. 9, Part 2 (*Aion. Beiträge zur Symbolik des Selbst*), p. 63, § 96. (English translation: "Christ, a Symbol of the Self," in *The Collected Works of C.G. Jung*, vol. 9, Part 2 (*Aion: Researches into the Phenomenology of the Self*), p. 53, § 96.)

[89]   C.G. Jung, "Versuch einer psychologischen Deutung des Trinitätsdogmas," in his *Gesammelte Werke*, vol. 11 (*Zur Psychologie westlicher und östlicher Religion*), p. 185, §

own rejection of "metaphysics," as it attempts to argue to the nature of God from observations of the world. Jung is on stronger ground if his remarks about the evil in God's nature are taken as remarks about the God-image. For the God of the Bible (in the New Testament as well as the Old) does seem to have a distinctly demonic edge to him, and the efforts by orthodox theologians to reconcile the goodness of the biblical God with his violence, from the destruction of Sodom and Gomorrah in the book of Genesis to the final apocalypse in the book of Revelation, have a distinctly disingenuous ring to them. Liberal theologians typically set aside the demonic aspects of God as distorted representations of his true nature, but Jung, while maintaining his "official" agnosticism on this issue,[90] insists on the integrity of the God-image found in the Bible, which he also finds in other myths and religions, and considers to be an archetype deeply rooted in the Collective Unconscious.

If Jung is not intending to refer to God's intrinsic nature, then his claim that God (the God-image) is partly evil does not directly contradict Kierkegaard's belief that God (in his real, intrinsic nature) is wholly good. But a great difference does remain between them. For Kierkegaard does not even take God-as-represented-in-the Bible to be (partly) evil. This claim might be challenged, for his most famous book, *Fear and Trembling*, is a meditation on Abraham's response to one of the more strikingly "demonic" commands of the biblical God—that he sacrifice Isaac. But although Johannes de silentio does entertain the possibility of God suspending the ethical and commanding the killing of the innocent, he is concerned with the existential horror of Abraham's predicament, not with judging God to be evil.[91] Indeed, his emphasis is on Abraham's faith; he prepares to sacrifice Isaac, not out of terrified submission to arbitrary power, or in a spirit of Dionysian identification with that sublimely amoral power, but in a spirit of trust that all will ultimately be well, that God, despite all appearances, is not demanding of him something wicked and cruel. Certainly, religion is presented as transcending the merely ethical, and in that Kierkegaard can be said to take a step in the direction of Jung's position. But it remains crucial for Kierkegaard, as we saw above, that the teleological aim of the self is towards

---

249. (English translation: "A Psychological Approach to the Dogma of the Trinity," in *The Collected Works of C.G. Jung*, vol. 11 (*Psychology and Religion: West and East*), p. 169, § 249.)

[90]   "Analysis of the unconscious has long since demonstrated the existence of these powers in the form of archetypal images which, be it noted, are not identical with the corresponding intellectual concepts. One can of course, believe that the concepts of the conscious mind are, through the inspiration of the Holy Ghost direct and correct representations of their metaphysical referent. But this conviction is only possible for one who already possesses the gift of faith." See Jung, "Religion und Psychologie: Eine Antwort an Martin Buber," in his *Gesammelte Werke*, vol. 18 (*Das symbolische Leben*), tome 2, p. 712, § 1505. ("Religion and Psychology: Reply to Martin Buber," in *The Collected Works of C.G. Jung*, vol. 18 (*The Symbolic Life*), p. 665, § 1505.)

[91]   That the work is pseudonymous is worth remembering. I shall not attempt to consider the complex question of how Kierkegaard's own attitude relates to that of Johannes. But Johannes himself, it should be noted, comes to no positive conclusion. He repeatedly insists that he cannot understand Abraham (*SKS* 4, 132 / *FT*, 26. *SKS* 4, 200 / *FT*, 112) and even that he is appalled by him (*SKS* 4, 153 / *FT*, 60).

a real and wholly good God. Jung, however, dismisses such ontological claims as unknowable, and focuses instead on our need to come to terms with the powerfully numinous, but also terrifying, God-image within. It should be stressed though, that this is *not* a call for us to imitate that terrifying inner deity. (One might say, "Be ye therefore evil as your Father is evil.") Jung's response to the dark side of the biblical God, expressed most nakedly in *Answer to Job*, is one of indignation and anger. Far from recommending that we worship or try to model ourselves on an image of cruel and arbitrary power, he protests vehemently against it.

This brings us to the final, ethical, criticism of Jung, that he relativizes good and evil. This is, I think, a misunderstanding, though one for which the lack of clarity in Jung's own language is in part responsible.[92] For Jung is by no means attempting to promote an antinomian acceptance of evil as legitimate, or to reject the normative distinction between good and evil.[93] Rather, his call to us to integrate our "shadows" has two main aspects. Firstly, we should accept those aspects of ourselves which have been repressed due to social influences, or the accidents of our personal histories, and which are indeed potentially dangerous—but also potentially valuable and life-giving (for example, sexuality, assertiveness, individual creativity). These need to be integrated with the other aspects of the personality (which does not, of course, mean that they should take over the personality and then, in their turn, repress the other aspects); the harm that they may do is more likely to occur if we continue to repress them, and thus leave them to fester in crude, un-integrated forms in the unconscious. This, of course, concerns not the integration of what really is evil, but merely of what is conventionally (and too narrowly) labeled as such. But, secondly, Jung does want us to acknowledge our propensity to real evil-doing. To become aware of that, though, is not to celebrate it, but to increase the possibility of bringing it more under conscious control. If it is left unacknowledged, we are in great danger of self-righteousness and of projecting the evil in ourselves onto another, who can then become a convenient scapegoat, an object of persecution. As Lammers puts it: "For Jung, the inclusion of evil and darkness cannot be a blind enactment of the shadow. Rather, it must be a process of becoming conscious of evil, and bearing one's own share of it."[94] The demand to integrate—that is, to recognize as part of oneself and

---

[92]   Lammers says that Jung's arguments will be found "hopelessly confusing" if we do not make explicit a distinction that is left implicit in his work, between the "evil of myth"— the potentially creative shadow—and the "evil of history"—the actual cruelties and atrocities which people commit and to which Jung responded with as much outrage as anyone. See Lammers, *In God's Shadow: The Collaboration of C.G. Jung and Victor White*, pp. 180–1.

[93]   As Jung says, alluding to, and rejecting, Nietzsche: "Even on the highest peak, we shall never be 'beyond good and evil.' " See Jung, "Versuch einer psychologischen Deutung des Trinitätsdogmas," in his *Gesammelte Werke*, vol. 11 (*Zur Psychologie westlicher und östlicher Religion*), p. 196, § 267. ("A Psychological Approach to the Dogma of the Trinity," in *The Collected Works of C.G. Jung*, vol. 11 (*Psychology and Religion: West and East*), p. 180, § 267.)

[94]   Lammers notes that Jung's case against the God of Job is that His arbitrary cruelty is due precisely to His lack of awareness of His shadow. See Lammers, *In God's Shadow: The Collaboration of C.G. Jung and Victor White*, p. 174.

not project onto others—one's capacity to do evil, is itself a moral demand, not a license to indulge ones evil tendencies:

> If you imagine someone who is brave enough to withdraw all these projections, then you get an individual who is conscious of a pretty thick shadow….Such a man knows that whatever is wrong in the world is in himself, and if he only learns to deal with his own shadow, he has done something real for the world….[The] social problems of today…are mostly so difficult because they are poisoned by mutual projections. How can anyone see straight when he does not even see himself and the darkness he unconsciously carries with him in all his dealings?[95]

This view does not, as far as I can see, include anything that would not be in principle acceptable to Kierkegaard. It is indeed a position deeply rooted in the Christian (and particularly Lutheran) tradition, according to which we are all sinners and need to be deeply aware of the dangers of Phariseeism or moralistic confidence in our own power to do good. What it does lack, of course, is the Lutheran assurance that we are upheld by the grace of a good God, despite our evil. I do not want to underestimate the importance of that belief for Kierkegaard. But however deep his ultimate divergence from Jung may be, the difference between them is not the difference that would separate Kierkegaard from a Nietzschean amoralist.

---

[95]   Jung, "Psychologie und Religion," in his *Gesammelte Werke*, vol. 11 (*Zur Psychologie westlicher und östlicher Religion*), p. 91, § 140. ("Psychology and Religion," in *The Collected Works of C.G. Jung*, vol. 11 (*Psychology and Religion: West and East*), p. 83, § 140.)

Bibliography

I. References to or Uses of Kierkegaard in Jung's Corpus

"Über die Archetypen des kollektiven Unbewußten," *Eranos-Jahrbuch*, vol. 2, 1934 (*Ostwestliche Symbolik und Seelenführung*), ed. by Olga Fröbe-Kapteyn, Zurich: Rhein-Verlag 1934, pp. 179–229, see p. 185 (a revised version published in his *Von den Wurzeln des Bewusstseins. Studien über den Archetypus*, Zurich: Rascher Verlag 1954, see p. 10; in his *Gesammelte Werke*, vols. 1–20, Olten: Walter Verlag 1971–94, vol. 9, Part 1 (*Die Archetypen und das kollektive Unbewußte*), p. 18, § 11; English translation: "The Archetypes and the Collective Unconscious," in *The Collected Works of C.G. Jung*, vols. 1–20, ed. by Herberg Read, Michael Fordham, and Gerhard Adler, trans. by R.F.C. Hull, Princeton, New Jersey: Princeton University Press 1953–79, vol. 9, Part 1 (*The Archetypes and the Collective Unconscious*), p. 8, § 11.)

"Psychologischer Kommentar zu Das tibetanische Buch der grossen Befreiung," in his *Gesammelte Werke*, vols. 1–20, Olten: Walter Verlag 1971–94, vol. 11 (*Zur Psychologie westlicher und östlicher Religion*), p. 519, § 772. (English translation: "Psychological Commentary on the Tibetan Book of the Great Liberation," in *The Collected Works of C.G. Jung*, vols. 1–20, ed. by Herberg Read, Michael Fordham, and Gerhard Adler, trans. by R.F.C. Hull, Princeton, New Jersey: Princeton University Press 1953–79, vol. 11 (*Psychology and Religion: West and East*), p. 482, § 772.)

Briefe, vols. 1–3, ed. by Aniela Jaffé and Gerhard Adler, Olten: Walter Verlag 1972–73, vol. 1, p. 294; p. 410; p 492; vol. 2, p. 366. (English translation: *Letters*, vols. 1–2, ed. by Gerhard Adler and Aniela Jaffé, trans. by R.F.C. Hull, Princeton, New Jersey: Princeton University Press 1973–75, vol. 1, p. 231; pp. 331–2; p. 399; vol. 2, p. 145.)

II. Sources of Jung's Knowledge of Kierkegaard

Barth, Karl, *Der Römerbrief*, 2nd ed., Munich: Kaiser 1922, pp. v–vi; p. xii; pp. 15–16; p. 71; p. 75; p. 77; pp. 85–9; p. 93; p. 96; pp. 98–9; p. 114; p. 141; p. 145; p. 236; p. 261; p. 264; p. 267; p. 319; p. 325; p. 381; p. 400; pp. 426–7; p. 455; p. 481; pp. 483–4.

— *Die Kirchliche Dogmatik*, vols. I–IV, Zollikon-Zürich: Zürich 1932–70, I/1, p. 19; II/2, p. 338; III/2, p. 22; pp. 133–4; III/3, p. 428; IV/I, p. 165; p. 381; p. 769; p. 828; p. 844; IV/2, p. 125; pp. 848–9; p. 886; IV/3, 1st half, p. 467; IV/3, 2nd half, p. 572.

Binswanger, Ludwig, *Einführung in die Probleme der allgemeinen Psychologie*, Berlin: Springer 1922, p. 225; p. 296; p. 322; p. 324.

— "Welche Aufgaben ergeben sich für die Psychiatrie aus den Fortschritten der neueren Psychologie?," *Zeitschrift für gesamte Neurologie und Psychiatrie*, vol. 91, nos. 3–5, 1924, pp. 402–36, see p. 402.

— "Erfahren, Verstehen, Deuten in der Psychoanalyse," *Imago*, vol. 12, nos. 2–3, 1926, pp. 223–37, see p. 224.

— *Wandlungen in der Auffassung und Deutung des Traumes von den Griechen bis zum Gegenwart*, Berlin: Springer 1928, p. 68.

— "Traum und Existenz," *Neue Schweizer Rundschau*, vol. 23, 1930, pp. 673–85; pp. 766–79, see p. 673; p. 772; p. 776.

— "Über Ideenflucht," in *Schweizer Archiv für Neurologie und Psychiatrie*, vol. 27, 2, 1932, pp. 203–17; vol. 28, nos. 1–2, 1932, pp. 18–26; pp. 183–202; vol. 29, no. 1, 1932, pp. 193ff.; vol. 30, no. 1, 1933; pp. 68–85, see vol. 28, no. 2, 1932, p. 201; vol. 29, no. 1, 1932, p. 25; vol. 29, no. 2, 1932, p. 222.

— "Das Raumproblem in der Psychopathologie," *Zeitschrift für die gesamte Neurologie und Psychiatrie*, vol. 145, 1933, pp. 598–647, see p. 620.

— "Heraklits Auffassung des Menschen," *Die Antike*, vol. 9, no. 1, 1935, pp. 1–38, see p. 6; p. 12; p. 13; pp. 36–7.

— "Freuds Auffassung des Menschen im Lichte der Anthropologie," *Nederlands Tijdschrift voor de Psychologie*, vol. 4, nos. 5–6, 1936, pp. 266–301, see p. 297.

— *Grundformen und Erkenntnis menschlichen Daseins*, Zürich: Niehans 1942, p. 58; p. 123; pp. 128–9; p. 189; p. 236; p. 243; p. 246; p. 400; p. 420; p. 422; p. 473; pp. 480–1; p. 498; pp. 545–8; p. 552; p. 562; p. 605; p. 639; p. 682.

— "Der Fall Ellen West. Eine anthropologisch-klinische Studie," *Schweizer Archiv für Neurologie und Psychiatrie*, vol. 53, 1944, pp. 255–77; vol. 54, 1944, pp. 69–117; pp. 330–60; and vol. 55, 1945, pp. 16–40, see vol. 54, 1944, p. 95; p. 96; pp. 100–2; p. 106; p. 108; p. 343; p. 360; vol. 55, 1945, p. 31.

— "Wahnsinn als lebensgeschichtliches Phänomen und als Geisteskrankheit," *Monatsschrift für Psychiatrie und Neurologie*, vol. 110, 1945, pp. 129–60, see p. 160.

— "Der Fall Jürg Zünd," *Schweizer Archiv für Neurologie und Psychiatrie*, vol. 56, 1946, pp. 191–220; vol. 58, 1947, pp. 1–43; and vol. 59, 1947, pp. 21–36, see vol. 58, 1947, p. 2; p. 29; pp. 36–8.

— "Über die daseinsanalytische Forschungsrichtung in der Psychiatrie," *Schweizer Archiv für Psychiatrie und Neurologie*, vol. 57, 1946, pp. 209–35, see p. 225.

— "Über den Satz von Hofmannsthal: 'Was Geist ist, erfaßt nur der Bedrängte,' " *Studia Philosophica*, vol. 8, 1948, pp. 1–11; see p. 3.

— "Die Bedeutung der Daseinsanalytik Martin Heideggers für das Selbstverständnis der Psychiatrie," in Carlos Astrada et al., *Martin Heideggers Einfluß auf die Wissenschaften*, Bern: Francke 1949, pp. 58–72, see p. 70.

— *Henrik Ibsen und das Problem der Selbstrealisation in der Kunst*, Heidelberg: Lambert Schneider 1949, pp. 10–11; pp. 35–6; p. 39; p. 54; p. 79.

— "Studien zum Schizophrenienproblem. Der Fall Lola Voss," *Schweizer Archiv für Neurologie und Psychiatrie*, vol. 63, 1949, pp. 29–97, see pp. 50–2; p. 59; p. 65; pp. 69–70; p. 76.

— "Daseinsanalytik und Psychiatrie," *Der Nervenarzt*, vol. 22, 1951, pp. 1–10, see p. 2.

— "Der Fall Suzanne Urban," *Schweizer Archiv für Neurologie und Psychiatrie*, vol. 69, 1952, pp. 36–77; vol. 70, 1952, pp. 1–32; and vol. 71, 1952, pp. 57–96, see vol. 69, 1952, p. 58.

— *Drei Formen missglückten Daseins*, Tübingen: Niemeyer 1956, see p. X; p. 115; p. 149; p. 155; p. 187; p. 189.

— "Der Mensch in der Psychiatrie," *Schweizer Archiv für Neurologie und Psychiatrie*, vol. 77, 1956, pp. 123–38, see pp. 123–5; pp. 134–6.

— *Melancholie und Manie. Phänomenologische Studien*, Pfullingen: Neske 1957, see p. 60.

Broch, Hermann, *Die Schlafwandler. Eine Romantrilogie*, vols. 1–3, Munich and Zürich: Rhein Verlag 1931–32.

— "Das Böse im Wertsystem der Kunst," *Die neue Rundschau*, vol. 44, no. 2 (August 1933), pp. 157–91.

Heidegger, Martin, *Sein und Zeit*, Halle: Niemeyer 1927, pp. 175–96, see also p. 190, note 1; p. 235, note 1; and p. 338, note 1.

Przywara, Erich, *Das Geheimnis Kierkegaards*, Munich and Berlin: Verlag von R. Oldenbourg 1929.

— *Analogia Entis. Metaphysik. Ur-Struktur und All-Rhythmus*, Munich: Kösel 1932, p. 7.

— "End-Zeit," *Stimmen der Zeit*, vol. 119, 1930, p. 353.

— "Essenz- und Existenz-Philosophie. Tragische Identität oder Distanz der Geduld," *Scholastik*, vol. 14, 1939, p. 517.

III. Secondary Literature on Jung's Relation to Kierkegaard

Bertelsen, Jes, *Ouroboros. En undersøgelse af selvets strukturer*, Copenhagen: Borgen 1974.

Burrell, David B., *Exercises in Religious Understanding*, Notre Dame, Indiana: University of Notre Dame Press 1974, pp. 143–240.

Casement, Ann, "The Qualitative Leap of Faith: Reflections on Kierkegaard and Jung," in *Post-Jungians Today*, ed. by Ann Casement, London: Routledge 1998, pp. 67–80.

Hitchcock, John Lathrop, *A Comparison of "Complementarity" in Quantum Physics with Analogous Structures in Kierkegaard's Philosophical Writings, from a Jungian Point of View*, Ph.D. Thesis, Graduate Theological Union, New York 1975.

Johnson, Bill, "Gender. A Perceptual Frame for Viewing Kierkegaard and Jung," *Journal of Psychology and Christianity*, vol. 7, no. 4, 1988, pp. 7–17.

Klindt-Jensen, Henrik, "Krisen som erkendelsesbetingelse hos Hegel—med sideblik til Kierkegaard og Jung," *Philosophia*, vol. 19, nos. 3–4, 1990, pp. 134–48.

— "Personbegrebet hos Kierkegaard og C.G. Jung," *Dansk Udsyn*, vol. 71, 1991, pp. 144–59.

Anthony Rudd

Koskinen, Lennart, *Søren Kierkegaard och existentialismen—om tiden, varat och evigheten*, Nora: Nya Doxa 1994, p. 93.

Künzli, Arnold, *Die Angst als Abendländische Krankheit: dargestellt am Leben und Denken Soeren Kierkegaards*, Zürich: Rascher Verlag 1948.

Pattison, George, "Jung, Kierkegaard and the Eternal Feminine," *Theology*, vol. 90, 1987, pp. 430–40.

Sobosan, Jeffrey G., "Kierkegaard and Jung on the Self," *Journal of Psychology and Theology*, vol. 3, 1975, pp. 31–5.

Julia Kristeva:

Tales of Horror and Love

Edward F. Mooney

I. Introduction

Julia Kristeva (b. 1941) is a Paris-based psychoanalyst, novelist, and prolific contributor to debates about subjectivity and its intersections with matters of gender, writing, and religion. She has large intellectual debts to Freud and Jacques Lacan. Their presence in her writing is pervasive even as she differs from them significantly on particular issues. Kristeva figures persons as subjectivities always at risk and in process, lacking anything like assured or reliable identities. This places her as a formidable critic of French structuralist essentialism and of any psychoanalytic theory that takes "the ego," say, or a particular adult psychic formation, say of "the feminine," as anything fixed in the individual or "the same" across subjectivities. She has been a major figure defining what has come to be known as third-wave feminism, which denies rigid identity constructions or fixed differences and instead endorses openness to a fluid range of gender identities across biological males and females.

Kristeva was raised and educated in Bulgaria in Roman Catholic institutions. Religious narratives, devotional images and art, in her view, serve to elaborate the place of subjects in ongoing relations to others, the world, and the limit conditions of birth and death. These images and narratives are part of what she calls "the imaginary"—the field of psychological and cultural symbols and practices that make distinctively human existence possible. Her psychoanalytic interpretations tie religious art and experience to facts of affliction and death, of mother–child and paternal relations. Her aim is not to deflate the religious but to vivify its tales of terror, hope, and saving attachment in order to illuminate and ameliorate the pain of human life.

Kristeva's writing ranges from her striking religious meditation, "Stabat Mater," to her *Revolution in Poetic Language*.[1] Its span and tonality show in a sample of her titles: *Desire in Language*; *Powers of Horror*; *In the Beginning was Love: Psychoanalysis and Faith*; *Tales of Love*; *Black Sun: Depression and Melancholia*;

---

[1] Julia Kristeva, *La Révolution du langage poétique. L'avant-garde à la fin du XIXe siècle: Lautréamont et Mallarmé*, Paris: Éditions du Seuil 1974. (English translation: *Revolution in Poetic Language*, trans. by Margaret Waller, New York: Columbia University Press 1984.)

Strangers to Ourselves, and *New Maladies of the Soul*.[2] Since the mid-1970s she has taught at Columbia University, as well as holding a chair in linguistics at University of Paris VII. In 1979 she completed training and began practice as a psychoanalyst. Her *oeuvre* is still growing.

Under a strong verificationist interpretation of "historical reception" there is little to say about Kristeva's reception of Kierkegaard. She has neither cited nor discussed him (to my knowledge) in her works. However, a lenient interpretation of "reception" allows us to make fruitful inferences about Kierkegaard's impact on Kristeva. There are powerful but indirect and unacknowledged channels of cultural transmission. Kafka says little directly about Kierkegaard, but surely Kierkegaard is an enormous presence in his work. Kierkegaard was a dominant presence in the Parisian milieu Kristeva entered in her formative years. That Kierkegaard infiltrates her works becomes more than plausible in view of the cultural complex within which she produced and in view of deep thematic convergences that resound as we listen to Kristeva through Kierkegaard's inventions.

Ernest Becker (1924–74) suggests that Kierkegaard's discussions of despair within a dynamic self-structure of relations makes him an important precursor of psychoanalytic thought.[3] The American psychoanalyst Erik Erikson (1902–94)

---

[2]   Julia Kristeva, *Séméiôtiké: recherches pour une sémanalyse*, Paris: Edition du Seuil 1969 (English translation: *Desire in Language: A Semiotic Approach to Literature and Art*, trans. by Leon S. Roudiez, New York: Columbia University Press 1980); Julia Kristeva, *Pouvoirs de l'horreur. Essai sur l'abjection*, Paris: Edition du Seuil 1980 (English translation: *Powers of Horror: An Essay on Abjection*, trans. by Leon S. Roudiez, New York: Columbia University Press 1982); Julia Kristeva, *Au commencement était l'amour. Psychanalyse et foi*, Paris: Hachette 1985 (English translation: *In the Beginning was Love: Psychoanalysis and Faith*, trans. by Arthur Goldhammer, New York: Columbia University Press 1987); Julia Kristeva, "*Stabat Mater*," in *Histoires d'amour*, Paris: Danoël 1983, pp. 225–47 (English translation: "Stabat Mater," in *Tales of Love*, trans. by Leon S. Roudiez, New York: Columbia University Press 1987, pp. 234–63); Julia Kristeva, *Soleil noir. Dépression et mélancolie*, Paris: Gallimard 1987 (English translation: *Black Sun: Depression and Melancholia*, trans. by Leon S. Roudiez, New York: Columbia University Press 1989); Julia Kristeva, *Étrangers à nous-mêmes*, Paris: Fayard 1988 (English translation: *Strangers to Ourselves*, trans. by Leon S. Roudiez, New York: Columbia University Press 1991); Julia Kristeva, *Les Nouvelles Maladies de l'âme*, Paris: Fayard 1993 (English translation: *New Maladies of the Soul*, trans. by Ross Guberman, New York: Columbia University Press 1995). See also Julia Kristeva, *La génie feminine*, vols. 1–3, Paris: Fayard 1999–2002 (English translation: *Female Genius: Life, Madness, Words: Hannah Arendt, Melanie Klein, Colette: A Trilogy*, vols. 1–3, trans. by Ross Guberman, New York: Columbia University Press 2001–04); Julia Kristeva, *Crise du sujet européen*, New York: Autre serrent 2000 (English translation: *Crisis of the European Subject*, trans. by Susan Fairfield, New York: Other Press 2000); Julia Kristeva, "Lecture de la bible," in *Le lecteur post-moderne de bible*, ed. by David Jobling, Reinette de Tina, and Ronald Schleifer, Oxford: Blackwell 2001, pp. 92–101 (English translation: "Reading the Bible," in *The Postmodern Bible Reader*, ed. by David Jobling, Tina Pippin, and Ronald Schleifer, Oxford: Blackwell 2001, pp. 92–101; and *The Kristeva Reader*, ed. by Toril Moi, Oxford: Basil Blackwell 1986.

[3]   Ernest Becker, "The Psychoanalyst Kierkegaard," (chapter 5) in his *The Denial of Death*, New York: Simon and Schuster 1973, pp. 67–92.

freely acknowledges large debts to Kierkegaard.[4] Kierkegaard's Parisian presence included widespread appreciation of his championing a relational self, always at risk. There is every reason to suppose that Kristeva took this in. Kierkegaard's relational self could even be a resource for Kristevan feminist thought, as Tamsin Lorraine has shown.[5] Bergson, not to mention Sartre and Proust, could contribute to her emerging formulation of a fluid self-at-risk. Her notion is culturally over-determined, but Kierkegaard was surely an inescapable force to be reckoned with.

As a young intellectual newly arrived in Parisian café life in the mid-1960s, Kristeva "cut her teeth" as an animated participant in ongoing debates centered on Lacan and Freud, with the thought of Sartre, Marx, Heidegger, and Lévinas playing a role as well. Discussions of subjectivity and of the place and responsibility of the individual person were conducted under the shadows of the Holocaust and of French resistance (and non-resistance) to the German occupation. These broadly existentialist concerns were gradually superseded by what came to be known as French Structuralism, spearheaded by the anthropologist Claude Lévi-Strauss (b. 1908). Its focus on broad, apparently universal, social and linguistic structures overshadowed the post-war individualism of Sartre and others. Kristeva arrived having adopted Russian formalism and became attracted to the structuralism of Lacan and others. She seems to have taken it as a starting point in the 1970s even as she was developing critiques that eventuated in her becoming a leading post-structuralist. On her arrival in Paris, she also became engaged by the work of Roland Barthes (1915–80) and others in developing semiotics as a theoretical approach to language, literature, and culture.

These Parisian debates in the 1960s and 1970s were in many ways a continuation of seminal pre-war discussions that placed Kierkegaard, Hegel, Heidegger, and Marx in complex, many-sided debates.[6] At stake were conflicting imperatives: the humanist imperatives of individual liberation from the suffocation of bourgeois conformity and fascist regimentation; the structural imperatives of a minimal social order providing stable institutions; the liberatory imperatives of social change and political revolution; the rational imperatives of science and critique in the formation of a viable society and culture; and the ever-present cultural imperatives of art and religion as these intersected social, political, and scientific imperatives. After 1945, Kierkegaard was a less obvious presence. Sartre's early atheistic humanism and later Marxism, Heidegger's anti-humanism, various forms of phenomenology, structuralism, post-structuralism, and the increasing influence of Lacan and Foucault seemed to dominate the French milieu and put Kierkegaard in partial eclipse.

---

[4]   See Lawrence J. Friedman, *Identity's Architect: A Biography of Erik Erikson*, New York: Scribners 1999, pp. 372–3; pp. 448–9; see also the article on Erikson in this volume.

[5]   Tamsin Lorraine, "Amatory Cures for Material Dis-ease. A Kristevian Reading of 'The Sickness unto Death,' " in *Feminist Interpretations of Søren Kierkegaard*, ed. by Céline Léon and Sylvia Walsh, University Park, Pennsylvania: Pennsylvania State University Press 1997, pp. 307–28.

[6]   See Samuel Moyn, *The Origins of the Other*, Ithaca: Cornell University Press 2005, pp. 164–94.

There was no city more intellectually adventurous, darkly flamboyant, and chaotic than Paris between the World Wars and in the decades after its liberation in 1944. Kristeva arrived there in 1965, having fled communist Bulgaria, where she had been writing a Ph.D. on inter-textuality in the work of the Russian literary theorist Mikhail Bakhtin (1895–1975).[7] Lucien Goldmann (1913–70), who had fled Rumania in the mid-1930s and knew the burdens of exile, became a mentor and friend. A decade later he was forced out of Paris by the Nazi occupation. Goldmann shared Kristeva's deep interests in literature. He had a passion for Kant and Marx as defenders of a socialist humanism. Kristeva made a name for herself fairly quickly with a widely discussed paper on Bakhtin that focused on his development of the dual themes of polyphony and the carnivalesque, especially in Dostoevsky's work.

II. Polyphony and Carnival

Bakhtin argues that the polyphony of voices in a novel like *The Brothers Karamazov* marks a polyphony of authorial standpoints. Accordingly, the assumption of a unitary authorial voice becomes problematic. To attempt to find Dostoevsky himself, his true voice, behind the voice of one or another of the brothers, is ill conceived. The author becomes not a singular voice but a multiplex spread throughout and between the voices of the characters so vividly delivered. The absence of a unified authorial identity will have its parallel in the absence, more generally, of a unified self, agent, or subjectivity. This is the issue Kierkegaard scholars face in their attempts to find a unitary authorial voice among the plurality of pseudonymous and veronymous writers in Kierkegaard's productions.[8] Kristeva develops Bakhtin's insight in her psychoanalytic writings by transporting his multiplicity of voices inward. The plurality of contesting voices assumed in the novel becomes, in her account of personal unfolding, a fluid, elusive self whose putative unity is in fact a fragile multiplicity, a loose-knit polyphony.[9] This is reminiscent of the polyphony of voices in the lyric sections of the pseudonym Johannes de silentio's *Fear and Trembling*. Johannes is a garrulous writer who remains silent about many things, including his true center. Lacking a unitary center of stability, "the" self, for Kristeva, becomes a Kierkegaard-like ensemble of dialogical internal relations, reflecting an unfolding matrix of interpersonal child–parent and self–other relations.

The other focus of Kristeva's first paper is Bakhtin's figuration of the carnivalesque, a strange mixture of the grotesque, sensational, and satirically

---

[7]   Kristeva and Tzvetan Todorov brought Bakhtin to the attention of the Francophone world, and beyond. See Mikhail Bakhtin, *Problems of Dostoyevsky's Poetics*, trans. by and ed. by Caryl Emerson, Minneapolis: University of Minnesota Press 1984.

[8]   See Joseph Westfall, *The Kierkegaardinan Author: Authorship and Performance in Kierkegaard's Literary and Dramatic Criticism*, Berlin and New York: Walter de Gruyter 2007 (*Kierkegaard Studies Monograph Series*, vol. 15) and my review in *Philosophy and Social Criticism*, vol. 35, no. 7, 2009, pp. 869–82.

[9]   I interpret the field of self-relations in *The Sickness unto Death* as a leaderless musical ensemble in Edward F. Mooney, *Selves in Discord and Resolve: Kierkegaard's Moral-Religious Psychology*, New York: Routledge 1996, Chapter 8.

comedic in Dostoevesky. The undercurrents of showmanship and spectacle are underappreciated features of the first third of *Fear and Trembling*. Copenhagen's Tivoli Gardens, an ongoing carnival, opened in 1843, the year *Fear and Trembling* was published. Johannes de silentio, its pseudonymous author, does not spare us the frankly theatrical, macabre celebration of the sensational, horrific, and grotesque in the story of Isaac about to be slain. Johannes presents four tableaux of the horror that might mimic the carnival excitements and spectacles on display in the just-opened Tivoli. Perhaps Johannes de silentio is a carnival barker for a kind of freak show— as if Abraham were a three-headed monster providing an occasion for gawkers to scream and crowds to line up for a view. [10] Of course, there is a legitimate religious horror to consider. But the story is retold with a carnivalesque sensationalism that satirically blurs sacred and profane, and that indulges the excitement of a horror story. As her career proceeds, Kristeva will elaborate what we could fairly call the psychoanalytic carnivalesque of the inner life.

III. Speaking Beings

Before she turned to psychoanalytic theory and practice, Kristeva wrote on language and literature as modes of signification. She held that language and signification have two faces. Words can operate as general signifiers, where their meaning is relatively independent of personal engagement or context. Alternatively, words can signify in a personally charged situation to express a particular speaker's desires or needs or passions. Some levels of language can be stripped free of any embodied expression of an individual speaking being. Newspaper accounts of humdrum events can signify without my needing to focus on the writer as a speaking embodied presence. On the other hand, hearing my daughter relay a painful episode at school will focus my attention on her quite particular embodied presence—the pace and pitch of her words, the look of her eyes as she speaks, a trembling or stiffness in her limbs. Kristeva calls the first face of signification—the relatively disembodied and detached—the symbolic, and she calls the second—the embodied expression of a singular being—the semiotic.

Kristeva's two faces of signification have a striking resemblance to Kierkegaard's two faces of communication, what he calls the contrast between direct and indirect communication. Indirect communication resembles Kristeva's semiotic signification, the embodied speech and gesture that impart a particular individual's feeling and passion. The contrast would be an occurrence of disembodied abstract words reporting banal facts or objective directions. Such information or prescription unhooked from any particular speaker or writer Kierkegaard calls direct communication and Kristeva calls the symbolic. [11] Both notice the ease with which theorists overlook the

---

[10] I explore this possibility in "*Fear and Trembling*: Spectacular Diversions" in Edward F. Mooney, *On Søren Kierkegaard: Dialogue, Polemics, Lost Intimacy, and Time*, Aldershot: Ashgate 2007, Chapter 8.

[11] The qualifier "indirect" can be misleading. The pathos of a cry for help—the urgency of its affect, not its informational content—can be direct, immediate, in its impact. Of course much pathos simmers inwardly, and our knowing what exactly that

particularities of embodied communication, the non-propositional imparting and transfer of affect, pathos, and individualized perspective.

In *Revolution and Poetic Language*, Kristeva argues that despite their attention to "the subject" and "language," neither Husserl nor Saussure has a place for embodied speech, the voice of *this* person, speaking in *this* tone of voice—in *this* physical posture, with *this* gesture, among *these* attentive *particular* (embodied) listeners. To give language a sort of theoretical and abstract sheen excises the dramatic, even theatrical context of living speech and expression. What most often gets theorized, as Kristeva sees it, is disembodied writing or speech—delivered *from* nowhere in particular, *to* no one in particular, the impersonal tightly secured at each pole of a communication. But living speech has its genesis in a baby's coos, eyes fixed on a mom, who returns the look and the coo. Later, it will emerge in an orator's sweaty or calming exhortations, eyes fixed on the mesmerized crowd. To insist on passion and embodiment is not to denigrate the symbolic but to resist the eclipse of particular speaking beings who avail themselves of the symbolic *and* the semiotic. Performing well in a physics exam requires considerable mastery of the symbolic. Teaching physics to an aversive, distracted student requires considerable mastery of the semiotic as well as the symbolic.

Kierkegaard uses pseudonyms, dramatic narrative, and a variety of genres to set words in living motion in particular contexts, uttered by singular, passionate souls. If he valorizes the singular individual, it is an *embodied* individual to whom he gives voice in the figures of Judge Wilhelm, Don Juan, the young man of *Repetition*, the seducer, and the professorial anti-professor, Johannes Climacus. And of course, it is the singular, embodied individual that Kierkegaard's writings will address: "My dear reader," as he would say. Kristeva has no use for a theory of language "removed from historical turmoil" written from a position "midair" and uttered, as she puts it, by "a sleeping body."[12]

As Kristeva sees it, humans participate in signifying practices from early on. The first babbles and cries of an infant are pre-symbolic, but they signify—convey, perhaps—a delight in the world or the pain of abandonment. Semiotic signification is altogether pertinent. Drives or passions are already present, as well as rhythmic and tonal modulation of expression.[13] The semiotic communication of embodied significance continues even as symbolic capacities emerge. It never diminishes, despite increasing dependence on the symbolic. Linguistic competence is marked by handling simple names, simple words for wants, simple words that "point to facts." Kristeva calls this second layer of human signifying "symbolic" because the simple

---

"inwardness" is meant to convey may be available only, as Kierkegaard has it, "indirectly" through subtle interpretations. See my discussion in *On Søren Kierkegaard: Dialogue, Polemics, Lost Intimacy, and Time*, Chapter 11.

[12]   Kristeva, *La Révolution du langage poétique. L'avant-garde à la fin du XIXe siècle: Lautréamont et Mallarmé*, p. 11. (*Revolution in Poetic Language*, p. 13.)

[13]   Lacan's "semiotic" encompasses both of the fields that Kristeva has subdivided; it is wider than her "semiotic" and is equivalent to her "signification." Kristeva's semiotic draws on what Freud designated as the pre-Oedipal phase of infant development, and Lacan calls the pre-mirror stage. It is elaborated by Melanie Klein and Object Relation psychoanalysis as a field of passion and primitive drives.

sounds that at first conveyed mostly pathos now do that, and in addition, become words that link up with things—that are "symbols" pointing roughly to things. Signification can have a referential target (asking for *that* apple). Poetry, of course, picks up words and combinations of them that have ordinary "symbolic" meaning ("the apple of my eye"), and much more. Poetry orders its words and sounds in ways that mimic the rhythmic cooing or delight of a child, or evoke shrieking, pleading, or enticing, or enact the calm of a lyric. The semiotic and symbolic merge.

The symbolic can veer toward a limit of mere information "peeled off" the affections, desires, commitments, and feelings of any particular speaker or writer (look at a restaurant's printed menu, and subtract your desires). The semiotic can veer toward a limit of non-verbal wheezing or coughing. Signifying in either dimension presupposes that the infant—then the child, then the youth—will separate itself, say from its mother, or its peers. It will come to know that its pain, hunger, interests, and desires are not directly its mother's. From this vantage, patterns of verbal and non-verbal signification signal modes of coping with separation and difference. Only a speaking being has issues of identity and difference. And only a speaking being has the subtlety of differentiated human desire.

As children become youths and adolescents become adults the semiotic develops accordingly to carry embodied feelings and desires of considerable complexity. I *insinuate scornfully* to the waiter that the salmon *served* is not the salmon *ordered*, *implying, threatening*, that he should return from the kitchen with something *better*. My embodied complex of affect and desire has a more or less banal content—I refuse the dish and demand another. But that relative banality must be learned, and becomes artfully (or clumsily) transformed in the rhythm and pitch of my utterance, in the mocking stress on certain syllables, in a measure of anger or condescension, in a look that could kill, and in a dismissive wave of the hand from a body that has stiffened in outraged resolve (or mild rebuke or exasperated condescension).

In living practice, the semiotic and the symbolic are interwoven. If one were learning the Chinese for "failing-grade salmon," perhaps a purely symbolic meaning could free up from semiotic residues—our hearing the Chinese for "D-grade salmon" would not be encumbered by a rasp of dismay or disgust. But "D-grade" typically carries a negative charge of affect or emotion. Affect or pathos can be conveyed in ways that circumvent the simply propositional or symbolic.[14]

---

[14] A Kierkegaardian might at this point launch into a theory of "indirect communication" of affect or emotion. If we undergo a sense of revulsion, disappointment, or disgust at the sight of rotten salmon, our emotion or pathos will be directly evident to others. However, in more complex cases I may want to instill affect in another by other means. My disgust might be modulated in a manner that opened to the recipient of my communication of it a chance to register *her own* disgust (or *Schadenfreude*, perhaps, or indifference, or contempt-for-my-disgust). My point in registering an emotion would be to evoke a proper emotion in another. And there is no acceptably direct way of evoking something like reverence or gratitude in another. It is not like fear, which I can evoke—*cause*—by popping a bag behind an unsuspecting child.

IV. Kant's Sublime, Kristeva's Horror

Horror plays a major role in the doing and undoing of a fluid, fragile identity or self. But Kristeva will hesitate to speak of "the" self, or "identity," for it is exactly traditional notions of these that she labors to challenge and revise. Perhaps the self is little more than the site of a complex of copings and undergoings whose description, for Kristeva, is pitched at an unusually high intensity of interest. Nearly always, once we think of it, identity *matters*! Her figuration of self-identity in frames of horror or a dispersal or shattering of "the" self can be made less strange by providing a tentative genealogy. Such a tracing of roots of Kristeva's figurations of self would run back from her immediate engagements with Lacan and Barthes to more mediated engagements with Freud and Heidegger, and then back further a century and more. Her sense of the uncanny and horror infusing and suffusing "the" self comes from Burke and Kant, who evoke the grotesque and the sublime as they unsettle the self.

Unheimlichkeit, an uncanny sense of displacement from home, is implicit in Kant's notion of the sublime, and prominent in Kierkegaard's notion of anxiety and restlessness of soul. It crisscrosses German Romanticism, and flows through Hegel, Marx, Nietzsche, and Freud. In its twentieth-century French and American guise, estrangement or alienation becomes a ubiquitous literary and philosophical trope, especially after World War II. Wholeness or home might be regained by a return to poetry as a way of life, or by a stint of psychoanalysis, or by social revolution. Or deep alienation might be figured as an inescapable feature of the human condition. In any case, from Kant through Kierkegaard to Kristeva, the site of the sublime and grotesque shifts from wild nature—alpine peaks, ocean storms, gnarled tree trunks—to tumult and danger within the ambit of the self.

The sublime unseats us with a frightening sense of finitude. A clap of thunder jolts us forbiddingly. For Kant, a frightening impact is followed by a bracing sense of our infinitude, by the wonder that *it is I*, a creature of *rational dignity*, who is privileged to access sublimity. Dogs shake in fright, or flee; humans stand upright. Rational judgment prevails. Existential *angst* is no doubt harder to dispel. Infinite reason is replaced by infinite passion in Kristeva's account. Subjectivity unfolds under the duress of terrible interruptions that appear like sublime interventions, constantly upending fledgling and partial identities.[15] Anxiety punctuates time, and intermittency replaces uniformity and continuity. We live episodically, our time punctuated by intrusions of the horrific.

---

[15]   Thunder snaps us out of routine identities—and then lets us return, refreshed. A sublime encounter—the peal of thunder—shatters pre-reflective ways of perception and orientation. See Chapter 4 ("On Death and the Sublime") in my *On Søren Kierkegaard: Dialogue, Polemics, Lost Intimacy, and Time.* Kant distinguished the "dynamic sublime" (encountered in views of ocean storms or alpine peaks) from the "mathematical sublime" (encountered, for example, in the infinite sky, sprinkled with stars). And there might be an (un-Kantian) nonspectacular "indifferent sublime," as when Camus' Meursault basks in "the benign indifference of the universe." Of course "the" sublime is not a well-defined "thing" like a tree or mountain any more than "the" self is. The term calls up a broad and loosely knit family of strange, uncanny, or startling phenomena traditionally arising in nature, but also arising in cities, and yet again in the streets and alleyways of one's inner world.

In *'Poor Paris!': Kierkegaard's Critique of the Spectacular City*, George Pattison argues that the nineteenth-century European city became a site of disruptive anxiety and what he calls the urban sublime.[16] A sense of anxious finitude is triggered by flashing night lights, hectic crowds, jarring traffic, tall buildings and banks of reflecting windows—not to mention the proliferation of media-distributed tales of violence and scandal. Cognitive and emotional overloads feed depression and neurasthenia, panic and paralysis. One might try throwing oneself into the whirl, the way a surfer casts herself into the wildness of crashing waves. One might try casting responsibilities aside for the whirl of color and taste. As a hedge on anxiety, a *flaneur*, street-poet, or sex-cruiser takes on the city as a feast to devour. Early in her career, among anxious Parisian spectacles, Kristeva draws directly from Guy Debord (1931–94), whose *The Society of the Spectacle* was first published in 1967.[17] Her *Black Sun: Depression and Melancholia*, and her *Strangers to Ourselves*, by titles alone, announce the Kierkegaardian themes of angst, despair, and estrangement. Suffering *das Unheimliche*, the uncanny or unhome-like, the German Romantics turned to art, especially poetry, to make suffering less insufferable by "living poetically." In the dark years just before and following World War I, this Romantic trope and life-strategy became suspect. In that period both Freud and Heidegger wrote of the uncanny but neither held out hope for "poetic living."[18] At best, it would be a cry of pain. Rilke declares, "Beauty is nothing but the beginning of terror, which we are still just able to endure."[19]

If Kant's dynamic sublime—lightening, or thunder—comes and goes, for Rilke or Kristeva, the uncanny seems sustained and inescapable, a pervasive malaise linked to the devastations of World War I (for Rilke), and to the even deeper horrors of World War II and the camps (for Kristeva).[20] However, the horror she typically delineates after her turn to psychoanalysis is less overtly social or political than lodged in the dynamics of infant and child development. Early imprints of horror are occasioned by repeated separation from a mother—from a personal and reliable source of comfort and nurture. They do not disappear with adulthood but live on in subterranean secrecy and power. Kristeva finds irremediable horror at the center of the psyche, where it pulls "ordinary life" apart at the seams. At best, she hopes to

---

[16] George Pattison, *'Poor Paris!': Kierkegaard's Critique of the Spectacular City*, Berlin and New York: Walter de Gruyter 1999 (*Kierkegaard Studies Monograph Series*, vol. 2), pp. 69–71. Kierkegaard's critique of the city parallels those we find in Rousseau, Thoreau, and early Marx.

[17] Guy Debord, *The Society of the Spectacle*, trans. by Donald Nicholson-Smith, London: Zone Books 1995.

[18] Yet Heidegger's writing after 1935 seems to turn to the Romantic option of poetic living.

[19] See Rilke's first "Duino Elegy."

[20] Kierkegaard meant to make the trauma of Abraham on Moriah emblematic of the human condition. It is as if that horror was visited on survivors of the Wars and camps, not least, Parisian survivors. These horrors led Adorno to famously declare that lyrical poetry could no longer exist.

replace a Cartesian "subordination of passions to thought" with the "experience of a loving subject," related to others reciprocating such affection.[21]

V. Father–Son, Mother–Infant

Take moral orientation to be that sensibility, outlook, or attunement that holds a person more or less together, as well as can be expected in always troubled times. It is a sensibility built on trust and a sense of purpose, for example, though too often it is identified exclusively with explicit principles or ideals that a rational adult might embrace. The emerging sensibility of interest here can include a sense of rules and obligations but also a variegated sense of good and bad, better and worse, disgusting and attractive, as these play out in a shared way of life.

Moral sensibility (or a moral-aesthetic sensibility) is ballast against those intrusions that disrupt the risky momentum of "the" self. It can manifest in an embrace (or rejection) of etiquette, in displays of good character (or of great failures to stand up). It can appear in the "aesthetic" predilections of one's life, in its pace and ease (or restless scurrying), in one's love of cats or smiles at strangers or attention to the fact that one's niece loves purple. There is an aesthetic cast to one's sense of good and bad, better and worse, disgusting and attractive: the good overlaps the beautiful or alluring, just as the bad overlaps the repulsive or ugly. Moral sensibility or attunement then looks like the human way of being in the world, a way that permeates our political or religious sensibilities, as well. Kristeva locates such orientations in the field of "the imaginary." Kierkegaard's *Fear and Trembling* is a classic depiction of wholesale threat to "normal" moral sensibility. Abraham on Moriah puts at risk hallowed modes of father–son, father–God, and husband–wife relations. Like Kristeva, Kierkegaard assumes a relational self-in-process under threat of rupture, upsetting the very assumption of stable moral sensibility. Like Kristeva's *Powers of Horror*, *Fear and Trembling* conjures a sublime disruption of interpersonal psychic orientation.

As a psychoanalyst, Kristeva is exquisitely attuned to the generative and dangerous drama of interlocking fathers, mothers, infants, and children. If thunder awakens us to mortality, finitude, and grandeur, and the chaos of cities awakens us to loss of a stable place, the family scenario awakens us also to the horrific, generative, and rejuvenating. Readers of Kierkegaard will appreciate elaborating Kristeva's schemas of familial tensions in terms of *Fear and Trembling*'s familial scenarios of trauma, near-death, and rebirth.[22] As Johannes de silentio stages it, the *Genesis* story becomes a collection of theatrical possibilities, even a collection of

---

[21]   Julia Kristeva, "Un pur silence: la perfection de Jeanne Guyo," in *Histoires d'amour*, p. 277. (English translation: "A Pure Silence: The Perfection of Jeanne Guyon," in *Tales of Love*, p. 297.)

[22]   I discuss these scenarios in Chapter 8 in my *On Søren Kierkegaard: Dialogue, Polemics, Lost Intimacy, and Time*, and in *Knights of Faith and Resignation: Reading Kierkegaard's Fear and Trembling*, Albany, New York: State University of New York Press 1991, pp. 25–31.

dreams, that awaken us to nightmarish undercurrents in father–son, mother–infant, and God–subject relations and hold out an "absurd" hope for their "resolution."

Early on, Johannes sketches four versions of the God–Abraham–Isaac ensemble, framed as musings, almost daydreams, of an old man remembering a childhood story, as if to offer them to an attentive analyst's ear. Each frightening tableaux has an underlying caption containing reflections on a mother weaning her infant, transposing Abraham severing his relation to Isaac into a complementary version of Sarah severing her relation to Isaac. These transpositions away from nightmarish fright to a calmer setting, domesticate the horror of the near-sacrifice of the son. But the juxtaposition of a knife and weaning also increases the momentousness, even terror, of maternal severing. Handling this severing smoothly is of world-shattering import exactly on a par with the father's flirtation with a near-murderous sacrifice-to-be. A dreamy mother–infant scenario matches a dreamy father–son scenario—both dreamed under the demanding gaze of God. The expectation of Isaac that his father will protect him, or of Abraham, that his God will protect him, or of a nursing infant, that its mother will protect her, are placed at catastrophic risk. Apart from grand moral theory, be it Christian, Kantian, or Hegelian, any decent middle-class burgher's moral sensibility—sense of up and down, good and bad, God and subjects, faith and reason—will be thrown into disarray. Yet we awake from these nightmares to a world more or less restored.

Kristeva's writes on "the imaginary father" (colloquially, a "father figure") and the powerful yet expelled "mother figure." Both are larger-than-life impostors with counterparts in Father-God, weaning-Mother, and knife-wielding Abraham. Viewed from the positions of an infant or Isaac or Abraham as under duress, the near-destructions and wondrous escapes imply a divine Wholly Other. The nightmare of God's demand is the fright of mammoth waves, and the release from terror mimics awakening from a bad dream, awakening, in the best of times, to a rejuvenating wonder and delight—*jouissance*.

VI. Abjection

With the exception of her introduction of "abjection" and "the abject," for the most part Kristeva avoids technical jargon. Facing a world of things, a subject takes them in, throws them out, or is thrown by them. In dejection we are thrown out of sorts, out of place. In introjection, we take in something and "throw" it inward. Thus a child might ward off fears of the dark by introjecting the image of a protective, powerful father or a nurturing, loving mother. These "introjects" become present for the child even if no adults are in the room. A child may "project" a pet as friendly—throw a "friendliness wrap" over the pup that otherwise might appear dangerous. In abjection, a child may throw out or expel something taken as disgusting or repulsive—again, as a protective tactic. Fearing a mother's rejection, say, during weaning, a child may "abject" or expel the mother. Verb then becomes noun, a repulsing creating something repulsive. Repulsing a mother is repulsing the repulsive, just as hating the father is hating the hateful. Abjection or expulsion of the mother becomes abjecting the abject. She is thrown out because in fright the child takes her as intermittently withholding warmth or nourishment or protection from pain.[23]

What can be exiled or expelled, in the fantasy of the child, cannot harm. Snakes or feces may become "abjects," colored with disgust. A culture's taboo behaviors isolate "abjects," things that are abjected. Some things are treated with disgust because they can harm (snakes or rotten fish or excrement), but other things are found fearful and rejected because they lack determinate boundaries: they are blobs, or slime balls. Ordinary things or objects usually have relatively secure borders or outlines, visually, tactilely, cognitively, and emotively. We like things that way, neat and clean. What Kristeva calls an "abject" is not "neat and clean" but a squirrelly indeterminately fluid mess that has threateningly shifting non-boundaries—semen, jellyfish, slugs, guts, spittle. But abjecting is seldom fully satisfying or successful. A teenager desires to expel a mother but cannot. One turns from a rotting corpse, but it continues to haunt. Abjects can survive even as we institute rituals of cleansing. The mother unreliable and rejected has as its inevitable counterpart, *Stabat Mater*.

Lacan's "*objet petit a*," an elusive ever-receding allure, allows one to reconcile and organize desires, facilitating stability in the symbolic order of meanings. In contrast, the abject undermines meaning-as-order. As Kristeva sees it, the abject "draws me toward the place where meaning collapses."[24] In disgust or horror, self-other boundaries collapse, the repulsive "thing" is both inside and outside oneself. Rotting flesh triggers vomiting, as if throwing up lunch throws out the repulsiveness, and cleans out the world. A corpse reminds us of our death and the deaths of friends and lovers, a thought we would just as soon expel. Accordingly, we preemptively denude it of allure, letting it cause—and be—vomit.

A corpse lies dangerously close in Johanes de silentio's Abraham–Isaac scenarios. The climb to Moriah can be a nightmare of infanticide, an image of the disgusting-to-be-expelled. In *Fear and Trembling*, the tale is framed as a childhood memory in the mode of a beautiful fairy-tale. Thus by inversion we handle our fears. But the possibility that God could make such a demand and that a father could heed it, remain disgusting, taboo, like mangled flesh.[25] These are thoughts to vomit out, but they remain powerfully there, marking the possibility of breakdown of meaning, a fate to which any self is heir. Expelling the horrific (than which no greater can be conceived) is fantasized protection. Writing and rewriting this disgusting possibility is Johannes' purifying rite to rid himself of exactly that possibility.

From a different angle, Moriah might be emblematic of a crisis of separation (and separation-survival). Abraham's freedom might require casting off his internalized Isaac, setting Isaac free of him, and freeing him from Isaac; and it might also require letting God cast off his (Abraham's) God-relation—temporarily suspending it. Just so, an infant's independence rests on a mother's severance or casting off at weaning. A son's survival requires a father's and mother's ever-greater relinquishment of control and sovereignty—without relinquishing love. It is as if these difficult

---

[23]   See Kristeva, *Pouvoirs de l'horreur* (*Powers of Horror*), Chapter 1.

[24]   Kristeva, *Pouvoirs de l'horreur*, p. 9. (*Powers of Horror*, p. 2.)

[25]   In *Powers of Horror*, Kristeva incorporates the anthropologist Mary Douglas' work on rites of purity and pollution.

relinquishments were collapsed into three days approaching Moriah and a moment of restoration, freedom, and independence.

Kristeva unabashedly defends the necessity of matricide—surely a hyperbole.[26] Yet that is exactly the hyperbole at work in the Moriah tales of near-infanticide. Matricide is the necessity that the child separate from its mother in the name of independence: there is the necessary severing of the umbilical cord, and the later severing at weaning. Each of these cuts are at the initiative of the mother, however, not of a matricidal child. Johannes gives primary initiative to the mother who blackens her breast (rather than to the infant). Likewise, Abraham's ordeal begins on the initiative of the Father who orders fathers. God thus flirts with the death of Abraham, at least with the death of Abraham as father of faith. Abraham is set a dilemma that can kill faith. By any reasonable light, he will die of grief and betrayal whether he obeys or disobeys, whether he loses Isaac (and retains God) or loses God (and retains Isaac). But perhaps there is method in this madness. In the *Concluding Unscientific Postscript*, Kierkegaard says that God's interest is in giving independence to persons over against himself.[27] God's various withdrawals, including apparent withdrawal of all succor to Abraham, might be severings in a *libratory* vein.

From yet another angle, the infant-weaning scenarios seem to highlight natality. Kristeva seems to privilege the moment of separation that is death, and the wide-screen drama of Isaac and Abraham haunts us as a moment of death. But there is the moment of life that occurs as the infant's cord is severed in birth and as the breast is blackened at weaning, not to mention the moment of rebirth at Isaac's restoration. If we figure separation not in mortality alone but in natality, then the infant's weaning becomes a foretaste of life, and the weaning of Isaac and Abraham, a foretaste of rebirth, as in the return of Isaac from the dead.

VII. Chora: The Place of Unnamable Swirl?

How are we to imagine the "roots" of becoming, the "place" from which emerges all that has been, and all that is and will be? A hopeless question, perhaps, but it is hard to abandon. All tales of origins or genesis are uttered hope against hope. Not just philosophers or priests but all of us can wonder where everything came from, or why there is something rather than nothing, or whether order or chaos is at the bottom of things, or whether creation is a muscular making or a matter of subtle midwifery. At one point, Genesis has creation begin in answer to a sovereign proclamation: "Let there be light!" But it is also figured there as handiwork, as the waters above are separated from the waters below. Initially it seems that God peers into emptiness, or into a formless void, or as Robert Alter renders "*tohu vabohu*," into "welter and waste," or as Catherine Keller has it, the "face of the deep."[28] But is it desert in which welter and waste reside? As Melville might ask, what holds the watery deep? Does a womb-like bowl hold all that becomes, and God reaches into it to touch and deliver?

---

[26]   See Kristeva, *Soleil noir*, pp. 38–41. (*Black Sun*, pp. 27–30.)

[27]   *SKS* 7, 237, note / *CUP1*, 260–1, note.

[28]   Robert Alter, *Genesis: Translation and Commentary*, New York: W.W. Norton 1997, p. 3; Catherine Keller, *The Face of the Deep*, New York: Routledge 2003, pp. 4–5.

Chora is a word Kristeva favors for the place (or abyss, or bowl, or womb-like wilderness) from which all things are born. *Chora* is a Platonic term for a matrix-like nourishing expanse that is unnamable and prior to any *individual* thing, place, person, or process. Kristeva borrows the term to gesture toward a primal frame, the source of the pre-symbolic semiotic, the non-individuated place of all places and things.[29] Heady stuff, poetic through and through. But hardly anyone fully escapes wandering, at one time or another, toward such enigmas of beginnings.

It is striking that Kristeva ventures beneath language, signification, psycho-analysis, and politics, to hazard an image of primal place. It is daring to venture beneath those discourses, disciplines, cultural practices, and institutions that crystallize, mold, shape, articulate, or edit our worlds—to imagine an unimaginable bottom line. *Chora* is not the *stuff* that creation (cultural, psychological, or otherwise) edits, organizes, or constructs. It is whatever *holds* or *contains* that stuff—is whatever "stuff" and its processes are "placed in." It is easy to remember that stuff is born from its predecessor, generative stuff. But Plato and Kristeva venture further to think that it is also primally born from a womb that holds both it and its generative-regenerative processes.

Socrates is midwife, male and female. He brings souls to birth, helps them emerge as individuals, emerge, that is, from *wombs*. Kristeva is enough of a Bakhtinian and Socratic dialogical thinker to take psychoanalysis as a midwife's venture. Insight comes as she helps readers or clients trace a genealogy of formative mothers, fathers, siblings, teachers, and neighbors—trace generative ensembles working in embodied, speaking space. These deeply rooted familial and wider ensembles are all held in play in an unnamable place of fright, but also of nurture and rejuvenation. Kierkegaard would call it the place of God. Kristeva lets it be the place of primal natality that answers the pain of separation, dispersal and mortality's abyss.

---

[29]   In *New Maladies*, p. 204, Kristeva characterizes Plato's *chora* approvingly as "a matrixlike space that is nourishing, unnameable, prior to the One and to God, and that thus defies metaphysics." See *Timaeus* 50–52. In *Revolution*, p. 25, however, she defines *chora* as "a nonexpressive totality formed by the drives and their stases in a motility that is as full of movement as it is regulated." In *Revolution*, therefore, *chora* does not defy metaphysics. It is (impossibly) located in a prior meta-psychology (or metaphysics) of drives.

Bibliography

I. References or Uses of Kierkegaard in Kristeva's Corpus

La Révolution du langage poétique. L'avant-garde à la fin du XIXe siècle:
Lautréamont et Mallarmé, Paris: Éditions du Seuil 1974, p. 117. (English
translation: *Revolution in Poetic Language*, trans. by Margaret Waller, New
York: Columbia University Press 1984, p. 127.)
Histoires d'amour, Paris: Danoël 1983, p. 187. (English translation: *Tales of Love*,
trans. by Leon S. Roudiez, New York: Columbia University Press 1987, p. 191.)
Le génie féminin. La vie, la folie, les mots, tome 1, *Hannah Arendt*, Paris: Fayard
1999, p. 36. (English translation: *Female Genius: Life, Madness, Words*, vol.
1, *Hannah Arendt*, trans. by Ross Guberman, New York: Columbia University
Press 2001, p. 13.)

II. Sources of Kristeva's Knowledge of Kierkegaard

Barthes, Roland, *Fragments d'un discours amoureux*, Paris: Éditions du Seuil 1977,
p. 248.
— *Leçon*, Paris: Éditions du Seuil 1978, pp. 15–16; pp. 27–8.
— *Sollers écrivain*, Paris: Éditions du Seuil 1979, p. 31.
Bataille, Georges, *L'Expérience intérieure*, Paris: Gallimard 1943, p. 29; p. 72;
p. 170, note (in *Œuvres Complètes*, vols. 1–12, Paris: Gallimard 1970–88, vol. 5,
p. 24; p. 56; p. 128, note).
Beauvoir, Simone de, *Le Deuxième sexe*, vols. 1–2, Paris: Gallimard 1949, vol. 1,
p. 236; p. 295, p. 387; vol. 2, p. 7; pp. 213–14; p. 564.
Blanchot, Maurice, *Faux Pas*, Paris: Gallimard 1943, p. 10; pp. 18–19; pp. 25–30.
— *La Part du feu*, Paris: Gallimard 1949, p. 65.
— *L'espace littéraire*, Paris: Gallimard 1955, p. 57; p. 103; p. 123; p. 141.
— *L'Entretiens Infini*, Paris: Gallimard 1969, pp. 3–4; pp. 211–12; p. 217.
— *L'Ecriture du désastre*, Paris: Gallimard 1980, p. 185.
Camus, Albert, *Le Mythe de Sisyphe*, Paris: Gallimard 1942, p. 39; pp. 42–3; p. 51;
pp. 56–61; p. 65; pp. 69–72.
Deleuze, Gilles, *Nietzsche et la philosophie*, Paris: Presses Universitaires de France
1962, pp. 41–3, 107, note 2.
— *Le bergsonisme*, Paris: Presses Universitaires de France 1966, p. 38, note 2; p. 53.
— *Différence et répétition*, Paris: Presses Universitaires de France 1968, pp. 12–20;
p. 38; p. 39, note 1; pp. 126–7; p. 289, note 1; pp. 347–8; p. 377; p. 397.
— *Logique du sens*, Paris: Minuit 1969, p. 349.
— *Cinéma 1. L'image-mouvement*, Paris: Minuit 1983, pp. 158–64; pp. 184–5.

— *Cinéma 2. L'image-temps*, Paris: Minuit 1985, p. 224, note 30; pp. 227–8; pp. 230–1.

— *Pourparlers 1972–1990*, Paris: Minuit 1990, p. 84.

Derrida, Jacques, *L'écriture et la différence*, Paris: Seuil 1967, p. 51; p. 143; pp. 161–5.

— *Glas*, Paris: Galilée 1974, pp. 224–5; pp. 258–9.

— *Passions*, Paris: Éditions Galilée 1993, pp. 57–8; p. 84.

— *Force de loi*, Paris: Galilée 1994, p. 58.

— *Adieu à Emmanuel Lévinas*, Paris: Galilée 1997, p. 24; pp. 166–7; p. 209.

— *Donner la mort*, Paris: Galilée 1999.

Heidegger, Martin, *Sein und Zeit*, Halle: Niemeyer 1927, pp. 175–96, see also p. 190, note 1; p. 235, note 1; and p. 338, note 1.

Kierkegaard, Søren, *Af Søren Kierkegaards Efterladte Papirer*, vols. 1–9, ed. by H.P. Barfod and Hermann Gottsched, Copenhagen: C.A. Reitzel 1869–81.

— *Oeuvres Complètes*, vols. 1–20, trans. and ed. by Paul-Henri Tisseau and Else-Marie Jacquet-Tisseau, Paris: Éditions de l'Orante 1966–86.

Lacan, Jacques, *Le Séminaire. Livre II. Le Moi dans la théorie de Freud et dans la technique psychanalytique. 1954–1955*, Paris: Le Seuil 1978, pp. 110; pp. 124–5.

— *Le Séminaire. Livre X. L'Angoisse. 1962–1963*, Paris: Éditions de Seuil 2004, p. 385.

— *Le Séminaire. Livre XI. Les Quatre Concepts fondamentaux de la psychanalyse*, Paris: Le Seuil 1974, p. 59.

— *Le Seminaire. Livre XVII. L'envers de la psychanalyse*, Paris: Le Seuil 1991, pp. 51–2; pp. 168–9.

Lukács, Georg, "Das Zerschellen der Form against Leben: Søren Kierkegaard und Regine Olsen," in *Die Seele und die Formen: Essays*, Berlin: Fleischel 1911, pp. 61–91.

Merleau-Ponty, Maurice, *Phénoménologie de la perception*, Paris: Gallimard 1945, p. 8; p. 100.

— "Complicité objective," in *Les Temps modernes*, no. 34, 1948, pp. 1–11.

— "La querelle de l'existentialisme," in his *Sens et non-sens*, Paris: Nagel 1948, pp. 141–64, see p. 151; p. 158 (originally published in *Le Temps modernes*, no. 2, 1945, pp. 344–56).

— "L'Existentialisme chez Hegel," in his *Sens et non-sens*, Paris: Nagel 1948, pp. 125–39, see pp. 127–8 (originally published in *Les Temps modernes*, no. 7, 1946, pp. 1311–19).

— "Foi et bonne foi," in his *Sens et non-sens*, Paris: Nagel 1948, pp. 351–70, see p. 359 (originally published in *Les Temps modernes*, no. 5, 1946, pp. 769–82).

— *Les aventures de la dialectique*, Paris: Gallimard 1955, p. 148.

Sartre, Jean-Paul, *L'être et le néant. Essai d'ontologie phénoménologique*, Paris: Gallimard 1943 (*Bibliothèque des Idées*), pp. 58–84; pp. 94–111; pp. 115–49; pp. 150–74; pp. 291–300; pp. 508–16; pp. 529–60; pp. 639–42; pp. 643–63; pp. 669–70; pp. 720–22.

— *L'existentialisme est un humanisme*, Paris: Nagel 1946, pp. 27–33.

— *Critique de la raison dialectique*, vol. 1, *Théorie des ensembles pratiques*, Paris: Gallimard 1960, p. 117, note 1.

— *Les carnets de la drôle de guerre. Novembre 1939–Mars 1940*, Paris: Gallimard 1983, pp. 333–7; pp. 342–7; pp. 348ff.; p. 352; pp. 382–3.

III. Secondary Literature on Kristeva's Relation to Kierkegaard

Lorraine, Tamsin, "Amatory Cures for Material Dis-ease. A Kristevian Reading of 'The Sickness unto Death,' " in *Kierkegaard in Post/Modernity*, ed. by Martin J. Matuštík and Merold Westphal, Bloomington, Indiana: Indiana University Press 1995, pp. 98–109 (reprinted in *Feminist Interpretations of Søren Kierkegaard*, ed. by Céline Léon and Sylvia Walsh, University Park, Pennsylvania: Pennsylvania State University Press 1997, pp. 307–28).

Jacques Lacan:

Kierkegaard as a Freudian Questioner of the Soul *avant la lettre*

J.D. Mininger

I. Introduction to Lacan's Relationship to Kierkegaard

At first glance Jacques Lacan (1901–81) and Søren Kierkegaard do not seem a very well-paired intellectual couple. Despite Kierkegaard's attack upon the church establishment, his dedication to a pure, if impossible brand of Christianity might lead some to label him a religious fanatic. In general the psychoanalytic tradition looks very skeptically (and perhaps with good reason) at the established institutions of the Judeo-Christian traditions and at religious fervor (let alone zealotry), perhaps especially in resonance with the outspoken atheism of its movement's intellectual father, Sigmund Freud (1856–1939). Lacan, whose "return to Freud" in his psychoanalytic labors placed him firmly within the Freudian camp both in spite of and because of his almost obsessively close readings of the Freudian texts, would seem to easily fit the mold of a potentially harsh critic of religion. And, at times he is; but, of course, so too was Kierkegaard. Although both men surely understood religiosity, its manifold appearances and possibilities, and its varying motives and motivations in significantly divergent ways, if Lacan's early education is any indicator, then it may be the case that the two men possessed both a talent and an appreciation for unusual, even radical forms of religiosity.

Lacan received a Catholic school education in Paris: the prestigious Collège Stanislas. He was a good student, but a not a great one. However, in pairing Lacan with Kierkegaard it may be relevant to note that young Jacques' greatest academic successes in school came in the fields of religious studies and Latin. However, his schooling came far too early to include the name of Kierkegaard. The French reception of Kierkegaard was a slow process indeed, with perhaps the first major event in this development occurring only first in 1938, with Jean Wahl's publication of *Études kierkegaardiennes*. Lacan most likely first came to Kierkegaard indirectly, through the rising popularity of Heidegger in France in the 1930s. But even if his encounters with Kierkegaardian texts clearly germane to psychoanalysis such as *Concept de l'angoisse* and *La Répétition* came much later in his intellectual development—in the 1930s and possibly even the 1940s—Lacan nonetheless shared with Kierkegaard a passion for pushing the envelope of the intersections of religiosity and philosophy.

In his introductory book on Lacan, Sean Homer cites a telling anecdote about Lacan's school days at the Collège Stanislas: young Lacan chose to decorate his room with perhaps the ultimate (philosophical) act of provocation: a diagram of Spinoza's *Ethics*.[1] Just like Lacan himself, whose battles with the psychoanalytic establishment in France are legendary, Spinoza's controversial status as heretic-hero has inspired many to critical fury and still more to fierce loyalty. For Lacan, Spinoza clearly instilled in him the latter sentiment. In his eleventh seminar, *The Four Fundamental Concepts of Psychoanalysis*, Lacan even likens himself to a modern Spinoza, excommunicated from the "church" of French psychoanalysis. Probably Lacan felt similar admiration for Kierkegaard's biography upon learning about it.

Though this is admittedly little more than speculation, Lacan's clear admiration for Kierkegaard found in the relatively rare instances in which Lacan directly references the Dane would seem to indicate some sort of affinity beyond the strictly scientific. Lacan does use theological terminology (for example, sin) at times, and Kierkegaard is an occasional reference Lacan leans on to buffer the entrance of such terms into his psychoanalytic discourse. Nevertheless, in addition to this more speculative affinity, the following simple factual statement may perhaps best introduce Lacan's relationship to the work of Søren Kierkegaard: Lacan's references to Kierkegaard are relatively rare in the larger scheme of his (Lacan's) body of work, and these references repeatedly (though with some exceptions) point in the direction of two major themes: repetition and anxiety.

II. Repetition

Of the more than twenty references to Søren Kierkegaard scattered throughout Lacan's published articles and the transcripts of his seminars, nearly half pertain to the topic of repetition. It would be an unjustified exaggeration to claim that Lacan prefers to explain the concept of repetition by way of reference to Kierkegaard; a reference to the Dane does not accompany every instance in which Lacan addresses the topic in his seminars and writings. However, it is not inappropriate to suggest that Kierkegaard's treatment of repetition in his book of the same title holds a privileged place in Lacan's accounts of repetition and, in particular, his explication(s) of Freud's notion of repetition compulsion (*Wiederholungszwang*). In several of his most significant engagements with the concept, most famously described by Freud in *Beyond the Pleasure Principle* (1920),[2] Lacan appeals directly to Kierkegaard's writings to support both his interpretation of Freud and the overarching importance of repetition for the study and practice of psychoanalysis.

The first mention of Kierkegaard's notion of repetition is crucial not so much for the significance of the treatment of the topic, but for its occurrence in one of Lacan's landmark texts. In "The Function and Field of Speech and Language in

[1]   Sean Homer, *Jacques Lacan*, London and New York: Routledge 2005, p. 3.

[2]   Sigmund Freud, *Jenseits des Lustprinzips*, Vienna: n.p. 1920. (English translations: *Beyond the Pleasure Principle*, trans. by C.M.J. Hubback, London and Vienna: International Psycho-Analytical Press 1922; a new translation was made by James Strachey, London: Hogarth Press & Institute of Psycho-Analysis 1950 (several later editions).)

Psychoanalysis," written for and delivered at the Rome congress in September, 1953, Lacan for the first time includes a direct reference to Kierkegaard in a commentary on the topic of repetition. In this text Lacan offers "Kierkegaardian repetition" as the appropriate contrast to Platonic reminiscence with respect to the dialectic of self-consciousness.[3]

In the section of the essay in which this reference appears, Lacan's overarching concern is the radical shift in the understanding of the subject that Freud's discovery of the unconscious makes possible. Though it is in and through speech that, in works such as *The Psychopathology of Everyday Life*, Freud placed in question the sovereignty of self-consciousness, Lacan suggests that the principles that govern the effects of speech are "nothing but the dialectic of self-consciousness, as it is realized from Socrates to Hegel, beginning with the ironic assumption that all that is rational is real, only to precipitate into the scientific judgment that all that is real is rational."[4] Plato's notion of reminiscence suggests a subject who is whole and without contradiction, since the Platonic subject achieves self-consciousness by a process of recollecting the original and genuine form from which he originated. The same wholeness may be claimed for the Hegelian subject, insofar as, with the benefit of an appeal to the future (in the form of the phenomenological development of Spirit toward absolute knowing), this subject finds in the Hegelian dialectic a methodical process of recollection in which the past is neatly synthesized in the self-consciousness of the present. Though Lacan follows the Hegelian phenomenological structure to some degree,[5] he insists that "it is certainly psychoanalysis that provides

---

[3]   Jacques Lacan, "Fonction et champ de la parole et du langage en psychanalyse," in his *Écrits*, Paris: Le Seuil 1966, p. 293. (English translation: "The Function and Field of Speech and Language in Psychoanalysis," in his *Écrits: The First Complete Edition in English*, trans. by Bruce Fink in collaboration with Héloïse Fink and Russell Grigg, New York: W.W. Norton 2006, p. 242.)

[4]   Lacan, "Fonction et champ de la parole et du langage en psychanalyse," p. 292. ("The Function and Field of Speech and Language in Psychoanalysis," p. 241.)

[5]   See, for example, Jacques Lacan, "Le stade du miroir comme formateur de la fonction du Je," in *Écrits*, pp. 93–100. (English translation: "The Mirror Stage as Formative of the I Function as Revealed in Psychoanalytic Experience," in *Écrits: The First Complete Edition in English*, pp. 75–81.) Lacan likes Kierkegaardian repetition because it offers a counter-concept to Hegelian understandings of movement and knowledge, in spite of the fact that Lacan remains indebted to Hegel's thought in many respects, which Lacan himself is quick to acknowledge. In fact, Lacan's pre-1950s and early 1950s accounts of repetition borrow epistemological assumptions from Hegel, against whom the critique will eventually, in part, be directed. This is strikingly similar to how Kierkegaard initially draws out his own theory of repetition vis-à-vis Hegel. In *Kierkegaard's Relations to Hegel Reconsidered*, Jon Stewart explains this relationship in the following passage: "What Kierkegaard calls 'repetition,' at least in this context, is what Hegel means by the relation of universality to particularity. The only way one can recognize a sensible particular as a repetition is by virtue of a universal concept that one already possesses. Without universals there would be no repetition since there would only be a plurality of dissimilar particulars. By the same token, without particulars there would be no repetition since there would be only eternal universals, which could never repeat. Thus, repetition can take place only in the relationship between the two. This can be regarded as the epistemological groundwork for the notion of repetition, a groundwork

[Hegel's concept of identity] with its paradigm by revealing the structure in which this identity is realized as disjunctive of the subject, and without appealing to the future."[6] Lacan stresses that, according to Freud's method, the process of authenticating the self through the dialectic of self-consciousness—a procedure of recognition achieved through the medium of language in analysis—effectively de-centers the subject from the very self-consciousness that the reconstruction initially endeavored to achieve. In short, the discourse of the unconscious intervenes, as it were, in the space between the "I" who speaks and the "I" who is the subject of that speech. Lacan appreciates the category of Kierkegaardian repetition precisely because it provides a kind of absolute distance from the Platonic version of the subject which ignores this crucial fracture in the subject—this irreconcilable lack—which conditions the function of repetition.

The contrast between Plato and Kierkegaard, which turns out to be an antinomy between reminiscence and repetition, is paradigmatic for Lacan's concept of repetition. A year after the reference to Kierkegaard in his Rome Report, Lacan again turns to Kierkegaard in order to address this antinomy, this time in his seminar of 1954–55, dedicated to the Freudian ego theory and psychoanalytic technique. In this work Lacan offers a slightly more sustained commentary on Kierkegaardian repetition than we find in most all other comparable places in his teachings on repetition. This is really saying something, considering Lacan typically uses Kierkegaard only in passing reference.

Lacan's point in the immediate context of the two Kierkegaard references in this seminar is to explain Freud's theories regarding the ego's dependence upon repetition as a structuring feature. As with seemingly all of his work, Lacan is drawing out a theory of his own by returning to Freud's texts, here specifically *Project for a Scientific Psychology* (1895).[7] Freud, says Lacan, distinguishes between two key ways in which human experience is structured:

> one which, along with Kierkegaard, I called *ancient*, based on reminiscence, presupposing agreement, harmony between man and the world of his objects, which means that he recognises them, because in some way, he has always known them—and, on the contrary, the conquest, the structuration of the world through the effort of labour, along the path of repetition. To the extent that what appears to him corresponds only

---

that Kierkegaard borrows from Hegel. This conclusion—that the notion of repetition arises from an analysis of Hegel's discussion of consciousness—is striking since Kierkegaard seems ultimately to want to use the notion of repetition to criticize Hegel's notion of mediation." Jon Stewart, *Kierkegaard's Relations to Hegel Reconsidered*, Cambridge and New York: Cambridge University Press 2002, p. 288.

6   Lacan, "Fonction et champ de la parole et du langage en psychanalyse," p. 292. ("The Function and Field of Speech and Language in Psychoanalysis," p. 242.)

7   Sigmund Freud, "Entwurf einer Psychologie," in *Aus den Anfängen der Psychoanalyse*, ed. by Marie Bonaparte, Anna Freud, and Ernst Kris, London: Imago 1950, pp. 371–466. (English translation: "Project for a Scientific Psychology," in *The Origins of Psycho-Analysis*, trans. by James Strachey, ed. by Marie Bonaparte, Anna Freud, and Ernst Kris, New York: Basic Books 1954, pp. 347–445.)

partially with what has already gained him satisfaction, the subject engages in a quest, and repeats his quest indefinitely until he rediscovers this object.[8]

In other words, repetition is when the subject substitutes new and different particular objects and contexts into (unconsciously) repeated patterns of behavior.

Lacan aligns Freud and Kierkegaard on the topic of repetition because, in Lacan's reading, despite the seemingly disparate purposes of their writing, both thinkers understand that repetition is always repetition with a difference, even at the most basic levels. In *Repetition*, Kierkegaard writes of simple repetition: "the dialectic of repetition is easy, for that which is repeated has been—otherwise it could not be repeated—but the very fact that it has been makes the repetition into something new."[9] In Freud's explanation, the subject repeats the same behavioral patterns because that subject is not conscious of the original impulses or experiences which initially structured this pattern of behavior. Therefore, every repetition is both a process of a consciously lived new experience and an unconsciously relived experience.[10]

For his contrast between reminiscence and repetition, Lacan says he agrees with Kierkegaard's category of reminiscence as correctly described by the term "ancient." This comment clearly points to Kierkegaard's analysis in the opening of *Repetition* about how repetition must be distinguished from recollection: "repetition is a crucial expression for what 'recollection' was to the Greeks. Just as they taught that all knowing is a recollecting, modern philosophy will teach that all life is a repetition."[11] The ancient conception of the subject, and in particular Plato's epistemology, is linked to recollection by Kierkegaard and to reminiscence by Lacan, but both use the term "repetition" to define the modern view.

In Kierkegaard's commentary Lacan finds the opportunity to emphasize the *modern* conception both of humanity and of the subject, of which Freud's work is his definitive model. In another article written in 1955 Lacan writes about this distinction:

> This is how Freud situates himself right from the outset in the opposition Kierkegaard taught us about, regarding whether the notion of existence is founded upon reminiscence or repetition. If Kierkegaard admirably discerns in that opposition the difference between Antiquity's conception of man and the modern conception of man, it appears

---

[8]   Jacques Lacan, *Le Séminaire. Livre II. Le Moi dans la théorie de Freud et dans la technique psychanalytique. 1954–1955*, Paris: Le Seuil 1978, pp. 124–5. (English translation: *The Seminar of Jacques Lacan. Book II. The Ego in Freud's Theory and in the Technique of Psychoanalysis 1954–1955*, trans. by Sylvana Tomaselli, Cambridge: Cambridge University Press 1988, p. 100.)

[9]   *SKS* 4, 25 / *R*, 149.

[10]   From this one might assume that the point of analysis is to consciously relive past experiences, but this is not at all what Lacan understands to be the purpose of psychoanalysis. Such analytic methods of catharsis resound more with the theories of Josef Breuer (1842–1925).

[11]   *SKS* 4, 9 / *R*, 131.

that Freud makes the latter take its decisive step by ravishing the necessity included in this repetition from the human agent identified with consciousness.[12]

The nod to Kierkegaard helps buoy Lacan's claims for the radically modern view that Freud and psychoanalysis bring to science via the study of the unconscious. Though Lacan correctly understands Kierkegaard's category of repetition as modern, or at the very least as Christian as opposed to pagan, there remains the slight irony that Kierkegaard's concept of repetition constitutes one of the few points in his body of work in which the term "modern" is viewed with anything other than suspicion by Kierkegaard.

In addition to the historically inflected contrast between reminiscence and repetition, Lacan's Kierkegaard-influenced distinction links reminiscence to the imaginary order and repetition to the symbolic order. Along with the real, these make up the three crucial dimensions of experience in Lacanian psychoanalysis. The imaginary is the order of the image, of illusion, of lures, and of the ego. Reminiscence belongs to the imaginary in that it involves reliving past experiences and really feeling those emotions and revisiting those thoughts and impulses that had occurred previously In contrast, repetition occurs as an "intrusion of the symbolic register."[13] The symbolic register is so named for its reference to symbols that are signifiers, such as may be understood from structural linguistics and such thinkers as Ferdinand de Saussure (1857–1913) and Roman Jakobson (1896–1982). The interplay of these signifiers, based on principles of oppositional meaning laid out in structural linguistics, help to determine the order of the subject. The unconscious manifests itself in the signifying chain, and repetition is the essential motor of that chain. It is in this context that Lacan speaks of the circuit, in which certain key signifiers continue to return to the subject, in spite of defenses and resistances. Thus, for analysis repetition must be studied as a symbolic phenomenon. Certain master signifiers must be charted through analysis, and the analysand must reconstruct or rewrite his or her own history by virtue of noting these symbolic repetitions. Though this may involve intense emotion, the source of the repetitions is not the imaginary order—it is precisely the emotions and feelings of the imaginary order that might hide the true nature of the symbolic repetition.

It is from the platform of hunting for these symbolic repetitions that Lacan briefly glosses his own summary of the opening action of Kierkegaard's *Repetition*. Lacan notes that this shift from reminiscence to repetition, from imaginary to symbolic, from ancient to modern, is precisely what links the insights of Kierkegaard and Freud. Upon recommending Kierkegaard's book to his auditors, imploring those with little time to at least read the first part of it, Lacan explains:

---

[12]   Jacques Lacan, "Le séminaire sur la 'Lettre vole,' " in *Écrits*, p. 46. (English translation: "Seminar on 'The Purloined Letter,' " in *Écrits: The First Complete Edition in English*, p. 34.)

[13]   Lacan, *Le Séminaire. Livre II. Le Moi dans la théorie de Freud et dans la technique psychanalytique. 1954–1955*, p. 110. (*The Seminar of Jacques Lacan. Book II. The Ego in Freud's Theory and in the Technique of Psychoanalysis 1954–1955*, p. 88.)

Kierkegaard wants to avoid precisely those problems which stem from his accession to a new order, and he encounters the dam of his own reminiscences, of who he thinks he is and of what he knows he will never be able to become. He then tries the experiment of repetition. He returns to Berlin where, during his previous stay he had experienced infinite pleasure, and he retraces his own steps. You will see what happens to him, seeking his well-being in the shadow of his pleasure. The experiment fails totally. But as a result of that, he puts us on the track of our problem, namely, how and why everything which pertains to an advance essential to the human being must take the path of a tenacious repetition.[14]

From the very start, Lacan conflates Kierkegaard and the "author" of *Repetition*, Constantin Constantius. In his later work, when Lacan returns to Kierkegaard (in passing) in contexts other than that of the concept of repetition, he will also allude to Kierkegaard's biography. However, regardless of the most correct authorial referent, what matters most for Lacan in the story of *Repetition* is that the attempt at repetition fails. It fails precisely because it attempts reminiscence, the former and inappropriate order, in the place where repetition and its symbolic and unconscious status are the more appropriate. In other words, for Lacan, Kierkegaard's book constitutes an example of illustrating Freudian theory *avant la lettre*, as if Kierkegaard were the first to "get it."

In 1964 Lacan returns to this same topic in his seminar *The Four Fundamental Concepts of Psychoanalysis*. Although what Lacan says in these lectures about repetition with respect to Kierkegaard is not at bottom divergent from his coverage of the same territory in his 1954–55 seminar, his thematic repetition does choose different details to emphasize as entry points to explaining repetition as the formal tool whereby the unconscious manifests itself and the subject constitutes itself. Perhaps most notable in this mention of Kierkegaard is Lacan's tone of admiration. Lacan introduces Kierkegaard to his audience as "the most acute of the questioners of the soul before [Freud]."[15] As in his seminar from 1954–55, Lacan urges his auditors "to re-read Kierkegaard's essay on *Repetition*, so dazzling in its lightness and ironic play, so truly Mozartian in the way, so reminiscent of *Don Giovanni*, it abolishes the mirages of love."[16] Lacan goes on to explore the relationship between repetition and love, in particular first loves. Kierkegaard's story, says Lacan, emphasizes "with great acuteness and in a quite unanswerable way,"[17] that the young man in love only relates himself to this love through memory. In other words, his approach is solely through the imaginary order of reminiscence. As with his commentary ten years earlier, Lacan uses Kierkegaard's story as an illustration of a subject's failure

---

[14]   Jacques Lacan, *Le Séminaire. Livre II. Le Moi dans la théorie de Freud et dans la technique psychanalytique. 1954–1955*, p. 110. (*The Seminar of Jacques Lacan. Book II. The Ego in Freud's Theory and in the Technique of Psychoanalysis 1954–1955*, pp. 87–8.)

[15]   Jacques Lacan, *Le Séminaire. Livre XI. Les Quatre Concepts fondamentaux de la psychanalyse*, Paris: Le Seuil 1974, p. 59. (English translation: *The Seminar of Jacques Lacan. Book XI. The Four Fundamental Concepts of Psychoanalysis*, trans. by Alan Sheridan, New York and London: W.W. Norton 1981, pp. 60–1.)

[16]   Lacan, *Le Séminaire. Livre XI. Les Quatre Concepts fondamentaux de la psychanalyse*, p. 59. (*The Seminar of Jacques Lacan. Book XI. The Four Fundamental Concepts of Psychoanalysis*, p. 61.)

[17]   Ibid.

to achieve true repetition. The young man has created false, narcissistic demands that fuel his ideal ego,[18] instead of understanding repetition in the symbolic sense, as a repetition that involves and makes manifest unconsciously repeated impulses. Repetition always demands a difference, and this "most radical diversity constituted by repetition itself"[19] is the kinship with his own understanding of repetition that Lacan seems to see in Kierkegaard's, which the story of *Repetition* points up *ex negativo* through the failures of Constantin Constantius and the young man to achieve "true repetition."

Though Lacan's concept of repetition undergoes several shifts throughout his teachings, he continues to occasionally refer his auditors and readers to Kierkegaard on the subject. As Dylan Evans explains in *An Introductory Dictionary to Lacanian Psychoanalysis*, Lacan's emphasis in the 1950s on repetition as the insistence of the letter (that is, the signifying chain) begins to change by the end of the 1960s.[20] In his seminar of 1969–70, *The Other Side of Psychoanalysis*, Lacan introduces the concept of repetition once again. This time, however, he explains the concept in relation to *jouissance*. As usual, Lacan is in the midst of explaining Freud—here the text in question is *Beyond the Pleasure Principle*. In this book Freud asks why people repeat destructive, unpleasant behavior if humans are supposedly guided by the pleasure principle. What emerges in Freud's text in answer to his own question is his theory of the death instinct. Lacan understands these repetitions as the return of the excess of enjoyment in the subject, namely, *jouissance*: "repetition is based on the return of *jouissance*."[21] Whereas pleasure remains tethered to the laws of the greatest possible relief and satisfaction, *jouissance* transgresses this law, existing beyond the pleasure principle.

Lacan notes that he has already gone over this territory of Freudian repetition before in his seminars, in particular via reference to Kierkegaard: "At the time, here, I pointed out the kinship with remarks by Kierkegaard. By virtue of being expressed and as such repeated, of being marked by repetition, what is repeated cannot be

---

[18]   In *On Anxiety*, Renata Selacl gives a succinct account of the concept of an ideal ego in the following passage: "Lacan distinguishes between ego-ideal, which is on the side of the symbolic and ideal ego, which is on the side of the imaginary. The subject often identifies with some ego-ideal (i.e. authority or ideals that are respected in his or her culture) in order to acquire a symbolic identity, which will inscribe them in a desirable way into society. The identification with the ego-ideal is always a primary one, occurring before the imaginary identification with some ideal ego (i.e. with some image in which the subject appears likeable to themselves)." Renata Salecl, *On Anxiety*, London and New York: Routledge 2004, p. 145.

[19]   Lacan, *Le Séminaire. Livre XI. Les Quatre Concepts fondamentaux de la psychanalyse*, p. 59. (*The Seminar of Jacques Lacan. Book XI. The Four Fundamental Concepts of Psychoanalysis*, p. 61.)

[20]   Dylan Evans, *An Introductory Dictionary to Lacanian Psychoanalysis*, London and New York: Routledge 1996, p. 167.

[21]   Jacques Lacan, *Le Seminaire. Livre XVII. L'envers de la psychanalyse*, Paris: Le Seuil 1991, p. 51. (*The Seminar of Jacques Lacan. Book XVII. The Other Side of Psychoanalysis*, New York and London: W.W. Norton 2007, p. 46.)

anything other," in relation to what it repeats, than a loss."[22] Lacan sees Kierkegaard's story of *Repetition* as illustrating these moments of loss in the form of what in the story is understood as a failure to achieve repetition. Proper repetition, which by necessity involves a loss,[23] must be understood according to Lacan as bearing witness to the limit of knowledge and of the subject's conscious memory. The *jouissance* that is lost in repetition roughly corresponds in Freud to the lost object,[24] which sustains the structure of the ego as organized around a trauma.[25] For Lacan, this lost object, in its relation to the *jouissance* that it instantiates for the subject, becomes a very important definition of the *objet a*, the object-cause of desire.

In total there are eight significant direct references to Kierkegaard among the various places in Lacan's writings and teachings where he addresses the concept of repetition. Two instances in particular stand out for their slightly more detailed commentary on Kierkegaard, consisting in both cases still of no more than a half-page of remarks directed in particular to Kierkegaard and his work.[26] In the final analysis, however, merely the number of appearances of Kierkegaard's name tells relatively little; more crucial is speculation on the guiding question: why does Lacan favor Kierkegaard's *Repetition* so much? Beyond what has already been said above and which was more easily supported by overt textual evidence, two further and more speculative answers to this question present themselves for consideration.

The first answer involves the nature of Kierkegaard's program of indirect communication as evidenced in *Repetition*. In *Repetition* not only does a pseudonym sign the book, but the reader is presented with different voices: for example, Constantin Constantius, the young man, the possibility of Kierkegaard's (the "real" author's) voice, and Job (in the form of intertextuality). The authority of the narrative voice is more tenuous than many of the other pseudonymous writings. This form underscores the tense and problematic issue of representing religious repetition—something which supposedly cannot be thought or captured statically and scientifically, but only individually manifested, shown, pointed to—in language and in thought. Though it would be incorrect to assume a homology between what

---

[22]   Lacan, *Le Seminaire. Livre XVII. L'envers de la psychanalyse*, p. 51. *The Seminar of Jacques Lacan. Book XVII. The Other Side of Psychoanalysis*, p. 46.)

[23]   It involves a loss by necessity because, in Kierkegaard's terms, repetition is acted forwards, into the future, instead of being recollected backwards in a desperate move to hold on to the past.

[24]   Or, understood alternately: the repressed, unconscious, or otherwise unknown origins of the original impulses of the repeated pattern of behavior.

[25]   For an outstanding analysis of Freud's *Hemmung, Symptom und Angst* (Leipzig et al.: Internationaler Psychoanalytischer Verlag 1926; English translation: *Inhibitions, Symptoms and Anxiety*, trans. by Alix Strachey, revised and ed. by James Strachey, New York: W.W. Norton 1989) that explains anxiety in its relationship to an original trauma, see Samuel Weber, *The Legend of Freud*, Stanford: Stanford University Press 2000 [1982].

[26]   See Lacan, *Le Séminaire. Livre II. Le Moi dans la théorie de Freud et dans la technique psychanalytique. 1954–1955*, p. 110. (*The Seminar of Jacques Lacan. Book II. The Ego in Freud's Theory and in the Technique of Psychoanalysis 1954–1955*, p. 87); and Lacan, *Le Séminaire. Livre XI. Les Quatre Concepts fondamentaux de la psychanalyse*, p. 59 (*The Seminar of Jacques Lacan. Book XI. The Four Fundamental Concepts of Psychoanalysis*, p. 61).

Lacan calls the return of the real and Kierkegaard's version of religious repetition, there is clearly an affinity of sorts between the religious repetition that Kierkegaard suggests and what in the psychoanalytic register (as if this were analysis) would be a piercing of the fabric of the imaginary by the real, or what might also more simply be called the action of the unconscious, namely, the return of the repressed. On a related note, a more far-flung and greatly speculative explanation would be that the kind of distance created by indirect communication mirrors the position of the analyst with respect to the reader-author. However, following this logic, even Constantin Constantius in his role as midwife, Socrates figure, and observer who helps the young man but is neither a new object nor a creator, begins to show outlines of an analyst figure, if even allegorically. The fatuous nature of the narrative voice in *Repetition* sustains the possibility of these speculations, but it is also this fact that undermines them, for the question of transference in analysis simply cannot be explained via simple comparison to the literary context, in spite of the seemingly formidable fact of reading understood as comprehension, activation, interpretation, and even a kind of re-writing process.

The second speculative answer to why Lacan admires Kierkegaard's *Repetition* is that perhaps he sees in *Repetition* a kind of affinity to his own strategy and method of reading Freud. Kierkegaard's theory of repetition as a continuity maintained precisely by always accepting some new element can be seen as a kind of model for Lacan's "return to Freud" in his own work.

III. Anxiety

Lacan's first mention of Kierkegaard in print occurs 1948 in "Aggressiveness in Psychoanalysis."[27] Kierkegaard's name emerges at the end of the article in relation to the topic of anxiety. Lacan has just finished discussing the relation between space and the possible tensions at work in the subject due to its irreducibly spatial dimension. The proper name sponsoring the discussion is Hegel, though this treatment clearly has in mind Heidegger's categories from *Being and Time*. Lacan notes that this spatial dimension intersects and correlates with the temporal dimension, which is the crucial factor in anxiety. Though he chooses not to go into it, Lacan mentions that were he to more fully attend to this question of time and anxiety, he would proceed by "using the contemporary significations of two philosophies that would seem to correspond to the philosophies I just mentioned: that of Bergson, owing to its naturalistic inadequacy, and that of Kierkegaard owing to its dialectical signification."[28] Though this does not provide details, it does serve as a hint that Lacan has read (or at least read about) *The Concept of Anxiety* and that he understands the significance of Kierkegaard's treatment of that topic to be related to the dialectical emergence of anxiety from the matrix of temporality. Lacan, it seems, appreciated Kierkegaard's

---

[27]   Jacques Lacan, "L'agressivité en psychanalyse," in *Écrits*, pp. 101–24. (English translation: "Aggressiveness in Psychoanalysis," in *Écrits: The First Complete Edition in English*, pp. 82–101.)

[28]   Lacan, "L'agressivité en psychanalyse," p. 123. ("Aggressiveness in Psychoanalysis," p. 100.)

reading of Adam and the entrance of sin, the existence of which anxiety's presence serves to prove (according to Kierkegaard).

Of the remaining four significant instances of the appearance of Kierkegaard's proper name in relation to anxiety in Lacan's texts, the obvious choice to begin a more proper discussion of Lacan's reception of Kierkegaard's theories of anxiety comes from his seminar of 1969–70, *The Other Side of Psychoanalysis*. On May 13, 1970, the Law Faculty in rue Saint-Jacques, where the seminar was to be held, was closed, and so a question-and-answer session with Lacan took place on the Steps of the Pantheon instead of a typical seminar meeting. Parts of the exchange from this unique gathering are transcribed in the published version of the seminar as chapter X: "Interview on the Steps of the Pantheon."[29] Fortunately, one of the specific exchanges to survive is on Lacan's relationship to Kierkegaard concerning anxiety—just the question to which this section seeks an answer. The unnamed questioner inquires: "What do you think of the relations that exist between you and Kierkegaard concerning anxiety?"[30] Lacan responds:

> No one can yet imagine the extent to which people attribute thoughts to me. I only have to mention someone and I am said to be condescending. It's the very model of academic vertigo. Why in fact wouldn't I speak about Kierkegaard? It's clear that if I place all this emphasis on anxiety in the economy, for it's a question of economy, it's obviously not in order to neglect the fact that at a certain moment there was someone who represents the emergence, the coming into being, not of anxiety but of the concept of anxiety, as Kierkegaard himself explicitly calls one of his works. It's not for nothing that historically this concept emerged at a certain moment. This is what I was counting on expounding for you this morning.[31]

The second half of the answer to the question, which has not been reproduced above, consists mostly of a digression in which Lacan mentions a recently published book in which his work is discussed and in which Kierkegaard is also named, though not necessarily in connection to one another.[32] Lacan's chief concern in his response is to defend his emphasis in past teachings and writings on anxiety as *the* foundational affect. In order to support his claim as to the centrality of anxiety for the subject, Lacan appeals to Kierkegaard. In particular, he indirectly suggests that there is a historical dimension to the intellectual study of anxiety that has apparently been neglected. Published in 1844, Kierkegaard's *The Concept of Anxiety* is the first focused and direct treatment (in monograph form) of the topic of anxiety that, as Lacan points out, more scientifically approaches anxiety.[33] Since the possible

---

[29]   Lacan, *Le Séminaire. Livre XVII. L'envers de la psychanalyse*, pp. 167–74. (*The Seminar of Jacques Lacan. Book XVII. The Other Side of Psychoanalysis*, pp. 143–9.)

[30]   Lacan, *Le Séminaire. Livre XVII. L'envers de la psychanalyse*, p. 168. (*The Seminar of Jacques Lacan. Book XVII. The Other Side of Psychoanalysis*, p. 144.)

[31]   Lacan, *Le Séminaire. Livre XVII. L'envers de la psychanalyse*, pp. 168–9. (*The Seminar of Jacques Lacan. Book XVII. The Other Side of Psychoanalysis*, pp. 144–5.)

[32]   Lacan is referring to Manuel de Dieguez, *Science et nescience*, Paris: Gallimard 1970.

[33]   As has been pointed out more than once in the critical literature, *The Concept of Anxiety* may very well also constitute a rather devastating parody of the very scientifically minded textbook style of nineteenth-century scholarship that endeavored to conceptualize the

applications of psychoanalysis to cultural criticism, politics, aesthetics, philosophy, and other discourses outside of the practice of psychoanalysis are the supposed focus of the 1969–70 seminar, Lacan's oblique reference to the emergence of anxiety in the mid-nineteenth century as a concept points to the possibility of a grand generalization about intellectual history and the development of modernity. "It's not for nothing," as Lacan says, that anxiety should become the focus of some attention at that time. Perhaps it is the result of two concomitant forces inherent in the Enlightenment project: the secularization of society, achieved by replacing the essential anchor of truth that had been God with reason and science, on the one hand; on the other hand, the intensifying class struggles brought on by the open-ended and emergent nature of industrial capitalism. These conflicts were to reach a fever pitch only four years after the publication of Kierkegaard's *The Concept of Anxiety*, in the form of the failed socialist uprisings of 1848 which occurred spontaneously all across Europe. This same anxiety-ridden spiritual impoverishment induced by the convergence of hyper-rationalized, over-academicized science and the quickly transformative conditions of industrial capitalism can already be sensed in the quip *ein wirklicher Ausverkauf* which Kierkegaard's pseudonym Johannes de silentio bitterly pens in the preface of *Fear and Trembling* (1843).

Beyond the historical speculation, there is another matter with greater evidence that Lacan is pointing to in his answer to the questioner. What he is indicating about anxiety with respect to Kierkegaard is that conceptuality is precisely the difficulty when trying to make sense of the problem of anxiety. In other words, Lacan understands that part of Kierkegaard's massive insight into the topic of anxiety, and what brings Kierkegaard into the discourse of psychoanalysis as a productive reference, is on the point that anxiety may lose itself or its truth at the very moment it is captured by intellectual or conceptual labor. As Jacques-Alain Miller explains in Lacanian terms: "the concept [is] the instrument of the symbolic grip on the real."[34] It may be that, by speaking about anxiety and turning it into a mere signifier, a symbol, we immediately devalue it of the existential power that we otherwise wish to find in it. After all, according to Kierkegaard, Freud, and Lacan, perhaps anxiety's most telling trait is its ambiguity and conceptual slipperiness.

In the opening session of his seminar of 1962–63, *L'angoisse*, dedicated to the topic of anxiety, Lacan warns that he (and, with him, his audience) must not come to terms with anxiety too quickly. There is something of the Kierkegaardian inherent in his warning—a hesitation grounded in the thought that anxiety may deceive the theoretician. Also in this opening session Lacan makes reference to Kierkegaard as well as the existentialist tradition, when noting previous attempts at accounting

---

entire world of existence. Certainly it was of paramount importance to much of Kierkegaard's work to, at pains, point out both the fact of existence and its potential resistance to intellectual capture and mastery. At so many points he sought to thematize this very problem of the non-thematic nature of existence through irony and indirect communication. For more on the parodic aspects of *The Concept of Anxiety*, see Roger Poole's wonderful and provocative *Kierkegaard: The Indirect Communication*, Charlottesville and London: University Press of Virginia 1993, pp. 83–107.

[34]   Jacques-Alain Miller, "Introduction to Reading Jacques Lacan's Seminar on Anxiety," *lacanian ink*, vol. 26, 2005, p. 31.

more fully for anxiety. But, as Samuel Weber in *Return to Freud* is quick to point out, the fact that Lacan wishes to distance himself and his efforts in his seminar from those of existentialist philosophy "does not alter the fact that the name of the Danish writer recurs throughout these lectures whenever the theoretical status of anxiety is at issue."[35] Although Lacan does appreciate certain small details of Kierkegaard's *The Concept of Anxiety*,[36] one thing he clearly greatly prizes about the book is that it places in question the very status of anxiety as an object of investigation.

In the final session of his anxiety seminar, Lacan returns to the topic of anxiety's possible conceptuality, stating:

> I don't know if you have been sufficiently aware of Kierkegaard's audacity in speaking of [the concept of anxiety]. What can this possibly mean if not the affirmation that, either the concept functions in a Hegelian manner, symbolically entailing a true grasp of the real; or, the sole grasp that we can have—and it is here that one must choose—is that afforded us by anxiety, the sole and thus ultimate apprehension of all reality.[37]

Lacan applauds Kierkegaard's intellectual courage, understanding *The Concept of Anxiety* as the ultimate methodological and epistemological throwing-down of the gauntlet: if we deign to understand and explain anxiety, then we also simultaneously claim to understand the real, the unconscious, or what in the Kierkegaardian register must surely be translated as the religious; otherwise, we must settle for understanding anxiety outside the symbolic order, solely through the experience of the affect. These are the ultimate stakes for a scholar, since the scholar stands to be subjected to the supreme deception: claiming absolute knowledge of an object, which, in truth, cannot but engender ignorance. The risk is nothing short of absolute alienation.

However, interestingly, the complete opposite is true for the person who experiences anxiety solely in its role as affect. Two years later, in his seminar on the four fundamental concepts of psychoanalysis, Lacan dramatically assures his audience that "anxiety is that which does not deceive."[38] Anxiety is a kind of warning signal, which is one of the insights offered by Freud in *Inhibitions, Symptoms, and Anxiety* (1926).[39] What Lacan adds to that insight is that anxiety is a warning signal—a guarantee—of the proximity of the real.[40]

It is, at least in part, with respect to this claim that Lacan reverses the canonical interpretation of anxiety as objectless, or having (the) nothing as its object, which is consistent from Kierkegaard to Freud to existentialism to nearly all modern standard

---

[35]   Samuel Weber, *Return to Freud: Jacques Lacan's Dislocation of Psychoanalysis*, Cambridge: Cambridge University Press 2008, p. 162.

[36]   See, for example, sin.

[37]   Jacques Lacan, *Le Séminaire. Livre X. L'Angoisse. 1962–1963*, Paris: Éditions de Seuil 2004, p. 385. (Translated and quoted in Samuel Weber, *Return to Freud*, p. 162.)

[38]   Lacan, *Le Séminaire. Livre XI. Les Quatre Concepts fondamentaux de la psychanalyse*, p. 40 (*The Seminar of Jacques Lacan. Book XI. The Four Fundamental Concepts of Psychoanalysis*, p. 41).

[39]   Freud, *Hemmung, Symptom und Angst*. (*Inhibitions, Symptoms and Anxiety*).

[40]   Lacan, *Le Séminaire. Livre X. L'Angoisse. 1962–1963*, especially pp. 185–98. To date, no published English translation exists of this seminar.

psychology textbooks. Lacan instead claims that anxiety is not without object. It is just that its object is a very particular, unique object: namely, the real.[41] Lack occurs, says Lacan in his anxiety seminar, when lack is lacking—that is, when the structure of desire has been disrupted. This is why Lacan's notion of the *objet a*—the object-cause of desire—is also a possible "object" of anxiety.

While Lacan may invert Kierkegaard's rhetoric on this point of lack of object, it is clear he still maintains close proximity to Kierkegaard's analysis of anxiety's relationship to the subject, in particular in his account of the entrance of sin. At several points Lacan aligns himself with Kierkegaard's understanding of sin as introduced in *The Concept of Anxiety* (though never naming the book in those places). Just as Kierkegaard's pseudonym Haufniensis emphasizes the radical break in the self that the entrance of sin introduces, Lacanian theory too, in a somewhat structurally analogous manner, explains the subject's entrance into the symbolic order as the introduction of lack into the subject, which is, most properly, the very condition of possibility of the subject. The Other (*grand Autre*) disrupts the originary unity assumed (retroactively, it must be pointed out) within the imaginary register (by the ego) to have existed prior to the assertion of the function of the Other. In Kierkegaard's account, the entrance of original sin[42] occurs in similar fashion, insofar as sin appears as a kind of third term that disrupts the purity of the self/world (some might prefer self/nature) dyad. Kierkegaard refers to this retroactively attributed original state as innocence.

Though this link between Other and sin may be somewhat hasty and not entirely correct, it is also not without warrant, for Lacan himself suggests this conceptual affinity. In the passage from his lectures in his 1954–55 seminar in which he invokes Kierkegaard apropos of repetition and the intrusion of the symbolic order as that which sets the structure of repetition in motion, Lacan gives a direct account of sin—one linked explicitly to the Kierkegaardian account. "Kierkegaard," he says,

> discussed the difference between the pagan world and the world of grace, which Christianity introduces. Something of the ability to recognize his natural object, so

---

[41]   Already as early as 1955 Lacan had stated as much. When glossing the Freudian analysis of the dream of Irma's injection, commenting in particular on the abyssal object represented by the anxiety-provoking look at the back of the throat, Lacan says: "there's an anxiety-provoking apparition of an image which summarizes what we can call the revelation of that which is least penetrable in the real, of the real lacking any possible mediation, of the ultimate real, of the essential object which isn't an object any longer, but this something faced with which all words cease and all categories fail, the object of anxiety *par excellence*." See Lacan, *Le Séminaire. Livre II. Le Moi dans la théorie de Freud et dans la technique psychanalytique. 1954–1955*, p. 196. (*The Seminar of Jacques Lacan. Book II. The Ego in Freud's Theory and in the Technique of Psychoanalysis 1954–1955*, p. 164.)

[42]   *Arvesynden* (German: *Erbsünde*) presents difficulty for English translation in the context of Kierkegaard's *Begrebet Angest* (*The Concept of Anxiety*). Literally translated it is "hereditary sin," thus *Arvesynden* alludes to an original sin passed down through flesh. However, "original sin" is the traditional English term. Kierkegaard is, in effect, arguing against sin as both hereditary and original (in the sense of first). I have chosen to use "original sin" because it resonates well with a realignment of the concept as entering "originally" in every individual. Regrettably, something is inevitably lost in either choice of translation.

apparent in animals, is present in man. There is being captured by form, being seized by play, being gripped by the mirage of life. That is what a theoretical, or theorial, or contemplative, or Platonic thought refers itself to, and it isn't an accident that Plato places reminiscence at the center of his entire theory of knowledge. The natural object, the harmonic correspondent of the living being, is recognizable because its outline has already been sketched. And for it to have been sketched, it must already have been within the object which is going to join itself to it. That is the relation of the dyad....But for certain specific reasons, a change occurred. Sin is from then on present as the third term, and it is no longer by following the path of reminiscence, but rather in following that of repetition, that man finds his way.[43]

Although repetition is the apparent concept in Lacan's crosshairs here, he manages to effectively kill two birds with one stone, in the sense that his appeal to Kierkegaard also allows him the opportunity to mention the term "sin" as a historical marker of one way of understanding the entrance into the symbolic order. Slavoj Žižek gives us a clue as to why Lacan privileges Kierkegaard's version of sin among others, when he compares Lacan's relations to Kierkegaard and Heidegger, respectively: "No wonder, then, that, with regard to anxiety, Lacan prefers Kierkegaard to Heidegger: he perceives Kierkegaard as the anti-Hegel for whom the paradox of Christian faith signals a radical break with the ancient Greek ontology."[44] Lacan prefers the term "sin" because of the radicality of the lack, or separation, that it entails. Like Kierkegaard, Lacan too understands anxiety to be proof of a fundamental lack at the heart of the subject—the Other.

The connections between these two thinkers' theories of anxiety do not stop there. Both also posit the possibility of overcoming anxiety. For Kierkegaard, anxiety can be the very platform upon which one may stand in order to achieve a certain kind of religious consciousness. To achieve this is rare, of course, and this category of anxiety as saving through faith may be as much a regulative principle or ideal as anything. But the same holds true for Lacan, in principle. In the final session of the anxiety seminar, Lacan claims that "anxiety is only surmounted when the Other names itself."[45] What saves one from anxiety, according to Lacan, is the protective power of the law as created by and invested in the symbolic order. Instead of the separation from nature or from the mother acting as the cause of anxiety, anxiety instead erupts in the renewed proximity to that lost wholeness. This may be a bit closer to Kierkegaard's own account of the appearance of anxiety than it may at first appear. In Kierkegaard, it is not the "nothing" that our finitude confronts which causes anxiety; rather, it is the structure of freedom occasioned and constructed by (spatial and temporal) finitude that causes anxiety.

Lacan's rhetoric of anxiety differs slightly, since according to him anxiety occurs when lack is lacking. According to the logic of this version anxiety, the typical

---

[43]   Lacan, *Le Séminaire. Livre II. Le Moi dans la théorie de Freud et dans la technique psychanalytique. 1954–1955*, p. 110. (*The Seminar of Jacques Lacan. Book II. The Ego in Freud's Theory and in the Technique of Psychoanalysis 1954–1955*, p. 87.)

[44]   Slavoj Žižek, "Language, Violence, and Non-Violence," *International Journal of Žižek Studies*, vol. 2, no. 3, 2008, p. 8.

[45]   Lacan, *Le Séminaire. Livre X. L'Angoisse. 1962–1963*, especially p. 390.

understanding of anxiety as produced by separation gets inverted: the possible (re-) union with the (symbolic) mother threatens oppressively. In other words, while that supposed original unity with the mother conditions the circuit of desire, Lacan's theory takes careful account of the fact that by any merging of the subject (or self) with this original unity would, of course, equally be the erasure and loss of the subject (or self). Oddly enough, in this sense the symbolic order becomes a defense against anxiety, and not vice-versa. Castration does in fact produce "positive" results. Authority, in the form of the father's law, provides a certain shelter from anxiety. Accepting this protection, however, has its price: sin.

The invocation of the father, in particular the Lacanian notion of the Name-of-the-Father, completes the conceptual triad around which Lacan's reception of Kierkegaard with respect to *The Concept of Anxiety* revolves: anxiety, sin, and the father. The symbolic role of the Name-of-the-Father is eventually to act as a kind of buffer between the subject and the real in which, through (symbolic) law the structure of desire is sustained. But, nevertheless, the inheritance of the father, as Lacan notes in *The Four Fundamental Concepts of Psychoanalysis*, "is that which Kierkegaard designates for us, namely, his sin."[46] Just as for Kierkegaard anxiety is proof of original sin, for Lacan anxiety is evidence of the functioning of the Other in the symbolic order. That function is filled by the Name-of-the-Father, the master signifier that both confers identity and delivers the Oedipal prohibition.

Given the interconnected nature of anxiety, sin, and the role of the symbolic father, it should come as no surprise that the seminar which Lacan had originally planned to follow his anxiety seminar was to be on the Name-of-the-Father. This seminar never happened—or, rather, it lasted only a single day, a single session. What intervened was a scandal whereby Lacan was, as he calls it, "excommunicated" from the Société Française de Psychanalyse by virtue of that body's acceptance into the International Psychoanalytic Association on the condition that Lacan (and one or two others) be removed from membership. This seminar on the Name-of-the-Father was to have contained a significant engagement with Kierkegaard, in particular *Repetition* and, most importantly, *Fear and Trembling*. While the one existing session of the Name-of-the-Father seminar addresses the story of Abraham's sacrifice, Kierkegaard is not significantly confronted there. But, as François Sauvagnat argues, Lacan surely had Kierkegaard's *Fear and Trembling* in mind.[47]

The session consists largely of Lacan's commentary on the various names for God used in the Bible, as well as in certain philosophical discourses, such as Pascal's writings. For Lacan, anxiety is clearly a key reference point on the topic, because the God of Abraham, of Isaac, and of Jacob is an inaccessible God, a God located in field of the real. By setting down the law, the Name-of-the-Father structures the symbolic

---

46   Lacan, *Le Séminaire. Livre XI. Les Quatre Concepts fondamentaux de la psychanalyse*, p. 35. (*The Seminar of Jacques Lacan. Book XI. The Four Fundamental Concepts of Psychoanalysis*, p. 34.)
47   François Sauvagnat, "Hvorledes J. Lacan var inspireret af Søren Aabye Kierkegaard og Anton Tjekhov. Eller: Faderens begær hos Kierkegaard og Anton Tjekhov," *Drift*, nos. 1–2, 2005, p. 138.

order of signifiers, structuring desire through prohibition.[48] This effectively controls anxiety and keeps it in check.

At one moment in a very late seminar Lacan points up the role of the father's authority as buffer against anxiety by mentioning Kierkegaard's own biographical relationship to his father.[49] Lacan names the problematic place of the father as the node where repetition and existence converge—the point where, not unlike the role of the real, anxiety cannot meet the subject. Lacan suggests that *jouissance* is the field of this problematic place. Drawing ostensibly from passages in Kierkegaard's journals, Lacan claims that the father–son relationship as the link between existence and repetition is well exemplified by Kierkegaard's relationship to his own father.

Another late reference to Kierkegaard in which Lacan turns once more to the biography occurs in the well-known twentieth seminar, *Encore*. In this complex and notoriously difficult seminar, Lacan sets out to, among other goals, renegotiate the terms of love and of the psychoanalytic perspective on woman, on so-called feminine *jouissance*. Lacan works toward the fleeting thesis that Kierkegaard reduces Regine to pure *objet a* in the act of renouncing his love and intent to marry.[50] According to Lacan, Kierkegaard attempts to reduce the Other (woman/Regine as Other) to *objet a*. In making this case, Lacan conflates Kierkegaard with the seducer from "The Seducer's Diary," as well as to some degree with the young man in *Repetition*. This is, claims Lacan, a renunciation whose goal is to rescue existence, and for which Kierkegaard himself, he insinuates, is responsible.[51]

A final telling reference to Kierkegaard can be found in the late seminars, specifically, *Les Non-dupes errent*, 1973–74. Lacan refers to *Works of Love* during a discussion of the New Testament call to love thy neighbor. While this does not relate immediately to the topic of anxiety, it is ancillary to the topic in the sense that it has to do with a certain articulation of desire. In short, Lacan claims that, in the dictum "love thy neighbor," confusion is created between means and end. By inserting the love of God, the structure of desire becomes the final goal: "it is the definition of teleology in itself."[52] Yves Depelsenaire comments on this passage,[53] explaining that Christian love inserts in the place of desire a knot, traversed by the symbolic significations of love under the Name-of-the-Father as God, that ties together the real of death with the imaginary of the body. Kierkegaard is less a mined resource in this lecture than a passing reference to an important text of which his auditors should be aware. Nevertheless, for those seeking further connections with Lacan's

---

[48]   And, thereby, the guilt will be produced that will serve as the source of the super-ego function.

[49]   Yves Depelsenaire, *Une analyse avec Dieu*, Brussels: La Lettre volée 2004, p. 20.

[50]   Jacques Lacan, *Le Séminaire. Livre XX. Encore*, Paris: Le Seuil 1975, p. 71. (English translation: *The Seminar of Jacques Lacan. Book XX. Encore. On Feminine Sexuality, the Limits of Love and Knowledge. 1972–1973*, New York: W.W. Norton 1998, p. 77.)

[51]   For a slightly more detailed treatment of this, see Depelsnaire, *Une analyse avec Dieu*, p. 20.

[52]   Jacques Lacan, *Le Séminaire. Livre XXI. Les Non-dupes errent*, leçon du 23 avril 1974, inédite. Quoted in Depelsenaire, *Une analyse avec Dieu*, p. 22.

[53]   Depelsenaire, *Une analyse avec Dieu*, p. 22.

comments on love in Kierkegaard, Depelsenaire's *Une analyse avec Dieu* is a good starting point.

IV. Secondary Literature on Lacan's Relationship to Kierkegaard

Although a number of sources that study Lacan's relationship to Kierkegaard have been named in the sections above, it is worth collecting these references into a compendious if brief closing section. At the time of writing (summer 2009), the rather recondite trajectory of scholarly inquiry on Lacan's relationship to Kierkegaard remains limited to three or four major studies and a handful of articles. Certainly none of these dedicated book-length studies[54] can be considered ultimately definitive, in particular because the relationship between the two proper names too often shifts ground, at times all too quickly, between inquiring into how Lacanian theory might newly illuminate Kierkegaardian philosophy and applying Lacanian analytic tendencies and concepts to a kind of pop analysis of Kierkegaard's biography. In many respects, the latter project is merely an extension of one of the liveliest trends in Kierkegaard scholarship over the years, namely, applying insights or analyses from Kierkegaard's biography to his philosophical and theological writings. The former arc of inquiry holds great potential for renewing Kierkegaardian motifs and ideas. Sophie Wennerscheid's *Das Begehren nach der Wunde* is an excellent example of new potential for reinvigorating Kierkegaard's texts through the application of Lacanian psychoanalytic perspectives.[55] As for the full-length books by Adam and Depelsenaire, both are certainly worthwhile, though many of the interpretations from Depelsenaire's book tend to fall back on the field of biographically oriented analysis, even when the initial questions appear to be textually motivated.[56]

Not surprisingly, many of the article-length studies concentrate on the topics of repetition and anxiety. On the topic of anxiety, Ed Cameron's "The Ethical Paradox in Kierkegaard's *Concept of Anxiety*"[57] contains an excellent assessment and comparison of Kierkegaard's theory of anxiety in relationship to Lacan's understanding of anxiety. Also on the topic of anxiety, Samuel Weber's "Beyond Anxiety: the Witch's Letter," in *Return to Freud*, contains clear and concise comparisons of Kierkegaard in relation to Freud and Lacan. On the topic of repetition, Marcus Pound's "Repetition,"[58] along with Depelsenaire's "Répétition dans la Répétition," in *Une analyse avec*

---

54   See Rodolphe Adam, *Lacan et Kierkegaard*, Paris: Presses Universitaires de France 2005; Depelsenaire, *Une analyse avec Dieu*; Marcus Pound, *Theology, Psychoanalysis, and Trauma*, London: SCM Press 2007; Elisabeth Strowick, *Passagen der Widerholung. Kierkegaard—Lacan—Freud*, Stuttgart: Metzler 1999.

55   Sophie Wennerscheid, *Das Begehren nach der Wunde*, Berlin: Matthes & Seitz 2008.

56   Depelsenaire, *Une analyse avec Dieu*. See especially chapters 3–5, pp. 53–102.

57   Ed Cameron, "The Ethical Paradox in Kierkegaard's *Concept of Anxiety*," *Colloquy Text Theory Critique*, vol. 13, 2007, pp. 93–113.

58   Marcus Pound, "Repetition," in *Theology, Psychoanalysis, and Trauma*, pp. 56–72.

Dieu,[59] offer carefully organized studies of Lacan's conception of repetition and its correspondences in Kierkegaard.

Slavoj Žižek proves himself to be one of the most interesting scholars working in the Kierkegaard–Lacan nexus. An example of his provocative and insightful pairing of Kierkegaard and Lacan can be found in "Anxiety: Kierkegaard with Lacan."[60] This essay covers the topic of anxiety, but also extends to parts of the Lacan–Kierkegaard relationship that remain otherwise underappreciated, including: the god-relationship, freedom, guilt, and sacrifice. Although the article eventually digresses into an interpretation of a Henry James novel, there is much to recommend in this essay (including the James reading, though not necessarily because it weds Kierkegaard's foci to Lacan's work). Another refreshing intervention from Žižek can be found buried in "Burned by the Sun," in *Lacan: The Silent Partners*.[61] In this essay, Žižek at one point turns to Kierkegaard's "On the Difference between a Genius and an Apostle" in order to arrive at a plausible response to the question: what is the subject of the unconscious?[62] Žižek suggests that the Lacanian answer is "that the Freudian 'subject of the unconscious' (or what Lacan calls 'subject of the signifier') has the structure of the Kierkegaardian apostle: he is witness to an 'impersonal' Truth."[63] As one of the most formidable and popular Lacan scholars, especially in his role as philosopher and cultural critic, Žižek's texts on Kierkegaard should be read carefully.

In the direction of theology or more theologically oriented commentary, Marcus Pound's *Theology, Psychoanalysis, and Trauma* is the best book to date on Lacan and Kierkegaard.[64] In fact, it is to date probably the best work in English on the topic of "Lacan avec Kierkegaard" period. Along with Žižek's Apostle commentary, Pound is the only scholar to invert the typical pattern in the secondary literature of applying Lacan to Kierkegaard. Pound's book quite successfully applies Kierkegaard to Lacan. He blends insightful and well-organized thought with dedication not merely to the Lacanian theories but to the practical goals of psychoanalysis and therapy more generally. His book brings much needed clarity to the theological dimensions of trauma, among other contributions, by reading Lacan through the lens of Kierkegaardian texts and themes, for example, repetition.

---

[59]   Yves Depelsenaire, "Répétition dans la Répétition," in *Une analyse avec Dieu*, pp. 31–52.

[60]   Slavoj Žižek, "Anxiety: Kierkegaard with Lacan," *lacanian ink*, vol. 26, 2005, pp. 102–117.

[61]   Slavoj Žižek, "Burned by the Sun," in *Lacan: The Silent Partners*, ed. by Slavoj Žižek, London and New York: Verso 2006, pp. 217–30.

[62]   Ibid., pp. 219–21.

[63]   Ibid., p. 219.

[64]   Pound, *Theology, Psychoanalysis, and Trauma*, see especially chapter 2, "Repetition," pp. 56–72, and chapter 4, "Stages on the Way from Kierkegaard to Lacan," pp. 101–17.

Bibliography

I. References to or Uses of Kierkegaard in Lacan's Corpus

"Le séminaire sur la 'Lettre vole,' " in his *Écrits*, Paris: Le Seuil 1966, pp. 45–6. (English translation: "Seminar on 'The Purloined Letter,' " in his *Écrits: The First Complete Edition in English*, trans. by Bruce Fink in collaboration with Héloïse Fink and Russell Grigg, New York: W.W. Norton 2006, p. 34.)

"L'agressivité en psychanalyse," in his *Écrits*, Paris: Le Seuil 1966, p. 123. (English translation: "Aggressiveness in Psychoanalysis," in his *Écrits: The First Complete Edition in English*, trans. by Bruce Fink in collaboration with Héloïse Fink and Russell Grigg, New York: W.W. Norton 2006, p. 100.)

"Fonction et champ de la parole et du langage en psychanalyse," in his *Écrits*, Paris: Le Seuil 1966, p. 293. (English translation: "The Function and Field of Speech and Language in Psychoanalysis," in his *Écrits: The First Complete Edition in English*, trans. by Bruce Fink in collaboration with Héloïse Fink and Russell Grigg, New York: W.W. Norton 2006, p. 242.)

"D'un dessein," in his *Écrits*, Paris: Le Seuil 1966, p. 367. (English translation: "On a Purpose," in his *Écrits: The First Complete Edition in English*, trans. by Bruce Fink in collaboration with Héloïse Fink and Russell Grigg, New York: W.W. Norton 2006, p. 307.)

"D'une question préliminaire à tout traitement possible de la psychose," in his *Écrits*, Paris: Le Seuil 1966, p. 519. (English translation: "The Instance of the Letter in the Unconscious," in his *Écrits: The First Complete Edition in English*, trans. by Bruce Fink in collaboration with Héloïse Fink and Russell Grigg, New York: W.W. Norton 2006, p. 432.)

"A la mémoire d'Ernest Jones: Sur sa théorie du symbolisme," in his *Écrits*, Paris: Le Seuil 1966, pp. 716–17. (English translation: "In Memory of Ernest Jones: On His Theory of Symbolism," in his *Écrits: The First Complete Edition in English*, trans. by Bruce Fink in collaboration with Héloïse Fink and Russell Grigg, New York: W.W. Norton 2006, p. 600.)

Le Séminaire. Livre II. Le Moi dans la théorie de Freud et dans la technique psychanalytique. 1954–1955, Paris: Le Seuil 1978, pp. 110; pp. 124–5. (English translation: *The Seminar of Jacques Lacan. Book II. The Ego in Freud's Theory and in the Technique of Psychoanalysis 1954–1955*, trans. by Sylvana Tomaselli, Cambridge: Cambridge University Press 1988, pp. 87–8; p. 100.)

Le Séminaire. Livre X. L'Angoisse. 1962–1963, Paris: Éditions de Seuil 2004, p. 385. (Translated and quoted in Samuel Weber, *Return to Freud: Jacques Lacan's Dislocation of Psychoanalysis*, Cambridge: Cambridge University Press 2008, p. 162.)

Le Séminaire. Livre XI. Les Quatre Concepts fondamentaux de la psychanalyse, Paris: Le Seuil 1974, p. 35; p. 59. (English translation: *The Seminar of Jacques Lacan. Book XI. The Four Fundamental Concepts of Psychoanalysis*, trans. by Alan Sheridan, New York and London: W.W. Norton 1981, p. 34; pp. 60–1.)

Le Seminaire. Livre XVII. L'envers de la psychanalyse, Paris: Le Seuil 1991, pp. 51–2; pp. 168–9. (*The Seminar of Jacques Lacan. Book XVII. The Other Side of Psychoanalysis*, New York and London: W.W. Norton 2007, p. 46; pp. 144–5.)

II. Sources of Lacan's Knowledge of Kierkegaard

Merleau-Ponty, Maurice, *Phénoménologie de la perception*, Paris: Gallimard 1945, p. 8; p. 100.

— "La querelle de l'existentialisme," in his *Sens et non-sens*, Paris: Nagel 1948, pp. 141–64, see p. 151; p. 158 (originally published in *Le Temps modernes*, no. 2, 1945, pp. 344–56).

— "L'Existentialisme chez Hegel," in his *Sens et non-sens*, Paris: Nagel 1948, pp. 125–39, see pp. 127–8 (originally published in *Les Temps modernes*, no. 7, 1946, pp. 1311–19).

— *Le visible et l'invisible*, Paris: Gallimard 1964, p. 234.

— "La philosophie dialectique" (1955–56), in his *Résumés de cours. Collège de France 1952–1960*, Paris: Gallimard 1968, pp. 75–87, see pp. 79–80; p. 83.

Sartre, Jean-Paul, *L'être et le néant. Essai d'ontologie phénoménologique*, Paris: Gallimard 1943 (*Bibliothèque des Idées*), pp. 58–84; pp. 94–111; pp. 115–49; pp. 150–74; pp. 291–300; pp. 508–16; pp. 529–60; pp. 639–42; pp. 643–63; pp. 669–70; pp. 720–22.

— *L'existentialisme est un humanisme*, Paris: Nagel 1946, pp. 27–33.

— "Un nouveau mystique," in his *Situations I*, Paris: Gallimard 1947, pp. 143–88, see pp. 154–5; pp. 162–3; pp. 168ff.

— *Critique de la raison dialectique*, vol. 1, *Théorie des ensembles pratiques*, Paris: Gallimard 1960, pp. 15–32; p. 117, note 1.

— "Kierkegaard: L'universal Singulier," in *Kierkegaard vivant. Colloque organisé par l'Unesco à Paris du 21 au 23 avril 1964*, Paris: Gallimard 1966, pp. 20–63.

III. Secondary Literature on Lacan's Use of Kierkegaard

Adam, Rodolphe, *Lacan et Kierkegaard*, Paris: Presses Universitaires de France 2005.

Berghe, Paul Vanden, "Het tragische blijft toch altijd het tragische. Kierkegaard en Lacan over een moderne Antigone," in *Tragisch. Over tragedie en ethiek in de 21e eeuw.*, ed. by Paul Vanden Berghe et al., Budel: Damon 2005, pp. 119–35.

Cameron, Ed. "The Ethical Paradox in Kierkegaard's *Concept of Anxiety*," *Colloquy Text Theory Critique*, vol. 13, 2007, pp. 93–113.

Depelsenaire, Yves, *Une analyse avec Dieu: le rendez-vous de Lacan et de Kierkegaard*, Brussels: La Lettre volée 2004.

Duquette, Elizabeth M., "Pour faire une hamlette. Freud, Kierkegaard, Lacan," *Literature and Psychology*, 49, 2003, pp. 1–38.

Gorog, Françoise, "Kierkegaard avec Lacan," *Hérédité. Revue de psychanalyse*, no. 2, 2001, pp. 47–59.

Pepper, Thomas Adam, "Fleisch und das Vergessen des Blickes," *Vom Nutzen des Vergessens*, trans. by Johanna Bodenstaub and Hans Werner Zerrahn, ed. by Hinderk Emrich and Gary Smith, Berlin: Akademie Verlag 1996, pp. 185–207.

Pound, Marcus, *Theology, Psychoanalysis, and Trauma*, London: SCM Press 2007.

Rasmussen, René and Tommy Thambour (eds.), *Angst hos Lacan og Kierkegaard*, Vanløse: Forlaget Drift 2005.

Ruprecht, Clifford Holt, *Language, Subjectivity and Absolute Possibility in Kierkegaard and Lacan*, Ph.D. Thesis, University of Chicago, Chicago 1995.

Sauvagnat, François, "Hvorledes J. Lacan var inspireret af Søren Aabye Kierkegaard og Anton Tjekhov. Eller: Faderens begær hos Kierkegaard og Anton Tjekhov," *Drift*, nos. 1–2, 2005, pp. 135–43.

Shepherdson, Charles, "A Pound of Flesh: Lacan's Reading of *The Visible and the Invisible*," *Diacritics*, vol. 27, no. 4, 1997, pp. 70–86.

Strowick, Elisabeth, *Passagen der Widerholung. Kierkegaard—Lacan—Freud*, Stuttgart: Metzler 1999.

Weber, Samuel, *Return to Freud: Jacques Lacan's Dislocation of Psychoanalysis*, Cambridge: Cambridge University Press 2008, pp. 152–67.

Wennerscheid, Sophie, *Das Begehren nach der Wunde*, Berlin: Matthes & Seitz 2008, pp. 27–41.

Rollo May:

Existential Psychology

Poul Houe

I. General Introduction

American psychologist, psychoanalyst, psychotherapist, and author Rollo May was born in Ada, Ohio in 1909. The son of Earl May, a field secretary for YMCA, and his wife Matie Boughton, May moved with his family to Michigan while he was still a child. His parents later divorced, and while his sister suffered a psychotic breakdown, he himself had personal difficulties both in school and with his anti-intellectual father at home. After high school, May initially attended Michigan State College but was soon asked to leave because of his involvement with a controversial college magazine. He graduated in 1930 from Ohio's more liberal Oberlin College with a major in English and a minor in Greek history and literature. After college he taught English at Anatolia College, the American College at Salonika, for three years. While in Greece he frequently traveled to Vienna and attended the seminars of Alfred Adler (1870–1937), but he also experienced a nervous breakdown.[1] When he returned to the USA, his burning interest in existential and religious matters led him to enroll at Union Theological Seminary in New York City, one of the few places where such issues were seriously dealt with. At Union he befriended and received lasting impulses from Professor Paul Tillich (1886–1965), the noted existentialist theologian and expatriate from Nazi Germany. Pursuant to his divinity degree from the Seminary in 1938, May was active as a Congregationalist minister in New Jersey for two years before he lost his faith and took up psychology as his primary field of inquiry.[2] He began at the White Institute and continued at the graduate program at Columbia University where in 1949 he received, with highest honors, the first Ph.D. in clinical psychology ever granted by that institution.

---

[1]   Kirk J. Schneider, "Rollo May: Liberator and Realist," in *Humanistic and Transpersonal Psychology: A Historical and Biographical Sourcebook*, ed. by Donald Moss, Westport, Connecticut: Greenwood Press 2001, p. 350.

[2]   Robert H. Abzug, "*Love and Will*: Rollo May and the Seventies' Crisis of Intimacy," in *The Lost Decade: America in the Seventies*, ed. by Elsebeth Hurup, Aarhus: Aarhus University Press 1996, pp. 82–3.

While working on his dissertation, which dealt with theories of anxiety and which was later published as *The Meaning of Anxiety* (1950),[3] May contracted tuberculosis and spent 18 months in an upstate New York sanatorium. This life-threatening illness—in combination with his professional training at Union and Columbia and Paul Tillich's personal example bringing "doubt to the faithful and faith to the doubters"—likely inspired May's orientation towards existentialism and humanism and informed the contradictory holism of his therapeutic approach.[4] May served for many years as a faculty member at the William Alanson White Institute of Psychiatry, Psychology and Psychoanalysis in Manhattan and as a lecturer at the New School for Social Research in New York, and he held visiting professorships at Harvard, Yale, and Princeton. By the time of his official retirement in the late 1970s, he had for two decades been one of the foremost existential and humanistic psychologists in the USA. An originator of the humanistic psychology movement and a co-founder of the Association for Humanistic Psychology, May co-edited the widely translated volume *Existence: A New Dimension in Psychiatry and Psychology* (1958),[5] which is generally considered the first American book on existential psychology. He also edited the papers from the American Psychological Association's 1959 symposium *Existential Psychology*,[6] published under this title the following year. May, who received the Association's Gold Medal and numerous other honors, was married three times and divorced twice. He died from congestive heart failure in his home in Tiburon, California in 1994.

Rollo May's existential and humanistic leanings must be seen against the background of the triumphant roles that scientific and experimental approaches played within the young disciplines of psychology and psychotherapy in America in the early half of the twentieth century. Behaviorism and technical versions of Freudian psychoanalysis had captured professional and public imaginations alike, and laboratory experiments and quantitative formulas were broadly applied, from personality classifications to treatment of shell-shocked soldiers to mass-market self-help books. Yet the more widely this net was cast, the more apparent it became to a small group of dissenting practitioners—May among them—that its objectified approach was severely reductive and that its narrowly quantified masks failed to capture the most essential component of all psychic life: human existence itself.[7] Hence, May and like-minded colleagues shifted the paradigm to put *einmalig* human existence and the individual client center stage in psychological discourse and therapeutic treatment. Not *what* the "I" is, or how the "I" functions, but *that* the "I" is, became the constitutive formula for his and other existentialist psychologists' locus of understanding.[8] Perhaps the "I" itself escapes comprehension, yet an

---

3   Rollo May, *The Meaning of Anxiety*, New York: Ronald Press 1950 (revised ed., New York: W.W. Norton 1977).

4   Schneider, "Rollo May: Liberator and Realist," pp. 347–8; pp. 350–1.

5   Rollo May, *Existence: A New Dimension in Psychiatry and Psychology*, New York: Basic Books 1958.

6   See *Existential Psychology*, ed. by Rollo May, New York: Random House 1960 (2nd ed., 1969).

7   Abzug, "*Love and Will*: Rollo May and the Seventies' Crisis of Intimacy," p. 80.

8   Kuno Poulsen, "Eksistentiel psykologi," *Dansk Udsyn*, vol. 47, 1967, p. 367.

understanding of everything else issues from the "I."[9] Therapeutically speaking, arriving at a sense of being precedes any cure or renders it superfluous.[10] And describing the consciousness of an actual human being (as existentialist psychologists do as they render pre-conscious experiences conscious) is to proceed in accordance with phenomenological principles—not so much to establish causal connections as to operate in a synchronic and structural mode. It is not a matter of deciding between empirical options, but rather of conjoining alternative human attitudes.[11]

There was still room for certain aspects of Freud's teachings within this epistemology, but primarily only for the branch of psychoanalysis that was grounded in Heidegger's philosophy of existence from 1927.[12] It has even been argued that "existentialism replaced Christianity as his [May's] explanatory framework, the existentialism of Kierkegaard and Nietzsche rather than that of Sartre. May's existentialism was the Christianity of Tillich but without Christ."[13]

What this and the earlier allusion to Paul Tillich suggest is how May's ideas about psychology and psychotherapy are as paradoxical and conflicted as they are holistic and comprehensive. In his edited volume *Existence* from 1958, and reiterated 25 years later in *The Discovery of Being* under the heading "Of Time and History,"[14] May writes of the simultaneous fragmentation of time and the capacity to transcend time that are unique to human existence. The human "being-in-the-world" exists in the three Heideggerian temporal *modi*. In the *Umwelt* a human being is in measurable " 'clock time'...an analogy from space...acted upon by instinctual drives,"[15] while in *Mitwelt* "quantitative time has much less to do with the significance of an occurrence";[16] what matter here are "personal relations and

---

[9]   Ibid., p. 367; Jørn Vosmar, "Forord," in Rollo May, *Eksistentiel Psykologi*, trans. by Kresten Nordentoft, Copenhagen: Gyldendal 1966, p. 11.

[10]   Poulsen, "Eksistentiel psykologi," p. 373.

[11]   Vosmar, "Forord," pp. 10–12.

[12]   Poulsen, "Eksistentiel psykologi," p. 359; Vosmar, "Forord," p. 9, calls May a model introducer to "the existential movement within depth psychology" but also points to what separates the concreteness of existential psychology and its interest in the single individual from the abstractions of existentialist philosophers (Heidegger not excluded).

[13]   Abzug, "*Love and Will*: Rollo May and the Seventies' Crisis of Intimacy," p. 83. In his "Introduction" to Jean-Paul Sartre, *Existential Psychoanalysis*, trans. by Hazel E. Barnes, Chicago: Henry Regnery, 1962, pp. 1–17 (reprinted as chapter 9 in Rollo May, *Psychology and the Human Dilemma*, New York: W.W. Norton 1967), May essentially credits this work for its ontology, "the necessary basis for psychoanalysis," and for not offering "an alternative form of psychoanalysis." It is Sartre's criticism of "modern psychology, and Freud's determinism, in particular," that elicits May's approval—along with his stress on "the individual's *choice of being*...the subjective choice by which each living person makes himself a person" and his "endeavor to find principles for psycho-analysis which will do justice to what man genuinely *is*, the *human* being." May even cites Tillich in support of these efforts by Sartre: "Man becomes truly human only at the moment of decision" (p. 14).

[14]   Rollo May, *The Discovery of Being: Writings in Existential Psychology*, New York: W.W. Norton 1983, pp. 133–42.

[15]   Ibid., p. 137.

[16]   Ibid.

love,"[17] that is, qualities that all but suspend quantity time. "Finally, the *Eigenwelt*, the own world of self-relatedness, self-awareness, and insight into the meaning of an event for one's self," has its locus in the "instantaneous, immediate—and the moment of awareness has its significance for all time."[18]

In appropriating these existential modi of time (and space), for which May is also indebted to Binswanger, Minkowski, and other colleagues, he approaches human existence as multifaceted. The human self is potentially embedded as an active, decision-making, and responsible subject in the forcefield of powers beyond its physical reach. As little as humans can control these powers per se, they can control their own attitude to them. In doing so, they express a wish or an intention to see the nexus between self and world unfold in a particular direction—and they lay the ground for realizing this wish or intention by creatively and imaginatively exercising their human will.

May's bestselling *Love and Will* from late 1969 became trendsetting for America's up-and-coming cultural transitions in the 1970s. Its notion of will departed from prevailing nineteenth-century concepts of voluntaristic "will-power," chiefly a conscious, rational, and instrumental function; but it also disputed Freud's relegation of the will to the unconscious. May's idea of intentionally freeing up the imagination to be willfully acted upon by the subject itself was beholden to the unconscious but not at the expense of human choice, for which "little room existed…in Freudian or behaviorist theory."[19]

As for love, the other part of May's poignant title, the multi-sidedness of this concept was no less evident.[20] After discussing "four types of human love: sex or *libido*, *eros*, *philia*, and *agape*…May proposed that authentic human love, in its fullest sense, was a 'blending' of all four. The modern age had distorted, trivialized, and alienated one manifestation of love from another."[21] As May restores balance to both love and will and to their mutual contribution to the freeing of the imagination and the self, inherent contradictions are not assuaged; rather, they are authenticated in a departure from conventional wisdom in psychotherapy. Human choice and decision-making, both decisive for the arrival at existential truth, are no longer based upon knowledge but are the basis for seeking knowledge.[22] May—speaking in his own words but with reference to a rich repository of philosophical and theological texts, classical literature and mythology, and the history of ideas—ends up rejecting "the untenable position in therapy of assuming that the patient develops a sense of identity and *then* acts. On the contrary, he experiences the identity *in* the action, or at least the possibility for it."[23] Again and again, for example, in *Freedom and Destiny*, he similarly proclaims that "freedom is possibility" and that "freedom is continually

---

[17]   Ibid.

[18]   Ibid.

[19]   Abzug, "*Love and Will*: Rollo May and the Seventies' Crisis of Intimacy," p. 86.

[20]   This in contrast to Heidegger's analysis, which is said to focus on anxiety at the expense of love (cf. Vosmar, "Forord," p. 8).

[21]   Abzug, "*Love and Will*: Rollo May and the Seventies' Crisis of Intimacy," p. 84.

[22]   Poulsen, "Eksistentiel psykologi," p. 370.

[23]   Rollo May, *Love and Will*, New York: W.W Norton 1969, p. 244.

creating itself."[24] His work and practice rely on the interplay of freedom and anxiety in the constitution of the self, and on therapies enabling such self-constitution; the self of an existing being dawns as it relates to itself in the active process of becoming. May has elsewhere spelled out that "Existentialism involves centering upon the *existing* person and emphasizes the human being as he is *emerging, becoming*."[25]

Thus, "holism, for May, meant optimizing our contradictoriness, our limitations as well as our freedom."[26] All one-sidedness turns neurotic, be it anxiety that neglects hope or creativity, or zest or boldness that neglect "anxieties of living, and limits."[27] "In short, *Love and Will* reflected and organized the contradictory impulses of the age and forged them into a message of dark hope."[28] In this and in most of Rollo May's other endeavors, Kierkegaard proved an indispensible aid.

II. Kierkegaard in Rollo May's Works

May's first book, *The Art of Counseling*, came out in 1939, while May was still a Congregationalist minister; given both the book's title and its author's occupation, Kierkegaard's absence from its list of referenced philosophers and psychologists of note (the top ten being Descartes, Spinoza, Rousseau, Schopenhauer, Nietzsche, Freud, Jung, Adler, Rank, and Tillich) is conspicuous.[29] The Danish thinker also goes unmentioned in May's second book, *The Springs of Creative Living*, which could be attributable to its year of publication, 1941, when May had left his ministry. Even so, the volume's subtitle, "A Study of Human Nature and Gods," as well as chapter headings like "Creativity and Sin" and "Grace and Clarification," might well have justified mention of Kierkegaard's religious work.[30] Its continued omission from May's early bibliography suggests that he had not yet warmed up to Kierkegaard's influence, perhaps even that the part of Kierkegaard upon which May would later rely the most for support was not the Dane's Christian thinking but his existentialist probing of human psychology.

By contrast, when May's Ph.D. dissertation in clinical psychology from Columbia (1949) appeared in print as the lengthy *The Meaning of Anxiety* in 1950, Kierkegaard (along with Freud and Kurt Goldstein) was its most cited name, and *The Concept of Anxiety* its seminal point of reference. Moreover, the third part of May's second chapter, entitled "Kierkegaard: Anxiety in the Nineteenth Century," was the longest

---

[24]   Rollo May, *Freedom and Destiny*, New York: W.W. Norton 1981, p. 10; p. 53.

[25]   *Existential Psychology*, ed. by May, 2nd ed. 1969 [1960], p. 11.

[26]   Schneider, "Rollo May: Liberator and Realist," p. 350.

[27]   Ibid., p. 351.

[28]   Abzug, "*Love and Will:* Rollo May and the Seventies' Crisis of Intimacy," p. 83.

[29]   Rollo May, *The Art of Counseling*, New York: Abingdon Press 1939.

[30]   Rollo May, *The Springs of Creative Living*, New York: Abingdon-Cokesbury Press 1941.

such section in the entire book.[31] Kierkegaard had become a pillar of Rollo May's psychological construction.[32]

Kierkegaard's influence begins with his definition of anxiety as the "fear of nothingness"[33] and his statement that the more the concept is addressed with abstract clarity, the less certitude ensues.[34] As nineteenth-century "cultural *compartmentalization*" entailed that a seventeenth century "*belief in the rational control*" of the emotions had now become the *habit of repressing* the emotions,"[35] Kierkegaard's dynamic definitions of 'self' and 'truth' and of subjectivity as the "genuine objectivity"[36] aimed instead at restoring "*unity*" to "*the individual as a living, experiencing*" being.[37] He (and other nineteenth-century existentialists) were the first to put anxiety "*directly into the foreground as a specific problem*,"[38] and May proceeds to detail his forerunner's anthropology of anxiety in a series of formulations from *The Concept of Anxiety* that were to become set phrases in his own work: "Freedom is the goal of personality development," "the good is freedom," and "Kierkegaard defines freedom as *possibility*," thus "whenever [he] writes 'spirit.' "[39] Indeed, "he describes anxiety as 'the possibility of freedom.' "[40] "There is anxiety in any actualizing of possibility," in passing possibility "over into actuality."[41] As May renders Kierkegaard, "In the state of innocence, individuation is a potentiality, which has not yet become self-conscious....Individuation (becoming a self) is gained at the price of confronting the anxiety inherent in taking a stand *against* as well as *with* one's environment."[42] Later, "Kierkegaard makes it clear that selfhood depends on the individual's capacity to *confront anxiety and move ahead despite it*."[43] Elsewhere, May explains how Kierkegaard arrives at this crucial double movement, upon which self-realization depends, in a polemic against Hegel. In *Love and Will*, for example, he writes that "Kierkegaard mocked Hegel's...oversimplified and intellectualistic solution that 'potentiality goes over into actuality' when he proclaimed that potentiality does go into actuality, *but the intermediate variable is*

---

31   Rollo May, *The Meaning of Anxiety*, pp. 32–51.
32   Kresten Nordentoft in his *Kierkegaard's Psychology*, trans. by Bruce H. Kirmmse, Pittsburgh: Duquesne University Press 1978, p. xix, mentions how "existential psychology" overall "has used Kierkegaard profitably as a critique of the conceptions of man held by psychoanalysis and experimental psychology, which ignore the concrete and historical character of existence"; he also writes (p. xx) that "a first attempt at a complete presentation of Kierkegaard's psychological theories was made by Rollo May in *The Meaning of Anxiety*."
33   May, *The Meaning of Anxiety*, p. 15.
34   Ibid., p. 20.
35   Ibid., p. 33. Emphasis in this and all subsequent quotations from May is original.
36   Ibid., p. 36.
37   Ibid.
38   Ibid.
39   Ibid., p. 37.
40   Ibid., p. 38.
41   Ibid.
42   Ibid., p. 39.
43   Ibid., p. 40.

anxiety." [44] Adds May, "We could rephrase it, 'potentiality is experienced as *mine—my power, my question*—and, therefore, whether it goes over into actuality depends to some extent on me'...What happens in human experience is 'I conceive—I can—I will—I am.' " [45] And we have come full circle as the structure of a principal tenet in *Love and Will* has found support in Kierkegaard.

May, not surprisingly, reminds us, in italics, that in Kierkegaard, "*Freedom... depends on how one relates oneself to oneself at every moment in existence.*" [46] This "idea of the *self* is only partially contained in the psychological term *ego*," [47] and he sets the "qualitative leap" "into self-awareness...against a backdrop of innocence." [48] But "as a consequence of this 'leap'...anxiety becomes reflective," [49] and so, "self-awareness makes possible not only self-directed individual development, but also self-conscious historical development....Through self-awareness man can mold and to an extent transform his present historical development." [50] " 'Every individual begins in a historical nexus,' Kierkegaard writes,...But what is of crucial significance is how a person relates himself to his historical nexus." [51]

Kierkegaard's thinking on the relation between freedom and history, and its involvement of anxiety, is crucial to May. For one thing, it connects individual history to history-at-large. May sums up Kierkegaard's argument by noting that following innocence, "there occurs the possibility of separation as an individual. Anxiety is now reflective; and the individual can through self-awareness partially direct his own development as well as participate in the history of the race." [52] Such reflective "anxiety involves inner conflict" to which the neurotic individual responds by retrenching to a " 'shut-in' condition, sacrificing his freedom," but to which a more healthy individual responds by moving "ahead despite the conflict, actualizing his freedom." [53]

The fact that May never tires from celebrating anxiety as an individual's optimal opportunity to realize his or her freedom, only throws freedom's relation to history into relief (by breaching the relation!), especially if the situation is viewed through Kierkegaard's lens. The focal point here is creativity, as when May says that in Kierkegaard,

> one has anxiety because it is possible to create...in every experience of creativity something in the past is killed so that something new in the present may be born. Hence, for Kierkegaard, guilt feeling is always a concomitant of anxiety: both are aspects of

---

[44]   May, *Love and Will*, p. 243. The exact same point and reference to Kierkegaard is made in Rollo May, *Power and Innocence: The Sources of Violence*, New York: W.W. Norton 1972, p. 122.

[45]   May, *Love and Will*, p. 243.

[46]   May, *The Meaning of Anxiety*, p. 41.

[47]   Ibid.

[48]   Ibid.

[49]   Ibid.

[50]   Ibid.

[51]   Ibid., p. 42.

[52]   Ibid.

[53]   Ibid., pp. 42–3.

experiencing and actualizing possibility....According to Kierkegaard, one is, or ought to be, continually creating his own every instant of his life.[54]

"The greater the anxiety the greater the man,"[55] was Kierkegaard's message; this also implied what May routinely states, that "anxiety is an even better teacher than reality, for one can temporarily evade reality...but anxiety is a source of education always present because one carries it within."[56] Near the conclusion of his Kierkegaard section, May even writes: "This is the way one becomes educated to maturity as a self."[57]

If indeed it was Kierkegaard's achievement that "despite his lack of the tools for interpreting unconscious material—which tools have been available in their most complete form only since Freud—he so keenly and profoundly anticipated modern psychoanalytic insight into anxiety," his own maturity as a Danish thinker is no pittance either. For "at the same time he placed these insights in the broad context of a poetic and philosophical understanding of human experience."[58]

---

[54]   Ibid., pp. 44–5. What applies to creativity applies to love as well, as May repeatedly makes clear. In his *The Courage to Create*, New York: W.W. Norton 1975, we read that "As Kierkegaard well said, the self is only that which is in the process of becoming" (p. 99) and "What Kierkegaard said about love is also true of creativity: every person must start at the beginning" (p. 26). But May addresses the issue already in *Love and Will*. "The individual completes the creative work vastly relieved and more a person than before—but also maimed," and one such maimed individual was Kierkegaard. "It is the danger of the razor-blade edge of heightened consciousness on which the creative person lives" (p. 171). Love, too, is a wide-ranging, transformative experience, as stated next in familiar terms: " 'In love every man starts from the beginning'....This beginning is the relationship between people which we term care. Though it goes beyond feeling, it begins there" (p. 303). Conversely, when we are alerted to Kierkegaard's distinction between the shut-upness of unfreedom and the "ever increasing communicativeness" of freedom (*The Meaning of Anxiety*, p. 46), it is easy to appreciate May's concern, for example, in his *My Quest for Beauty*, San Francisco: Saybrook 1985, about the evil that locks the individual up "with himself alone...shut up *from* his life, not, as Kierkegaard puts it in contrast, shut up *with* something—which latter may instead be constructive solitude. Diabolism refers to evil inherent in the process of being torn apart, the spreading of calumny" (p. 158; see also *Psychology and the Human Dilemma*, p. 69). May's belief in human creativity and its link to freedom was an article of faith to which Kierkegaard lent credence. *The Meaning of Anxiety*, p. 113, states it as follows: "When Kierkegaard says, 'Anxiety is the dizziness of freedom,' he is saying something that every artist and every man of letters knows..."

[55]   May, *The Meaning of Anxiety*, p. 49.

[56]   Ibid.; see also ibid., p. 365 and p. 376.

[57]   Ibid., p. 51.

[58]   Ibid. This is the ultimate conclusion to the *The Meaning of Anxiety*'s Kierkegaard section as it spells out the proximity between May and his Danish source of inspiration and/ or elected affinity. That May's own holistic broad-mindedness as a psychologist is akin to Kierkegaard's, he made evident on several occasions, e.g., in his presentation to the 1959 APA symposium on *Existential Psychology*: "The existential approach in psychology as elsewhere is *not to be rationalistic or antirationalistic, but to seek the ground on which both reason and unreason are based.* This is what was sought by Kierkegaard, who was marvelously gifted

The themes introduced in *The Meaning of Anxiety*'s section on Kierkegaard keep surfacing in the book, notably in the form of elaborations on previous claims. First, the summary description of anxiety as "fear of nothingness" is now matched by the italicized notion that *"anxiety is objectless because it strikes at that basis of the psychological structure on which the perception of one's self as distinct from the world of objects occur."*[59] Second, May has more explanatory formulations of anxiety as a teacher and quotes directly from *The Concept of Anxiety*:

> Anxiety is afraid, yet it maintains a sly intercourse with its object, cannot look away from it, indeed will not…[Anxiety] is a desire for what one dreads, a sympathetic antipathy. Anxiety is an alien power which lays hold on an individual, and yet one cannot tear oneself away, nor has a will to do so; for one fears, but what one fears one desires. Anxiety then makes the individual impotent.[60]

And to illustrate how anxiety puts humans between a rock and a hard place, May writes: " 'To venture causes anxiety, but not to venture is to lose oneself,' Kierkegaard puts it pithily."[61]

Anxiety, on both Kierkegaard's and May's view, marks the boundary between self and world, but as significantly problematic, at once risky and alluring. It must be both respected and disrespected by the borderline self in order for this self to increase its self-awareness, transcend itself, and enter the world. To this end, creativity is pivotal. "The more creative the individual, the more possibilities he or she has and the more they are confronted with anxiety and its concomitant responsibility and guilt feeling. Or, as Kierkegaard again phrases it: 'The more consciousness, the more self.' "[62] Using italics one last time, May concludes his paragraph—and the entire book—thus: *"the positive aspects of selfhood develop as the individual confronts, moves through, and overcomes anxiety-creating experiences."*[63] He could just as well have cited the quotation his mentor Paul Tillich put on the flyleaf of the copy of *The Courage to Be* he gave to him, and which May cites in his *Paulus*: "The self is the stronger the more non-being it can take into itself."[64] Anxiety is a reality to

---

logically and intellectually but preferred to be called a poet." (*Existential Psychology*, ed. by May, p. 46)

[59] May, *The Meaning of Anxiety*, p. 207.

[60] Ibid., p. 247.

[61] Ibid., p. 392.

[62] Ibid., p. 393.

[63] Ibid.

[64] Rollo May, *Paulus: Tillich as Spiritual Teacher*, Dallas: Saybrook 1973 (revised ed. 1988), p. 83; p. 122. Tillich himself found peace in "seeing meaning in the most chaotic states, a peace which comes from the courage to meet the 'devils' head on. Modern Art such as that of Pollock and Motherwell appealed to him. They literally paint tension, and their paintings are never quiet but have a peace which comes only from dynamic equilibrium." (p. 46) It seems fair to say that May here remembers his teacher and friend (*Paulus*'s 1st ed was titled *Reminiscences of a Friendship*) as an admirable modern embodiment of Kierkegaard's dictum that only when anxiety is taken on whole-heartedly can the possibility of true self-realization become reality. Conversely, says May, "The avoidance of the anxiety of solitude by constant agitated diversion is what Kierkegaard, in a nice smile, likened to the settlers in the early days

be experienced and overcome; it guards a border between being and non-being that is indistinguishable from the one between being and the world. The risk for self-effacement is identical with the prospect for self-hood; this is the dizzying reality to which Kierkegaard alerted Rollo May.

In his next book, *Man's Search for Himself* (1953), May begins where he left off in *The Meaning of Anxiety*. Viewing Kierkegaard as one of "the true prophets …[who] foresaw the destruction of values which would occur in our time, the loneliness, emptiness and anxiety which would engulf us in the twentieth century,"[65] he cites Kierkegaard's words about anxiety as a double-edged sword that robs the "I" of self if the individual dodges it but puts the "I" on a risky path to selfhood if instead the individual confronts it.[66] The bottom line, to repeat Kierkegaard, is "The more consciousness,…the more self."[67] And "Choosing One's Self," which May later uses as a heading, is yet another phrase from Kierkegaard meant "to affirm one's responsibility for one's self and one's existence."[68] We are finally reminded of Kierkegaard's "Purity of Heart Is to Will One Thing" when May enlists this author's concept of freedom in "an ethics of inwardness";[69] he arrives at "the truth in the 'inner light' tradition in religious history,"[70] which is "that one must always begin with himself.…Relating this truth to Socrates, Kierkegaard writes, 'In the Socratic view each individual is his own center, and the entire world centers in him, because his self-knowledge is a knowledge of God.' "[71] Consistent with May's biography, his appeal to religion persists; what is now on his mind, however, is no longer the Christian faith of his youth, but rather the repository for moral guidance for which Socrates is emblematic in Kierkegaard.[72]

May's next single-authored book with a substantial Kierkegaardian component, *Psychology and the Human Dilemma* (1967), fittingly strikes an immediate note in accord with the Socratic tone of its 1953 precursor. Hence the first chapter's epigraph, quoted from Kierkegaard's *Fragments*: "one should not think slightingly of the paradoxical; the paradox is the source of the thinker's passion, and the thinker without paradox is like a lover without feeling: a paltry mediocrity."[73] The question of the chapter's title, "What Is the Human Dilemma?" is answered accordingly: "My freedom, in any genuine sense, lies not in my capacity to live as 'pure subject,'

---

of America who used to beat on pots and pans at night to make enough din to keep the wolves away." (May, *The Courage to Create*, p. 67; for an earlier version of this statement, see Rollo May, *Man's Search for Himself*, New York: W.W. Norton 1953, p. 30)

65   May, *Man's Search for Himself*, pp. 53–4.

66   Ibid., p. 9.

67   Ibid., p. 116.

68   Ibid., pp. 168–9.

69   Ibid., p. 221.

70   Ibid., p. 222.

71   Ibid.

72   See also ibid., pp. 190–1, where May sees the executions of both Jesus and Socrates as the outcome of warfare between "ethical leaders and existing religious institutions" with "the ethical leader often attacking the church and the church as frequently branding the other an enemy," cf. Kierkegaard's own *Attack on Christendom*.

73   May, *Psychology and the Human Dilemma*, p. 3.

but rather in my capacity to experience *both* modes, to live in the dialectical relationship."[74] A note reminds us that this means the "dizziness of freedom" that is anxiety.[75] Like Nietzsche, Kierkegaard stresses the *commitment* to choose in the paradox;[76] and to specify the bottom line, May brings even Tillich into the equation: "The loss of experience of one's own significance leads to the kind of anxiety that Paul Tillich called the anxiety of meaninglessness, or what Kierkegaard terms anxiety as the fear of nothingness."[77] In subsequent passages May recalls in slightly different wording Kierkegaard's lesson about anxiety as the preeminent teacher of life: "learning to know anxiety is an adventure which every man has to affront if he would not go to perdition either by not having known anxiety or by sinking under it. He therefore who has learned rightly to be anxious has learned the most important thing."[78] It turns out that May, as he visits theories of anxiety from Spinoza via Kierkegaard to Freud, heads for the conclusion that each theory "is designed to illuminate the anxiety-creating experiences of people at that particular stage in the historical development of the culture."[79] What Kierkegaard (along with Marx and Nietzsche) described as technical and instrumental reason sidetracking autonomous reason in the nineteenth century were "the fissures in contemporary cultural [*sic!*] which were later to generate widespread anxiety."[80] Eventually Kierkegaard and Freud, like Schopenhauer and Nietzsche before them, "sought in different ways to rediscover the repressed dynamic, unconscious, so-called 'irrational' springs of man's behavior, and to unite these with man's rational functions."[81] May has a vested interest in this endeavor, with the lion's share of the investment going Kierkegaard's way.

In his book's fourth chapter, "Historical Roots of Modern Anxiety Theories," May elaborates key points from his earlier *The Meaning of Anxiety*. His response to the central human dilemma in the present volume truly bears the trademark of conflicted holism. As a case in point, he writes that "a distinct characteristic of man is his capacity for *awareness* of his own possibilities. This brings Kierkegaard to his important concept of the relation of *conflict* to anxiety."[82] With the "development of self-awareness,"[83] the maturing individual realizes that "conscious choice...may involve clashes with parents and defiance of them.... This self-awareness is the basis in the growing individual for responsibility, inner conflict, and guilt feeling."[84] Such conflicted states of mind, which Kierkegaard believed are "always a concomitant of creativity,"[85] unless the individual succumbs to his or her fear of freedom, are called

---

74   Ibid., p. 9.
75   Ibid., p. 21.
76   Ibid., p. 20.
77   Ibid., p. 37.
78   Ibid., p. 49; identically repeated p. 81.
79   Ibid., p. 56.
80   Ibid., p. 64.
81   Ibid., p. 65.
82   Ibid., p. 68.
83   Ibid.
84   Ibid.
85   Ibid.

in the present volume a *"retrenchment"* that spurs *"neurotic anxiety."*[86] In the instance where creative self-production is thwarted, conflict remains, but within an imploding framework. In place of "freedom…continually communicating" as "concentric circles of the widening and deepening self involv[ing] at the same time expanding circles of meaningful relations with one's fellowmen,"[87] the result is neurotic, or what Kierkegaard called *"shut-upness*. The shut-up person is not shut up *with* himself, but *from* himself, as well as from others."[88] In this case, neurotic anxiety's barren conflicts have replaced normal anxiety's fertile ones, and what one might call self-reduction has been substituted for potential self-production. May elevates the distinction—between deadening passivity and risk-taking initiative in the face of anxiety—from its historical grounding in Kierkegaard to its employment in topical analyses of culture and therapeutic practice; in fact he reveals its importance both in his "Introduction" to Sartre's *Existential Psychoanalysis* and in his mention of Sartre in *Psychology and the Human Dilemma*.[89] In both instances he claims that Sartre— "given added conviction by the passionate beliefs of Kierkegaard and Nietzsche"[90]— has identified a meaningful structure in Western bourgeois society against which one can powerfully fight. The example suggests how conflictual sources of mental health can energize individuation by actually transcending the individual and incorporating him or her in a larger production of meaning. Regardless of whether the dual effect is merely a simultaneity or springs from a cause-and-effect interrelationship, its holistic scope clearly goes to the bottom of Kierkegaard's deep psychological thinking and to the heart of Rollo May's broad conception of existential psychology.

In *Freedom and Destiny* (1981) May continues drilling the concept of freedom so as to reach further into Kierkegaard's psychological vocabulary. In the process, he also distinguishes Kierkegaard, and by association himself, from Freud. "When Kierkegaard points out again and again that 'freedom depends on how the self relates to itself at every moment,' he is speaking of the psyche-self in relation to the ego. The self relating to itself was the aspect of selfhood that Freud never understood."[91] Beyond that, he brings to the fore two contrasting Kierkegaardian concepts not previously subjected to scrutiny: spirit and despair. In Kierkegaard, not only is the self self-relating, it is identified with spirit, which in turn is identified with man, of whom Kierkegaard speaks as "a synthesis of the finite and the infinite, of the temporal and the eternal, of freedom and necessity."[92] Despair, by contrast, is the dark side of the synthesis, "a failure of spirit, a spiritlessness."[93] It is "a desperate refusal to be oneself. Kierkegaard puts it well, citing the different levels of 'despair at not willing to be one's self, or still lower, despair at not willing to be a self; or lowest of all, despair at willing to be another than himself.' "[94] Ultimately, and in

---

[86]   Ibid.
[87]   Ibid., p. 69.
[88]   Ibid.
[89]   May, "Introduction," p. 8 and May, *Psychology and the Human Dilemma*, p. 141.
[90]   Ibid.
[91]   May, *Freedom and Destiny*, p. 178.
[92]   Ibid., p. 220.
[93]   Ibid., p. 238.
[94]   Ibid., pp. 237–8.

italics, Kierkegaard proclaims: "*In unconsciousness of being in despair a man is the furthest from being conscious of himself as spirit.*"[95]

As its subtitle, *Writings in Existential Psychology*, intimates, *The Discovery of Being* (1983) is simultaneously a collection of older studies and Rollo May's last major exposition in single-authored book-form of Kierkegaard's impact on his writing. Only its "Foreword" and first chapter (of a total of 12), "Bases of Psychotherapy," are new; the rest of its contents harks back to May's contributions to the two anthologies he (co-) edited in 1958 and 1960: chapter 2 to *Existence* (1958) and chapters 3–12 to *Existential Psychology* (1960). Consequently, the backbone of this publication can be considered an assemblage of May's cardinal ideas and observations of the human as a being, as reflected in his anthologies from around 1960 and in several of his single-authored books before and after that time. The gist of the volume and its title is set forth in the "Foreword":

> I believe it is by discovering and affirming the being in ourselves that some inner certainty will become possible. In contrast to the psychologies that conclude with theories about conditioning, mechanisms of behavior, and instinctual drives, I maintain that we must go below these theories and discover the person, *the being to whom these things happen.*[96]

The ulterior motive for the whole text is said to be a desire by the author to counter "the severest threat in history to human survival," to which end it seems to him especially appropriate to contrast "our possible annihilation" with "the possibilities of being" that had been at the center of his professional interest for decades.[97]

Kierkegaard's relevance to May's attention to current affairs functions on a fairly general level of cultural criticism; for instance, May says that

> the existential way of understanding human beings has some illustrious progenitors in Western history....But it arose specifically just over a hundred years ago in Kierkegaard's violent protest against the reigning rationalism of his day....Kierkegaard proclaimed that Hegel's identification of abstract truth with reality was an illusion and amounted to trickery. "Truth exists," wrote Kierkegaard, "only as the individual himself produces it in action."[98]

In compatible terms,

> Kierkegaard, Nietzsche and those who followed them accurately foresaw this growing split between truth and reality in Western culture, and they endeavored to call Western man back from the delusion that reality can be comprehended in an abstracted, detached way....Kierkegaard and the existential thinkers appealed to a reality *underlying both subjectivity and objectivity*. We must not only study a person's experience as such, they held, but even more we must study the man to whom the experience is happening, the one who is doing the experiencing.[99]

---

[95]   Ibid., p. 238.
[96]   May, *The Discovery of Being: Writings in Existential Psychology*, p. 10.
[97]   Ibid., p. 10.
[98]   Ibid., p. 49.
[99]   Ibid., pp. 52–3.

This, in turn, leads May to acknowledge that

> Kierkegaard and Nietzsche did not underestimate the importance of the specific
> psychological analysis; but they were much more concerned with understanding *man
> as the being who represses*, the being who surrenders self-awareness as a protection
> against reality and then suffers the neurotic consequences....Kierkegaard and Nietzsche
> were keenly aware that the "sickness of soul" of Western man was a deeper and more
> extensive morbidity than could be explained by the specific individual and social
> problems.[100]

Considering that the cultural-historical criticism attributed to Kierkegaard (and
Nietzsche) in these passages indeed defies individual and social specification; it
comes as a small surprise that May tempers the almost explicit generality of his
discourse by turning his attention to Ludwig Binswanger's famous case story
of Ellen West (who suffered from what Kierkegaard had described as "Sickness
unto Death") as a bridge to return to Kierkegaard for insights in truly individual
psychology.[101] Like Nietzsche and Freud, Kierkegaard based his knowledge "chiefly
on the analysis of one case"[102]—to wit, himself: "The central psychological endeavor
of Kierkegaard may be summed up under the heading of the question he pursued
relentlessly: How can you become an individual?"[103] The rational absoluteness and
the lack of passion that drowned out individuality in nineteenth-century culture
triggered, in May's rendition of a passage from the *Postscript*, an alternative notion
of "*relational truth...*truth as *inwardness*"[104] in Kierkegaard, "or, as Heidegger puts
it, truth as freedom."[105]

    May notes that "roughly speaking, Kierkegaard speaks out of a time when God
is dying, Nietzsche when God is dead,"[106] and that the two thinkers' shared respect
for man's nobility led the former to speak of the "true individual" and the latter
to counter with his "man of power."[107] May then seeks to subsume their different
positions under his one holistic project—and to interlace its broader socio-cultural
and historical criticism with its enduring respect for the deeper nature of existential
individuation. The result, taking even Freud into account, can be read in sentences
like these: "The fact that Kierkegaard, Nietzsche, and Freud all dealt with the same
problems of anxiety, despair, fragmentalized personality, and the symptoms of these
bears out our earlier thesis that psychoanalysis and the existential approach to human
crises were called forth by and were answers to the same problems."[108] Altogether,
"Kierkegaard and Nietzsche, and the existentialists who followed them perdurably

---

[100]   Ibid., p. 65.
[101]   Ibid., p. 68.
[102]   Ibid., pp. 68–9.
[103]   Ibid., p. 69.
[104]   Ibid., p. 70.
[105]   Ibid.
[106]   Ibid., p. 76.
[107]   Ibid., p. 77.
[108]   Ibid., p. 84.

pointed out that the two chief sources of modern Western man's anxiety and despair were, first, his loss of sense of being and, second, his loss of his world."[109]

At this point, disruptions and conflicts prevail: between the individual and the rest of the world and Western culture; between this individual's loss of self and world; and between psychoanalytic and existentialist responses to all such discrepancies. Yet while these conflicts are reconfigured in an orderly way under May's problem-identifying and problem-unifying umbrella, history remains only an outcast:

> The existential analysts take history very seriously, but they protest against any tendency to evade the immediate, anxiety-creating issues in the present by taking refuge behind the determinism of the past. They are against the doctrines that historical forces carry the individual along automatically....Kierkegaard was very emphatic on this point.[110]

The concept of history in question is a particular one, to be sure.[111] Nevertheless, the historical is as good a reason as any to conclude this discussion of Kierkegaard's place in May's *Discovery of Being* with a comment on the book's first (and only new) chapter. In it, the author reflects on his first "existentialist" book, *The Meaning of Anxiety*, which he was working on while hospitalized in the tuberculosis sanatorium and "had a great deal of time to ponder the meaning of anxiety."[112] He situates his own book and title in the context of its only two predecessors, Kierkegaard's *The Concept of Anxiety* and Freud's *The Problem of Anxiety*. His conclusion on these reflections reads:

> What powerfully struck me then was that Kierkegaard was writing about *exactly what my patients and I were going through*...Kierkegaard was portraying what is immediately experienced by human beings in crisis...Freud was writing on the technical level, where his genius was supreme...he *knew about* anxiety. Kierkegaard, a genius of a different order, was writing on the existential, ontological level; he *knew anxiety*.[113]

With these words, May comes close to calling Kierkegaard's text on anxiety performative, one that *is* what it supposedly *is about*. That May gives it preference over Freud's (while paying Freud the respect his work is due) caps May's own edgy

---

[109]   Ibid., p. 118.

[110]   Ibid., pp. 140–1.

[111]   Referring in a note (p. 182) to a cited passage from *Fear and Trembling*, May underscores that Kierkegaard was not disputing technical progress in history; but the notion of existential beginnings could not be historically compromised. In another context, his "Introduction" to R. Patton Howell, *War's End: The Revolution of Consciousness in the European Community 1992*, San Francisco: Saybrook 1989, p. 15, May suggests, in accordance with his Sartrean idea of the historical as a site of meaning we need to challenge, that "we need to confront, for example, the *historical dimension* of ourselves and the human beings we read about, as well as the history of the culture in which we live and move and have our being. It is a failure to see things in their historical inner dimension which has made us blind to the dangers in our phenomenal growth."

[112]   May, *The Discovery of Being: Writings in Existential Psychology*, p. 14.

[113]   Ibid., pp. 14–15.

and holistic, discriminating and inclusive, cultured and experiential sense of being that justifies the label "existential psychology."

His last book, *The Cry for Myth* (1991), certifies the scope of this line of inquiry. The qualified totalization that marks the tortured and upbuilding process of self-realization, of becoming a self, is the one that cries for myth to sustain it: "The most powerful influence is that which grasps us as a totality, on levels Jung would call the collective unconscious."[114] But conversely, "the lost self is the central theme in Kierkegaard: his greatest condemnation is directed to 'the conforming citizen.' "[115] The eminent case in point is the title figure of Ibsen's *Peer Gynt*; "in Kierkegaard's terms, the Peer Gynts try to *be* without ever *choosing* themselves."[116] This ethical level of Kierkegaard's thinking, to which May adheres (without sharing in Sartre's atheist humanism), is what has him enroll Kierkegaard among those who emphatically "*saw that the error of the Enlightenment was that it lacked a devil.*"[117] Existentially speaking—as May has been speaking since his grappling with "anxiety" in 1950 and until his crying for myth in 1991—a harmonious concord without a discord is a falsehood, not a selfhood.

III. General Interpretation

Rollo May is a humanistic psychologist whose intellectual interests and orientation span wide swaths of psychology, philosophy, religion, mythology, and literary tradition from classical antiquity to European and American modernism. At the same time, his respect for the individual human being's lived experience and existential authenticity is unfailing. The two traits are as interwoven and counterbalanced in his writings as are so many other opposites on his agenda. There is even, as Jørn Vosmar has stressed, a Kierkegaardian and Socratic dimension to this suspenseful equilibrium. Kierkegaard worried that his reader would "accept what was said as an intellectual explanation—without acknowledging it as a personally committing reality."[118] May and other existential psychologists had similar concerns; they, too, wanted their communications to be personally engaging. But the strategy these therapists employed to reach their goal was different from the indirect communication used in Socrates' dialogues and Kierkegaard's pseudonymous works to fend off purely intellectual receptions. May instead presented his patients with "a purely formal view of existence"[119] that did afford practical application, but left it up "to the reader how he would practically apply it."[120]

For all his informed and open-minded disposition, May was an eclectic rather than profoundly discriminating importer of Kierkegaardian ideas and impulses. The fact that Kierkegaard's *oeuvre* displays as many disciplinary intersections and at

---

114   Rollo May, *The Cry for Myth*, New York: W.W. Norton 1991, p. 171.
115   Ibid.
116   Ibid., p. 179.
117   Ibid., p. 283.
118   Vosmar, "Forord," p. 15.
119   Ibid.
120   Ibid.

least as many approaches as May's own certainly did not bar the Dane from serving the American as an elected affinity, especially since the former epitomized an intellectual whose every pursuit was subjected to existential (and religious) passion. All the same, May's application of Kierkegaard is limed to relatively few of the philosopher's texts and a limited part of his conceptual inventory. *The Concept of Anxiety* is the mainstay, with occasional digressions to *The Sickness unto Death* and a rare mention of *Fear and Trembling, Philosophical Fragments, Postscript*, and the collection known as *Attack on Christendom*. Now and then, May refers to Robert Bretall's (ed.) *A Kierkegaard Anthology* and, for secondary literature, to Walter Lowrie's *A Short Life of Kierkegaard.*[121] His focal point is clearly Kierkegaard's psychology, while the Christian thinking, for instance, is marginal to his sphere of interest. Correspondingly, May most often resorts to psychological takes on existential categories like anxiety and despair, whereas a host of ethically and religiously attuned concepts, such as sin, admission, and forgiveness, go unnoticed. Even within this limited scope, his reading of Kierkegaard shows a preponderance of eye-catching phrases—like "anxiety is the dizziness of freedom"—and a sparser effort at real intercourse with Kierkegaard's primary texts. Almost without exception, his exposition of the material is uncritical, if not laudatory. There is little doubt that Kierkegaard was a real source of inspiration for May, though in the restricted sense that May usually distilled from the source material what directly boosted his own agenda. That even holds true in *The Meaning of Anxiety*, where the objective is an examination of various anxiety theories.

All in all, it is difficult to determine whether or not the intertextual configuration involving May and Kierkegaard amounts to "influence." If treated the way this unwieldy term usually is in traditional comparative studies of literature—that is, as

---

[121]   May, *The Discovery of Being: Writings in Existential Psychology*, p. 175: "[Kierkegaard's] two most important psychological books are *The Concept of Anxiety* and *The Sickness unto Death*." May generally quotes Kierkegaard, *The Concept of Dread*, trans. by Walter Lowrie, Princeton, New Jersey: Princeton University Press 1944; but in a note to the 1977 rev. ed. of *The Meaning of Anxiety*, pp. 36–7, May discusses the terms "dread" vs. "anxiety" and concludes by praising the translators for having restored " 'anxiety' to its rightful place." Here he refers enigmatically to *The Concept of Anxiety*, ed. and trans. by Howard V. Hong and Edna H. Hong, Northfield, Minnesota 1976. However, this edition does not seem to exist. In the "Historical Introduction" to *The Concept of Anxiety* (*CA*, p. xvii), the editor/translator Reidar Thomte (and Albert B. Anderson) writes of *The Meaning of Anxiety* that "Rollo May emphasizes that anxiety is not an affect among other affects, such as pleasure and sadness. It is an ontological characteristic of man, rooted in his very existence. Fear is a threat to the periphery of one's existence and can be studied as an affect among other affects. Anxiety is a threat to the foundation and center of one's existence. It is ontological and can be understood only as a threat to *Dasein*. If the individual did not have some measure of freedom, there could be no experience of anxiety." See also May, *The Discovery of Being: Writings in Existential Psychology*, pp. 110–11. For the other texts, May used the following translations: *Sickness unto Death*, trans. by Walter Lowrie, Princeton, New Jersey: Princeton University Press 1941 and *The Sickness unto Death*, trans. by Walter Lowrie, New York: Doubleday 1954; *"Fear and Trembling" and "Sickness unto Death,"* New York: Doubleday 1954; Walter Lowrie, *A Short Life of Kierkegaard*, Princeton: Princeton University Press 1942; and *A Kierkegaard Anthology*, ed. Robert Bretall, Princeton: Princeton University Press 1951.

an operation meant to detect similarities penetrating integral complexes and their dominating features[122]—May has obviously ignored too many of the interconnections that constitute Kierkegaard's "authorship" as a whole to be considered having been under his direct "influence." But bearing in mind how many disciplinary branches are at work in this author's compositions, it may not be justified to apply an entirely literary definition of "influence." Suffice it to say that parts of Kierkegaard's production seem to have helped inspire the design of May's psychological toolbox; few other cultural personalities—Freud and Tillich among them—take up comparable positions in May's work. Yet, for all his reservations against instrumental reason, many of which were engendered by Kierkegaard, May's approach to Kierkegaard actually suggests that he did not refrain from instrumentalizing his Danish role model to serve this critical purpose. The irony inevitably raises the question whether May has facilitated an updating of Kierkegaard or if he has rather outdated him, which in turn hinges on May's own currency.

Kirk Schneider, in a chapter titled "Rollo May: Liberator and Realist," opines that "the embracing of life's paradoxes and the maximizing of freedom [that] are Rollo May's prime psychological legacies"[123] currently face "three major threats…: scientistic reductionism; psychospiritual absolutism; and postmodern relativism."[124] May was not adverse to all these positions, "but what he could not countenance was their extremity (as he viewed it) and their neglect, thereby, of life's complexity."[125] That said, Schneider's view is that an even larger question than how May's legacy will fare vis-à-vis these challenges "is just beginning to be posed by [his] successors: will society change? Will culture and the vast socio-economic machine that fuels it open themselves to [his] insights?"[126]

While Schneider saw experiential contact and client awareness as integral to May's therapeutic process of healing,[127] Kuno Poulsen, writing decades earlier about the first translation of cardinal texts by May into Danish, questions the relevance of existential psychology to healing and therapy. He suggests that May and psychologists of his ilk should distinguish more clearly between, say, anxiety as an existential disposition and a mental illness, and that only the former version be reserved for the client's own decision-making. That such distinctions between health and disease are rarely made in full, Poulsen attributes to the fact that existential psychology "doesn't consider healing people its task at all."[128]

Robert H. Abzug, who considered May's influence to be at its peak in the 1960s and 1970s[129] and who wrote an essay about May's 1969 bestseller *Love and Will*, would not disagree that the author's principal impact, even therapeutically, was on

---

[122]   For this definition, see Johan Fjord Jensen's seminal comparative study, *Turgenjev i dansk åndsliv. Studier i dansk romankunst 1870–1900*, Copenhagen: Gyldendal 1961, p. 21.

[123]   Schneider, "Rollo May: Liberator and Realist," p. 352.

[124]   Ibid.

[125]   Ibid.

[126]   Ibid., p. 353.

[127]   Ibid., p. 352.

[128]   Poulsen, "Eksistentiel psykologi," p. 376.

[129]   See Eric Pace, "Dr. Rollo May Is Dead at 85; Was Innovator in Psychology," *New York Times*, October 24, 1994.

culture at large, rather than on specific cases of mental disease and illness. Issues such as sex and intimacy, love and death, art and creativity, tradition and modernity, are front and center in this book, and Abzug gets it right when he writes: "One can read *Love and Will* for its insights concerning sexuality, love, and personal regeneration, concentrating on what is said to the individual, pure and simple. Yet for a fleeting moment in cultural history, its multiple levels brought together an otherwise unlikely set of readers, devotees of past, present, and future."[130] And in conclusion: "In retrospect, we may view *Love and Will* and other, later works of Rollo May as some of the last to integrate the search for intimacy with the great themes of the pre-1970s West."[131]

By taking a last stand for the grand cultural narrative, May's position has been called the "existentialism of Kierkegaard and Nietzsche rather than that of Sartre," and an "existentialism [that] was the Christianity of Tillich but without Christ."[132] How could a patient on a couch possibly be cured by such big gestures or gesturers? "Kierkegaard [who] is clearly no ordinary religious author,"[133] and certainly no ordinary psychotherapist, may be the best to answer this question on Rollo May's behalf, at least if one is to believe Neil Pembroke's article "Kierkegaard as a Paradoxical Therapist."[134]

Its title alludes to the notion of self-realization Kierkegaard so resoundingly pronounced: that adversity must be embraced if the self is to mature. Choosing despair is to enlist an ally "rather than an enemy. In embracing her despair, a person is able to shatter the illusion of freedom that is restricting her development in selfhood."[135] It is Kierkegaard's belief, in *The Sickness unto Death*, that "by the aid of the eternal the self has courage to lose itself in order to gain itself."[136] Choosing despair is to move from outward illusion to inward reflection and from unfreedom to hope. It is the therapy of courageously moving through paradox, as most existentialists acknowledge. Tillich (Paulus) would quote Kierkegaard's "To venture causes anxiety, but not to venture is to lose one's self"[137]; and May would write that "whenever I was in despair myself I longed to be near Paulus, for I knew that no matter how deep my discouragement, he had gone deeper."[138] In his last book, *The Cry for Myth*, May speaks of the creative person's "struggle with the daimonic" and of "catharsis in the struggle with evil."[139] His terminology and scenarios may vary, but the points he makes are much the same.

---

130   Abzug, "*Love and Will:* Rollo May and the Seventies' Crisis of Intimacy," p. 87.

131   Ibid., p. 88. To his closing remark, Abzug adds the note about May's *Freedom and Destiny* and its author's "continued use of the western tradition, as well as May's own recognition that the cultural field was narrowing dangerously." (p. 88)

132   Ibid., p. 83.

133   Neil Pembroke, "Kierkegaard as a Paradoxical Therapist," *Pacifica*, vol. 18, no. 1, February 2005, p. 53.

134   Ibid., pp. 53–66.

135   Ibid., p. 55.

136   Ibid., p. 66.

137   May, *Paulus: Tillich as Spiritual Teacher*, p. 122.

138   Ibid., p. 46.

139   May, *The Cry for Myth*, p. 282.

Rollo May, the existential psychologist, may not have been a therapist for all ages. But he was an outspoken therapeutic voice of his own times, which he would not have been without Kierkegaard as his sounding board and without a few kindred voices of the twentieth century with whom this nineteenth-century Dane also resonated.

Bibliography

I. References to or Uses of Kierkegaard in May's Corpus

The Meaning of Anxiety, revised ed., New York: W.W. Norton 1977 [1950], pp. xiv–xv; p. xxi; p. 15; pp. 20–1; pp. 26–8; pp. 32–51; pp. 58–9; pp. 65–6; p. 99; p. 113; p. 123; p. 125; p. 133; p. 151; p. 158; p. 192; p. 207; pp. 218–20; p. 229; p. 244; p. 247; p. 265; p. 365; p. 370; p. 376; p. 379; pp. 384–5; p. 390; pp. 392–3.
Man's Search for Himself, New York: W.W. Norton 1953, p. 30; pp. 53–4; p. 101; p. 116; pp. 168–70; p. 191; pp. 221–2.
Psychology and the Human Dilemma, New York: W.W. Norton 1967, p. 3; p. 9; pp. 20–1; p. 37; p. 49; pp. 55–6; pp. 64–9; p. 81; p. 129; p. 137; p. 141; p. 179; p. 189.
The Courage to Create, New York: W.W. Norton 1975, p. 26; p. 29; p. 67; p. 88; p. 99; p. 108.
Freedom and Destiny, New York: W.W Norton 1981, p. 10; p. 21; p. 53; p. 63; p. 169; p. 172; p. 178; pp. 185–6; p. 220; pp. 226–7; pp. 237–8.
The Discovery of Being: Writings in Existential Psychology, New York: Norton 1983, pp. 14–15; p. 17; p. 30; p. 49; pp. 52–4; pp. 60–2; pp. 65–7; pp. 83–6; pp. 110–12; p. 118; pp. 126–7; p. 131; pp. 139–42; p. 149; pp. 165–6.
The Cry for Myth, New York: W.W. Norton 1991, p. 15; p. 74; p. 132; pp. 170–1; p. 179; p. 207.
May, Rollo et al. (eds.), *Existence: A New Dimension in Psychiatry and Psychology*, New York: Touchstone/Simon and Schuster 1958, pp. 11–12; pp. 14–15; pp. 19–20; pp. 22–30; pp. 33–5; pp. 51–2; p. 56; pp. 61–2; p. 65; pp. 69–71; p. 75; p. 87.
May, Rollo (ed.), *Existential Psychology*, 2nd ed., New York: Random House 1969 [1961], pp. 2–3; p. 6; p. 8; pp. 11–12; pp. 46–7; p. 79.

II. Sources of May's Knowledge of Kierkegaard

Bretall, Robert (ed.), *A Kierkegaard Anthology*, Princeton, New Jersey: Princeton University Press 1946 (1951).
Kierkegaard, Søren, *The Sickness unto Death*, trans. by Walter Lowrie, Princeton, New Jersey: Princeton University Press 1941.
— *The Concept of Dread*, trans. by Walter Lowrie, Princeton, New Jersey: Princeton University Press 1944.
— *Fear and Trembling*, trans by. Walter Lowrie, New York: Doubleday 1954.
— *"Fear and Trembling" and "Sickness unto Death,"* trans. by Walter Lowrie, New York: Doubleday 1954.
— *The Sickness unto Death*, trans. by Walter Lowrie, New York: Doubleday 1954.

Lowrie, Walter, *A Short Life of Kierkegaard*, Princeton, New Jersey: Princeton University Press 1942 (1944).

Tillich, Paul, *The Courage to Be*, New Haven: Yale University Press 1952.

III. Secondary Literature on May's Relation to Kierkegaard

Poulsen, Kuno, "Eksistentiel psykologi," *Dansk Udsyn*, vol. 47, 1967, pp. 359–76.

Vosmar, Jørn, "Forord," in Rollo May, *Eksistentiel psykologi*, trans. by Kresten Nordentoft, Copenhagen: Gyldendal 1966, pp. 7–15.

Carl R. Rogers:

"To Be That Self Which One Truly Is"

Simon D. Podmore

I. Introduction: Carl Rogers and the Person-Centered Revolution

One of the most influential, contested, and embraced figures in twentieth century psychology, and arguably America's most widely disseminated psychologist, Carl Ransom Rogers (1902–87) exerted an influence in humanistic thinking and action which extended far beyond the academic and the clinical *milieu*. Rogers' psychology of human potential and actualization has gained significant recognition beyond the mainstream of Anglo-American academic psychology, penetrating the domains of education, health care, community action and social agency, child and adult development, communications training, parenting education, and pastoral care, as well as psychotherapy and counseling. Although a former President of the American Psychological Association—by whom he had also been honored with the Distinguished Scientific Contribution Award in 1956, and a Professional Achievement Award in 1972—Rogers' influence managed to reach the lives of "ordinary" individuals and practitioners. Rogers worked not only with patients, students, and psychologists; he was also involved in peace initiatives between Catholics and Protestants in Northern Ireland and between rival ethnic sides in South Africa. During his final ten years of life, Rogers traveled and spoke across Western and Eastern Europe, Japan, China, Brazil, Mexico, Venezuela, Kenya, and Zimbabwe. His cross-cultural conflict resolution led to Rogers being nominated for the Nobel Peace Prize in 1987—news of which only arrived after his death on February 4, 1987.

Given the extent of Rogers' influence—particularly contrasted with Kierkegaard's own rather parochial self-confinement—it is tempting to wonder about the extent to which Rogers may, if only unconsciously, have brought the thoughts and feelings of Kierkegaard into the lives of numerous unsuspecting clients, listeners, students, and practitioners. This possible dissemination appears especially intriguing when one considers the simple yet abundantly fertile maxim that Rogers carried with him and which apparently translated across so many cultural and ideological borders: "to be that self which one truly is." The reference is to the work of Kierkegaard's very own physician of the soul, Anti-Climacus, *The Sickness unto Death: A Christian Psychological Exposition for Upbuilding and Awakening.*[1]

Carl Rogers was born on January 8, 1902 in Oak Park, Illinois, a suburb of Chicago in the United States. Rogers endured a fairly strict Christian upbringing, with his mother the most devout presence in the household. He was a prodigious young child, reading from an early age, but becoming increasingly isolated and independent in his adolescence. Having moved to a family farm at the age of 12, Rogers went on to major in agriculture at the University of Wisconsin. However, the austere religious-ethical environment of his youth had not deterred Rogers from studying religion. Following a change from agriculture to history, Rogers finally majored in religion, with an eventual view to a life of ministry. In 1920, at the age of 20, Rogers was one of ten students to be selected to attend the World Student Christian Federation Conference for six months in Beijing, China. Rather than intensifying his convictions, however, this broadening environment caused Rogers to question the authority and veracity of his previously accepted Christian claims to absolute truth.

After graduating from the University of Wisconsin, Rogers defied his parent's wishes and married Helen Elliot, moving to New York City, to attend Union Theological Seminary, where Paul Tillich (1886–1965) later taught between 1933 and 1955, and where a more liberal attitude to religion prevailed. However, enrolling in a student-led seminar was to emphasize his doubts—somewhat ironically titled "Why am I entering the Ministry?" Rogers' response to this question was, as for many who attended, confirmed in the negative.

Subsequently changing tact to study clinical and educational psychology at Teachers College, Columbia University, Rogers achieved an M.A. (1928) and a Ph.D. (1931), becoming particularly informed by the thought of the post-Freudian Otto Rank (1884–1939)—also an important influence for the existentialist psychologist and close friend of Paul Tillich, Rollo May (1909–94)—and the

---

[1]   Rogers' reference is to Walter Lowrie's translation, *The Sickness unto Death*, Princeton, New Jersey: Princeton University Press 1941, p. 29. The Hong and Hong translation reads: "to be that self that he is in truth." *SKS* 11, 136 / *SUD*, 20. As Robert Perkins summarizes, "Kierkegaard's view of the self has been one of his most fruitful ideas in the areas of psychotherapy and counseling, *The Sickness unto Death* frequently being read. The wealth of comment on Kierkegaard by practitioners and scholars in these areas is pertinent and perceptive." See Robert L. Perkins, "Introduction," in *The Sickness unto Death*, ed. by Robert L. Perkins, Macon, Georgia: Mercer University Press 1987 (*International Kierkegaard Commentary*, vol. 19), p. 3. Charles Carr claimed in 1973 that the "penetrating quality of Kierkegaard's insights into guilt, dread, sin, and despair also render him worthy of recognition as the father of modern therapeutic psychology." Charles Carr, "Kierkegaard: On Guilt," *Journal of Psychology and Theology*, vol. 1, no. 3, p. 16. Carr also asserts that "Kierkegaard was the first to transfer psychology from the physiological laboratory to a truly personal context. He bridged the gap between the psychology of his day which focused primarily on the observation of external phenomena and the application of these techniques to his own self-understanding. Through his writings and self-analysis, Kierkegaard preceded Freud, Jung, and Rogers on subjects such as the unconscious, introversion, and self, ideal-self conflict" (ibid.).

American pragmatist John Dewey (1859–1952). It was during his doctoral research in education that Rogers engaged in what was to become for him a formative child study. Rogers began his clinical work at the Rochester Society for the Prevention of Cruelty to Children, serving as director of the Society in 1930. Between 1935 and 1940 he lectured at the University of Rochester. During this period Rogers wrote his first major work deriving from his experience working with children, *The Clinical Treatment of the Problem Child* (1939).[2]

In 1940 Rogers became a full professor of clinical psychology at Ohio State University, where he wrote *Counseling and Psychotherapy* (1942).[3] In this work, Rogers begins to formulate his most significant contribution to therapeutic practice, suggesting that it is through an inter-personal relationship with an accepting therapist that the client can be best equipped to understanding and resolving their difficulties. In 1945 the unique invitation to establish a new counseling center at the University of Chicago was embraced by Rogers. He remained professor of psychology from 1945 to 1957, conducting numerous studies in the center, continually assessing, as scientifically as possible, the efficacy of his clinical practices. Many of the findings of these studies were crystallized in Rogers' major 1951 work *Client-Centered Therapy*[4] and his subsequent *Psychotherapy and Personality Change* (1954).[5] Rogers summarized his approach at this innovative period with the reflection that "I have come to trust the capacity of persons to explore and understand themselves and their troubles, and to resolve those problems, in any close, continuing relationship where I can provide a climate of real change and understanding."[6] This trust was even extended to his academic colleagues ("Authority has been given to me, and I am going to give it to them"),[7] and also to his students: "I am going to experiment with putting trust in students, in class groups, to choose their own directions and to evaluate their progress in terms of their own choosing."[8]

After 12 years of formative work at the University of Chicago, Rogers was appointed to a teaching position at the University of Wisconsin in 1957. However, the return to his alma mater also coincided with a time of internal conflicts and tensions within the Department of Psychology. Rogers became increasingly disillusioned by the frictions of higher education and even the efficacy of teaching itself.[9] Despite this

---

[2]   Carl R. Rogers, *The Clinical Treatment of the Problem Child*, London: Allen & Unwin 1939.

[3]   Carl R. Rogers, *Counseling and Psychotherapy: Newer Concepts in Practice*, Boston: Houghton Mifflin and Co. 1942.

[4]   Carl R. Rogers, *Client-Centered Therapy*, Boston: Houghton Mifflin and Co. 1951.

[5]   Carl R. Rogers, *Psychotherapy and Personality Change*, Chicago: University of Chicago Press 1954.

[6]   Carl R. Rogers, "My Philosophy of Interpersonal Relationships and How It Grew," *Journal of Humanistic Psychology*, vol. 13, no. 2, 1973, p. 13 (reprinted in his *A Way of Being*, Boston: Houghton Mifflin and Co. 1995, p. 38).

[7]   Ibid.

[8]   Ibid.

[9]   See further Carl R. Rogers, "Personal Thoughts on Teaching and Learning," *Merrill-Palmer Quarterly*, vol. 3, 1957, pp. 241–3 (reprinted in his *On Becoming a Person: A Therapist's View of Psychotherapy*, London: Constable 1967 [1961], pp. 273–8).

disenchantment, Rogers produced one of his most renowned works, a collection of essays under the pithy title *On Becoming a Person* (1961).[10] Rogers remained in his position until 1963, when he was contented to accept a resident research position at the Western Behavioral Studies Institute (WBSI) in La Jolla, California. In 1968, he and several colleagues left WBSI to form the Center for Studies of the Person (CSP). Carl Rogers remained a resident of La Jolla for the rest of his life, practicing therapy, writing, and delivering speeches, and travelling widely until his sudden death in 1987. Word of his nomination for the Nobel Peace Prize arrived shortly afterwards.

Rogers was the innovator of a new theoretical approach in psychology which he successfully developed into the foundation of a system of psychotherapy. This approach came to be known as an influential form of "person-centered" therapy which today is one of the most widely disseminated practices in Anglo-American psychotherapy and counseling. Rogers had initially identified his approach as "non-directive," referring to the manner in which the therapist would seek not to direct or guide the "client" (rather than "patient") through the therapeutic process. Such a stance of non-direction signified a departure from the implicit, or sometimes far too explicit, dynamics of power, expertise, and authority which Rogers believed to be excessively—even detrimentally so—prominent within therapeutic relationships. By contrast to a more typically Freudian approach, Rogers developed his "non-directive" stance into what he came to refer to as a "client-centered" therapy: a therapeutic relationship in which the *relationality* between therapist and "client" is emphasized, as an alternative to the hierarchical binary of therapist and "patient." Rogers later supplemented "client" with "person," thereby rendering more explicit his desire to situate the interpersonal at the heart of the therapeutic relationship. The patient may well be a client, insofar as a therapeutic contract of goals, outcome, boundaries, and expectations is negotiated (one which exceeds the reductive dynamic of "therapist-patient"), but the therapy itself is established upon the recognition that engagement is *person-to-person*.

This empathic approach, established upon a refusal to identify the patient as object, has gained significant credence over the years. However, Rogers himself encountered serious opposition from the disciplines of medicine and psychiatry. In fact, as Irvin D. Yalom explains, "these were once such novel ideas that Rogers had to bludgeon the profession to take note of them."[11] In concordance with Kierkegaard's emphasis upon subjectivity, Rogers esteemed the therapeutic value of human insight and will over the medicalization of the patient *mit Pulver und mit Pillen* (with powder and with pills).[12] For many, Rogers' controversial emphasis upon human choice placed him more within the genealogy of humanist existentialism than Freudian psychoanalysis:

> Rogers often spoke of his belief in the existence of a formative impulse (counterbalancing an entropic force) in all organic life. In his belief in an actualizing tendency he joined the ranks of a skein of humanistic thinkers like Nietzsche, Kierkegaard, Adler, Goldstein,

---

10   Carl R. Rogers, *On Becoming a Person: A Therapist's View of Psychotherapy*, London: Constable 1961.

11   Irvin D. Yalom, "Introduction," in Rogers, *A Way of Being*, p. x.

12   *SKS* 4, 413 / *CA*, 121.

Maslow, and Horney, who believed in the existence within each individual of a vast potential for self-understanding and personal change.[13]

It is this privileging of the interpersonal therapeutic relationship that provides the most fertile line of exploration for this essay, since it is through this dynamic that Rogers' Kierkegaardian maxim can be most authentically realized: "to be that self which one truly is."[14]

II. Rogers' Recognition of Kierkegaard: "A home-grown brand of existentialism"

Rogers' own output was prolific and testament to an energy and focus which continued unabated into his eighties. Working tirelessly, he authored or co-authored around twenty books and over two hundred articles. Along with Rollo May, whom Rogers referred to as "the leading scholar of humanistic psychology,"[15] Rogers nurtured the humanistic approach to therapy—though May made more explicit recourse to philosophy, and Rogers to empirical research.[16] Rogers regarded scholarly learning ("the printed page") as "much further down the scale" of the sources of his learnings (below both "Clients and Group Participants" as well as "Younger Colleagues"). "Reading, I fear, has most of its value for me in buttressing my views," Rogers reflects. "I realize I am not a scholar, gaining my ideas from the writings of others."[17] However, there are a few notable exceptions who managed to draw Rogers out beyond himself—albeit by initially corroborating that which he already thought to be true. "Occasionally, however, a book not only confirms me in what I am tentatively thinking, but lures me considerably further. Søren Kierkegaard, Martin Buber, and Michael Polanyi, for example, would fall into that category."[18]

It is notable that Kierkegaard is the first in Rogers' rarified shortlist. Buber was known to Rogers through his writings, but also personally, to the extent that dialogue between the two is a matter of record.[19] The same is true of the polymathic Michael

---

[13]   Yalom, "Introduction," in Rogers, *A Way of Being*, p. xi.

[14]   Rogers, "What It Means to Become a Person," in *The Self*, ed. by C.E. Moustakas, [New York]: Harper and Brothers 1956, p. 197 (in *On Becoming a Person*, p. 110).

[15]   Carl R. Rogers, "Notes on Rollo May," *Perspectives*, Humanistic Psychology Institute, vol. 2, no. 1, 1981 (special number on Rollo May), p. 1 (reprinted in *Carl Rogers—Dialogues: Conversations with Martin Buber, Paul Tillich, B.F. Skinner, Gregory Bateson, Michael Polanyi, Rollo May, and others*, ed. by Howard Kirschenbaum and Valerie Land Henderson, London: Constable 1989, p. 237). May studied under Paul Tillich at the Union Theological Seminary in New York in the 1930s, and himself became a "scholar" of Nietzsche, Camus, and Kierkegaard. See further Poul Houe's article on Rollo May in the present volume.

[16]   Yalom, "Introduction," in Rogers, *A Way of Being*, p. x.

[17]   Carl R. Rogers, "In Retrospect: Forty-Six Years," *American Psychologist*, vol. 29, no. 2, 1974, pp. 115–23, see p. 121 (in *A Way of Being*, p. 63).

[18]   Rogers, "In Retrospect: Forty-Six Years," p. 121 (in *A Way of Being*, p. 63).

[19]   Rogers and Buber's recorded dialogue does not explicitly mention Kierkegaard however. They do discuss one another's work but not the work of one of their greatest mutual influences (the same is true with Tillich, even though the themes of the demonic, forgiveness and self-acceptance which they discuss are evidently indebted to Kierkegaard). This is a

Polanyi (1891–1976).[20] In fact, Rogers is recorded in dialogue with a number of notable contemporaries who have significant debts to Kierkegaard.[21] But here Rogers by-passes the likes of Tillich[22] and privileges Kierkegaard, with whom, of course, it was not possible to experience a dialogue in the embodied interpersonal sense.

For Rogers, scholarship was as much a question of the accidental as the avid pursuit of lines of research. "I must confess that when I wish to be scholarly, serendipity plays a very important part. Serendipity, in case you have forgotten, is 'the faculty of making fortunate and unexpected discoveries by accident.' "[23] It was at the University of Chicago that Rogers became more acquainted with some of the philosophical sources who had also informed Rollo May.[24] The enormous trust that Rogers placed in his students was reciprocated as they in turn recommended Buber and Kierkegaard to him. Rogers acceded to their urging and found that both thinkers confirmed much of his thinking. It was through this that Rogers came to recognize his thought as what he called "a home-grown brand of existentialism."[25]

Indeed, the parallels do not end there. When referring to the ambivalence of academic psychology towards his own position, Rogers describes how he was regarded as a "gadfly" or "respected gadfly": a term that endeared Rogers to his outsider situation—like that of Socrates and Kierkegaard—on the peripheries of mainstream thought.[26] A superficial search encompassing Rogers and Kierkegaard

---

frustrating omission given Buber's critique of Kierkegaard's individualism and Rogers' esteem for Buber's dialogical "I–Thou" principle. See Rob Anderson and Kenneth N. Cissna, *The Martin Buber–Carl Rogers Dialogue: A New Transcript with Commentary*, Albany, New York: State University of New York Press 1997.

[20]   See, for example, "Michael Polanyi and Carl Rogers: A Dialogue." Recorded at KPBS television, San Diego, California, March 5, 1966, and published in *Man and the Science of Man*, ed. by William R. Coulson and Carl R. Rogers, Columbus, Ohio: Charles E. Merrill Publishing 1968, pp. 193–201.

[21]   See, for example, *Carl Rogers—Dialogues*.

[22]   Rogers and Tillich do not, however, discuss Kierkegaard in their dialogue—though they do refer to Augustine and Sartre. See further, "Paul Tillich and Carl Rogers: A Dialogue," *Pastoral Psychology*, vol. 19, no. 2, 1968, pp. 55–64.

[23]   Rogers, "In Retrospect: Forty-Six Years," p. 121 (in *A Way of Being*, p. 64).

[24]   See Rogers, "My Philosophy of Interpersonal Relationships and How It Grew," *Journal of Humanistic Psychology*, 1973, vol. 13, no. 2, pp. 3–15 (in *A Way of Being*, pp. 38–9): "Chicago was a time of great learning for me....By 1957 I had developed a rigorous theory of therapy and the therapeutic relationship. I had set forth the 'necessary and sufficient conditions of therapeutic personality change' [Rogers, "The necessary and sufficient conditions of therapeutic personality change," *Journal of Consulting Psychology*, vol. 21, 1957, pp. 95–103], all of them personal attitudes, *not* professional training. This was a rather presumptuous paper, but it presented hypotheses (38) to be tested and sparked much research over the next fifteen years, which has in general been confirming."

[25]   Carl R. Rogers, "My Philosophy of Interpersonal Relationships and How It Grew," in *Journal of Humanistic Psychology*, vol. 13, no. 2, 1973, p. 13 (in *A Way of Being*, p. 39): "It was a period when, at the urging of my students, I became acquainted with Martin Buber (first in his writings and then personally) and with Søren Kierkegaard. I felt greatly supported in my new approach, which I found to my surprise was a home-grown brand of existentialism."

[26]   Rogers, "In Retrospect: Forty-Six Years," p. 117 (*A Way of Being*, p. 53).

will quickly reveal the assumption that both were in some sense "humanistic psychologists," each committed to the liberation of the self from the dehumanizing intellectual practices of modernity. However, when searching for secondary literature on this relation, one can find several passing references to Kierkegaard's importance for Rogers, but nothing of sustained depth.[27] The extent and detail of Rogers' debt to Kierkegaard remains opaque, thanks in no small part to Rogers himself.

However, the explicit references to Kierkegaard within Rogers' works give at least a glimpse of the depths of his indebtedness. For example, in a controversial statement on "student-centred learning," "Personal Thoughts on Teaching and Learning"—"[o]ne of the earliest and most important of Rogers' statements on education"[28]—Rogers refers only once to another writer: Kierkegaard. As Paul Maharg maintains:

> It is significant that the only reference Rogers makes to another author is to Søren Kierkegaard: what Rogers gives us is in one sense an existential view of education, one which relies heavily on his firmly held view that teachers and therapists achieve most when they are attentive, as facilitators, to the learning experience, rather than overt teachers.[29]

Rogers included this short piece in 1961's *On Becoming a Person*, describing in the new preface how at the time of deliberating the content of his lecture he "immersed [himself] in the writings of Søren Kierkegaard."[30] Rogers reflected that "I am sure that his willingness to call a spade a spade influenced me more than I realized."[31] When this essay was again republished in Rogers' 1969 collection, *Freedom to Learn*, Rogers again commented that "[i]f the style, and the attempt to be as honest as possible, smacks of Kierkegaard, this is not a coincidence. I had spent much of

---

27   Rodriguez J. Alvarez and Silva S. Alvarez, "Sören Kierkegaard, Carl Rogers y la relación terapéutica," (Sören Kierkegaard, Carl Rogers and Therapeutic Relation), *Anales de psiquiatria*, vol. 18, no. 8, 2002, pp. 375–7, is possibly one notable, if rather brief, exception. The authors "conclude that the Danish philosopher already advances the main features that will appear one hundred years later in Carl Rogers' papers, defining the therapeutic relation" (p. 375). However, while features of Rogers' approach may have been anticipated by Kierkegaard, many of the incompatibilities and disparities—particularly those which are theologically grounded—tend to remain under-acknowledged.

28   Paul Maharg, "Rogers, Constructivism and Jurisprudence: Educational Critique and the Legal Curriculum," *International Journal of the Legal Profession*, vol. 7, no. 3, 2000, p. 189: "First delivered in 1952 at a conference in Harvard during a session on 'Classroom Approaches to Influencing Human Behavior,' and widely circulated, then published in 1957, this controversial piece was extensively re-published."

29   Maharg, "Rogers, Constructivism and Jurisprudence: Educational Critique and the Legal Curriculum," p. 193.

30   Rogers, "Personal Thoughts on Teaching and Learning," p. 241 (in *On Becoming a Person*, p. 273).

31   Ibid.

my time on this trip [to Mexico, where the paper was written] reading, digesting and appreciating his work."[32]

However, despite his reflections on his immersion in Kierkegaard, Rogers' retrospective avowal of Kierkegaard's influence is not matched by direct documentation or referencing of Kierkegaard's work. Nonetheless when it comes to articulating the crucial distinction between "the teacher" and "the learner" in this work it becomes obvious that Rogers has *Philosophical Fragments* in mind. Much to the consternation of his audience, however, Rogers delivered a surprisingly disillusioned assessment of teaching and learning. "*My experience has been that I cannot teach another person how to teach. To attempt it is for me, in the long run, futile.*"[33] Given the pertinence of Rogers' work to perspectives on "student-centered learning" this was not at all what his audience were expecting. And yet, when he confesses that "I have come to feel that the only learning which significantly influences behavior is self-discovered, self-appropriated learning,"[34] Rogers invokes the name and motifs of Kierkegaard:

> *Such self-discovered learning, truth that has been personally appropriated and assimilated in experience, cannot be directly communicated to the other.* As soon as an individual tries to communicate such experience directly, often with quite natural enthusiasm, it becomes teaching, and its results are inconsequential. It was some relief recently to discover that Søren Kierkegaard, the Danish philosopher, had found this too, in his own experience, and stated it very clearly a century ago. It made it seem less absurd.[35]

This statement typifies Rogers' overall approach to receiving Kierkegaard. Kierkegaard is read as an antecedent thinker who anticipates and therefore confirms that which Rogers has discovered for himself. As shall be elucidated further below, while this connectivity creates fertile ground for the generation of synchronicity, it is not without its problems. In the above statement, Rogers has clearly recognized the Kierkegaardian relation between learning and self-discovery, the need for personal appropriation: for Truth as subjectivity. He also identifies the impossibility of "direct communication" of such truth. But Rogers has only acknowledged that which he believes himself and Kierkegaard to have mutually recognized. The notion of "self-discovered learning" operates within the Socratic paradigm of subjectivity: a paradigm which for Kierkegaard is described as ultimately *provisional*.[36] Rogers

---

[32]   Carl R. Rogers, *Freedom to Learn: A View of What Education Might Become*, Columbus, Ohio: Charles E. Merrill Publishing 1969, p. 151.

[33]   Rogers, "Personal Thoughts on Teaching and Learning," p. 242 (in *On Becoming a Person*, p. 276).

[34]   Ibid.

[35]   Ibid. (emphasis original).

[36]   *SKS* 24, 425, NB24:159 / *JP* 4, 3902: "Paganism required: Know yourself. Christianity declares: No, that is provisional—know yourself—and look at yourself in the mirror of the Word in order to know yourself properly. No true self knowledge without God knowledge or before God. To stand before the mirror means to stand before God."

fails, or refuses to contrast this with the truth that can only be received in relation to the revelation of "the god" who *is* the truth.[37]

In the Socratic model of learning, the teacher becomes essentially incidental to the *maieutic* delivery of truth. But when it comes to therapeutic practice Rogers wishes to place the therapeutic *relation* between therapist and client at the center of his psychological framework. In this sense, the *maieutic* practice of therapy is one in which the therapist seeks to indirectly awaken and deliver the client of a self-appropriated truth: a truth that can only be realized through the heightened experience of subjectivity. Rogers explains this difference more clearly in another essay in which he again avows his debt to Kierkegaard, "Person or Science? A Philosophical Question":

> But in the significant learning which takes place in therapy, one person *cannot* teach another. The teaching would destroy the learning.[38] Thus I might teach a client that it is safe for him to be himself, that freely to realize his feelings is not dangerous, etc. The more he learned this, the less he would have learned it in the significant, experiential, self-appropriating way. Kierkegaard regards this latter type of learning as true subjectivity, and makes the valid point that there can be no direct communication of it, or even about it. The most that one person can do to further it in another is to create certain conditions which make this type of learning *possible*. It cannot be compelled.[39]

The Rogerian model certainly resonates with a Kierkegaardian notion of subjectivity; however, as shall be explored further below, Rogers is not especially interested in remaining faithful to the essentially theological spirit of Kierkegaard.

Despite this, the most valorized acknowledgement of Kierkegaard also appears in Rogers' 1961 collection of essays *On Becoming a Person*. In "What It Means to Become a Person," originally given as a talk to a meeting at Oberlin College in 1954, Rogers describes "the process of becoming" as involving a need for "getting behind the mask."[40] For a person unwilling to become himself a mask can be

> [a] façade, a front, behind which he has been hiding. He discovers how much of his life is guided by what he thinks he *should* be, not by what he is. Often he discovers that he exists only in response to the demands of others, that he seems to have no self of his own, that he is only trying to think, and feel, and behave in the way that others believe he ought to think and feel and behave.[41]

Such a critique of inauthenticity could easily be traced from Judge William's admonishment of the young seducer A in *Either/Or*.[42] And yet, though he does not

---

[37]   *SKS* 4, 246ff. / *PF*, 59ff.
[38]   See, for example, *SKS* 4, 236 / *PF*, 30.
[39]   Carl R. Rogers, "Person or Science? A Philosophical Question," *American Psychologist*, vol. 10, no. 7, 1955, pp. 267–78, see p. 269 (in *On Becoming a Person*, pp. 204–5).
[40]   Rogers, "What It Means to Become a Person," p. 198 (in *On Becoming a Person*, p. 110).
[41]   Ibid.
[42]   For example, *SKS* 3, 190ff. / *EO2*, 196ff.

invoke it by name, Rogers is clearly more conscious of the anatomy of despair outlined in *The Sickness unto Death*:

> In this connection I have been astonished to find how accurately the Danish philosopher, Søren Kierkegaard, pictured the dilemma of the individual more than a century ago, with keen psychological insight. He points out that the most common despair is to be in despair at not choosing, or willing, to be oneself; but that the deepest form of despair is to choose "to be another than himself." On the other hand "to will to be that self which one truly is, is indeed the opposite of despair," and this choice is the deepest responsibility of man.[43]

Indeed, such is Rogers' esteem for Kierkegaard's insight into the relation between freedom and the self that he continues with the remark: "As I read some of his writings I almost feel that he must have listened in on the statements made by our clients as they search and explore for the reality of the self—often a painful and troubling search."[44]

This valorization of Kierkegaard the psychologist reaches its most explicit zenith in his famous 1957 lecture at Wooster College, Ohio, " 'To Be That Self Which One Truly Is': A Therapist's View of Personal Goals." Rogers prefaces the version of this lecture which appears in *On Becoming a Person* with a personal defense of philosophy's pertinence to psychology.[45] Here Rogers proposes a somewhat perennialist view of philosophical truth "and the existential quality of satisfying living, a theme presented by some of our most modern philosophers, which was however beautifully expressed more than twenty-five centuries ago by Lao-tzu, when he said, "The way to do is to *be*." '[46] As shall be discussed to some extent below, such perennialism raises significant problems for Rogers' reception of Kierkegaard, particularly with regard to Rogers' translation of Kierkegaard's avowedly *Christian* psychology into an existential humanism. Nonetheless, Rogers' reading of Kierkegaard as a respondent to the inherent questions "What is my goal in life?," "What am I striving for?," "What is my purpose?" certainly broadens the accessibility of Kierkegaard's thought, thereby rendering him pertinent and intelligible to a wider and existentially engaged audience:

> Indeed the opening phrase in the title I have chosen for this paper is taken from the writings of a man who wrestled with these questions more than a century ago…as I have worked for many years with troubled and maladjusted individuals I believe that I can

---

[43]   Rogers, "What It Means to Become a Person," p. 198 (in *On Becoming a Person*, p. 110).

[44]   Ibid.

[45]   Carl R. Rogers, " 'To Be That Self Which One Truly Is': A Therapist's View of Personal Goals," in *On Becoming a Person*, p. 163: "In these days most psychologists regard it as an insult if they are accused of philosophical thoughts. I do not share this reaction. I cannot help but puzzle over the meaning of what I observe. Some of these meanings seem to have exciting implications for the modern world."

[46]   Ibid., pp. 163–4.

discern a pattern, a trend, a commonality, an orderliness, in the tentative answers to these questions which they have found for themselves.[47]

Rogers later reiterates that "[a]s I watch person after person struggle in his therapy hours to find a way of life for himself, there seems to be a general pattern emerging.... The best way I can state this aim of life, as I see it coming to light in my relationship with my clients, is to use the words of Søren Kierkegaard—'to be that self which one truly is.' "[48]

Rogers devotes the rest of this important lecture to an explication of the meaning of this maxim; but exact references to Kierkegaard's works are virtually absent. Kierkegaard is generally allowed to saturate and synchronize the text without much specificity. The only other exception to this is a citation from the *Concluding Unscientific Postscript* which is invoked to describe the positive moment when the client moves towards a recognition of their "move toward more openly being a process, a fluidity, a changing"[49]:

> He is beginning to appreciate himself as a fluid process, at first in the therapy hour, but later he will find this true in his life. I cannot help but be reminded of Kierkegaard's description of an individual who really exists. "An existing individual is constantly in process of becoming...and translates all his thinking into terms of process. It is with (him)...as it is with a writer and his style; for he only has a style who never has anything finished, but he 'moves the waters of the language' every time he begins, so that the most common expression comes into being for him with the freshness of a new birth." I find this catches excellently the direction in which clients move, toward being a process of potentialities being born, rather than being or becoming some fixed goal.[50]

Rogers concludes that "to be that self which one truly is," while therapeutically and existentially desirable, is "not an easy direction to move, nor one which is ever completed. It is a continuing way of life."[51] But Rogers' stance is not reducible to the rhetoric of existential philosophy. He also remains an empirical scientist: an ambivalence which he seeks to address in a paper also included in *On Becoming a Person*, titled "Person or Science? A Philosophical Question." In his retrospective preface, Rogers perceives "a growing puzzlement and conflict within myself"[52]:

---

[47]   Ibid., p. 164.

[48]   Ibid., p. 166.

[49]   Rogers, " 'To Be That Self Which One Truly Is': A Therapist's View of Personal Goals," p. 171.

[50]   Rogers, " 'To Be That Self Which One Truly Is': A Therapist's View of Personal Goals," pp. 171–2. Again this is Walter Lowrie's translation, *Concluding Unscientific Postscript*, Princeton, New Jersey: Princeton University Press 1941, p. 79. See *SKS* 7, 114 / *CUP1*, 86.

[51]   Rogers, " 'To Be That Self Which One Truly Is': A Therapist's View of Personal Goals," p. 181.

[52]   Rogers, "Person or Science? A Philosophical Question," p. 267 (in *On Becoming a Person*, p. 199). The preface from the version of the paper in *American Psychologist* differs from that in *On Becoming a Person* and does not mention Kierkegaard. However, I have provided page references for comparison.

As I look back on it I can recognize the origin of the conflict. It was between the logical positivism in which I was educated, for which I had deep respect, and the subjectively oriented existential thinking which was taking root in me because it seemed to fit so well with my therapeutic experience.[53]

Rogers confirms that "I am not a student of existential philosophy,"[54] and reiterates how he first made the acquaintance of Kierkegaard and Martin Buber "at the insistence of some of the theological students who were taking work with me. They were sure that I would find the thinking of these men congenial, and in this they were largely correct."[55] And yet, while saying nothing further on Buber (to whom he also refers in the preceding paper), Rogers continues to describe a little more about his ambivalence and his debt to Kierkegaard:

While there is much in Kierkegaard, for example, to which I respond not at all, there are, every now and then, deep insights and convictions which beautifully express views I have held but never been able to formulate. Though Kierkegaard lived one hundred years ago, I cannot but regard him as a sensitive and highly perceptive friend. I think this paper shows my indebtedness to him, mostly in the fact that reading his work loosened me up and made me more willing to trust and express my own experience.[56]

This is the most crystallized formulation of his relation to Kierkegaard which Rogers offers us. There is much in Kierkegaard, Rogers reveals, "to which I respond not at all" (I shall explore this below). And yet he is "a sensitive and highly perceptive friend," who above all "loosened me up and made me more willing to trust and express my own experience." In other words, Rogers is fairly honest about the fact that there are significant amounts of Kierkegaard that do not speak to him; and yet what does speak to him is that which he recognizes as already within himself—if not yet fully articulated. As such, I will suggest below that Rogers' relationship to Kierkegaard gives more recognition to the Socratic elements than to the explicitly and inexorably Christian relation between the learner and the teacher.

III. The Transparent Self

Perhaps Rogers' direct but succinct statements on Kierkegaard deliver the first and final word on all discussion of influence: it is vast, deep-seated, but ultimately too general, diffuse, or even saturating to warrant further exploration. Kierkegaard is for Rogers a debt that cannot be fully expressed because his heritage pervades and corroborates so much of the latter's view. As such, it is not the purpose of this article to speculate *ad infinitum* about the possible Kierkegaardian links, traces, and genealogies of Rogers' theory. I will here in conclusion—and hopefully in

---

[53]   Ibid.
[54]   Rogers, "Person or Science? A Philosophical Question," p. 267 (in *On Becoming a Person*, pp. 199–200).
[55]   Ibid.
[56]   Ibid.

provocation of new and deeper lines of enquiry—offer an interpretation of a central aspect of Rogers' reception of Kierkegaard: the question of becoming a self.

In general, Kierkegaard confirms or provides synchronicity for what Rogers already knows or has observed for himself in the therapeutic relationship. And this is both the strength and the weakness of Rogers' appropriation. That which Rogers does not respond to within Kierkegaard is not explored by him but is merely allowed to remain unacknowledged, a silent lacuna in Rogers' reception of "the Danish philosopher." However, by acknowledging key notions in Kierkegaard's writings which Rogers does not, I believe that we can move towards a clearer sense of this appropriation.

From the experientialist perspective, Rogers identified the dangers to authentic selfhood inherent in science's tendency to transform the person into its object. There is a risk "that a developing social science (as now conceived and pursued) leads to a social dictatorship and individual loss of personhood. The dangers perceived by Kierkegaard a century ago in this respect seem much more real now, with the increase of knowledge, than they could have then."[57] As such, Rogers regards Kierkegaard's as a prophetic voice in the existential dissent and resistance against the dehumanizing and objectifying machinations of science's omniscience. But this is not the only social dimension of Kierkegaard's polemic. His desire to electrify the bourgeois façade of Christendom, to hold up the mirror of authentic Christianity, is not shared or even acknowledged by Rogers. This is, I suggest, because Rogers' concern with the social status of Christianity does not cohere with Kierkegaard's own. Notwithstanding the laborious piety of his upbringing and his renunciation of a desire to pursue ordination, Rogers' concerns become resolutely humanistic, as he explains in dialogue with Paul Tillich:

> I realize very well that I and many other therapists are interested in the kind of issues that involve the religious worker and the theologian, and yet, for myself, I prefer to put my thinking on those issues in humanistic terms, or to attack those ideas through the channels of scientific investigation. I guess I have some real sympathy for the modern view that is sort of symbolized in the phrase that "God is dead"; that is, that religion no longer *does* speak to people in the modern world.[58]

Indeed, Rogers' sympathy with the symbolic maxim that "God is dead" renders his unapologetically unbalanced reception of Kierkegaard far clearer. The "much in Kierkegaard to which I respond not at all" is evidently that which predates the "modern view" symbolized by the death of God.[59] Rogers was happy to appropriate

---

[57]   Rogers, "Person or Science? A Philosophical Question," p. 273 (in *On Becoming a Person*, p. 214).

[58]   Carl R. Rogers, "Paul Tillich," in *Carl Rogers—Dialogues*, p. 72.

[59]   As in dialogue with Tillich so also with the theologian Reinhold Niebuhr (1892–1971), who was Professor of Practical Theology at Union Theological Seminary in New York from 1928 to 1960. Rogers affirms no explicit parallel to the doctrine of sin outlined in Niebuhr's *The Nature and Destiny of Man*, his 1941 Gifford Lectures. This is notable when one considers the Kierkegaardian roots of Niebuhr's psychology of sin. As Walter M. Horton observes, "This analysis [of sin] (surely the definitive statement of Niebuhr's position)

theological interpretations of love,[60] and to acknowledge his esteem for Buber's dialogic principle of "I–Thou" and its pertinence to the therapeutic relationship.[61] However, he is resistant to the more negative theological diagnoses of humanity's inherent sinfulness or fallenness. Rogers remains optimistic about the self's capacity to overcome itself—something which remained problematic to Kierkegaard. Indeed, when considering the objection that "to be that self which one truly is" "would mean to be bad, evil, uncontrolled, destructive,"[62] Rogers is confident that even the most selfish urges can be understood and harmonized within the self.[63] In fact, in potential contrast to Anti-Climacus' diagnosis of "in despair to will to be oneself,"[64] Rogers contends that to be all of oneself "is not synonymous with being evil or uncontrolled. It is instead to feel a growing pride in being a sensitive, realistic, inner-directed member of the human species."[65]

The decisive difference between Rogers and Kierkegaard's physician of the soul, Anti-Climacus,[66] is in their final diagnoses of despair. For Rogers and for Anti-Climacus, the will to be that self which one truly is, is the opposite of despair. In this

---

starts interestingly enough with a psychological insight borrowed from Kierkegaard to whom Carl Rogers, from a different angle, has also acknowledged a great debt." See "Reinhold Niebuhr and Carl R. Rogers. A Discussion by Bernard M. Loomer, Walter M. Horton, and Hans Hofmann," *Pastoral Psychology*, vol. 9, no. 5, 1958, p. 22.

[60]   Carl R. Rogers, "The Interpersonal Relationship: The Core of Guidance," *Harvard Educational Review*, vol. 32, no. 4, 1962, pp. 416–29, see p. 419 (in *A Way of Being*, p. 94): "It means a kind of love for the client as he is, providing we understand the word love as equivalent to the theologian's term *agape*, and not in its usual romantic and possessive meanings."

[61]   Rogers, "Person or Science? A Philosophical Question," p. 268 (in *On Becoming a Person*, p. 202): "In these moments there is, to borrow Buber's phrase, a real 'I–Thou' relationship, a timeless living in the experience which is *between* the client and men. It is at the opposite pole from seeing the client, or myself, as an object. It is the height of personal subjectivity."

[62]   Rogers, " 'To Be That Self Which One Truly Is': A Therapist's View of Personal Goals," p. 177.

[63]   Ibid., p. 178: "Fully to be one's own uniqueness as a human being, is not, in my experience, a process which would be labeled bad. More appropriate words might be that it is a positive, or a constructive, or a realistic, or a trustworthy process."

[64]   *SKS* 11, 181–7 / *SUD*, 67–74.

[65]   Rogers, " 'To Be That Self Which One Truly Is': A Therapist's View of Personal Goals," p. 181.

[66]   In an unused draft of *The Sickness unto Death*, Kierkegaard writes: "It does indeed seem as if the book were written by a physician. But he who is a physician is someone who is no one; he does not say to any single human being: You are sick. Nor does he say it to me; he merely describes the sickness while he at the same time continually defines what 'faith' is…. On the other hand, I do all I can so that I might be the one he means—as if I were the one, the sick person, of whom he speaks—by at least striving to be the one who honestly strives." *Pap.* X-5 B 19 / *SUD*, Supplement, p. 160f. I discuss the relationship between Kierkegaard and Anti-Climacus, as patient and physician of the soul in greater depth in my "Kierkegaard as Physician of the Soul: On Self-Forgiveness & Despair," *Journal of Psychology & Theology*, vol. 37, no. 3, 2009, pp. 174–85. I contend that "by presenting this integrative notion of self-knowledge through the 'higher' Christian pseudonym of Anti-Climacus, Kierkegaard is

there is coherence between the Rogerian and the Anti-Climacean diagnosis of "in despair not to will to be oneself."[67] However, the point of departure can be found in Anti-Climacus' definition of sin as despair: "Sin is: *before God, or with the conception of God, in despair not to will to be oneself, or in despair to will to be oneself.*"[68] Of course, the form of "in despair to will to be oneself" only exists insofar as the relation of the self "before God" exists and exerts primacy. But for Rogers the sense that "God is dead" prevails over any sense of God as the establishing power of selfhood.

The difference between these positions can be further elucidated with reference to the differing functions of the term "transparency" in each psychological structure. For Anti-Climacus, "Faith is: that the self in being itself and in willing to be itself rests transparently [*gjennemsigtigt*—see-through] in God."[69] In this relation, the self opens itself to the divine gaze, becoming "transparent" [*gjennemsigtigt*] and thereby, via a profound movement of resignation, allowing the divine to "illuminate [*gjennemlyse*] him so that he resembles God."[70]

"Transparency" also emerges as an important concept in Rogers' structure; though, while it appears within the context of the Kierkegaardian motto "to be that self which one truly is," there is no explicit ascription of the term to *The Sickness unto Death*. In fact, it becomes clear that it operates within a different dynamic for Rogers' relational self than it does for Anti-Climacus' self before God. Rather than the sick self becoming transparent before God—surrendering itself to the divine—it is the task of the *therapist* to become "transparent" to the client. In this Rogers seeks to subvert the Freudian power dynamics of the psychoanalyst: the one who remains inaccessible to the client, whose insights are hidden behind the veneer of expertise and authority, the other who, in Derridean terms, watches me behind my back.[71] In its place Rogers seeks to bring the therapist into a face-to-face, I–Thou encounter with the client. It is in this open, honest relational space that therapy is encouraged to flourish. It is this which Rogers identifies as "congruence"—as opposed to the "incongruous" and discrepant relationship between "analyst" and "patient." This congruence is essentially characterized by the *transparency*, rather than the heteronomous detachment, of the therapist:

> I have sometimes thought that the word transparency helps to describe this element of personal congruence. If everything going on in me which is relevant to the relationship can be seen by my client, if he can see "clear through me," and if I am *willing* for this realness to show through in the relationship, then I can be almost certain that this will be a meaningful encounter in which we both learn and develop.[72]

---

indicting his own resistances to accepting divine forgiveness and thereby operating—via a 'higher' pastoral identity—as a physician to his own soul" (p. 174).

[67]   *SKS* 11, 164–81 / *SUD*, 49–67.

[68]   *SKS* 11, 191 / *SUD*, 77.

[69]   *SKS* 11, 197 / *SUD*, 82.

[70]   *SKS* 5, 380 / *EUD*, 399.

[71]   Jacques Derrida, *The Gift of Death*, trans. by David Wills, Chicago and London: University of Chicago Press 1996, p. 91.

[72]   Carl R. Rogers, "The Interpersonal Relationship: The Core of Guidance," in Carl R. Rogers and Barry Stevens, *Person to Person: The Problem of Being Human*, London:

When a gap persists between the real self and the ideal self (the "I am" and the "I should"), even in the therapist, an *incongruity* will emerge analogous to Kierkegaardian despair. On the other hand, "congruence" and "transparency" are formative to the "authenticity" of the therapist: the *conditio sine qua non of acceptance and empathy*."[73] This "authenticity" constitutes *the way of communicating between persons where the other is truly acknowledged as an Other (in the sense of encounter philosophy), who is opening up, revealing himself—or herself*."[74] All these notions are epitomized for Rogers by the Kierkegaardian maxim "to be that self which one truly is," in which "self-actualising tendency and actualising tendency coincide. There is congruence between awareness and organism, self and person."[75]

Decisively, however, authenticity, congruence, and transparency are for Rogers derived from self-authorship; whereas for Anti-Climacus the self receives its authenticity from beyond itself: from God, *before God*. Becoming transparent before God thus constitutes a self-negation, a death to self in which the self is delivered from the despair of the sickness unto death. Whereas for Rogers the transparency of the therapist is a relational attitude of openness towards the client, renouncing the power dynamic of the analyst; for Anti-Climacus transparency is not primarily a self-revelation to another self, but a disavowal of "the self which in despair wills to be itself" before the gaze of a Holy Other God, whose knowledge of the self necessarily exceeds the noetic capacities of the subject. The self is revealed to itself by an Other who transcends and yet is intimately bound up with it.

The decisive point of divergence is, inevitably, a theological one, namely, sin and forgiveness, *both* of which are expressions of the "infinite qualitative difference" between the self and God.[76] Rogers advocates the therapeutic movement towards self-acceptance as a necessary and integral moment in becoming that self which one truly is.[77] As observed previously, Rogers effectively rejects the theological idiom

---

Souvenir Press 1973, p. 92. Contrast also with Kierkegaard's veiling of himself behind the higher pseudonym of Anti-Climacus. See further my "Kierkegaard as Physician of the Soul," p. 177.

[73]   Germain Lietaer, "Being Genuine as a Therapist: Congruence and Transparency," in *Congruence*, ed. by Gill Wyatt, Ross-on-Wye: PCCS Books 2001 (*Rogers' Therapeutic Conditions: Evolution, Theory and Practice*, vol. 1), p. 37.

[74]   Peter F. Schmid, "Authenticity: the Person as His or Her Own Author. Dialogical and Ethical Perspectives on Therapy as an Encounter Relationship. And Beyond," in *Congruence*, ed. by Wyatt, p. 312.

[75]   Ibid., p. 216.

[76]   I explore this dialectical understanding of the infinite qualitative difference further my "The (Im)possibility of Forgiveness," in *Kierkegaard and Christianity*, ed. by Roman Králik et al., Šaľa: Kierkegaard Society in Slovakia et al., 2008 (*Acta Kierkegaardiana*, vol. 3), pp. 117–31.

[77]   Rogers, " 'To Be That Self Which One Truly Is': A Therapist's View of Personal Goals," p. 173: "This does not occur easily. Often as the client senses some new facet of himself, he initially rejects it. Only as he experiences such a hitherto denied aspect of himself in an acceptance climate can he tentatively accept it as part of himself."

of sin which forms such a central part of Anti-Climacus' Christian psychology.[78] For Anti-Climacus, despair is sin and as such can only be fully overcome by the acceptance of forgiveness—provided that the self does not despair *over* or *of* the forgiveness of sins.[79] The self must accept the forgiveness which comes to itself as a gift from God: a God whose capacity to forgive and accept *infinitely* exceeds the self's capacity for self-acceptance (or even the therapist's capacity for acceptance of the client for that matter). In this respect, a further contrast emerges between Rogers' notion of the transparent therapist and Anti-Climacus' vision of the self before God. Roger's therapist Socratically, incidentally, and indirectly seeks to "deliver" the client of the truth of self-acceptance, Anti-Climacus' self before God, on the other hand, is revealed to itself, and becomes *transparent*, through its relation to the Teacher who *is* the Truth. From the Kierkegaardian perspective, therefore, one may wish to ask whether a deeper self-acceptance can derive its basis from the authenticity of the therapist. Or does this once again return us to a therapeutic power-dynamic implicitly dependent upon the therapist's capacity to elicit self-knowledge? Does the sickness of the self as despair (sin) require an infinitely different physician of the soul?

This variance becomes clearer when Rogers' Kierkegaardian maxim is revisited in its entirety. "To be that self which one truly is" is merely a fragment of a wider sentence which reveals those theological commitments of Anti-Climacus which Rogers allows to dissolve away. The full sentence reads: "The self that he despairingly wants to be is a self that he is not (for *to will to be the self that he is in truth* is the very opposite of despair), that is, he wants to tear himself away from the power that established it."[80] The key divergences reside in the notions of *truth* and *the Power that established* the self (Lowrie's translation capitalizes "Power" thus rendering it even more dominant).

For Rogers, the truth of the self is a question of its authenticity, its self-authorship, and self-reflected knowledge of itself, drawn out (Socratically and indirectly) through the relation with the transparent therapist. Ultimately for Kierkegaard, such self-reflection is provisional. If there were no establishing power—and for Rogers "God is dead"—then there can only be "despair *not* to will to be oneself." But since for Anti-Climacus there *is* a power that establishes the self, the possibility of an *inauthentic* self arises: a self which seeks to derive itself apart from the relation to God. The self in truth, for Anti-Climacus, is a self which relates itself to itself through the power (the Absolute Truth) which establishes it. In other words, the self that wills to become "authentic" through becoming "transparent" *before God*. From this relation the self receives itself as the gift of divine acceptance: an acceptance which is infinitely greater even than the self's capacity to accept itself.

---

[78] It is interesting to note that in his dialogue with Rogers, Paul Tillich, in advocating "the courage to accept acceptance," disavows the theological language of "fallen" or "sinful men," even when referring to "the demonic." See Rogers, "Paul Tillich," p. 69.

[79] *SKS* 11, 223 / *SUD*, 113. Tillich also notes to Rogers that "I have not used often anymore the word 'forgiveness,' because this often produces a bad superiority in him who forgives and the humiliation of him who is forgiven." Rogers, "Paul Tillich," pp. 71–2.

[80] *SKS* 11, 136 / *SUD*, 20 (my emphasis).

Bibliography

I. References to or Uses of Kierkegaard in Rogers' Corpus

"Persons or Science? A Philosophical Question," *American Psychologist*, vol. 10, no. 7, 1955, pp. 267–78 (reprinted in his *On Becoming a Person: A Therapist's View of Psychotherapy*, London: Constable 1967, pp. 199–224).

"What It Means to Become a Person," In *The Self*, ed. by C.E. Moustakas, New York: Harper and Brothers 1956, pp. 195–211 (reprinted in his *On Becoming a Person: A Therapist's View of Psychotherapy*, London: Constable 1967, pp. 107–24).

"Personal Thoughts on Teaching and Learning," *Merrill-Palmer Quarterly*, vol. 3, 1957, pp. 241–3 (reprinted in his *On Becoming a Person: A Therapist's View of Psychotherapy*, London: Constable 1967, pp. 273–8).

"The Interpersonal Relationship: The Core of Guidance," *Harvard Educational Review*, vol. 32, no. 4, 1962, pp. 416–29 (reprinted in Carl R. Rogers and Barry Stevens, *Person to Person: The Problem of Being Human*, London: Souvenir Press 1973, pp. 89–104).

" 'To Be That Self Which One Truly Is': A Therapist's View of Personal Goals," in his *On Becoming a Person: A Therapist's View of Psychotherapy*, London: Constable 1967, pp. 163–82.

Freedom to Learn: A View of What Education Might Become, Columbus, Ohio: Charles E. Merrill Publishing 1969, pp. 151–3.

"My Philosophy of Interpersonal Relationships and How It Grew," *Journal of Humanistic Psychology*, vol. 13, no. 2, 1973, pp. 3–19.

A Way of Being, Boston: Houghton Mifflin 1995, pp. 27–45; pp. 46–69; pp. 113–36.

II. Sources of Roger's Knowledge of Kierkegaard

Buber, Martin, *I and Thou*, trans. by Ronald Gregor Smith, Edinburgh: T. and T. Clark 1937.

Kierkegaard, Søren, *Concluding Unscientific Postscript*, trans. by Walter Lowrie, Princeton, New Jersey: Princeton University Press 1941.

— *Philosophical Fragments*, trans. by Walter Lowrie, Princeton, New Jersey: Princeton University Press 1941.

— *The Sickness unto Death*, trans. by Walter Lowrie, Princeton, New Jersey: Princeton University Press 1941.

May, Rollo, *The Meaning of Anxiety*, revised ed., New York: W.W. Norton 1977 [1950], pp. xiv–xv; p. xxi; p. 15; pp. 20–1; pp. 26–8; pp. 32–51; pp. 58–9; pp. 65–6; p. 99; p. 113; p. 123; p. 125; p. 133; p. 151; p. 158; p. 192; p. 207;

pp. 218–20; p. 229; p. 244; p. 247; p. 265; p. 365; p. 370; p. 376; p. 379; pp. 384–5; p. 390; pp. 392–3.

Niebuhr, Reinhold, *The Nature and Destiny of Man: A Christian Interpretation*, *Vol. 1: Human Nature*, New York: Charles Scribner's Sons 1941, p. 44; p. 75; p. 81; p. 163; pp. 170–1; p. 182; pp. 242–3; p. 245; pp. 251–2; p. 254; p. 263.

— *The Nature and Destiny of Man: A Christian Interpretation*, *Vol. 2: Human Destiny*, New York: Charles Scribner's Sons 1943, p. 38; p. 57; p. 61.

Tillich, Paul, *The Courage to Be*, New Haven, Connecticut: Yale University Press 1952, pp. 125–6; p. 134; p. 137; p. 140.

III. Secondary Literature on Rogers' Relation to Kierkegaard

Alvarez, Rodriguez J. and Silva S. Alvarez, "Sören Kierkegaard, Carl Rogers y la relación terapéutica" (Sören Kierkegaard, Carl Rogers and therapeutic relation), *Anales de psiquiatria*, vol. 18, no. 8, 2002, pp. 375–7.

Carr, C., "Kierkegaard: On Guilt," *Journal of Psychology and Theology*, vol. 1, no. 3, 1973, pp. 15–21.

Maharg, Paul, "Rogers, Constructivism and Jurisprudence: Educational Critique and the Legal Curriculum," *International Journal of the Legal Profession*, vol. 7, no. 3, 2000, pp. 189–204.

Max Weber:

Weber's Existential Choice

Dustin Feddon

In his article on the reception of Kierkegaard in Germany and Austria, Heiko Schulz distinguishes various modes of receptions ranging from productive receptions to unproductive receptions. In what follows, I will place Max Weber's (1864–1920) reception of Kierkegaard under what Schulz termed an "unproductive reception." Schulz describes this form of reception as follows: "author A has evidently been taken note of by author B (be it ever so sporadically or briefly)," and that "this reception has left at best marginal (explicit or implicit) traces in B's writings (of course, such traces can be of the affirmative or of the critical sort)."[1] In the case of Weber's reception, A's writings (that is, Kierkegaard's) are never specifically referenced or used, rather author B (Weber) merely cites Kierkegaard as representative of the conflict between the individual and ethics in his revisions to *The Protestant Ethic and the Spirit of Capitalism* which was reprinted in 1920: "The conflict between the individual and the ethic (in Søren Kierkegaard's sense) did not exist for Calvinism, although it placed the individual entirely on his own responsibility in religious matters."[2] With this one brief remark aside, another quotation may be more promising regarding the extent of Kierkegaard's influence on Weber.

Uncovering any influence Kierkegaard may have had on Weber necessitates that we approach this reception through his friendship with Georg Lukács (1885–1971) just before World War I. The one place we can find a connection between Kierkegaard, Lukács, and Weber is from Lukács' onetime student Ágnes Heller (b. 1929). An obscure footnote in Heller's book *A Theory of Modernity* hints at what may have been a fairly remarkable influence Kierkegaard had on European intelligentsia before the Great War.[3] Heller informs us that she knew "from Lukács'

---

[1] See Heiko Schulz, "Germany and Austria: A Modest Head Start: The German Reception of Kierkegaard," *Kierkegaard's International Reception*, Tome I, *Northern and Western Europe*, ed. by Jon Stewart, Aldershot: Ashgate 2009 (*Kierkegaard Research: Sources, Reception and Resources*, vol. 8), p. 309.

[2] See Max Weber, "Die protestantische Ethik und der 'Geist' des Kapitalismus," in *Gesammelte Aufsätze zur Religionssoziologie*, vols. 1–3, Tübingen: Mohr 1920–21, vol. 1, p. 101. (Originally published in *Archiv für Sozialwissenschaften und Sozialpolitik*, vol. 20, no. 1, 1904, pp. 1–54 and vol. 21, no. 1, 1905, pp. 1–110 (n.b. this passage does not appear in the first printing); English translation: *The Protestant Ethic and the Spirit of Capitalism*, trans. by Talcott Parsons, New York: Charles Scribner's Sons 1958, p. 109.)

[3] See Ágnes Heller, *A Theory of Modernity*, Malden, Massachusetts: Blackwell 1999.

personal communication that Kierkegaard's concept of existential choice was widely discussed in the Weber circle."[4] This statement is a critical clue regarding what Kierkegaard's "existential-choice" meant to Weber and others at a time wrought with ethical, political, and philosophical significance. In his post-World War I essay, "Politics as Vocation," Weber prioritized existential choice as essential to one's ethics, vocation, and political involvement amidst the collapse of Imperial Germany. How people, particularly those seeking a profession in politics, attempted to establish personal values in times of great crisis concerned Weber enough for him to focus on how the modern individual might face human finitude and political uncertainty with some bravado. Charles Turner takes up the possible influence of Kierkegaard on Weber in the following:

> Weber himself employs the term "ethics of conviction" and "ethic of responsibility." But when he does so he writes not as an "ethical rigorist enthusiastic about a formal, abstract freedom" but as one who believes that "every human being, no matter how slightly gifted he is, no matter how subordinate his position may be, has a natural need to formulate a life-view, a conception of the meaning of life and its purpose." These are the words of Kierkegaard, whose influence on Weber remains virtually unexplored but whose formulation of the relationship between the ethical and the continuity of practice and the idea of the total personality, finds its way in Weber's analyses at numerous points.[5]

Weber's emphasis on the formation of a life-view, as Taylor suggests, is made clearer when we consider the Weber–Lukács nexus.

It is well-noted that Lukács was instrumental in the reception of Kierkegaard in the German-speaking world.[6] What is not well-noted is that Lukács' reception brought Kierkegaard to the famed Heidelberg circle, as one of its members, Paul Honigsheim (1885–1963), recalled: "His book on soul and forms (*Die Seele und die Formen*) appeared shortly before he came to Heidelberg and met Max Weber. This is one of the first places Kierkegaard, who was almost completely forgotten, experienced a resurrection."[7] This resurrection took place when many of Europe's renowned theorists weighed issues related to ethical subjectivity as defining one's role in the socio-political realm. The moral crisis over the loss of an evaluative standard for ethical judgments was at the forefront of concern for this circle in the years preceding World War I. Theorists like Weber and Lukács exposed the mechanisms driving culture and its discontents, which they felt were in danger of erasing an ethically engaged populace. Like Weber, who in his *Protestant Ethic* set out to discern equally the influence that religious consciousness and the material causes had on life, culture, and national character, Lukács also shared similar ambitions to

---

4   Ibid., p. 247. This is a footnote to her discussion on Weber's value-spheres. The value-spheres—science, politics, art, religion, law, and economy—are individualized through one choosing oneself as one committed to this or that value-sphere.

5   Charles Turner, *Modernity and Politics in the Works of Max Weber*, London: Routledge 1992, p. 106

6   See Habib C. Malik, *Receiving Søren Kierkegaard*, Washington D.C.: Catholic University of America Press 1997, pp. 354–7.

7   Paul Honigsheim, *On Max Weber*, New York: The Free Press 1968, p. 17.

understand what drives modernity. To make this crisis germane to the reception in question, I will focus on Weber's dichotomy between an ethic of responsibility and an ethic of conviction, since it is here we will see how existential choice directly related to Weber's modern ethic. The ethic of responsibility, for Weber, entails moral conviction about the need for action and decision, yet is cognizant that the ethical subject is ensnared in a world devoid of ultimate meaning. The absence of transcendent values guiding human action renders the individual responsible for taking consequences into consideration before making any judgment. The ethic of conviction is similar to the ethic of responsibility insofar as it views the material world as irrational, but unlike the ethic of responsibility it does not take consequences into consideration in order to determine ethical actions. Rather, it acts from conscience alone, regardless of external factors. While Weber leaned more toward an ethic of responsibility (though he understood the profound conflict between the two), Lukács established an ethic of conviction which is evident from his final essay in what he considered his "Kierkegaard phase": "Why should Goodness concern itself with the consequences?"[8] To get at the role of Kierkegaard's existential choice at this particular point of the resurrection, it will be important to show how Kierkegaard functioned for the early Lukács as one exhibiting the ethic of conviction.[9] If one wants a full account of Weber's existential reading of the ethical dilemma facing his generation, and thus what existential choice might have meant to him, then one should consider what was at stake in his relation to Lukács since both men grappled with the question "On what, or in what way, does one base one's ethical judgment?." Regardless of their clear differences, both Lukács and Weber understood that in an instrumentalist society the one thing remaining entirely unique for the ethical subject was a choice which required the entirety of one's existence. This means that ethical choice reflected people's commitment to their respective life conviction apart from external sources. In this way human existence was redeemed from the perceived demonic forces operative in a bureaucratic age, as it committed itself to acting in a world devoid of ultimate meaning. And so in this way, these two thinkers, who would end up at radically different political positions regarding revolution, democracy, and almost all other political matters facing post-war Europe, shared similar existential, ethical concerns about the fate of the ethical subject.

I. Context

The disenchantment was the sense among some that the state threatened to do nothing less than absolve the citizen from having any positive ethical meaning for society

---

[8]   Georg Lukács, "On Poverty of Spirit," in *The Lukács Reader*, ed. by Arpad Kadarkay, Oxford: Blackwell 1995, p. 45. The German version of this essay, which Weber read, was published as "Von der Armut am Geiste: Ein Gespräch und ein Brief," *Neue Blätter*, no. 2, 1912, pp. 67–92. For Lukács' titling this period of his authorship as his "Kierkegaard phase," see Georg Lukács, *Curriculum Vitae*, ed. by János Ambrus, Budapest: Magvető 1982, p. 12.

[9]   Karl Mannheim, a member of Lukács' circle at the time, listed among their patron saints and ideals: Dostoevsky's concept of life and Kierkegaard's ethical convictions. See *The Lukács Reader*, p. 144.

apart from the instrumentalism extant in the socio-political order: society and state were constructed around rational capitalism and legal-rational concerns relativizing the identity of the self to means-based existence. This was apparent in the context of redefining vocation as externally valued in relation to the elite's interest, rooted in economics and social power, as opposed to the self's own autonomously developed ethical goals. The reduction of vocation to means-based existence troubled many of the thinkers in the Heidelberg circle. This economic-political reduction of vocation troubled Weber to the extent that he wrote in *The Protestant Ethic* that "one's duty in a calling is what is most characteristic of the social ethic of capitalistic culture," and that this calling is present in spite of "whether it appears on the structure as a utilization of his personal powers, or only of his material possessions."[10] The ascetic pursuit of one's calling enabled the subject to base its decisions on something apart from the world of means-based existence. The waning of religion and metaphysics brought to light for those concerned about the hollowing out of ethical subjectivity the need for re-evaluating the sources necessary to ensure moral conviction regarding ethical duties. This led some to create new means in order to give an account of the individual as distinct from the economic-political orders otherwise known as and henceforth termed *Zweckrationalität*.[11]

Lukács' essays "Søren Kierkegaard and Regine Olsen: The Foundering of Form against Life," in his *Soul and Form* and his 1911 (published in German in 1912) essay "On Poverty of Spirit," catapulted him from obscurity in Hungary to an enthused reception among the wider European intelligentsia.[12] His numerous essays written before the War explored various tragic figures in order to realize their alienated existence as sources for ethico-political reflection. These pariahs (mostly poets, mystics, philosophers, and other eccentrics) were ideal *types* for Lukács to observe an ascetic ethic take form in an imperative life-ethics, as they sought their ethic apart from the emerging utilitarian culture. Lukács, in a sense, was in search of his own puritan ethic in order to identify new ethico-political developments on the horizon. Weber also considered aesthetics a field of study to be mined for its socio-

---

[10]   Weber, "Die protestantische Ethik und der 'Geist' des Kapitalismus," in *Gesammelte Aufsätze zur Religionssoziologie*, vol. 1, p. 36. (*The Protestant Ethic and the Spirit of Capitalism*, p. 54.)

[11]   Defined as purpose-rationality.

[12]   György Lukács, "Sören Kierkegaard és Regine Olsen," *Nyugat*, vol. 1, no. 6, 1910, pp. 378–87. (English translation: "Sören Kierkegaard and Regina Olsen: The Foundering of Form against Life," in *Soul and Form*, trans. by Anna Bostock, London: Merlin Press 1974, pp. 28–41; German translation: *Die Seele und die Formen: Essays*, Berlin: Fleischel 1911, pp. 61–91.) The essay was first published in the Hungarian literary periodical, and shortly after in German. Michael Löwy describes the power these German academics possessed in that they "enjoyed an especially privileged social position during the nineteenth century. A relatively homogeneous and well-integrated community, marked by social prestige, influence and status, these 'mandarins' held a dominant position in Germany's system of stratification." Löwy goes on to write that they were the "most prestigious representative of a whole 'cultured elite' stretching into the liberal professions, the bureaucracy, the army, and so on." See Michael Löwy, *Georg Lukács, from Romanticism to Bolshevism*, trans. by Patrick Camiller, London: NLB 1979, pp. 26–8.

political impact. Weber wrote at this time: "The relationship between a religious ethic and art will remain harmonious as far as art is concerned for so long as the creative artist experiences his work as resulting either from a charisma of 'ability' or from spontaneous play...intellectualism and the rationalization of life change this situation."[13] Art has the luxury to have its own ends, without respect to its surrounding instrumentalist society. The "spontaneous play" in art is entirely indifferent to consequences or external evaluations. Weber argued that the increasingly secularized world of *Zweckrationalität* forced ethics, religion, and aesthetics to express their autonomy primarily in intimate spheres of existence rather than those beholden to rationalization. On this point, as we will see, Weber and Lukács agreed. Yet, and this is where these two thinkers will diverge, Lukács remained unconvinced that it was necessary to banish ethics from political existence. For those inclined toward renewing the ethico-political order, the first stage of any revolt required developing a narrative of the collapse of society and its tragic state of alienation, before then signaling how the self could in fact transcend the state through various performances of existential choice: artistic expression, mystical experience, or ethical sacrifice. This would mean rethinking the ethical as religious insofar as it transcended the socio-political realm through forms of self-transcendence and yet also the religious as ethical in its reinscribing the self back to a socio-political existence. For Weber and Lukács the estranged subject was of utmost concern, yet how this subject would reinscribe itself back into the socio-political was where differences between the two would surface.

II. Weber and Lukács in Heidelberg

Before attending to the Heidelberg circle, I should first briefly establish the Lukács reception which preceded the Kierkegaard resurrection Honigsheim mentioned in his reflections on Weber. The essays published in *Soul and Form* tapped into personalized stories of disenchantment which elicited positive reactions among thinkers like Max Weber, Georg Simmel (1858–1918), Ernst Troeltsch (1865–1923), Thomas Mann (1875–1955), and Martin Buber (1878–1965). Troeltsch's letter is the most telling. He wrote to Lukács after reading the essays: "you intended to penetrate contemporary intellectual life and its most significant *types* in order to arrive at your own position in the reigning odd mixture of decay and forward-looking political-economic forces."[14] Troeltsch's response is significant in that he sees the political dimension at play in Lukács' work as one mining these figures for possible political trends in development: namely, proto-revolutionary types. Concerning the genre of

---

[13]   Max Weber, "Zwischenbetrachtung: Theorie der Stufen und Richtungen religiöser Weltablehnung," in *Gesammelte Aufsätze zur Religionssoziologie*, vols. 1–3, Tübingen: J.C.B. Mohr 1920–21, vol. 1, pp. 436–73, see p. 555. (English translation: "Religious Rejections of the World and their Directions," in *From Max Weber*, trans. and ed. by H.H. Gerth and C. Wright Mills, New York: Oxford University Press 1946, pp. 341–2.)

[14]   Letter from Ernst Troeltsch to Lukács on August 1, 1912, in *Georg Lukács Selected Correspondence 1902–1920*, ed. and trans. by Judith Marcus and Zoltán Tar, New York: Columbia University Press 1986, p. 205.

the essay, Margit Koves writes: "The essay brings into play a number of genres like the letter, stories, dialogues, and confessions directed towards modern man who searches for substance."[15] This I believe captures Lukács' essay on Kierkegaard insofar as it lacked any direct exposition of Kierkegaard's life and thought. Rather, Lukács wrote the essay in piecemeal fashion focusing on distinct moments in the relationship between Kierkegaard and Regine Olsen (1822–1904), intermixed with brief excerpts from Kierkegaard's writings, then providing at times his own analysis. This to say the essay is not a systematic reading of Kierkegaard. Again, as Troeltsch's response suggested, Lukács was one searching for possibilities: experiences that might provide political insight for a disenchanted class of aesthetes. Important here is how Kierkegaard is emerging as a type for the intended audience of Lukács' essays: aesthetes who were potential political revolutionaries. In a few short years, as we will see in the Ernst letters, Lukács would begin to make explicit statements regarding the need for revolutionary figures.

When Lukács arrived in Heidelberg in 1912 he had ended his so-called Kierkegaard phase, Weber was drafting his sociology of religion for his compendium *Economy and Society*, and various other notable theorists such as Karl Jaspers (1883–1969) were present in this circle. This particular resurrection of Kierkegaard is best described as taking place when the men of culture abandoned the socio-political realm to "mere" specialists, thus leading those troubled by the bureaucratization of the university to search for heroic existences who established their world-view apart from elite interests: that is, existentially choosing their vocation. In addition to the numerous and disparate avant-garde movements in early twentieth-century Europe, there were rigorous intellectual engagements with the human sciences by poets, mystics, philosophers, artists, and self-proclaimed prophets and Messiahs. For these new types their singular mission was to rebuild Western democratic society under a mythico-religious framework that resembled either past pre-modern societies or new utopian societies on the horizon: to restore a social existence founded upon virtue as opposed to a utilitarian ethic. The Heidelberg circle was known for its interest in religious mysticism, Russian literature, and sundry other neo-Romantic sources, which sought further to understand the evolving disenchantment. The fact that Kierkegaard intrigued this circle speaks to the importance Lukács' appropriation had on the greater Kierkegaard reception.

It is important to pause here to take up the extent to which Weber was likely to have encountered Kierkegaard prior to Lukács. Habib Malik wrote that Weber was probably already familiar with the standard read of Kierkegaard as critic of the State Church.[16] Yet, as Malik points out, his exposure to Kierkegaard, "did not amount to much."[17] Malik situates Weber's early exposure to Kierkegaard at the time when Weber contributed to the periodical *Die Wahrheit*. The periodical was edited by Kierkegaard's future premier German translator, Christoph Schrempf (1860–1944). This is helpful insofar as we know that Weber was at minimum sympathetic to the

---

[15]   Margit Koves, "Anthropology in the Aesthetics of the Young Lukács," *Social Scientist*, vol. 29, nos. 7–8, 2001, pp. 68–81, see p. 73.

[16]   Malik, *Receiving Søren Kierkegaard*, p. 335.

[17]   Ibid.

concerns shared by the avant-garde critics of the State Church, making it likely he was already familiar with Kierkegaard in this capacity. Malik speculates that the reason for the scant attention given to Kierkegaard from theorists like Weber, Tönnies, and Troeltsch during the turn of the century is more than likely the result of staying clear of individualism. Malik's chronicling of Kierkegaard's reception at the turn of the century up to the outbreak of World War I consists more of celebrity sighting—notable poets striving to attain individuality find their respective polestars to an authentic existence in Kierkegaard—than of anything as substantive as that which we find in Lukács' critical reception. Antecedent to the crisis at hand, those theorists inquiring into social mechanisms underlying the rapidly emerging nation-state in Imperial Germany would find little to nothing of import in Kierkegaardian individualism. However, signs of increasing discontent would alter this omission.

Lukács arrived in Heidelberg just after completing his essay "On Poverty of Spirit." This essay, autobiographical in content, addressed in existentialist prose the conflict involved as one seeks to choose their life-ethic amidst what was otherwise a culture warped by a formulaic approach to ethical reasoning. Marianne Weber (1870–1954) wrote concerning her husband's appreciation for Lukács' essay: the "creative power of love that brings salvation is conceded the right to break through the ethical norm."[18] In Arthur Mitzman's (b. 1931) historical interpretation of Weber, he pointed out that Lukács' essay came close to expressing Weber's concept of charisma and the importance for the individual to find their daemon, or in the vein of the *Protestant Ethic*, their calling.[19] Mitzman wrote that this essay "probably reveals the kind of discussions occurring in the Weber-Kries at that time."[20] Mitzman went on to write that charisma was ethically important for Weber because while Weber denied that value choices could be objectively justified, "the necessity of choice, of commitment to one's daemon, was an ethical imperative."[21] Lukács' initial influence on the Webers was his knack for stylizing life in intimate and particularized essays such as the ones found in *Soul and Form*. Marianne Weber makes mention of the fact that while Weber was on vacation in Italy he asked that she send him Lukács' *Soul and Form*.[22] His request, Mitzman notes, was likely due to the fact Weber was reading Charles-Louis Philippe's *Marie Donadieu*: one of the essays in *Soul and Form* is on Philippe.[23] Lukács' use of intimate, particular, and stylized existences was in line with what Weber wrote concerning art as taking over the function of "this-worldly salvation," which "provides a salvation from the routines of everyday life."[24] Honigsheim mentions as well that the two men "discussed many things,

---

[18]   Marianne Weber, *Max Weber*, trans. by Harry Zohn, New York: Wiley 1974, p. 466.

[19]   Arthur Mitzman, *The Iron Cage: An Historical Interpretation of Max Weber*, New York: Knopf 1969, pp. 273–6.

[20]   Ibid, p. 273.

[21]   Ibid., p. 229.

[22]   Marianne Weber, *Max Weber*, p. 488.

[23]   Mitzman, *The Iron Cage: An Historical Interpretation of Max Weber*, p. 276. The Charles-Louis Philippe essay was first published in German in 1911 in *Die neue Rundschau*, vol. 22, 1911, pp. 192ff.

[24]   Weber, "Zwischenbetrachtung: Theorie der Stufen und Richtungen religiöser Weltablehnung," p. 555. ("Religious Rejections of the World and their Directions," p. 342.)

particularly esthetic problems."[25] The relation between aesthetics and ethics, for Weber, is evident in his speech in Munich, titled "Science as a Vocation," delivered a few short years after his time with Lukács in Heidelberg:

> It is not accidental that our greatest art is intimate and not monumental, nor is it accidental that today only within the smallest and intimate circles, in personal human situations, in *pianissimo*, that something is pulsating that corresponds to the prophetic *pneuma*, which in former times swept through the great communities like a firebrand, wedding them together.[26]

This from Weber underlines the distinct value he placed on both life and art as sources for forming one's ethical life-view. Maybe then we would not think it odd that one who succeeded in critical aesthetics would lead theorists like Weber, Simmel, and Troeltsch to evaluate the situation in Imperial Germany with Kierkegaard and Dostoevsky in mind. For example, Mitzman believes that Lukács' influence probably contributed to Weber's renewed interest "in Slavic culture as an anti-modernist challenge to his earlier values."[27] If Lukács' influence on the Weber circle is as Mitzman argues, then the question about existential choice probably came from this renewal of anti-modernist challenges as well.

Marianne Weber also provides clues to not only Lukács' political thought but also his evaluation of existential choice when she wrote that Lukács' eschatological Manichaeism came through his stressing human choice:

> For Lukács the splendor of inner-worldly culture, particularly its esthetic side, meant the Antichrist, the "Luciferian" competition against God's effectiveness. But there was to be a full development of this realm, the individual's choice between it and the transcendent must not be facilitated. The final struggle between God and Lucifer is still to come and depends on the *decision* of mankind. The ultimate goal is salvation from the world, not, as for [Stefan] George and his circle, fulfillment in it.[28]

This quotation shows us how Lukács' acosmism eventually led to a form of decisionism. Lukács had already began to argue that only apart from a world ordered rationally and instrumentally can an authentic life, oriented around unflinching existential conviction, emerge. This is an important breaking point because from here we can see the divide between Weber and Lukács. Weber, in his essay on "Religious Rejections of the World and their Directions," makes clear his skepticism concerning Lukács' pseudo-religious politics. Weber wrote that the organic world of the religious is no longer possible in present-day culture, that tragically "the cultivated man who strives for self-perfection, in the sense of acquiring or creating 'cultural values,' cannot do this. He can become 'weary of life' but he cannot become 'satiated with

---

25   Honigsheim, *On Max Weber*, p. 27.
26   Weber, "Wissenschaft als Beruf," in *Gesammelte Aufsätze zur Wissenschaftslehre*, Tübingen: J.C.B. Mohr 1922, pp. 524–55, see p. 554 (delivered as a speech in 1918; English translation: "Science as a Vocation," in *From Max Weber*, p. 155).
27   Mitzman, *The Iron Cage: An Historical Interpretation of Max Weber*, p. 271.
28   Marianne Weber, *Max Weber*, p. 466.

life' in the sense of completing a cycle."[29] The mystic's religious need for salvation is repeatedly frustrated in the particularized and relativized aspects yielded by modern culture. Weber wrote: "It thus becomes less and less likely that culture and the striving for culture can have any inner-worldly meaning for the individual."[30] This frustration either led one to abandoning the world, or to use "religious ethics practically and ethically to rationalize the world."[31] Employing religious ethics to rationalize the world is another way of describing what is underneath the ethic of conviction. These two paths were often the ones young neo-Romantics, many of which passed through Weber's circle in Heidelberg, were forced to choose between. On one hand, Lukács and others were appropriating mysticism and socialism commonly found in those seeking an otherworldly retreat from the political, while, on the other hand, they used apocalyptic, anarchic, and eschatological rhetoric for political redemption. In essence, their tragic vision, according to Weber, was that they retained the need for absolute satiation in an otherworldly mysticism, while intent on realizing these ideals amidst the plurality of values extant in a modern, post-metaphysical culture. Weber is essentially arguing that this form of political Romanticism is likely to end with greater disenchantment once assuredly the ideals fail to materialize.

The differences between Weber and Lukács concerning where one goes after the existential choice, is made clearer in Weber's distinction between two types of acosmism, and thus again stressing the tragic either/or young Romantics were finding themselves in regarding the socio-political realm. Both types of acosmism have a *meta* concern motivating their ethic. Weber's political realism refused any rational certainty, or religious conviction, that the means will justify the ends: all rational action remained inescapably bound to finite conditions. Weber writes that the "sublimated and thoroughgoing search for salvation may lead to an acosmism increasing to the point where it rejects purposive-rational action *per se*, and hence all action in terms of means–ends relations, for it considers them tied to worldly things and thus estranged from God."[32] The first form of acosmism culminated in some form of Romantic retreat from any participation in the socio-political sphere. This was one temptation facing the current generation of intellectuals. The second form of acosmism is oriented towards a this-worldly salvation. Weber notes this political transition in mysticism:

> possession of God to possession by God…is meaningful and possible when eschatological expectations of an immediate beginning and of the millennium of acosmic brotherliness are flaming up, hence, when the belief is dropped that an everlasting tension exists between the world and the irrational metaphysical realm of salvation.[33]

---

29   Weber, "Zwischenbetrachtung: Theorie der Stufen und Richtungen religiöser Welt-ablehnung," p. 570. ("Religious Rejections of the World and their Directions," p. 356.)
30   Ibid.
31   Weber, "Zwischenbetrachtung: Theorie der Stufen und Richtungen religiöser Welt-ablehnung," p. 571. ("Religious Rejections of the World and their Directions," p. 357.)
32   Weber, "Zwischenbetrachtung: Theorie der Stufen und Richtungen religiöser Welt-ablehnung," p. 553. ("Religious Rejections of the World and their Directions," p. 339.)
33   Weber, "Zwischenbetrachtung: Theorie der Stufen und Richtungen religiöser Welt-ablehnung," pp. 553–4. ("Religious Rejections of the World and their Directions," p. 340.)

The active form of acosmism is where "the radical rejection of the world easily turns into radical *anomism*. The commands of the world do not hold for the man who is assured in his obsession...and is thereby saved, the manner of action is without significance for salvation."[34] The ascetic or mystic denial of the world is antinomian, yet the danger is when in this antinomian instance the individual or group posits absolute imperatives for the socio-political sphere, which again for Weber operates out of indifference to the ultimate ends posited from either aesthetic or religious ideals. It is interesting to note how, while Weber was an enthused fan of Lukács' aesthetic writings, he was troubled by any attempt to play these theories out in the political realm. Lukács' politics would intensify in the coming years as is evident in some of his wartime correspondence. In these letters we can see the intensification of his belief that the pending crises will only be resolved through an ethic of conviction. Take, for example, when Lukács wrote to the German dramatist Paul Ernst (1866–1933) at the outset of World War I that the idea of terrorism "is really close to my heart because I happen to believe we are now faced with a new type of man that we should become familiar with."[35] Already at this point the seeds for his eventual support of the Bolshevik revolution were sown. His wartime correspondence with Ernst is useful since these letters were written days after Lukács transitioned from his work on aesthetics in Heidelberg with Weber, to taking up ethico-political issues in his Sunday Circle in Budapest.[36] These letters, I believe, will help explain why Weber was able to converse and sympathize with those, like Lukács, who were more and more becoming estranged from the increasing disenchanting political environment, and yet Weber refused the means by which they would want to resist and overcome the existing powers. In the end, as we will see, for Weber it would come down to an existential choice, either one would choose the ethic of responsibility or the ethic of conviction.

III. Post Heidelberg

The political outcome of Lukács' Kierkegaard phase is evident six years after the essays were published in letters written at the start of World War I. These letters, I believe, will provide a good lead up to Weber's final take on existential choice. The most expressive letters, revealing the influence of a Kierkegaardian conviction in their starkest manner, are his wartime correspondence with Paul Ernst. These letters suggest that the metaphysical concepts of existence and choice, which were at stake in his essays on Kierkegaard, were preserved after his years in Heidelberg. The issue is to what extent elevating the state as the valuator in human society has resulted in the cheapening of human existence. We see this explicitly when Lukács contends with utopian-like "power structures" that deceptively elevate *Zweckrationalität* to the point it represents "the existing reality more accurately than does the really

---

34   Weber, "Zwischenbetrachtung: Theorie der Stufen und Richtungen religiöser Welt-ablehnung," p. 554. ("Religious Rejections of the World and their Directions," p. 340.)

35   See *Georg Lukács Selected Correspondence 1902–1920*, p. 245.

36   For more on this circle see Mary Gluck, *Georg Lukács and His Generation 1900–1918*, Cambridge, Massachusetts: Harvard University Press 1985.

existent [essence]."³⁷ The war exposed for Lukács the ethical consequences when the nation-state baptizes itself as the *de facto* valuator regarding human issues. The consequences of this freedom of supreme right are of ethical concern, especially when the state turned against those who are "really existent" in the state of total war. Lukács distinguished the state as not existing (abstract, inorganic) and the individual as that which exists. Up to this point, Weber would agree. Lukács' critique of the nation-state was as much a philosophical critique on the de-essentializing effect that *Zweckrationalität* had on the individual as it was a political critique concerning the current events surrounding the war. Lukács implicated positivism, relativism, and nihilism as producing the post-metaphysical environment which "has administered sanctification to all power."³⁸ The irony was how *Zweckrationalität*, which for Lukács and other Romantic anti-capitalists was merely mechanistic and therefore unable to represent human interest, transformed its nature from function to essence: that which in reality is mere means is now valued *as if* it contained an essence. The only way to limit the faulty empowering of the state was to reinstate the individual over the state. This will entail showing how individuals possess the "ethical means" in challenging this deception.³⁹ Lukács continued the discussion with Ernst a month later, now stating explicitly that the soul alone "possesses a metaphysical reality."⁴⁰

At another point in this letter to Ernst, Lukács uncovered the root of the problem concerning the undermining of individuality in inverting value and *Zweckrationalität*: "I certainly don't deny that there are people whose soul…is ready and willing to enter into a relationship to the objective spirit and its structures."⁴¹ Lukács' contention was rather "against those who consider this relationship to be the norm and claim that everyone should associate the destiny of his soul with it."⁴² So at the core of his argument was the Romantic critique of capitalism, perceived by Lukács as the sole valuator which estranges the individual from its essence, when it is given the power to determine worth and value especially in times of war. Again, both Weber and Lukács shared a similar Romantic criticism concerning the limits extant in the political sphere, especially a socio-political sphere defined by instrumental rationality. But, Lukács wanted to extend ethics beyond the reach of the existing political sphere. This is what framed the political effect that Kierkegaard's existential choice had on Lukács: it emphasized the role of self-agency in the ethic of conviction which would elevate self-agency over and above the existing socio-political orders. Lukács wrote: "Here the soul must be sacrificed in order to save the soul. One must become a cruel *Realpolitiker* out of a mystical ethic and has to violate the absolute ethic."⁴³

Three years after these letters were written, Lukács took another step toward realizing the ethical ideals of social democracy by joining the Bolshevist party. He

---

³⁷	See *Georg Lukács Selected Correspondence 1902–1920*, p. 246.
³⁸	Ibid.
³⁹	Ibid., p. 247.
⁴⁰	Ibid., p. 248.
⁴¹	Ibid.
⁴²	Ibid.
⁴³	Ibid.

wrote in Kierkegaardian terms of an either/or that "when the moment of decision arrives—and the moment has arrived—one must decide whether socialism indeed personifies the will and power to redeem this world—or whether socialism is really just an ideological cover for class interest."[44] The dilemma, much in the same way Weber would see it, was whether or not one decides to act out of conviction or if one settles on compromise in standard democratic fashion. Lukács chose the former:

> The question of faith therefore, like every ethical question, involves a choice between two alternatives....In Bolshevism the individual can, if he so desires, preserve—no matter at what cost—the apparent unity of his conviction. In democracy, the individual consciously surrenders his conviction so that, though he sacrifices himself, social democracy as a whole can be realized.[45]

After Lukács' break with the Heidelberg circle his explicit involvement in political circles led to his eventual participation and support for the Bolshevik Revolution. Not long after the Revolution, Weber would deliver his lecture on "Politics as Vocation" to students in Munich in 1919. I will finish by showing how in this lecture we can see the influence of what Heller noted as Kierkegaard's existential choice, as Weber addressed students who shared Lukács' enthusiasm for revolution. Weber and Lukács agreed that the antihuman qualities of rationalization required some form of an authentic ethic, though they were unable to agree on the prospects for renewing the ethico-political order. In this lecture Weber reduced all ethical conduct to either an ethic of conviction or the ethic of responsibility, saying it "may be guided by one of two fundamentally differing and irreconcilably opposed maxims: conduct can either be oriented to an 'ethic of ultimate ends' or to an 'ethic of responsibility.' "[46] This, for Weber, was an ethical paradox precluding any rationalizing of one over the other, thus necessitating that those seeking a future in politics make an existential choice as to which attitude they would base their ethical actions on. In other words, there was no objective standard to which the subject could make an appeal, one must make a choice. Weber said:

> Whoever wants to engage in politics at all, and especially in politics as a vocation, has to realize these ethical paradoxes. He must know that he is responsible for what may become of himself under the impact of these paradoxes. I repeat, he lets himself in for the diabolical forces lurking in all violence....The genius or demon of politics lives in an inner tension with the god of love....This tension can at any time lead to an irreconcilable conflict.[47]

Ethics, for Weber, is never free from consequences. The wheat and tares are not to be separated in the political sphere, so to speak. Those seeking to act for the sake of ultimate ends will always, tragically, find their aims undone. You might say

---

[44]   Georg Lukács, "Bolshevism as an Ethical Problem," in *The Lukács Reader*, p. 218.

[45]   Ibid., p. 220

[46]   Max Weber, "Politik als Beruf," in his *Gesammelte politische Schriften*, Munich: Drei Masken Verlag 1921, pp. 396–450, see p. 441. ("Politics as a Vocation," in *From Max Weber*, p. 120.)

[47]   Weber, "Politik als Beruf," p. 447. ("Politics as a Vocation," pp. 125–6.)

that the true ethical moment for Weber is when one takes up responsibility—"what may become of himself"—by participating in the political sphere. That is, the young politician choosing to bear the weight of good and bad consequences resulting from their participation in the socio-political sphere had for Weber a distinct moral quality.

These two standards represent their respective replies to the modern crisis of ethical judgments in a world given over to human calculation and instrumental reason. For Lukács, the free, ethical subject alone validated ethical actions without respect to reasons or consequences. His ethical subject, freed from external influence, can then posit its pure intention out of conviction alone. Weber countered Lukács' ethic of conviction by arguing that those who sought political redemption ignored the fundamental power-based function of the state which undermined the pure intention operative in any ends-based ethic. He responded to Lukács' ethic of conviction after the Bolshevik Revolution with his own existential choice expressed in the ethic of responsibility that situates the chooser in tragic but human tones. In prose suggesting something of a proto-existentialist, Weber said to the students in Munich, no doubt tempted by revolution, that,

> it is immensely moving when a mature man—no matter whether old or young in years— is aware of a responsibility for the consequences of his conduct and really feels such responsibility with heart and soul...that is something human...every one of us who is not spiritually dead must realize the possibility of finding himself in that position.[48]

Is it, then, not likely in the light of this that Kierkegaard's existential choice is at play in Weber's description of what is at stake in a vocation of politics since one must choose, apart from any objective standards or elite interest, between responsibility and conviction? Whereas Weber remained skeptical that any ethic could ever reach its intended goal in the political sphere whose *modus operandi* was *Zweckrationalität*, Lukács staked his professional career on the possibility of establishing a new world order where ethics strengthened the political through ethically engaged subjects. In spite of their respective differences, however, each saw a fork in the road necessitating an existential choice.

---

[48]   Weber, "Politik als Beruf," pp. 448–9. ("Politics as a Vocation," p. 127.)

Bibliography

I. References to or Uses of Kierkegaard in Weber's Corpus

"Die protestantische Ethik und der 'Geist' des Kapitalismus," in *Gesammelte Aufsätze zur Religionssoziologie*, vols. 1–3, Tübingen: Mohr 1920–21, vol. 1, p. 101. (English translation: *The Protestant Ethic and the Spirit of Capitalism*, trans. by Talcott Parsons, New York: Charles Scribner's Sons 1958, p. 109.)

II. Sources of Weber's Knowledge of Kierkegaard

Lukács, Georg, *Die Seele und die Formen*, Berlin: Fleischel 1911, pp. 61–91.
— "Von der Armut am Geiste: Ein Gespräch und ein Brief," *Neue Blätter*, vol. 2, 1912, pp. 67–92.

III. Secondary Literature on Weber's Relation to Kierkegaard

Baumgarten, Eduard, "Für und wider das radikale Böse. Meditationen über wesentliche Differenzen zwischen Jaspers und Max Weber; zwischen Jaspers, Kant, Goethe, Kierkegaard und Nietzsche," in *Karl Jaspers*, ed. by Paul Arthur Schilpp, Stuttgart: Kohlhammer 1957 (*Philosophen des 20. Jahrhunderts*), pp. 323–3.
Heller, Ágnes, *A Theory of Modernity*, Malden, Massachusetts: Blackwell 1999, p. 247.
Honigsheim, Paul, *On Max Weber*, New York: The Free Press 1968, p. 27.
Lehmann, Günther K., *Ästhetik der Utopie. Arthur Schopenhauer, Sören Kierkegaard, Georg Simmel, Max Weber, Ernst Bloch*, Stuttgart: Neske 1995.
Malik, Habib, *Receiving Søren Kierkegaard*, Washington D.C.: Catholic University of America Press 1997, p. 335; p. 354.
Turner, Charles, *Modernity and Politics in the Works of Max Weber*, London: Routledge 1992, pp. 106–9.

Irvin Yalom:

The "Throw-Ins" of Psychotherapy

Almut Furchert

Irvin D. Yalom (b. 1931) is one of the best-known and most widely read American psychiatrists in the contemporary world. He is not only a psychoanalyst and professor emeritus at Stanford, but a vivid story-teller with a passion to reach beyond scientific reductionism and disciplinary boundaries to point to the existential realms of life. He has published two widely read psychotherapy textbooks, as well as a wide range of medical journal articles and case studies.[1] But he became famous through his gift of psychological story-telling displayed in such books as *When Nietzsche Wept* and *The Schopenhauer Cure.* He has been influential in his field for his work in group psychotherapy. His textbook, written in 1970, is now in its fifth edition.[2] More to the point of this article, Yalom is recognized as perhaps the most influential advocate for existential psychotherapy in the United States.[3]

Although Yalom counts Kierkegaard as one of the forefathers of existential psychotherapy, no deeper exploration of his Kierkegaardian connection can be found, either in Yalom's own writings or in writings about Yalom.[4] This article is

---

[1]   For a bibliographical overview of Yalom's writings see Ruthellen Josselson, *Irvin D. Yalom: On Psychotherapy and the Human Condition*, New York: Jorge Pinto Books 2007, pp. 127–31.

[2]   Irvin D. Yalom, *The Theory and Practice of Group Psychotherapy*, 5th ed., New York: Basic Books 2005 [1970].

[3]   For a very brief introduction to Yalom's approach see Emmy van Deurzen and Raymond Kenward, *Dictionary of Existential Psychotherapy and Counseling*, Thousand Oaks, California: Sage 2005, p. 218. Van Deurzen and Kenward view Yalom from the European understanding of existential psychotherapy which wants to go beyond medical models and psychopathological diagnostics. Even if they give Yalom credit for having done much to popularize the existential approach, they criticize him for still clinging to a Freudian psychodynamic. Introductions in more depth into Yalom and his work can be found in various handbooks, e.g. Russel A. Walsh and Brian McElwain, "Existential Psychotherapies," in *Humanistic Psychotherapies: Handbook of Research and Practice,* ed. by David Cain and Julius Seeman, Washington D.C.: American Psychological Association 2002, pp. 253–78; *Handbook of Experimental Existential Psychology*, ed. by Jeff Greenberg, Sander L. Koole, and Tom Pyszczynski, New York: Guilford 2004.

[4]   A search in November 2010 of 8 indexes (ERIC, 1966–Current; CSA Linguistics and Language Behavior Abstracts, 1973-Current; MEDLINE, 2000–Current; MLA International Bibliography, 1926–Current; Philosopher's Index, 1940–Current; PsycINFO, 1806–Current;

therefore a first attempt to trace back to Kierkegaard those thoughts which can be found in Yalom's writings, concentrating primarily on direct references. We will find, however, that Yalom's Kierkegaard is mostly seen through the lenses of his intellectual teachers such as Rollo May (1909–94), Paul Tillich (1886–1965), and Ernest Becker (1924–74). My article therefore can be read as an initial tracing of the influence of these authors (who are discussed in this volume) on Yalom's thought. After giving a brief introduction to Yalom's life and work I will focus mainly on his *Existential Psychotherapy*, which holds nearly all Kierkegaard references in the Yalom *corpus*.[5] Using this text as our focus will also provide a better understanding of Yalom's existential psychotherapy approach.

I. A Brief Outline of Yalom's Life and Work

Born in 1931 into a family of Russian Jews who had immigrated to Washington D.C., Yalom grew up in a rough neighborhood. His parents, both shopkeepers, were usually busy when little Irv was heading home on his bike to read the books he schlepped from the nearby library.[6] He read what he could get in the small library, but it was mainly in fiction where he found a refuge and a source of inspiration and wisdom: "Sometime early in life I developed the notion—one which I have never relinquished—that writing a novel is the very finest thing a person can do."[7] With this attitude, he eagerly explored the worlds of authors such as Lyev Nikolayevich Tolstoy (1828–1910) and Fyodor Mikhaylovich Dostoevsky (1821–81). His early interest would eventually make him one of the most widely read psychological novelists. In Ruthellen Josselson's 2007 biographical interview, Yalom pictures himself in hindsight as a young man looking for a mentor for guidance but unable to find one. So he mainly taught himself through the art of story-telling—through the stories he read and the stories he recounted from his own life. One story from childhood left a significant impression on him: it is about the medical doctor Benjamin Manchester, a kind man who rushed to the Yalom family when the father had a heart attack. Irv, barely 14 and anxiously watching the scene, was blamed by his frightened mother: his troublemaking might have "killed" his father. It was not merely the arrival of the doctor with "his round friendly face" that relieved the anxious boy but also *how* the doctor treated him. He was "wonderfully reassuring," tousling the boy's hair and letting him listen to the father's stabilized heartbeat through the stethoscope. Yalom

---

Social Services Abstracts, 1979–Current; and Sociological Abstracts, 1952–Current) for all occurrences of "Kierkegaard" and "Yalom" anywhere in the record yielded 128 unique references. Most of these simply cited both in the references, but did not connect them at all. Only five did more than simply mention that Yalom relied on Kierkegaard for some concepts. These five are included in this article.

5   Irvin D. Yalom, *Existential Psychotherapy*, New York: Basic Books 1980.

6   The following bibliographical information is taken from Yalom's autobiography as found in Josselson, *Irvin D. Yalom: On Psychotherapy and the Human Condition*.

7   For these biographical accounts see also Yalom's webpage. The quotation is taken from Jason Merchey, *Values of the Wise: Aspiring to "The Life of Value*," Haverford, Pennslyvania: Infinity Publishing 2004, p. 187.

recounts, "there I made the decision that I was going to go to medical school and try to offer others what Dr. Manchester had offered."[8]

When he finally made it to Boston University School of Medicine, his gift of story-telling became itself a turning point. Having to present a psychiatric case to a large group of faculty members, mostly psychoanalysts, the young student got frightened as the presenters before him were painfully tested by the analysts' criticism. When it was his turn, Yalom got up and did what he could do best: story-telling. He forgot about his notes and what was taught about case presentations; instead, he recalled the story of his client, a story of each trying to understand the other:

> At the end of my talk there was a loud long total silence. I was puzzled. I had done something that was extremely easy and natural for me. And, one by one, the analysts—those guys who couldn't stop one-upping each other—said things to the effect of, "Well, this presentation speaks for itself. There's nothing we can say. It's a remarkable case. A startling and tender relationship." And all I had done was simply tell a story, which felt so natural and effortless for me. That was definitely an eye-opening experience: Then and there I knew I had found my place in the world.[9]

Another important figure helping him find his place in the world was Marilyn, his high-school love. She was a gifted student of comparative literature and became a treasured friend and partner for the young Yalom, remaining so until today.

In medical school Yalom started reading Sigmund Freud (1856–1939), whom he acknowledges as a "master story teller."[10] John Whitehorn, the chairman of psychiatry at Johns Hopkins Hospital, Baltimore, where Yalom spent three years of residency, also left a deep impression on the young psychiatrist. Whitehorn was primarily interested in the client's story, not in pressing on them any therapeutic formula. During this residency Yalom read other authors such as Harry Stack Sullivan (1892–1949), Karen Horney (1885–1952), Erich Fromm (1900–80), and Otto Rank (1884–1939). These authors "brought some old world wisdom into their perspective, and they weren't reductionistic."[11] But it was first of all Rollo May's book *Existence* which enticed him to take philosophy courses at Johns Hopkins University.[12] Later, a professor at Stanford, he audited courses about Edmund Husserl (1859–1938), Martin Heidegger (1889–1976), Friedrich Nietzsche (1844–1900), Kierkegaard, Jean-Paul Sartre (1905–80), Plato and Aristotle.[13] During this time Rollo May became his academic mentor and therapist and soon also a friend. In his latest book *Staring at the Sun* Yalom shares the last minutes he spent with his dying friend.[14]

---

[8] Josselson, *Irvin D. Yalom: On Psychotherapy and the Human Condition*, p. 7.
[9] Ibid., p. 15.
[10] Ibid., p. 24.
[11] Ibid., pp. 30–1.
[12] Ibid., p. 2.
[13] Ibid., p. 33.
[14] Irvin D. Yalom, *Staring at The Sun*, New York: Jossey-Bass/Wiley 2008, p. 174.

In 1998 Yalom produced an anthology of his own writing called *The Yalom Reader*.[15] This reader offers a helpful overview of his work as well as an idea of those texts the author came to understand as most central to his work. In new introductions to those selected texts, Yalom also provides an account of how he sees himself as an author over time. Yalom has structured his own *corpus* into three sections: I. Group psychotherapy, II. Existential Psychotherapy, and III. Psychological Story-Telling. Since nearly all Yalom's references to Kierkegaard appear in his Existential Psychotherapy (and interestingly reappear in *The Yalom Reader*), the following account will focus on the second section of Yalom's *corpus: Existential Psychotherapy*.[16]

Before we explore the Yalom–Kierkegaard connection more closely I shall give a brief overview of American existential therapy approaches. It is commonly accepted that Rollo May brought existential psychology to the United States.[17] May regards Kierkegaard as one of the most remarkable psychologists of all time, who not only anticipated Freud's theory of the unconsciousness but at the same time went beyond it. May especially depended on Kierkegaard's concepts of anxiety and selfhood.[18] Yalom and May together co-authored the introductory article "Existential Psychotherapy" in the third edition of the Corsini textbook *Current Psychotherapies*. Here also Kierkegaard holds the first place in the line of precursors to existential therapies.[19]

Though both begin with Kierkegaard, the Americans' path of existential approaches to psychotherapy has developed somewhat differently from their European contemporaries. This might be attributed to their more positive-humanistic and pragmatic way of thinking.[20] Emmy van Deurzen (b. 1951), one of the best-known existential therapy advocates in Great Britain, criticizes these American pragmatist tendencies for detaching the existential concepts from their philosophical roots. Still, all existential approaches share some sympathy for philosophical

---

[15]   Irvin D. Yalom, *The Yalom Reader: Selections from the Work of a Master Therapist and Storyteller*, ed. by Ben Yalom, New York: Basic Books 1998.

[16]   Yalom mentions Kierkegaard four times in *The Schopenhauer Cure*, New York: HarperCollins 2005, and once each in *The Gift of Therapy*, New York: HarperCollins 2002; *Staring at The Sun*, as well as in *Lying on the Couch*, New York: Basic Books 1996. Usually those references mention Kierkegaard in a list of other important thinkers.

[17]   See *Existence: A New Dimension in Psychiatry and Psychology*, ed. by Rollo May et al., New York: Touchstone/Simon and Schuster 1958 and *Existential Psychology*, ed. by Rollo May, New York: Random House 1961.

[18]   For a distinctive account on the May–Kierkegaard connection see Poul Houe's article, "Rollo May: Existential Psychology," in this volume.

[19]   Rollo May and Irvin Yalom, "Existential Psychotherapy," in *Current Psychotherapies*, ed. by Raymond Corsini, Itasca, Illinois: Peacock 1984, pp. 354–91.

[20]   For a further introduction to the field see Mick Cooper, *Existential Therapies*, Thousand Oaks, California: Sage 2003, pp. 63ff. Also Ed Mendelowitz and Kirk Schneider, "Existential Psychotherapy," in *Current Psychotherapies*, ed. by Raymond Corsini and Danny Wedding, Belmont, California: Thomson/Brooks/Cole 2009, pp. 295–327; Gerald Corey, *Theory and Practice of Counseling and Psychotherapy*, Thomson/Brooks/Cole 2009, p. 138; Walsh and McElwain, "Existential Psychotherapies," pp. 253ff.

reflection rather than mere psychological technique and are informed by thinkers such as Kierkegaard, Nietzsche, Sartre, Karl Jaspers (1883–1969), Martin Buber (1878–1965), Maurice Merleau-Ponty (1907–61), Tillich, and Emmanuel Levinas (1906–95) among others. These authors have in common that they grapple with human existence, but like the existential therapists, they often come to different conclusions. Thus existential therapies are mainly anti-systematic—considering themselves an approach to doing therapy rather than an independent school of therapy.[21] Attempts to summarize existential therapy approaches often underline common essential themes: human freedom and its attenuation, intersubjectivity, temporality, being as becoming, existential anxiety and guilt, and authenticity, as well as emphasizing the therapeutic relationship, mutual understanding, liberation, and the therapist's flexibility.[22]

Yalom is widely praised for undertaking the effort to bring these scattered existential attempts in the therapeutic field together. His 1980 book *Existential Psychotherapy* greatly influenced the development of existential thinking and practice in today's American psychotherapeutic scene.[23] Yet Yalom has not made it easy for the scholar who wants to trace his central concepts to their origins. He builds his approach on many thoughts from many thinkers, usually without exploring the roots of those thoughts further. Yalom has written his book for practitioners rather than philosophers, and does not waste time with philosophical finesse or exploration. Yalom has widely read philosophers, theologians, and novelists and is not shy to quote them as original sources even though he finds them in other authors (e.g. Kierkegaard as quoted by Tillich). His excursions into philosophy are "brief and pragmatic,"[24] and he tests philosophical "wisdom" with the empirical reality a therapist faces day by day. His textbook pragmatically relies on a wide range of authors: Freud, Rank, May, Becker, Kierkegaard, Tillich, also Buber, Jaspers, Viktor Frankl (1905–97), Erich Fromm (1900–80), Dostoevsky, Tolstoy, Ernest Hemingway (1899–1961), as well as Nietzsche, Heidegger, Sartre, and Albert Camus (1913–60) would head the list.[25] And he leans heavily on his own practice as a psychiatrist and group therapist.

---

[21]   Therefore it would be best "to speak of existential psychotherapies rather than of a single existential psychotherapy," suggest Walsh and McElwain in their overview, "Existential Psychotherapies," p. 254.

[22]   Ibid.

[23]   Corey, *Theory and Practice of Counseling and Psychotherapy*, p. 138.

[24]   Yalom, *Existential Psychotherapy*, p. 16.

[25]   Corey's textbook provides a first attempt to structure and systemize the many different voices to whom Yalom's approach refers. According to his introductory chapter on "Existential Psychotherapy," p. 138, Yalom's approach is based on the following authors and themes: From Kierkegaard Yalom has taken themes such as creative anxiety, despair, fear and dread, guilt, and nothingness, from Nietzsche death, suicide and will, from Heidegger authentic being, caring, death, guilt, individual responsibility, and isolation, from Sartre, meaninglessness, responsibility and choice, from Buber the importance of interpersonal relationship, the I–Thou perspective, and self-transcendence as well as from Viktor Frankl the emphasise on meaning. Even if Corey misses many of the important influences, his attempt suggests that main themes of Yalom's *Existential Psychotherapy* such as anxiety, despair, guilt and nothingness could be traced back to the Danish thinker.

Yalom starts his journey into *Existential Psychotherapy*, as described in his introductory chapter, with an encounter in a cookery class. Wondering why the cook's meal is always better than his own using the same recipe, he watched the process more carefully. What he saw became a fundamental metaphor for his therapeutic approach: It was not just the recipe which made the dish. In the end of his preparation, the cook gave the meal to his assistant, who, before putting the meal in the oven, threw some spices on it. There it was, the vision for a more realistic therapy approach: it is not just a good theory that makes good therapy, but the "Throw Ins" which give it its real taste. "Yet, I believe," Yalom states, "that, when no one is looking, the therapist throws in the 'real thing.' "[26] These "critical ingredients" from the therapy session should be incorporated in the theory, but more importantly, the therapist should be able to employ "existential insight" into the uniqueness of the individual case. What makes existential psychotherapy existential is not a certain theory, school, or technique. Instead it is the therapist's awareness of those concerns "that are rooted in the individual's existence." In this way Yalom understands his *Existential Psychotherapy* as a first attempt to provide a framework for those "extras of therapy."[27]

II. Making it more Difficult—Kierkegaard in Yalom's Existential Psychotherapy

The interpreter of Yalom has the advantage of his hindsight view on his authorship and its influences as described in his 1998 *Yalom Reader*:

> In the process of writing the textbook *Existential Therapy*, I immersed myself for years in the work of the great existential philosophers—Sartre, Heidegger, Camus, Jaspers, Kierkegaard, Nietzsche. Of these thinkers, I found Nietzsche to be the most creative, the most powerful, and the most relevant for psychotherapy.[28]

It was this reading, and particularly his regard for Nietzsche, that led Yalom to write his bestselling 1991 novel: *When Nietzsche Wept*. This is a thought experiment about one of the founding fathers of psychoanalysis Josef Breuer (1842–1925) and Friedrich Nietzsche, the great but deeply despairing thinker, performing some sort of "talking cure" with each other. In the *Yalom Reader* Yalom recounts that he reads Nietzsche not as a destroyer or nihilist but rather as a "therapist" and "healer" who well understands that "one can build a self only on the ashes of the old."[29] Thus in reflecting on his *Existential Psychotherapy* and his story-telling engagement with Nietzsche and Breuer, Yalom gives pride of place to Nietzsche. Despite this claim, a simple comparison of the indexes in *Existential Psychotherapy* reveals that Kierkegaard holds up well against Nietzsche and provides at least double the amount of direct references (not to count his second-hand influences through the existential psychologists Yalom cites). This happily means that Nietzsche and Kierkegaard,

---

[26]   See Yalom, *Existential Psychotherapy*, p. 3.
[27]   Ibid., pp. 4–5.
[28]   Yalom, *The Yalom Reader*, p. 375.
[29]   Ibid., pp. 375–6.

who did not meet in life, now sit together in *Existential Psychotherapy*—though they are still not really speaking to each other.

A. Climacus, the Forerunner

When Yalom began his work on *Existential Psychotherapy* he was aware that this approach would become a "homeless waif"—not welcome in the "better academic neighborhoods."[30] It would neither produce a formal school nor be able to depend upon a stable institution. Instead, the existential approaches leap into the gap where therapy and philosophy meet in their existential concern about the human being. Thus Yalom, like previous existential-humanist therapists, introduced his approach with a view backwards to its "ancestral home."[31] He begins with the anecdote of a cigar-smoking Dane who was himself quite familiar with the troubles of intellectual homelessness: hanging out in a cafe somewhere in the streets of Copenhagen in the 1830s the young Dane wonders about the disarray of the present age and how to contribute to it. Søren Kierkegaard, the hidden dramatist behind the scene, produces here the remarkable plot that allows his pseudonymous Johannes Climacus to reflect in his unique, ironic way on his own awakening moment as an author.[32] And those playful words of the "experiential humorist psychologist," as Climacus likes to introduce himself, have made their unlikely way 150 years later into the introduction of a psychiatrist's textbook. In a time when the "benefactors of the age" want to make everything in life "easier," Yalom quotes Climacus:

> "some by railways, others by omnibuses and steamboats, others by telegraph, others by easily apprehended compendiums and short recitals of everything worth knowing, and finally the true benefactors of the age who by virtue of thought make spiritual existence systematically easier and easier,"
>
> someone has to make a difference, Climacus reflects:
>
> "You must do something but inasmuch as with your limited capacities it will be impossible to make anything easier than it has become, you must, with the same humanitarian enthusiasm as the others, undertake to make something harder."[33]

This fellow who wants to make it harder somehow clicked with the psychotherapist Yalom; this anecdote constitutes the longest quotation of a Kierkegaard text in the entire Yalom *corpus*. Yalom has taken the passage from *A Kierkegaard Anthology*, edited by Robert Bretall.[34] Bretall has selected the relevant text from Kierkegaard's *Concluding Unscientific Postscript to the Philosophical Fragments* and titled the piece "How Climacus Became an Author."[35] Yalom himself does not mention the

---

[30]   Yalom, *Existential Psychotherapy*, p. 14.

[31]   As does, for example, May in "The Emergence of Existential Psychology" in his *Existential Psychology*, pp. 1ff. as well as Emmy van Deurzen-Smith in her *Everyday Mysteries: Existential Dimensions of Psychotherapy*, London: Routledge 1997.

[32]   Cf. *SKS* 7, 185–7 / *CUP1*, 186–7.

[33]   Yalom, *Existential Psychotherapy*, p. 15.

[34]   *A Kierkegaard Anthology*, ed. by Robert Bretall, Princeton, New Jersey: Princeton University Press 1946.

[35]   Ibid., pp. 193–4.

pseudonymous construction of the text but introduces the cigar-smoking Dane as Kierkegaard himself. Still, he gets Climacus' significant point here, namely to become a reminder of the existential problem. While Climacus likes to make it *more* difficult[36] for those intellectuals of his time who have built themselves a comfortable home of speculative thoughts in the midst of the Christian bourgeoisie, Yalom aims to challenge the secular psychologists and medical practitioners of the twentieth century who were too comfortable with their diagnostic schemes and techniques. "And which difficulties?," asks Yalom, summarizing his encounter with the cigar-smoking Dane: "They were not hard to find. He had only to consider his own situation in existence, his own dread, his choices, his possibilities and limitations."[37] Concluding this excursion into the ancestry of existential psychotherapy, Yalom gives Kierkegaard credit for devoting his short life to exploring the "existential situation," something which later found "fertile soil," he states, in authors such as Martin Heidegger and Karl Jaspers.[38]

B. The Givens of Existence—the Individual's Ultimate Concern

Yalom postulates the human task just as Climacus did in a familiar sort of anthropological contemplation, namely, facing one's own existential situation and its "givens." "And I mean by 'givens' of existence," Yalom explains, "certain ultimate concerns, certain intrinsic properties that are part, and an inescapable part of the human being's existence in the world."[39] And as it reads further: "*This book deals with four ultimate concerns: death, freedom, isolation, and meaninglessness.* The individual's confrontation with each of these facts of life constitutes the content of the existential dynamic conflict."[40] Before we can explore this dynamic conflict further the term "ultimate concern" needs some exploration. Yalom uses the term as a synonym for the "givens of existence." Both refer to those "facts of life" the existing person cannot always escape from. That these concerns really make the backbone of Yalom's approach is also evident in the author's comment in *The Yalom Reader* nearly twenty years later. Here Yalom summarizes his *Existential Psychotherapy* as an attempt to discuss the field "in terms of four deep, ever present, and clinically relevant ultimate concerns of human life."[41] Yalom has borrowed the term "ultimate concern" from the theologian Paul Tillich, the teacher of his mentor Rollo May.[42] But his secular, psychological reuse of the term misses its theological essence as well as allowing the troublesome cigar-smoking Dane to sneak through the backdoor right into the center of his theoretical approach. The door is left open because Tillich

---

[36]   This is how the Hongs translate here, see *SKS* 7, 172 / *CUP1*, 186. The phrase reads in Danish: *at gjøre Noget sværere.*
[37]   Yalom, *Existential Psychotherapy*, p. 15.
[38]   Ibid.
[39]   Ibid., p. 8.
[40]   Ibid. (emphasis in original).
[41]   Yalom, *The Yalom Reader*, p. 168.
[42]   Van Deurzen-Smith, *Everyday Mysteries*, p. 158.

refers directly to Kierkegaard when he explains his understanding of the "ultimate concern":

> The word "concern" points to the "existential" character of religious experience....That which is ultimate gives itself only to the attitude of ultimate concern. It is the correlate of an unconditional concern,...the object of total surrender, demanding also the surrender of our subjectivity while we look at it. It is a matter of infinite passion and interest (Kierkegaard), making us its object whenever we try to make it our object.[43]

Tillich presumes here that the reader of his *Systematic Theology* knows of Kierkegaard's concept of existential pathos. In his *Concluding Unscientific Postscript to the Philosophical Fragments*[44] the difficulty-seeking Johannes Climacus explores the passion of the individual towards the infinite and *how* one can relate to what is infinite. Therefore what concerns us as ultimate is an "object of theology," Tillich concludes, because the ultimate has an infinite claim. Yalom does not use the term "ultimate concern" as such a singular striving towards the ultimate as do Tillich and Kierkegaard. Instead he postulates *plural* ultimate concerns which mark those "boundary situations" which confront the individual with the givens of existence. It is, Yalom explains, when "we reflect deeply upon our 'situation' in the world, upon our existence, our boundaries, our possibilities, if we arrive at the ground that underlies all other ground, we invariably confront the givens of existence, the 'deep structures,' which I shall henceforth refer to as 'ultimate concerns.' "[45] Without having the place to explore this issue deeper here, it seems that Yalom understands "ultimate concerns" as fundamental *existential concerns*: concerns which are essentially related to the very existence of the individual. Those concerns confront the individual with the givens and boundaries of existence and therefore also with one's finitude. Whether this encounter *leads one* to a concern towards the infinite or *leads one* to explore the "ground that underlies all other ground" (see above)[46] or, as we will see later, into avoidance and fear, seems to be a question of how one makes meaning out of such an encounter. Within the framework of the spiritual

---

[43]   Paul Tillich, *Systematic Theology*, vol. 1, *Reason and Revelation. Being and God*, Chicago: University of Chicago Press 1951, p. 12. For an extensive exploration of the Tillich–Kierkegaard connection see Lee C. Barrett's article: "Paul Tillich: An Ambivalent Appropriation, in *Kierkegaard's Influence on Theology*, ed. by Jon Stewart, Aldershot: Ashgate 2012 (*Kierkegaard Research: Sources, Reception and Resources*, vol. 10), forthcoming.

[44]   In the *Postscript* Kierkegaard's Climacus analyzes the existential pathos at length. With existential pathos Climacus describes the relationship of the individual towards an absolute *telos*, the infinite truth, the eternal. He starts: "Esthetic pathos expresses itself in words and can in its truth signify that the individual abandons himself in order to lose himself in the idea, whereas existential pathos results from the transforming relation of the idea to the individual's existence." Therefore such pathos towards the highest truth expresses itself in a "transformation by which the existing person in existing changes everything in his existence in relation to that highest good." (*SKS* 7, 352–3 / *CUP1*, 387 and *SKS* 7, 354 / *CUP1*, 389.)

[45]   Yalom, *Existential Psychotherapy*, p. 8.

[46]   Using this phrase Yalom might have been inspired again by Tillich. Tillich speaks about "the ground of all being," in his *Systematic Theology*, vol. 1, p. 112 and also pp. 155–6: "The religious word for what we called the ground of being is God."

thinkers Tillich and Kierkegaard, the givens of existence awaken one's ultimate concern but do not provide its content. This is because the risk of ultimate concern is that the person may become ultimately concerned with something which cannot bear the weight of an ultimate claim. Therefore the individual comes into "conflict," as Tillich concludes with recourse to Kierkegaard, when something finite is given "infinite significance." The conflict arises because "the absolute element of man's ultimate concern demands absolute intensity, infinite passion (Kierkegaard), in the religious relation."[47]

C. Existential Psychodynamics—Anxiety vs. Fear

While Tillich describes the inner conflict of the individual concerning the ultimate within a theistic framework, Yalom embeds his four *ultimate concerns* in a psychodynamic conflict model.[48] To help understand this model I first will give a brief overview of the content of those concerns.[49] The first concern or given of existence in Yalom's approach is *Death*, which is the "most easily apprehended ultimate concern"[50] because it simply seems obvious that everyone has to die at one point or another. Usually people respond to this fact with "mortal terror."[51] (We will later see that this mortal terror also descends from Kierkegaard.) With *Freedom* as the second concern, Yalom refers to an existential awareness of the "absence of external structure."[52] Such awareness concludes that one finds oneself responsible for one's "world, life design, choices, and actions."[53]This fact is closely connected to the third concern called *Existential Isolation.* Yalom builds here on a fundamental existential claim, namely, that one has to face the "final, unbridgeable gap" between individuals who must "enter" and "depart" existence "alone."[54] As the fourth and last ultimate concern Yalom introduces *Meaninglessness*, and concludes that this "existential dynamic conflict" is based on the dilemma that we are a "meaning-seeking creature who is thrown into a universe that has no meaning."[55] Unfortunately, Yalom does not provide us with a further explanation of this claim. It blends different thoughts from different authors—one might first think of Heidegger, Camus, and Nietzsche.

---

[47]   Tillich, *Systematic Theology*, vol. 1, p. 13; p. 215. Also Yalom is aware of such mismatch, for example, when he describes the idea of "the ultimate rescuer" as a defense mechanism against existential anxiety which projects ultimate meaning into another thing or person. See Yalom, *Existential Psychotherapy*, pp. 129ff.

[48]   See Yalom, *Existential Psychotherapy*, pp. 8–9.

[49]   For a helpful introduction to those concerns see also "Existential Psychotherapy" by Rollo May and Irvin Yalom in Corsini, *Current Psychotherapies*, pp. 367–70. Yalom comes back to them also in the *Yalom Reader*, pp. 167–8 as well as in his latest book *Staring at the Sun*, pp. 201–2.

[50]   Yalom, *Existential Psychotherapy*, p. 8.

[51]   Ibid.

[52]   Ibid.

[53]   Ibid., p. 9.

[54]   Ibid.

[55]   Ibid., pp. 8–9.

Still, one might wonder if "meaninglessness" describes the concern or is instead an attempt to resolve that concern by claiming there is no meaning.[56]

How are these concerns now added to the psychodynamic model? Yalom joins them into the formula of psychodynamics by replacing Freud's concept of particular drives with his concept of ultimate concerns: "An existential paradigm assumes that anxiety emanates from the individual's confrontation with the ultimate concerns in existence."[57] In this way the "awareness of ultimate concern" becomes the force which provokes anxiety which then can lead to defense mechanisms. "Both formulas assume that anxiety is the fuel of psychopathology," Yalom comments. Yet the difference is "that Freud's sequence begins with 'drive,' whereas an existential framework begins with awareness and fear."[58] To understand this postulate it is important to distinguish between anxiety and fear. Here Yalom has further recourse to Kierkegaard:[59]

> Kierkegaard was the first to make a clear distinction between fear and anxiety (dread); he contrasted fear that is fear of *some* thing with dread that is fear of *no* thing—"not," as he wryly noted, "a nothing with which the individual has nothing to do." One dreads (or is anxious about) losing oneself and becoming nothingness. This anxiety cannot be located. As Rollo May says, "it attacks us from all sides at once."…How can we combat anxiety? *By displacing it from nothing to something*. This is what Kierkegaard meant by "the nothing which is the object of dread becomes, as it were, more and more something." It is what Rollo May means by "anxiety seeks to become fear." If we can transform a fear of nothing to a fear of something, we can mount some self-protective campaign—that is, we can either avoid the thing we fear, seek allies against it, develop magical rituals to placate it, or plan a systematic campaign to detoxify it.[60]

This passage opens up three important aspects of Yalom's existential psychodynamic: first the distinction between anxiety (*Angest*) vs. fear (*Frygt*), which leads second to the understanding of anxiety on a deeper existential level, and third the attempt to combat anxiety (for example, by avoiding or projecting it into *some*thing which seems to be easier to control). For Yalom and for his teacher May those aspects are deeply interwoven with their adoption of Kierkegaard's *The Concept of Dread*. In his extensive study about *The Meaning of Anxiety* Rollo May gives Kierkegaard credit for

---

[56]   One can find this also in chapters 10 and 11 in which Yalom explores the problem of meaning more closely. He simply assumes that "the existential concept of freedom" knows only one absolute truth, namely, "that there are no absolutes." (Yalom, *Existential Psychotherapy*, p. 423) Surely this claim counts for some existential thinkers Yalom mentions such as Camus, Nietzsche, Sartre, etc. But other authors such as Tillich, Kierkegaard, Becker, Jaspers, Buber, and Frankl would probably not agree with that claim.

[57]   Yalom, *Existential Psychotherapy*, p. 110. In *Everyday Mysteries*, p. 158, Emy van Deurzen-Smith has criticized Yalom for simply replacing Freud's strivings but keeping the mechanical idea of repression.

[58]   Yalom, *Existential Psychotherapy*, pp. 9–10.

[59]   Ibid. , p. 43. Yalom quotes from Søren Kierkegaard, *The Concept of Dread*, trans. by Walter Lowrie, Princeton: Princeton University Press 1957, p. 55; compare *SKS* 4, 366.

[60]   Yalom, *Existential Psychotherapy*, p. 43 (emphasis original). The quotations of Rollo May refer to *The Meaning of Anxiety*, rev. ed., New York: W.W. Norton 1977, p. 207.

having explored the phenomenon in depth even before Freud had laid the groundwork for understanding the processes of the unconscious. Thereby Kierkegaard sees not only the mere fears but also into the deeper layers of anxiety.[61] While fear can be understood on the level of symptoms, just like we have a certain fear of *something*, anxiety refers to a deeper level, to the essential ground of being: we cannot even say what we are afraid of. May explains it this way: "Hence Kierkegaard's statement that anxiety is the 'fear of nothingness' means in this context the fear of becoming nothing."[62]

This brings us finally to the second part of *Existential Psychotherapy* which gives a closer exploration of the first ultimate concern: Death. "I shall argue that the fear of death is a primal source of anxiety,"[63] Yalom proclaims. The awareness of our finitude confronts us with the "fragility of being (Jaspers)," which Yalom also refers to as "ontological anxiety (Tillich)" or "dread of nonbeing (Kierkegaard)."[64] That also means anxiety on the *ontological* level is not merely a byproduct of repression but is immanent in the existential situation: it is embedded in the paradoxical structure of the self and comes with our freedom to extend or to restrict ourselves. Rollo May has emphasized the relationship between freedom and anxiety as a "keystone" of Kierkegaard's study of anxiety: "Anxiety is the state of man, says Kierkegaard, when he confronts his freedom."[65] But "this is 'normal anxiety,' and is not to be confused with 'neurotic anxiety.' " May clarifies further: "Kierkegaard makes it clear that neurotic anxiety is a more constrictive and uncreative form of anxiety which results from the individual's failure to move ahead in situations of normal anxiety."[66] May has laid out this distinction between normal and neurotic anxiety at length in his *Meaning of Anxiety*.[67] This is also central to Yalom's approach. In his chapter "Death and Psychotherapy" Yalom reminds the therapist that death anxiety "is *both*, neurotic and normal," because "all human beings experience death anxiety."[68] That means the question is not *if* anxiety belongs to our human condition but rather *how* we are able to deal with it. As May puts it: "Kierkegaard makes it clear that selfhood depends upon the individual's capacity to confront anxiety and move ahead despite it."[69] This *creative* view of anxiety has laid the ground for the existential psychotherapeutic conviction that anxiety can have an awakening function to develop a truer and more courageous self. In this way anxiety is no longer seen as a mere symptom to be cured, but also as an important tool, a "new possibility," towards a fuller life. "This is, what Kierkegaard called creative anxiety," comments Yalom.[70] So what May and Yalom have appropriated from Kierkegaard is also a more optimistic view on

---

61   Rollo May, *The Meaning of Anxiety*, New York: The Ronald Press Company 1950, p. 100.
62   Ibid., p. 193.
63   Yalom, *Existential Psychotherapy*, p. 42.
64   Ibid.
65   May, *The Meaning of Anxiety*, 1950, p. 32; p. 33.
66   Ibid., p. 33.
67   Ibid., pp. 193ff.
68   Yalom, *Existential Psychotherapy*, p. 207.
69   May, *The Meaning of Anxiety*, 1950, p. 56.
70   Yalom, *Existential Psychotherapy*, p. 166.

anxiety, namely that it can "self-strengthen" the individual and "educate it towards maturity."[71]

As we can see, Kierkegaard's concept of *Angest*,[72] especially through May's readings, has become central to Yalom's understanding of existential anxiety. Such anxiety occurs, he concludes in his *Existential Psychotherapy*, "when fear of some thing…is understood for what it truly is—a fear of *no* thing."[73] But because such anxiety threatens the basis of our selfhood and shakes our very foundation, we are tempted to combat anxiety by turning it from the fear of *no*thing into a fear of *some*thing we hope we can better control.

D. Avoiding Dread—Existential Psychopathology

The attempt to avoid the deeper layers of anxiety by projecting them into something else could also be understood as the transition zone where "normal anxiety" turns into "neurotic anxiety." To cope with our existential fears, Yalom says, "we erect defenses against death awareness, defenses that are based on denial."[74] In this way Yalom's first ultimate concern has somewhat of a prior place in the list of concerns. It is not only the "primordial source of anxiety" but as such also the "primary fount of psychopathology."[75] Psychopathology is an "*ineffective* defense mode," Yalom explains referring to Kierkegaard for illustration: "Kierkegaard knew that man limited and diminished himself in order to avoid perception of the 'terror, perdition and annihilation that dwell next door to any man.' "[76] Yalom took this Kierkegaard quotation from Ernest Becker's book *The Denial of Death*.[77] This Pulitzer Prize winning book depends heavily on Søren Kierkegaard's thoughts as well as their connections to the ideas of the psychoanalyst Otto Rank (1884–1939).[78] Laying out his understanding of the *ineffective defense*, Yalom merges the ideas of several thinkers: we find beside Kierkegaard and Becker also Rank and Tillich cited in the same paragraph. It is the avoidance of the everyday "terror" of existing which Kierkegaard adds to the picture and which has been appropriated by Becker, and thus Yalom. Yalom also brings in Becker's comment on the ironic situation that man wants to be free of death anxiety but at the same time "it is life itself which awakens it and so we must shrink from being fully alive."[79] In his *The Courage to Be* Tillich

---

[71]   See May, *The Meaning of Anxiety*, 1950, p. 45.

[72]   There has been difficulty finding a proper translation of the Danish term *Angest*. This difficulty is reflected in the different titles of the different translations. While Lowrie decided in 1944 to translate this term with "dread," the Hongs translate with "anxiety." See also May's comment on it in his *The Meaning of Anxiety, 1950*, p. 32 n. 45.

[73]   Yalom, *Existential Psychotherapy*, p. 48.

[74]   Ibid.

[75]   Ibid., p. 29.

[76]   Ibid., p. 111.

[77]   Ernest Becker, *The Denial of Death*, New York: Free Press 1973, p. 70.

[78]   For a deeper exploration of the Becker–Kierkegaard connection see also the article by Rick Anthony Furtak, "Ernest Becker: A Kierkegaardian Theorist of Death and Human Nature" in this volume.

[79]   Cited from Becker, *The Denial of Death*, p. 44.

gives a familiar understanding of the neurotic as "the way of avoiding non-being by avoiding being."[80] Surely the Dane is here sneaking in again behind Tillich. In many long passages, Tillich's chapter "Being, Nonbeing and Anxiety" reads like a comment on Kierkegaard's concept of anxiety.[81] Rank has previously described the neurotic person in a familiar way: as one "who refused the loan (life) in order to avoid the payment of the debt (death)."[82] Yalom has mainly taken the dialectics of life and death anxiety from Rank: "That's why I've always been intrigued with Otto Rank's formulation of going back and forth between the poles of life anxiety and death anxiety. And also Ernest Becker, who is very Rankian, and developed Rank's ideas in his wonderful book, *The Denial of Death*."[83] It is worth mentioning that Becker, in *Denial of Death,* titles his chapter on Rank "Otto Rank and the Closure of Psychoanalysis on Kierkegaard."[84]

Yalom uses death anxiety as a paradigm for psychopathology. Because the problem is not that we are afraid of death but rather that we try to avoid and neglect this fact by any means: "Primary anxiety is transformed into something less toxic for the individual," Yalom explains, and such transformation then becomes the source of the psychological defenses.[85] Even if the individual "restricts" himself or herself this way—here Yalom comes back to the idea he has earlier quoted from Kierkegaard, it has a protective function, namely, to avoid the terror of death anxiety.[86]

But what are the costs of such "neurotic adaptation"?[87] One fails to live one's life fully, Yalom answers, one does not live to one's full potential. By doing so one also becomes guilty against oneself: "It was Kierkegaard, and later Rank and Tillich, who called attention to another source of guilt—the transgression against oneself, the failure to live the life allotted to one," Yalom states. Therefore "repression is this double-edged sword; it provides safety and relief from anxiety, while at the same time it generates life restriction and a form of guilt, henceforth referred to as "existential guilt."[88] Yalom comes back to the guilt theme later when he presents the second ultimate concern: freedom. Here he explores the existential dimension of guilt: "Of all existential philosophers Kierkegaard and then Heidegger most fully developed this concept." Later Tillich and Buber also contributed to this "extraordinarily important concept."[89] Here Yalom appears quite aware of Tillich's appropriation of Kierkegaard's thoughts:

---

[80]   Cited from Paul Tillich, *The Courage to Be*, New Haven and London: Yale University Press 1952, p. 66.

[81]   Ibid., pp. 32ff.

[82]   Cited from Otto Rank, *Will Therapy and Truth and Reality*, New York: Alfred A. Knopf 1945, p. 126.

[83]   Josselson, *Irvin D. Yalom: On Psychotherapy and the Human Condition*, p. 114.

[84]   Becker, *The Denial of Death*, pp. 159–76.

[85]   Yalom, *Existential Psychotherapy*, p. 45.

[86]   Ibid., p. 49.

[87]   Ibid., p. 146.

[88]   Ibid., p. 147.

[89]   Ibid.

Tillich's view that man is "asked to make of himself what he is supposed to become, to fulfill his destiny" derives from Kierkegaard who described a form of despair that emerged from not being willing to be oneself. Self-reflection (awareness of guilt) tempers the despair, whereas not to know that one is in despair is a deeper form of despair yet.[90]

The person who is not willing to be himself or herself is "twice in despair," says Yalom, echoing Kierkegaard, "to begin with, in a fundamental existential despair, and then further in despair because, having sacrificed self-awareness, they do not even know they are in despair."[91] Twice in despair means, in the Kierkegaardian sense, that a person does not want to be himself or herself, does not want to face their existential dilemmas, does not want to awake to full consciousness. Therefore the despair about such deficient self-relation is not conscious either; the person despairs without being aware of it. Such unconsciousness of despair is like unconsciousness of dread, comments Kierkegaard's Anti-Climacus in *The Sickness unto Death*, referring to Vigilius Haufniensis, the pseudonym writer of *The Concept of Anxiety*. This is because by avoiding consciousness of the self as spirit one can also avoid the dread which comes with it by keeping a "spiritless sense of security."[92]

E. The Highest Venture—Becoming Conscious of Oneself

Yalom illustrates the human task of becoming oneself with a famous hasidic story told by Martin Buber. It is about the rabbi Susya who said shortly before his death: "When I get to heaven they will not ask me 'Why were you not Moses?' Instead they will ask: 'Why were you not Susya? Why did you not become what only you could become?' "[93] But what is so difficult about becoming oneself? "[I]t is a dangerous venture," Yalom answers with Kierkegaard:

And why? Because one may lose. Not to venture is shrewd. And yet, by not venturing, it is so dreadfully easy to lose that which it would be difficult to lose in even the most venturesome venture....one's self. For if I have ventured amiss—very well, then life helps me by its punishment. But if I have not ventured at all—who then helps me? And moreover, if by not venturing at all in the highest sense (*and to venture in the highest*

---

[90]   Ibid., pp. 277–8. This paragraph refers to Tillich, *The Courage to Be*, p. 52 as well as to Søren Kierkegaard's *Fear and Trembling and The Sickness unto Death*, translated with Introductions and Notes by Walter Lowrie, Garden City, New York: Doubleday Anchor Books 1954, pp. 186–7.

[91]   Yalom, *Existential Psychotherapy*, p. 374. Yalom cites from Kierkegaard, *Fear and Trembling and The Sickness unto Death*, p. 177. Yalom uses this theme also in his novel *The Schopenhauer Cure*, p. 84: Here the main figure brings in a thought from Kierkegaard about the "double despair," when one is in despair but "too self-deceived" to know even that one is in despair.

[92]   *SKS* 11, 159 / *SUD*, 44. Anti-Climacus refers here to Haufniensis' "anxiety of spiritlessness" (*Aandløshedens Angest*), *SKS* 4, 396–7 / *CA*, 93ff.

[93]   Yalom, *Existential Psychotherapy*, p. 278. Yalom cites from Michael Friedman's introduction to Martin Buber in *Between Man and Man*, New York: Macmillan 1965, p. xix.

sense is precisely to become conscious of oneself) I have gained all earthly advantages…
and lose myself. What of that?[94]

Yalom has borrowed this Kierkegaard quotation from a footnote in May's *The Meaning of Anxiety*. The quotation itself is taken from *The Sickness unto Death*, part I section C in which Anti-Climacus introduces the forms of despair in regard to the structure of the self.[95] This is based on the Kierkegaardian anthropology that the self is a synthesis of finitude and infinitude, possibility and necessity, and that despair occurs as result of a misrelation in this very synthesis. The first form is "despair of infinity" [*Uendelighedens Fortvivlese*] and describes a "fantastical" state in which one gets carried away from oneself and loses oneself in the fantastic: "The self thus leads a fantastic existence in abstract endeavor after infinity, or in abstract isolation, constantly lacking itself, from which it merely gets further and further away."[96] This way one can also "infinitize" one's God relationship by losing oneself in its abstract illusion instead of "to exist before God." Such despair, therefore, can be described as a "lack of finitude."[97] The other side of this despair Anti-Climacus describes as the "despair of finitude" [*Endelighedens Fortvivlelse*].[98] This form of despair is the context for the above passage to which Yalom is referring. Such despair is lost in pure worldliness which lacks infinitude and therefore meaning. Anti-Climacus pictures it thus:

> This form of despair is hardly ever noticed in the world. Such a man, precisely by losing his self in this way, has gained perfectibility in adjusting himself to business, yea, in making a success in the world. Here there is no hindrance, no difficulty, occasioned by his self and his infinitization, he is ground smooth as a pebble, courant as a well-used coin.[99]

Such a man who has lost himself this way, "forgets himself, forgets what his name is (in the divine understanding of it), does not dare to believe in himself, finds it too venturesome a thing to be himself, far easier and safer to be like the others, to become an imitation, a number, a cipher in the crowd."[100]

Having taken the quotation about the dreadful venture from May, Yalom does not comment here on the context of Kierkegaard's analysis of despair. He uses the quotation to contrast "the perils of 'venturing' (emergence, individuation,

---

[94]   Yalom, *Existential Psychotherapy*, p. 130. Yalom cites this Kierkegaard passage from May, *The Meaning of Anxiety*, p. 38. May has taken it from Kierkegaard, *The Sickness unto Death*, trans. by Walter Lowrie, Princeton: Princeton University Press 1941, p. 52 and added the italics.

[95]   See *SKS* 11, 145ff. / *SUD*, 29ff.

[96]   I quote here from Lowrie's translation of *The Sickness unto Death*, p. 48, which was the relevant source for May and Yalom; Cf. *SKS* 11, 148 / *SUD*, 32.

[97]   Ibid.

[98]   Kierkegaard, *The Sickness unto Death*, trans. by Lowrie, p. 49; Cf. *SKS* 11, 149 / *SUD*, 33.

[99]   Kierkegaard, *The Sickness unto Death*, trans. by Lowrie, p. 51; Cf. *SKS* 11, 149–50 / *SUD*, 32–3.

[100]   Ibid.

specialness) and not venturing (fusion, embeddedness, belief in ultimate rescuer)."[101] What are those perils? The individual can lose either way, by venturing or not. In addition, venturing can be understood in different ways. One can keep oneself busy venturing in the worldly sense and still not venturing in the highest sense. What then is it to venture in the "highest sense"? For Anti-Climacus it is not about rushing from one thing to another or collecting earthly goods and purposes. Instead, the *highest venture* happens mostly unseen from the world. It is when one starts to walk inwardly and becomes more and more conscious of oneself. Or as Yalom puts it with another Kierkegaard reference (again, via May): the true vocation of the human being is "to will to be oneself."[102] But Kierkegaard's challenge *at ville være sig selv* is truly dialectical, since it points to the boundary situation in which the individual can lose or gain the very self:[103] because one can desperately not want to be oneself ("weakness") or one can want to be oneself desperately ("defiance"). One can lose oneself in mere infinitude (the fantastic) or in mere finitude. One can win all "worldly advantage" but lose one's spiritual health. Since such despair can appear quite successful in the world, Anti-Climacus never tires of stressing the downside of mere self-actualization: the one who has lost himself this way may even

> be praised by men, be honored and esteemed, and pursue all the aims of temporal life. What is called worldliness is made up of just such men, who (if one may use the expression) pawn themselves to the world. They use their talents, accumulate money, carry on worldly affairs, calculate shrewdly, etc., etc., are perhaps mentioned in history, but themselves they are not; spiritually understood, they have no self, no self for whose sake they could venture everything, no self before God—however selfish they may be for all that.[104]

As we see, for Kierkegaard the striving towards a truer self, *the highest venture*, is embedded in the paradoxical structure of the self, infinity embodied in finitude, a tension which the individual has somehow to hold together. Coming back to the beginning of this section and to the trouble-seeking Dane, he indeed has made it difficult because it is not only about becoming oneself; instead, it is about becoming oneself by holding the paradoxical dimensions of the self together. That means for the Dane the dialectical structure of the self is itself a given of existence.

Even if Yalom and Kierkegaard might differ in their particular understanding of the givens of existence (and even more about "the giver"), they share common ground in this: both seek to help and foster the individual's encountering and coping with the threats of existence. "[T]he confrontation with the givens of existence is painful but ultimately healing," Yalom states.[105] And just like Kierkegaard, Yalom is not shy about bringing both experts together for this task: "the task of the philosopher, and of the therapist as well, is to de-repress, to reacquaint the individual with something he

---

[101]   Yalom, *Existential Psychotherapy*, p. 130.
[102]   Ibid., p. 285, Yalom quotes again from May, *The Meaning of Anxiety*, 1977, p. 40.
[103]   Cf. *SKS* 11, 164–5 / *SUD*, 49–50.
[104]   Kierkegaard, *The Sickness unto Death*, trans. by Lowrie, p. 53; Cf. *SKS* 11, 150–1 / *SUD*, 35–7.
[105]   Yalom, *Existential Psychotherapy*, p. 14.

or she has known all along."[106] For this both "must encourage the individual to look within and to attend to his or her existential situation."[107]

F. Finding Meaning Despite the Threat

But how one can come to terms with the fundamental threats of existence? This question leads us to the concern for meaning that Yalom explores in the fourth part of his book. No direct references to Kierkegaard can be found in this section, but if we are generous, we can allow the Dane to sneak through the back door twice more. In discussing man's search for meaning, Yalom comes back to his concept of psychopathology as an "ineffective mode of death transcendence."[108] One can only transcend death *"by finding a meaning for his life,"* a meaning which can hold up to the threats of our existence, Yalom quotes from Becker.[109] This also means such "transcending" must be different from simple transformation in the sense of projecting the threat into something else, because it reaches beyond oneself and leads the self towards something which is outside or "above" the self. The Dane sneaks in thus: Yalom draws this point from Becker, who in turn points to Kierkegaard for illustration: If failure is to not transcend the terror of death, the "healthy person, the true individual, the real man" would be one "who has *transcended* himself."[110] But how can one do exactly this? Becker offers the way with his reading of Kierkegaard: "by realizing the truth of our condition we can transcend ourselves."[111] Since becoming aware of our "creatureness" overwhelms us with anxiety we have to accept the fact to conquer its threat: "The flood of anxiety is not the end for man. It is, rather, a 'school' that provides man with the ultimate education, the final maturity."[112] This idea of being educated by anxiety we have also found in May's Kierkegaard readings, and thus in Yalom. And by giving in to our creatureness, Becker goes further with Kierkegaard here; one becomes aware of one's finitude and the need to reach beyond it.[113]

According to Yalom, the search for meaning goes beyond mere self-interest by *striving* "toward something or someone outside or 'above' oneself."[114] This means also the search for meaning is radically different from mere drive theories, which see man only *driven* by the search for pleasure. Yalom returns several times to the "hedonistic paradox" which he illustrates with Viktor Frankl, the main advocate for

---

[106]   Ibid., p. 340.

[107]   Ibid., p. 16.

[108]   Ibid., p. 27.

[109]   Ibid., p. 465. Yalom quotes from Ernest Becker, *Escape from Evil*, New York: Free Press 1975, p. 3 (emphasis original).

[110]   Becker, *The Denial of Death*, p. 86 (emphasis original).

[111]   Ibid, p. 86; p. 87.

[112]   Ibid., p. 87. Becker refers here to Kierkegaard's *The Concept of Dread*, trans. by Lowrie, pp. 140ff.; Cf. *SKS* 4, 455ff. / *CA*, 156ff. where Kierkegaard speaks about being educated by anxiety as a "school of possibility."

[113]   Becker, *The Denial of Death*, p. 89.

[114]   Yalom, *Existential Psychotherapy*, p. 439.

and author of *Man's Search for Meaning*.[115] "Earlier I described Frankl's dictum, that 'happiness cannot be pursued, it can only ensue,' "[116] he states, and he recounts at another place: "Happiness ensues; it cannot be pursued."[117] Here also Kierkegaard sneaks through the back door since Frankl most often illustrates this dictum with Kierkegaard: "Kierkegaard speaks analogously when he notes that the door to happiness opens outward; it closes itself all the more tightly as we try to push our way into happiness. We could say that the hunt for happiness scares it away—the fight for pleasure chases it away."[118] The Kierkegaard that Frankl has appropriated from a simple aphorism and changed over time now finds its way into Yalom's approach:

> Earlier I discussed the hedonistic paradox that the more we explicitly search for pleasure, the more it eludes us. Frankl argues that pleasure is a by-product of meaning, and that one's search should be directed towards the discovery of meaning. I believe that the search for meaning is similarly paradoxical: the more we rationally seek it, the less we find it; the question that one can pose about meaning will always outlast the answers. Meaning, like pleasure, must be pursued obliquely.[119]

Having taken Frankl's dictum to heart, Yalom advises the therapist to help the meaning-seeking client to "look *away* from the question"[120] and instead to engage in and embrace life and thereby find meaning on the way. He concludes his *Existential Psychotherapy* with the help of the Buddha: "One must immerse oneself in the river of life and let the question drift away."[121]

III. Ultimate Concerns and the Concern for the Ultimate: Some Concluding Thoughts

As we have seen, Kierkegaard's influence is widely appropriated in the field of existential psychotherapy and intermingled with Yalom's approach as well as with that of many of the authors he has read. This makes it difficult and sometimes

---

[115]   Viktor Emil Frankl, *Man's Search for Meaning*, Boston: Beacon Press 1963.

[116]   Yalom, *Existential Psychotherapy*, p. 472.

[117]   Ibid., p. 472; p. 444; see also ibid., p. 482.

[118]   Viktor Emil Frankl, *On the Theory and Therapy of Mental Disorders: An Introduction to Logotherapy and Existential Analysis*, ed. by James M. DuBois, trans. by James M. DuBois with Kateryna Cuddeback, New York and Howe: Brunner–Routledge, p. 126. Indeed Frankl uses several versions of this door metaphor from Kierkegaard throughout his writings. It is taken from "Diapsalmata" (*SKS* 2, 32 / *EO1*, 23): "Alas, fortune's [*Lykkens*] door doesn't open inward so that one can push it open by rushing at it; but it opens outward, and therefore one can do nothing about it." In his book *Der leidende Mensch. Anthropologische Grundlagen der Psychotherapie*, Munich, Zürich: Piper 1990 Frankl uses the metaphor twice, in the introduction p. 11 and in objection to the mere pleasure principle (*Lustprinzip*) of psychoanalysis, p. 281: "*Kierkegaard sagte einmal, die Tür zum Glück gehe nach außen auf: wer hineinzustürmen versucht—dem verschließt und versagt es sich.*"

[119]   Yalom, *Existential Psychotherapy*, p. 482.

[120]   Ibid., p. 483.

[121]   Ibid.

impossible to trace certain concepts back to their origins. Many of Kierkegaard's thoughts form the basis and the underpinnings of existential psychotherapy and have also today become "common sense." Still we have been able to trace back the main Kierkegaard references in Yalom's writings, most of them directly quoted, but some sneaking in through the back door.

(1) Yalom starts his introduction into the field with the difficulty-seeking Climacus to illustrate the importance of considering one's existential situation: one's dreads, one's choices, one's possibilities and limitations. This has led him (2) to define four existential "ultimate concerns," a term which is taken from the theistic concept of the passion towards the ultimate as described by Tillich and Kierkegaard. Yalom reuses the term to point to the essential themes or concerns of existence. (3) Both Yalom and Kierkegaard, are aware that existential anxiety (*Angest*) is provoked by the givens of the existential situation. At the same time the confrontation with existential anxiety also connects the individual with the deeper layers, the ground of being. As we saw, the meaning of anxiety as used by authors such as May, Tillich, Becker, and Rank are intimately intertwined with the concepts of the Dane, and thus with Yalom. The distinction between normal and neurotic anxiety is particularly based on Kierkegaard's analysis. (4) Yalom also relies on Kierkegaard to illustrate one's tendency to avoid those threats of existence by repressing or transforming the fear of nothing into a fear of something. Kierkegaard and his many pseudonyms have richly portrayed the many ways the individual tries to avoid the terror of finitude. Such a defense can lead one into an anxious state of despair and one transgresses against oneself by not willing to be oneself. Both concepts, that is, despair and "existential guilt," became key concepts in Yalom's understanding of individuation and psychopathology. (5) Both authors also share the conviction that the terror of existence can only be overcome by confronting and processing existential anxiety. They think about such processing as a life-long journey through which one grows into the self one is supposed to be. Yalom also relies on Kierkegaard's expression of the "highest venture" as becoming conscious of oneself and one's situation. (6) Last but not least, coming to terms with the threats of existing depends on the capacity of the individual not only to deal with anxiety but also to transcend it and move into meaning.

Both authors have in common their concern about the human condition and their art of midwifery, namely, to help the individual into an encounter with their existential situation. But Yalom and Kierkegaard differ in their understanding of what that situation actually is, and how one lives one's life fully. While Yalom interprets the highest venture in a secular humanist frame, for Kierkegaard the highest venture also embeds the striving for the highest, which means to become conscious of oneself as a spiritual creature. While for Yalom the ultimate concern is concerned with our finite existence, for the Dane the ultimate concern makes one concerned about the ultimate and how one can relate to what is ultimate. In Kierkegaard's understanding, contemplating the givens of one's existential situation not only confronts one with one's finite existence but points at the same time to the infinite world from which spirit and freedom arises. While Yalom came to believe that, for example, love obsession comes "from the same stuff as religion,"[122] his sources of that concept such as Rank and Becker come to a contradictory conclusion: it is the lack of the ultimate in the life of a person which makes him or her search for the ultimate in finite objects.[123]

It was Ernest Becker who brought thinkers such as Freud, Rank, Tillich, and Kierkegaard together in their concern about the ultimate: while for Freud man's God relation is seen as mostly masochistic, for Rank it also "represents in the contrary the furthest reach of the self, the highest idealisation man can achieve."[124] And as Becker goes further:

> It represents the fulfillment of the Agape love-expansion, the achievement of the truly creative type. Only this way, says Rank, only by surrendering to the bigness of nature on the highest, least—fetishized level, can man conquer death....Therefore man is a "theological being" concludes Rank, and not a biological one. In all this it is as though Tillich were speaking and, behind him, Kierkegaard and Augustine; but what makes it uncanny in the present world of science is that these are the conclusions of the lifework of a psychoanalyst, not a theologian.[125]

Therefore leaving out the spiritual dimension of man is not only a problem of anthropological foundation. It also makes it difficult in the therapeutic field to differentiate between natural and neurotic ways of spiritual engagement. Omitting the spiritual dimension of man also risks that psychotherapy itself becomes the promised land and the therapeutic relationship is expected to be ultimately healing.

Despite these differences in their anthropological foundation, the Dane himself would likely honor Yalom as a Socratic teacher who reminds us of our finitude, and stresses the existential dilemma as far as he can. It was Climacus himself who reminded his reader that existential work is the hard work which has to be done before one should start to grapple with the religious.

---

[122]   Josselson, *Irvin D. Yalom*, p. 116.

[123]   For an attempt to bring Yalom's approach into discussion with a theistic framework see Jeremy D. Bartz, "Theistic Existential Psychotherapy," in *Psychology of Religion and Spirituality*, vol. 1, no. 2, 2009, pp. 69–80.

[124]   Becker, *The Denial of Death*, p. 174.

[125]   Ibid., pp. 174–5.

Bibliography

I. Works by Yalom that Refer to Kierkegaard

Existential Psychotherapy, New York: Basic Books 1980, p. 15; p. 42; p. 43; p. 111; pp. 130–1; p. 147; p. 162; p. 166; p. 277; p. 278; p. 285; p. 360; p. 374; p. 380.

Lying on the Couch, New York: Basic Books 1996, p. 2.

The Yalom Reader: Selections from the Work of a Master Therapist and Storyteller, ed. by Ben Yalom, New York: Basic Books 1998, pp. 177–8; p. 192; pp. 193–4; p. 203; pp. 220–1; p. 233; p. 237; p. 340; p. 375.

The Schopenhauer Cure, New York: HarperCollins 2005, p. 84; p. 108; p. 298; p. 324.

Staring at the Sun, New York: Jossey-Bass/Wiley 2008, p. 200.

II. Sources of Yalom's Knowledge of Kierkegaard

Becker, Ernest, *The Denial of Death*, New York: Free Press 1973, pp. 67–92; pp. 159–75; pp. 196–8; p. 205.

— *Escape from Evil*, New York: Free Press 1975, p. 61; p. 162.

Kierkegaard, Søren, *Fear and Trembling and The Sickness unto Death*, trans. by Walter Lowrie, Garden City, New York: Doubleday Anchor Books 1954 (originally published by Princeton University Press 1941).

— *A Kierkegaard Anthology*, ed. by Robert Bretall, Princeton, New Jersey: Princeton University Press 1946.

— *The Concept of Dread*, trans. by Walter Lowrie, Princeton: Princeton University Press 1957.

May, Rollo, Ernest Angel, and Henry F. Ellenberger (eds.), *Existence: A New Dimension in Psychiatry and Psychology*, New York: Basic Books 1958, pp. 11–12; p. 14; p. 15, note; pp. 19–20; pp. 22–30; pp. 33–5; pp. 51–2; p. 56; p. 61; p. 62, note; p. 65; p. 69; pp. 70–1; p. 75; p. 87; p. 92; pp. 117–18; p. 236; p. 292; p. 294; pp. 297–9; p. 303; p. 305; p. 326, note; p. 341; p. 356.

May, Rollo, *The Meaning of Anxiety*, revised ed., New York: W.W. Norton 1977, p. xv; p. xix; p. xxi; pp. 20–1; p. 26; p. 28; pp. 32–51; p. 60; p. 65; p. 99; p. 113; p. 123; p. 125; p. 133; p. 143; p. 151; p. 158; p. 162; p. 175; p. 186; p. 207; p. 212; p. 220; p. 226; p. 229; p. 244; p. 265; p. 320; p. 370; p. 376; p. 379; p. 384; p. 385; p. 387; p. 390; pp. 392–3.

Tillich, Paul, *The Courage to Be*, New Haven and London: Yale University Press 1952, pp. 32–40; p. 125; p. 135; p. 138; p. 142.

III. *Secondary Literature on Yalom's Relation to Kierkegaard*

Bartz, Jeremy D., "Theistic Existential Psychotherapy," *Psychology of Religion and Spirituality*, vol. 1, no. 2, 2009, pp. 69–80; see p. 69; p. 71.

Corey, Gerald, *Theory and Practice of Counselling and Psychotherapy*, Belmont, California: Thomson/Brooks/Cole 2009, p. 138.

Slavoj Žižek:
Mirroring the Absent God

Leo Stan

When crossing ways with any written testimony of Slavoj Žižek's thought, the unwarned reader may be baffled by the broad ideational terrain and seamless eclecticism unfolding before one's eyes. Equally controversial and captivating, Žižek's *corpus* nonchalantly sails through numerous heterogeneous disciplines, unrelated historical epochs, and radically disparate ways of thinking. As Sarah Kay observes: "Reading Žižek is like taking an exhilarating ride on a roller-coaster through anecdote, Kant, popular film, science, religion, smut, current affairs, modern art, Derrida, political correctness, canonical literature, cyberspace, etc., etc., being constantly buffeted as you do so in the twists and turns of Hegelian dialectic and Lacanian theory."[1] Slavoj Žižek was born on March 21, 1949 in Ljubljana, Slovenia. His first doctoral degree on German idealism was received in his hometown, while the second, on Lacan and Hegel, was completed in Paris. The vast recognition Žižek enjoys today is due to both his gigantesque work (over fifty singly authored books translated into twenty languages) and an assiduous lecturing activity. A visiting professor at numerous North American universities, Žižek holds permanent positions at the Institute for Sociology, Ljubljana, and at the European Graduate School. He is also the founder and president of the Society for Theoretical Psychoanalysis, Ljubljana. Currently, he serves as International Director of the Birkbeck Institute for the Humanities at the University of London. His latest interests orbit around such socio-political topics as globalization, multiculturalism, ideology, Leninism, while his increasing concern for ethics, theology, and even opera adds an interesting twist to the communist-revolutionary ideals he proudly upholds. The superlative appraisals of his authorship did not lag behind.[2]

Regarding Žižek's mentors, Hegel and Marx occupy the foreground, followed closely by Kant and Schelling. However, the *axis mundi* of his theoretical cosmos remains the unorthodox French psychoanalyst, Jacques Lacan. Generally speaking,

---

[1]   Sarah Kay, *Žižek: A Critical Introduction*, Cambridge: Polity Press 2003, p. 1.
[2]   For illuminating discussions of Žižek's theories, philosophical or otherwise, see Tony Myers, *Slavoj Žižek*, London and New York: Routledge 2003; Ian Parker, *Slavoj Žižek: A Critical Introduction*, London and Sterling: Pluto Press 2004. See also Sarah Kay, *Žižek: A Critical Introduction*, p. 1.

Slavoj Žižek advocates an essentialism or an ontology of the void.[3] That is to say, he inoculates the language of essentiality with constant references to gaps, splits, and various other instantiations of non-identity. For him, reality "is never a complete, self-enclosed, positive order of being,"[4] but rather the timeless "ontological gap"[5] in the very heart of existence. Therefore, truth should be predicated only on "the interstice, the non-self-coincidence of Being, that is, [on] the ontological nonclosure of the order of Being."[6] However, Žižek's ontology is suffused with such concepts as impossibility, primordial trauma, and unbearable surplus. In this line of thinking, every structured pattern appears as "precariously balanced on a seething morass of disorder, and at the same time incomprehensibly penetrated by it, so that, in the midst of the order there always persists an 'indivisible remainder' of chaos."[7] In the following, we shall see how this unique mélange of essentialism, pathological bellicosity, and subtle nihilism insinuates itself into Žižek's reading of Kierkegaard.

For the purposes of this study, we should also keep in mind that, although not a bitter attacker of religion, Žižek strips Christianity of any spiritual, transcendent, and eschatological connotation. This may go hand in hand with the fact that the prophets of his idiosyncratic religiosity are Nietzsche and a Freudian Schelling, whereas its apostles are Lacan, Marx, and Lenin. Sarah Kay's observation that Žižek's view of Christianity combines an indirect animosity towards Catholicism and Eastern Orthodoxy with an open enthusiasm for radical Protestantism is not sufficient.[8] To the Protestant tenor I would add the suspicion-driven, libido-oriented, and even scatological dimension[9] of Žižek's incursions into Christian theology. With that in mind, Žižek deploys the major doctrinal postulates of Christianity only to uncover the

---

[3]   For illustration see Slavoj Žižek, *The Puppet and the Dwarf: The Perverse Core of Christianity*, Cambridge, Massachusetts and London: MIT Press 2003, p. 152; Slavoj Žižek, *Enjoy Your Symptom!*, New York and London: Routledge 1992, pp. 46–50; p. 53; Slavoj Žižek, *Tarrying with the Negative:. Kant, Hegel, and the Critique of Ideology*, Durham: Duke University Press, 1993, p. 25; p. 31; Slavoj Žižek, *The Fragile Absolute*, London and New York: Verso 2000, p. 8. For the coevally Cartesian-Lacanian and Kantian background of Žižek's view of subjectivity, see Kay, *Žižek*, pp. 117–18. See also Slavoj Žižek, *The Parallax View*, Cambridge, Massachusetts and London: MIT Press 2006, pp. 20–3; pp. 90–4; 244; Slavoj Žižek, *On Belief*, London and New York: Routledge 2001, pp. 139–40; Žižek, *Enjoy Your Symptom!*, pp. 179–84; Žižek, *Tarrying with the Negative*, pp. 12–20; pp. 45–56; pp. 108–14; p. 173. Not to be ignored either is Schelling's decisive place in this composite picture.
[4]   Žižek, *The Parallax View*, p. 242.
[5]   Ibid.
[6]   Ibid., p. 167; see also ibid, p. 281.
[7]   Kay, *Žižek*, p. 113.
[8]   Ibid., p. 126.
[9]   Žižek rests assured that there is "no pure, rational, self-transparent spirituality without the accompanying stain of an obscene, uncanny, spectral pseudo-materiality." See Slavoj Žižek, *The Metastases of Enjoyment*, London and New York: Verso 1994, p. 194. On excrement as the externalization of "our innermost intimacy," see Žižek, *On Belief*, pp. 59–60. In *The Parallax View*, Martin Luther appears as the proponent of an "excremental" anthropology, see Žižek, *The Parallax View*, p. 187. Within the same mind frame, Žižek goes so far as to parallel Christian worship with the male's fascination for his partner's vagina, see Žižek, *On Belief*, pp. 94–5 and Kay, *Žižek*, p. 125. See also note 117 below.

repressed truths of the human condition. For instance, Žižek's Christ will reconfirm the interminable circularity of the subject's drive, of the individual's endless, albeit enjoyable, confrontation with a horrifying nothingness or an unconscious discord.[10] Viewed psychoanalytically, the postulates of the Christian religion are, on Žižek's estimation, mere indicators of the paradoxical *jouissance* that the subject experiences upon facing its immemorial traumas and the ontological void. Moreover, Christ, according to Žižek, reveals that God, if anyone, is divided against himself, and that serves only as a *metaphor* or *analogy* for the constitution of human subjectivity. Through his self-sacrificial acts—which Žižek calls ethical—Christ coevally offers a way out of our deep-seated antagonism, and thus announces a novel understanding of sociality. Briefly, the Judeo-Christian deity matters to Žižek primarily because it lays bare the conflictual-pathological crux of our nature.

I. Enter Kierkegaard

That said, it is no surprise that Žižek does not appropriate his composite sources with an eye to historical strictures. The ever-shifting palimpsest of his exegeses is continually fuelled by decontextualized formalizations and structural-integrative analogies.[11] His commentaries on Kierkegaard will make no exception. In principle, they are continually filtered through Lacan,[12] Hegel,[13] Schelling,[14] Marx,[15] Chesterton,[16] and sometimes Kant.[17] Of all these figures, Lacan by far holds the reins, although Schelling and Chesterton come very close behind. My analysis will start from Žižek's marginal references to Kierkegaard. The next sections will develop the frontal encounter with Kierkegaard.

The history of Kierkegaard research has been indelibly marked by an interpretive tradition initiated by Georg Brandes and resuscitated today by Joakim Garff, which teaches us that Kierkegaard's authorship is inextricable from his personal life. Regardless of the indubitable limitations of this approach, it remains a mystery why Slavoj Žižek, a philosopher intensely preoccupied with the emergence, internal dialectics, and a subterranean universe of subjectivity, is completely uninterested in the founding events of Kierkegaard's biography. Indeed, for an author who

---

[10]   See Žižek, *The Parallax View*, pp. 61–3; Žižek, *On Belief*, p. 98; and Žižek, *Enjoy Your Symptom!*, p. 48.

[11]   For an example of Žižek's formalist tactics, see his *Tarrying with the Negative*, p. 170. We shall soon see that structural analogies are endlessly deployed in Žižek's reception of Kierkegaard. By integrative I simply mean the incorporation of completely dissimilar tropes for the sake of a unified theory on subjectivity, ethics, politics, religion, and so on.

[12]   Žižek, *Enjoy Your Symptom!*, p. 78; p. 79; p. 95; p. 102; Kay, *Žižek*, p. 112.

[13]   Žižek, *Enjoy Your Symptom!*, p. 84; p. 109, note 33; Žižek, *Tarrying with the Negative*, p. 28; p. 243, note 28.

[14]   Žižek, *The Parallax View*, p. 31; Kay, *Žižek*, pp. 112–17.

[15]   Žižek, *Enjoy Your Symptom!*, p. 81.

[16]   Ibid., p. 83. Žižek, *The Puppet and the Dwarf*, pp. 14–15.

[17]   For example, Žižek, *The Parallax View*, p. 21. See also Slavoj Žižek, *The Indivisible Remainder*, London and New York: Verso 1996, p. 185, note 95.

holds Freud and Lacan in high esteem, it is rather odd that he leaves untouched Kierkegaard's rapports with paternal authority, the troubling absence of his mother from the journals, the trauma caused by the broken engagement,[18] and the clash with the ecclesiastical establishment. Instead, Žižek mentions only *en passant* Kierkegaard's addiction to theatrical performances, attended, he holds, as a temporary relief from "the extreme effort of thought."[19] In addition, for obvious reasons Žižek admiringly notes how "towards the end of his life Kierkegaard himself was compelled to admit that he was not a believer."[20]

The second object of Žižek's brief references concerns the complex constellation of anxiety, fantasy, and the void.[21] Thirdly, Žižek appreciates Kierkegaard's expostulation on the superiority of possibility over actuality as a prerequisite to the genuine comprehension of human freedom.[22] Probably in line with a certain hermeneutics of suspicion, Žižek conceives the tension between necessity and possibility—originally thematized by Kierkegaard in a relatively *religious* setting[23]—as most relevant within a *societal* perspective. To be precise, he alleges that Kierkegaard is valuable for trying to come to terms with the way in which every new social pact (possibility) will fatally exhaust all of its potentialities, thereby attaining an inevitable closure (the stage of necessity).[24]

Another topic surfacing time and again pertains to the concept of becoming. Kierkegaardian reflections in this regard help Žižek understand issues as disparate as the dialectic between law and violence,[25] the rift between thought and practice,[26] the body's interaction with the mind,[27] and even Heidegger's "worlding of the world."[28] The opposition Kierkegaard set between being and becoming proves equally fruitful when Žižek considers "the ultimate *undecidability*"[29] intrinsic to every historical

---

[18]   Just a passing allusion to this event is made in Mladen Dolar and Slavoj Žižek, *Opera's Second Death*, New York and London: Routledge 2002, p. 153.

[19]   Žižek, *The Parallax View*, p. 273.

[20]   Žižek, *The Indivisible Remainder*, p. 185, note 95. What Žižek refuses to remember, however, is that Kierkegaard's earnest self-criticisms were expressed in full accord with the never contested absoluteness of Christianity's salvific truth. Beyond that, upon reading Emil Boesen's confessions regarding the last days of Kierkegaard's life, we get a completely different picture of his faith. See *Encounters with Kierkegaard: A Life as Seen by His Contemporaries*, ed. by Bruce H. Kirmmse, Princeton: Princeton University Press 1996, pp. 121–8.

[21]   See, for instance, Žižek, *The Parallax View*, p. 61.

[22]   Žižek, *On Belief*, p. 105.

[23]   *SKS* 11, 151–7 / *SUD*, 35–42.

[24]   Slavoj Žižek, *The Universal Exception: Selected Writings*, vols. 1–2, London and New York: Continuum 2006, vol. 2, p. 15. In a similar sense, Žižek mentions Kierkegaard when arguing that a "singular point of exception" (illustrated by Christ's singularity, in which universality as such is *aufgehoben*) lies at the root of every universal norm and therefore, of all endeavors to regulate interpersonal relations. See Žižek, *The Puppet and the Dwarf*, p. 17.

[25]   Žižek, *Enjoy Your Symptom!*, p. 82.

[26]   Žižek, *The Parallax View*, p. 6. Žižek, *Enjoy Your Symptom!*, p. 54.

[27]   Žižek, *The Parallax View*, p. 178.

[28]   Žižek, *Tarrying with the Negative*, p. 269, note 42.

[29]   Ibid., p. 155 (emphasis original).

process, or the abysmal connection between Good and Evil.[30] Further, Žižek proves very creative in coining new categories out of Kierkegaard's philosophical arsenal. In this respect, he speaks of a "Christianity-in-becoming"[31] to describe the way in which St. Paul made a violent break with his Judaic roots and established the new Christian dogma. Žižek also hints at a "Universality-in-becoming,"[32] whereby Kierkegaard putatively employs "the power of negativity"[33] to undermine "the fixity of every particular constellation."[34]

Lastly, Žižek cherishes Kierkegaard's religious *Aufhebung* of the ethical.[35] Typically enough, however, his goal in doing so is to bring further insight into Berthold Brecht's communist reveries[36] and Lenin's frenzied critique of "formal freedom."[37] No wonder, then, that Žižek avails himself of the same reference to *Fear and Trembling* to advocate the necessity of a "political suspension of the Ethical"[38] as an authentic act to be pursued by the Left in the age of globalization. Perhaps, for the same reason and no less provocatively, Žižek interprets the revolutionary violence condoned and even prescribed by Lenin as a truly Kierkegaardian "work of love."[39]

II. On Unsurpassable Deadlocks and Religious Impossibilities

A substantial part of Žižek's reception of Kierkegaard can be found in *Enjoy Your Symptom!*[40] The context is a discussion of repetition, pursued by Žižek in negative

---

[30]   Ibid., pp. 96–7; Žižek, *The Puppet and the Dwarf*, p. 88.

[31]   Žižek, *The Puppet and the Dwarf*, p. 10. See also Slavoj Žižek, "Dialectical Clarity versus the Misty Conceit of Paradox," in Slavoj Žižek and John Milbank, *The Monstrosity of Christ: Paradox or Dialectic?*, ed. by Creston Davis, Cambridge, Massachusetts and London: MIT Press 2009, p. 292.

[32]   Žižek, *The Universal Exception*, vol. 2, pp. 121–2 note 23.

[33]   Ibid.

[34]   Ibid.

[35]   Žižek dwells a great deal on this Kierkegaardian theme. Žižek, *Enjoy Your Symptom!*, p. 177. Žižek, *The Puppet and the Dwarf*, p. 19. Žižek, *The Parallax View*, p. 132.

[36]   Žižek, *Enjoy Your Symptom!*, p. 177.

[37]   Žižek, *On Belief*, p. 149. On the opposition between formal and actual freedom, see ibid, pp. 116–22.

[38]   Žižek, *The Universal Exception*, vol. 2, p. 177.

[39]   Žižek, *The Puppet and the Dwarf*, p. 30. Žižek, *The Parallax View*, p. 282. For Christ as a forerunner of Che Guevara, see Žižek, *The Puppet and the Dwarf*, p. 6; p. 9; p. 30. As to Kierkegaard himself, his Christian "overorthodox" qualities, Žižek claims, continually prompt him to "subvert the ruling ideology by taking it more literally than it is ready to take itself." Slavoj Žižek, *The Plague of Fantasies*, London and New York: Verso 1997, p. 77. Kierkegaard's subversiveness can be inferred in yet another sense. Žižek remarks that in commenting upon Matt 21:28–31, Kierkegaard paradoxically praises the son who promises to unconditionally acquiesce to his father's command, but does not actually do what he is asked Žižek, *The Fragile Absolute*, pp. 147–8. SKS 9, 97–8 / WL, 91–2.

[40]   See Žižek, *Enjoy Your Symptom!*, pp. 78–80. For another short discussion of the same theme with similar results, see Dolar and Žižek, *Opera's Second Death*, pp. 151–3.

terms, that is to say, along the lines of impossibility, impasse, *aporia*. Taking *Repetition* as a landmark, Žižek considers that Kierkegaard's aesthete comes up against the impossibility of repetition through "the imaginary deadlocks that [he] encounters when he endeavors to resuscitate the fullness of past pleasures."[41] Every aesthetic attempt to fully relive a pleasant experience by reconstituting its original milieu to the minutest detail is doomed to fail. Since the aesthete's effort to cancel this impediment by a free exercise of fantasy turns out to be futile, a melancholy disappointment will get the better of him.

Kierkegaard's ethics is estimated by Žižek as a tentative endeavor to surmount the hedonistic impulses and the nostalgic-fantasmatic escapism of aesthetics. In living ethically, Žižek writes, "the subject has learned to avoid the twin traps of impatient hope in the New and of nostalgic memory of the Old."[42] The ethical self encounters repetition every time he must appropriate the given "universal norms of conduct."[43] However, failure seems to be the inexorable nemesis of the ethical existence due to a vicious circularity. Specifically, Žižek asserts that, even if he embraces the golden middle—that is, he avoids both unreal expectations as well as rhapsodic self-withdrawal—the ethicist cannot fully dispense with hopes and memories, in general. Hence the following dead-end of Kierkegaard's ethics: "the ideal point between hope and memory *is present precisely and only in the mode of hope or memory*."[44] Unfortunately, Žižek stops his argumentation here.[45] Implicitly, he then ignores the other side of Judge William's ethics, devised to offer an existential cure for aesthetic despair through a repentant self-choice.

Since the failure of repetition afflicts the ethical existence as much as aestheticism, a third stage becomes necessary. This is how, according to Žižek, we cross the threshold of religion. Žižek's thesis is that the Kierkegaardian religiousness disinclines the subject to reiterate past pleasures and to prevail over the predicaments of the ethical repetition. Instead, continues Žižek, religion enables the individual to experience repetition but in a very restricted sense. That is, when existing religiously, the impossibility that stood in the way of aesthetic enjoyment and ethical maturation is to be fully and deliberately internalized. In Žižek's phrasing, "insofar as repetition is not possible, it *is* possible to repeat this very experience of impossibility, i.e., the failure to attend the Object."[46] As such, Kierkegaard's religious repetition necessitates not only the sacrifice of "the particular 'aesthetic' content for the sake

---

[41]   Žižek, *Enjoy Your Symptom!*, p. 78.

[42]   Ibid.

[43]   Ibid.

[44]   Ibid., p. 79 (emphasis original).

[45]   What we are told is that "the ideal point at which we overcome the futile yearning for the New without falling into a nostalgic backward-directed attitude, is never present as such." Ibid., p. 78.

[46]   Ibid., p. 79. In *Opera's Second Death*, Žižek addresses the way impossibility is reflected in each Kierkegaardian stage from the standpoint of sexuality. The point he makes—namely, that "the aesthetic-ethical-religious triad provides the matrix for the three versions of the impossibility of sexual relationship"—is purely Lacanian. Dolar and Žižek, *Opera's Second Death*, p. 153.

of the universal ethical Law,"[47] but also the suspension of "this Law itself."[48] As depicted by Kierkegaard, religion harbors the possibility to willfully acknowledge, and hereby inwardly repeat, the unavoidable *aporiae* of aesthetic and ethical repetition.[49] But does that exhaust the full meaning of Kierkegaard's religiousness, according to Žižek?

After some brief remarks about Kierkegaard's insistence on the "abyss of free decision"[50] and historical becoming, Žižek suddenly veers towards a discussion of Christ. His (disenchanting) claim, most probably driven by an elusive hermeneutic of suspicion, is that as "a temporal Event...which, in its very singularity, provides the only gateway to Eternity,"[51] Incarnation represents, for Kierkegaard, the ingenuous third solution in the confrontation of two incompatible outlooks on history: the historicist approach, whereby different subjective stances towards life and existence are reduced to the social constellations they arose from, and the metaphysical-quietist angle, which is liable to deprecate everything related to this world. Žižek's reading has nothing to do with the soteriological, suffering-laden, and mimetic framework of Kierkegaard's Christianity. Instead, he uses the Kierkegaardian God-man to argue that a genuine grasp of historicity requires "the presence of an *unhistorical kernel*."[52] How so? When read correctly, argues Žižek, Kierkegaard's reflections on the embodied God reveal that "the only way to save historicity from the fall into historicism, into the notion of the linear succession of 'historical epochs,' is to conceive these epochs as a series of ultimately failed attempts to deal with the same 'unhistorical' traumatic kernel."[53] In principle, Kierkegaard's Christianity seems to rely on "an impossible demand that a priori cannot be complied with."[54] Once more, Žižek leaves the discussion at this declaratory level. We do not find out what exactly is the "traumatic kernel" concealed by the Incarnation or why Christ places

---

[47]   Žižek, *The Indivisible Remainder*, p. 121. Žižek suspects that this particular point brings Kierkegaard very close to Hegel.

[48]   Ibid.

[49]   We should not ignore either that Žižek sets religious repetition in opposition to remembrance. See Žižek, *Enjoy Your Symptom!*, p. 79. In dealing with remembrance (or what Kierkegaard called recollection), Žižek has in mind *Philosophical Fragments* which, he states, should "be read as the *repetition* of Plato's *Symposium*." His justification is that both texts show how love (or "transference" in psychoanalytical jargon) requires a relationship to the teacher (or the analyst) as "subject supposed to know." See Žižek, *Enjoy Your Symptom!*, p. 92. Besides, Žižek sees the Socratic truth in Kierkegaard's depiction as implying a universal meaningfulness (the truth) which is impervious to its position of enunciation (the teacher). By contrast, the Christian truth seems profoundly "dependent on the event of its enunciation," that is, on the personality of its proclaimer. See Žižek, *Enjoy Your Symptom!*, p. 93. See also Slavoj Žižek, "The Fear of Four Words: A Modest Plea for the Hegelian Reading of Christianity," in Žižek and Milbank, *The Monstrosity of Christ*, p. 37.

[50]   Žižek, *Enjoy Your Symptom!*, p. 79.

[51]   Žižek, *The Plague of Fantasies*, p. 52.

[52]   Žižek, *Enjoy Your Symptom!*, p. 81 (emphasis original).

[53]   Ibid.

[54]   Žižek, *The Indivisible Remainder*, p. 185, note 95.

us before "an impossible demand." This aspect may become more clear when we discuss Žižek's particular understanding of God or divine transcendence.

For now, two cursory observations are in order. First, we should note that the unhistorical is projected by Žižek into a pathological horizon: it testifies to or lies at the origin of, an originary disturbance. Second, on Žižek's account, Kierkegaard's Christianity never goes beyond the barrier of impossibility; that is, it remains incapable of offering a way beyond the constitutive obstacles of the ethical and the aesthetic. However, Žižek seems to forget that Kierkegaard's expatiations on Christianity are built on the conviction that for God everything is possible, and that the maniac dwelling on the impossibility of overcoming despair is tantamount to the demonic. Nevertheless, these are exceptionally theological clarifications which Žižek would treat with distrust.

Whereas Kierkegaard's Christianity seems relevant to Žižek because of its negativity (that is, pathology), things are no different with religious belief, which is equally incapable of conveying any positive content. For Žižek, the ruling principle of Kierkegaard's faith is that "I can never be quite sure that I truly believe."[55] That is why Žižek thinks highly of Kierkegaard's connection between belief and uncertainty. What he maintains is that, insofar as sinfulness concerns the open refusal to believe, the self, on Kierkegaard's portrayal, appears ceaselessly caught between the abyss of uncertainty and the pressing need to believe in order to avoid ungodliness.[56] At the same time, since Kierkegaard's merit is to have taught us that the Christian faith envisages primarily the personhood of Christ,[57] Žižek appreciates "the properly Kierkegaardian paradox, according to which Eternity is grounded in a concrete temporal, historical deed."[58] However, Christian fideism remains essentially vacuous: that is, it is reduced to the empty gesture of believing. Since believing "in Christ because we consider him wise and good is a dreadful blasphemy—it is, on the contrary, *only the act of belief itself* which can give us an insight into his goodness and wisdom."[59]

Žižek draws two specific conclusions from the intricate argument presented above. In the first place, he states that Kierkegaard's existential spheres can never be existentially synchronized. In Žižek's words, "we choose either within the first 'either/or,' that is, between the *esthetical* and the *ethical*, or within the second 'either/or,' that is, between the *ethical* and the *religious*."[60] In other words, the intersection between aesthetics and religion remains unconceivable to Žižek.[61] The second

---

[55]   Ibid. See also Žižek, *Tarrying with the Negative*, p. 247, note 53. However, this might be at odds with Žižek's awareness that belief is strong enough to generate existence. See Žižek, *Tarrying with the Negative*, p. 202.

[56]   Žižek, *The Indivisible Remainder*, p. 186, note 95.

[57]   Žižek, *Enjoy Your Symptom!*, p. 93.

[58]   Žižek, *The Plague of Fantasies*, p. 83, note 9.

[59]   Slavoj Žižek, *The Sublime Object of Ideology*, London and New York: Verso 1989, p. 37 (emphasis original). See also Žižek, *The Plague of Fantasies*, p. 108.

[60]   Žižek, *Enjoy Your Symptom!*, p. 82 (emphasis original).

[61]   Kierkegaard would drastically amend this reading. See, for example, the quasi-religious attitude of the merman and the aesthetic pleasures experienced by the knight of faith in *Fear and Trembling*. I have attempted to delineate the aesthetic dimension of Kierkegaard's

conclusion is that Kierkegaard's goal was to reaffirm Christianity and its fideism as an *act* which precedes its sedimentation into the reign of institutional order. In this limited sense, Kierkegaard's ultimate lesson is that the Christian religion still has the potential to show that "the *ethical* attitude is the only true subversion."[62] Otherwise stated—and this is Žižek's central contention—if Christianity still speaks to our secularized world, it is only because it champions the pursuance of a revolutionary creed (in Lenin's sense), deriving its gusto from a series of gratuitous self-sacrifices that are antithetical to aesthetic delusions, ethical complacency, and ossified normativity.

Without explicitly admitting it, Žižek's approach to religion is heavily indebted to the demythologizing tactics of Marxism and psychoanalysis. True enough, the primacy of subjective appropriation over the appropriated content, in conjunction with the paradoxical coincidence between the lowest and the highest in the historical existence of the God-man, whose truth is accessible solely through faith, have ensured Kierkegaard an immortal place in history of Western theology and philosophy. But in religious matters Žižek follows a different path. We have already seen that, when expanding on Christianity, his intention is chiefly to gain a fresh insight into the philosophy of history, to uncover a desirable meaning of sociality in contemporary cyber-age, and most significantly, to pinpoint the perverse entanglements of human nature. Žižek's hermeneutic is thus dominated by a thorough anthropologization: what he undertakes is to delineate the extent to which Christian transcendence validates that humanity is at the mercy of a *jouissant* superego, of a repressed primordial antagonism, and of the drive's infernal machinations.

III. On the Difference between a Savior and an Apostle

Kierkegaard's name surfaces in connection with another leitmotif of Žižek's *corpus*: namely, the roots and status of authority. In this regard, the Slovenian commentator embarks upon a close reading of Kierkegaard's classical piece "The Difference between a Genius and an Apostle,"[63] which was originally elaborated on the occasion of pastor Adolph Peter Adler's (1812–69) mischance in the arena of divine revelation. Although completely uninterested in the text's original context, and thus quite far from Kierkegaard's primary goals, Žižek's discussion is not without originality. To Žižek the first element of great import appears to be Kierkegaard's realization that "we obey a person in whom authority is vested irrespective of the content of his statements (authority ceases to be what it is the moment we make it dependent on the quality of its content), [and] yet [that] this person retains authority only insofar

---

religiosity in Leo Stan, "The Lily in the Field and the Bird of the Air: An Endless Liturgy in Kierkegaard's Authorship," in *Kierkegaard and the Bible*, Tome II, *The New Testament*, ed. by Lee C. Barrett and Jon Stewart, Aldershot: Ashgate 2010 (*Kierkegaard Research: Sources, Reception and Resources*, vol. 1), pp. 55–78.

62   Žižek, *Enjoy Your Symptom!*, p. 83 (emphasis original).

63   *SKS* 11, 95–111 / *WA*, 91–108.

as he is reduced to a neutral carrier, bearer of some transcendent message."[64] As in the case of religious faith, Žižek has a high opinion of Kierkegaard for having realized that "the ultimate and only support of a statement of authority is its own act of enunciation."[65] If that is true, then Kierkegaard can be considered "the first [thinker] to render visible the outlines of 'pure' authority."[66] On this ground, Žižek finds that the way Kierkegaard describes Abraham's unconditional obedience to a sacred authority—that is, as contingent upon a trans-ethical sacrifice—is fully analogous to the reverence of *every* individual for *any* authority, which arises from a similar suspension of ethics.[67] However, Žižek's reading acquires a critical tone when ascertaining an alleged contradiction in Kierkegaard's ratiocination. Whereas in *Philosophical Fragments* Kierkegaard tends to prioritize the teacher's personality and to discount the content of his teaching, upon expounding the stakes of the apostolic authority, Kierkegaard does the very opposite: he deems primary the *content* of divine commandments and is indifferent to the contingent identity of their proclaimer.[68]

One way to tackle Žižek's objection is by a rigorous contextualization. As envisaged by Kierkegaard, the aim of "The Difference between a Genius and an Apostle" was to bring into the open the spiritual summons, dogmatic presuppositions, and existential implications of *divine revelation*. To put it shortly, its chief subject matter is the way in which the absolute truth is given to, and adequately received by, the human subject. Kierkegaard's more general question is how we could rightly discern between a genuine witness to God and a false messenger. Pastor Adler's particular plight has urged Kierkegaard to reflect on the interconnection between the receipt of a transcendent message and the subsequent conduct of its receiver. What seriously compromised Adler's dramatic confrontation with the Church was, on Kierkegaard's judgment, the significant discrepancy between the messenger's stance toward the establishment and the original impetus of this stance (that is, a supposedly genuine theophany)—hence, Kierkegaard's disappointment at Adler's doubts about the truthfulness of his revelation after the clash with the official church. Such is the context in which Kierkegaard puts forward the thesis that the apostle's injunctions (which are, indeed, immune to the threats of secular society and its institutions) are enough for the communication of truth. Given its heteronomous roots, the apostle's act of enunciation should be sufficient to incite the compliance of others. However, to extend this fact to any type of authority, as Žižek does, is a move which Kierkegaard would probably not warrant.[69]

---

[64]   Žižek, *Enjoy Your Symptom!*, p. 95. See also Žižek, *The Parallax View*, p. 149. Tellingly enough, Žižek prefers the genius against the apostle. Žižek, *The Parallax View*, p. 148.

[65]   Žižek, *Enjoy Your Symptom!*, p. 94.

[66]   Ibid., p. 91.

[67]   Ibid., pp. 83–4.

[68]   Ibid., p. 94.

[69]   For the inevitable clash between the political and the transcendent authority, see *SKS* 11, 37 / *WA*, 34. *SKS* 13, 330 / *M*, 271. *SKS* 13, 332–3 / *M*, 274. On the importance of politics in Kierkegaard's authorship the literature is already substantial and still growing. For orientation, see Bruce H. Kirmmse, *Kierkegaard in Golden Age Denmark*, Bloomington,

One may also dispel Žižek's quandary through a Christological argument. Here it is absolutely vital to realize that in his interpretation of "The Difference between a Genius and an Apostle," Žižek adopts a disputable position on the difference, from the standpoint of authority, between Christ and all other humans. After he cites Kierkegaard's insistence on the "eternal qualitative difference"[70] between the affirmation of eternal life by Christ and by an ordinary theology student, Žižek conjectures that the same dissimilarity applies to the genius and the apostle. Kierkegaard, in Žižek's reading, posits thus a qualitative disparity between the apostle, who "is sustained by a transcendent authority,"[71] and the genius, who "represents the highest intensification of the immanent human capacities (wisdom, creativity, and so forth)."[72] Here, Žižek passes too quickly over the fact that, for Kierkegaard, Christ is the *absolute* truth and that only for him the teaching perfectly coincides with his existence. In the same vein, Kierkegaard is adamant in disallowing the reader to ignore Christ's infinite qualitative heterogeneity with respect to *all humans* (apostles and geniuses included). By way of consequence, a genius *can never* differ from an apostle in the same sense in which the God-man differs from humankind *per se*.[73] That is also why in Christ's case only, the carrier of the message is what matters the most. Moreover, the content of Christ's message coincides with his concrete historical being—that is, with his atoning sufferings—while his admonitions are authoritative to a supreme degree because in contrast to humanity as a whole, he is the God-man.

So, unlike the apostle, Kierkegaard's Christ could (and should) never be "reduced to a neutral carrier, bearer of some transcendent message."[74] The self-obliteration of the apostle occurs precisely due to the transcendent substratum of his proclamations, a substratum which has been revealed only in and through the Savior. Moreover, the contingent existence of the apostle must needs be overshadowed not solely because the message he delivers comes from an infinitely different authority, but also because his life is not divine in the sense that Christ's was. Even more, by his self-sacrificial conduct, the apostle tries to witness unconditionally to God's revelation so as to make others follow it for the sake of their deliverance. In conclusion, for Kierkegaard, the content of the apostolic interpellation is always already *Christocentric*. If this conclusion is valid, it is not immediately clear, as Žižek portends, that an apostle is the embodiment of "a pure representative"[75] in the service of a transpersonal authority.

Indiana: Indiana University Press 1990; Bruce H. Kirmmse, "On Authority and Revolution: Kierkegaard's Road to Politics," in *Kierkegaard Revisited*, ed. by Niels Jørgen Cappelørn and Jon Stewart, New York and Berlin: Walter de Gruyter 1997 (*Kierkegaard Studies Monograph Series*, vol. 1), pp. 254–73.

[70]   See *SKS* 11, 105–6 / *WA*, 101–2.

[71]   Žižek, *Enjoy Your Symptom!*, p. 93.

[72]   Ibid.

[73]   Whereas, for Žižek, "Adam and Christ are *one and the same*." See Žižek, *The Puppet and the Dwarf*, pp. 87–8.

[74]   Žižek, *Enjoy Your Symptom!*, p. 95.

[75]   Ibid.

A similar reduction operates in Žižek's hypothesis that there is no difference between Christ's apostle, Marx, Freud, and Lacan. The reason is that they all "opened up a new theoretical field which sets the very criteria of veracity,"[76] and therefore, they should be taken as infallible and simultaneously seditious, truth authorities.[77] Moreover, in his own way each of them helps us become aware of "the unbreakable link connecting the doctrine to the contingent person of the teacher i.e., to the teacher *qua* material surplus that sticks out from the neutral edifice of knowledge."[78] And because, for Kierkegaard, "our belief in the person of the Savior is the absolute, not abolishable condition of our access to truth,"[79] that is to say, because the "eternal truth itself clings to this contingent material externality,"[80] Žižek contends that with the loss of "this 'little piece of the real'…the entire edifice of Christian knowledge crumbles."[81] It is on this very ground that Kierkegaard's Christology can be read as a corrective to, and "materialist reversal"[82] of, Hegel.

IV. Love versus Jouissance: A False Dilemma?

We have said earlier that, as contemplated by Žižek, Lenin's revolutionarism is equivalent with a Kierkegaardian "work of love."[83] Yet, Žižek's encounter with Kierkegaard's theory on human affectivity is not limited to this surprising statement. Somewhat similarly to Kierkegaard, Žižek warns that the erotic should not be confounded with carnal lust. Rather, eros is an indication of "the kindness and care that are part of one's nature, and whose accomplishment delivers its own satisfaction."[84] For Žižek, the need to express and fulfill one's concern for the other is a given of human nature. However, in the erotic affection the disavowed part is that self-giving is contingent upon the vague, yet deeply instilled, expectation that the other will respond at some point with a matching solicitude. This idea bears striking similarities with the hidden egotism that Kierkegaard detected at the root of all erotic relationships (friendship included).[85]

---

[76]   Ibid., p. 100.

[77]   For instance, "Lacan's scandal," Žižek writes, "is that he repeated the Kierkegaardian gesture in relationship to his followers: what he demanded of them was not fidelity to some general theoretical propositions, but precisely fidelity to his person." See Žižek, *Enjoy Your Symptom!*, p. 100.

[78]   Ibid. Yet, Žižek forgets that, as he himself brought to our attention, before the transcendent authority of the message, the apostle's personality is reduced to a neutral (faceless) carrier. That aside, my point is that, according to Kierkegaard, only Christ enjoys the privilege that Žižek assigns to Lacan, Freud, and Marx.

[79]   Ibid., p. 101.

[80]   Ibid.

[81]   Ibid.

[82]   Ibid., pp. 99–102. Moreover, Žižek claims that Hegel "ultimately stays within the boundary of the 'Socratic' universe" (ibid, p. 101), which conflicts with Žižek's own interpretation of Hegel from *The Parallax View*.

[83]   Žižek, *The Puppet and the Dwarf*, p. 30.

[84]   Žižek, *The Fragile Absolute*, p. 100.

[85]   See, for instance, *SKS* 9, 59–64 / *WL*, 52–8. *SKS* 9, 264 / *WL*, 264–5.

However, concerning the trope of Christian love, the closeness between our thinkers is rather ambiguous. To begin with, in complete disagreement with Kierkegaard, Žižek detects a certain interdependence between the putative cruelty of the Jewish Law and Christian agape.[86] Another non-Kierkegaardian tenet entertained by Žižek is that Christianity possesses a proclivity "to reduce agape to an imaginary reconciliation,"[87] thereby "[obfuscating] the Otherness of the divine Thing."[88]

Žižek is also enticed to decrypt, of course critically, the Kierkegaardian principle that true love is only of a dead neighbor,[89] which he regards as "the ultimate form of intolerance towards the Other's enjoyment."[90] His argument is that, because Kierkegaard expects the Christian lover to dismiss "the particular idiosyncrasy of the Other's enjoyment,"[91] and because he reduces the love of the Other to "the empty universality of death,"[92] the Danish thinker can be seen as a precursor of contemporary political correctness which masks its intolerant penchants under the ideal of universal tolerance.[93] Nevertheless, Žižek does not dwell for too long on this criticism. Instead, he focuses on Kierkegaard as a resolute advocate of the Pauline assumption that love is "the force of the real that resists the law."[94] The subversiveness of agape, as arguably endorsed by Kierkegaard, is quite precious to Žižek.[95] In what sense? He argues—in an exceptionally *non*-Kierkegaardian fashion—that Christian love "singles out, focuses on, a finite temporal object which 'means more than anything else.' "[96] Subsequently, he reminds us that the discontents of modernity can be overcome only through *ethico-sacrificial acts*, most probably in the nature of Abraham's willingness to sacrifice Isaac. And since Kierkegaard, continues Žižek, "enjoins a true Christian believer to hate [i.e., to sacrifice] the beloved himself out of love,"[97] he might open for us a genuine ethical path beyond the hindrances of modern normativity.

---

[86]   Žižek, *The Parallax View*, p. 187; p. 280.

[87]   Žižek, *On Belief*, p. 142.

[88]   Ibid., p. 142. Needless to add that for Kierkegaard, agape, far from dissolving God's alterity, does justice to it, and that in a supreme sense.

[89]   Žižek, *The Parallax View*, p. 309. See also Slavoj Žižek, *How to Read Lacan*, London: Granta Books 2006, p. 101.

[90]   For details, see Žižek, *The Puppet and the Dwarf*, p. 61.

[91]   Slavoj Žižek and Glyn Daly, *Conversations with Žižek*, Cambridge and Malden: Polity Press 2004, pp. 116–17.

[92]   Ibid., p. 117.

[93]   See Žižek, *Tarrying with the Negative*, pp. 213–14.

[94]   Kay, *Žižek*, p. 121. That is because, "[if] the affirmative value of love, rather than the negative power of prohibition, becomes the motive for action, then we can hope to interrupt the vicious circle of law and sin and achieve freedom." Ibid., p. 120.

[95]   What Žižek forgets is that, for Kierkegaard, Christ overcame the Law because *he fulfilled it perfectly*. It is not a subversion by denial as is the case of all revolutionaries. Christ dissolves the Law, so to speak, by flawlessly bringing it to fruition. In other words, the requirements of the old Law do not apply to him anymore. Žižek also disregards Kierkegaard's reluctance to assign humans, who are first and foremost sinful, a similar capacity to "abolish" the Law.

[96]   Žižek, *The Fragile Absolute*, p. 96. For Kierkegaard, this constitutes the preferential dimension which is an exclusive attribute of eros not agape.

[97]   Ibid., p. 154. For an extremist version of the same idea, see Žižek, "Dialectical Clarity versus the Misty Conceit of Paradox," in Žižek and Milbank, *The Monstrosity of Christ*, p.

In view of the hateful potential of agape, Žižek affirms that what I am expected to detest in the beloved is only "his inscription into the socio-symbolic structure."[98] Furthermore, I hate the socially integrated other "on behalf of my very love for him as a unique person,"[99] as "a singular member of the community of believers (of the 'Holy Ghost')."[100] Thus, Žižek's Kierkegaard teaches us to sacrifice the *societal* dimension of the neighbor in order to let the latter's *subjective particularity* shine forth. (An interesting question here would be how this differs from Kierkegaard's thesis that only by loving the neighbor as if dead can the lover surmount the temptations of preferentiality and love the other for what he or she truly is, that is, an irreplaceable individual.) So, whereas Kierkegaard's love for the dead neighbor awakens Žižek's disquietude, the incipient hatred of the same agape will harvest Žižek's praise because it advances a truly revolutionary ethics. Otherwise stated, on the one hand, the love of the dead neighbor occasions Žižek's critique that Kierkegaard anticipates postmodern intolerance. On the other hand, Žižek uses the hostility against the symbolically integrated other, in tandem with the Pauline injunction to die to the law,[101] to delineate the contours of an authentic ethics. The tension here resides in understanding Kierkegaard's agape as an inadequate relation to others and also as the advisable ethical stance towards human alterity. Moreover, Žižek does not clarify whether in turning the other into "a singular member of the community of believers,"[102] the true lover comes to efficiently deal with the other's enjoyment. For if ethics requires me to sacrifice the other's inscription into the socio-symbolic structure, why would the Other's enjoyment thereby lose its menacing potential?[103] Besides, how does the annihilation of the symbolic other avoid intolerance?

V. The Materialist Virtues of the Parallax

Perhaps, the ambiguities and tensions made explicit so far will acquire a certain validity if set against the following epistemic statement: "There is a truth…but this truth is the truth of the perspectival distortion as such."[104] The perspectival distortion, to which Žižek assigns an indubitable heuristic value is called parallax. If an object can be contemplated through a dual perspective, the parallax represents, according to Žižek, the passage from (or the distortive gap between) one perspective and the other. Consequently, if two elements appear to us as entirely different, it is because "they are one and the same element in two different spaces."[105] The latter

---

254.

[98]   Žižek, *The Fragile Absolute*, p. 126.
[99]   Ibid.
[100]   Ibid., p. 127.
[101]   Ibid., p. 100. Rom 7:5.
[102]   Ibid., p. 127.
[103]   For details on the continual threat of others' enjoyment, see Žižek, *The Puppet and the Dwarf*, p. 61; Žižek, *On Belief*, p. 47; Žižek, *Enjoy Your Symptom!*, p. 134; Žižek, *Tarrying with the Negative*, p. 212; and Žižek, *The Fragile Absolute*, p. 8.
[104]   Žižek, *The Parallax View*, p. 281.
[105]   Ibid., p. 159.

are separated precisely by a parallactic gap, that is, by an invisible, "irreducible and insurmountable"[106] crack, by an "unfathomable X which forever eludes the symbolic grasp, and thus causes the multiplicity of symbolic perspectives."[107] Worthy of note is that these perspectives, while "radically incommensurable,"[108] are also asymmetrical.[109] Thus seen, the parallax will give Žižek the means to reinscribe the antagonism between different entities within one of those entities;[110] and consequently, to thematize "the speculative identity of the highest and the lowest."[111] To offer one example, Žižek goes to great lengths to show that by virtue of Jesus Christ, "the difference between God and man [can be] transposed into man himself,"[112] as well as into God.[113] In addition, Christ's nature will attest to the unfathomable identity between the holy, the sublime, the absolute, on the one hand, and the profane, the abject, the contingent, on the other.[114]

That is the notional and ideational framework of Žižek's most extensive commentary on Kierkegaard.[115] In general, Žižek can be said to seek to bring into focus (A) the "unexpected continuity between German idealism and Kierkegaard,"[116] a continuity which, when projected within a parallactic vista, becomes coterminous with "dialectical materialism proper";[117] (B) the fact that for an "anti-philosopher"[118] like Kierkegaard, "the most radical authentic core of being human is perceived as a *concrete practico-ethical engagement and/or choice which precedes (and*

---

[106]   Ibid., p. 10.

[107]   Ibid., p. 18.

[108]   Ibid.

[109]   See ibid., p. 29.

[110]   For instance, transcendence, writes Žižek, represents "a kind of perspective illusion, the way we (mis)perceive the gap/discord that inheres to immanence itself." and he continues: "In the same way, the tension between the Same and the Other is secondary with regard to the noncoincidence of the Same with itself." See Žižek, *The Parallax View*, p. 36. For the Lacanian undertones of this thesis, see ibid., p. 353. Žižek, *The Metastases of Enjoyment*, p. 122.

[111]   Žižek, *The Parallax View*, p. 5.

[112]   Ibid., p. 6.

[113]   As Žižek states about Schelling's monism, "there is only One, the gap is inherent to this One itself." See Žižek, *The Parallax View*, p. 36. See also Žižek, *On Belief*, p. 146.

[114]   Žižek claims that the first to realize this impenetrable conjunction was not Kierkegaard but Hegel, whose notion of "infinite judgment" represents "the paradoxical conjunction of the Universal with the 'lowest' singularity." See Žižek, *The Parallax View*, p. 76. Žižek takes this logic to its furthest limit when he audaciously writes that Protestant Christianity conceived Christ "as a God who, in his act of Incarnation, freely *identified himself with his own shit*, with the excremental Real that is man...." See ibid., p. 187. In the same perspective, Žižek sees Christ as "the ultimate diabolic figure." See ibid., p. 99.

[115]   Ibid., pp. 75–80.

[116]   Ibid., p. 75.

[117]   Ibid. Sarah Kay pertinently remarks that "Christianity is thus paradoxically pressed into service by Žižek as an argument *against* faith in spiritual reality, and *in favour of* a dialectical materialism whereby the armature of our thought is shaped by the irreducible real of the body." See Kay, *Žižek*, p. 124.

[118]   Žižek, *The Parallax View*, p. 75.

grounds) every 'theory' ";[119] and (C) "the hidden materialist content of Kierkegaard's religious sacrifice."[120] Briefly stated, Žižek will suggest that the proper philosophical perspective on Kierkegaard is not to be found in the commonsensical opposition between static idealism and dialectical materialism, but in the parallactic hiatus that conceals the disturbing *identity* of the latter two.

The type of idealism Žižek favors is of Hegelian extraction.[121] However, Žižek reads Hegel in an unusual manner. His starting premise is that Hegelian idealism "explodes the coordinates of the standard Aristotelian ontology which is structured around the vector running from possibility to actuality."[122] By contrast, Hegel posits "at the very heart of actuality, a secret striving toward potentiality."[123] Žižek presumes that, thus understood, idealism illumines Kierkegaard's thinking[124] and connects it irrevocably, as if through a Moebius strip, with materialism.

The first feature that Kierkegaard shares with the idealist philosophy of Kant and Fichte is, according to Žižek, the unambiguous rebuttal of theory for the sake of an ethical decisionalism, whose main concern and milieu are practice, concreteness, and historicity. What Kierkegaard has rightly understood is that "only subjectivity designates a domain which is *in itself* 'open' "*;[125] the result of this is, "his effort to break this Hegelian closed circle, and open up the space for contingent cuts, 'jumps,' intrusions, which undermine the field of what appears to be possible."[126] However, Kierkegaard's prevalent criticisms notwithstanding, Hegel endeavors "to *reintroduce the openness of the future into the past, to grasp that-which-was in its process of becoming,* to see the contingent process which generated existing necessity."[127] And since he set in opposition the dynamism of subjectivity and the fixed completeness of objectivity, Kierkegaard, claims Žižek, must be thought as fully Hegelian in spirit. In other words, whenever he turned against Hegel for propounding an all-embracing, impersonal, and rationally teleological conception of *Geist*, Kierkegaard aimed at a straw man.

But in what sense does Kierkegaard's theology represent "the extreme point of idealism,"[128] while his ontology is intimately materialist? *Prima facie*, Žižek's answers seem both byzantine and speculative, although not bereft of interpretive

---

[119]   Ibid. (emphasis original).

[120]   Ibid., p. 81.

[121]   For more details, see Žižek, *Enjoy Your Symptom!*, pp. 46–55.

[122]   Žižek, *The Parallax View*, p. 78.

[123]   Ibid.

[124]   In fact, Žižek advances the tenet that Kierkegaard might be more Hegelian than he had wished. See Žižek, *The Parallax View*, pp. 76–8. However, the contours of the Kierkegaard-Hegel rapports on Žižek's account are far from being unequivocal. I refer here to Žižek's intention to show that Kierkegaard is simultaneously a materialist *reversal* of Hegel (see Žižek, *Enjoy Your Symptom!*, p. 101) and a full-fledged Hegelian (Žižek, *The Parallax View*, pp. 75ff. Žižek, *Tarrying with the Negative*, p. 243, note 28).

[125]   Žižek, *The Parallax View*, p. 76; p. 77.

[126]   Ibid., p. 77.

[127]   Ibid., p. 78 (emphasis original).

[128]   Ibid., p. 79.

value. However, their sinuousness makes their faithful translation an almost impossible task. What follows is my own provisional reconstruction.

Before anything else, one should be aware that Žižek expects the true materialist "to discern the void that separates material reality from itself that makes it 'non-all.' "[129] Materialist is thus every affirmation of "the non-All of Becoming, in its openness and uncertainty."[130] Žižek purports that Kierkegaard's theology is ultimately materialist because it is patterned on a deity who is just "the name for the Absolute Other against which we can measure the thorough contingency of reality."[131] In other words, Kierkegaard operates with a notion of God that is "strictly correlative to the ontological openness of reality."[132] To substantiate this hypothesis, Žižek turns to the problem of religious sacrifice, hoping to establish that the latter's ultimate object does not actually exist. Kierkegaard's religious sacrifice, he states, is an act by which "we give up everything, all that really matters, *for nothing*."[133] That being the case, God is reduced to a mere "name for the purely negative gesture of meaningless sacrifice,"[134] while the infinite qualitative difference between the immanent and the transcendent is indicative of Kierkegaard's awareness of this frightening possibility.

To reinforce this point, Žižek suggests that the economy of religious renunciation is haunted not solely by God's absence but also by the specter of irrationalism. In order to function properly, the sacrifice, warns Žižek, "must be in a way 'meaningless,' a gesture of 'irrational,' useless expenditure or ritual."[135] Thus, Kierkegaard's unswerving stress on the bond between madness and faith is testimony to the *lack* of any guarantee whatsoever to sacrifice. Žižek's conclusion—which, again, runs against the very core of Kierkegaard's edifying intentions—is that every religious gift *can occur only as a kind of empty gesture in a Godless universe*."[136] Welcome to the desert of disenchantment!

After pointing out that Kierkegaard's view of self-sacrifice necessitates a minimal rectification to become part of a "proper materialist theory of subjectivity,"[137] Žižek's discussion is abruptly redirected toward an oblique discussion of anxiety, innocence, the Fall, and the prohibitions of the Law. Hegel, Nietzsche, and Descartes seem to lurk in the background of this shift. The materialist corrective pursued by Žižek is Nietzschean to the extent that "our life needs no transcendent Measure to confer meaning on its totality,"[138] that human existence remains "a creative play of incessantly creating new meanings and values."[139] A consistent (Nietzschean-Hegelian) materialist should accept "Kierkegaard's point about the primacy of

---

[129]   Ibid., p. 383.
[130]   Ibid., p. 84.
[131]   Ibid., p. 79.
[132]   Ibid.
[133]   Ibid., p. 81.
[134]   Ibid., p. 75.
[135]   Ibid., p. 85.
[136]   Ibid., p. 81 (emphasis original).
[137]   Ibid., p. 86.
[138]   Ibid., p. 84.
[139]   Ibid.

Becoming in human life,"[140] and, as already stated, "joyously *affirm* the non-All of Becoming, in its openness and uncertainty."[141]

To this eclectic anatomy, Žižek adds a Cartesian dash. He observes that similarly to Descartes, Kierkegaard's reflections emerge from a comparable radical doubt. However, in contrast to Descartes, Žižek's Kierkegaard transplants uncertainty from the realm of knowledge into the terrain of existing selfhood. Epistemological skepticism becomes thus the existential despair which prompts the individual to stoic resignation, if not to a relentless search for meaning.[142] Even if Žižek admits that such total and despair-generating doubt is "resolved through reference to God,"[143] while faith seems "the only truly viable answer,"[144] the materialist relevance of this point is not clarified within the confines of *The Parallax View*. Žižek's argument looks as though the "God solution" is something that the self could come up with in an *unassisted* fashion.[145] Consequently, an authentically materialist-ethical subjectivity is faced with the unenviable perspective of the skeptic who resolutely and exuberantly has to affirm the incomplete and endless becoming. It is only against this backdrop that a superfluous self-sacrifice can be contemplated as the ultimate ethical act.

From the abyss of despair Žižek passes to Kierkegaard's perusal of anxiety. What holds his attention is the fact that anxiety permits one to subvert traditional ethics defined in terms of (superegotized) Law, Universality, or Prohibition. This subversive possibility encapsulates the ethical import of anxiety. At the same time, Žižek discusses Kierkegaard's anxiety with reference to the biblical narrative of the Fall. However, his approach remains eclectic since the jargon and dialectic are clearly Hegelian, while the last word belongs to Schelling.[146]

Schelling's thought (from *The Ages of the World*) is appropriated by Žižek as a novel and critical way to examine Kierkegaard's concept of anxiety, but also as a correlative theory on the constitution of subjectivity, in general.[147] Our cultural

---

[140]   Ibid.

[141]   Ibid. (emphasis original)

[142]   Ibid., p. 86.

[143]   Ibid.

[144]   Ibid.

[145]   My claim is that Žižek hereby rejects the possibility of divine revelation which would be the properly Kierkegaardian response to the despairing doubt. Kierkegaard nowhere argues that the self could ever find God or attain faith if the transcendent had not already opened itself to the immanent. See in this sense, *Philosophical Fragments* (on which Žižek bases part of his argument) and *The Sickness unto Death*.

[146]   For Žižek's extensive treatment of Schelling, see Žižek, *The Indivisible Remainder*, pp. 13–91. See also Iain Hamilton Grant, "The Insufficiency of Ground: On Žižek's Schellingianism," in *The Truth of Žižek*, ed. by Paul Bowman and Richard Stamp, London and New York: Continuum 2007, pp. 82–98.

[147]   Kay notices that "Žižek finds in Schelling, as he did in Kierkegaard, a conception of human freedom and agency that repeats divine freedom and agency." Therefore, Žižek reads Schelling as if his "account of the emergence of the world from chaos, and of history from eternity, were an account of the emergence of the human subject (specifically of the imposition of the symbolic on the real)." See Kay, *Žižek*, p. 113. See also Žižek, *The Indivisible Remainder*, pp. 20–1; p. 42.

theorist analyzes the emergence of the culpable and anxiety-ridden selfhood through a formal transposition of Schelling's pre-creation theology, but implicitly refrains from any affirmation of transcendence.[148] After observing that Kierkegaard clearly appropriates the first and third stage of Schelling's dialectic, Žižek finds fault with the former for passing too quickly from the anxiety of the "dreaming spirit"[149] to the advent of (and perverse interaction between) Prohibition and desire, or Law and sin.[150] Thus, argues Žižek, Kierkegaard skips Schelling's second level, namely, the "primordial egotistic contraction"[151] (*Zusammenziehung*), whereby an inner deadlock is projected as "an external impediment"[152] and "inherent obstacle,"[153] which are later turned into the object of Prohibition. However, anxiety which occurs when the individual feels not only repelled, but also attracted by an apparently external impasse,[154] indicates that the impasse belongs to one's innermost core. For Žižek, Kierkegaard's reasoning is erred through the unwarranted leap from the "primordial repose"[155] to the emergence of objective universal norms. Hereby Kierkegaard turns a blind eye to the fact that normativity is a mere flight into exteriority, intended to counteract the inevitable tribulations of free singularity.

At this juncture, Žižek turns to the Judeo-Christian paradise narrative. His surmise is that, contrary to what Kierkegaard thought, "*the function of* [God's] *Prohibition is not to introduce disturbance into the previous repose of paradisiacal innocence, but, on the contrary, to resolve some terrifying deadlock* [within God himself]."[156] By implication, Žižek will argue—*contra* Kierkegaard, who saw in the emergence of sin the indication of a radical qualitative dissimilarity between the creature and the Creator—that sinfulness is just a self-deluding escape from the subject's constitutive trauma.[157] Sin is the vain refuge into an authoritarian superego and the perverse enjoyment of an endless guilt.[158] Simultaneously, Žižek seems to embrace a *felix culpa* perspective—which comes as no surprise, given his Hegelian bias—by openly claiming that the Fall is just "the first step toward liberation."[159]

---

[148] Žižek, *The Parallax View*, p. 89.

[149] *SKS* 4, 347–50 / *CA*, 48–9. *SKS* 4, 354 / *CA*, 48–9.

[150] For more on the malign dialectic between normativity and sinfulness, and therefore, the allegedly perverse crux of Christianity, see Žižek, *The Parallax View*, p. 90; p. 100. See also Žižek, *The Puppet and the Dwarf*, p. 15; p. 49.

[151] Žižek, *The Parallax View*, p. 89.

[152] Ibid.

[153] Ibid.

[154] Žižek, *The Puppet and the Dwarf*, p. 79.

[155] Žižek, *The Parallax View*, p. 96.

[156] Ibid., p. 89. See *SKS* 4, 347 / *CA*, 41. *SKS* 4, 350 / *CA*, 44–5. *SKS* 4, 365–6 / *CA*, 61.

[157] Žižek, *On Belief*, p. 86.

[158] See Žižek, *The Parallax View*, p. 334; p. 337; p. 338. See also Žižek and Daly, *Conversations*, pp. 127–8; p. 131; Žižek, *The Metastases of Enjoyment*, p. 61; p. 69; p. 194; and Žižek, *The Puppet and the Dwarf*, p. 103.

[159] Žižek, *The Parallax View*, p. 96. See also Žižek, *The Puppet and the Dwarf*, p. 88. Žižek's interpretation of the Fall narrative is conspicuously Hegelian. Žižek, *The Fragile Absolute*, pp. 88–9.

What Žižek wishes to establish through all these zigzagging detours and insufficiently developed insights is that Kierkegaard's understanding of the paradisiacal prohibition, original sin, anxiety, and despair enables us to pierce through the enigma of subjectivity. Similar results will be reached by Žižek in a second encounter with Christ, when Kierkegaard's atypical association of incarnation with humor will evince its inestimable worth, however, within the same, unabashedly godless, panorama.

VI. Christ as Divine Comedian

In an essay provocatively entitled "The Comedy of Incarnation," Žižek lends supplementary support to his thesis that Kierkegaard's authorship is favorable to a paradoxical approach, whereby theological reflections could be seen as purely materialistic.[160] We have said that the parallax has the distinctive capacity to reveal the complete coincidence between two regimens of being, which are usually opposed to one another. As in the previous section, the parallactic view will allow us to glance into the impenetrable fold wherein Kierkegaard's Christology appears indistinguishable from Žižek's materialism.[161]

The re-encounter with the tutelary figure of Christ takes over a principle set in motion in *Enjoy Your Symptom!*. The principle stipulated that the eternal truth needs a "contingent material externality,"[162] a mere "material surplus,"[163] or a "dumb material weight,"[164] to which it attaches itself with all its might. We also remember that Žižek frames his discussion of materialism in step with the following coordinates: noncoincidence, openness, uncertainty, and constitutive fissures.[165] Within the bounds of *The Parallax View*, while applying these two points to Kierkegaard's Christ, Žižek claims that the latter confirms that the eternal (or God) needs a material remainder, an irreducible remnant to exist and compensate for its inherently non-substantial condition.[166] Concisely put, the heavy and lowly materiality of the Son is indicative of the void within the Father.[167] Kierkegaard thus assists Žižek in realizing that the function of Christ's corporeality is to mask the internal and frightening non-coincidence of the transcendent.[168]

---

[160]   Žižek, *The Parallax View*, pp. 103–11. For more substantial developments of the continuity between Christianity and dialectical materialism in the Marxian-Leninist sense, see Žižek's *The Fragile Absolute* and *On Belief*.

[161]   A few concise definitions of materialism can be found in Žižek, *The Parallax View*, p. 17; p. 168. For an example of a materialist twist to Kierkegaard's notion of infinite resignation, see Žižek, *The Parallax View*, p. 84.

[162]   Žižek, *Enjoy Your Symptom!*, p. 100; p. 101.

[163]   Ibid., p. 100.

[164]   Ibid., p. 101.

[165]   Žižek, *The Parallax View*, p. 79; p. 168.

[166]   Ibid., p. 79.

[167]   Ibid., p. 6. For the postulation of a similar hiatus, this time within subjectivity, see ibid., pp. 353.

[168]   Žižek, *The Puppet and the Dwarf*, p. 24; p. 78. See also Žižek, *The Parallax View*, p. 36; p. 184. On the imperfection(s) of God, see Žižek, *The Puppet and the Dwarf*, p. 89.

The Kierkegaard student might expect Žižek to address the notion of the infinite qualitative difference, which sustains almost the entire edifice of Kierkegaard's Christian soteriology. But even if this expectation does not come to fruition, the unforeseen turn of Žižek's reading will, indeed, make one quickly forget the disappointment. Žižek argues that the inherent split within the absolute deity becomes visible when contemplating the narrative of Christ's existence as part and parcel of a comic screenplay. With this particular goal in mind, he relies on Kierkegaard's insight that the connection between humor and religiousness should be taken seriously.

Taking a quick detour, Žižek draws a distinction between comedy and what he calls non-tragedy. To explicate the meaning of the latter, he considers the teleological suspension of the ethical from *Fear and Trembling* in concert with the imaginary modern rendition of Antigone from *Either/Or*, Part 1. In a certainly debatable move, Žižek juxtaposes Abraham with Sophocles' heroine and finds that they share an incommunicable "accursed knowledge."[169] In other words, there is no significant difference between Antigone, who could never confide that her father committed the most abominable crimes—parricide and incest—and the father of (the Judeo-Christian) faith, who was likewise marked by an unspeakable and absurd ordeal (Isaac's sacrifice). Both Abraham and Antigone lack the distinctive features of a tragic persona[170] on account of the inevitable isolation entailed by their incommunicable cognizance. Furthermore, the Kierkegaardian duo of Abraham and Antigone anticipates, in Žižek's reading, the humorous kernel of Christianity.

Unfortunately, the specifics regarding the transition from non-tragedy to comedy remain to be guessed.[171] Žižek's commentary returns to Kierkegaard's stages and purports that they could be profitably evaluated from a parallactic vantage part. In the first section of this article we have seen how Žižek conceived religious repetition as a willful appropriation of the impossibilities and impasses posed by the ethico-aesthetical existence. Here Žižek rephrases the same idea arguing that, whereas in aestheticism and ethics "the subject wants to live a consistent mode of existence, and thus disavows the radical antagonism of the human situation,"[172] in religion the self comes face to face with this antagonism. In this way, Kierkegaard's religious stage can be viewed as "the radical assertion of the parallax gap."[173] What is more, according to Žižek, at the center of religious life lies not the ideal of faith but rather the realistic and limitless validity of *doubt*. As Žižek abstrusely puts it:

God's impotence and nonexistence are announced in Žižek, *The Puppet and the Dwarf*, pp. 126–9; p. 137; p. 171. On these points, Žižek claims to have been influenced by G.K. Chesterton. See Žižek, *The Puppet and the Dwarf*, pp. 14–15. For the Hegelian provenience of this self-martial view of the absolute see Žižek, *The Puppet and the Dwarf*, p. 28; p. 66.

[169]   Žižek, *The Parallax View*, p. 104.

[170]   However, in *On Belief*, pp. 91–2, while opposing tragedy to comedy, Žižek sees Antigone as a tragic character.

[171]   We may assume, albeit not without risks, that Abraham, Antigone, and Christ share a certain awareness of their inward void, which is manifest in their silence.

[172]   Žižek, *The Parallax View*, p. 105.

[173]   Ibid.

We are never safely within the Religious, doubt forever remains, the same act can be seen as religious or as aesthetic,[174] in a parallax split which can never be abolished, since the "minimal difference" which transubstantiates (what appears to be) an aesthetic act into a religious one can never be specified, located in a determinate property.[175]

I have already clarified that the parallax brings to light the ultimate *coincidence* between two opposites. I also said that the same parallax bespeaks a distortive gap which *veils* the unfathomable identity between antipodes. When viewing Kierkegaard's Savior through these lenses, as Žižek wants us to, the conclusion we reach is that in Christ the highest intersects the wretchedness of a human being that walked the earth two millennia ago. Žižek's main point is that, if we take comedy as being contingent upon the convergence between total meaningfulness and utter absurdity, between spirit and corporeality, or between holiness and excrement, then a parallactic rendition of the God-man renders him as the supreme comedian, in whom divinity is inseparable from filth. "[Is] there anything more comical," asks Žižek, "than Incarnation, this ridiculous overlapping of the Highest and the Lowest, the coincidence of God, creator of the universe, and a miserable man?"[176]

Žižek's reflections take their impetus from Kierkegaard's juxtaposition between the humorous potential of religion and the paradoxical coincidence within Christ of the non-substantial God and the density of the human body. Moreover, according to Žižek, whereas the comical appearance of Kierkegaard's Christ introduces us to the (materialist) identity of the zenith and the nadir, Christ's crucifixion unveils the non-coincidence of God with himself, that is to say, the internal antagonism which renders the Christian deity absolutely indistinguishable from every single human subject. God's inner and conflictual gulf is generalized in this manner to the entire domain of human ontology.[177]

Despite its cogency, the argument may be just partly Kierkegaardian. I defend this claim because it is rather difficult to understand how Kierkegaard could be seen as an early proponent of the parallax view while inflexibly defending the unsurpassable and even irreducible difference between the human and the divine. My conjecture is reinforced by the fact—which is largely ignored by Žižek—that in Kierkegaard's Christianity, there exists an even lower level than Christ's "miserable" corporeality, which is human sinfulness. What is more, like every other consistent Christian thinker, Kierkegaard unambiguously rejects the presence of sin in Christ. Thus, if we are to speak about a truly parallactic identity in Žižek's sense, that should be the one between the holy and the sinful, and that coincidence is exceptionally *absent* from Kierkegaard's deliberations on the God-man.[178]

Despite all the inconsistencies and differences made explicit throughout this article, four particular points, I suggest, should be valued in Žižek's dialogue with

---

[174]   Contrast this point with the thesis that Kierkegaard's religion and aesthetics can never be brought together; Žižek, *Enjoy Your Symptom!*, p. 82.

[175]   Žižek, *The Parallax View*, p. 105.

[176]   Ibid.

[177]   Ibid., pp. 106–7; p. 109.

[178]   Whereas Žižek does believe that Christ was a sinner as any other human. See Žižek, *The Puppet and the Dwarf*, p. 15.

Kierkegaard. First and most noteworthy is the discussion of Kierkegaard's religious psychology within the horizon of Lacanian psychoanalysis. Secondly, one can find in Žižek an important re-evaluation of Kierkegaard's relation to Hegel, obviously in continuance with Jon Stewart's outstanding efforts in the same direction.[179] Next, Žižek's endeavor to read the Kierkegaardian Christ in a materialistic optic remains notable inasmuch as it accounts for certain issues so far understudied in Kierkegaard research. Here I refer particularly to the relation between the Savior's Gethsemane agony and his omniscience, but also to the endlessness of spiritual struggles and the fine balance between the resolute certainty of faith and the continual awareness of sin. Even if he mainly deals with all these issues in the secularized setting of Freudian-Lacanian psychoanalysis, Žižek succeeds in thematizing the role of negativity in Kierkegaard's theo-Christology. Finally, our interpreter should be complimented for having reopened the subject of Kierkegaard's political relevance for the Left, a topic with an already tormented past.[180] As for the future, his competence in this direction would certainly allow him to expose unexplored pathways in Kierkegaard's social thought, though their course may be anything but straight.

---

[179]   Jon Stewart, *Kierkegaard's Relations to Hegel Reconsidered*, Cambridge and New York: Cambridge University Press 2003.

[180]   See in this sense András Nagy, "Kierkegaard in Russia. The Ultimate Paradox: Existentialism at the Crossroads of Religious Philosophy and Bolshevism," in *Kierkegaard Revisited*, pp. 107–38; András Nagy, "Abraham the Communist," in *Kierkegaard: The Self in Society*, ed. by George Pattison and Steven Shakespeare, Basingstoke: Macmillan 1998, pp. 196–220. A Marxian analysis of Kierkegaard's ethico-religious thought is proposed by Mark Dooley in *The Politics of Exodus: Søren Kierkegaard's Ethics of Responsibility*, New York: Fordham University Press 2001.

Bibliography

I. References to or Uses of Kierkegaard in Žižek's Corpus

The Sublime Object of Ideology, London and New York: Verso 1989, pp. 36–7.
Enjoy Your Symptom!, New York and London: Routledge 1992, p. 52; pp. 78–84; p. 91; pp. 92–6; pp. 99–102; p. 105; p. 177.
Tarrying with the Negative: Kant, Hegel, and the Critique of Ideology, Durham: Duke University Press 1993, p. 1; p. 83; pp. 96–7; p. 155; p. 178; p. 188; pp. 192–3; pp. 227–8; p. 243, note 28; p. 244, note 36; p. 247, note 53; p. 269, note 42; pp. 284–5, note 34.
The Indivisible Remainder, London and New York: Verso 1996, pp. 185–6, note 95.
The Plague of Fantasies, London and New York: Verso 1997, p. 52; p. 77; p. 83, note 9; p. 108; p. 152.
The Fragile Absolute, London and New York: Verso 2000, pp. 126–7; pp. 147–8; p. 154.
On Belief, London and New York: Routledge 2001, p. 45; p. 77; p. 105; p. 148; p. 149.
The Puppet and the Dwarf: The Perverse Core of Christianity, Cambridge, Massachusetts and London: MIT Press 2003, p. 10; pp. 17–19; p. 30; p. 88.
Conversations with Žižek, Cambridge and Malden: Polity Press 2004, pp. 116–18.
"Filozofija, teologija, etika: nekaj odprtih vprašanj" [Philosophy, Theology, Ethics: Some Open Questions], in *Filozofski Vestnik*, vol. 26, no. 3, 2005, pp. 7–21.
The Parallax View, Cambridge, Massachusetts and London: MIT Press 2006, p. 6; pp. 51–2; pp. 75–80; pp. 84–90; p. 96; p. 99; pp. 103–11; p. 117; p. 132; pp. 148–50; p. 178; p. 198; p. 273; p. 282; p. 309; p. 353.
The Universal Exception: Selected Writings, vols. 1–2, London and New York: Continuum 2006, vol. 2, p. 15; pp. 121–2, note 23; p. 177.
How to Read Lacan, London: Granta Books 2006, p. 99; p. 101.

II. Sources of Žižek's Knowledge of Kierkegaard

Dolar, Mladen, "The Opera in Philosophy: Mozart and Kierkegaard," in Mladen Dolar and Slavoj Žižek, *Opera's Second Death*, New York and London: Routledge 2002, pp. 50–8.
Huntington, Patricia, "Heidegger's Reading of Kierkegaard Revisited: From Ontological Abstraction to Ethical Concretion," in *Kierkegaard in Post/Modernity*, ed. by Martin Matustik and Merold Westphal, Bloomington: Indiana University Press 1995, pp. 43–65.

Kierkegaard, Søren, *Either/Or—A Fragment of Life*, trans. by Alastair Hannay, Harmondsworth: Penguin Books 1992.

— *Fear and Trembling*, trans. by. Howard and Edna Hong, Princeton, New Jersey: Princeton University Press 1983.

— *Repetition*, trans. by Howard and Edna Hong, Princeton, New Jersey: Princeton University Press 1983.

— *Fear and Trembling*, trans. by Alastair Hannay, Harmondsworth: Penguin 1985.

— *Philosophical Fragments*, trans. by Howard and Edna Hong, Princeton, New Jersey: Princeton University Press, 1985.

— *Works of Love*, trans. by Howard and Edna Hong, New York: Harper Torchbooks, 1962.

— "Of the Difference between a Genius and an Apostle," in *The Present Age*, trans. by Alexander Dru, New York: Harper Torchbooks 1962, pp. 87ff.

III. Bibliography of Secondary Literature on Kierkegaard and Žižek

Holbo, John, "On Žižek and Trilling," *Philosophy and Literature*, vol. 28, no. 2, 2004, pp. 430–40.

Index of Persons

Abraham, 62, 69, 73, 132, 170, 181, 186-9, 210, 306, 309-317.

Abzug, Robert H., 234, 235.

Adam, 21, 130, 205, 212.

Adler, Adolph Peter (1812-69), Danish pastor, 305, 306.

Adler, Alfred (1870-1937), Austrian medical doctor, psychotherapist, 217, 221, 242.

Adorno, Theodor W. (1903-69), German philosopher, 3, 7, 73, 109.

Alexandrescu, Sorin (b. 1937), Romanian literary critic and semiotician, 56, 63, 64.

Amiel, Henri Frédéric (1821-81), Swiss philosopher, poet and critic, 57.

Antigone, 317.

Aristotle, 45, 85, 275.

Artaud, Antonin (1896-1948), French playwright, poet, actor and theater director, 3.

Augustine of Hippo (354-430), church father, 37, 40, 47, 101, 169, 293,

Bakhtin, Mikhail (1895-1975), Russian philosopher, literary critic, 180, 181, 190.

Barth, Karl (1886-1968), Swiss Protestant theologian, 165.

Barthes, Roland (1915-80), French writer, 2, 3, 138, 179, 184.

Bataille, Georges (1897-1962), French writer, 1, 3, 7.

Baudrillard, Jean (1929-2007), French sociologist, philosopher, cultural theorist, xii, 1-16.

Becker, Ernest (1924-74), American cultural anthropologist, xii, 17-27, 97, 178, 274, 277, 283, 285, 286, 290, 292, 293.

Beckett, Samuel (1906-89), Irish novelist, playwright, theater director, and poet, 133.

Benedict, Ruth (1887-1948), American anthropologist, 84.

Bergman, Ingmar (1918-2007), Swedish director, writer and producer, 90.

Bergson, Henri (1859-1941), French philosopher, 97, 179, 204.

Binswanger, Ludwig (1881-1966), Swiss psychiatrist, xi, 29-53, 161, 220, 230.

Bleuler, Eugen (1857-1939), Swiss psychiatrist, 32.

Borges, Jorge Luis (1899-1986), Argentine writer, 3.

Bourdieu, Pierre (1930-2002), French sociologist, 2.

Brandes, Georg (1842-1927), Danish author and literary critic, ix, 57, 81, 299.

Brecht, Bertolt (1898-1956), German poet, 1, 2, 301.

Bretall, Robert, 233, 279.

Breuer, Josef (1842-1925), Austrian physician, 199, 278.

Bruner, Jerome (b. 1915), American psychologist, 92.

Buber, Martin (1878-1965), German philosopher, 65, 73, 165, 166, 168-70, 243, 244, 250, 252, 263, 277, 283, 286, 287.

Buddha, 104, 291.

Index of Subjects

College Lane, Hatfield, Herts. AL10 9AB
Information Hertfordshire
Services and Solutions for the University

For renewal of Standard and One Week Loans,
please visit the web site http://www.voyager.herts.ac.uk

This item must be returned or the loan renewed by the due date.
A fine will be charged for the late return of items.